Trade conflicts between developing nations and industrial nations

Trade problems of the developing nations—Ch. 7

Economic growth strategies—import substitution versus export-led growth—Ch. 7

Can all developing nations achieve export led growth?—Ch. 7

China enters the WTO—Ch. 7

Do advanced nations gain from trade liberalization with developing nations?—Ch. 7

Do U.S. multinationals exploit foreign workers?—Ch. 9

[**Trade Conflicts**]

Liberalizing trade: The WTO versus regional trading arrangements

From GATT to the WTO—Ch. 6

Does the WTO reduce national sovereignty?—Ch. 6

Regional integration versus multilateralism—Ch. 8

The European Union—Ch. 8

The North American Free Trade Agreement (NAFTA)—Ch. 8

[**Liberalizing Trade**]

The dollar as a key currency

Euro and dollar compete for supremacy—Ch. 8

NAFTA: An optimum currency area?—Ch. 8

Preventing currency crises: Currency boards versus dollarization—Ch. 15

For Argentina, no panacea in dollarization—Ch. 15

U.S. pressures China to revalue its yuan—Ch. 15

[**Key Currency**]

tenth edition

International Economics

Robert J. Carbaugh

Professor of Economics
Central Washington University

THOMSON
SOUTH-WESTERN

Australia · Canada · Mexico · Singapore · Spain · United Kingdom · United States

International Economics, 10e
Robert J. Carbaugh

VP/Editorial Director:
Jack W. Calhoun

VP/Editor-in-Chief:
Dave Shaut

Sr. Acquisitions Editor:
Michael W. Worls

Sr. Developmental Editor:
Susanna C. Smart

Sr. Marketing Manager:
John Carey

Sr. Production Editor:
Elizabeth A. Shipp

Sr. Technology Project Manager:
Peggy Buskey

Sr. Manufacturing Coordinator:
Sandee Milewski

Art Director:
Michelle Kunkler

Production House:
Rebecca Gray Design

Internal Designer:
Lou Ann Thesing (Cincinnati, Ohio)

Cover Designer:
Laura Brown (Cincinnati, Ohio)

Cover Image:
© Brand X Pictures/Alamy

Printer:
Courier Westford

For permission to use material from
this text or product, contact us by
Tel (800) 730-2214
Fax (800) 730-2215
http://www.thomsonrights.com

For more information
contact South-Western,
5191 Natorp Boulevard,
Mason, Ohio 45040.
Or you can visit our Internet site at:
http://www.swlearning.com

Contents in Brief

Contents

chapter 3

Sources of Comparative Advantage 63

chapter 4

Tariffs 101

chapter 7

Trade Policies for the Developing Nations

chapter 8

Regional Trading Arrangements 253

chapter 9

International Factor Movements and Multinational Enterprises 289

Part 2: International Monetary Relations

chapter 10

The Balance of Payments

chapter 11

chapter 12

chapter 13

Balance-of-Payments Adjustments

chapter 14

Exchange-Rate Adjustments and the Balance of Payments

chapter 15

Exchange-Rate Systems and Currency Crises 442

chapter 16

Macroeconomic Policy in an Open Economy 474

chapter 17

International Banking: Reserves, Debt, and Risk 490

Preface

Preface

My belief is that the best way to motivate students to learn a subject is to demonstrate how it is used in practice. The first nine editions of *International Economics* reflected this belief and were written to provide a serious presentation of international economic theory with an emphasis on current applications. Adopters of these editions strongly supported the integration of economic theory with current events.

This edition has been revised with an eye toward improving this presentation and updating the applications as well as toward including the latest theoretical developments. Like its predecessors, this edition is intended for use in a one-quarter or one-semester course for students who have no more background than principles of economics. This book's strengths are its clarity and organization and its applications, which demonstrate the usefulness of theory to students. The revised and updated material in this edition emphasizes current applications of economic theory and incorporates recent theoretical and policy developments in international trade and finance.

International Economics Themes

This edition highlights five themes that are widely discussed by the news media: (1) globalization of economic activity; (2) the controversy over free trade—the gap between economists and the general public; (3) trade conflicts between developing nations and industrial nations; (4) liberalizing trade—the WTO versus regional trading arrangements; and (5) the dollar as a key currency. These themes are emphasized throughout the text as follows:

- **Globalization of economic activity**
  - Waves of globalization—Ch. 1
  - Why globalization is important—Ch. 1

- Globalization and competitiveness—Ch. 1
- Has globalization gone too far?—Ch. 1
- Terrorism jolts the global economy—Ch. 1 and Ch. 3
- Job outsourcing and free trade—Ch. 2
- The anxiety behind globalization—Ch. 2
- Free trade and the law of comparative advantage—Ch. 2

- **Free trade and quality of life issues**
  - Do low-skilled jobs have to shift overseas?—Ch. 2
  - Does trade make the poor even poorer?—Ch. 3
  - Sweatshop labor competes against American workers—Ch. 3
  - Does wage insurance make free trade more acceptable to workers?—Ch. 6
  - Free trade policies and the environment—Ch. 6
  - Is the Kyoto Protocol a lot of hot air?—Ch. 6

- **Trade conflicts between developing nations and industrial nations**
  - Trade problems of the developing nations—Ch. 7
  - Economic growth strategies—import substitution versus export-led growth—Ch. 7
  - Can all developing nations achieve export-led growth?—Ch. 7
  - China enters the WTO—Ch. 7
  - Do advanced nations gain from trade liberalization with developing nations?—Ch. 7
  - Do U.S. multinationals exploit foreign workers?—Ch. 9

- **Liberalizing trade: The WTO versus regional trading arrangements**
  - From GATT to the WTO—Ch. 6
  - Does the WTO reduce national sovereignty?—Ch. 6
  - Regional integration versus multilateralism—Ch. 8

- The European Union—Ch. 8
- The North American Free Trade Agreement —Ch. 8

- **The dollar as a key currency**
  - Euro and dollar compete for supremacy— Ch. 8
  - NAFTA: An optimum currency area?—Ch. 7
  - Stabilizing currencies of developing countries: Currency boards versus dollarization— Ch. 15
  - For Argentina, no panacea in dollarization —Ch. 15

Besides emphasizing several contemporary themes, the tenth edition of this text contains many new or substantially revised topics such as:

- Cloth Imports from China Threaten Italy's Textile Makers—Ch. 1
- The Fruits of Global Trade—Ch. 1
- Maytag Slashes Costs to Survive in a Global Market—Ch. 2
- Babe Ruth and the Principle of Comparative Advantage—Ch. 2
- Why Factor Prices Don't Equalize—Ch. 3
- Should Tariffs Be Placed on Steel Imports to Protect National Security?—Ch. 4
- Should Retaliatory Tariffs Be Used for WTO Enforcement?—Ch. 7
- The World Bank and International Monetary Fund—Ch. 7
- U.S. Farm Subsidies and Developing Countries —Ch. 7
- U.S.–Chile Free Trade Agreement—Ch. 8
- Does U.S. Immigration Policy Harm Domestic Workers?—Ch. 9
- How Markel Co. Rides Foreign-Exchange Fluctuations—Ch. 11
- The Ups and Downs of the Dollar—Ch. 12
- Does the U.S. Current Account Deficit Weigh on the Dollar?—Ch. 12
- Exchange Rate Pass-Through—Ch. 14
- Japanese Firms Move Output Overseas to Limit Effects of Strong Yen—Ch. 14
- Is Exchange Rate Stabilization Effective?— Ch. 15
- International Currency Crises—Ch. 16

Organizational Framework

Although instructors generally agree on the basic content of the international economics course, opinions vary widely about what arrangement of material is appropriate. This book is structured to provide considerable organizational flexibility. The topic of international trade relations is presented before international monetary relations, but the order can be reversed by instructors who choose to start with monetary theory. Instructors can begin with Chapters 10–17 and conclude with Chapters 2–9. Those who do not wish to cover all the material in the book can easily omit all or parts of Chapters 6–9 and Chapter 13 and Chapters 15–17 without loss of continuity.

In response to the comments of adopters of previous editions, the tenth edition of *International Economics* streamlines its presentation of theory so as to provide greater flexibility for instructors. First, the major topics of Chapters 2 and 3 of the previous edition are combined into a single chapter, Chapter 2, in the tenth edition, with the indifference curve material now in an appendix. Much of the IMF and World Bank coverage from old Chapter 18 "International Banking" is moved to Chapter 7 "Trade Policies for Developing Nations" and expanded. Some of the more rigorous theoretical material is now placed into appendices or streamlined within the chapters.

Also, the new edition makes greater use of "Exploring Further" sections at the end of chapters to discuss more advanced theoretical topics. These revisions enhance the ability of instructors to emphasize contemporary applications of international economics if they desire. At the same time, more advanced theoretical topics are available to those instructors who wish to include them in their courses.

Supplementary Materials

International Economics Web Site (http://carbaugh.swlearning.com)

In this age of technology, no text package would be complete without Web-based resources. An international economics Web site is offered with the tenth edition. This site, **http://carbaugh.swlearning. com**, contains many useful pedagogical enrichment features including NetLink Exercises, which draw upon the expanded NetLinks feature at the end of each chapter. While the NetLinks direct the student to an appropriate international economics Web site to gather data and other relevant information, the NetLink Exercises allow students to access these Web sites to answer pertinent and practical questions that relate to international economics. As an added enrichment feature, a Virtual Scavenger Hunt engages and encourages students to search for international economics answers at various Internet Web sites. These features are found within the Interactive Study Center section of the Carbaugh Web site.

In addition, students and instructors alike can address questions and provide commentary directly to the author with the Talk to the Author feature.

For other high-tech study tools, visit the South-Western Economics Resource Center at **http://economics.swlearning.com**.

Carbaugh Xtra! (http://carbaughxtra.swlearning.com)

Carbaugh Xtra! can be packaged with the textbook or access can be purchased separately by students online at **http://carbaughxtra.swlearning.com**.

Carbaugh Xtra! offers a variety of online learning enhancements, including tutorials that cover the most difficult concepts for students, such as graphing and derivatives. These tutorials, created by Koushik Ghosh of Central Washington University, walk students through extensive graphing and derivatives exercises that correspond to exercises found within the book.

Carbaugh Xtra! also offers links to "Economic Applications" (EconNews, EconData, and EconDebate online features that closely relate concepts discussed in the text to the latest contemporary applications); these applications are highlighted in the margins throughout the text. In addition, Xtra! quizzing is available, which offers you an opportunity to practice for midterms and finals by taking interactive quizzes.

PowerPoint Slides

The tenth edition also includes PowerPoint slides created by Steve Norton of Okno Consulting Group, Ann Arbor, Michigan. These slides can be easily downloaded from the Carbaugh Web site (**http://carbaugh.swlearning.com**) within "Instructor Resources." The slides offer professors flexibility in enhancing classroom lectures. Slides may be edited to meet individual needs. They also serve as a study tool for students.

Instructor's Manual

To assist instructors in the teaching of international economics, I have written an *Instructor's Manual with Test Bank* (ISBN: 0-324-22203-3) that accompanies the tenth edition. It contains (1) brief answers to end-of-chapter study questions; (2) multiple-choice questions for each chapter; and (3) true-false questions for each chapter. The *Instructor's Manual with Test Bank* is available for download for qualified instructors from the Carbaugh Web site (**http://carbaugh.swlearning.com**) under "Instructor Resources."

Study Guide

To accompany the tenth edition of the international economics text, Professor Jim Hanson of Willamette University has prepared a *Study Guide* (ISBN: 0-324-32020-5) for students. This guide reinforces key concepts by providing a review of the text's main topics and offering practice problems, true-false and multiple-choice questions, and short-answer questions.

InfoTrac College Edition

An InfoTrac College Edition 4-month subscription card is automatically packaged free with new copies of this text. With InfoTrac College Edition, journals like *Business Week*, *Fortune*, and *Forbes* are just a click away! InfoTrac College Edition provides students with anytime, anywhere access to 20 years' worth of full-text articles (*more than 10 million!*) from nearly *4,000* scholarly and popular sources! In addition to receiving the latest business news as reported in the popular business press, students also have access to many other journals, among them those that are particularly valuable to the economics discipline—including the *Economist (US)*, *American Economist*, *Economic Review*, and *Quarterly Journal of Economics*. For more information on InfoTrac College Edition, visit **http://infotrac.thomsonlearning.com/index.html**.

TextChoice

TextChoice is the home of Thomson Learning's online digital content. TextChoice provides the fastest, easiest way for you to create your own learning materials. South-Western's Economic Issues and Activities content database includes a wide variety of high-interest, current event/policy applications as well as classroom activities designed specifically to enhance economics courses. Choose just one reading, or many—even add your own material—to create an accompaniment to the textbook that is perfectly customized to your course. Contact your Thomson sales representative for more information.

Acknowledgments

I am pleased to acknowledge those who aided me in preparing the current and past editions of this textbook. Helpful suggestions and often-detailed reviews were provided by:

- Burton Abrams, University of Delaware
- Richard Adkisson, New Mexico State University
- Richard Anderson, Texas A&M
- Brad Andrew, Juniata College
- Richard Ault, Auburn University
- Robert Blecker, Stanford University
- John Charalambakis, Asbury College
- Charles Chittle, Bowling Green University
- Susan Christofferson, Philadelphia University
- Christopher Cornell, Fordham University
- Barbara Craig, Oberlin College
- Elanor Craig, University of Delaware
- Manjira Datta, Arizona State University
- Gopal Dorai, William Paterson College
- Veda Doss, Wingate University
- Seymour Douglas, Emory University
- Daniel Falkowski, Canisius College
- Patrice Franko, Colby College
- Norman Gharrity, Ohio Wesleyan University
- Sucharita Ghosh, University of Akron
- Thomas Grennes, North Carolina State University
- Jim Hanson, Willamette University
- Bassam Harik, Western Michigan University
- John Harter, Eastern Kentucky University
- Phyllis Herdendorf, Empire State College (SUNY)
- Pershing Hill, University of Alaska–Anchorage
- William Lynn Holmes, Temple University
- Robert Jerome, James Madison University
- Mohamad Khalil, Fairmont State College
- Wahhab Khandker, University of Wisconsin–La Crosse
- Jacqueline Khorassani, Marietta College
- Robin Klay, Hope College
- William Kleiner, Western Illinois University
- Anthony Koo, Michigan State University
- Faik Koray, Louisiana State University
- Peter Karl Kresl, Bucknell University
- Edhut Lehrer, Northwestern University
- Jim Levinsohn, University of Michigan
- Susan Linz, Michigan State University
- Andy Liu, Youngstown State University
- Mike Marks, Georgia College School of Business
- Al Maury, Texas A&I University
- Jose Mendez, Arizona State University
- John Muth, Regis University
- Mary Norris, Southern Illinois University
- John Olienyk, Colorado State University
- Terutomo Ozawa, Colorado State University
- Gary Pickersgill, California State University, Fullerton
- Chuck Rambeck, St. John's University
- James Richard, Regis University
- Malcolm Robinson, Thomas More College
- Daniel Ryan, Temple University
- Nindy Sandhu, California State University, Fullerton
- Anthony Scaperlanda, Northern Illinois University
- Ben Slay, Middlebury College (now at PlanEcon)

- Robert Stern, University of Michigan
- Howard Wachtel, American University
- Darwin Wassink, University of Wisconsin–Eau Claire
- Peter Wilamoski, Seattle University
- Harold Williams, Kent State University
- Hamid Zangeneh, Widener University

I would like to thank my colleagues at Central Washington University—Tim Dittmer, David Hedrick, Koushik Ghosh, Richard Mack, Peter Saunders, Chad Wassell—for their advice and help while I was preparing the manuscript. I am also indebted to Shirley Hood, who provided advice in the manuscript's preparation.

It has been a pleasure to work with my editors, Susan Smart and Mike Worls, who provided many valuable suggestions and assistance in seeing this edition to its completion. Special thanks is given to Libby Shipp, who orchestrated the production of this book in conjunction with Rebecca Gray, project manager at Rebecca Gray Design. I also appreciate the meticulous efforts that Rebecca Roby took in the copyediting of this textbook. Moreover, John Carey did a fine job in advertising and marketing the tenth edition. Finally, I am grateful to my students, as well as students at other universities, who provided helpful comments on the material contained in this new edition.

I would appreciate any comments, corrections, or suggestions that faculty or students wish to make so I can continue to improve this text in the years ahead. Please contact me! Thank you for permitting this text to evolve to the tenth edition.

Bob Carbaugh
Department of Economics
Central Washington University
Ellensburg, Washington 98926
Phone: (509) 963-3443
Fax: (509) 963-1992
E-mail: Carbaugh@cwu.edu

Introduction

chapter 1

The International Economy and Globalization

In today's world, no nation exists in economic isolation. All aspects of a nation's economy—its industries, service sectors, levels of income and employment, living standard—are linked to the economies of its trading partners. This linkage takes the form of international movements of goods and services, labor, business enterprise, investment funds, and technology. Indeed, national economic policies cannot be formulated without evaluating their probable impacts on the economies of other countries.

The high degree of **economic interdependence** among today's economies reflects the historical evolution of the world's economic and political order. At the end of World War II, the United States was economically and politically the most powerful nation in the world, a situation expressed in the saying, "When the United States sneezes, the economies of other nations catch a cold." But with the passage of time, the U.S. economy became increasingly integrated into the economic activities of foreign countries. The formation in the 1950s of the European Community (now known as the European Union), the rising importance of multinational corporations in the 1960s, the 1970s market power in world oil markets enjoyed by the Organization of Petroleum Exporting Countries (OPEC), and the creation of the euro at the turn of the twenty-first century all resulted in the evolution of the world community into a complicated system based on a growing interdependence among nations.

Recognizing that world economic interdependence is complex and its effects uneven, the economic community has made efforts toward international cooperation. Conferences devoted to global economic issues have explored the avenues through which cooperation could be fostered between the industrial and the developing nations. The efforts of the developing nations to reap larger gains from international trade and to participate more fully in international institutions have been hastened by the impact of the global recession on manufacturers, industrial inflation, and the burdens of high-priced energy.

In the past 50 years, the world's market economies have become increasingly integrated. Exports and imports as a share of national output have risen for most industrial nations, while foreign investment and international lending have expanded. This closer linkage of economies can be mutually advantageous for trading nations. It permits producers in each nation to take advantage of specialization and efficiencies of large-scale production. A nation can consume a wider variety of products at a cost less than that which could be achieved in the absence of trade. Despite these advantages, demands have grown for protection against imports. Protectionist pressures have been strongest during periods of rising unemployment caused by economic recession. Moreover, developing nations often maintain that the so-called liberalized trading system called for by industrial nations serves to keep the developing nations in poverty.

Economic interdependence also has direct consequences for a student taking an introductory course in international economics. As consumers, we can be affected by changes in the international values of currencies. Should the Japanese yen or British pound appreciate against the U.S. dollar, it would cost us more to purchase Japanese television sets or British automobiles. As investors, we might prefer to purchase Swiss securities if Swiss interest rates rise above U.S. levels. As members of the labor force, we might want to know whether the president plans to protect U.S. workers producing steel or automobiles from foreign competition.

In short, economic interdependence has become a complex issue in recent times, often resulting in strong and uneven impacts among nations and among sectors within a given nation. Business, labor, investors, and consumers all feel the repercussions of changing economic conditions and trade policies in other nations. Today's global economy requires cooperation on an international level to cope with the myriad issues and problems.

Globalization of Economic Activity

When listening to the news, we often hear about globalization. What does this term mean? **Globalization** is the process of greater interdependence among countries and their citizens. It consists of increased integration of product and resource markets across nations via trade, immigration, and foreign investment—that is, via international flows of goods and services, of people, and of investment such as equipment, factories, stocks, and bonds. It also includes noneconomic elements such as culture and the environment. Simply put, globaliza-

tion is political, technological, and cultural, as well as economic.

In terms of people's daily lives, globalization means that the residents of one country are more likely now than they were 50 years ago to consume the products of another country, to invest in another country, to earn income from other countries, to talk on the telephone to people in other countries, to visit other countries, to know that they are being affected by economic developments in other countries, and to know about developments in other countries.

What are the forces driving globalization?[1] The first and perhaps most profound influence is technological change. Since the industrial revolution of the late 1700s, technical innovations have led to an explosion of productivity and slashed transportation costs. The steam engine preceded the arrival of railways and the mechanization of a growing number of activities hitherto reliant on muscle power. Later discoveries and inventions such as electricity, the telephone, the automobile, container ships, and pipelines altered production, communication, and transportation in ways unimagined by earlier generations. More recently, rapid developments in computer information and communications technology have further shrunk the influence of time and geography on the capacity of individuals and enterprises to interact and transact around the world. As technical progress has extended the scope of what can be produced and where it can be produced, and advances in transport technology have continued to bring people and enterprises closer together, the boundary of tradable goods and services has been greatly extended.

Also, continuing liberalization of trade and investment has occurred as the result of multilateral trade negotiations. For example, tariffs in industrial countries have come down from high double digits in the 1940s to about 5 percent in the early 2000s. At the same time, most quotas on trade, except for those imposed for health, safety, or other public policy reasons, have been removed. Globalization has also been promoted by the widespread liberalization of investment

[1]World Trade Organization, *Annual Report*, 1998, pp. 33–36.

Trade Conflicts

Cloth Imports from China Threaten Italy's Textile Makers

The Italian textile industry illustrates the notion of globalization and how producers react to foreign competitive pressure.

For more than six centuries, the waters that flow through Biella, Italy, have provided cost savings for weavers, who use the fast-flowing rivers to power looms and clean wool. Located in the foothills of the snow-capped Alps, this region manufactures some of the most famous brands in Italian clothing, including Zegna and Cerruti. But now a competitor has emerged: China.

Home to more than half of Europe's textile producers—along with other low-tech manufacturers, such as shoes—Italy is in the path of advancing Chinese producers. The competitive threat of the Chinese threatens Biella and other towns that have contributed to the prosperity of Italy. Italian industries founded on craftmanship and quality, such as leather and cashmere, became the powerhouse of Europe, and for

years they ignored the threat from low-wage, foreign countries. But now they face intense price competition, as well as quality competition, as China slashes production costs and narrows the quality gap.

In the past, Biella's cloth producers relied on unity and shared efficiencies. However, fears of competition from the Chinese have scattered Biella's producers in different directions. Some have moved more production in-house to promote high quality and have laid off workers. Others have slashed costs by moving much of their production to low-wage countries in the Far East, including China. Analysts predict that in the future, firms will replace "Made in Italy" with "Created in Italy" labels to denote that their designs, if not production, continue to come from local craftspeople.

The American economy's size, flexibility, and enthusiasm for technology have permitted it to

transactions and the development of international financial markets. These factors have facilitated international trade through the more ready availability and affordability of financing.

Lower trade barriers and financial liberalization have allowed more and more companies to globalize production structures through investment abroad, which in turn has provided a further stimulus to trade. On the technology side, increased information flows and the greater tradability of goods and services have profoundly influenced production location decisions. Businesses are increasingly able to locate different components of their production processes in various countries and regions and still maintain a single corporate identity. As firms subcontract part of their production processes to their affiliates or other enterprises abroad, jobs, technologies, capital, and skills are transferred around the globe.

Fewer and fewer products can be produced competitively today solely on the basis of national inputs. For the production of a particular car, for example, manufactured by one of the large U.S. auto firms, no fewer than nine countries are

involved in some aspect of production, marketing, and selling. Thirty percent of the car's value goes to South Korea for assembly, 17.5 percent to Japan for components and advanced technology, 7.5 percent to Germany for design, 4 percent to Taiwan and Singapore for minor parts, 2.5 percent to the United Kingdom for advertising and marketing services, and 1.5 percent to Ireland and Barbados for data processing. This means that only 37 percent of the production value of this "American" car is generated in the United States.

How significant is production sharing in world trade? Researchers have estimated production sharing by calculating the share of components and parts in world trade. They conclude that global production sharing accounts for about 30 percent of world trade in manufactured goods. Moreover, trade in components and parts is growing significantly faster than trade in finished products, highlighting the increasing interdependence of countries through production and trade.[2]

[2]A. Yeats, *Just How Big Is Global Production Sharing?* World Bank, Policy Research Working Paper No. 1871, 1998, Washington, DC.

absorb the impact of China's arrival, through relocating production or exporting more goods to China. For Italy, China's emergence is more difficult. Inflexible labor laws limit the ability of Italian firms to fire workers and shift jobs abroad. Also, most Italian firms are family-run outfits with fewer than100 employees. Moving to distant countries is not a possibility for many. And Italian firms generally believe that what makes their products attractive, whether a Gucci bag or a Versace dress, is that they have "Made in Italy" tags.

Europe felt the first competitive threat from China in the 1980s, when it increased production of silks, a traditional Chinese product. The resulting excess supply drove some European companies out of business, but many buyers rejected the Chinese silks for their inferior quality. The Italian companies sustained a decline in sales and then prospered. At the turn of the century, the Chinese

returned with much higher quality, placing additional competitive pressure on the Italians.

To survive, Bella textile makers improved operating efficiencies and informed customers of the quality and standards behind their textiles, including better working conditions and environmental practices at their factories, compared with those in China. Some Italian producers revised up to 70 percent of their product line in a period of two years, introducing new blends, dyes, and fibers. In the past, such a modification would have taken a decade. Rapid changes of product line are intended to restrict the ability of Chinese firms from copying their product. It remains to be seen whether the family-run textile producers of Italy will survive the competitive attack of China.

Source: "Threat from China Starts to Unravel Italy's Cloth Trade," *The Wall Street Journal*, December 17, 2003, pp. A–1 and A–8.

Waves of Globalization

In the past two decades, there has been pronounced global economic integration. Economic integration occurs through trade, labor migration, and capital (investment) flows such as corporation stocks and government securities. Let us consider the major waves of globalization that have occurred in recent history.[3]

First Wave of Globalization: 1870–1914

The first wave of global integration occurred from 1870 to 1914. It was sparked by decreases in tariff barriers and new technologies that resulted in declining transportation costs, such as the shift from sail to steamships and the advent of railways. Therefore, exports as a share of world income nearly doubled to about 8 percent while per capita incomes, which had risen by 0.5 percent per

year in the previous 50 years, rose by an annual average of 1.3 percent. The countries that actively participated in globalization, such as the United States, became the richest countries in the world.

However, the first wave of globalization was brought to an end by World War I. Also, during the Great Depression of the 1930s, governments responded by protectionism: a futile attempt to enact tariffs on imports to shift demand into their domestic markets, thus promoting sales for domestic companies and jobs for domestic workers. For the world economy, increasing protectionism caused exports as a share of national income to fall to about 5 percent, therefore undoing 80 years of technological progress in transportation.

Second Wave of Globalization: 1945–1980

The horrors of the retreat into nationalism provided renewed incentive for internationalism following World War II. The result was a second wave of globalization that took place from 1945 to 1980.

[3]This section draws from World Bank, *Globalization, Growth and Poverty: Building an Inclusive World Economy*, 2001.

Falling transportation costs continued to foster increased trade. Also, nations persuaded governments to cooperate to decrease trade barriers they had previously established.

However, trade liberalization discriminated both in terms of which countries participated and which products were included. By 1980, trade between developed countries in manufactured goods had been largely freed of barriers. However, barriers facing developing countries had been eliminated for only those agricultural products that did not compete with agriculture in developed countries. For manufactured goods, developing countries faced sizable barriers. For developed countries, however, the slashing of trade barriers between them greatly increased the exchange of manufactured goods, thus helping to raise the incomes of developed countries relative to the rest.

The second wave of globalization introduced a new kind of trade: rich country specialization in manufacturing niches that gained productivity through **agglomeration economies**. Increasingly, firms clustered together, some producing the same product and others connected by vertical linkages. Japanese auto companies, for example, became famous for insisting that their parts manufacturers locate within a short distance of the main assembly plant. For companies such as Toyota and Honda, this decreases the costs of transport, coordination, monitoring, and contracting. Although agglomeration economies benefit those in the clusters, they are bad news for those left out. A region may be uncompetitive simply because not enough firms have chosen to locate there. Thus, a divided world may emerge, in which a network of manufacturing firms is clustered in some high-wage region, while wages in the remaining regions stay low. Firms will not shift to a new location until the discrepancy in production costs becomes sufficiently large to compensate for the loss of agglomeration economies.

During the second wave of globalization, most developing countries did not participate in the growth of global manufacturing and services trade. The combination of continuing trade barriers in developed countries, and unfavorable investment climates and antitrade policies in developing countries, confined them to dependence on agricultural and natural-resource products.

Although the second globalization wave succeeded in increasing per capita incomes within the developed countries, developing countries as a group were being left behind. World inequality fueled the developing countries' distrust of the existing international trading system, which seemed to favor developed countries. Therefore, developing countries became increasingly vocal in their desire to be granted better access to developed-country markets for manufactured goods and services, thus fostering additional jobs and rising incomes for their people.

Latest Wave of Globalization

The latest wave of globalization, which began about 1980, is distinctive. First, a large number of developing countries broke into world markets for manufacturers. Second, other developing countries became increasingly marginalized in the world economy and realized decreasing incomes and increasing poverty. Third, international capital movements, which were modest during the second wave of globalization, again became significant.

Of major significance for third wave globalization is that some developing countries succeeded for the first time in harnessing their labor abundance to provide them a competitive advantage in labor-intensive manufactures. Examples of developing countries that have shifted into manufactures trade include China, Bangladesh, Malaysia, Turkey, Mexico, Hungary, Indonesia, Sri Lanka, Thailand, and the Philippines. This shift is partly due to tariff cuts that developed countries have made on imports of manufactured goods. Also, many developing countries liberalized barriers to foreign investment, which encouraged firms such as Ford Motor Company to locate assembly plants within their borders. Moreover, technological progress in transportation and communications permitted developing countries to participate in international production networks. However, the dramatic increase in exports of manufactures from developing countries has contributed to protectionist policies in developed countries. With so many developing countries emerging as important trading countries, reaching further agreements on multilateral trade liberalization has become more complicated.

Although the world has become more globalized in terms of international trade and capital flows compared to 100 years ago, the world is less globalized when it comes to labor flows. The United States, for example, had a very liberal immigration policy in the late 1800s and early 1900s, and large flows of people entered the country, primarily from Europe. As a large country with a lot of room to absorb newcomers, the United States also attracted foreign investment throughout much of this period, which meant that high levels of migration went hand in hand with high and rising wages. Since World War I, however, immigration has been a disputed topic in the United States, and restrictions on immigration have tightened. In contrast to the largely European immigration in the 1870 to 1910 globalization wave, contemporary immigration into the United States comes largely from Asia and Latin America.

Another aspect of the most recent wave of globalization is foreign outsourcing, in which certain aspects of a product's manufacture are performed in more than one country. As travel and communication got easier in the 1970s and 1980s, manufacturing increasingly moved wherever costs were lowest. For example, U.S. companies shifted the assembly of autos and the production of shoes, electronics, and toys to low-wage developing countries. This resulted in job losses for blue-collar workers producing these goods and cries for the passage of laws to restrict outsourcing.

When passengers travel in a Boeing 777, for example, they are riding in a global jetliner. About 35 percent of its parts are manufactured in foreign nations, as seen in Table 1.1. The same applies to the jetliners produced by Airbus. Airbus has more than 1,500 suppliers in 27 countries, and cooperative agreements exist with aerospace industries in 19 countries. An estimated 100,000 employees internationally are involved in production for Airbus' program. According to Airbus, about 40 percent of an Airbus A330 is provided by parts coming from the United States. Thousands of U.S. citizens earn their livelihoods working for more than 800 Airbus suppliers in 40 states.

By the 2000s, the Information Age resulted in the foreign outsourcing of white-collar work. Today, many companies' locations hardly matter. Work is connected through digitization, the Internet, and high-speed data networks around the world. Companies now can send office work anywhere, and that means places like India, Ireland, and the Philippines, where for $1.50 to $2 per hour companies can hire college graduates to do

Visit EconNews Online
International Trade

TABLE 1.1

Suppliers of Components for the Boeing 777

Boeing	U.S. Suppliers	Japanese Suppliers	Other International Suppliers*	
Nose section	Fixed trailing edge	Cargo doors	Radome	Aileron
Trailing edge panels	Floor beams	Fuselage panels	Dorsal fin	Wingtip assembly
Vertical fin	Spoilers	Wing-to-body-fairing	Rudder	Main landing gear
Horizontal stabilizer	Inboard flaps	In-spar ribs	Elevator	Engine
Fixed leading edge	Leading edge flaps	Wing center section	Flaperon	Nose landing gear
Wing box	Engine	Main landing gear doors	Flap support fairings	Nose landing gear doors
Struts and fairings		Passenger doors	Outboard flap	

*France, Canada, China, Italy, Australia, South Korea, United Kingdom.

Source: Boeing News Releases. See also Airbus Company of North America, Inc., *The Last Frontier?* (Herndon, VA, 1998), and *About Airbus* at http://www.airbus.com.

the jobs that could go for $12 to $18 in the United States. Simply put, a new round of globalization is sending upscale jobs offshore, including accounting, chip design, engineering, basic research, and financial analysis, as seen in Table 1.2. Analysts estimate that foreign outsourcing can allow companies to reduce costs of a given service 30 percent to 50 percent.

For example, Boeing uses aeronautics specialists in Russia to design luggage bins and wing parts on its jetliners. Having a master's degree or doctorate in math or aeronautics, these specialists are paid $650 per month in contrast to a monthly salary of $6,000 for an American counterpart. Similarly, engineers in China and India, earning $1,000 a month, develop chips for Texas Instruments and Intel; their American counterparts are paid $7,000 a month. However, companies are likely to keep crucial research and development and the bulk of office operations close to home. Many jobs can't go anywhere because they require face-to-face contact with customers. Economists note that the vast majority of the jobs in the United States consist of services such as retail, restaurants and hotels, personal care services, and the like. These services are necessarily produced and consumed locally, and thus cannot be offshored.

Besides saving money, foreign outsourcing can enable companies to do things they simply couldn't do before. For example, a consumer product company in the United States found it impractical to chase down tardy customers buying less than $1,000 worth of goods. When this service was run in India, however, the cost dropped so much the company could profitably follow up on bills as low as $100.

Although the Internet makes it easier for U.S. companies to remain competitive in an increasingly brutal global marketplace, is foreign outsourcing good for white-collar workers? A case can be made that Americans will benefit from this process. In the 1990s, U.S. companies had to import hundreds of thousands of immigrants to ease engineering shortages. Now, by sending routine service and engineering tasks to nations with a surplus of educated workers, U.S. labor and capital can be shifted to higher-value industries and cutting-edge research and development.

However, a question remains: What happens if displaced white-collar workers can't find greener pastures? The truth is that the rise of the global knowledge industry is so recent that most economists have not begun to figure out the implications. But people in developing nations like India see foreign outsourcing as a bonus because it helps spread wealth from rich nations to poor nations. Among its many other virtues, the Internet may turn out to be a great equalizer. Outsourcing will be further discussed at the end of Chapter 2.

TABLE 1.2

Globalization Goes White Collar

U.S. Company	Number of Workers and Country	Type of Work Moving
Accenture	5,000 in the Philippines	Accounting, software, office work
Conseco	1,700 in India	Insurance claim processing
Delta Air Lines	6,000 in India, Philippines	Airline reservations, customer service
Fluor	700 in Philippines	Architectural blueprints
General Electric	20,000 in India	Finance, information technology
Intel	3,000 in India	Chip design, tech support
Microsoft	500 in China, India	Software design
Philips	700 in China	Consumer electronics, R&D
Procter & Gamble	800 in Philippines, China	Accounting, tech support

Source: Drawn from "Is Your Job Next?" *Business Week*, February 3, 2003, pp. 50–60.

The United States as an Open Economy

It is generally agreed that the U.S. economy has become increasingly integrated into the world economy (become an open economy) in recent decades. Such integration involves a number of dimensions, including trade of goods and services, financial markets, the labor force, ownership of production facilities, and dependence on imported materials.

Trade Patterns

To appreciate the globalization of the U.S. economy, go to a local supermarket. Almost any supermarket doubles as an international food bazaar. Alongside potatoes from Idaho and beef from Texas, stores display melons from Mexico, olive oil from Italy, coffee from Colombia, cinnamon from Sri Lanka, wine and cheese from France, and bananas from Costa Rica. Table 1.3 shows a global fruit basket that is available for American consumers.

The grocery store isn't the only place Americans indulge their taste for foreign-made products. We buy cameras and cars from Japan, shirts from Bangladesh, videocassette recorders from South Korea, paper products from Canada, and fresh flowers from Ecuador. We get oil from Kuwait, steel from China, computer programs from India, and semiconductors from Taiwan.

Most Americans are well aware of our desire to import, but they may not realize that the United States ranks as the world's greatest exporter, selling personal computers, bulldozers, jetliners, financial services, movies, and thousands of other products to just about all parts of the globe. Simply put, international trade and investment are facts of everyday life.

As a rough measure of the importance of international trade in a nation's economy, we can look at the nation's exports and imports as a percentage of its gross domestic product (GDP). This ratio is known as **openness**.

$$\text{Openness} = \frac{(\text{Exports} + \text{Imports})}{\text{GDP}}$$

Table 1.4 on page 10 shows measures of openness for selected nations as of 2002. In that year, the United States exported 9 percent of its GDP while imports were 13 percent of GDP; the openness of the U.S. economy to trade thus equaled 22 percent. Although the U.S. economy is significantly tied to international trade, this tendency is even more striking for many smaller nations, as seen in the table. Simply put, large countries tend to be less reliant on international trade because many of their companies can attain an optimal production

TABLE 1.3

The Fruits of Free Trade: A Global Fruit Basket

On a trip to the grocery store, consumers can find goods from all over the globe.

Apples	New Zealand	Limes	El Salvador
Apricots	China	Oranges	Australia
Bananas	Ecuador	Pears	South Korea
Blackberries	Canada	Pineapples	Costa Rica
Blueberries	Chile	Plums	Guatemala
Coconuts	Philippines	Raspberries	Mexico
Grapefruit	Bahamas	Strawberries	Poland
Grapes	Peru	Tangerines	South Africa
Kiwifruit	Italy	Watermelons	Honduras
Lemons	Argentina		

Source: "The Fruits of Free Trade," *Annual Report*, Federal Reserve Bank of Dallas, 2002, p. 3.

TABLE 1.4

Exports and Imports of Goods and Services as a Percentage of Gross Domestic Product (GDP), 2002

Country	Exports as Percentage of GDP	Imports as Percentage of GDP	Exports Plus Imports as Percentage of GDP
Netherlands	53	46	99
Canada	37	33	70
Germany	31	25	56
South Korea	27	26	53
Norway	31	18	49
France	22	21	43
United Kingdom	18	21	39
United States	9	13	22
Japan	10	8	18

Source: International Monetary Fund, *International Financial Statistics*, January 2004, and *Economic Report of the President*, 2004.

size without having to export to foreign nations. Therefore, small countries tend to have higher measures of openness than do large ones.

Figure 1.1 shows the openness of the U.S. economy from 1890 to 2002. One significant trend is that the United States became less open to international trade between 1890 and 1950. Openness was relatively high in the late 1800s due to the rise in world trade resulting from technological improvements in transportation (steamships) and communications (trans-Atlantic telegraph cable). However, two world wars and the Great Depression of the 1930s caused the United States to reduce its dependance on trade, partly for national security reasons and partly to protect its home industries from import competition. Following World War II, the United States and other countries negotiated reductions in trade barriers, which contributed to rising world trade. Technological improvements in shipping and communications also bolstered trade and the increasing openness of the U.S. economy.

The relative importance of international trade for the United States has increased by about 50 percent during the past century, as seen in Figure 1.1. But a significant fact is hidden by these data. In 1890, most U.S. trade was in raw materials and agricultural products;

manufactured goods and services dominate U.S. trade flows today. Therefore, American producers of manufactured products are more affected by foreign competition than they were a hundred years ago.

The significance of international trade for the U.S. economy is even more noticeable when specific products are considered. For example, we would have fewer personal computers without imported components, no aluminum if we did not import bauxite, no tin cans without imported tin, and no chrome bumpers if we did not import chromium. Students taking an 8 A.M. course in international economics might sleep through the class (do you really believe this?) if we did not import coffee or tea. Moreover, many of the products we buy from foreigners would be much more costly if we were dependent on our domestic production.

With which nations does the United States conduct trade? As seen in Table 1.5, Canada, Mexico, Japan, and China head the list. Other leading trading partners of the United States include Germany, France, Italy, and the Netherlands.

Labor and Capital

Besides trade of goods and services, movements in factors of production are a measure of economic

FIGURE 1.1

Openness of the U.S. Economy, 1890–2002

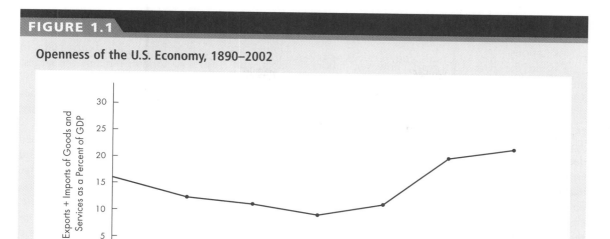

The figure shows that for the United States the importance of international trade has increased by about 50 percent from 1890 to the early 2000s.

Source: U.S. Census Bureau, Foreign Trade Division, *U.S. Trade in Goods and Services, 1960–2002* at http://www.census.gov/foreign-trade/statistics, and *Economic Report of the President, 2002.*

TABLE 1.5

Leading Trading Partners of the United States, 2002

Country	Value of U.S. Exports (in Billions of Dollars)	Value of U.S. Imports (in Billions of Dollars)	Total Value of Trade (in Billions of Dollars)
Canada	160.8	213.9	374.7
Mexico	97.5	136.1	233.6
Japan	51.4	124.6	176.0
China	22.1	133.5	155.6
Germany	26.6	63.9	90.5
France	19.3	29.0	48.3
Italy	10.1	25.4	35.5
Netherlands	18.3	10.3	28.6
Venezuela	4.5	15.8	20.3
Australia	13.1	6.8	19.9
Belgium/Luxembourg	13.8	4.4	18.2

Source: U.S. Department of Commerce, Bureau of Economic Analysis, *U.S. Transactions by Area* at http://www.bea.gov. See also International Monetary Fund, *Direction of Trade Statistics.*

integration. As nations become more interdependent, labor and capital should move more freely across nations.

During the past 100 years, however, labor mobility has not risen for the United States. In 1900, about 14 percent of the U.S. population was foreign born. From the 1920s to the 1960s, however, the United States sharply curtailed immigration. This resulted in the foreign born U.S. population declining to 6 percent of the total population. During the 1960s, the restrictions were liberalized and the flow of immigrants increased. By 2003, about 12 percent of the U.S. population was foreign born while foreigners made up about 14 percent of the labor force. People from Latin America accounted for about half of this figure while Asians accounted for another quarter. These immigrants contributed to economic growth in the United States by taking jobs in labor-scarce regions and filling the types of jobs native workers often shun.

Although labor mobility has not risen for the United States in recent decades, the country has become increasingly tied to the rest of the world in capital (investment) flows. Foreign ownership of U.S. financial assets has risen since the 1960s. During the 1970s, the oil-producing nations of the Middle East recycled many of their oil dollars by making investments in U.S. financial markets. The 1980s also witnessed major flows of investment funds to the United States as Japan and other nations, with dollars accumulated from trade surpluses with the United States, acquired U.S. financial assets, businesses, and real estate. Consuming more than it was producing, by the late 1980s, the United States became a net borrower from the rest of the world to pay for the difference. Increasing concerns were raised about the interest cost of this debt to the U.S. economy and about the impact of this debt burden on the living standards of future U.S. generations.

The process of globalization has also increased international banking. The average daily turnover in today's foreign-exchange market (where currencies are bought and sold) is estimated at more than $1.5 trillion, compared to $205 billion in 1986. The global trading day begins in Tokyo and Sydney and, in a virtually unbroken 24-hour cycle, moves around the world through Singapore and Hong Kong to Europe and finally across the United States before being picked up again in Japan and Australia. London remains the largest center for foreign-exchange trading, followed by the United States; significant volumes of currencies are also traded in the Asian centers, Germany, France, Scandinavia, Canada, and elsewhere.

In commercial banking, U.S. banks developed worldwide branch networks in the 1960s and 1970s for loans, payments, and foreign-exchange trading. Foreign banks also increased their presence in the United States throughout the 1980s and early 1990s, reflecting the multinational population base of the United States, the size and importance of U.S. markets, and the role of the U.S. dollar as an international medium of exchange and reserve currency. Today, more than 250 foreign banks operate in the United States; in particular, Japanese banks have been the dominant group of foreign banks operating in the United States. Like commercial banks, securities firms have also globalized their operations. In the 1970s, U.S. securities firms began to establish operations in Europe and Tokyo. Table 1.6 profiles the world's top public financial companies.

By the 1980s, U.S. government securities were traded on virtually a 24-hour basis. Foreign investors purchased U.S. treasury bills, notes, and bonds, and many desired to trade during their own working hours rather than those of the United States. Primary dealers of U.S. government securities opened offices in such locations as Tokyo and London. Stock markets became increasingly internationalized, with companies listing their stocks on different exchanges throughout the world. Financial futures markets also spread throughout the world.

Why Is Globalization Important?

Because of trade, individuals, firms, regions, and nations can specialize in the production of things they do well and use the earnings from these activities to purchase from others those items for which

TABLE 1.6

The World's Largest Public Financial Companies,* 2002

Company (Country)	Assets (Millions of Dollars)
Mizuho Financial Group (Japan)	$1,128,174
Citigroup (U.S.)	1,097,190
Allianz (Germany)	893,722
Fannie Mae (U.S.)	887,515
Sumitomo Mitsui Financial Group (Japan)	880,497
UBS (Switzerland)	852,618
Deutsche Bank (Germany)	791,348
HSBC Holdings (U.K.)	759,246
J.P. Morgan Chase (U.S.)	758,800
ING Group (Netherlands)	751,400

*Banks and financial-services firms.

Source: Data taken from "World Business," *The Wall Street Journal,* September 23, 2003, p. R–10.

they are high-cost producers. Therefore, trading partners can produce a larger joint output and achieve a higher standard of living than would otherwise be possible. Economists refer to this as the law of comparative advantage, which will be further discussed in Chapter 2.

According to the **law of comparative advantage**, the citizens of each nation can gain by spending more of their time and resources doing those things where they have a relative advantage. If a good or service can be obtained more economically through trade, it makes sense to trade for it instead of producing it domestically. It is a mistake to focus on whether a good is going to be produced domestically or abroad. The central issue is how the available resources can be used to obtain each good at the lowest possible cost. When trading partners use more of their time and resources producing things they do best, they are able to produce a larger joint output, which provides the source for mutual gain.

International trade also results in gains from the competitive process. Competition is essential to both innovation and efficient production.

International competition helps keep domestic producers on their toes and provides them with a strong incentive to improve the quality of their products. Also, international trade usually weakens monopolies. As countries open their markets, national monopoly producers face competition from foreign firms.

For example, during the 1950s General Motors (GM) was responsible for 60 percent of all passenger cars produced in the United States. Although GM officials praised the firm's immense size for providing economies of scale in individual plant operations, skeptics were concerned about the monopoly power resulting from GM's dominance of the auto market. Some argued that GM should be broken up into several independent companies to inject more competition into the market. Today, however, stiff foreign competition has resulted in GM's share of the market currently standing at less than 30 percent. Also, foreign competition has forced GM to work hard to improve the quality of its vehicles. Therefore, the reliability of the automobiles and light trucks available to American consumers—including those produced by domestic manufacturers—is almost certainly higher than would have been the case in the absence of competition from abroad.

Not only do open economies have more competition, but they also have more firm turnover. Being exposed to competition around the globe may result in high-cost domestic producers exiting the market. If these firms were less productive than remaining firms, then their exits represent productivity improvements for the industry. The increase in exits is only part of the adjustment. The other side is that there are new firms entering the market, unless there are significant barriers. With this comes more labor market churning as workers formerly employed by obsolete firms must now find jobs in emerging ones. However, inadequate education and training may make some workers unemployable for emerging firms creating new jobs we often can't yet imagine. This is probably the key reason why workers often find globalization to be controversial. Simply put, the higher turnover of firms is an important source of the dynamic benefits of globalization. In general, dying firms

Are Detroit's Big Three Heading for a Crash?

U.S. Automobile Market: Market Shares: January 2004

Manufacturer	Percentage Share of U.S. Market	Manufacturer	Percentage Share of U.S. Market
General Motors*	26.4	Hyundai	2.1
Ford*	20.4	Mazda	1.7
DaimlerChrysler*	14.4	Mitsubishi	1.4
Toyota*	12.8	Subaru*	1.2
Honda*	8.0	Suzuki*	0.5
Nissan*	6.4		

*Vehicles built in the United States, Canada, and Mexico for sale in the United States.

Source: Data taken from *The Wall Street Journal*, February 4, 2004 p. A–9. This table appears in *The Wall Street Journal* during the first week of the month, in section A or B.

The history of the U.S. automobile industry can be divided into the following distinct eras: the emergence of Ford Motor Company as a dominant producer in the early 1900s; the shift of dominance to General Motors in the 1920s; and the rise of foreign competition in the 1970s.

As a share of the U.S. market, foreign nameplate autos expanded from 0.4 percent in the late 1940s to more than 25 percent by the 1990s. Foreign producers have been effective competitors for the U.S. auto oligopoly, which used to be largely immune from market pressures (such as costs and product quality). Increased competitiveness has forced U.S. auto companies to alter price policies, production methods, work rules, and product quality. Japanese firms are the largest source of the competition.

The competitive success of foreign car makers in the U.S. market has led to the deconcentration of the domestic industry. Although the Big Three (GM, Ford, DaimlerChrysler) controlled more than 90 percent of the U.S. market in the 1960s, their collective market share has greatly diminished because of foreign competition. As seen in the table, in 2004, the Big Three accounted for about 61 percent of U.S. auto sales. For decades,

have falling productivity, and new firms tend to increase their productivity over time.

International trade may also help stabilize a company. Consider the case of Eaton, Inc., a U.S. manufacturer of truck and auto components. Foreign competition has forced the firm to become nimble and productive. By the early 2000s, the firm paid out as much as 4 percent more each year for labor and materials, but raised prices by less than 1 percent. To remain in business, the firm had to continue driving down its overall costs through new technologies and man-

agement methods. In effect, foreign competition resulted in the firm's absorbing inflation.

Another example is Invacare Corporation, an Ohio-based manufacturer of wheelchairs and other health-care equipment. For the wheelchairs it sells in Germany, the electronic controllers come from the firm's New Zealand factories; the design is largely American; and the final assembly is done in Germany, with parts shipped from the United States, France, and the United Kingdom. By purchasing parts and components worldwide, Invacare can resist suppliers' efforts to increase foreign manufacturers emphasized the small-car segment of the market; their impact on U.S. auto-company deconcentration has been greatest in this segment. Now, Detroit faces ruthless competition on the lucrative turf of pickup trucks, minivans, and sport-utility vehicles.

Perhaps the biggest problem is that the Big Three is saddled with large unfunded pension obligations and health-care costs for hundreds of thousands of retirees, while their own employee base is shrinking. Almost 500,000 retirees now collect benefits from the Big Three, compared with just 300,000 active employees. Of Ford's $2.8 billion health bill, 70 percent goes to retirees. Japanese auto companies have dodged such burdens by generally employing younger, nonunionized workers. For GM, about $1,200 of each car it sold in 2003 went to pay for health care alone. That is money that GM can't pour into features that make vehicles more competitive—everything from fancy engines to smooth suspensions and tailored interiors.

As competition in the auto market has become truly international, it is highly unlikely that GM, Ford, and DaimlerChrysler will ever regain the dominance that once allowed them to dictate which vehicles Americans bought and at what prices. There is speculation that when the day of reckoning comes, two choices will emerge: bankruptcy and bailout. Some policy makers will desire market forces to guide the

evolution to an auto industry that is dramatically downsized and predominantly Japanese owned. They would tolerate a bankruptcy or two, permitting the severing of contractual obligations to retirees, and also extensive production outsourcing to China and other countries where costs are much lower.

But other policy makers will favor sizable government aid conditioned on substantial corporate restructuring. The Big Three and the unions would have to agree to shut down many more plants and to increase their investment in more competitive technologies. Health-care benefits for current workers and obligations to retirees would be gradually reduced, but far less radically than in the case of bankruptcy. Considerable foreign outsourcing will be permitted, but within limits. In return, the federal government would provide certain tax breaks, loan guarantees, and protection from imports, and assume some pension and health-care obligations.

The global marketplace requires players to be hypercompetitive. With or without Washington's help, the restructuring that may lie ahead for Detroit could be deep and painful.

Source: Jeffrey Garten, "Detroit's Big Three Are Heading for a Pileup," *Business Week*, September 1, 2003, p. 24; "America's Car Industry: Still Power in the Union?" *The Economist*, August 20, 2003, p. 45.

prices for aluminum, steel, rubber, and other materials. By selling its products in 80 nations, Invacare can maintain a more stable workforce in Ohio than if it were completely dependent on the U.S. market; if sales decline anytime in the United States, Invacare has an ace up its sleeve: exports.

However, globalization can make the domestic economy vulnerable to disturbances initiated overseas. For example, the economic downturn that occurred in East Asia from 1997 to 1999 resulted in declining exports for Boeing, Bethlehem Steel, and other American companies. U.S. financial markets

also felt the impact of East Asia's downturn. Major banks, such as Citibank and Chase Manhattan, suffered losses on loans made in East Asia.

Common Fallacies of International Trade

Despite the gains derived from international trade, fallacies abound.[4] One fallacy is that trade

[4]*Twelve Myths of International Trade*, U.S. Senate, Joint Economic Committee, June 1999, pp. 2–4.

is a zero-sum activity—if one trading party gains, the other most lose. In fact, just the opposite occurs—both partners gain from trade. Consider the case of trade between Brazil and the United States. These countries are able to produce a larger joint output when Brazilians supply coffee and Americans supply wheat. The larger production will make it possible for Brazilians to gain by using revenues from their coffee sales to purchase American wheat. At the same time, Americans will gain by doing the opposite, by using revenues from their wheat sales to purchase Brazilian coffee. In turn, the larger joint output provides the basis for the mutual gains achieved by both. By definition, if countries specialize in what they are comparatively best at producing, they must import goods and services that other countries produce best. The notion that imports are "bad" while exports are "good"—popular among politicians and the media—is incorrect.

Another fallacy is that imports reduce employment and act as a drag on the economy, while exports promote growth and employment. This fallacy stems from a failure to consider the link between imports and exports. For example, American imports of German machinery provide Germans with the purchasing power to buy our computer software. If Germans are unable to sell as much to Americans, then they will have fewer dollars with which to buy from Americans. Thus, when the volume of U.S. imports decreases, there will be an automatic secondary effect—Germans will have fewer dollars with which to purchase American goods. Therefore, sales, production, and employment will decrease in the U.S. export industries.

Finally, people often feel that tariffs, quotas, and other import restrictions will save jobs and promote a higher level of employment. Like the previous fallacy, this one also stems from the failure to recognize that a reduction in imports does not occur in isolation. When we restrict foreigners from selling to us, we are also restricting their ability to obtain the dollars needed to buy from us. Thus, trade restrictions that reduce the volume of imports will also reduce exports. As a result, jobs saved by the restrictions tend to be offset to jobs lost due to a reduction in exports.

Why don't we use tariffs and quotas to restrict trade among the 50 states? After all, think of all the jobs that are lost when, for example, Michigan "imports" oranges from Florida, apples from Washington, wheat from Kansas, and cotton from Georgia. All of these products could be produced in Michigan. However, the residents of Michigan generally find it cheaper to "import" these commodities. Michigan gains by using its resources to produce and "export" automobiles, and other goods it can produce economically, and then using the sales revenue to "import" goods that would be expensive to produce in Michigan. Indeed, most people recognize that free trade among the 50 states is a major source of prosperity for each of the states. Similarly, most recognize that "imports" from other states do not destroy jobs—at least not for long.

The implications are identical for trade among nations. Free trade among the 50 states promotes prosperity; so, too, does free trade among nations. Of course, sudden removal of trade barriers might harm producers and workers in protected industries. It may be costly to transfer quickly the protected resources to other, more productive activities. Gradual removal of the barriers would minimize this shock effect and the accompanying cost of relocation.

Does Free Trade Apply to Cigarettes?

When President George W. Bush pressured South Korea in 2001 to cease from imposing a 40 percent tariff on foreign cigarettes, administration officials said the case had nothing to do with public health. Instead, it was a case against protecting the domestic industry from foreign competition. However, critics maintained that with tobacco nothing is that simple. They recognized that free trade, as a rule, increases competition, lowers prices, and makes better products available to consumers, leading to higher consumption. Usually, that's a good thing. With cigarettes, however, the result can be more smoking, disease, and death.

About 4 million people globally die each year from lung cancer, emphysema, and other smoking-related diseases, making cigarettes the largest single cause of preventable death. By 2030, the annual number of fatalities could hit 10 million, according to the World Health Organization. That has antismoking activists and even some economists arguing that cigarettes are not normal goods but are, in fact, "bads" that require their own set of regulations. They contend that the benefits of free trade do not apply for cigarettes: They should be treated as an exception to trade rules.

This view is finding favor with some governments, as well. In recent talks of the World Health Organization, dealing with a global tobacco-control treaty, a range of nations expressed support for provisions to emphasize antismoking measures over free-trade rules. The United States, however, opposed such measures. In fact, the United States, which at home has sued tobacco companies for falsifying cigarettes' health risks, has promoted freer trade in cigarettes. For example, President Bill Clinton demanded a sharp reduction in Chinese tariffs, including those on tobacco, in return for supporting China's entry into the World Trade Organization. Those moves, combined with free-trade pacts that have decreased tariffs and other barriers to trade, have helped stimulate international sales of cigarettes.

The United States, under President Clinton and then President Bush, has said it challenges only rules imposed to aid local cigarette makers, not nondiscriminatory measures to protect public health. The United States opposed South Korea's decision to impose a 40 percent tariff on imported cigarettes because it was discriminatory and aimed at protecting domestic producers and not at protecting the health and safety of the Korean people, according to U.S. trade officials. However, antismoking activists maintain that's a false distinction: Anything that makes cigarettes more widely available at a lower price is harmful to public health. However, cigarette makers oppose limiting trade in tobacco. They maintain that there is no basis for creating new regulations that weaken the principle of open trade protected by the World Trade Organization.

Current trade rules permit countries to enact measures to protect the health and safety of their citizens, as long as all goods are treated equally, tobacco companies argue. For example, a trade-

dispute panel notified Thailand that, although it could not prohibit foreign cigarettes, it could ban advertisements for both domestic and foreign-made smokes. But tobacco-control activists worry that the rules could be used to stop governments from imposing antismoking measures. They contend that special products need special rules, pointing to hazardous chemicals and weapons as goods already exempt from regular trade policies. Cigarettes kill more people every year than AIDS. Antitobacco activists think it's time for health concerns to be of primary importance in the case of smoking, too.

International Competitiveness

International competitiveness is a hot issue these days. Intense debate has focused on how firms based in a particular nation can create and maintain competitiveness against the world's leaders in a particular industry. Let us consider the meaning of competitiveness and how it applies to firms, industries, and nations.[5]

Firm (Industry) Competitiveness

Competitiveness refers to the extent to which the goods of a firm or industry can compete in the marketplace; this competitiveness depends on the relative prices and qualities of products. If Toyota can produce a better automobile at a lower price than General Motors, it is said to be more competitive; if the U.S. steel industry can produce better steel at a lower price than Brazil's steel industry, it is said to be more competitive. Governments are concerned about the competitiveness of their firms and industries because it is difficult for uncompetitive ones to survive.

The long-run trend in a firm's productivity (output per worker hour) relative to those of other firms is a key indicator of changing competitiveness. If the productivity of Honda workers increases at a faster rate than the productivity of Ford workers, then Honda's cost per unit of output will

[5]See Michael Porter, *The Competitive Advantage of Nations* (New York: The Free Press, 1990), Chapter 2.

decrease over time relative to Ford's cost per unit. How much physical output a worker produces, on average, in an hour's work depends on (1) what the output is; (2) the worker's motivation and skill; (3) the technology, plant, and equipment in use, as well as the parts and raw materials; (4) the scale of production; (5) how easy the product is to manufacture; and (6) how the many tasks of production are organized in detail.

The structural characteristics of an economy also influence the competitiveness of a firm or industry. These characteristics include an economy's assets, such as infrastructure, and institutions, such as the educational system. These factors determine whether a nation's business environment is fertile for developing competitiveness for its firms and industries.

A Nation's Competitiveness

Although one can assess the competitiveness of a firm or industry, assessing the competitiveness of a nation is more difficult. What criteria underlie a nation's international competitiveness? For a nation to be competitive, must all of its firms and industries be competitive? Even economic powerhouses like Japan and Germany have economies in which large segments cannot keep pace with foreign competitors. Does a nation have to export more than it imports to be competitive? Nations such as the United States have realized increasing national income in spite of imports exceeding exports. Is a competitive nation one that creates jobs for its citizens? Although this ability is important, the creation of jobs in itself is not the critical issue; what matters most is the creation of high-paying jobs that improve a nation's standard of living. If the goal of domestic policy were to maximize jobs, today we would have thriving horse-drawn-carriage and blacksmith industries. By keeping the same jobs we have always had, we discourage the development of new high-skill jobs that add to the stock of knowledge and generate innovation and growth. Finally, is a competitive nation one in which wage rates are low? Low wages are not the key to exporting. If they were, nations such as Haiti and Bangladesh would be great exporters. The truth is exactly the opposite. High-wage nations such as the United States are the world's largest exporters. Clearly,

none of these explanations for national competitiveness is fully satisfactory.

A primary economic objective of a nation is to generate a high and increasing standard of living for its people. Accomplishing this goal depends not on the vague notion of maintaining national competitiveness, but rather on achieving high productivity of its employed resources. Over time, productivity is a major determinant of a nation's standard of living because it underlies per capita income. Besides supporting high incomes, high productivity allows people the option of choosing more leisure instead of working long hours. Productivity also creates the national income that can be taxed to pay for public services that enhance the standard of living.

International trade allows a nation to increase its productivity by eliminating the need to produce all goods and services within the nation itself. A nation can thus specialize in those industries in which its firms are relatively more productive than foreign rivals and can import the goods and services in which its firms are less productive. In this way, resources are channeled from low-productivity uses to high-productivity uses, thus increasing the economy's average level of productivity. Both imports and exports are necessary for rising productivity. This conclusion contradicts the sometimes popular notion that exports are good and imports are bad.

No nation can be competitive in, and thus be a net exporter of, everything. Because a nation's stock of resources is limited, the ideal is for these resources to be used in their most productive manner. Even nations that are desperately bad at making everything can expect to gain from international competition. By specializing according to their comparative advantage, nations can prosper through trade regardless of how inefficient, in absolute terms, they may be in their chosen specialty.

Competition, Productivity, and Economic Growth

Does exposure to competition with the world leader in a particular industry improve a firm's productivity? The McKinsey Global Institute has addressed this question by examining labor productivity in manufacturing industries in Japan, Germany, and

Competition in the World Steel Industry

Cost per Ton of Steel, 2003

Cost Components*	United States	Japan	South Korea	Brazil	China
Labor cost					
Labor hours per ton	3.51	3.04	3.93	4.4	12.6
Employee cost per hour	$ 39	$37.50	$ 15	$ 10	$1.75
Labor cost**	$137	$ 114	$ 59	$ 44	$ 22
Material costs	279	263	261	221	301
Depreciation expense	23	40	30	25	30
Interest expense	13	15	10	35	15
Total cost per ton	$452	$432	$360	$325	$368

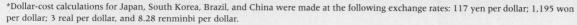

*Dollar-cost calculations for Japan, South Korea, Brazil, and China were made at the following exchange rates: 117 yen per dollar; 1,195 won per dollar; 3 real per dollar, and 8.28 renminbi per dollar.

**The product of labor-hours-per-ton times employee-cost-per-hour.

Source: Data taken from Peter F. Marcus and Karlis M. Kirsis, "World Steel Dynamics," *Steel Strategist #29*, June 2003.

During the 1960s and 1970s, the relatively low production costs of foreign steelmakers encouraged their participation in the U.S. market. In 1982, the average cost per ton of steel for integrated U.S. producers was $685 per ton—52 percent higher than for Japanese producers, the highest of the Pacific Rim steelmakers. This cost differential was largely due to a strong U.S. dollar and higher domestic costs of labor and raw materials, which accounted for 25 percent and 45 percent, respectively, of total cost. Moreover, domestic operating rates were relatively low, resulting in high fixed costs of production for each ton of steel.

The cost disadvantage encouraged U.S. steelmakers to initiate measures to reduce production costs and regain competitiveness. Many steel companies closed obsolete and costly steel mills, coking facilities, and ore mines. They also negotiated long-term contracts permitting materials, electricity, and natural gas to be obtained at lower prices. Labor contracts were also renegotiated, with a 20-to-40 percent improvement in labor productivity. However, U.S. steel companies are burdened with large unfunded pension obligations and health-care costs for hundreds of thousands of retirees, while their own employee base is shrinking.

By the turn of the century, the U.S. steel industry had substantially reduced its cost of producing a ton of steel, as seen in the table. U.S. steelworker productivity was estimated to be higher than that of most foreign competitors, a factor that enhanced U.S. competitiveness. But semi-industrialized nations, such as South Korea, Brazil, and China, had labor-cost advantages because of lower wages and other employee costs. Overall, the cost disadvantage of U.S. steel companies narrowed considerably from the 1980s to the early 2000s. The table shows the costs of producing a ton of steel for selected nations in 2003.

the United States. Its study concluded that global competitiveness is a bit like golf. You get better by playing against people who are better than you.[6]

[6]McKinsey Global Institute, *Manufacturing Productivity* (Washington, DC: McKinsey Global Institute, 1993), p. 3. See also William Lewis, "The Secret to Competitiveness," *The Wall Street Journal*, October 22, 1993, p. A–14.

Comparing the labor productivity of nine industries in 1990, the Institute found that Japan led in five industries: autos, auto parts, consumer electronics, metalworking, and steel. The United States led in four industries: computers, processed food, soap and detergent, and beer. In none of the industries surveyed was Germany the most productive. The weighted average of Japanese workers' productivity in these industries was 17 percent below that in the United States, and German workers' productivity was 21 percent below U.S. levels.

The McKinsey researchers analyzed the sources of productivity differences among these nations in the industries investigated. They found that, whether in the auto industry in Japan or the food industry in the United States, managers and engineers do not achieve innovations because they are smarter, work harder, or are better educated than their peers. They do so because they are subjected to intense global competition, where improving labor productivity is the key to success. Conversely, government trade restrictions have protected most productivity laggards from the painful rigors of global competition. Of the three nations studies, the United States was the most exposed to international competition. The McKinsey study provides evidence that the surest path to high productivity, and thus to high living standards, is to open markets to trade, investment, and ideas from the most advanced nations and to permit vigorous competition with firms that have implemented leading-edge technologies.

Also, economists at the World Bank have found that economic growth rates are closely related to openness to trade, education, and communications infrastructure. As the boxes in Figure 1.2 show, a country can foster its growth rate by increasing its openness to international trade, the education of its people, and its supply of telecommunications infrastructure. That impact on growth can perhaps be as much as 4 percentage points for a country that moves from significantly below the average to significantly above the average on all of these indicators.

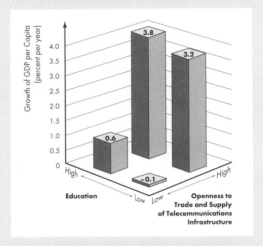

FIGURE 1.2

The Impact of Education, Openness to Trade, and Telecommunications Infrastructure on Economic Growth for 74 Countries

Each bar represents the average growth rate for a group of countries over the period 1965–1995. As the figure shows, moving from low (below average) to high (above average) on these determinants of growth leads to higher growth rates.

Source: Adapted from The World Bank, *World Development Report* (Washington, DC: The World Bank, 1999), p. 23.

Is International Trade an Opportunity or a Threat to Workers?

• Tom lives in Chippewa Falls, Wisconsin. His former job as a bookkeeper for a shoe company, where he was employed for many years, was insecure. Although he earned $100 a day, promises of promotion never panned out, and the company eventually went bankrupt as cheap imports from Mexico forced shoe prices down. Tom then went to a local university, earned a degree in management information systems, and was hired by a new machine-tool firm that exports to Mexico. He now enjoys a more comfortable living even after making the monthly payments on his government-subsidized student loan.

- Rosa and her family recently moved from a farm in southern Mexico to the country's northern border, where she works for a U.S.–owned electronics firm that exports to the United States. Her husband, Jose, operates a janitorial service and sometimes crosses the border to work illegally in California. Rosa and Jose and their daughter have improved their standard of living since moving out of subsistence agriculture. However, Rosa's wage has not increased in the past year; she still earns about $2.25 per hour with no future gains in sight.

Workers around the globe are living increasingly intertwined lives. Most of the world's population now live in countries that either are integrated into world markets for goods and finance or are rapidly becoming so. Are workers better off as a result of these globalizing trends? Stories about losers from international trade are often featured in newspapers: how Tom lost his job because of competition from poor Mexicans. But Tom currently has a better job, and the U.S. economy benefits from his company's exports to Mexico. Producing goods for export has led to an improvement in Rosa's living standard, and her daughter can hope for a better future. Jose is looking forward to the day when he will no longer have to travel illegally to California.

International trade benefits many workers. It enables them to shop for consumption goods that are cheapest and permits employers to purchase the technologies and equipment that best complement their workers' skills. Trade also allows workers to become more productive as the goods they produce increase in value. Moreover, producing goods for export generates jobs and income for domestic workers. Workers in exporting industries appreciate the benefits of an open trading system.

But not all workers gain from international trade. The world trading system, for example, has come under attack by some in industrial countries where rising unemployment and wage inequality have made people feel apprehensive about the future. Some workers in industrial countries are threatened with losing their jobs because of cheap exports produced by lower-cost, foreign workers. Others worry that firms are relocating abroad in search of low wages and lax environmental standards or fear that masses of poor immigrants will be at their company's door, offering to work for lower wages. Trade with low-wage developing countries is particularly threatening to unskilled workers in the import-competing sectors of industrial countries.

As an economy opens up to international trade, domestic prices become more aligned with international prices; wages tend to increase for workers whose skills are more scarce internationally than at home and to decrease for workers who face increased competition from foreign workers. As the economies of foreign nations open up to trade, the relative scarcity of various skills in the world marketplace changes still further, harming those countries with an abundance of workers who have the skills that are becoming less scarce. Increased competition also suggests that unless countries match the productivity gains of their competitors, the wages of their workers will deteriorate. It is no wonder that workers in import-competing industries often lobby for restrictions on the importation of goods so as to neutralize the threat of foreign competition. Slogans such as "Buy American" and "American goods create American jobs" have become rallying cries among many U.S. workers.

Keep in mind, however, that what is true for the part is not necessarily true for the whole. It is certainly true that imports of steel or automobiles can eliminate American steel or automobile jobs. But it is not true that imports decrease the total number of jobs in a nation. A large increase in U.S. imports will inevitably lead to a rise in U.S. exports or foreign investment in the United States. In other words, if Americans suddenly wanted more European autos, eventually American exports would have to increase to pay for these products. The jobs lost in one industry are replaced by jobs gained in another industry. The long-run effect of trade barriers is thus not to increase total domestic employment, but at best to reallocate workers away from export industries and toward less efficient, import-competing industries. This reallocation leads to a less efficient utilization of resources.

Simply put, international trade is just another kind of technology. Think of it as a machine that adds value to its inputs. In the United States, trade is the machine that turns computer software, which the United States makes very well, into CD players, baseballs, and other things that it also wants, but does not make quite so well. International trade does this at a net gain to the economy as a whole. If somebody invented a device that could do this, it would be considered a miracle. Fortunately, international trade has been developed.

If international trade is squeezing the wages of the less skilled, so are other kinds of advancing technology, only more so. Yes, you might say, but to tax technological progress or put restrictions on labor-saving investment would be idiotic: that would only make everybody worse off. Indeed it would, and exactly the same goes for international trade—whether this superior technology is taxed (through tariffs) or overregulated (in the form of international efforts to harmonize labor standards).

This is not an easy thing to explain to American textile workers who compete with low-wage workers in China, Malaysia, and the like. However, free-trade agreements will be more easily reached if those who may lose by new trade are helped by all of the rest of us who gain.

Backlash Against Globalization

Proponents of globalization note how it has helped the United States and other countries prosper. Open borders permit new ideas and technology to flow freely around the world, fueling productivity growth and increases in living standards. Moreover, increased trade helps restrain consumer prices, so inflation becomes less likely to disrupt economic growth.

ECONOMIC *Applications*

Visit EconDebate Online for a debate on this topic

In spite of the advantages of globalization, critics maintain that U.S. policies primarily benefit large corporations rather than average citizens—of the United States or any other country. Environmentalists argue that elitist trade organizations, such as the World Trade Organization, make undemocratic decisions that undermine national sovereignty on environmental regulation. Also, unions maintain that unfettered trade permits unfair competition from countries that lack labor standards. Moreover, human rights activists contend that the World Bank and International Monetary Fund support governments that allow sweatshops and pursue policies that bail out governmental officials at the expense of local economies. Put simply: A gnawing sense of unfairness and frustration has emerged about trade policies' ignoring the concerns of the environment, American workers, and international labor standards.

The noneconomic aspects of globalization are at least as important in shaping the international debate as are the economic aspects. Many of those who object to globalization resent the political and military dominance of the United States, and they resent also the influence of foreign (mainly American) culture, as they see it, at the expense of national and local cultures.

The World Trade Organization's summit meeting in Seattle, Washington, in 1999 attests to a globalization backlash in opposition to continued liberalization of trade, foreign investment, and foreign immigration. The meeting was characterized by shattered storefront windows, looting, tear gas, pepper spray, rubber bullets, shock grenades, and a midnight to dawn curfew. Police in riot gear and the National Guard were called in to help restore order. About 100,000 antiglobalization demonstrators swamped Seattle to vocalize their opposition to the policies of the World Trade Organization.

Such backlash reflects concern about globalization, and these perceptions appear to be closely related to the labor-market pressures that globalization may be imparting on American workers. First, public opinion surveys note that many Americans are aware of both the benefits and costs of integration with the world economy, but they consider the costs to be more than the benefits. Second, these policy preferences cut most strongly across labor-market skills. Less-skilled workers are much more likely to oppose freer trade and immigration than their more-skilled counterparts. Third, the skills-preferences gap may reflect very different wage-growth levels across skill groups in the U.S. labor market since the early 1970s. Less-skilled American workers, a group that still constitutes the majority of the U.S. labor force, have had close to zero or even negative real wage growth and have also seen sharp declines in their wages relative to more-skilled workers. While concerns about the effect of globalization on the environment, human rights, and other issues are an important part of the politics of globalization, it is the tie between policy liberalization, worker interests, and individual opinions that forms the foundation for the backlash against liberalization in the United States.[7] Table 1.7 summarizes some of the pros and cons of globalization.

Terrorism Jolts the Global Economy

Some critics point to the terrorist attack on the United States on September 11, 2001, as what can occur when globalization ignores the poor people of the world. The terrorist attack resulted in a tragic loss of life for thousands of innocent Americans. It also jolted America's golden age of prosperity, and the promise it held for global growth, that existed throughout the 1990s. Because of the threat of terrorism, Americans became

[7]Kenneth Scheve and Matthew Slaughter, *Globalization and the Perceptions of American Workers* (Washington, DC: Institute for International Economics, 2001).

TABLE 1.7

Advantages and Disadvantages of Globalization

Advantages	Disadvantages
Productivity increases faster when countries produce goods and services in which they have a comparative advantage. Living standards can increase more rapidly.	Millions of Americans have lost jobs because of imports or shifts in production abroad. Most find new jobs that pay less.
Global competition and cheap imports keep a constraint on prices, so inflation is less likely to disrupt economic growth.	Millions of other Americans fear getting laid off, especially at those firms operating in import-competing industries.
An open economy promotes technological development and innovation, with fresh ideas from abroad.	Workers face demands of wage concessions from their employers, which often threaten to export jobs abroad if wage concessions are not agreed to.
Jobs in export industries tend to pay about 15 percent more than jobs in import-competing industries.	Besides blue-collar jobs, service and white-collar jobs are increasingly vulnerable to operations being sent overseas.
Unfettered capital movements provide the United States access to foreign investment and maintain low interest rates.	American employees can lose their competitiveness when companies build state-of-the-art factories in low-wage countries, making them as productive as those in the United States.

Source: "Backlash Behind the Anxiety over Globalization" *Business Week*, April 24, 2000, p. 41.

increasingly concerned about their safety and livelihoods.

As the United States retaliated against Osama bin Laden and his band of terrorists, analysts were concerned that this conflict might undo a decades-long global progression toward tighter economic, political, and social integration—the process known as globalization. Fueled by trade, globalization has advanced the ambitions, and boosted the profits, of some of the world's largest corporations, many of them based in the United States, Europe, and Japan. Indeed, companies such as General Electric, Ford Motor Company, and Coca-Cola have been major beneficiaries of globalization. Also, globalization has provided developing countries a chance to be included in the growing global economy and share in the wealth. In many developing countries, it has succeeded: Life expectancies and per capita income have increased, and local economies have flourished.

But the path to globalization has been rocky. Critics have argued that it has excluded many of the world's poor, and that the move toward prosperity has often come at the expense of human rights and the quality of the environment. For many Islamic fundamentalists, globalization represents an intolerable secularization of society, and it must be prevented. This contrasts with much of the criticism in the West, which calls for reform of globalization—not its undoing.

Globalization certainly isn't going to disintegrate—the world's markets are too integrated to roll back now. But globalization could well become slower and costlier. With continuing terrorism, companies will likely have to pay more to insure and provide security for overseas staff and property. Heightened border inspections could slow shipments of cargo, forcing companies to stock more inventory. Tighter immigration policies could reduce the liberal inflows of skilled and blue-collar laborers that permitted companies to expand while keeping wages in check. Moreover, a greater preoccupation with political risk has companies greatly narrowing their horizons when making new investments. Put simply, what has driven the rapid expansion in trade and capital flows in the past was the notion that the world was becoming a

seamless, frictionless place. With continuing terrorism, all of these things are imperiled, and this puts sand in the gears of globalization.

Many economists view international trade to be a long-run weapon in the war against terrorism. They maintain that expanded trade wraps the world more tightly in a web of commerce, lifting living standards in impoverished regions and eliminating an important cause of war and terror. For example, following the 2001 terrorist attack against the United States, the U.S. government negotiated trade deals with Jordan and Vietnam and began advising Russia on joining the World Trade Organization. Put simply, trade cannot make peace, but trade can help. If you look at history, strong trading relationships have rarely led to conflict. Of course, trade needs to be accompanied by other factors, such as strong commitments to universal education and well-run governments, to promote world peace.

However, these economists note that a trade-based strategy to unite the world would require a far greater investment of money and political capital than the United States and Europe have demonstrated. Moreover, they argue that the United States and Europe must push for massive debt relief for impoverished nations. They also recommend that industrial countries slash tariffs and quotas for the steel, textiles, clothing, and crops produced by poor nations, even though increased imports could harm U.S. and European producers. Indeed, these recommendations invite much debate concerning the political and economic stability of the world.

The Plan of This Book

This book examines the functioning of the international economy. Although it emphasizes the theoretical principles that govern international trade, it also gives considerable coverage to empirical evidence of world trade patterns and to trade policies of the industrial and developing nations. The book is divided into two major parts. Part One deals with international trade and commercial policy; Part Two stresses the balance of payments and adjustment in the balance of payments.

Chapters 2 and 3 deal with the theory of comparative advantage, as well as theoretical extensions and empirical tests of this model. This topic is followed by a treatment of tariffs, nontariff trade barriers, and contemporary trade policies of the United States in Chapters 4 through 6. Discussions of trade policies for the developing nations, regional trading arrangements, and international factor movements in Chapters 7 through 9 complete the first part of the text.

The treatment of international financial relations begins with an overview of the balance of payments, the foreign-exchange market, and exchange-rate determination in Chapters 10 through 12. Balance-of-payments adjustment under alternate exchange-rate regimes is discussed in Chapters 13 through 15. Chapter 16 considers macroeconomic policy in an open economy, and Chapter 17 analyzes the international banking system.

Summary

1. Throughout the post–World War II era, the world's economies have become increasingly interdependent in terms of the movement of goods and services, business enterprise, capital, and technology.
2. The United States has seen growing interdependence with the rest of the world in its trade sector, financial markets, ownership of production facilities, and labor force.
3. Largely owing to the vastness and wide diversity of its economy, the United States remains among the countries for which exports constitute a small fraction of national output.
4. Proponents of an open trading system contend that international trade results in higher levels of consumption and investment, lower prices of commodities, and a wider range of product choices for consumers. Arguments against free trade tend to be voiced during periods of excess production capacity and high unemployment.
5. International competitiveness can be analyzed in terms of a firm, an industry, and a nation. Key to the concept of competitiveness is productivity, or output per worker hour.
6. Researchers have shown that exposure to competition with the world leader in an industry improves a firm's performance in that industry. Global competitiveness is a bit like sports: You get better by playing against folks who are better than you.
7. Although international trade helps workers in export industries, workers in import-competing industries feel the threat of foreign competition. They often see their jobs and wage levels undermined by cheap foreign labor.
8. Among the challenges that the international trading system faces are dealing with fair labor standards and concerns about the environment.

Key Concepts and Terms

- Agglomeration economies (page 6)
- Economic interdependence (page 2)
- Globalization (page 3)
- Law of comparative advantage (page 13)
- Openness (page 9)

Study Questions

1. What factors explain why the world's trading nations have become increasingly interdependent, from an economic and political viewpoint, during the post–World War II era?
2. What are some of the major arguments for and against an open trading system?
3. What significance does growing economic interdependence have for a country like the United States?
4. What factors influence the rate of growth in the volume of world trade?
5. Identify the major fallacies of international trade.
6. What is meant by international competitiveness? How does this concept apply to a firm, an industry, and a nation?
7. What do researchers have to say about the relation between a firm's productivity and exposure to global competition?
8. When is international trade an opportunity for workers? When is it a threat to workers?
9. Identify some of the major challenges confronting the international trading system.
10. What problems does terrorism pose for globalization?

netlink

1.1 The Economic Report of the President contains a wealth of information about the U.S. and world economies, as well as recent and historical international trade statistics. Visit

http://w3.access.gpo.gov/eop

1.2 The U.S. Census Bureau has extensive recent and historical data on U.S. exports, imports, and trade balances with individual countries. It has also developed a profile of U.S. exporting companies. Go to

http://www.census.gov/ftp/pub/foreign-trade/www

1.3 Honda maintains both American and Japanese Web sites. For a better understanding of economic interdependence and the concept of what makes a company

"American," visit and compare these Web sites:

http://www.hondacars.com
(American site)
and

http://www.honda.co.jp (Japanese site)

1.4 The World Bank Briefing Papers on "Assessing Globalization" tries to answer three dominant questions: Is globalization increasing world poverty? Is it increasing world inequality by destroying jobs and lowering wages among the poor and unskilled? Is it causing deterioration in environmental standards? Go to

http://www1.worldbank.org/economic
policy/globalization
and click on "Issue Briefs."

To access NetLink Exercises and the Virtual Scavenger Hunt, visit the Carbaugh Web site at http://carbaugh.swlearning.com.

Xtra! CARBAUGH Log onto the Carbaugh Xtra! Web site (http://carbaughxtra.swlearning.com) for additional learning resources such as practice quizzes, help with graphing, and current events applications.

part 1

International Trade Relations

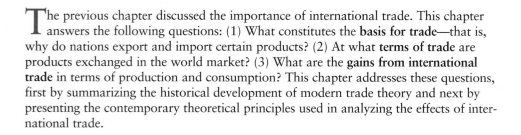

chapter 2

Foundations of Modern Trade Theory: Comparative Advantage

The previous chapter discussed the importance of international trade. This chapter answers the following questions: (1) What constitutes the **basis for trade**—that is, why do nations export and import certain products? (2) At what **terms of trade** are products exchanged in the world market? (3) What are the **gains from international trade** in terms of production and consumption? This chapter addresses these questions, first by summarizing the historical development of modern trade theory and next by presenting the contemporary theoretical principles used in analyzing the effects of international trade.

Historical Development of Modern Trade Theory

Modern trade theory is the product of an evolution of ideas in economic thought. In particular, the writings of the mercantilists, and later those of the classical economists—Adam Smith, David Ricardo, and John Stuart Mill—have been instrumental in providing the framework of modern trade theory.

The Mercantilists

During the period 1500–1800, a group of writers appeared in Europe who were concerned with the process of nation building. According to the **mercantilists**, the central question was how a nation could regulate its domestic and international affairs so as to promote its own interests. The solution lay in a strong foreign-trade sector. If a country could achieve a *favorable trade balance* (a surplus of exports over imports), it would realize net payments received from the rest of the world in the form of gold and silver. Such revenues would contribute to increased spending and a rise in domestic output and employment. To promote a favorable trade balance, the mercantilists advocated government regulation of trade. Tariffs, quotas, and other commercial policies were proposed by the mercantilists to minimize imports in order to protect a nation's trade position.[1]

---

[1]See E.A.J. Johnson, *Predecessors of Adam Smith* (New York: Prentice Hall, 1937).

By the eighteenth century, the economic policies of the mercantilists were under strong attack. According to David Hume's **price-specie-flow doctrine**, a favorable trade balance was possible only in the short run, for over time it would automatically be eliminated. To illustrate, suppose England were to achieve a trade surplus that resulted in an inflow of gold and silver. Because these precious metals would constitute part of England's money supply, their inflow would increase the amount of money in circulation. This would lead to a rise in England's price level relative to that of its trading partners. English residents would therefore be encouraged to purchase foreign-produced goods, while England's exports would decline. As a result, the country's trade surplus would eventually be eliminated. The price-specie-flow mechanism thus showed that mercantilist policies could provide at best only short-term economic advantages.[2]

The mercantilists were also attacked for their *static view* of the world economy. To the mercantilists, the world's wealth was fixed. This meant that one nation's gains from trade came at the expense of its trading partners; not all nations could simultaneously enjoy the benefits of international trade. This view was challenged with the publication in 1776 of Adam Smith's *Wealth of Nations*. According to Smith (1723–1790), the world's wealth is not a fixed quantity. International trade permits nations to take advantage of specialization and the division of labor, which increase the general level of productivity within a country and thus increase world output (wealth). Smith's dynamic view of trade suggested that *both* trading partners could simultaneously enjoy higher levels of production and consumption with trade. Smith's trade theory is further explained in the next section.

Why Nations Trade: Absolute Advantage

Adam Smith, a classical economist, was a leading advocate of **free trade** (open markets) on the grounds that it promoted the international division of labor. With free trade, nations could concentrate their production on goods they could make most cheaply, with all the consequent benefits of the division of labor.

Accepting the idea that *cost differences* govern the international movement of goods, Smith sought to explain why costs differ among nations. Smith maintained that *productivities* of factor inputs represent the major determinant of production cost. Such productivities are based on natural and acquired advantages. The former include factors relating to climate, soil, and mineral wealth, whereas the latter include special skills and techniques. Given a natural or acquired advantage in the production of a good, Smith reasoned that a nation would produce that good at lower cost, becoming more competitive than its trading partner. Smith thus viewed the determination of competitiveness from the *supply side* of the market.[3]

Smith's concept of cost was founded upon the **labor theory of value**, which assumes that within each nation, (1) labor is the only factor of production and is homogeneous (of one quality) and (2) the cost or price of a good depends exclusively upon the amount of labor required to produce it. For example, if the United States uses less labor to manufacture a yard of cloth than the United Kingdom, the U.S. production cost will be lower.

Smith's trading principle was the **principle of absolute advantage**: in a 2-nation, 2-product world, international specialization and trade will be beneficial when one nation has an absolute cost advantage (that is, uses less labor to produce a unit of output) in one good and the other nation has an absolute cost advantage in the other good. For the world to benefit from specialization, each nation must have a good that it is absolutely more efficient in producing than its trading partner. A nation will *import* those goods in which it has an absolute cost *disadvantage*; it will *export* those goods in which it has an absolute cost *advantage*.

An arithmetic example helps illustrate the principle of absolute advantage. Referring to Table 2.1 on page 30, suppose workers in the United States can produce 5 bottles of wine or 20 yards of cloth in an hour's time, while workers in the United Kingdom

---

[2]David Hume, "Of Money," *Essays*, Vol. 1 (London: Green and Co., 1912), p. 319. Hume's writings are also available in Eugene Rotwein, *The Economic Writings of David Hume* (Edinburgh: Nelson, 1955).

[3]Adam Smith, *The Wealth of Nations* (New York: Modern Library, 1937), pp. 424–426.

TABLE 2.1

A Case of Absolute Advantage When Each Nation Is More Efficient in the Production of One Good

World Output Possibilities in the
Absence of Specialization

Nation	Output per Labor Hour	
	Wine	Cloth
United States	5 bottles	20 yards
United Kingdom	15 bottles	10 yards

can produce 15 bottles of wine or 10 yards of cloth in an hour's time. Clearly, the United States has an absolute advantage in cloth production; its cloth workers' productivity (output per worker hour) is higher than that of the United Kingdom, which leads to lower costs (less labor required to produce a yard of cloth). In like manner, the United Kingdom has an absolute advantage in wine production.

According to Smith, each nation benefits by specializing in the production of the good that it produces at a lower cost than the other nation, while importing the good that it produces at a higher cost. Because the world uses its resources more efficiently as the result of specializing, there occurs an increase in world output, which is distributed to the two nations through trade. All nations can benefit from trade, according to Smith.

Why Nations Trade: Comparative Advantage

According to Smith, mutually beneficial trade requires each nation to be the *least-cost producer* of at least one good that it can export to its trading partner. But what if a nation is more efficient than its trading partner in the production of *all* goods? Dissatisfied with this looseness in Smith's theory, David Ricardo (1772–1823) developed a principle to show that mutually beneficial trade can occur even when one nation is absolutely more efficient in the production of all goods.[4]

[4]David Ricardo, *The Principles of Political Economy and Taxation* (London: Cambridge University Press, 1966), Chapter 7. Originally published in 1817.

Like Smith, Ricardo emphasized the supply side of the market. The immediate basis for trade stemmed from cost differences between nations, which were underlaid by their natural and acquired advantages. Unlike Smith, who emphasized the importance of absolute cost differences among nations, Ricardo emphasized *comparative* (relative) cost differences. Ricardo's trade theory thus became known as the **principle of comparative advantage.** Indeed, countries often develop comparative advantages, as shown in Table 2.2.

According to Ricardo's comparative-advantage principle, even if a nation has an absolute cost disadvantage in the production of *both* goods, a basis for mutually beneficial trade may still exist. The *less efficient* nation should specialize in and export the good in which it is relatively less inefficient (where its absolute disadvantage is least). The *more efficient* nation should specialize in and export that good in which it is relatively more efficient (where its absolute advantage is greatest).

To demonstrate the principle of comparative advantage, Ricardo formulated a simplified model based on the following *assumptions*:

1. The world consists of two nations, each using a single input to produce two commodities.
2. In each nation, labor is the only input (the labor theory of value). Each nation has a fixed endowment of labor, and labor is fully employed and homogeneous.

TABLE 2.2

Examples of Comparative Advantages in International Trade

Country	Product
Canada	Lumber
Israel	Citrus fruit
Italy	Wine
Jamaica	Aluminum ore
Mexico	Tomatoes
Saudi Arabia	Oil
China	Textiles
Japan	Automobiles
South Korea	Steel, ships
Switzerland	Watches
United Kingdom	Financial services

Babe Ruth and the Principle of Comparative Advantage

Babe Ruth was the first great home-run hitter in baseball history. His batting talent and vivacious personality attracted huge crowds wherever he played. He made baseball more exciting by establishing homers as a common part of the game. Ruth set many major league records, including 2,056 career bases on balls and 72 games in which he hit two or more home runs. He had a .342 lifetime batting average and 714 career home runs.

George Herman Ruth (1895–1948) was born in Baltimore. After playing baseball in the minor leagues, Ruth started his major league career as a left-handed pitcher with the Boston Red Sox in 1914. In 158 games for Boston, he compiled a pitching record of 89 wins and 46 losses, including two 20-win seasons—23 victories in 1916 and 24 victories in 1917.

On January 2, 1920, a little more than a year after Babe Ruth had pitched two victories in the Red Sox World Series victory over Chicago, Ruth became violently ill. Most suspected that The Babe, known for his partying excesses, simply had a major league hangover from his New Year's celebrations. The truth was, though, that Ruth had ingested several bad frankfurters while entertaining youngsters the day before, and his symptoms were misdiagnosed as being life-threatening. The Red Sox management, already strapped for cash, thus sold its ailing player to the Yankees the very next day for $125,000 and a $300,000 loan to the owner of the Red Sox.

Ruth eventually added five more wins as a hurler for the New York Yankees and ended his pitching career with a 2.28 earned run average. Ruth also had three wins against no losses in World Series competition, including one stretch of 29$\frac{2}{3}$ consecutive scoreless innings. Ruth evolved to become the best left-handed pitcher in the American league.

Although Ruth had an absolute advantage in pitching, he had even greater talent at the plate. Simply put, Ruth's comparative advantage was in hitting. As a pitcher, Ruth had to rest his arm between appearances, and thus could not bat in every game. To ensure his daily presence in the lineup, Ruth gave up pitching to play exclusively in the outfield.

In Ruth's 15 years with the Yankees, Ruth dominated professional baseball. He teamed with Lou Gehrig to form what became the greatest one-two hitting punch in baseball. Ruth was the heart of the 1927 Yankees, a team regarded by some baseball experts as the best in baseball history. That year, Ruth set a record of 60 home runs; at that time, a season had 154 games as compared to 162 games of today. He attracted so many fans that Yankee Stadium, which opened in 1923, was nicknamed "The House That Ruth Built." The Yankees released Ruth after the 1934 season, and he ended his playing career in 1935 with the Boston Braves. In the final game he started in the outfield for Boston, Ruth hit three home runs.

The advantages to having Ruth switch from pitching to batting were enormous. Not only did the Yankees win four World Series during Ruth's tenure, but they also became baseball's most renowned franchise. Ruth was elected to the Baseball Hall of Fame in Cooperstown, New York, in 1936.

Source: Paul Rosenthal, "America at Bat: Baseball Stuff and Stories," *National Geographic*, 2002; Geoffrey Ward and Ken Burns, *Baseball: An Illustrated History* (Knoph, 1994); and Keith Brandt, *Babe Ruth: Home Run Hero* (Troll, 1986).

3. Labor can move freely among industries within a nation but is incapable of moving between nations.

4. The level of technology is fixed for both nations. Different nations may use different technologies, but all firms within each nation utilize a common production method for each commodity.

5. Costs do not vary with the level of production and are proportional to the amount of labor used.

6. Perfect competition prevails in all markets. Because no single producer or consumer is large enough to influence the market, all are price takers. Product quality does not vary among nations, implying that all units of each

product are identical. There is free entry to and exit from an industry, and the price of each product equals the product's marginal cost of production.

7. Free trade occurs between nations; that is, no government barriers to trade exist.

8. Transportation costs are zero. Consumers will thus be indifferent between domestically produced and imported versions of a product if the domestic prices of the two products are identical.

9. Firms make production decisions in an attempt to maximize profits, whereas consumers maximize satisfaction through their consumption decisions.

10. There is no money illusion; that is, when consumers make their consumption choices and firms make their production decisions, they take into account the behavior of all prices.

11. Trade is balanced (exports must pay for imports), thus ruling out flows of money between nations.

Table 2.3 illustrates Ricardo's comparative-advantage principle when one nation has an absolute advantage in the production of both goods. Assume that in one hour's time, U.S. workers can produce 40 bottles of wine or 40 yards of cloth, while U.K. workers can produce 20 bottles of wine or 10 yards of cloth. According to Smith's principle of absolute advantage, there is no basis for mutually beneficial specialization and trade, because the United States is more efficient in the production of both goods.

Ricardo's principle of comparative advantage, however, recognizes that the United States is four times as efficient in cloth production (40/10 = 4) but only twice as efficient in wine production (40/20 = 2). The United States thus has a *greater absolute advantage* in cloth than in wine, while the United Kingdom has a *smaller absolute disadvantage* in wine than in cloth. Each nation specializes in and exports that good in which it has a *comparative* advantage—the United States in cloth, the United Kingdom in wine. The output gains from specialization will be distributed to the two nations through the process of trade.

TABLE 2.3

A Case of Comparative Advantage When the United States Has an Absolute Advantage in the Production of Both Goods

World Output Possibilities in the Absence of Specialization

Nation	Output per Labor Hour	
	Wine	Cloth
United States	40 bottles	40 yards
United Kingdom	20 bottles	10 yards

Like Smith, Ricardo asserted that both nations can gain from trade.

Concerning U.S. trade patterns during the 1980s and 1990s, in which the United States realized large trade deficits (imports exceeded exports) with Japan, some doomsayers appeared to believe that Japan could outproduce the United States in virtually everything. Those who foresaw a flood of imports from Japan causing the United States to deindustrialize and become a nation of fast-food restaurants seemed to be suggesting that the United States did not have a comparative advantage in anything.

It is possible for a nation not to have an absolute advantage in anything; but it is not possible for one nation to have a comparative advantage in everything and the other nation to have a comparative advantage in nothing. That's because comparative advantage depends on *relative* costs. As we have seen, a nation having an absolute disadvantage in all goods would find it advantageous to specialize in the production of the good in which its absolute disadvantage is *least*. There is no reason for the United States to surrender and let Japan produce all of everything. The United States would lose and so would Japan, because world output would be reduced if U.S. resources were left idle. The idea that a nation has nothing to offer confuses absolute advantage and comparative advantage.

Although the comparative-advantage principle is used to explain international trade patterns, people are not generally concerned with which nation has a comparative advantage when they purchase something. A person in a candy store does not look at Swiss chocolate and U.S. chocolate and say, "I wonder which nation has the comparative advantage in chocolate production?" The buyer relies on price, after allowing for quality differences, to tell which nation has the comparative advantage. It is helpful, then, to illustrate how the principle of comparative advantage works in terms of money prices, as seen in "Exploring Further 2.1" at the end of this chapter.

Production Possibilities Schedules

Ricardo's law of comparative advantage suggested that specialization and trade can lead to gains for both nations. His theory, however, depended on the restrictive assumption of the labor theory of value, in which labor was assumed to be the only factor input. In practice, however, labor is only one of several factor inputs.

Recognizing the shortcomings of the labor theory of value, modern trade theory provides a more generalized theory of comparative advantage. It explains the theory using a **production possibilities schedule**, also called a transformation schedule. This schedule shows various alternative combinations of two goods that a nation can produce when *all* of its factor inputs (land, labor, capital, entrepreneurship) are used in their most efficient manner. The production possibilities schedule thus illustrates the maximum output possibilities of a nation. Note that we are no longer assuming labor to be the only factor input, as Ricardo did.

Figure 2.1 on page 34 illustrates hypothetical production possibilities schedules for the United States and Canada. By fully using all available inputs with the best available technology during a given time period, the United States could produce either 60 bushels of wheat or 120 autos or certain combinations of the two products. Similarly, Canada could produce either 160 bushels of wheat or 80 autos or certain combinations of the two products.

Just how does a production possibilities schedule illustrate the concept of comparative cost? The

answer lies in the slope of the production possibilities schedule, which is referred to as the **marginal rate of transformation (MRT)**. The *MRT* shows the amount of one product a nation must sacrifice to get one additional unit of the other product:

$$\text{MRT} = \frac{\Delta Wheat}{\Delta Autos}$$

This rate of sacrifice is sometimes called the *opportunity cost* of a product. Because this formula also refers to the slope of the production possibilities schedule, the *MRT* equals the absolute value of the production possibilities schedule's slope.

In Figure 2.1, the *MRT* of wheat into autos gives the amount of wheat that must be sacrificed for each additional auto produced. Concerning the United States, movement from the top endpoint on its production possibilities schedule to the bottom endpoint shows that the relative cost of producing 120 additional autos is the sacrifice of 60 bushels of wheat. This means that the relative cost of each auto produced is 0.5 bushel of wheat sacrificed (60/120 = 0.5)—that is, the *MRT* = 0.5. Similarly, Canada's relative cost of each auto produced is 2 bushels of wheat—that is, Canada's *MRT* = 2.

Trading Under Constant-Cost Conditions

This section illustrates the principle of comparative advantage under **constant opportunity costs**. Although the constant-cost case may be of limited relevance to the real world, it serves as a useful pedagogical tool for analyzing international trade. The discussion focuses on two questions. First, what are the *basis for trade* and the *direction of trade*? Second, what are the potential *gains from trade*, for a single nation and for the world as a whole?

Referring to Figure 2.1, notice that the production possibilities schedules for the United States and Canada are drawn as straight lines. The fact that these schedules are linear indicates that the relative costs of the two products do not change as the economy shifts its production from all wheat to all autos, or anywhere in between. For the United States, the relative cost of an auto is 0.5 bushel of

FIGURE 2.1

Trading Under Constant Opportunity Costs

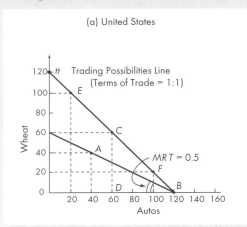
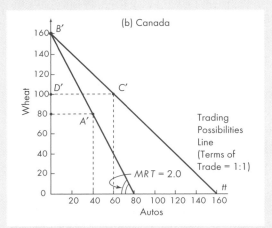

With constant opportunity costs, a nation will specialize in the product of its comparative advantage. The principle of comparative advantage implies that with specialization and free trade, a nation enjoys production gains and consumption gains. A nation's trade triangle denotes its exports, imports, and terms of trade. In a 2-nation, 2-product world, the trade triangle of one nation equals that of the other nation; one nation's exports equal the other nation's imports, and there is one equilibrium terms of trade.

wheat as output expands or contracts; for Canada, the relative cost of an auto is 2 bushels of wheat as output expands or contracts.

There are *two reasons* for constant costs. First, the factors of production are perfect substitutes for each other. Second, all units of a given factor are of the same quality. As a country transfers resources from the production of wheat into the production of autos, or vice versa, the country will not have to resort to resources that are less well suited for the production of the good. Therefore, the country must sacrifice exactly the same amount of wheat for each additional auto produced, regardless of how many autos it is already producing.

Basis for Trade and Direction of Trade

Let us now examine trade under constant-cost conditions. Referring to Figure 2.1, assume that in

autarky (the absence of trade) the United States prefers to produce and consume at point *A* on its production possibilities schedule, with 40 autos and 40 bushels of wheat. Assume also that Canada produces and consumes at point *A′* on its production possibilities schedule, with 40 autos and 80 bushels of wheat.

The *slopes* of the two countries' production possibilities schedules give the *relative cost* of one product in terms of the other. The relative cost of producing an additional auto is only 0.5 bushel of wheat for the United States but is 2 bushels of wheat for Canada. According to the principle of comparative advantage, this situation provides a basis for mutually favorable specialization and trade owing to the differences in the countries' relative costs. As for the direction of trade, we find the United States specializing in and exporting autos and Canada specializing in and exporting wheat.

Production Gains from Specialization

The law of comparative advantage asserts that with trade each country will find it favorable to specialize in the production of the good of its comparative advantage and will trade part of this for the good of its comparative disadvantage. In Figure 2.1, the United States moves from production point *A* to production point *B*, totally specializing in auto production. Canada totally specializes in wheat production by moving from production point *A'* to production point *B'* in the figure. Taking advantage of specialization can result in **production gains** for both countries.

We find that prior to specialization, the United States produces 40 autos and 40 bushels of wheat. But with complete specialization, the United States produces 120 autos and no wheat. As for Canada, its production point in the absence of specialization is at 40 autos and 80 bushels of wheat, whereas its production point under complete specialization is at 160 bushels of wheat and no autos. Combining these results, we find that both nations together have experienced a net production gain of 40 autos

and 40 bushels of wheat under conditions of complete specialization. Table 2.4(a) summarizes these production gains.

Consumption Gains from Trade

In the absence of trade, the consumption alternatives of the United States and Canada are limited to points *along* their domestic production possibilities schedules. The exact consumption point for each nation will be determined by the tastes and preferences in each country. But with specialization and trade, the two nations can achieve posttrade consumption points *outside* their domestic production possibilities schedules; that is, they can thus consume more wheat and more autos than they could consume in the absence of trade. Thus, trade can result in **consumption gains** for both countries.

The set of posttrade consumption points that a nation can achieve is determined by the rate at which its export product is traded for the other country's export product. This rate is known as the terms of trade. The terms of trade defines the relative prices at which two products are traded in the marketplace.

TABLE 2.4

Gains from Specialization and Trade: Constant Opportunity Costs

(a) Production Gains from Specialization

	Before Specialization		After Specialization		Net Gain (Loss)	
	Autos	Wheat	Autos	Wheat	Autos	Wheat
United States	40	40	120	0	80	−40
Canada	40	80	0	160	−40	80
World	80	120	120	160	40	40

(b) Consumption Gains from Trade

	Before Trade		After Trade		Net Gain (Loss)	
	Autos	Wheat	Autos	Wheat	Autos	Wheat
United States	40	40	60	60	20	20
Canada	40	80	60	100	20	20
World	80	120	120	160	40	40

Under constant-cost conditions, the slope of the production possibilities schedule defines the domestic rate of transformation (domestic terms of trade), which represents the relative prices at which two commodities can be exchanged at home. For a country to consume at some point *outside* its production possibilities schedule, it must be able to exchange its export good internationally at a terms of trade more favorable than the domestic terms of trade.

Assume that the United States and Canada achieve a terms-of-trade ratio that permits both trading partners to consume at some point outside their respective production possibilities schedules (Figure 2.1). Suppose that the terms of trade agreed on is a 1:1 ratio, whereby 1 auto is exchanged for 1 bushel of wheat. Based on these conditions, let line *tt* represent the international terms of trade for both countries. This line is referred to as the **trading possibilities line** (note that it is drawn with a slope having an absolute value of 1).

Suppose now that the United States decides to export, say, 60 autos to Canada. Starting at post-specialization production point *B* in the figure, the United States will slide along its trading possibilities line until point *C* is reached. At point *C*, 60 autos will have been exchanged for 60 bushels of wheat, at the terms-of-trade ratio of 1:1. Point *C* then represents the U.S. *posttrade consumption point*. Compared with consumption point *A*, point *C* results in a consumption gain for the United States of 20 autos and 20 bushels of wheat. The triangle *BCD* showing the U.S. exports (along the horizontal axis), imports (along the vertical axis), and terms of trade (the slope) is referred to as the **trade triangle**.

Does this trading situation provide favorable results for Canada? Starting at postspecialization production point *B'* in the figure, Canada can import 60 autos from the United States by giving up 60 bushels of wheat. Canada would slide along its trading possibilities line until it reached point *C'*. Clearly, this is a more favorable consumption point than point *A'*. With trade, Canada experiences a consumption gain of 20 autos and 20 bushels of wheat. Canada's trade triangle is denoted by *B'C'D'*. Note that in our 2-country model,

the trade triangles of the United States and Canada are identical; one country's exports equal the other country's imports, which are exchanged at the equilibrium terms of trade. Table 2.4(b) summarizes the consumption gains from trade for each country and the world as a whole.

One implication of the foregoing trading example was that the United States produced only autos, whereas Canada produced only wheat—that is, **complete specialization** occurs. As the United States increases and Canada decreases the production of autos, both countries' unit production costs remain constant. Because the relative costs never become equal, the United States does not lose its comparative advantage, nor does Canada lose its comparative disadvantage. The United States therefore produces only autos. Similarly, as Canada produces more wheat and the United States reduces its wheat production, both nations' production costs remain the same. Canada produces only wheat without losing its advantage to the United States.

The only exception to complete specialization would occur if one of the countries, say Canada, is too small to supply the United States with all of the U.S. needs for wheat. Then Canada would be completely specialized in its export product, wheat, while the United States (large country) would produce both goods; however, the United States would still export autos and import wheat.

Distributing the Gains from Trade

Our trading example has assumed that the terms of trade agreed to by the United States and Canada will result in both trading partners' benefiting from trade. But where will this terms of trade actually lie?

A shortcoming of Ricardo's principle of comparative advantage was its inability to determine the actual terms of trade. The best description that Ricardo could provide was only the *outer limits* within which the terms of trade would fall. This is because the Ricardian theory relied solely on domestic cost ratios (supply conditions) in explaining trade patterns; it ignored the role of demand.

To visualize Ricardo's analysis of the terms of trade, recall our trading example of Figure 2.1. We

Maytag Slashes Costs to Survive in Global Appliance Market

Maytag dishwashers have Mexican wiring, Chinese motors, and are assembled in a gigantic factory in Jackson, Tennessee. Although this three-tiered method of manufacturing is known as a "triad strategy," Maytag refers to it as attempting to survive in a competitive global market.

For a many years, Maytag's bulky appliances—like refrigerators and washing machines—were relatively insulated from foreign competition because their large size made them expensive to transport across the ocean. By 2003, however, declining labor and production costs in Asia offset high shipping costs, permitting some imported appliances to be marketed in the United States at lower prices.

On this side of the ocean, Maytag's American competitors—Whirlpool and General Electric (GE)—turned Mexico into a strategic site for producing appliances for the U.S. market. In Mexico, GE owns almost half of the largest appliance manufacturer and Whirlpool has full control of the second-largest. Both companies are shipping Mexican-manufactured appliances to the United States by the truckload, suggesting that Maytag's largest import threat is its own American rivals.

Because of low-priced imports, Maytag had to rethink how and where to manufacture dishwashers, washing machines, and refrigerators. It knew its triad strategy resulted in efficiencies, but in order to avert a massive relocation of production out of the United States, and slash American jobs, Maytag wanted to remain as close to its retail market as possible. In producing dishwashers, Maytag purchases motors from a GE plant in China because China provides the lowest price, and wires harnesses for dishwashers in Mexico because rapid changes in demand make it efficient to supply from a close location.

Maytag's new method of production began in the late 1990s, when other companies had already located in Mexico. Instead of constructing a factory there, Maytag rented a small plant and instructed each division to ascertain what amounts of their subassembly work could be sent there. Subassembly work is generally labor intensive, but not very skill intensive. This strategy reduced Maytag's costs because Mexican workers earn lower wages than U.S. workers. Since then, the company has purchased another plant in Mexico for subassembly work.

Maytag does the same cost calculations with its other products. It disassembled one of GE's side-by-side refrigerators manufactured in Mexico and concluded that it could not compete with GE without building its side-by-sides in Mexico as well. As a result, Maytag built a factory in Mexico that produces only those models. In another case, profit margins on refrigerators with the freezer on top were so small due to inexpensive imports that Maytag decided to stop producing them. Instead, it licensed a company in South Korea to make this particular model and ship them to America under the Maytag name. This strategy was tied to the closing of a refrigerator factory in Illinois, where those models had been produced.

Source: "Three Countries, One Dishwasher," *The Wall Street Journal*, October 6, 2003, pp. B–1 and B–8.

assumed that for the United States the relative cost of producing an additional auto was 0.5 bushels of wheat, whereas for Canada the relative cost of producing an additional auto was 2 bushels of wheat. Thus, the United States had a comparative advantage in autos, whereas Canada had a comparative advantage in wheat. Figure 2.2 on page 38 illustrates these domestic cost conditions for the two countries. For each country, however, we have translated the domestic cost ratio, given by the neg-atively sloped production possibilities schedule, into a *positively sloped* cost-ratio line.

According to Ricardo, the domestic cost ratios set the **outer limits for the equilibrium terms of trade.** If the United States is to export autos, it should not accept any terms of trade less than a ratio of 0.5:1, indicated by its domestic cost-ratio line. Otherwise, the U.S. posttrade consumption point would lie inside its production possibilities schedule. The United States would clearly be better

FIGURE 2.2

Equilibrium Terms-of-Trade Limits

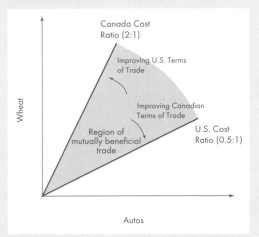

The supply-side analysis of Ricardo describes the outer limits within which the equilibrium terms of trade must fall. The domestic cost ratios set the outer limits for the equilibrium terms of trade. Mutually beneficial trade for both nations occurs if the equilibrium terms of trade lies between the two nations' domestic cost ratios. According to the theory of reciprocal demand, the actual exchange ratio at which trade occurs depends on the trading partners' interacting demands.

off without trade than with trade. The U.S. domestic cost-ratio line therefore becomes its **no-trade boundary.** Similarly, Canada would require a minimum of 1 auto for every 2 bushels of wheat exported, as indicated by its domestic cost-ratio line; any terms of trade less than this rate would be unacceptable to Canada. The no-trade boundary line for Canada is thus defined by its domestic cost-ratio line.

For gainful international trade to exist, a nation must achieve a posttrade consumption location at least equivalent to its point along its domestic production possibilities schedule. Any acceptable international terms of trade has to be more favorable than or equal to the rate defined

by the domestic price line. The **region of mutually beneficial trade** is thus bounded by the cost ratios of the two countries.

Equilibrium Terms of Trade

As noted, Ricardo did not explain how the actual terms of trade would be determined in international trade. This gap was filled by another classical economist, John Stuart Mill (1806–1873). By bringing into the picture the intensity of the trading partners' demands, Mill could determine the actual terms of trade for Figure 2.2. Mill's theory is known as the **theory of reciprocal demand.**[5] It asserts that within the outer limits of the terms of trade, the actual terms of trade is determined by the relative strength of each country's demand for the other country's product. Simply put, production costs determine the outer limits to the terms of trade, while reciprocal demand determines what the actual terms of trade will be within these limits.

Referring to Figure 2.2, if Canadians are more eager for U.S. autos than Americans are for Canadian wheat, the terms of trade would end up close to the Canadian cost ratio of 2:1. Thus, the terms of trade would improve for the United States. However, if Americans are more eager for Canadian wheat than Canadians are for U.S. autos, the terms of trade would fall close to the U.S. cost ratio of 0.5:1, and the terms of trade would improve for Canadians.

The reciprocal-demand theory best applies when both nations are of equal economic size, so that the demand of each nation has a noticeable effect on market price. If two nations are of unequal economic size, however, it is possible that the relative demand strength of the smaller nation will be dwarfed by that of the larger nation. In this case, the domestic exchange ratio of the larger nation will prevail. Assuming the absence of monopoly elements working in the markets, the small nation can export as much of the commodity as it desires, enjoying large gains from trade.

Consider trade in crude oil and autos between Venezuela and the United States before the rise of

[5]John Stuart Mill, *Principles of Political Economy* (New York: Longmans, Green, 1921), pp. 584–585.

the OPEC (Organization of Petroleum Exporting Countries) oil cartel. Venezuela, as a small nation, accounted for only a very small share of the U.S.–Venezuelan market, whereas the U.S. market share was overwhelmingly large. Because Venezuelan consumers and producers had no influence on market price levels, they were in effect price takers. In trading with the United States, no matter what the Venezuelan demand was for crude oil and autos, it was not strong enough to affect U.S. price levels. As a result, Venezuela traded according to the U.S. domestic price ratio, buying and selling autos and crude oil at the price levels existing within the United States.

The example just given implies the following generalization: If two nations of approximately the *same size* and with similar taste patterns participate in international trade, the gains from trade will be shared about *equally* between them. However, if one nation is significantly larger than the other, the *larger* nation attains *fewer* gains from trade while the *smaller* nation attains *most* of the gains from trade. This situation is characterized as the **importance of being unimportant**. What's more, when nations are very dissimilar in size, there is a strong possibility that the larger nation will continue to produce its comparative-disadvantage good because the smaller nation is unable to supply all of the world's demand for this product.

Terms-of-Trade Estimates

As we have seen, the terms of trade affect a country's gains from trade. How are the terms of trade actually measured?

The **commodity terms of trade** (also referred to as the *barter terms of trade*) is a frequently used measure of the international exchange ratio. It measures the relationship between the prices a nation gets for its exports and the prices it pays for its imports. This is calculated by dividing a nation's export price index by its import price index, multiplied by 100 to express the terms of trade in percentages:

$$\text{Terms of Trade} = \frac{\text{Export Price Index}}{\text{Import Price Index}} \times 100$$

An *improvement* in a nation's terms of trade requires that the prices of its exports rise relative to the prices of its imports over the given time period. A smaller quantity of export goods sold abroad is required to obtain a given quantity of imports. Conversely, a *deterioration* in a nation's terms of trade is due to a rise in its import prices relative to its export prices over a time period. The purchase of a given quantity of imports would require the sacrifice of a greater quantity of exports.

Table 2.5 gives the commodity terms of trade for selected countries. With 1995 as the base year (equal to 100), the table shows that by 2002 Norway's index of export prices was 108, an

TABLE 2.5

Commodity Terms of Trade, 2002 (1995 = 100)

Country	Export Price Index	Import Price Index	Terms of Trade
Norway	108	70	154
China	87	84	104
Argentina	83	82	101
United States	95	94	101
Australia	84	84	100
Germany	68	70	97
France	62	64	97
Japan	71	81	88

Source: International Monetary Fund, *IMF Financial Statistics* (Washington, DC, December 2003).

increase of 8 percent. During the same period, the index of Norway's import prices fell by 30 percent, to a level of 70. Using the terms-of-trade formula, we find that Norway's terms of trade *rose* by 54 percent [(108/70) × 100 = 154] over the period 1995–2002. This means that to purchase a given quantity of imports, Norway had to sacrifice 54 percent *fewer* exports; conversely, for a given number of exports, Norway could obtain 54 percent *more* imports.

Although changes in the commodity terms of trade indicate the direction of movement of the gains from trade, their implications must be interpreted with caution. Suppose there occurs an increase in the foreign demand for U.S. exports, leading to higher prices and revenues for U.S. exporters. In this case, an improving terms of trade implies that the U.S. gains from trade have increased. However, suppose that the cause of the rise in export prices and terms of trade is falling *productivity* of U.S. workers. If this results in reduced export sales and less revenue earned from exports, we could hardly say that U.S. welfare has improved. Despite its limitations, however, the commodity terms of trade is a useful concept. Over a long period, it illustrates how a country's share of the world gains from trade changes and gives a rough measure of the fortunes of a nation in the world market.

Dynamic Gains from Trade

The previous analysis of the gains from international trade stressed specialization and reallocation of *existing* resources. However, these gains can be dwarfed by the effect of trade on the country's growth rate and thus on the volume of additional resources made available to, or utilized by, the trading country. These are known as the **dynamic gains from international trade**, as opposed to the static effects of reallocating a fixed quantity of resources.

We have learned that international trade tends to be about a more efficient use of an economy's resources, which leads to higher output and income. Over time, increased income tends to result in more saving and, thus, more investment in equipment and manufacturing plants. This additional invest-

ment generally results in a higher rate of economic growth. Moreover, opening an economy to trade may lead to imported investment goods, such as machinery, which fosters higher productivity and economic growth. In a roundabout manner, the gains from international trade grow larger over time. Empirical evidence has shown that countries that are more open to international trade tend to grow faster than closed economies.[6]

Free trade also increases the possibility that a firm importing a capital good will be able to locate a supplier who will provide a good that more nearly meets its specifications. The better the match, the larger is the increase in the firm's productivity, which promotes economic growth.

Economies of large-scale production represent another dynamic gain from trade. International trade allows small and moderately sized countries to establish and operate many plants of efficient size, which would be impossible if production were limited to the domestic market. For example, the free access that Mexican and Canadian firms have to the U.S. market, under the North American Free Trade Agreement (NAFTA), allows them to expand their production and employ more specialized labor and equipment. This has led to increased efficiency and lower unit costs for these firms.

Finally, increased competition can be a source of dynamic gains from trade. For example, General Motors had extensive monopoly power in the U.S. automobile market during the 1950s–1960s. Lack of effective competition allowed it to become lethargic in terms of innovation and product development. The advent of foreign competition in subsequent decades forced General Motors to increase its productivity and reduce unit costs. This has resulted in lower prices and a greater diversity of vehicles that Americans could purchase.

Simply put, besides providing static gains rising from the reallocation of existing productive resources, trade might also generate dynamic gains by stimulating economic growth. Proponents of free trade note the many success stories of growth

[6]D. Dollar and A. Kraay, "Trade, Growth, and Poverty," *Finance and Development*, September 2001, pp. 16–19, and S. Edwards, "Openness, Trade Liberalization, and Growth in Developing Countries," *Journal of Economic Literature*, September 1993, pp. 1358–1393.

through trade. However, the effect of trade on growth is not the same for all countries. In general, the gains tend to be less for a large country such as the United States than for a small country such as Belgium.

Changing Comparative Advantage

Although international trade can promote dynamic gains in terms of increased productivity, the comparative advantage realized by producers of a particular good can vanish over time when productivity growth falls behind that of foreign competitors. In the post–World War II era, for example, many U.S. steel companies produced steel in aging plants in which productivity lagged behind that of foreign companies. This contributed to U.S. steel companies' loss of market share to foreign firms. Other U.S. industries that went the way of steel were machine tools and consumer electronics. By the 1990s, Japanese computer suppliers had begun to compete effectively with U.S. producers in markets including printers, floppy-disk drives, and dynamic random-access memory chips. This was particularly disturbing to

those who considered computers to be a treasure of U.S. technology and a hallmark of U.S. competitiveness. Let us see how changing comparative advantage relates to our trade model.

Figure 2.3 illustrates the production possibilities schedules, for computers and automobiles, of the United States and Japan under conditions of constant opportunity cost. Note that the *MRT* of automobiles into computers initially equals 1.0 for the United States and 2.0 for Japan. The United States thus has a comparative advantage in the production of computers and a comparative disadvantage in auto production.

Suppose both nations experience productivity increases in manufacturing computers but no productivity change in manufacturing automobiles. Assume that the United States increases its computer-manufacturing productivity by 50 percent (from 100 to 150 computers) but that Japan increases its computer-manufacturing productivity by 300 percent (from 40 to 160 computers).

Because of these productivity gains, the production possibilities schedule of each country rotates outward and becomes flatter. More output can now be produced in each country with the same amount of resources. Referring to the new production possibilities schedules, the *MRT* of automobiles into

FIGURE 2.3

Changing Comparative Advantage

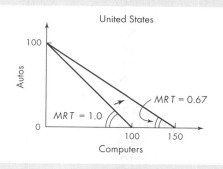
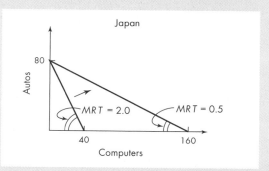

If productivity in the Japanese computer industry grows faster than it does in the U.S. computer industry, the opportunity cost of each computer produced in the United States increases relative to the opportunity cost of the Japanese. For the United States, comparative advantage shifts from computers to autos.

computers equals 0.67 for the United States and 0.5 for Japan. The comparative cost of a computer in Japan has thus fallen below that in the United States. For the United States, the consequence of lagging productivity growth is that it loses its comparative advantage in computer production. But even after Japan achieves comparative advantage in computers, the United States still has a comparative advantage in autos; the change in manufacturing productivity thus results in a change in the direction of trade. The lesson of this example is that producers who fall behind in research and development, technology, and equipment tend to find their competitiveness dwindling.

It should be noted, however, that all countries realize a comparative advantage in some product or service. For the United States, the growth of international competition in industries such as steel may make it easy to forget that the United States continues to be a major exporter of aircraft, paper, instruments, plastics, and chemicals.

Trading Under Increasing-Cost Conditions

The preceding section illustrated the comparative-advantage principle under constant-cost conditions. But in the real world, a good's opportunity costs may *increase* as more of it is produced. Based on studies of many industries, economists think the opportunity costs of production increase with output rather than remain constant for most goods. The principle of comparative advantage must be illustrated in a modified form.

Increasing opportunity costs give rise to a production possibilities schedule that appears *concave*, or bowed outward from the diagram's origin. In Figure 2.4, with movement along the production possibilities schedule from *A* to *B*, the opportunity cost of producing autos becomes larger and larger in terms of wheat sacrificed. Increasing costs mean that the *MRT* of wheat into autos *rises* as more autos are produced. Remember that the *MRT* is measured by the absolute slope of the production possibilities schedule at a given point. With movement from production point *A* to production point *B*, the

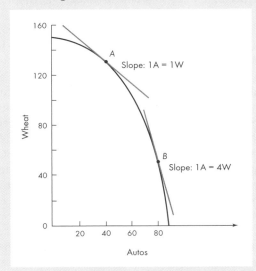

FIGURE 2.4

Production Possibilities Schedule Under Increasing-Cost Conditions

Increasing opportunity costs lead to a production possibilities schedule that is concave, viewed from the diagram's origin. The marginal rate of transformation equals the (absolute) slope of the production possibilities schedule at a particular point along the schedule.

respective tangent lines become *steeper*—their slopes increase in absolute value. The *MRT* of wheat into autos rises, indicating that each additional auto produced requires the sacrifice of increasing amounts of wheat.

Increasing costs represent the usual case in the real world. In the overall economy, increasing costs may result when inputs are imperfect substitutes for each other. As auto production rises and wheat production falls in Figure 2.4, inputs that are less and less adaptable to autos are introduced into that line of production. To produce more autos requires more and more of such resources and thus an increasingly greater sacrifice of wheat. For a *particular product*, such as autos, increasing cost is explained by the principle of diminishing marginal productivity. The addition of successive units of labor (variable input) to capital (fixed input) beyond some point results in decreases in the marginal production of autos that is attributable to each additional unit of labor. Unit production costs thus rise as more autos are produced.

Under increasing costs, the slope of the concave production possibilities schedule varies as a nation locates at different points on the schedule. Because the MRT equals the production possibilities schedule's slope, it will also be different for each point on the schedule. In addition to considering the *supply factors* underlying the production possibilities schedule's slope, we must also take into account the demand factors (tastes and preferences), for they will determine the point along the production possibilities schedule at which a country chooses to consume.

Increasing-Cost Trading Case

Figure 2.5 shows the production possibilities schedules of the United States and Canada under conditions of increasing costs. In Figure 2.5(a), assume that in the absence of trade the United

States is located at point A along its production possibilities schedule; it produces and consumes 5 autos and 18 bushels of wheat. In Figure 2.5(b), assume that in the absence of trade Canada is located at point A' along its production possibilities schedule, producing and consuming 17 autos and 6 bushels of wheat. For the United States, the relative cost of wheat into autos is indicated by the slope of line $t_{U.S.}$, tangent to the production possibilities schedule at point A (1 auto = 0.33 bushels of wheat). In like manner, Canada's relative cost of wheat into autos is denoted by the slope of line t_C (1 auto = 3 bushels of wheat). Because line $t_{U.S.}$ is *flatter* than line t_C, autos are relatively cheaper in the United States and wheat is relatively cheaper in Canada. According to the law of comparative advantage, the United States will export autos and Canada will export wheat.

As the United States specializes in auto production, it slides downward along its production possibilities schedule from point A toward point B. The relative cost of autos (in terms of wheat) rises, as implied by the increase in the (absolute) slope of the production possibilities schedule. At the same

FIGURE 2.5

Trading Under Increasing Opportunity Costs

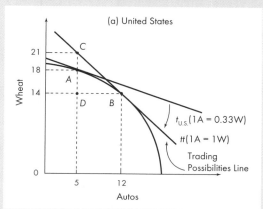
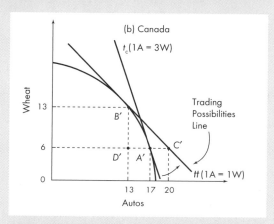

With increasing opportunity costs, comparative product prices in each country are determined by both supply and demand factors. A country tends to partially specialize in the product of its comparative advantage under increasing-cost conditions.

time, Canada specializes in wheat. As Canada moves upward along its production possibilities schedule from point A' toward point B', the relative cost of autos (in terms of wheat) decreases, as evidenced by the decrease in the (absolute) slope of its production possibilities schedule.

The process of specialization continues in both nations until (1) the relative cost of autos is identical in both nations and (2) U.S. exports of autos precisely equal Canada's imports of autos, and conversely for wheat. Assume that this situation occurs when the domestic rates of transformation (domestic terms of trade) of both nations converge at the rate given by line tt. At this point of convergence, the United States produces at point B, while Canada produces at point B'. Line tt becomes the international terms-of-trade line for the United States and Canada; it coincides with each nation's domestic terms of trade. The international terms of trade are favorable to both nations because tt is steeper than $t_{U.S.}$ and flatter than t_C.

What are the *production gains* from specialization for the United States and Canada? Comparing the amount of autos and wheat produced by the two nations at their points prior to specialization with the amount produced at their postspecialization production points, we see that there are gains of 3 autos and 3 bushels of wheat. The production gains from specialization are shown in Table 2.6(a).

What are the *consumption gains* from trade for the two nations? With trade, the United States can choose a consumption point along international terms-of-trade line tt. Assume that the United States prefers to consume the same number of autos as it did in the absence of trade. It will export 7 autos for 7 bushels of wheat, achieving a posttrade consumption point at C. The U.S. consumption gains from trade are 3 bushels of wheat, as shown in Figure 2.5(a) and also in Table 2.6(b). The U.S. *trade triangle*, showing its exports, imports, and terms of trade, is denoted by triangle BCD.

In like manner, Canada can choose to consume at some point along international terms-of-trade line tt. Assuming that Canada holds constant its consumption of wheat, it will export 7 bushels of

TABLE 2.6

Gains from Specialization and Trade: Increasing Opportunity Costs

(a) Production Gains from Specialization

	Before Specialization		After Specialization		Net Gain (Loss)	
	Autos	Wheat	Autos	Wheat	Autos	Wheat
United States	5	18	12	14	7	−4
Canada	17	6	13	13	−4	7
World	22	24	25	27	3	3

(b) Consumption Gains from Trade

	Before Trade		After Trade		Net Gain (Loss)	
	Autos	Wheat	Autos	Wheat	Autos	Wheat
United States	5	18	5	21	0	3
Canada	17	6	20	6	3	0
World	22	24	25	27	3	3

wheat for 7 autos and wind up at posttrade consumption point C'. Its consumption gain of 3 autos is also shown in Table 2.6(b). Canada's *trade triangle* is depicted in Figure 2.5(b) by triangle $B'C'D'$. Note that Canada's trade triangle is identical to that of the United States.

In this chapter, we discussed the autarky points and posttrade consumption points for the United States and Canada by assuming "given" tastes and preferences (demand conditions) of the consumers in both countries. In "Exploring Further 2.2" at the end of this chapter, we introduce indifference curves to show the role of each country's tastes and preferences in determining the autarky points and how gains from trade are distributed.

Partial Specialization

One feature of the increasing-cost model analyzed here is that trade generally leads each country to specialize only partially in the production of the good in which it has a comparative advantage. The reason for **partial specialization** is that increasing costs constitute a mechanism that forces costs in two trading nations to converge. When cost differentials are eliminated, the basis for further specialization ceases to exist.

Figure 2.5 assumes that prior to specialization the United States has a comparative cost advantage in producing autos, whereas Canada is relatively more efficient at producing wheat. With specialization, each country produces more of the commodity of its comparative advantage and less of the commodity of its comparative disadvantage. Given increasing-cost conditions, unit costs rise as both nations produce more of their export commodities. Eventually, the cost differentials are eliminated, at which point the basis for further specialization ceases to exist.

When the basis for specialization is eliminated, there exists a strong probability that both nations will produce some of each good. This is because costs often rise so rapidly that a country loses its comparative advantage vis-à-vis the other country before it reaches the endpoint of its production possibilities schedule. In the real world of increasing-cost conditions, partial specialization is a likely result of trade.

Comparative Advantage Extended to Many Products and Countries

In our discussion so far, we have used trading models in which only two goods are produced and consumed and in which trade is confined to two countries. This simplified approach has permitted us to analyze many essential points about comparative advantage and trade. But the real world of international trade involves more than two products and two countries; each country produces thousands of products and trades with many countries. To move in the direction of realism, it is necessary to understand how comparative advantage functions in a world of many products and many countries. As we will see, the conclusions of comparative advantage hold when more realistic situations are encountered.

More Than Two Products

When a large number of goods are produced by two countries, operation of comparative advantage requires that the goods be ranked by the degree of comparative cost. Each country exports the product(s) in which it has the greatest comparative advantage. Conversely, each country imports the product(s) in which it has greatest comparative disadvantage.

Figure 2.6 on page 46 illustrates the hypothetical arrangement of six products—chemicals, jet planes, computers, autos, steel, and semiconductors—in rank order of the comparative advantage of the United States and Japan. The arrangement implies that chemical costs are lowest in the United States relative to Japan, whereas the U.S. cost advantage in jet planes is not quite as pronounced. Conversely, Japan enjoys its greatest comparative advantage in semiconductors.

This product arrangement clearly indicates that, with trade, the United States will produce and export chemicals and that Japan will produce and export semiconductors. But where will the cutoff point lie between what is exported and what is imported? Between computers and autos? Or will Japan produce computers and the United States produce only

FIGURE 2.6

Hypothetical Spectrum of Comparative Advantages for the United States and Japan

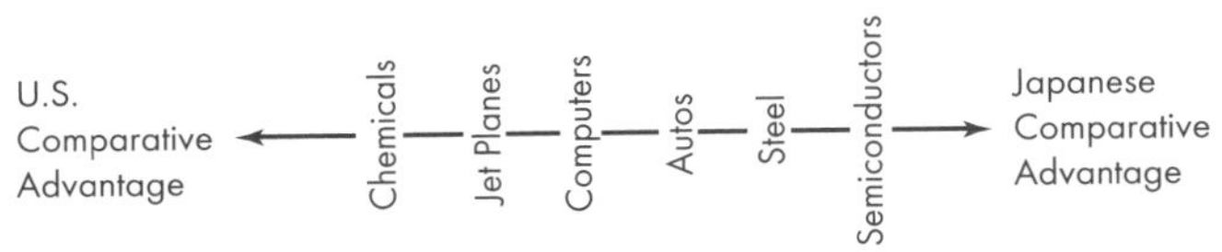

U.S.
Comparative
Advantage

← Chemicals Jet Planes Computers Autos Steel Semiconductors →

Japanese
Comparative
Advantage

When a large number of goods are produced by two countries, operation of the comparative-advantage principle requires the goods to be ranked by the degree of comparative cost. Each country exports the product(s) in which its comparative advantage is strongest. Each country imports the product(s) in which its comparative advantage is weakest.

chemicals and jet planes? Or will the cutoff point fall along one of the products rather than between them—so that computers, for example, might be produced in both Japan and the United States?

The cutoff point between what is exported and what is imported depends on the relative strength of international demand for the various products. One can visualize the products as beads arranged along a string according to comparative advantage. The strength of demand and supply will determine the cutoff point between U.S. and Japanese production. A rise in the demand for steel and semiconductors, for example, leads to price increases that move in favor of Japan. This leads to rising production in the Japanese steel and semiconductor industries.

More Than Two Countries

When many countries are included in a trading example, the United States will find it advantageous to enter into *multilateral trading relationships*. Figure 2.7 illustrates the process of multilateral trade for the United States, Japan, and OPEC. The arrows in the figure denote the directions of exports. The United States exports jet planes to OPEC, Japan imports oil from OPEC, and Japan exports semiconductors to the United States. The real world of international trade involves trading relationships even more complex than this triangular example.

FIGURE 2.7

Multilateral Trade Among the United States, Japan, and OPEC

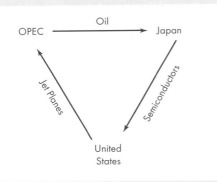

When many countries are involved in international trade, the home country will likely find it advantageous to enter into multilateral trading relationships with a number of countries. This figure illustrates the process of multilateral trade for the United States, Japan, and OPEC.

This example casts doubt upon the idea that *bilateral balance* should pertain to any two trading partners. Indeed, there is no more reason to expect bilateral trade to balance between nations than between individuals. The predictable result is that a nation will realize a trade surplus (exports of goods exceed imports of goods) with trading partners that buy a lot of the things that we supply at low cost. Also, a nation will realize a trade deficit (imports of goods exceed exports of goods) with trading partners that are low-cost suppliers of goods that we import intensely.

Consider the trade "deficits" and "surpluses" of a dentist who likes to snow ski. The dentist can be expected to run a trade deficit with ski resorts, sporting goods stores, and favorite suppliers of items like shoe repair, carpentry, and garbage collection. Why? The dentist is highly likely to buy these items from others. On the other hand, the dentist can be expected to run trade surpluses with his patients and medical insurers. These trading partners are major purchasers of the services provided by the dentist. Moreover, if the dentist has a high rate of saving, the surpluses will substantially exceed the deficits.

The same principles are at work across nations. A country can expect to run sizable surpluses with trading partners that buy a lot of the things the country exports, while trade deficits will be present with trading partners that are low-cost suppliers of the items imported.

What would be the effect if all countries entered into bilateral trade agreements that balanced exports and imports between each pair of countries? The volume of trade and specialization would be greatly reduced, and resources would be hindered from moving to their highest productivity. Although exports would be brought into balance with imports, the gains from trade would be lessened.

Exit Barriers

According to the principle of comparative advantage, an open trading system results in a channeling of resources from uses of low productivity to those of high productivity. Competition forces high-cost plants to exit, leaving the lowest-cost plants to operate in the long run. In practice, the restructuring of inefficient companies can take a long time because they often cling to capacity by nursing along antiquated plants. Why do companies delay plant clos-

ing when profits are subnormal and overcapacity exists? Part of the answer lies in the existence of **exit barriers**, various cost conditions that make lengthy exit a rational response by companies.

Consider the case of the U.S. steel industry. Throughout the past three decades, industry analysts maintained that overcapacity has been a key problem facing U.S. steel companies. Overcapacity has been caused by factors such as imports, reduced demand for steel, and installation of modern technology that allowed greater productivity and increased output of steel with fewer inputs of capital and labor.

Traditional economic theory envisions hourly labor as a *variable* cost of production. However, the U.S. steel companies' contracts with the United Steelworkers of America, the labor union, make hourly labor a *fixed* cost instead of a variable cost, at least in part. The contracts call for many employee benefits such as health and life insurance, pensions, and severance pay when a plant is shut down as well as unemployment benefits.

Besides employee benefits, other exit costs tend to delay the closing of antiquated steel plants. These costs include penalties for terminating contracts to supply raw materials and expenses associated with writing off undepreciated plant assets. Steel companies also face environmental costs when they close plants. They are potentially liable for cleanup costs at their abandoned facilities for treatment, storage, and disposal costs that can easily amount to hundreds of millions of dollars. Furthermore, steel companies cannot realize much by selling their plants' assets. The equipment is unique to the steel industry and is of little value for any purpose other than producing steel. What's more, the equipment in a closed plant is generally in need of major renovation because the former owner allowed the plant to become antiquated prior to closing. Simply put, exit barriers hinder the market adjustments that occur according to the principle of comparative advantage.

Empirical Evidence on Comparative Advantage

We have learned that Ricardo's theory of comparative advantage implies that each country will export goods for which its labor is relatively productive compared with that of its trading partners. Does his theory accurately predict trade patterns? A number of economists have put Ricardo's theory to empirical tests.

The first test of the Ricardian model was made by the British economist G.D.A. MacDougall in 1951. Comparing the export patterns of 25 separate industries for the United States and the United Kingdom for the year 1937, MacDougall tested the Ricardian prediction that nations tend to export goods in which their labor productivity is relatively high. Of the 25 industries studied, 20 fit the predicted pattern. The MacDougall investigation thus supported the Ricardian theory of comparative advantage. Using different sets of data, subsequent studies by Balassa and Stern also supported Ricardo's conclusions.[7]

A more recent test of the Ricardian model comes from Stephen Golub, who examined the relationship between relative unit labor costs (the ratio of wages to productivity) and trade for the United States vis-à-vis the United Kingdom, Japan, Germany, Canada, and Australia. He found that relative unit labor cost helps to explain trade patterns for these nations. The U.S. and Japanese results lend particularly good support for the Ricardian model, as shown in Figure 2.8. The figure displays a scatter plot of U.S.–Japan trade data showing a clear negative correlation between relative exports and relative unit labor costs for 33 industries investigated.

Although there is empirical support for the Ricardian model, it is not without limitations. Labor is not the only factor input. Allowance should be made where appropriate for production and distribution costs other than direct labor. Differences in product quality also explain trade patterns in industries such as automobiles and footwear. We should therefore proceed with caution in explaining a nation's competitiveness solely on

the basis of labor productivity and wage levels. The next chapter will further discuss this topic.

Outsourcing and Free Trade

Recall that the argument for free trade is founded on the theory of comparative advantage developed by David Ricardo in 1817. It states that if each nation produces what it does best and allows trade, all will realize lower prices and higher levels of output, income, and consumption than could be achieved in isolation. However, is free trade relevant in the 2000s?

When Ricardo formulated his theory, major factors of production—climate, soil, geography, and even most workers—could not move to other nations. However, critics of Ricardo note that in today's world, important resources—technology, capital, and ideas—can easily shift around the globe. Comparative advantage is weakened if resources can move to wherever they are most productive: in today's case, to a relatively few nations with abundant cheap labor. In this case, there are no longer shared gains—some nations win and others lose.[8]

Critics see a major change in the world economy caused by three developments. First, strong educational systems produce millions of skilled workers in developing nations, especially in China and India, who are as capable as the most highly educated workers in advanced nations but can work at a much lower cost. Second, inexpensive Internet technology allows many workers to be located anywhere. Third, new political stability permits technology and capital to move more freely around the globe.

Critics fear that the United States may be entering a new situation in which American workers will encounter direct world competition at almost every job category—from the machinist to the software engineer to the medical analyst. Anyone whose job does not entail daily face-to-

[7]G.D.A. MacDougall, "British and American Exports: A Study Suggested by the Theory of Comparative Costs," *Economic Journal* 61 (1951). See also B. Balassa, "An Empirical Demonstration of Classical Comparative Cost Theory," *Review of Economics and Statistics*, August 1963, pp. 231–238, and R. Stern, "British and American Productivity and Comparative Costs in International Trade," *Oxford Economic Papers*, October 1962.

[8]Charles Schumer and Paul Craig Roberts, "Second Thoughts on Free Trade," *The New York Times*, January 6, 2004, op ed. See also Paul Craig Roberts, "The Harsh Truth About Outsourcing," *Business Week*, March 22, 2004, p. 48.

FIGURE 2.8

Relative Exports and Relative Unit Labor Costs: U.S./Japan, 1990

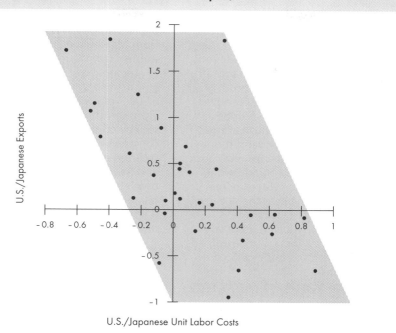

U.S./Japanese Exports (vertical axis)

U.S./Japanese Unit Labor Costs (horizontal axis)

The figure displays a scatter plot of U.S./Japan export data for 33 industries. It shows a clear negative correlation between relative exports and relative unit labor costs. A rightward movement along the figure's horizontal axis indicates a rise in U.S. unit labor costs relative to Japanese unit labor costs; this correlates with a decline in U.S. exports relative to Japanese exports, a downward movement along the figure's vertical axis.

SOURCE: S. Golub, *Comparative and Absolute Advantage in the Asia–Pacific Region*, Center for Pacific Basin Monetary and Economic Studies, Economic Research Department, Federal Reserve Bank of San Francisco, October 1995, p. 46.

face interaction may now be replaced by a lower-paid, equally skilled worker across the globe. American jobs are being sacrificed not because of competition from foreign firms, but because of multinational corporations, often headquartered in America, that are slashing expenses by locating operations in low-wage nations.

Advantage of Outsourcing

However, not everyone agrees with the claim that comparative advantage no longer applies in today's world. They note that it is technology, not the movement of labor, that is creating new opportunities for trade in services, and this does not negate the case for free trade and open markets.[9]

Technologies such as computers and the Internet have made the U.S. service sector a candidate for outsourcing on a global scale. High-tech

[9]Douglas Irwin, "Outsourcing Is Good for America," *The Wall Street Journal*, January 28, 2004. See also McKinsey Global Institute, *Offshoring: Is It a Win-Win Game?* (Washington, DC: McKinsey Global Institute, 2003) and "Who Wins in Offshoring?," *The McKinsey Quarterly*, November 2003.

Do U.S. Companies Have to Outsource Production to Low-Wage Countries to Remain Competitive?

In a global economy, trade with other countries tends to redirect people into the jobs that make best use of their productive abilities. Trade redirects people away from low-productive jobs in industries having cost disadvantages into high-productive jobs in industries having cost advantages. Low-productive jobs tend to disappear from the domestic economy and move abroad.

However, some economists wonder if this process always holds. It rests on the assumption that a low-skilled U.S. job shifted abroad would have remained low-skilled had it stayed home. But if U.S. companies could increase the skill level for such work and perform the task more efficiently, the advantages from moving production would decline. Simply put, if work can be upgraded, it's not so obvious which countries should do the exporting. Let us consider two cases of two U.S. companies, Fortune Brands and New Balance.

Fortune Brands Moves Production to Mexico

You may never have heard of Fortune Brands, but you probably are familiar with some of its products: Titleist golf clubs, Swingline staplers, Jim Beam whiskey, and Master Lock padlocks.

At the turn of the century, Fortune was implementing a cost-cutting program to improve its competitiveness. The firm expanded its manufacturing industrial park in Nogales, Mexico, which employed more than 3,000 people, most of them performing work Fortune used to do in the United States. Fortune moved several businesses into its 40-acre industrial park just south of the Arizona–Mexico border. For example, it brought Master Lock padlocks down from Milwaukee and Acco Industries' Swingline staplers from Queens, New York.

Locating in the Mexican industrial park was an effort to slash costs. It wasn't just a matter of taking advantage of low wages in Mexico—although that was a major factor—but of squeezing every possible cent out of costs. By constructing its own industrial park, Fortune reduced costs by obtaining its land all at once and lowered energy expenses by installing its own electric substation. Efficiencies were also gained by contracting single suppliers of packaging materials and components and having one waste-hauler for all of the campus' plants.

According to Fortune, the move to Nogales came at a crucial time when profit margins on its best-known products were under heavy pressure. Besides competition from U.S. manufacturers already in Mexico, as well as rivals in the Far East, the firm also faced demands for lower prices from its biggest customers. Buyers like Wal-Mart, Lowe's, and Home Depot increased their direct purchases of imports, forcing companies like Fortune to locate production abroad. Simply put, Fortune justified its move to Nogales on the grounds that if it didn't move abroad, its customers would find someone else who would.

New Balance Keeps Production in the United States

Now let us consider New Balance Athletic Shoe, Inc., headquartered in Boston, Massachusetts.

companies such as IBM can easily outsource software programming to India, and American medical centers are relying on Indian doctors to process data. Indeed, it seems that policy makers have few options to slow down this process of rapid technological change, although several state governments are considering laws that restrict contracting with businesses that outsource from low-wage countries.

Proponents of outsourcing maintain that it can create a win-win situation for the global economy. Obviously, outsourcing benefits a recipient country, say India. Some of its people work for, say, a subsidiary of Delta Airlines of the United States and make telephone reservations for Delta's travelers. Moreover, incomes increase for Indian vendors supplying goods and services to the subsidiary, and the Indian government receives addi-

As the firm's managers watched Nike, Reebok, and other rivals shift production abroad at the millennium, they came to think that producing close to their customers could give them an advantage in quick turnaround on new products and in fulfilling orders for shoe stores. How could New Balance manufacture shoes in the United States when Nike and Reebok couldn't? Mainly by using the latest production techniques adopted by American firms in higher-skilled industries. For example, in New Balance's factories workers operate shoe-stitching machines that use cameras to scan the edges of material. Working in small teams, staffers are trained to master a variety of skills. As a result, New Balance's U.S. factories, which manufacture 25 percent of its shoes, have little downtime.

To increase worker efficiency, New Balance trains its workers intensely, even enrolling them in 22-hour courses. The firm also makes large capital investments in its U.S. factories, including massive robots whose arms swing around the production floor, picking up shoe uppers, joining them with soles, and placing them on conveyor belts to be packaged. New Balance has also switched from incentive wages, based on the number of shoes workers produce, to hourly rates. Hourly rates allow staff to concentrate on training and upgrading their skills, and to internalize that the competition is workers in foreign plants, not other workers next to them.

The combination of technology and small teams has reduced the cost disadvantage of manufacturing shoes in the United States.

New Balance's American workers produce a pair of shoes in just 24 minutes, versus about 3 hours in the Chinese factories that manufacture the same product. If the American workers were no more productive than those in China, New Balance's labor costs in the United States, where it pays $14 an hour in wages and benefits, would be a noncompetitive $44 per pair of shoes. But the company has slashed the labor cost to $4 a pair versus $1.30 in China, where wages are about 40 cents an hour. The remaining $2.70 labor cost differential is a manageable 4 percent of a typical $70 pair of shoes, and it's offset by the advantages of producing in the United States, where New Balance can fill store orders faster than rivals and respond more quickly to new footwear trends.

Of course, many of the millions of American jobs that have moved abroad over the decades could probably never have been upgraded enough to offset the wide wage discrepancy with less-developed countries. But New Balance's experience provokes the question of whether Congress might offer tax credits or other incentives to U.S. companies that invest in training or technology for low-skilled production.

Sources: "Fortune Brands Moves Units to Mexico to Lower Costs," *The Wall Street Journal*, August 7, 2000, p. B2, and "New Balance Stays a Step Ahead," *U.S. News & World Report*, July 2, 2001, p. 34; "Low-Skilled Jobs: Do They Have to Move?" *Business Week*, February 26, 2001, pp. 94–95.

tional tax revenue. The United States also benefits from outsourcing in several ways:

- *Reduced costs and increased competitiveness for Delta, which hires low-wage workers in India to make airline reservations.* Also, whereas in the United States many of the offshored jobs are viewed as relatively undesirable or of low prestige, in India they are often considered attractive.

Thus, workers in India may have higher motivation and outproduce their counterparts in the United States. Higher productivity of Indian workers leads to falling unit costs for Delta.
- *New exports.* As business expands, Delta's Indian subsidiary may purchase additional goods from the United States, such as computers and telecommunications equipment. These purchases result in increased earnings

for U.S. companies such as Dell and AT&T and additional jobs for American workers.

- *Repatriated earnings.* Delta's Indian subsidiary returns its earnings to the parent company; these earnings are ploughed back into the U.S. economy. Many offshore providers are in fact U.S. companies that repatriate earnings.

Catherine Mann of the Institute for International Economics analyzed the outsourcing of manufactured components by U.S. telecommunications and computer firms in the 1990s. She found that outsourcing reduced the prices of computers and communications equipment by 10 percent to 30 percent. This stimulated the investment boom in information technology and fostered the rapid expansion of information technology jobs. Also, she contends that the offshoring of information technology services will have a similar effect, creating jobs for American workers to design and implement information technology packages for a range of industries and companies.[10]

Simply put, proponents of outsourcing contend that if U.S. companies can't locate work abroad they will become less competitive in the global economy as their competitors reduce costs by outsourcing. This will weaken the U.S. economy and threaten more American jobs. They also note that job losses tend to be temporary and that the creation of new industries and new products in the United States will result in more lucrative jobs for Americans. As long as the U.S. workforce retains its high level of skills and remains flexible as companies position themselves to improve their productivity, high-value jobs will not disappear in the United States.

Burdens of Outsourcing

Of course, these benefits to the United States do not eliminate the burden on Americans who lose their jobs or find lower-wage ones due to foreign outsourcing. American labor unions often lobby Congress to prevent outsourcing, and several U.S. states have considered legislation to severely restrict their governments from contracting with companies that move jobs to low-wage developing countries.

So far, the debate about the benefits and costs of outsourcing has emphasized jobs rather than wages. However, the risks to the latter may be more significant. Over the past three decades, the wages of low-skilled American workers, those with a high school education or less, decreased both in real terms and relative to the wages of skilled workers, especially those having a college education or higher. Technological change and outsourcing caused the demand for low-skilled American workers to decline. Now the outsourcing of high-skilled jobs threatens to shift demand away from high-skilled workers to cheaper substitutes in Asia. Like the assembly-line revolution that reduced demand for skilled artisan workers during England's industrial revolution, the new wave of outsourcing may prove to be a technical change that decreases demand for many U.S. skilled workers. Although the outsourcing of high-skilled American jobs may yield economic benefits for the nation, there may be a sizable number of losers as well.[11]

Many observers feel that the plight of the displaced worker must be increasingly addressed if free trade and outsourcing are to be widely accepted by the American public. Training programs and generous severance packages, accompanied by insurance programs, are among the measures that could lessen the adverse effects of people suffering job losses due to outsourcing. Some economists call for the insuring of full-time workers who lose jobs. The program would compensate those workers for, say, 70 percent of the wages they missed from the time they were laid off to the time they were reemployed, as well as offer health-care subsidies, for up to two years. The program would be funded by cost savings that companies realize when conducting outsourcing. U.S. government taxes are another possible source of funding for the program. The notion of this proposal is that if the U.S. economy as a whole benefits from outsourcing, some of the benefits should be shared with those whose lives are disrupted by it. As outsourcing grows, so will the importance of government policies in health-care insurance and pension portability, in education and training, and in unemployment-compensation programs that enhance the skills and mobility of American workers.

[10]Catherine Mann, *Globalization of IT Services and White-Collar Jobs: The Next Wave of Productivity Growth*, International Economics Policy Briefs (Washington, DC: Institute for International Economics, December 2003).

[11]Laura D'Andrea Tyson, "Outsourcing: Who's Safe Anymore?" *Business Week*, February 23, 2004, p. 26.

Summary

1. To the mercantilists, stocks of precious metals represented the wealth of a nation. The mercantilists contended that the government should adopt trade controls to limit imports and promote exports. One nation could gain from trade only at the expense of its trading partners because the stock of world wealth was fixed at a given moment in time and because not all nations could simultaneously have a favorable trade balance.

2. Smith challenged the mercantilist views on trade by arguing that, with free trade, international specialization of factor inputs could increase world output, which could be shared by trading nations. All nations could simultaneously enjoy gains from trade. Smith maintained that each nation would find it advantageous to specialize in the production of those goods in which it had an absolute advantage.

3. Ricardo argued that mutually gainful trade is possible even if one nation has an absolute disadvantage in the production of both commodities compared with the other nation. The less productive nation should specialize in the production and export of the commodity in which it has a comparative advantage.

4. Comparative costs can be illustrated with the production possibilities schedule. This schedule indicates the maximum amount of any two products an economy can produce, assuming that all resources are used in their most efficient manner. The slope of the production possibilities schedule measures the marginal rate of transformation, which indicates the amount of one product that must be sacrificed per unit increase of another product.

5. Under constant-cost conditions, the production possibilities schedule is a straight line. Domestic relative prices are determined exclusively by a nation's supply conditions. Complete specialization of a country in the production of a single commodity may occur in the case of constant costs.

6. Because Ricardian trade theory relied solely on supply analysis, it was not able to determine actual terms of trade. This limitation was addressed by Mill in his theory of reciprocal demand. This theory asserts that within the limits to the terms of trade, the actual terms of trade is determined by the intensity of each country's demand for the other country's product.

7. The comparative advantage accruing to manufacturers of a particular product in a particular country can vanish over time when productivity growth falls behind that of foreign competitors. Lost comparative advantages in foreign markets reduce the sales and profits of domestic companies as well as the jobs and wages of domestic workers.

8. In the real world, nations tend to experience increasing-cost conditions. Thus, production possibilities schedules are drawn concave to the diagram's origin. Relative product prices in each country are determined by both supply and demand factors. Complete specialization in production is improbable in the case of increasing costs.

9. According to the comparative-advantage principle, competition forces high-cost producers to exit from the industry. In practice, the restructuring of an industry can take a long time because high-cost producers often cling to capacity by nursing along obsolete plants. Exit barriers refer to various cost conditions that make lengthy exit a rational response by high-cost producers.

10. The first empirical test of Ricardo's theory of comparative advantage was made by MacDougall. Comparing the export patterns of the United States and the United Kingdom, MacDougall found that wage rates and labor productivity were important determinants of international trade patterns. A more recent test of the Ricardian model, done by Golub, also supports Ricardo.

Key Concepts and Terms

- Autarky *(page 34)*
- Basis for trade *(page 28)*
- Commodity terms of trade *(page 39)*
- Community indifference curve *(page 60)*
- Complete specialization *(page 36)*
- Constant opportunity costs *(page 33)*
- Consumption gains *(page 35)*
- Dynamic gains from international trade *(page 40)*
- Exit barriers *(page 47)*
- Free trade *(page 29)*
- Gains from international trade *(page 28)*
- Importance of being unimportant *(page 39)*
- Increasing opportunity costs *(page 42)*
- Indifference curve *(page 60)*
- Labor theory of value *(page 29)*
- Marginal rate of transformation (MRT) *(page 33)*
- Mercantilists *(page 28)*
- No-trade boundary *(page 38)*
- Outer limits for the equilibrium terms of trade *(page 37)*
- Partial specialization *(page 45)*
- Price-specie-flow doctrine *(page 29)*
- Principle of absolute advantage *(page 29)*
- Principle of comparative advantage *(page 30)*
- Production gains *(page 35)*
- Production possibilities schedule *(page 33)*
- Region of mutually beneficial trade *(page 38)*
- Terms of trade *(page 28)*
- Theory of reciprocal demand *(page 38)*
- Trade triangle *(page 36)*
- Trading possibilities line *(page 36)*

Study Questions

1. Identify the basic questions with which modern trade theory is concerned.
2. How did Smith's views on international trade differ from those of the mercantilists?
3. Develop an arithmetic example that illustrates how a nation could have an absolute disadvantage in the production of two goods and could still have a comparative advantage in the production of one of them.
4. Both Smith and Ricardo contended that the pattern of world trade is determined solely by supply conditions. Explain.
5. How does the comparative-cost concept relate to a nation's production possibilities schedule? Illustrate how differently shaped production possibilities schedules give rise to different opportunity costs.
6. What is meant by constant opportunity costs and increasing opportunity costs? Under what conditions will a country experience constant or increasing costs?
7. Why is it that the pretrade production points have a bearing on comparative costs under increasing-cost conditions but not under conditions of constant costs?
8. What factors underlie whether specialization in production will be partial or complete on an international basis?
9. The gains from specialization and trade are discussed in terms of *production gains* and *consumption gains*. What do these terms mean?
10. What is meant by the term *trade triangle*?
11. With a given level of world resources, international trade may bring about an increase in total world output. Explain.
12. **Xtra!** For a tutorial of this question, go to http://carbaughxtra.swlearning.com
The maximum amount of steel or aluminum that Canada and France can produce if they fully use all the factors of production at their disposal with the best technology available to them is shown (hypothetically) in Table 2.7.

TABLE 2.7

Steel and Aluminum Production

	Canada	France
Steel (tons)	500	1200
Aluminum (tons)	1500	800

Assume that production occurs under constant-cost conditions. On graph paper, draw the production possibilities schedules for Canada and France; locate aluminum on the horizontal axis and steel on the vertical axis of each country's graph. In the absence of trade, assume that Canada produces and consumes 600 tons of aluminum and 300 tons of steel and that France produces and consumes 400 tons of aluminum and 600 tons of steel. Denote these autarky points on each nation's production possibilities schedule.

a. Determine the *MRT* of steel into aluminum for each nation. According to the principle of comparative advantage, should the two nations specialize? If so, which product should each country produce? Will the extent of specialization be complete or partial? Denote each nation's specialization point on its production possibilities schedule. Compared to the output of steel and aluminum that occurs in the absence of trade, does specialization yield increases in output? If so, by how much?

b. Within what limits will the terms of trade lie if specialization and trade occur? Suppose Canada and France agree to a terms-of-trade ratio of 1:1 (1 ton of steel = 1 ton of aluminum). Draw the terms-of-trade line in the diagram of each nation. Assuming that 500 tons of steel are traded for 500 tons of aluminum, are Canadian consumers better off as the result of trade? If so, by how much? How about French consumers?

c. Describe the trade triangles for Canada and France.

13. **Xtra!** For a tutorial of this question, go to http://carbaughxtra.swlearning.com

The hypothetical figures in Table 2.8 give five alternate combinations of steel and autos that Japan and South Korea can produce if they fully use all factors of production at their disposal with the best technology available to them. On graph paper, sketch the production possibilities schedules of Japan and South Korea. Locate steel on the vertical axis and autos on the horizontal axis of each nation's graph.

a. The production possibilities schedules of the two countries appear concave, or bowed out, from the origin. Why?

b. In autarky, Japan's production and consumption points along its production possibilities schedule are assumed to be 500 tons of steel and 600 autos. Draw a line tangent to Japan's autarky point and from it calculate Japan's *MRT* of steel into autos. In autarky, South Korea's production and consumption points along its production possibilities schedule are assumed to be 200 tons of steel and 800 autos. Draw a line tangent to South Korea's autarky point and from it calculate South Korea's *MRT* of steel into autos.

c. Based on the *MRT* of each nation, should the two nations specialize according to the principle of comparative advantage? If so, in which product should each nation specialize?

d. The process of specialization in the production of steel and autos continues in Japan

TABLE 2.8

Steel and Auto Production

Japan		South Korea	
Steel (Tons)	Autos	Steel (Tons)	Autos
520	0	1200	0
500	600	900	400
350	1100	600	650
200	1300	200	800
0	1430	0	810

and South Korea until their relative product prices, or *MRT*s, become equal. With specialization, suppose the *MRT*s of the two nations converge at *MRT* = 1. Starting at Japan's autarky point, slide along its production possibilities schedule until the slope of the tangent line equals 1. This becomes Japan's production point under partial specialization. How many tons of steel and how many autos will Japan produce at this point? In like manner, determine South Korea's production point under partial specialization. How many tons of steel and how many autos will South Korea produce? For the two countries, do their combined production of steel and autos with partial specialization exceed their output in the absence of specialization? If so, by how much?

e. With the relative product prices in each nation now in equilibrium at 1 ton of steel equal to 1 auto (*MRT* = 1), suppose 500 autos are exchanged at this terms of trade.

(1) Determine the point along the terms-of-trade line at which Japan will locate after trade occurs. What are Japan's consumption gains from trade?

(2) Determine the point along the terms-of-trade line at which South Korea will locate after trade occurs. What are South Korea's consumption gains from trade?

14. **Xtra!** **For a tutorial of this question, go to http://carbaughxtra.swlearning.com**
Table 2.9 gives hypothetical export price indexes and import price indexes (1990 = 100) for Japan, Canada, and Ireland. Compute the commodity terms of trade for each country for the period 1990–2004. Which country's terms of trade improved, worsened, or showed no change?

15. Why is it that the gains from trade could not be determined precisely under the Ricardian trade model?

16. What is meant by the theory of reciprocal demand? How does it provide a meaningful explanation of the international terms of trade?

17. How does the commodity terms-of-trade concept attempt to measure the direction of trade gains?

TABLE 2.9

Export Price and Import Price Indexes

Country	Export Price Index		Import Price Index	
	1990	2004	1990	2004
Japan	100	150	100	140
Canada	100	175	100	175
Ireland	100	167	100	190

 **netlink**

2.1 For a look at some international data from the United Nations' home page, go to
http://unstats.un.org/unsd

2.2 The Web site of the World Trade Organization offers a number of avenues to explore, including a brief biographical sketch of David Ricardo, information on recent world trade and output growth, and a summary of the arguments in favor of free trade. You can find them at
http://www.wto.org

2.3 For a skeptical look at free trade, go to the United Auto Workers' home page and read some of the articles in the online magazines. Also, Ralph Nader's organization, Public Citizen Global Trade Watch, has created a site that supports this skepticism of free trade. These two sites can be found at
http://www.uaw.org
and
http://www.citizen.org/trade/index.cfm

To access NetLink Exercises and the Virtual Scavenger Hunt, visit the Carbaugh Web site at http://carbaugh.swlearning.com.

Xtra!
CARBAUGH

Log onto the Carbaugh Xtra! Web site (http://carbaughxtra.swlearning.com) for additional learning resources such as practice quizzes, help with graphing, and current events applications.

Comparative Advantage in Money Terms

To illustrate comparative advantage in money terms, refer to the comparative-advantage example of Table 2.3 (page 32), which assumes that labor is the only input and is homogeneous. Recall that (1) the United States has an absolute advantage in the production of both cloth and wine; and (2) the United States has a comparative advantage in cloth production, while the United Kingdom has a comparative advantage in wine production. This information is restated in Table 2.10. As we shall see, even though the United Kingdom is absolutely less efficient in producing both goods, it will export wine (the product of its comparative advantage) when its money wages are so much lower than those of the United States that it is cheaper to make wine in the United Kingdom. Let us see how this works.

Suppose the wage rate is $20 per hour in the United States, as indicated in Table 2.10. If U.S. workers can produce 40 yards of cloth in an hour, the average cost of producing a yard of cloth is $0.50 ($20/40 yards = $0.50 per

yard); similarly, the average cost of producing a bottle of wine in the United States is $0.50. Because Ricardian theory assumes that markets are perfectly competitive, in the long run a product's price equals its average cost of production. The prices of cloth and wine produced in the United States are shown in the table.

Suppose now that the wage rate is £5 (5 British pounds) per hour in the United Kingdom. Thus, the average cost (price) of producing a yard of cloth in the United Kingdom is £0.50 (£5/10 yards = £0.50 per yard), and the average cost (price) of producing a bottle of wine is £0.25. These prices are also shown in Table 2.10.

Is cloth less expensive in the United States or the United Kingdom? In which nation is wine less expensive? When U.S. prices are expressed in dollars and U.K. prices are expressed in pounds, we cannot answer this question. We must therefore express all prices in terms of one currency—say, the U.S. dollar. To do this, we must know the prevailing exchange

TABLE 2.10

Ricardo's Comparative-Advantage Principle Expressed in Money Prices

Nation	Labor Input	Hourly Wage Rate	Cloth (Yards)		Wine (Bottles)	
			Quantity	Price	Quantity	Price
United States	1 hour	$20	40	$0.50	40	$0.50
United Kingdom	1 hour	£5	10	£0.50	20	£0.25
United Kingdom*	1 hour	$8	10	$0.80	20	$0.40

*Dollar prices of cloth and wine, when the prevailing exchange rate is $1.60 = £1. This exchange rate was chosen for this example because at other exchange rates it would not be possible to have balanced trade and balance in the foreign-exchange market.

rate at which the pound and the dollar trade for each other.

Suppose the dollar/pound exchange rate is $1.60 = £1. In Table 2.10, we see that the U.K. hourly wage rate (£5) is equivalent to $8 at this exchange rate (£5 × $1.60 = $8). The average dollar cost of producing a yard of cloth in the United Kingdom is $0.80 ($8/10 yards = $0.80 per yard), and the average dollar cost of producing a bottle of wine is $0.40 ($8/20 bottles = $0.40 per bottle). Compared to the costs of producing these products in the United States, we see that the United Kingdom has lower costs in wine production but higher costs in cloth production. The United Kingdom thus has a comparative advantage in wine.

We conclude that even though the United Kingdom is not as efficient as the United States in the production of wine (or cloth), its lower wage rate in terms of dollars more than compensates for its inefficiency. At this wage rate, the U.K. average cost in dollars of producing wine is less than the U.S. average cost. With perfectly competitive markets, the U.K. selling price is lower than the U.S. selling price, and the United Kingdom exports wine to the United States.

Indifference Curves and Trade

In this section, we introduce indifference curves to show the role of each country's tastes and preferences in determining the autarky points and how gains from trade are distributed.

The role of tastes and preferences can be illustrated graphically by a consumer's indifference curve. An **indifference curve** depicts the various combinations of two commodities that are equally preferred in the eyes of the consumer—that is, yield the same level of satisfaction (utility). The term *indifference curve* stems from the idea that the consumer is indifferent among the many possible commodity combinations that provide identical amounts of satisfaction.

Figure 2.9 illustrates a consumer's indifference map, which consists of a set of indifference curves. Referring to indifference curve *I*, a consumer is just as happy consuming, say, 6 bushels of wheat and 1 auto at point *A* as consuming 3 bushels of wheat and 2 autos at point *B*. All combination points along an indifference curve are equally desirable because they yield the same level of satisfaction. Besides this fundamental characteristic, indifference curves have several other features:

- Indifference curves pass through every point in the figure;
- Indifference curves slope downward to the right;
- Indifference curves are bowed in (convex) to the diagram's origin;
- Indifference curves never intersect each other;
- Indifference curves lying farther from the origin (higher curves) represent greater levels of satisfaction.

FIGURE 2.9

A Consumer's Indifference Map

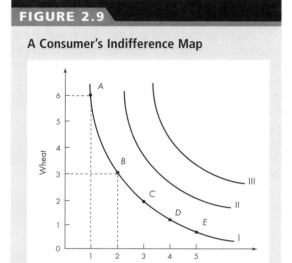

An indifference map is a graph that illustrates an entire set of indifference curves. Each higher indifference curve represents a greater level of satisfaction for the consumer. A community indifference curve denotes various combinations of two goods that yield equal amounts of satisfaction to the nation as a whole.

Having developed an indifference curve for one individual, can we assume that the preferences of all consumers in the entire nation could be added up and summarized by a **community indifference curve**? Strictly speaking, the answer is no, because it is impossible to make interpersonal comparisons of satisfaction. For example, person A may prefer a lot of coffee and little sugar, whereas person B prefers the opposite. The dissimilar nature of individuals' indifference curves results in their being noncomparable. Despite these theoretical problems, a community indifference curve can be used as a pedagogical device that depicts the role of consumer preferences in international trade.

Using indifference curves, let us now develop a trade example to restate the basis-for-trade and the gains-from-trade issues. Figure 2.10 depicts the trading position of the United States. The United States in the absence of trade will maximize satisfaction if it can reach the highest attainable indifference

FIGURE 2.10

Indifference Curves and Trade

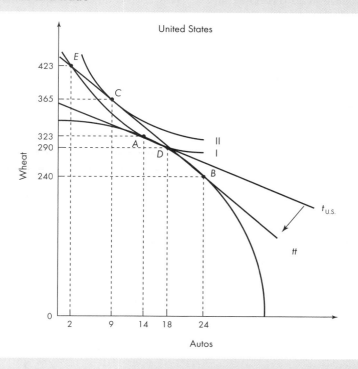

A nation benefits from international trade if it can achieve a higher level of satisfaction (indifference curve) than it can attain in the absence of trade. Maximum gains from trade occur at the point where the international terms-of-trade line is tangent to a community indifference curve.

curve, given the production constraint of its production possibilities schedule. This will occur when the U.S. production possibilities schedule is just tangent to indifference curve I, at point A. At this point, the U.S. relative price ratio is denoted by line $t_{U.S.}$, which equals the absolute slope of the production possibilities curve at that point.

Suppose that the United States has a comparative advantage vis-à-vis Canada in the production of autos. The United States will find it advantageous to specialize in auto production until the two countries' relative prices of autos equalize. Suppose this occurs at production point B, where the U.S. price rises to Canada's price, depicted by line tt. Also suppose that tt becomes the international terms-of-trade line. Starting at production point B, the United States will export autos and import wheat, trading along line tt. The immediate problem the United States faces is to determine the level of trade that will maximize its satisfaction.

Suppose that the United States exchanges 6 autos for 50 bushels of wheat at terms of trade tt. This would shift the United States from production point B to posttrade consumption point D. But the United States would be no better off with trade than it was in the absence of trade. This is because in both cases the consumption points are located along indifference curve I. Trade volume of 6 autos and 50 bushels

of wheat thus represents the minimum acceptable volume of trade for the United States. Any smaller volume would force the United States to locate on a lower indifference curve.

Suppose instead that the United States trades 22 autos for 183 bushels of wheat. The United States would move from production point B to posttrade consumption point E. With trade, the United States would again locate on indifference curve I, resulting in no gains from trade. From the U.S. viewpoint, trade volume of 22 autos and 183 bushels of wheat therefore represents the maximum acceptable volume of trade. Any greater volume would find the United States moving to a lower indifference curve.

Trading along terms-of-trade line tt, the United States can achieve maximum satisfaction if it exports 15 autos and imports 125 bushels of wheat. The U.S. posttrade consumption location would be at point C along indifference curve II, the highest attainable level of satisfaction. Comparing point A and point C reveals that with trade the United States consumes more wheat, but fewer autos, than it does in the absence of trade. Yet point C is clearly a preferable consumption location. This is because under indifference-curve analysis, the gains from trade are measured in terms of total satisfaction rather than in terms of number of goods consumed.

chapter 3

Sources of Comparative Advantage

As discussed in Chapter 2, the comparative-advantage principle can explain why residents of different nations trade. But what are the sources of a nation's comparative advantage? In this chapter, we first consider the leading theories that economists use to explain the sources of comparative advantage.

Factor Endowments as a Source of Comparative Advantage

Recall that David Ricardo thought that comparative advantage depended solely on relative differences in the productivity of labor. However, he did not explain the basis for these differences. Ricardo essentially assumed the existence of comparative advantage in his theoretical model. Moreover, Ricardo's assumption of a single factor of production (labor) ruled out an explanation of how trade affects the distribution of income within a nation and why certain groups favor free trade, whereas other groups oppose it.

In the 1920s and 1930s, the Swedish economists Eli Heckscher and Bertil Ohlin formulated a theory addressing two questions left largely unexplained by Ricardo: (1) What determines comparative advantage? (2) What effect does international trade have on the earnings of various factors of production (distribution of income) in trading nations? Because Heckscher and Ohlin maintained that factor endowments underlie a nation's comparative advantage, their theory became known as the **factor-endowment theory**. It is also known as the **Heckscher–Ohlin theory**[1], and Ohlin was awarded the 1977 Nobel prize in economics for his contribution to the theory of international trade.

The factor-endowment theory states that comparative advantage is explained exclusively by differences in relative national *supply conditions*. In particular, the theory highlights the role of nations' *resource endowments* as the key determinant of comparative advantage. The theory implies that Brazil exports coffee because it has an abundance of the soil and climatic conditions required for coffee's production; the United States and

---

[1]Eli Heckscher's explanation of the factor-endowment theory is outlined in his article, "The Effects of Foreign Trade on the Distribution of Income," *Economisk Tidskrift* 21 (1919), pp. 497–512. Bertil Ohlin's account is summarized in his *Interregional and International Trade* (Cambridge, MA: Harvard University Press, 1933).

63

Canada export wheat because they are endowed with an abundance of temperate-zone land, which is well suited for wheat production; and India and China are huge exporters of shoes and garments because they are heavily endowed with labor.

The factor-endowment theory relies on several simplifying assumptions: (1) nations have the same tastes and preferences (demand conditions); (2) they use factor inputs that are of uniform quality; and (3) they use the same technology. This last assumption is made explicitly to neutralize the possibility that trade is based on international technological variations in favor of the possibility that trade is based solely on differences in supplies of labor and capital.

According to the factor-endowment theory, relative price levels differ among nations because (1) the nations have different relative endowments of factor inputs and (2) different commodities require that the factor inputs be used with differing intensities in their production. Given these circumstances, a nation will *export* that commodity for which a large amount of the relatively *abundant* (cheap) input is used. It will *import* that commodity in the production of which the relatively *scarce* (expensive) input is used.

For example, refer to Table 3.1, which illustrates hypothetical resource endowments in the United States and China. The U.S. **capital/labor ratio** equals 0.5 (100 machines/200 workers = 0.5). In China, the capital/labor ratio is 0.02 (20 machines/1,000 workers = 0.02). Since the U.S. capital/labor ratio exceeds China's capital/labor ratio, we call the United States the capital-abundant country and China the capital-scarce country. On the other side of the coin, China is called the labor-abundant country and the United States the labor-scarce country.

TABLE 3.1

Factor Abundances in the United States and China

Resource	United States	China
Capital	100 machines	20 machines
Labor	200 workers	1,000 workers

Relative abundance of a resource suggests that its relative cost is less than in countries where it is relatively scarce. This means that before the two countries trade, capital would be less expensive in the United States and labor would be less expensive in China. Therefore, the United States will have a lower opportunity cost in goods, say, aircraft, that are produced using more capital and less labor. China's opportunity cost will be lower in goods that are produced using more labor and less capital, say, textiles.

Simply put, the Heckscher–Ohlin theory makes the following assertion: Given identical demand conditions and input productivities, differences in the relative abundance of resources determine relative price levels and the pattern of trade. Capital is relatively cheaper in the capital-abundant country, and labor is relatively cheaper in the labor-abundant country. *The capital-abundant country thus exports the capital-intensive product, and the labor-abundant country exports the labor-intensive product.*

Table 3.2 illustrates capital/labor ratios for selected countries in 1997. To permit useful international comparisons, capital stocks are shown in 1990 international dollar prices to reflect the actual purchasing power of the dollar in each country. We see that the United States had less capital per worker than many other industrial countries, but more capital per worker than the developing countries. According to the factor-endowment theory, we could conclude that the United States would have a comparative advantage in capital-intensive products in relation to developing countries, but not with many industrial countries.

Factor-Price Equalization

In Chapter 2, we learned that free trade tends to equalize commodity prices among trading partners. Can the same be said for factor prices?[2] A nation with trade finds output expanding in its comparative-advantage industry, which uses a lot of the cheap, abundant factor. As a result of the rise in demand for the abundant factor, its price increases.

[2]See Paul A. Samuelson, "International Trade and Equalization of Factor Prices," *Economic Journal*, June 1948, pp. 163–184, and "International Factor-Price Equalization Once Again," *Economic Journal*, June 1949, pp. 181–197.

TABLE 3.2

Capital Stock per Worker of Selected Countries in 1997*

Industrial Country	1997	Developing Country	1997
Japan	$77,429	South Korea	$26,635
Germany	61,673	Chile	17,699
Canada	61,274	Mexico	14,030
France	59,602	Turkey	10,780
United States	50,233	Thailand	8,106
Italy	48,943	Philippines	6,095
Spain	38,897	India	3,094
United Kingdom	30,226	Kenya	1,412

*In 1990 international dollar prices.

Source: A. Heston, R. Summers, and B. Aten, Penn World Table (January 2003, Version 6.0).

At the same time, the expensive, scarce factor is being released from the comparative-disadvantage industry; producers will not be induced to employ this factor unless its price falls. Because this process occurs at the same time in both nations, each nation experiences a *rise in the price of the abundant factor* and a *fall in the price of the scarce factor*. Trade therefore leads toward an equalization of the relative factor prices in the two trading partners.

In the preceding example, the Chinese demand for inexpensive American aircraft results in an increased American demand for its abundant factor, capital; the price of capital thus rises in the United States. As China produces fewer aircraft, its demand for capital decreases, and the price of capital falls. The effect of trade is thus to equalize the price of capital in the two nations. Similarly, the American demand for cheap Chinese textiles leads to China's demanding more labor, its abundant factor; the price of labor thus rises in China. With the United States producing fewer textiles, its demand for labor decreases, and the price of labor falls. With trade, the price of labor tends to equalize in the two trading partners. We conclude that by redirecting demand away from the scarce factor and toward the abundant factor in each nation, trade leads toward **factor-price equalization**. In each nation, the cheap factor becomes more expensive, and the expensive factor becomes cheaper.

An example of the tendency toward factor-price equalization is provided by the U.S. auto industry. By the early 1980s, the compensation of the U.S. autoworker was roughly double that of the Japanese autoworker. In 1981, the average General Motors worker earned hourly wages and benefits of $19.65, compared to the $10.70 earned by the average Japanese autoworker. Owing to the domestic (U.S.) recession, high gasoline prices, and other factors, the demand for U.S.–produced autos deteriorated. However, the U.S. consumer continued to purchase Japanese vehicles up to the limit permissible under the prevailing quota system. To save its members' jobs with struggling U.S. auto companies, the United Auto Workers (UAW) union reluctantly accepted wage cuts so that the companies could remain in business. It is no wonder that the UAW pushed for trade legislation to further restrict foreign autos entering the United States, thereby insulating the wages of domestic autoworkers from the market pressure created by foreign competition.

Although the tendency toward the equalization of factor prices may sound plausible, in the real world we do not see full factor-price equalization. Table 3.3 on page 66 shows indexes of hourly compensation for 11 countries in 2002. Notice that wages differed by a factor of more than 11, from workers in the highest-wage country (Norway) to

TABLE 3.3

Indexes of Hourly Compensation for Manufacturing Workers in 2002 (U.S. = 100)

Norway	128
Germany	118
Switzerland	113
United States	100
Japan	88
United Kingdom	82
Canada	75
Israel	57
South Korea	43
Hong Kong	27
Mexico	11

Source: U.S. Department of Labor, Bureau of Labor Statistics at http://www.bls.gov.

workers in the lowest-wage country (Mexico). There are several reasons why differences in factor prices exist.

Much income inequality across countries results from uneven ownership of human capital. The factor-endowment model assumes that all labor is identical. However, labor across countries differs in terms of human capital, which includes education, training, skill, and the like. We would not expect a computer engineer in the United States with a Ph.D. and 25 years' experience to be paid the same wage as would a college graduate taking her first job as a computer engineer in Peru.

Also, the factor-endowment model assumes that all countries use the same technology for producing a particular good. When a new and better technology is developed, it tends to replace older technologies. But this process can take a long time, especially between advanced and developing countries. Therefore, returns paid to resource owners across countries will not equalize when two countries produce some good using different technologies. Machinery workers using superior production technologies in Germany tend to be paid more than workers using inferior production technologies in Algeria.

Moreover, transportation costs and trade barriers may prevent product prices from equalizing. Such market imperfections reduce the volume of

trade, limiting the extent to which product prices and thus factor prices can become equal.

Simply put, that resource prices may not fully equalize across nations can be explained in part by the fact that the assumptions underlying the factor-endowment theory are not completely borne out in the real world.

Trade and the Distribution of Income

We have seen how specialization and trade can increase the level of output and income for all nations. Not only does trade affect a nation's aggregate income level, however; it also affects the internal **distribution of income** among the owners of resources. How does this occur?

The factor-endowment theory states that the export of commodities embodying large amounts of the relatively cheap, abundant factors makes those factors less abundant in the domestic market. The increased demand for the *abundant factor* leads to an *increase* in its return. At the same time, returns to the factor used intensively in the import-competing product (the *scarce factor*) *decrease* as its demand falls. The increase in the returns to each country's abundant factor thus comes at the expense of the scarce factor's returns.

In theory, increased trade could worsen inequalities in wages even while increasing national income. The U.S. economy, for example, has a relative abundance of skilled labor, and so its comparative advantage is in producing skill-intensive goods. The factor-endowment model suggests that the United States will tend to export goods requiring relatively large amounts of skilled labor and import goods requiring relatively large amounts of unskilled labor. International trade in effect increases the supply of unskilled labor to the U.S. economy, lowering the wages of unskilled American workers relative to those of skilled workers. Skilled workers—who are already at the upper end of the income distribution—find their incomes increasing as exports expand, while unskilled workers are forced into accepting even lower wages in order to compete with imports. According to the factor-endowment theory, then, international trade can aggravate income inequality, at least in a country

The Heckscher–Ohlin Theory: U.S.–China Trade

U.S.–China Trade: Top 10 Products, 2002 (in Millions of Dollars)

U.S. Exports to China		U.S. Imports from China	
Boilers, machinery	4,109,132	Sound equipment, TVs	24,203,918
Electrical machinery	3,950,078	Boilers, machinery	20,214,882
Aircraft, spacecraft	3,428,793	Toys, games, sporting equipment	14,440,857
Medical instruments	1,258,610	Footwear	10,226,857
Plastics	995,157	Furniture, bedding	9,922,790
Agricultural products	917,873	Apparel	4,478,787
Fertilizers	666,331	Leather products	3,909,098
Chemicals	618,408	Plastics	3,227,957
Iron and steel	494,006	Photo and optical equipment	2,758,628
Rawhides	441,625	Iron and steel	2,108,719

Source: U.S. Department of Commerce, International Trade Administration at http://www.ita.doc.gov. Scroll down to "Trade Stats-Express, National Trade Data" and to "Product Profiles of U.S. Merchandise Trade with China."

According to the Heckscher–Ohlin theory, factor endowments are the source of comparative advantage among nations. As we have learned, human capital (skills), scientific talent, and engineering talent are abundant in the United States, but unskilled labor is scarce. Conversely, China is rich in unskilled labor and scarce in scientific and engineering talent. Thus, the Heckscher–Ohlin theory predicts that the United States will export to China goods embodying large amounts of skilled labor and technology; China will export to the United States goods for which a large amount of unskilled labor is used.

The table lists the top 10 U.S. exports to China and the top 10 Chinese exports to the United States in 2002. The pattern of U.S.–China trade appears to fit quite well to the predictions of Heckscher–Ohlin. About 58 percent of U.S. exports to China were concentrated in higher skilled industries, including boilers, machinery, aircraft, and medical equipment. Conversely, Chinese exports to the United States tended to fall into the lower skill industries such as toys, sporting equipment, footwear, and sound equipment. However, note that this trade data provides only a rough overview of U.S.–Chinese trade patterns and does not prove the validity of the Heckscher–Ohlin theory.

Note: For a more sophisticated analysis of the relevance of the Heckscher–Ohlin theory to U.S.–China trade, see Jeffrey Sachs and Howard Shatz, "Trade and Jobs in U.S. Manufacturing," *Brookings Papers on Economic Activity* I (1994), pp. 18, 53.

such as the United States where skilled labor is relatively abundant.

From the perspective of an unskilled U.S. worker, it makes little difference whether his wages are driven down directly via relaxed immigration laws that let in more people from low-wage nations, or indirectly via the importation of products that make heavy use of unskilled labor. To the extent that import competition imposes hardship on suppliers of the scarce factor, those suppliers may desire tariffs or quotas on imports. This may explain why segments of the U.S. labor force (such as steelworkers or autoworkers) favor protection against import competition; labor is scarce relative to capital in the United States, compared with the rest of the world.

The notion that the abundant factor gains from free trade and that the relatively scarce factor loses is founded on the assumption that resources are completely mobile among industries within a country and completely immobile among countries. In the short run, however, the mobility of factors may be imperfect and the results quite different. "Exploring Further 3.1" at the end of this chapter discusses the effects of opening trade when resources are immobile in the short run.

Does Trade Make the Poor Even Poorer?

Are your wages pulled down by workers in Mexico or China? That question has underlined many Americans' fears about their economic future. They worry that the growth of trade with low-wage developing nations could reduce the demand for low-skilled workers in the United States and cause unemployment and wage decreases for U.S. workers.

The wage gap between skilled and unskilled workers widened in the United States during the past 40 years. This wider gap has destroyed the confidence of many Americans that the economic system works for them. For every dollar that a high-school graduate earned in 1973, a college graduate would have made $1.48. By 2000, the college graduate was making about $1.85 for every dollar earned by the high-school graduate. Over the same period, imports increased as a percentage of gross domestic product. These facts raise the question, is trade harming unskilled workers? If so, is this an argument for an increase in trade barriers?[3]

ECONOMIC *Applications*

Visit EconDebate Online for a debate on this topic

Explaining Wage Inequality

Economists agree that some combination of trade, technology, education, immigration, and union weakness has held down wages for unskilled American workers; but apportioning the blame is

tough, partly because income inequality is so pervasive. During the 1990s, economists attempted to disentangle the relative contributions of trade and other influences on the wage discrepancy between skilled workers and unskilled workers. Their approaches shared the analytical framework shown by Figure 3.1. This framework views wages of skilled workers "relative" to those of unskilled workers as the outcome of the interaction between supply and demand in the labor market.

The vertical axis of Figure 3.1 shows the wage ratio, which equals the wage of skilled workers divided by the wage of unskilled workers. The figure's horizontal axis shows the labor ratio, which equals the quantity of skilled workers available divided by the quantity of unskilled workers. Initially we assume that the supply curve of skilled workers relative to unskilled workers is fixed and is denoted by S_0. The demand curve for skilled workers relative to unskilled workers is denoted by D_0. The equilibrium wage ratio is 2.0, found at the intersection at the supply and demand curves: It suggests that the wages of skilled workers are twice as much as the wages of unskilled workers.

In the figure, a shift in either the supply curve or demand curve of skilled workers available relative to unskilled workers will induce a change in the equilibrium wage ratio. Let us consider factors that can affect wage inequality for the United States.

- *International trade and technological change.* Trade liberalization and falling transportation and communication costs result in an increase in the demand curve of skilled workers relative to unskilled workers, say, to D_1 in the figure. Assuming a constant supply curve, the equilibrium wage ratio rises to 2.5, suggesting that the wages of skilled workers are 2.5 times as much as the wages of unskilled workers. Similarly, skill-biased technological improvements lead to an increase in the demand for skilled workers relative to unskilled workers, thus promoting higher degrees of wage inequality.

- *Immigration.* Immigration of unskilled workers results in a decrease in the supply of skilled workers relative to unskilled workers. Assuming that the demand curve is constant, as the supply curve shifts from S_0 to S_2, the equi-

[3]Robert Lawrence and Matthew Slaughter, "International Trade and American Wages in the 1980s," *Brookings Papers on Economic Activity,* 1993.

FIGURE 3.1

Inequality of Wages Between Skilled and Unskilled Workers

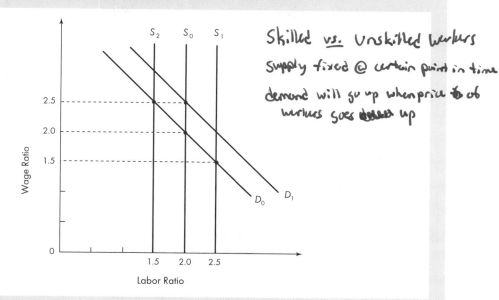

Handwritten notes: Skilled vs. Unskilled Workers
Supply fixed @ certain point in time
demand will go up when price of job
workers goes up

By increasing the demand for skilled relative to unskilled workers, expanding trade or technological improvements result in greater inequality of wages between skilled and unskilled workers. Also, immigration of unskilled workers intensifies wage inequality by decreasing the supply of skilled workers relative to unskilled workers. However, expanding opportunities for college education results in an increase in the supply of skilled relative to unskilled workers, thus reducing wage inequality. In the figure, the wage ratio equals wage of skilled workers/wage of unskilled workers. The labor ratio equals the quantity of skilled workers/quantity of unskilled workers.

librium wage ratio rises to 2.5, thus intensifying wage inequality.

- *Education and training.* As the availability of education and training increases, so does the ratio of skilled workers to unskilled workers, as seen by the increase in the supply curve from S_0 to S_1. If the demand curve remains constant, then the equilibrium wage ratio will fall from 2.0 to 1.5. Additional opportunities for education and training thus serve to reduce the wage inequality between skilled and unskilled workers.

Evidence on Wage Inequality

We have seen how trade and immigration can promote wage inequality. However, economists have found that their effects on the wage distribution have been small. In fact, the vast majority of wage inequality is due to domestic factors, especially technology.

One study, by William Cline, estimated that technological change was about four times more powerful in widening wage inequality in the United States between 1973 and 1993 than trade, and that trade accounted for only 7 percentage points of all the unequalizing forces at work during that period. That's only one study, but it is consistent with many studies. The consensus is that technological change has exerted a far stronger effect on wage inequality than trade.

The results of Cline's study are summarized in Table 3.4 on page 70. It found that between 1973

TABLE 3.4

Sources of the Increase in the Ratio of Skilled to Unskilled Wages in the United States, 1973–1993 (Percent)

A. Forces Causing Greater Inequality of Wages	
International trade	7
Lower transport and communication costs	3
Liberalization of trade barriers	3
Production sharing with other countries	1
Immigration	2
Stagnant minimum wage	5
Decline of labor unions	3
Skill-biased technological change	29
Unexplained	29
B. Forces Causing Greater Equality of Wages	
Increase in supply of skilled workers relative to unskilled workers	−40
C. Net Effect	18

Note: Percentages for unequalizing forces must be chained, not added, to equal total unequalizing effect. Similarly, "A" and "B" must be chained to calculate "C."

Source: William Cline, *Trade and Income Distribution*, Institute for International Economics, Washington, DC, 1997, p. 264.

and 1993, the ratio of skilled to unskilled wages increased by 18 percent. This was the net result of two opposing forces. First, there was an increase in the supply of skilled workers relative to the supply of unskilled workers, made possible by increased opportunities for education and training. The increased relative supply of skilled workers drove down the ratio of skilled to unskilled wages, thus promoting wage equality. But at the same time, a variety of forces promoted wage inequality, and these unequalizing forces overwhelmed the equalizing forces. This resulted in an 18 percent net increase in the ratio of skilled to unskilled wages. Besides trade and technology, these unequalizing forces included immigration, stagnant minimum wage, and decline of unions.

Two things are striking about Cline's data. First, trade has been relatively unimportant in widening wage inequality. Second, trade's impact on wage inequality is overwhelmed not just by technology but also by the main force operating in the opposite direction—education and training. Indeed, the shifts in labor demand, away from less educated workers, are the most important factors

behind the eroding wages of the less educated. Such shifts appear to be the result of economy-wide technological and organizational changes in how work is performed. The use of computers in the workplace has increased significantly in recent years. Not only has computerization led to the replacement of rote jobs (typing letters on an electric typewriter), but workers who use computers are also generally paid higher wages than those who do not.

The relatively small impact of trade on the inequality of skilled and unskilled wages means that skeptics of globalization miss the point if they are concerned mainly about the impact of globalization on adversely affected workers in wealthy countries.

Indeed, some workers in wealthy countries do lose out from a combination of trade and technology. Yet just as a crusade against technology is not the solution to increased inequality resulting from technological progress, most economists argue that increased trade protection will not raise the relative wages of unskilled workers. A better solution involves better education and increased training to allow low-wage workers to take advantage of the technological changes that increase productivity.

Are Actual Trade Patterns Explained by the Factor-Endowment Theory?

Following the development of the Heckscher–Ohlin theory, little empirical evidence was brought to bear about its validity. All that came forth were intuitive examples such as labor-abundant India exporting textiles, rugs, or shoes, or capital-abundant Germany and the United States exporting machinery and automobiles, or land-abundant Australia and Canada exporting wheat and meat. For some economists, such examples were sufficient to illustrate the validity of the Heckscher–Ohlin theory. However, others demanded stronger evidence.

The first attempt to investigate the factor-endowment theory empirically was undertaken by Wassily Leontief in 1954.[4] It had been widely recognized that in the United States capital was relatively abundant and labor was relatively scarce. According to the factor-endowment theory, the United States should export capital-intensive goods and its import-competing goods should be labor-intensive.

Leontief tested this proposition by analyzing the capital/labor ratios for some 200 export industries and import-competing industries in the United

[4]Wassily W. Leontief, "Domestic Production and Foreign Trade: The American Capital Position Reexamined," *Proceedings of the American Philosophical Society* 97, September 1953.

States, based on trade data for 1947. As shown in Table 3.5, Leontief found that the capital/labor ratio for U.S. export industries was lower (about $14,000 per worker year) than that of its import-competing industries (about $18,000 per worker year). Leontief concluded that exports were *less* capital-intensive than import-competing goods! These findings, which contradicted the predictions of the factor-endowment theory, became known as the **Leontief paradox**.

Some economists maintained that 1947 was not a normal year, because the World War II reconstruction of the global economy had not been corrected by that time. To silence his critics, Leontief repeated his investigation in 1956, using 1951 trade data. Leontief again determined that U.S. import-competing goods were more capital-intensive than U.S. exports.

Since Leontief's time, many other studies have tested the predictions of the factor-endowment model. Although the tests conducted thus far are not conclusive, they seem to provide support for a more generalized factor-endowment model that takes into account many subvarieties of capital, land, and human factors and recognizes that factor endowments change over time as a result of investment and technological advances.

The upshot of a generalized factor-endowment model can be seen by looking at some trading statistics of the United States. Table 3.6 on page 72 shows the shares of world resources for various

---

TABLE 3.5

Factor Content of U.S. Trade: Capital and Labor Requirements per Million Dollars of U.S. Exports and Import Substitutes

Empirical Study	Import Substitutes	Exports	Import/Export Ratio
Leontief			
Capital	$3,091,339	$2,550,780	
Labor (person years)	70	182	
Capital/person years	$18,184	$14,015	1.30

Source: W. Leontief, "Domestic Production and Foreign Trade: The American Capital Position Re-examined," *Economia Internazionale*, February 1954, pp. 3–32. See also W. Leontief, "Factor Proportions and the Structure of American Trade: Further Theoretical and Empirical Analysis," *Review of Economics and Statistics*, November 1956, pp. 386–407.

TABLE 3.6

Factor Endowments of Countries and Regions, as a Percentage of the World Total

Country/Region	Capital	Skilled Labor	Unskilled Labor	All Resources
United States	20.8%	19.4%	2.6%	5.6%
European Union	20.7	13.3	5.3	6.9
Japan	10.5	8.2	1.6	2.9
Canada	2.0	1.7	0.4	0.6
Mexico	2.3	1.2	1.4	1.4
China	8.3	21.7	30.4	28.4
India	3.0	7.1	15.3	13.7
Hong Kong, South Korea, Taiwan, Singapore	2.8	3.7	0.9	1.4
Eastern Europe, including Russia	6.2	3.8	8.4	7.6
OPEC	6.2	4.4	7.1	6.7
Rest of the world	17.2	15.5	26.6	24.8
Total	100.0	100.0	100.0	100.0

Source: Elaboration on W. R. Cline, *Trade and Income Distribution* (Washington, DC: Institute for International Economics, 1997) pp. 183–185.

countries and regions in 1993. The table shows that the United States had 20.8 percent of the world's capital, 19.4 percent of the world's skilled labor, and 2.6 percent of the world's unskilled labor. Because the United States has a relatively large share of capital, the factor-endowment model predicts that the United States should have a comparative advantage in goods and services that embody more scientific know-how and physical capital. This prediction is consistent with recent trade data for the United States. The United States has been a net exporter for technologically intensive manufactured goods (such as transportation equipment) and services (such as financial services and lending) that reflect U.S. technological know-how and past accumulation of physical capital. The United States is a net importer of standardized and labor-intensive manufactured goods (such as footwear and textiles).

Early versions of the Heckscher–Ohlin model emphasized relative endowments of capital, labor, and natural resources as sources of comparative advantage. More recently, researchers have increasingly focused on the importance of worker *skills* in the creation of comparative advantage. Investments

in skill, education, and training, which enhance a worker's productivity, create human capital in much the same manner that investments in machinery create physical capital. The United States is abundant in this human capital, including a well-educated and skilled labor force, relative to those of many other nations, as shown in Table 3.7. Therefore, the United States exports goods, such as jetliners and computer software, that use a highly skilled workforce intensively.

Researchers at the World Bank have analyzed the relationship between manufactures and primary products to relative supplies of skills and land, as shown in Figure 3.2 on page 74. Their study included export data for 126 industrial and developing nations in 1985. Values along the horizontal axis of the figure denote the ratio of a nation's average educational attainment to its land area; values along the vertical axis indicate the ratio of manufactured exports to exports of primary products. In the figure, the regression line relates the division of each nation's exports between manufactures and primary products to its relative supplies of skills and land. The regression line suggests that nations endowed with relatively large amounts

TABLE 3.7

U.S. Human Capital Relative to Those of Other Nations

Although education captures only one aspect of human capital, it is the easiest to measure.

	School Enrollment as a Percent of Age Group*		
	Primary Education	Secondary Education	Tertiary Education**
United States	100	96	81
Germany	100	95	31
China	100	70	53
Russia	100	88	49
Mexico	100	66	31
Cambodia	99	39	23
Chile	90	85	43
Chad	48	18	14
Ethopia	35	25	36

*Enrollment ratios may exceed 100 percent because some pupils are younger or older than the country's standard age for a particular level of education.

**Tertiary education includes all postsecondary schools such as technical schools, junior colleges, colleges, and universities.

Source: World Bank, *Human Development Report*, Washington, DC, 2003. See also World Bank, *World Development Report*.

of skilled workers tend to emphasize the export of manufactures. Conversely, land-abundant nations tend to emphasize exports of primary products.

Thus far, we have examined the two most popular theories of trade—the Ricardian theory, in which comparative advantage is based on labor productivities, and the Heckscher–Ohlin theory, in which factor endowments underlie comparative advantage. The Ricardian model is easier to empirically test because measuring labor productivity is easier than measuring factor endowments. Thus, it is no wonder that empirical tests of the Ricardian model have been more successful, as discussed in Chapter 2. In general, these tests support the notion that trade patterns between pairs of countries are largely determined by the relative differences in labor productivities.

However, tests of the Heckscher–Ohlin theory of trade have been mixed. Many empirical studies have raised questions about the validity of this theory. The consensus among economists appears to be that factor endowments explain only a portion of trade pat-

terns. Other determinants of comparative advantage include technology, economies of scale, governmental economic policies, and transportation costs, which we will examine throughout this chapter.

Increasing Returns to Scale and Specialization

Although comparative advantage theory has great appeal, it has little ability to explain why regions with similar productivity levels trade to the extent they do—why Europe and the United States, for example, trade in such great volume. Nor does it shed light on intraindustry trade: the fact that Germany and Japan will trade automobiles with each other.

In response to these weaknesses, economists developed a new theory of trade in the 1980s.[5]

[5]Paul Krugman, "New Theories of Trade Among Industrial Countries," *American Economic Review* 73, No. 2, May 1983, pp. 343–347, and Elhanan Helpman, "The Structure of Foreign Trade," *Journal of Economic Perspectives* 13, No. 2, Spring 1999, pp. 121–144.

FIGURE 3.2

Heckscher–Ohlin, Skills, and Comparative Advantage

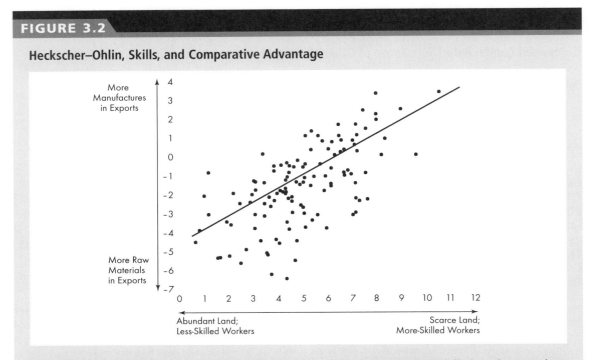

The regression line in the figure suggests that a nation endowed with more-skilled workers tends to have a comparative advantage in manufactures. Conversely, a land-abundant nation tends to have a comparative advantage in primary products.

Source: World Bank, *World Development Report 1995*, Geneva, World Bank, 1995, p. 59.

This "new trade theory" is founded on the notion of increasing returns to scale, also known as economies of scale. The increasing-returns explanation for trade does not attempt to replace the comparative advantage explanation; it just supplements it.

According to increasing-returns trade theory, nations with similar factor endowments, and thus negligible comparative-advantage differences, may nonetheless find it beneficial to trade because they can take advantage of massive economies of scale, a phenomenon prevalent in a number of industries. In the automobile and pharmaceutical industries, for example, the first unit is very expensive to produce, but each subsequent unit costs much less than the one before because the large setup costs can be spread across all units. Companies such as Toyota and Honda reduce costs by specializing in machin-

ery and labor and obtaining quantity discounts in the purchase of inputs.

Increasing-returns trade theory asserts that a nation can develop an industry that has economies of scale, produce that good in great quantity at low average costs, and then trade those low-cost goods to other nations. By doing the same for other increasing-returns goods, all trading partners can take advantage of economies of scale through specialization and exchange.

Figure 3.3 illustrates the effect of economies of scale on trade. Assume that a U.S. auto firm and a Mexican auto firm are each able to sell 100,000 vehicles in their respective countries. Also assume that identical cost conditions result in the same long-run average cost curve for the two firms, *AC*. Note that scale economies result in decreasing unit costs over the first 275,000 autos produced.

FIGURE 3.3

Economies of Scale as a Basis for Trade

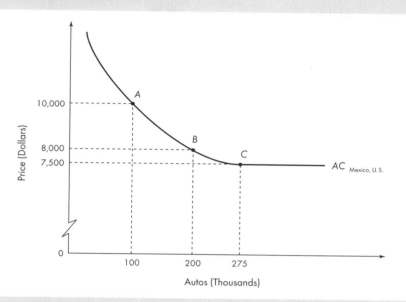

By adding to the size of the domestic market, international trade permits longer production runs by domestic firms, which can lead to greater efficiency and reductions in unit costs.

Initially, there is no basis for trade, because each firm realizes a production cost of $10,000 per auto. Suppose that rising income in the United States results in demand for 200,000 autos, while the Mexican auto demand remains constant. The larger demand allows the U.S. firm to produce more output and take advantage of economies of scale. The firm's cost curve slides downward until its cost equals $8,000 per auto. Compared to the Mexican firm, the U.S. firm can produce autos at a lower cost. With free trade, the United States will now export autos to Mexico.

Economies of scale thus provide additional cost incentives for *specialization* in production. Instead of manufacturing only a few units of each and every product that domestic consumers desire to purchase, a country specializes in the manufacture of large amounts of a limited number of goods and trades for the remaining goods. Specialization in a few products allows a manufacturer to benefit from longer production runs, which lead to decreasing average costs.

A key aspect of increasing-returns trade theory is the **home market effect**: Countries will specialize in products for which there is large domestic demand. Why? By locating close to its largest market, an increasing-scale industry can minimize the cost of shipping its products to its customers while still taking advantage of economies of scale. That is, auto companies will locate in Germany rather than France if it's clear that Germans are likely to buy more cars. That way the company can produce low-cost cars and not have to pay much to ship them to its largest market.

But the home market effect also has a disturbing implication. If increasing-scale industries tend to locate near their largest markets, what happens to small market areas? Other things equal, they're likely to become deindustrialized as factories and industries move to take advantage of scale economies and low transportation costs. Thus, trade could lead to small countries and rural areas becoming peripheral to the economic core, the backwater suppliers of commodities. As Canadian critics have phrased it, "With free trade, Canadians would become hewers of wood and drawers of water." However, other things are not strictly equal: Comparative-advantage effects exist alongside the influence of increasing returns, so the end result of open trade is not a foregone conclusion.

Overlapping Demands as a Basis for Trade

The home market effect has implications for another theory of trade, the so-called **theory of overlapping demands**. This theory was formulated by Staffan Linder, a Swedish economist, in the 1960s.[6] According to Linder, the factor-endowment theory has considerable explanatory power for trade in primary products (natural resources) and agricultural goods. But it does not explain trade in *manufactured goods* because the main force influencing manufactured-good trade is domestic *demand conditions*. Because much of international trade involves manufactured goods, demand conditions play an important role in explaining overall trade patterns.

Linder states that firms within a country are generally motivated to manufacture goods for which there is a large domestic market. This market determines the set of goods that these firms will have to sell when they begin to export. The foreign markets with greatest export potential will be found in nations with consumer tastes similar to those of domestic consumers. A nation's exports are thus an extension of production for the domestic market.

Going further, Linder contends that tastes of consumers are conditioned strongly by their income levels. Thus, a country's average or *per capita income* will yield a particular pattern of

tastes. Nations with high per capita incomes will demand high-quality manufactured goods (luxuries), while nations with low per capita incomes will demand lower-quality goods (necessities).

The Linder hypothesis explains which types of nations will most likely trade with each other. Nations with similar per capita incomes will have overlapping demand structures and will likely consume similar types of manufactured goods. Wealthy (industrial) nations will likely trade with other wealthy nations, and poor (developing) nations will likely trade with other poor nations.

Linder does not rule out all trade in manufactured goods between wealthy and poor nations. Because of unequal income distribution within nations, there will always be some overlapping of demand structures; some people in poor nations are wealthy, and some people in wealthy nations are poor. However, the potential for trade in manufactured goods is small when the extent of demand overlap is small.

Linder's theory is in rough accord with the facts. A high proportion of international trade in manufactured goods takes place among the relatively high-income (industrial) nations: Japan, Canada, the United States, and the European nations. Moreover, much of this trade involves the exchange of similar products: Each nation exports products that are much like the products it imports. However, Linder's theory is not borne out by developing country trade. The bulk of lower-income, developing countries tend to have more trade with high-income countries than with other lower-income countries.

Intraindustry Trade

The trade models considered so far have dealt with **interindustry trade**—the exchange between nations of products of different industries; examples include computers and aircraft traded for textiles and shoes, or finished manufactured items traded for primary materials. Interindustry trade involves the exchange of goods with *different* factor requirements. Nations having large supplies of skilled labor tend to export sophisticated manufactured products, while nations with large supplies of nat-

[6]Staffan B. Linder, *An Essay on Trade and Transformation* (New York: Wiley, 1961), Chapter 3.

ural resources export resource-intensive goods. Much of interindustry trade is between nations having vastly different resource endowments (such as developing countries and industrial countries) and can be explained by the principle of comparative advantage (the Heckscher–Ohlin model).

Interindustry trade is based on **interindustry specialization**: Each nation specializes in a particular industry (say, steel) in which it enjoys a comparative advantage. As resources shift to the industry with a comparative advantage, certain other industries having comparative disadvantages (say, electronics) contract. Resources thus move geographically to the industry where comparative costs are lowest. As a result of specialization, a nation experiences a growing *dissimilarity* between the products that it exports and the products that it imports.

Although some interindustry specialization occurs, this generally has not been the type of specialization that industrialized nations have undertaken in the post–World War II era. Rather than emphasizing entire industries, industrial countries have adopted a narrower form of specialization. They have practiced **intraindustry specialization**, focusing on the production of particular products or groups of products within a given industry (for example, subcompact autos rather than autos). With intraindustry specialization, the opening up of trade does not generally result in the elimination or wholesale contraction of entire industries within a nation; however, the range of products produced and sold by each nation changes.

Advanced industrial nations have increasingly emphasized **intraindustry trade**—two-way trade in a similar commodity. For example, computers manufactured by IBM are sold abroad, while the United States imports computers produced by Hitachi of Japan. Table 3.8 provides examples of intraindustry trade for the United States. As the table indicates, the United States is involved in two-way trade in many manufactured goods such as chemicals and motor vehicles.

The existence of intraindustry trade appears to be *incompatible* with the models of comparative advantage previously discussed. In the Ricardian and Heckscher–Ohlin models, a country would not simultaneously export and import the same product. However, California is a major importer of French wines as well as a large exporter of its own wines; the Netherlands imports Löwenbräu beer while exporting Heineken. Intraindustry trade involves flows of goods with *similar* factor requirements. Nations that are net exporters of manufactured goods embodying sophisticated technology also purchase such goods from other nations. Much of intraindustry trade is conducted among industrial

TABLE 3.8

Intraindustry Trade Examples: Selected U.S. Exports and Imports, 2002 (in Billions of Dollars)

Category	Exports	Imports
Motor vehicles	60.39	168.1
Electrical machinery	82.7	81.2
Office machines	39.7	76.9
Telecommunications equipment	24.9	66.3
Power-generating equipment	34.4	34.0
Industrial machinery	31.8	35.2
Scientific instruments	29.2	20.9
Transportation equipment	46.1	20.2
Chemicals	16.8	30.2
Apparel and clothing	8.0	63.8

Source: U.S. International Trade Administration, *U.S. Manufacturers Trade 1997–2002* at http://www.ita.doc.gov. See also U.S. Department of Commerce, Bureau of Economic Analysis, *U.S. Trade in Goods, 2000* at http://www.bea.doc.gov.

Nike and Reebok Respond to Sweatshop Critics: But Wages Remain at Poverty Level

Sweatshop Conditions in Chinese Factories Producing for U.S. Companies

U.S. Company/Product	Labor Problems in Chinese Factory
Huffy/bicycles	15-hour shifts, 7 days a week. No overtime pay.
Wal-Mart/handbags	Guards beat workers for being late.
Kathie Lee/handbags	Excessive charges for food and lodging mean some workers earn less than 1 cent an hour
Stride Rite/footwear	16-year-old girls apply toxic glues with bare hands and toothbrushes.
Keds/sneakers	Workers locked in factories behind 15-foot walls.
New Balance/shoes	Lax safety standards, no overtime pay as required by Chinese law.

Source: National Labor Committee, *Made in China*, May 2000.

Prodded by controversy over exploitation in foreign factories that make much of America's clothes and shoes, Nike, Reebok, and other U.S. corporations have pushed for sweatshop reforms. A sweatshop is characterized by the systematic violation of workers' rights that have been certified in law. These rights include the right to organize and bargain collectively, and the prohibition of child labor. Also, employers must pay wages that allow workers to feed, clothe, and shelter themselves and their families. The table provides examples of sweatshop conditions in Chinese factories producing for U.S. companies.

For example, a 1997 audit by the firm of Ernst & Young, commissioned by Nike, was leaked to reporters. The audit found that employees in a large Vietnam factory were exposed to the fumes of cancer-causing toluene and had a high incidence of respiratory problems. The audit also found that employees were required to work as long as 65-hour weeks, sometimes in unsafe conditions. Also, in 1999 Reebok released a study of two large Indonesian factories. The study uncovered substandard working conditions, sex bias, and health problems among workers.

Pressured by sweatshop critics, in 1999 Nike and Reebok initiated improvements in the wages and working conditions of its foreign workers. Nike and Reebok increased wages and benefits in their Indonesian footwear factories, which employed more than 100,000 workers, making base compensation 43 percent higher than the minimum wage. Also, Nike agreed to end health and safety problems at its 37 factories in Vietnam and other nations. Moreover, Reebok and Nike took unprecedented steps to defend labor rights activists, who have long been their adversaries. However, critics argued that these reforms left

countries, especially those in Western Europe, whose resource endowments are similar. The firms that produce these goods tend to be oligopolies, with a few large firms constituting each industry.

Intraindustry trade includes trade in homogeneous goods as well as in differentiated products. For *homogeneous goods*, the reasons for intraindustry trade are easy to grasp. A nation may export and import the same product because of *transportation costs*. Canada and the United States, for example, share a border whose length is several thousand miles. To minimize transportation costs (and thus total costs), a buyer in Albany, New York, may import cement from a firm in Montreal, Quebec, while a manufacturer in Seattle, Washington, sells cement to a buyer in Vancouver, British Columbia. Such trade can be explained by the fact that it is less expensive to transport cement from Montreal to Albany than to ship cement from Seattle to Albany.

much to be desired. For example, the Indonesia wage increases by Reebok and Nike put total minimum compensation at only 20 U.S. cents an hour, less than what is needed to support a family and well below the 27 cents per hour that Nike paid until Indonesia's economic crisis began in 1997.

Indeed, there simply is no excuse on humanitarian grounds for sweatshop conditions to prevail anywhere. But what is the best way of preventing sweatshops? Unions and human rights activists in the United States advocate imposing boycotts on imports from countries where sweatshops exist, to encourage those countries to improve working conditions. Although domestic unions may have legitimate concerns over the well-being of foreign workers, unions may benefit from a boycott of products produced by sweatshop workers. The demand for domestic union workers will increase and become more inelastic if the goods produced by low-wage sweatshop workers are no longer perceived as being close substitutes to the goods produced by union workers. Thus a boycott will be expected to increase the wage and employment for union workers.

Critics, however, contend that it makes no sense to impose sanctions on a whole country for labor standards violations by a relative few employers: That would punish the innocent along with the guilty. An alternative approach would be to boycott only the products of those companies that do not implement good labor practices. Yet implementing such selective sanctions would be difficult because it would require governments to devote sufficient resources to enable impartial inspectors to visit each company for purposes of certification.

At the turn of the century, dozens of U.S. universities jumped on the antisweatshop bandwagon, reacting to a growing student protest movement, and took steps to bar labor abuses in the manufacture of clothes that bear college logos. This led to a new White House–sponsored alliance, the Fair Labor Association (FLA), which consisted of 56 universities and corporations such as Nike, Reebok, Liz Claiborne, and Phillips-Van Hausen. The alliance is intended to set up an elaborate, worldwide factory-monitoring system to attempt to eliminate sweatshop abuses. Under its provisions, participating companies can use the FLA logo on their labels and in their advertising, helping portray the firms as ethical corporate citizens. Ethics-minded consumers, in turn, can look for the FLA logo while shopping to guarantee that what they purchase is free of moral stigma. Simply put, company executives hope that the FLA logo will improve their products' image and boost sales; critics of sweatshops hope that the logo will pressure nonparticipating companies into eliminating sweatshop abuses and join the FLA. The charter of the Fair Labor Association is available on the Internet at http://www.dol.gov/dol/esa/public/nosweat/partnership/aip.htm.

Source: Robert Collier, "U.S. Firms Reducing Sweatshop Abuses: But Wages Still at Poverty Level," *San Francisco Chronicle*, April 17, 1999, and "Reebok Finds Ills at Indonesian Factories," *The Wall Street Journal*, October 18, 1999. See also Edward Graham, *Fighting the Wrong Enemy*, Institute for International Economics, Washington, DC, 2000, Chapter 4.

Another reason for intraindustry trade in homogeneous goods is *seasonal*. The seasons in the Southern Hemisphere are opposite those in the Northern Hemisphere. Brazil may export seasonal items (such as agricultural products) to the United States at one time of the year and import them from the United States at another time during the same year. Differentiation in time also affects electricity suppliers. Because of heavy fixed costs in electricity production, utilities attempt to keep plants operating close to full capacity, meaning that it may be less costly to export electricity at off-peak times, when domestic demand is inadequate to ensure full-capacity utilization, and import electricity at peak times.

Although some intraindustry trade occurs in homogeneous products, available evidence suggests that most intraindustry trade occurs in *differentiated products*. Within manufacturing, the levels of intraindustry trade appear to be especially high in machinery, chemicals, and transportation equipment. A significant share of the output of modern economies consists of differentiated products within the same broad product group. Within the automobile industry, a Ford is not identical to a Honda, a Toyota, or a Chevrolet. Two-way trade flows can occur in differentiated products within the same broad product group.

For industrial countries, intraindustry trade in differentiated manufactured goods often occurs when manufacturers in each country produce for the "majority" consumer tastes within their country while ignoring "minority" consumer tastes. This unmet need is fulfilled by imported products. For example, most Japanese consumers prefer Toyotas to General Motors vehicles; yet some Japanese consumers purchase vehicles from General Motors, while Toyotas are exported to the United States. Intraindustry trade increases the range of choices available to consumers in each country, as well as the degree of competition among manufacturers of the same class of product in each country.

Intraindustry trade in differentiated products can also be explained by overlapping demand segments in trading nations. When U.S. manufacturers look overseas for markets in which to sell, they often find them in countries having market segments that are similar to the market segments in which they sell in the United States, for example, luxury automobiles sold to high-income buyers. Nations with similar income levels can be expected to have similar tastes, and thus sizable overlapping market segments, as envisioned by Linder's theory of overlapping demand; they would be expected to engage heavily in intraindustry trade.

Besides marketing factors, economies of scale associated with differentiated products also explain intraindustry trade. A nation may enjoy a cost advantage over its foreign competitor by specializing in a few varieties and styles of a product (for example, subcompact autos with a standard transmission and optional equipment), while its foreign competitor enjoys a cost advantage by specializing in other variants of the same product (subcompact autos with automatic transmission, air-conditioning, cassette player, and other optional equipment). Such specialization permits longer production runs, economies of scale, and decreasing unit costs. Each nation exports its particular type of auto to the other nation, resulting in two-way auto trade. In contrast to interindustry trade, which is explained by the principle of comparative advantage, intraindustry trade can be explained by *product differentiation and economies of scale*.

With intraindustry specialization, fewer adjustment problems are likely to occur than with interindustry specialization, because intraindustry specialization requires a shift of resources within an industry instead of between industries. Interindustry specialization results in a transfer of resources from import-competing to export-expanding sectors of the economy. Adjustment difficulties can occur when resources, notably labor, are occupationally and geographically immobile in the short run; massive structural unemployment may result. In contrast, intraindustry specialization often occurs without requiring workers to exit from a particular region or industry (as when workers are shifted from the production of large-size automobiles to subcompacts); the probability of structural unemployment is thus lessened.

The Product Cycle: A Technologically Based Theory of Trade

The explanations of international trade presented so far are similar in that they presuppose a *given* and unchanging state of technology. The basis for trade was ultimately attributed to such factors as differing labor productivities, factor endowments, and national demand structures. In a dynamic world, however, technological changes occur in different nations at different rates of speed. Technological innovations commonly result in new methods of producing existing commodities, in the production of new commodities, or in commodity improvements. These factors can affect comparative advantage and the pattern of trade.

Recognition of the importance of *dynamic* changes has given rise to another explanation of international trade in manufactured goods: the **product life cycle theory**. This theory focuses on the role of technological innovation as a key determinant of trade patterns in manufactured products.[7]

According to this theory, many manufactured goods such as electronic products and office machinery undergo a predictable *trade cycle*. During this cycle, the home country initially is an exporter, then loses its competitive advantage vis-à-vis its trading partners, and eventually may become an importer of the commodity. The stages that many manufactured goods go through include the following:

1. Manufactured good is introduced to home market.
2. Domestic industry shows export strength.
3. Foreign production begins.
4. Domestic industry loses competitive advantage.
5. Import competition begins.

The introduction stage of the trade cycle begins when an innovator establishes a technological breakthrough in the production of a manufactured good. At the start, the relatively small local market for the product and technological uncertainties imply that mass production is not feasible. The manufacturer will likely operate close to the local market to gain quick feedback on the quality and overall appeal of the product.

During the trade cycle's next stage, the domestic manufacturer begins to export its product to foreign markets having similar tastes and income levels. The local manufacturer finds that, during this stage of growth and expansion, its market becomes large enough to support mass-production operations and the sorting out of inefficient production techniques. The home-country manufacturer is therefore able to supply increasing amounts to the world markets.

As time passes, the manufacturer realizes that it must locate production operations closer to the foreign markets to protect its export profits. The domestic industry enters its mature stage as innovating businesses establish branches abroad. A reason for locating production operations abroad is that the cost advantage initially enjoyed by an innovator is not likely to last indefinitely. Over time, the innovating nation may find its technology

becoming more commonplace and transportation costs and tariffs playing an increasingly important role in influencing selling costs. The innovator may also find that the foreign market is large enough to permit mass-production operations.

Although an innovating nation's monopoly position may be prolonged by legal patents, it will likely break down over time, because in the long run knowledge tends to be a free good. The benefits an innovating nation achieves from its technological gap are short-lived, as import competition from foreign producers begins. Once the innovative technology becomes fairly commonplace, foreign producers begin to imitate the production process. The innovating nation gradually loses its comparative advantage, and its export cycle enters a declining phase.

The trade cycle is complete when the production process becomes so standardized that it can be easily used by other nations. The technological breakthrough therefore no longer benefits only the innovating nation. In fact, the innovating nation may itself become a net importer of the product as its monopoly position is eliminated by foreign competition. Textiles and paper products are generally considered to have run the full course of the trade cycle. The spread of automobile production into many parts of the world implies that its production process is close to becoming standardized.

Radios, Pocket Calculators, and the International Product Cycle

The experience of U.S. and Japanese radio manufacturers illustrates the product life cycle model. Following World War II, the radio was a well-established product. U.S. manufacturers dominated the international market for radios because vacuum tubes were initially developed in the United States. But as production technologies spread, Japan used cheaper labor and captured a large share of the world radio market. The transistor was then developed by U.S. companies. For a number of years, U.S. radio manufacturers were able to compete with the Japanese, who continued to use outdated technologies. Again, the Japanese imitated the U.S. technologies and were able to sell radios at more competitive prices.

[7]See Raymond Vernon, "International Investment and International Trade in the Product Life Cycle," *Quarterly Journal of Economics* 80, 1966, pp. 190–207.

Pocket calculators provide another illustration of a product that has moved through the stages of the international product cycle. This product was invented in 1961 by engineers at Sunlock Comptometer, Inc., and was marketed soon after at a price of approximately $1,000. Sunlock's pocket calculator was more accurate than slide rules (widely used by high school and college students at that time) and more portable than large mechanical calculators and computers that performed many of the same functions.

By 1970, several U.S. and Japanese companies had entered the market with competing pocket calculators; these firms included Texas Instruments, Hewlett-Packard, and Casio (of Japan). The increased competition forced the price down to about $400. As the 1970s continued, additional companies entered the market. Several began to assemble their pocket calculators in foreign countries, such as Singapore and Taiwan, to take advantage of lower labor costs. These calculators were then shipped to the United States. Steadily improving technologies resulted in product improvements and falling prices; by the mid-1970s, pocket calculators sold routinely for $10 to $20, sometimes even less. It appears that pocket calculators had reached the standardized-product stage of the product cycle by the late 1970s, with product technology available throughout the industry, price competition (and thus costs) of major significance, and product differentiation widely adopted. In a period of less than two decades, the international product cycle for pocket calculators was complete.

Dynamic Comparative Advantage: Industrial Policy

David Ricardo's theory of comparative advantage has influenced international trade theory and policy for almost 200 years. It implies that nations are better off by promoting free trade and allowing competitive markets to determine what should be produced and how.

Ricardian theory emphasizes specialization and reallocation of existing resources found domestically. It is essentially a *static* theory that does not allow for a dynamic change in industries' comparative advantage or disadvantage over the course of several decades. The theory overlooks the fact that additional resources can be made available to the trading nation because they can be created or imported.

The remarkable postwar economic growth of the East Asian countries appears to be based on a modification of the static concept of comparative advantage. The Japanese were among the first to recognize that comparative advantage in a particular industry can be created through the mobilization of skilled labor, technology, and capital. They also realized that, in addition to the business sector, government can establish policies to promote opportunities for change through time. Such a process is known as **dynamic comparative advantage**. When government is actively involved in creating comparative advantage, the term **industrial policy** applies.

In its simplest form, industrial policy is a strategy to revitalize, improve, and develop an industry. Proponents maintain that government should enact policies that encourage the development of emerging, "sunrise" industries (such as high technology). This strategy requires that resources be directed to industries in which productivity is highest, linkages to the rest of the economy are strong (as with semiconductors), and future competitiveness is important. Presumably, the domestic economy will enjoy a higher average level of productivity and will be more competitive in world markets as a result of such policies.

A variety of government policies can be used to foster the development and revitalization of industries; examples are antitrust immunity, tax incentives, R&D subsidies, loan guarantees, low-interest-rate loans, and trade protection. Creating comparative advantage requires government to identify the "winners" and encourage resources to move into industries with the highest growth prospects.

To better understand the significance of dynamic comparative advantage, we might think of it in terms of the classic example of Ricardo's theory of comparative advantage. His example showed that, in the eighteenth century, Portugal and England would each have gained by specializing respectively in the production of wine and cloth, even though Portugal might produce both cloth and wine more cheaply than England. According to static comparative-advantage theory, both nations would be better off by specializing in the product in which they had an existing comparative advantage.

By adhering to this prescription, however, Portugal would sacrifice long-run growth for short-run gains. Instead, if Portugal adopted a dynamic theory of comparative advantage, it would specialize in the growth industry of that time (cloth). The Portuguese government (or Portuguese textile manufacturers) would thus initiate policies to foster the development of its cloth industry. This strategy would require Portugal to think in terms of acquiring or creating strength in a "sunrise" sector instead of simply accepting the existing supply of resources and using that endowment as productively as possible.

Today, every industrialized country and many less-developed countries use industrial policies that encourage the development or revitalization of basic industries, including steel, autos, chemicals, transportation, and other important manufactures. Each of these industrial policies differs in character and approach; common to all is an active role for government in the economy. Usually, industrial policy is a strategy developed collectively by government, business, and labor through some sort of tripartite consultation process.

Advocates of industrial policy typically cite Japan as a nation that has been highly successful in penetrating foreign markets and achieving rapid economic growth. Following World War II, the Japanese were the high-cost producers in many basic industries (such as steel). In this situation, a static notion of comparative advantage would require the Japanese to look to areas of lesser disadvantage that were more labor intensive (such as textiles). Such a strategy would have forced Japan into low-productivity industries that would eventually compete with other East Asian nations having abundant labor and modest living standards.

Instead, the Japanese invested in basic industries (steel, autos, and later electronics, including computers) that required intensive employment of capital and labor. From a short-run, static perspective, Japan appeared to pick the wrong industries. But from a long-run perspective, those were the industries in which technological progress was rapid, labor productivity rose fast, and unit costs decreased with the expansion of output. They were also industries in which one would expect rapid growth in demand as national income increased.

These industries combined the potential to expand rapidly, thus adding new capacity, with the opportunity to use the latest technology and thus promote a strategy of cost reduction founded on increasing productivity. Japan, placed in a position similar to that of Portugal in Ricardo's famous example, refused to specialize in "wine" and chose "cloth" instead. Within three decades, Japan became the world's premier low-cost producer of many of the products for which it initially started in a high-cost position.

Critics of industrial policy, however, contend that the causal factor in Japanese industrial success is unclear. They admit that some of the Japanese government's targeted industries—such as semiconductors, steel, shipbuilding, and machine tools—are probably more competitive than they would have been in the absence of government assistance. But they assert that Japan also targeted some losers, such as petrochemicals and aluminum, for which the returns on investment were disappointing and capacity had to be reduced. Moreover, there are examples of successful Japanese industries that did not receive government assistance—motorcycles, bicycles, paper, glass, and cement.

Industrial-policy critics contend that if all trading nations took the route of using a combination of trade restrictions on imports and subsidies on exports, a "beggar-thy-neighbor" process of trade-inhibiting protectionism would result. They also point out that the implementation of industrial policies can result in pork-barrel politics, in which politically powerful industries receive government assistance. Finally, it is argued that in a free market, profit-maximizing businesses have the incentive to develop new resources and technologies that change a country's comparative advantage. This raises the question of whether the government does a better job than the private sector in creating comparative advantage.

Industrial Policies Support Boeing and Airbus

Industrial policy applies to the commercial jetliner industry, as seen in Boeing and Airbus. The world's manufacturers of commercial jetliners operate in an oligopolistic market that has been dominated by Boeing of the United States and the Airbus Company of Europe. During the1970s, Airbus sold less than 5 percent of the world's jetliners; today, it accounts for more than half of the world market.

The United States has repeatedly complained that Airbus receives unfair subsidies from governments of Europe, as seen in Table 3.9. U.S. officials argue that these subsidies place their company at a competitive disadvantage. Airbus allegedly receives loans for the development of new aircraft; these loans are made at below-market interest rates and can amount to 70 to 90 percent of an aircraft's development cost. Rather than repaying the loans according to a prescribed timetable as typically would occur in a competitive market, Airbus is allowed to repay them as it delivers an aircraft. Airbus is also alleged to benefit from debt forgiveness when it suffers losses. The United States maintains that these subsidies allow Airbus to set unrealistically low prices, offer concessions and attractive financing terms to airlines, and write off development costs.

Airbus has defended its subsidies on the grounds that they prevent the United States from holding a worldwide monopoly in commercial jetliners. In the absence of Airbus, European airlines would have to rely exclusively on Boeing as a supplier. Fears of dependence and the loss of autonomy in an area on the cutting edge of technology motivate European governments to subsidize Airbus.

Airbus also argues that Boeing benefits from government assistance. Rather than receiving direct subsidies like Airbus, Boeing receives indirect subsidies. For example, governmental research organizations support aeronautics and propulsion research that is shared with Boeing. Support for commercial jetliner innovation also comes from military-sponsored research and military procurement. Research financed by the armed services yields indirect but important technological spillovers to the commercial jetliner industry, most notably in aircraft engines and aircraft design. Also, Boeing subcontracts part of the production of its jetliners to nations such as Japan and China, whose producers receive substantial governmental subsidies. Boeing is thus able to purchase components from these producers at rel-

TABLE 3.9

Does Airbus Have an Unfair Advantage?

Government support of Airbus has long been a sore point for Boeing. Most of the support comes in the form of low-interest loans to develop new planes, and repayment does not begin until deliveries start. All figures in millions of dollars.

Airbus Aircraft Program	Government Loans	Total Cost to Airbus with Interest	Outstanding Repayments
A300/310	$ 888	$ 0	$ 0
A320	1,480	2,101	140
A330/340	2,671	3,306	0
A340-500	2,548	3,637	3,637
A380	2,450	3,351	3,351
Total	10,037	12,395	7,128

Source: European Aeronautic Defence and Space Company, *Bloomberg News*, Airbus, Boeing, Morgan Stanley.

atively low prices because of governmental subsidies, thus enhancing Boeing's competitiveness.

As a result of the subsidy conflict between Boeing and Airbus, the United States and Europe negotiated an agreement to curb subsidies for the two manufacturers. The principal element of the accord was a 33 percent cap on the amount of government subsidies that these manufacturers could receive for product development. In addition, the indirect subsidies were limited to 4 percent of a firm's commercial-jetliner revenue.

Although the subsidy agreement calmed trade tensions between the United States and Europe, by the early 2000s the subsidy dispute was heating up. The United States criticized the European Union for granting subsidies to Airbus and called for the European Union to renegotiate the 1992 subsidy deal.

What inspired the United States to renew its efforts to force European compliance with its interpretation of the subsidy pact was severe price discounting by Airbus. In 2003, for example, Airbus offered discounts of 40 to 45 percent off list price to win the contract to supply jetliners to airlines. Boeing contended that such discounts could not possibly occur without subsidies. Moreover, Airbus developed a new super-jumbo jetliner, the A380, capable of carrying 555 passengers. The Airbus jetliner would challenge the market supremacy of the Boeing 747 (with about 400 seats), the only other jumbo jet available for sale. To pay for the development costs of the A380, which could reach $15 billion, Airbus will get 40 percent of its funding from parts suppliers, 30 percent from government loans arranged by its partners, and the final chunk from its own resources. It remains to be seen how renewed tensions between Boeing and Airbus will be resolved.

Government Regulatory Policies and Comparative Advantage

Besides providing industrial policies to enhance competitiveness, governments impose regulations on business to pursue goals such as workplace safety, product safety, and a clean environment. In the United States, these regulations are imposed by the Occupational Safety and Health Administration, Consumer Product Safety Commission, and Environmental Protection Agency. Although government regulations may improve the well-being of the public, they can result in higher costs for domestic firms. According to the American Iron and Steel Institute, U.S. steel producers are today technologically advanced, low cost, environmentally responsible, and customer focused. Yet they continue to face regulatory burdens of the U.S. government that impair their competitiveness and trade prospects, as seen in Table 3.10 on page 86.

Strict government regulations applied to the production of goods and services tend to increase costs and erode an industry's competitiveness. This is relevant for both export- and import-competing firms. Even if government regulations are justified on social welfare grounds, the adverse impact on trade competitiveness and the associated job loss have long been a cause for policy concern. Let us examine how governmental regulations on business can affect comparative advantage.

Figure 3.4 on page 87 illustrates the trade effects of pollution regulations imposed on the production process. Assume a world of two steel producers, South Korea and the United States. The supply and demand schedules of South Korea and those of the United States are indicated by $S_{S.K.0}$ and $D_{S.K.0}$, and by $S_{U.S.0}$ and $D_{U.S.0}$. In the absence of trade, South Korean producers sell 5 tons of steel at $400 per ton, while 12 tons of steel are sold in the United States at $600 per ton. South Korea thus enjoys a comparative advantage in steel production.

With free trade, South Korea moves toward greater specialization in steel production, and the United States produces less steel. Under increasing-cost conditions, South Korea's costs and prices rise, while prices and costs fall in the United States. The basis for further growth of trade is eliminated when prices in the two countries are equal at $500 per ton. At this price, South Korea produces 7 tons, consumes 3 tons, and exports 4 tons, and the United States produces 10 tons, consumes 14 tons, and imports 4 tons.

Suppose that the production of steel results in discharges into U.S. waterways, leading the

TABLE 3.10

U.S. Steelmakers Complain About Regulatory Burdens

Here are some examples of U.S. regulations affecting domestic steel producers:

- **Alternative Minimum Tax.** The corporate alternative minimum tax (*AMT*) maintains slower depreciation methods than under the regular corporate tax. The *AMT* increases the cost of capital for steel by about 3.6 percent, acts as a disincentive to capital investment in steel, and harms the competitiveness of domestic steel companies.
- **Health Care.** U.S. steel companies spent more than $1.5 billion for health care in 2003—for workers, retirees, and dependents. This adversely affects the competitiveness of U.S. steel companies vis-à-vis foreign competitors, many of whose health-care costs are borne by government through general tax revenues.
- **OSHA.** The complexity and cost of compliance with Occupational Safety and Health Administration (OSHA) regulations continue to increase. Many OSHA rules do not have a sound scientific or medical basis and thus are impractical and cost ineffective.
- **Electricity Policy.** Electricity is a major component of steel-manufacturing costs, but it cannot be purchased on a competitive basis as are other commodities.
- **Global Climate Change.** Efforts by the United States to achieve a 7 percent decrease in greenhouse gas emissions from 1990 levels by the year 2012, as dictated by the Kyoto Protocol, could result in $5 billion in extra annual energy costs for U.S. steel companies.
- **Clean Air.** Proposed tighter standards for pollutants could place much of the United States—including many steel industry sites—in nonattainment areas. The result would be enormous new costs for steel, with no comparable requirements for U.S. trading partners.
- **Cleanup Standards.** Cleanup standards of manufacturing sites, as mandated by the Resource Conservation and Recovery Act, are cost ineffective. No comparable program exists in other nations. Likewise, U.S. steel companies are often stymied in their efforts to return former industrial properties to productive, job-creating use.

Source: *Domestic Policies that Impact American Steel's International Competitiveness,* American Iron and Steel Institute, Washington, DC, 2001, pp. 1–2.

Environmental Protection Agency to impose pollution regulations on domestic steel producers. Meeting these regulations adds to production costs, resulting in the U.S. supply schedule of steel shifting to $S_{U.S.1}$. The environmental regulations thus provide an additional cost advantage for South Korean steel companies. As South Korean companies expand steel production, say, to 9 tons, higher production costs result in a rise in price to $600. At this price, South Korean consumers demand only 1 ton. The excess supply of 8 tons is earmarked for sale to the United States. As for the United States, 12 tons of steel are demanded at the price of $600, as determined by

South Korea. Given supply schedule $S_{U.S.1}$, U.S. firms now produce only 4 tons of steel at the $600 price. The excess demand, 8 tons, is met by imports from South Korea. For U.S. steel companies, the costs imposed by pollution regulations lead to further comparative disadvantage and a smaller share of the U.S. market.

Environmental regulation thus results in a policy trade-off for the United States. By adding to the costs of domestic steel companies, environmental regulations make the United States more dependent on foreign-produced steel. However, regulations provide American households with cleaner water and air, and thus a higher quality of life.

FIGURE 3.4

Trade Effects of Governmental Regulations

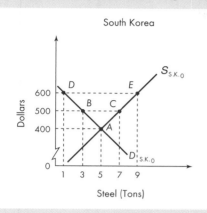
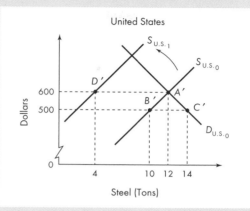

The imposition of government regulations (clean environment, workplace safety, product safety) on U.S. steel companies leads to higher costs and a decrease in market supply. This detracts from the competitiveness of U.S. steel companies and reduces their share of the U.S. steel market.

Also, the competitiveness of other American industries, such as forestry products, may benefit from cleaner air and water. These effects must be considered when forming an optimal environmental regulatory policy. The same principle applies to the regulation of workplace safety by the Occupational Safety and Health Administra-tion and the regulation of product safety by the Consumer Product Safety Commission.

Business Services and Comparative Advantage

The trading of products among countries is not confined to the exporting and importing of manufactured goods, but also includes a group of activities known as **business services**. In many cases, business services are nonstorable, in that they must be consumed as they are produced (for example, management consulting); unlike manufactured goods, business services cannot be maintained in inventories by producers. Examples of internation-

ally traded business services include items such as tourism, freight transportation, construction, banking, finance, insurance, information management, and medical and legal services. Table 3.11 on page 88 shows the world's leading exporters and importers of services.

Does the *theory of comparative advantage* apply to trade in business services? The theory suggests that trade between two countries creates mutual economic gains, provided that such trade is based on a competitive market. As a theoretical statement, the theory of comparative advantage should be equally valid whether the products involved are tradable merchandise (such as aircraft) or tradable services (such as accounting services). The wine and cloth in Ricardo's classic example of comparative advantage could easily have been replaced by wine and insurance policies without altering the validity of the comparative-advantage doctrine.

Similar to manufactured goods, business services are produced by combining resources to create something of value that can be bought or sold in the

TABLE 3.11

Top 10 Exporters and Importers of Business Services, 2002 (in Billions of Dollars)

Exporters	Value	Share*	Importers	Value	Share*
United States	$273.6	17.4%	United States	$205.6	13.3%
United Kingdom	123.1	7.8	Germany	149.1	9.6
Germany	99.6	6.3	Japan	106.6	6.9
France	85.9	5.5	United Kingdom	101.4	6.6
Japan	64.9	4.1	France	68.2	4.4
Spain	62.1	4.0	Italy	61.5	4.0
Italy	59.4	3.8	Netherlands	55.7	3.6
Netherlands	54.1	3.4	China	46.1	3.0
Hong Kong	45.2	2.9	Canada	41.9	2.7
China	39.4	2.5	Ireland	40.4	2.6

*Share of world exports or imports.

Source: World Trade Organization, *World Trade Statistics, 2003* at http://www.wto.org.

market. One would expect that the production and sale of services would follow a pattern of economic behavior similar to the production and sale of manufactured goods. The majority of researchers who have examined the applicability of the comparative-advantage principle to services have indicated that there is nothing in the theory that intrinsically makes it less applicable to services than to goods.

However, applying the comparative-advantage principle to services is difficult because they are such a *heterogeneous group*. The clear differences that exist among, say, banking services, air freight, and architecture services have led many to question whether the theory of comparative advantage can be a useful empirical guide for all service sectors. The heterogeneous nature of services makes it impossible to think of them as a single entity or for a nation to think of itself as having a competitive advantage in all services, any more than it can have a cost advantage in all manufactured goods.

It is unlikely that a single theory can encompass all the characteristics of international trade in services. However, researchers have identified a number of determinants underlying a nation's competitiveness in various services:

- Skills and capabilities of employees and employee wages
- A business's ability to organize a cooperative effort among workers with the right complementary skills
- Abundance of equipment, including communications facilities, data processing, and computers
- The institutional support provided by the legal system, practices, and traditions found in each nation
- The potential economies of scale afforded by a market's size

The export advantage in many services, as revealed by existing patterns of trade in services, appear to lie with the developed countries. Many traded services are intensive in the use of both technology and capital, whether human or physical. This seems to give the developed countries a competitive edge. The United States, for example, has often been characterized as having a comparative advantage in business services; this advantage reflects the long-standing position of the United States as a net exporter of technology and know-how.

Transportation Costs and Comparative Advantage

Besides embodying production costs, the principle of comparative advantage recognizes the costs of moving goods from one nation to another. **Transportation costs** refer to the costs of moving goods, including freight charges, packing and handling expenses, and insurance premiums. These costs can modify international trade patterns.

Trade Effects

The trade effects of transportation costs can be illustrated with a conventional supply and demand model based on increasing cost conditions. Figure 3.5(a) illustrates the supply and demand curves of autos for the United States and Canada. Reflecting the assumption that the United States has the comparative advantage in auto production, the U.S. and Canadian equilibrium locations are at points E and F, respectively. In the absence of trade, the U.S. auto price, $4,000, is lower than that of Canada, $8,000.

When trade is allowed, the United States will move toward greater specialization in auto production, whereas Canada will produce fewer autos. Under increasing-cost conditions, the U.S. cost and price levels rise, and Canada's price falls. The basis for further growth of trade is eliminated when the two countries' prices are equal, at $6,000. At this price, the United States produces 6 autos, consumes 2 autos, and exports 4 autos; Canada produces 2 autos, consumes 6 autos, and imports 4 autos. Thus, $6,000 becomes the equilibrium price for both countries because the excess auto supply of the United States just matches the excess auto demand in Canada.

The introduction of transportation costs into the analysis modifies the conclusions of this example. Suppose the per-unit cost of transporting an

FIGURE 3.5

Free Trade Under Increasing-Cost Conditions

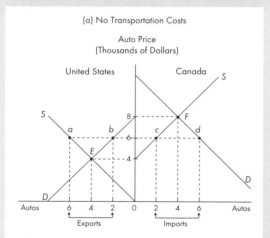

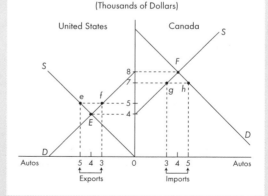

In the absence of transportation costs, free trade results in the equalization of the prices of the traded goods, as well as resource prices, in the trading nations. With the introduction of transportation costs, the low-cost exporting nation produces less, consumes more, and exports less; the high-cost importing nation produces more, consumes less, and imports less. The degree of specialization in production between the two nations decreases as do the gains from trade.

auto from the United States to Canada is $2,000, as shown in Figure 3.5(b). The United States would find it advantageous to produce autos and export them to Canada until its relative price advantage is eliminated. But when transportation costs are included in the analysis, the U.S. export price reflects domestic production costs *plus* the cost of transporting autos to Canada. The basis for trade thus ceases to exist when the U.S. auto price plus the transportation cost rises to equal Canada's auto price. This equalization occurs when the U.S. auto price rises to $5,000 and Canada's auto price falls to $7,000, the difference between them being the $2,000 per-unit transportation cost. Instead of a single price ruling in both countries, there will be two domestic auto prices, differing by the cost of transportation.

Compared with free trade in the absence of transportation costs, when transportation costs are included the high-cost importing country will produce more, consume less, and import less. The low-cost exporting country will produce less, consume more, and export less. *Transportation costs, therefore, tend to reduce the volume of trade, the degree of specialization in production among the nations concerned, and thus the gains from trade.*
The inclusion of transportation costs in the analysis modifies our trade-model conclusions. A product will be traded internationally as long as the pretrade price differential between the trading partners is *greater* than the cost of transporting the product between them. When trade is in equilibrium, the price of the traded product in the exporting nation is less than the price in the importing country by the amount of the transportation cost.

Transportation costs also have implications for the factor-price-equalization theory presented earlier in this chapter. Recall that this theory suggests that free trade tends to equalize commodity prices and factor prices so that all workers will earn the same wage rate and all units of capital will earn the same interest income in both nations. Free trade permits factor-price equalization to occur because factor inputs that cannot move to another country are implicitly being shipped in the form of commodities. Looking at the real world, however, we

see U.S. autoworkers earning more than South Korean autoworkers. One possible reason for this differential is transportation costs. By making low-cost South Korean autos more expensive for U.S. consumers, transportation costs reduce the volume of autos shipped from South Korea to the United States. This reduced trade volume stops the process of commodity- and factor-price equalization before it is complete. In other words, the prices of U.S. autos and the wages of U.S. autoworkers do not fall to the levels of those in South Korea. Transportation costs thus provide some relief to high-cost domestic workers who are producing goods subject to import competition.

The cost of shipping a product from one point to another is determined by a number of factors, including distance, weight, size, value, and the volume of trade between the two points in question. Table 3.12 shows the average importance of transportation costs for imports of the United States and other countries. Since the 1960s, the cost of international transportation has decreased significantly relative to the value of U.S. imports. From 1965 to 2000, transportation

TABLE 3.12

The Size of Transportation Costs for Selected Countries in 2002

Country	Freight and Insurance Costs as a Percent of Import Value*
Philippines	18.2
Poland	14.9
South Africa	12.9
Russia	9.9
New Zealand	7.1
Brazil	5.0
Australia	4.5
United States	3.3
Germany	2.8
Turkey	2.3
France	2.0

*The freight and insurance factor is calculated by dividing the value of a country's imports, including freight and insurance costs (the cost-insurance-freight value), by the value of its imports excluding freight and insurance costs (the free-on-board value).

Source: International Monetary Fund, *International Financial Statistics,* January 2004. See also International Monetary Fund, *International Financial Statistics Yearbook,* 1996, pp. 122–125.

costs as a percentage of the value of all U.S. imports decreased from 10 percent to less than 4 percent. This decline in the relative cost of international transportation has made imports more competitive in U.S. markets and contributed to a higher volume of trade for the United States. Falling transportation costs have been due largely to technological improvements, including the development of large dry-bulk containers, large-scale tankers, containerization, and wide-bodied jets. Moreover, technological advances in telecommunications have reduced the economic distances among nations.

Falling Transportation Costs Foster Trade Boom

If merchants everywhere appear to be selling imports, there is a reason. International trade has been growing at a startling pace. What underlies the expansion of international commerce? The worldwide decrease in trade barriers, such as tariffs and quotas, is certainly one reason. The economic opening of nations that have traditionally been minor players, such as Mexico and China, is another. But one factor behind the trade boom has largely been unnoticed: the declining costs of getting goods to the market.[8]

Today, transportation costs are a less severe obstacle than they used to be. One reason is that the global economy has become much less transport intensive than it once was. In the early 1900s, for example, manufacturing and agriculture were the two most important industries in most nations. International trade thus emphasized raw materials, such as iron ore and wheat, or processed goods such as steel. These sorts of goods are heavy and bulky, resulting in a relatively high cost of transporting them compared with the value of the goods themselves. As a result, transportation costs had much to do with the volume of trade. Over time, however, world output has shifted into goods whose value is unrelated to their size and weight. Finished manufactured goods, not raw commodities, dominate the flow of trade. Therefore, less transportation is required for every dollar's worth of exports or imports.

Consider the business of manufacturing disk drives for computers. Most of the world's disk-drive manufacturing occurs in East Asia, a situation that is possible only because disk drives, although valuable, are small and light and therefore cost little to transport. Computer manufacturers in the United States or Japan will not face hugely bigger freight bills if they import drives from Malaysia rather than purchasing them domestically. Distance thus presents no hindrance to the globalization of the disk-drive industry.

That the cost of shipping has decreased dramatically also accounts for the growth of international trade. In the early 1900s, the physical process of importing or exporting was difficult. Imagine a British textile firm desiring to sell its product in the United States. First, at the firm's loading dock, workers would have lifted bolts of fabric into the back of a truck. The truck would have headed to a port and unloaded its cargo, bolt by bolt, into a dockside warehouse. As a vessel prepared to set sail, dockworkers would have removed the bolts from the warehouse and hoisted them into the hold, where other dockworkers would have stowed them in place. When the cargo reached the United States, the process would have been reversed. Indeed, this sort of shipment was a complicated task, requiring much effort and expense.

Indeed, falling transport costs provided a boost to trade. In 1868, for example, it cost 177.5 pence to ship 8 bushels of wheat from Chicago to Liverpool. By 1902, it cost only 46.5 pence. Thanks to cheaper transport and lower tariffs, prices across the world converged. Whereas in 1870 wheat cost 58 percent more in Liverpool than in Chicago, by 1895 it cost only 18 percent more.

By the 1950s, changes had occurred in the transportation of goods when American shippers developed more efficient methods of moving goods. Under their original scheme, a truck trailer, wheels and all, was unhitched from the driver's cab and hoisted onto the deck of a ship, thus eliminating the need for longshoremen to handle the individual items inside the cargo compartment. This method soon evolved into the use of metal

[8]Drawn from "Delivering the Goods," *The Economist,* November 15, 1997, pp. 85–86.

containers that could be separated from the truck's trailer. With the trailer left at dockside, the containers could be stacked several high aboard the ship. As time passed, a container crane was invented, which made it possible to load and unload containers without capsizing a vessel. Moreover, the adoption of standard container sizes permitted almost any box to be transported on any vessel.

Although the shipping container transformed ocean shipping into a highly productive business, getting the cargo to and from the dock was another problem. National governments generally regulated the prices and shipping practices of domestic freight companies. New firms could enter the freight business only with great difficulty and were subject to tight restrictions. This situation started changing during the 1970s, when the United States began to deregulate its transportation industry. First airlines, then road shippers and railroads, were freed from regulations on what they could carry, where they could haul it, and what price they could charge. Trucks were no longer forced to run empty because they were licensed to ship goods on only one leg of a round-trip journey. Railways were no longer forced to maintain unprofitable branch lines, but could emphasize the shipping of freight in large volumes over long distances. Deregulation of the transportation industry resulted in increased efficiency and lower costs.

The freight revolution intensified during the 1980s, as deregulation and new technology eliminated the boundaries between different modes of transportation. For example, an electronics manufacturer in, say, Taiwan could request an ocean freight company to deliver its exports to the American Midwest. The ocean freighter might negotiate a deal with a railroad to ship the container from Oakland to Kansas City; hire a trucking firm to haul it from Kansas City to Topeka; assume responsibility for fulfilling delivery schedules at each stage of the journey; and send a single invoice for the entire shipment. Such intermodalism has resulted in freight companies such as United Parcel Service and Federal Express, which specialize in using a combination of aircraft and trucks to deliver freight quickly. It has also resulted in railroads' building tracks at dockside, so containers can be shipped directly from ships onto trains.

Terrorist Attacks Result in Added Costs and Slowdowns for U.S. Freight System: A New Kind of Trade Barrier?

Once in a great while, an event occurs that is so horrific that it sears its way into the national psyche. Such an event occurred on September 11, 2001, when terrorists launched an assault on the very symbols of American economic and military might—the twin towers of New York's World Trade Center and the Pentagon complex in Washington, DC.

Immediately following the terrorist attacks, Quality Carriers, Inc., the country's biggest liquid-bulk trucker, rehired the $5,000-a-month night-shift security guard it had previously let go at its tanker-truck terminal in Newark, New Jersey. The company also paid two drivers a total of $1,200 to re-park any vehicles loaded with chemicals in plain view and under security lights. To get in at night, the terminal's 52 drivers now must wait for supervisors to open the gate with new electronic gadgets. For Quality Carriers, extra security measures added to the firm's costs. Company officials noted that the carrier would try to pass along most of the added costs to its customers.

Also at risk were the nation's 361 public seaports, which handle more than 95 percent of overseas trade. Following the attacks, President George W. Bush instructed the U.S. Coast Guard to take additional measures to guard bridges in U.S. harbors and sites such as the Statue of Liberty. For example, Coast Guard personnel board each inbound cargo ship some 11 miles outside the harbor and inspect the ship's cargo. Once inside the harbor, ships must travel at slow speeds, flanked on each side by a tugboat, to prevent ships from ramming into bridge supports. Shipping companies are charged up to $1,500 for each tugboat escort. Once ships are at their berths, random containers are opened and their contents removed and inspected by government officials. Such tightened security measures add about two hours to each ship's arrival process. Table 3.13 summarizes some security measures taken to protect the U.S. freight system from terrorist attacks.

TABLE 3.13

Security Measures Taken to Protect the U.S. Freight System from Terrorist Attacks

Ships	Trains	Planes	Trucks
X-ray screening of cargo	Inspections of tracks, bridges, and tunnels	Earlier drop-off deadlines at airports	Background checks of drivers
Onboard Coast Guard inspections of crews and cargo	Strengthening critical buildings and communications facilities	Ban on shipments from unknown customers	Satellite-tracking systems that monitor exact location of trucks and trailers
Confining foreign crew members to their ships while docked		Waiting periods before shipments put on planes	New fences and alarm systems at freight terminals

Source: "After Terror Attacks, U.S. Freight Services Get Slower, Costlier," *The Wall Street Journal*, September 27, 2001, pp. A1 and A7.

Before the terrorist attacks on the World Trade Center and Pentagon, U.S. border enforcement overwhelming focused on limiting the inflow of illegal drugs and immigrants. However, the terrorist attack complicated business as usual along U.S. borders. This is because the cross-border transportation and communications networks used by terrorists are also the arteries of a highly integrated and interdependent economy. Analysts note that U.S. prosperity relies on its ready access to global networks of transport, energy, information, finance, and labor. It would be self-defeating for the United States to embrace security measures that isolate it from these networks.

The U.S. border security measures adopted since 2001 have consisted of taking the old drug and immigration enforcement infrastructure and adapting it to counterterrorism efforts. As understandable as these measures may be, a sustained crackdown at U.S. ports of entry risks a considerable impact on legitimate travel and trade. For example, the United States and Canada conduct more than $1.3 billion worth of two-way trade a day, most of which is transported by truck. Analysts estimate that a truck crosses this border every 2.5 seconds, amounting to 45,000 trucks and 40,000 commercial shipments every day. Immediately following the terrorist attacks of 2001 and the subsequent clampdown, the result was a drastic slowing of cross-border traffic. Delays for trucks hauling cargo across the U.S.–Canadian border rose from 1 to 2 minutes to 10 to 15 hours, stranding shipments of perishable goods and parts. Automobile firms, many of which produce parts in Ontario and ship them to U.S. assembly plants on a cost-efficient, just-in-time basis, were especially vulnerable. Ford closed an engine plant in Windsor and a vehicle plant in Michigan because of parts shortages. Extensive traffic jams and long delays also plagued the U.S.–Mexican border, where some 300 million people, 90 million cars, and 4.3 million trucks cross the border annually.

Although border delays are now not as long as immediately following the terrorist attacks, heightened security concerns can have an adverse effect on cross-border trade. Simply put, security can become a new kind of trade barrier. The U.S. response immediately following September 11, 2001, was the equivalent of imposing a trade embargo on itself. While the long-term process of North American integration has not been reversed, it has been complicated by the squeeze on the cross-border transportation arteries that provide its lifeblood.[9]

[9]Peter Andreas, "Border Security in the Age of Globalization," *Regional Review*, Federal Reserve Bank of Boston, Third Quarter, 2003, pp. 3–7.

Summary

1. The immediate basis for trade stems from relative commodity price differences among nations. Because relative prices are determined by supply and demand conditions, such factors as resource endowments, technology, and national income are important determinants of the basis for trade.

2. The Heckscher–Ohlin theory suggests that differences in relative factor endowments among nations underlie the basis for trade. The theory asserts that a nation will export that commodity in the production of which a relatively large amount of its abundant and cheap resource is used. Conversely, it will import commodities in the production of which a relatively scarce and expensive resource is used. The theory also states that with trade, the relative differences in resource prices between nations tend to be eliminated.

3. Contrary to the predictions of the Heckscher–Ohlin model, the empirical tests of Wassily Leontief demonstrated that for the United States exports are labor-intensive and import-competing goods are capital-intensive. His findings became known as the Leontief paradox.

4. By widening the size of the domestic market, international trade permits firms to take advantage of longer production runs and increasing efficiencies (such as mass production). Such economies of large-scale production can be translated into lower product prices, which improve a firm's competitiveness.

5. Staffan Linder offers two explanations of world trade patterns. Trade in primary products and agricultural goods conforms well to the factor-endowment theory. But trade in manufactured goods is best explained by overlapping demand structures among nations. For manufactured goods, the basis for trade is stronger when the structure of demand in the two nations is more similar—that is, when the nations' per capita incomes are similar.

6. Besides interindustry trade, the exchange of goods among nations includes intraindustry trade—two-way trade in a similar product. Intraindustry trade occurs in homogeneous goods as well as in differentiated products.

7. One dynamic theory of international trade is the product life cycle theory. This theory views a variety of manufactured goods as going through a trade cycle, during which a nation initially is an exporter, then loses its export markets, and finally becomes an importer of the product. Empirical studies have demonstrated that trade cycles do exist for manufactured goods at some times.

8. Dynamic comparative advantage refers to the creation of comparative advantage through the mobilization of skilled labor, technology, and capital; it can be initiated by either the private or public sector. When government attempts to create comparative advantage, the term *industrial policy* applies. Industrial policy seeks to encourage the development of emerging, sunrise industries through such measures as tax incentives and R&D subsidies.

9. The environmental laws of national governments can affect the competitive position of their industries. These laws often result in cost-increasing compliance measures, such as the installation of pollution-control equipment, which can detract from the competitiveness of domestic industries.

10. International trade includes the flow of services between countries as well as the exchange of manufactured goods. As with trade in manufactured goods, the principle of comparative advantage applies to trade in services.

11. Transportation costs tend to reduce the volume of international trade by increasing the prices of traded goods. A product will be traded only if the cost of transporting it between nations is less than the pretrade difference between their relative commodity prices.

Key Concepts and Terms

- Business services *(page 87)*
- Capital/labor ratio *(page 64)*
- Distribution of income *(page 66)*
- Dynamic comparative advantage *(page 82)*
- Economies of scale *(page 74)*
- Factor-endowment theory *(page 63)*
- Factor-price equalization *(page 65)*

- Heckscher–Ohlin theory *(page 63)*
- Home market effect *(page 75)*
- Increasing returns to scale *(page 74)*
- Industrial policy *(page 82)*
- Interindustry specialization *(page 77)*
- Interindustry trade *(page 76)*
- Intraindustry specialization *(page 77)*

- Intraindustry trade *(page 77)*
- Leontief paradox *(page 71)*
- Product life cycle theory *(page 80)*
- Specific-factors theory *(page 98)*
- Theory of overlapping demands *(page 76)*
- Transportation costs *(page 89)*

Study Questions

1. What are the effects of transportation costs on international trade patterns?

2. Explain how the international movement of products and of factor inputs promotes an equalization of the factor prices among nations.

3. How does the Heckscher–Ohlin theory differ from Ricardian theory in explaining international trade patterns?

4. The Heckscher–Ohlin theory demonstrates how trade affects the distribution of income within trading partners. Explain.

5. How does the Leontief paradox challenge the overall applicability of the factor-endowment model?

6. According to Staffan Linder, there are two explanations of international trade patterns—one for manufactures and another for primary (agricultural) goods. Explain.

7. Do recent world-trade statistics support or refute the notion of a product life cycle for manufactured goods?

8. How can economies of large-scale production affect world trade patterns?

9. Distinguish between intraindustry trade and interindustry trade. What are some major determinants of intraindustry trade?

10. What is meant by the term *industrial policy?* How do governments attempt to create comparative advantage in sunrise sectors of the economy? What are some problems encountered when attempting to implement industrial policy?

11. How can governmental regulatory policies affect an industry's international competitiveness?

12. International trade in services is determined by what factors?

13. **Xtra!** **For a tutorial of this question, go to** http://carbaughxtra.swlearning.com Table 3.14 on page 96 illustrates the supply and demand schedules for calculators in Sweden and Norway. On graph paper, draw the supply and demand schedules of each country.

   a. In the absence of trade, what are the equilibrium price and quantity of calculators produced in Sweden and Norway? Which country has the comparative advantage in calculators?

   b. Assume there are no transportation costs. With trade, what price brings about balance in exports and imports? How many calculators are traded at this price? How many calculators are produced and consumed in each country with trade?

TABLE 3.14

Supply and Demand Schedules for Calculators

| | Sweden | | | Norway | |
Price	Quantity Supplied	Quantity Demanded	Price	Quantity Supplied	Quantity Demanded
$ 0	0	1200	$0	—	1800
5	200	1000	5	—	1600
10	400	800	10	—	1400
15	600	600	15	0	1200
20	800	400	20	200	1000
25	1000	200	25	400	800
30	1200	0	30	600	600
35	1400	—	35	800	400
40	1600	—	40	1000	200
45	1800	—	45	1200	0

c. Suppose the cost of transporting each calculator from Sweden to Norway is $5. With trade, what is the impact of the transportation cost on the price of calculators in Sweden and Norway? How many calculators will each country produce, consume, and trade?

d. In general, what can be concluded about the impact of transportation costs on the price of the traded product in each trading nation? The extent of specialization? The volume of trade?

3.1 The Penn World Dataset provides statistics on 28 key economic variables for the world's major economies from 1950 to 1992, including GDP per capita adjusted for changes in terms of trade. Visit

http://www.bized.ac.uk/dataserv/

penndata/pennhome.htm

3.2 The home page of the Office of Trade and Economic Analysis of the U.S. Department of Commerce/International Trade Administration provides a variety of trade statistics for the United States by world, region, or country. Go to

http://www.ita.doc.gov/td/industry/otea

3.3 The U.S. Department of Labor/ Bureau of Labor Statistics maintains a home page that shows how the hourly compensation of U.S. workers in manufacturing compares to that of workers in other countries. Visit the site at

http://www.bls.gov/data/home.htm

To access NetLink Exercises and the Virtual Scavenger Hunt, visit the Carbaugh Web site at http://carbaugh.swlearning.com.

Xtra!
CARBAUGH

Log onto the Carbaugh Xtra! Web site (http://carbaughxtra.swlearning.com) for additional learning resources such as practice quizzes, help with graphing, and current events applications.

Exploring Further

Specific Factors—Trade and the Distribution of Income in the Short Run

The factor-price-equalization theory assumes that factor inputs are completely mobile among industries within a nation and completely immobile among nations. However, although factor mobility among industries may occur in the long run, many factors are immobile in the short run. Physical capital (such as factories and machinery), for example, is generally used for specific purposes; a machine designed for computer production cannot suddenly be used to manufacture jet aircraft. Similarly, workers often acquire certain skills suited to specific occupations and cannot immediately be assigned to other occupations. The so-called **specific-factors theory** analyzes the income-distribution effects of trade in the *short run* when factor inputs are *immobile* among industries—in effect, a short-run version of the factor-price-equalization theory.

Referring to Figure 3.6, suppose the United States produces steel and computers using labor and capital. Assume that labor is perfectly mobile between the steel and computer industries, but capital is industry-specific: Steel capital cannot be used in computer production, and computer capital cannot be used in steel production. Also assume that the total U.S. labor force equals 30 workers.

In each industry, labor is combined with a fixed quantity of the other factor (steel capital or computer capital) to produce the good.

Labor is thus subject to diminishing marginal productivity, and the labor demand schedule in each industry is downward-sloping.[10] The computer industry's labor demand schedule is denoted by $D_{L(C)}$, while $D_{L(S)}$ denotes the labor demand schedule in the steel industry. Because labor is assumed to be the mobile factor, it will move from the low-wage industry to the high-wage industry until wages are equalized. Let the equilibrium wage rate equal $15 per hour, seen at the intersection point *A* of the two labor demand schedules. At this wage, 14 workers are hired for computer production (reading from left to right) and 16 are used in steel production (reading from right to left).

Suppose the United States has a comparative advantage in computer production. With free trade and expanded output, the domestic price of computers increases, say, from $2,000 to $4,000 per unit, a 100 percent increase; the demand for labor in computer production increases by the same proportion as the computer price increase and is denot-

---

[10]The value of marginal product (*VMP*) refers to the price of a product (*P*) times the marginal product of labor (*MP*). The *VMP* schedule is the labor demand schedule. This is because a business hiring under competitive conditions finds it most profitable to hire labor up to the point at which the price of labor (wage rate) equals its *VMP*. The *VMP* schedule is downward sloping because of the law of diminishing returns: As extra units of labor are added to capital, beyond some point the marginal product attributable to each additional unit of labor will decrease. Because *VMP* = *P* × *MP*, falling *MP* means that VMP decreases as more units of labor are hired.

FIGURE 3.6

Relative Prices and the Specific-Factors Model

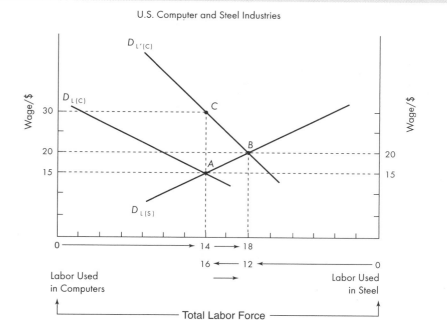

The computer labor demand schedule increases in proportion to the rise in the price of computers (100 percent); however, the wage rate increases less than proportionately (33 percent). Labor is transferred from steel to computer production. Output of computers thus increases, while output of steel falls.

ed by demand schedule $D_{L'(C)}$.[11] The result of the demand increase is a shift in equilibrium from point A to point B.

The increased demand for labor in computer production has two effects. First, the

equilibrium wage rate rises, from $15 to $20, which is a lesser increase (33 percent) than the computer price increase (100 percent). Second, the increased labor demand in computer production draws workers away from steel

[11]Because $VMP = P \times MP$, a 100 percent rise in computer prices (P) leads to a 100 percent increase in VMP. As a result, the labor demand schedule shifts upward by 100 percent from $D_{L(C)}$ to $D_{L'(C)}$ following the price increase. To visualize this shift, compare point A and point C along the two demand schedules. After the increase in

demand, computer firms will be willing to hire a given amount of labor, say 14 workers, at a wage rate of up to $30 instead of $15, a 100 percent increase. In like manner, all points along $D_{L'(C)}$ are located at a wage rate that is 100 percent greater than the corresponding wage rate along $D_{L(C)}$.

production. At the new equilibrium point *B*, 18 workers are employed in computer production and 12 workers are employed in steel manufacturing; compared to equilibrium point *A*, 4 workers are shifted from steel to computers. Output of computers thus rises, and output of steel falls.

How does trade affect the *distribution of income* for the three groups: workers, owners of computer capital, and owners of steel capital? Workers find that although their nominal wages are higher than before, their real wages (that is, the purchasing power of the nominal wage) have fallen relative to the price of computers but have risen relative to the price of steel, which is assumed to be unchanged. Given this information, we are uncertain whether workers are better off or worse off. Their welfare will rise, fall, or remain the same depending on whether they purchase computers or steel or a combination of the two goods.

Owners of computer capital, however, are better off with trade. More computers are being manufactured, and the price received per computer has risen more than the wage cost per unit. The difference between the price and the wage rate is the income of capital owners for each computer sold. Conversely, owners of steel capital are worse off as the rise in computer prices decreases the purchasing power of any given income—that is, real

income falls.[12] In general, owners of factors specific to *export* industries tend to *gain* from international trade, while owners of factors specific to *import-competing* industries *suffer*. International trade thus gives rise to potential conflict between different resource suppliers within a society.

The specific-factors theory helps to explain Japan's rice policy. Japan permits only small quantities of rice to be imported, even though rice production in Japan is more costly than in other nations such as the United States. It is widely recognized that Japan's overall welfare would rise if free imports of rice were permitted. However, free trade would harm Japanese farmers. Although rice farmers displaced by imports might find jobs in other sectors of Japan's economy, they would find changing employment to be time-consuming and costly. Moreover, as rice prices decrease with free trade, so would the value of Japanese farming land. It is no surprise that Japanese farmers and landowners strongly object to free trade in rice; their unified political opposition has influenced the Japanese government more than the interests of Japanese consumers.

---

[12]Not only do the real incomes of steel-capital owners fall, but so do their nominal incomes. Trade results in a decrease in their *VMP* due to a decline in their *MP*, even if the price of steel remains the same.

chapter 4

Tariffs

The conclusion of the principle of comparative advantage presented so far is that free trade and specialization lead to the most efficient use of world resources. With specialization, the level of world output is maximized. Not only do free trade and specialization enhance world welfare, but they can also benefit each participating nation. Every nation can overcome the limitations of its own productive capacity to consume a combination of goods that exceeds the best it can produce in isolation.

Despite the power of the free-trade argument, however, free-trade policies meet major resistance among those companies and workers who face losses in income and jobs because of import competition. Policy makers are torn between the appeal of greater global efficiency made possible by free trade and the needs of the voting public whose main desire is to preserve short-run interests such as employment and income. The benefits of free trade may take years to achieve and are spread out over wide segments of society, whereas the costs of free trade are immediate and fall on specific groups (for example, workers in the import-competing industry).

ECONOMIC *Applications*

Visit EconNews Online
International Trade

Researchers at Harvard University have investigated the factors that make people more likely to favor or oppose free trade. Analyzing a survey of more than 28,000 people in 23 countries, they found the expected result that well-educated people in well-educated countries are more likely to favor trade, while workers in industries exposed to foreign competition in any country are more likely to be against it. Surprisingly, however, even well-educated workers in poorer nations tend to be against free trade. This opposition, from those who might be expected to be allies of globalization, may make it more difficult to extend free trade. The researchers also found that high levels of nationalism and patriotism are associated with support for protectionism. That implies that continuing global conflict, which fosters nationalist fervor at home and abroad, could undermine support for free trade.[1]

This chapter considers barriers to free trade. In particular, it focuses on the role that tariffs play in the global trading system.

[1]Anna Mayda and Dani Rodrik, *Why Are Some People and Countries More Protectionist Than Others?* National Bureau of Economic Research, Working Paper 8461 (Cambridge, MA: 2001).

The Tariff Concept

A **tariff** is simply a tax (duty) levied on a product when it crosses national boundaries. The most widespread tariff is the *import tariff*, which is a tax levied on an imported product. A less common tariff is an *export tariff*, which is a tax imposed on an exported product. Export tariffs have often been used by developing nations. For example, cocoa exports have been taxed by Ghana, and oil exports have been taxed by the Organization of Petroleum Exporting Countries (OPEC) in order to raise revenue or promote scarcity in global markets and hence increase the world price.

Did you know that the United States cannot levy export tariffs? When the U.S. Constitution was written, southern cotton-producing states feared that northern textile-manufacturing states would pressure the federal government into levying export tariffs to depress the price of cotton. An export duty would lead to decreased exports and thus a fall in the price of cotton within the United States. As the result of negotiations, the Constitution was worded so as to prevent export taxes: "No tax or duty shall be laid on articles exported from any state."

Tariffs may be imposed for protection or revenue purposes. A **protective tariff** is designed to insulate import-competing producers from foreign competition. Although a protective tariff generally is not intended to totally prohibit imports from entering the country, it does place foreign producers at a competitive disadvantage when selling in the domestic market. A **revenue tariff** is imposed for the purpose of generating tax revenues and may be placed on either exports or imports.

Over time, tariff revenues have decreased as a source of government revenue for industrial nations, including the United States. In 1900, tariff revenues constituted more than 41 percent of U.S. government receipts; in 2001, the figure stood at 1 percent. However, many developing nations currently rely on tariffs as a major source of government revenue. Table 4.1 shows the percentage of government revenue selected nations derive from tariffs.

Types of Tariffs

Tariffs can be specific, ad valorem, or compound. A **specific tariff** is expressed in terms of a fixed amount of money per physical unit of the imported product. For example, a U.S. importer of a German computer may be required to pay a duty to the U.S. government of $100 per computer, regardless of the computer's price. An **ad valorem** (of value) **tariff**, much like a sales tax, is expressed as a fixed percentage of the value of the imported product. Suppose that an ad valorem duty of 15

TABLE 4.1

Tariff Revenues as a Percentage of Government Revenues, 2001: Selected Countries

Developing Countries	Percentage	Industrial Countries	Percentage
Ghana	74.65	Australia	2.56
The Bahamas	55.94	New Zealand	1.73
Sudan	51.94	Canada	1.32
Madagascar	51.86	Iceland	1.24
Uganda	49.82	Japan	1.24
Sierra Leone	48.60	Switzerland	1.02
Dominican Republic	42.74	United States	1.01
Jordan	31.85	Norway	0.49

Source: International Monetary Fund, *Government Finance Statistics Yearbook* (Washington, DC, 2002), pp. 4–5.

percent is levied on imported trucks. A U.S. importer of a Japanese truck valued at $20,000 would be required to pay a duty of $3,000 to the government ($20,000 × 15% = $3,000). A **compound tariff** is a combination of specific and ad valorem tariffs. For example, a U.S. importer of a television might be required to pay a duty of $20 plus 5 percent of the value of the television. Table 4.2 lists U.S. tariffs on certain items.

What are the relative merits of specific, ad valorem, and compound tariffs?

Specific Tariff

As a fixed monetary duty per unit of the imported product, a specific tariff is relatively easy to apply and administer, particularly to standardized commodities and staple products where the value of the dutiable goods cannot be easily observed. A main disadvantage of a specific tariff is that the degree of protection it affords domestic producers varies *inversely* with changes in import prices. For example, a specific tariff of $1,000 on autos will discourage imports priced at $20,000 per auto to a greater degree than those priced at $25,000. During times of rising import prices, a given specific tariff loses some of its protective effect. The result is to encourage domestic firms to produce less expensive goods, for which the degree of protection against imports is higher. On the other hand, a specific tariff has the advantage of providing domestic producers more protection during a business recession, when cheaper products are purchased. Specific tariffs thus cushion domestic producers progressively against foreign competitors who cut their prices.

Ad Valorem Tariff

Ad valorem tariffs usually lend themselves more satisfactorily to manufactured goods, because they can be applied to products with a wide range of grade variations. As a percentage applied to a product's value, an ad valorem tariff can distinguish among small differentials in product quality to the extent that they are reflected in product price. Under a system of ad valorem tariffs, a person importing a $20,000 Honda would have to pay a higher duty than a person importing a $19,900 Toyota. Under a system of specific tariffs, the duty would be the same.

Another advantage of an ad valorem tariff is that it tends to maintain a constant degree of protection for domestic producers during periods of changing prices. If the tariff rate is 20 percent ad valorem and the imported product price is $200, the duty is $40. If the product's price increases, say, to $300, the duty collected rises to $60; if the

---

TABLE 4.2

Selected U.S. Tariffs

Product	Duty Rate
Brooms	32 cents each
Fishing reels	24 cents each
Wrist watches (without jewels)	29 cents each
Ball bearings	2.4% ad valorem
Electrical motors	6.7% ad valorem
Bicycles	5.5% ad valorem
Wool blankets	1.8 cents/kg + 6% ad valorem
Electricity meters	16 cents each + 1.5% ad valorem
Auto transmission shafts	25 cents each + 3.9% ad valorem

Source: U.S. International Trade Commission, *Tariff Schedules of the United States* (Washington, DC: U.S. Government Printing Office, 2004); http://www.usitc.gov/taffairs.htm.

product price falls to $100, the duty drops to $20. An ad valorem tariff yields revenues proportionate to values, maintaining a constant degree of relative protection at all price levels. An ad valorem tariff is similar to a proportional tax in that the real proportional tax burden or protection does not change as the tax base changes. In recent decades, in response to global inflation and the rising importance of world trade in manufactured products, ad valorem duties have been used more often than specific duties.

Determination of duties under the ad valorem principle at first appears to be simple, but in practice it has suffered from administrative complexities. The main problem has been trying to determine the value of an imported product, a process referred to as **customs valuation**. Import prices are estimated by customs appraisers, who may disagree on product values. Moreover, import prices tend to fluctuate over time, which makes the valuation process rather difficult.

Another customs-valuation problem stems from variations in the methods used to determine a commodity's value. For example, the United States has traditionally used **free-on-board (FOB) valuation**, whereby the tariff is applied to a product's value as it leaves the exporting country. But European countries have traditionally used a **cost-insurance-freight (CIF) valuation**, whereby ad valorem tariffs are levied as a percentage of the imported commodity's total value as it arrives at its final destination. The CIF price thus includes transportation costs, such as insurance and freight.

Compound Tariff

Compound duties are often applied to manufactured products embodying raw materials that are subject to tariffs. In this case, the specific portion of the duty neutralizes the cost disadvantage of domestic manufactures that results from tariff protection granted to domestic suppliers of raw materials, and the ad valorem portion of the duty grants protection to the finished-goods industry. In the United States, for example, there is a compound duty on woven fabrics (48.5 cents per kilogram plus 38 percent). The specific portion of the duty (48.5 cents) compensates U.S. fabric manufacturers for tariff protection granted to U.S. cotton producers, while the ad valorem portion of the duty (38 percent) provides protection for their own woven fabrics.

Smuggled Steel Evades U.S. Tariffs

Manuel Ibanez smuggled 20,000 tons of steel into the United States in 2000. It was easy. All he did was modify the shipping documents on a product called "reinforcing steel bar" to make it appear that it was part of a shipment of another type of steel called "flat-rolled." This deception saved him about $38,000 in import duties. Multiply this tariff-evasion episode many times over and you have smuggled steel avoiding hundreds of thousands of dollars in duties in the past few years. The smuggling of steel concerns the U.S. government, which losses tariff revenue, and also the U.S. steel industry, which maintains that it cannot afford to compete with products made cheaper by tariff evasion.

Each year, about 38 million tons of steel with a value of about $12 billion is imported by the United States. About half of it is subject to tariffs that range from pennies to hundreds of dollars a ton. The amount of the tariff depends on the type of steel product (of which there are about 1,000) and on the country of origin (of which there are about 100). These tariffs are applied to the selling price of the steel in the United States. U.S. Customs Service inspectors scrutinize the shipments that enter the United States to make sure that tariffs are properly assessed. However, monitoring shipments is difficult given the limited staff of the customs service. Therefore, the risk of being caught and the odds of penalties being levied are modest.

Although larger importers of steel generally pay correct duties, it is the smaller, often fly-by-night importers that are more likely to try to slip illegal steel into the country. These traders use one of three methods to evade tariffs. One method is to falsely reclassify steel that would be subject to a tariff as a duty-free product. Another is to detach markings that the steel came from a country subject to tariffs and make it appear to have come from one that is exempt. A third method involves altering the chemical composition of a steel product enough so that it can be labeled duty-free.

For example, one importer purchased 20,000 tons of low-grade wire rod from a mill in Ukraine. He stated that the product was subject to a 10 percent tariff, which in effect made it unprofitable to sell in the United States. The importer then researched the laws and noticed that eight categories of high-grade wire rod did not have a tariff. So, he altered the classification codes that U.S. Customs uses to identify steel products to say he had high-quality wire rod. The deception, he estimates, saved him from having to pay $42,000 in tariffs, and he saw nothing wrong with that. He complained that U.S. trade laws are unfair and that the only way to make any money is by evading the laws. Although Customs agents did not know that Ukraine produces only low-quality wire rod, steel companies in the United States did. They contacted Customs agents, who tracked down the importer and fined him.

Although Customs inspectors attempt to scrutinize imports, once the steel gets by them they can do little about it. They cannot confiscate the smuggled steel because often it is already sold and in use. Meanwhile, the people buying the steel get a nice price break, and the American steel companies, who compete against smuggled steel, find their sales and profits declining.[2]

Effective Rate of Protection

A main objective of an import tariff is to protect domestic producers from foreign competition. By increasing the domestic price of an import, a tariff serves to make home-produced goods more attractive to resident consumers. Output in the import-competing industry can thus expand beyond what would exist in the absence of a tariff. The degree of protection afforded by a tariff reflects the extent to which domestic prices can rise above foreign prices before the home producers are priced out of the market.

The **nominal tariff rate** published in a country's tariff schedule gives us a general idea of the level of protection afforded the home industry. But it may not always truly indicate the actual, or effective, protection given. For example, it is not necessarily true that a 25 percent import tariff on an automobile provides the domestic auto industry a protective margin of 25 percent against foreign producers. This is because the nominal tariff rates apply only to the total value of the final import product. But in the production process, the home import-competing industry may use imported material inputs or intermediate products that are subject to a different tariff than that on the final product; in this case, the **effective tariff rate** will differ from the nominal tariff rate.[3]

The effective tariff rate is an indicator of the actual level of protection that a nominal tariff rate provides the domestic import-competing producers. It signifies *the total increase in domestic productive activities (value added) that an existing tariff structure makes possible*, compared with what would occur under free-trade conditions. The effective rate tells us how much more expensive domestic production can be relative to foreign production and still compete in the market.

Assume that the domestic radio industry adds value to imported inputs by assembling component radio parts imported from abroad. Suppose the imported components can enter the home country on a duty-free basis. Suppose also that 20 percent of a radio's final value can be attributed to domestic assembly activities (value added), the remaining 80 percent reflecting the value of the imported components. Furthermore, let the cost of the radio components be the same for both the domestic country and the foreign country. Finally, assume that the foreign country can produce a radio for $100.

Suppose the home country imposes a nominal tariff of 10 percent on finished radios, so that the domestic import price rises from $100 to $110 per unit (see Table 4.3 on page 106). Does this mean that home producers are afforded an effective rate of protection equal to 10 percent? Certainly not! The imported component parts enter the country duty-free (at a nominal tariff rate less than that on

---

[2]Drawn from "Steel Smugglers Pull Wool over the Eyes of Customs Agents to Enter U.S. Market," *The Wall Street Journal*, November 1, 2001, pp. A1 and A14.

[3]The effective tariff is a measure that applies to a single nation. In a world of floating exchange rates, if all nominal or effective tariff rates rose, the effect would be offset by a change in the exchange rate.

TABLE 4.3

The Effective Rate of Protection

Foreign Radio Import	Cost	Domestic Competing Radio	Cost
Component parts	$80	Component parts	$80
Assembly activity (value added)	20	Assembly activity (value added)	30 (?)
Nominal tariff	10	Domestic price	$110
Import price	$110		

the finished import product), so the effective rate of protection is 50 percent. Compared with what would exist under free trade, domestic radio producers can be 50 percent more costly in their assembly activities and still be competitive!

Table 4.3 shows the figures in detail. Under free trade (zero tariff), a foreign radio could be imported for $100. To meet this price, domestic producers would have to hold their assembly costs down to $20. But under the protective umbrella of the tariff, domestic producers can afford to pay up to $30 for assembly and still meet the $110 domestic price of imported radios. The result is that domestic assembly costs could rise to a level of 50 percent above what would exist under free-trade conditions: ($30 − $20)/$20 = 0.5.

In general, the effective tariff rate is given by the following formula:

$$e = \frac{(n - ab)}{(1 - a)}$$

where

e = the effective rate of protection
n = the nominal tariff rate on the final product
a = the ratio of the value of the imported input to the value of the final product
b = the nominal tariff rate on the imported input

When the values from the radio example are plugged into this formula, we obtain

$$e = \frac{0.1 - 0.8\ (0)}{1 - 0.8}$$
$$= 0.5$$

The nominal tariff rate of 10 percent levied on the final import product thus affords domestic production activities an effective degree of protection equal to 50 percent—five times the nominal rate.

Two consequences of the effective-rate calculation are worthy of mention. First, the degree of effective protection increases as the value added by domestic producers declines (the ratio of the value of the imported input to the value of the final product increases). In the formula, the higher the value of a, the greater the effective-protection rate for any given nominal tariff rate on the final product. Second, a tariff on imports used in the production process reduces the level of effective protection. The higher the value of b, the lower the effective-protection rate for any given nominal tariff on the final product. In the formula, as b rises, the numerator of the formula decreases and hence e decreases. Note that is possible for the effective-tariff rate to assume a negative value, depending on the values of the components in the formula for the calculation of the effective-tariff rate.

Generalizing from this analysis, *when material inputs or intermediate products enter a country at a very low duty while the final imported commodity is protected by a high duty, the result tends to be a high protection rate for the domestic producers.* The nominal-tariff rate on finished goods thus understates the effective rate of protection. But should a tariff be imposed on imported inputs that exceeds that on the finished good, the nominal-tariff rate on the finished product would tend to overstate its protective effect. Such a situation might occur if the home government desired to protect suppliers of raw materials more than domestic manufacturers.

Tariff Escalation

As illustrated in Table 4.4, in many industrialized nations the effective rate of protection is more than twice the nominal rate. An apparently low nominal tariff on a final import product may thus *understate* the effective rate of protection, which takes into account the effects of tariffs levied on raw materials and intermediate goods. In addition, the tariff structures of industrialized nations have generally been characterized by rising rates that give greater protection to intermediate and finished products than to primary commodities. This is commonly referred to as **tariff escalation.** Although raw materials are often imported at zero or low tariff rates, the nominal and effective protection increases at each stage of production. As seen in Figure 4.1 on page 108, tariffs often rise

significantly with the level of processing in many industrial countries. This is especially true for agricultural products.

The tariff structures of the industrialized nations may indeed discourage the growth of processing, thus hampering diversification into higher value-added exports for the less-developed nations. The industrialized nations' low tariffs on primary commodities encourage the developing nations to expand operations in these sectors, while the high protective rates levied on manufactured goods pose a significant entry barrier for any developing nation wishing to compete in this area. From the point of view of the less-developed nations, it may be in their best interest to discourage disproportionate tariff reductions on raw materials. The effect of these tariff reductions is to magnify the discrepancy between the nominal and effective tariffs of the industrialized nations, worsening the potential competitive position of the less-developed nations in the manufacturing and processing sectors.

TABLE 4.4

Nominal and Effective Tariff Rates[*]

Product	United States		Japan		European Union	
	Nominal Rate	Effective Rate	Nominal Rate	Effective Rate	Nominal Rate	Effective Rate
Agriculture, forestry, fish	1.8%	1.9%	18.4%	21.4%	4.8%	4.1%
Food, beverages, tobacco	4.7	10.6	25.4	50.3	10.1	17.8
Textiles	9.2	18.0	3.3	2.4	7.2	8.8
Wearing apparel	22.7	43.3	13.8	42.2	13.4	19.3
Leather products	4.2	5.0	3.0	−14.8	2.0	−2.2
Footwear	8.8	15.4	15.7	50.0	11.6	20.1
Wood products	1.6	1.7	0.3	−30.6	2.5	1.7
Furniture and fixtures	4.1	5.5	5.1	10.3	5.6	11.3
Paper and paper products	0.2	-0.9	2.1	1.8	5.4	8.3
Printing and publishing	0.7	0.9	0.1	−1.5	2.1	-1.0

[*]Following the completion of the Tokyo Round of Multilateral Trade Negotiations in 1979.

Source: Alan Deardorff and Robert Stern, "The Effects of the Tokyo Round on the Structure of Protection," in R. Baldwin and A. Krueger, *The Structure and Evolution of Recent U.S. Trade Policy* (Chicago: University of Chicago Press, 1984), pp. 368–377.

FIGURE 4.1

Tariff Escalation on Industrial Countries' Imports from Developing Countries

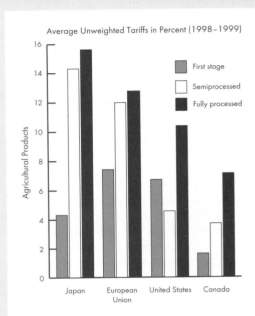

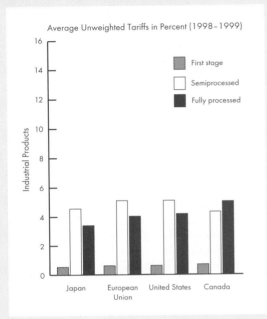

Tariffs often rise significantly with the level of processing (tariff escalation) in many industrial countries. This is especially true for agricultural products. Tariff escalation in industrial countries has the potential of reducing demand for processed imports from developing countries, hampering diversification into higher-value added exports.

Source: The World Bank, *Global Economic Prospects and the Developing Countries,* 2002, p. 45.

Production Sharing and Offshore-Assembly Provision

Production sharing, also known as outsourcing, is a key aspect of our global economy. Production sharing occurs when certain aspects of a product's manufacture are performed in more than one country. For example, electronic components made in the United States are shipped to a regionally accessible country with low labor costs, say, Singapore, for assembly into television sets. The assembled sets are then returned to the United States for further pro-

cessing or packaging and distribution. This *foreign assembly* type of production sharing has evolved into an important competitive strategy for many U.S. producers of low-cost, labor-intensive products. Market share, in the United States and abroad, can often be preserved as a result of improvements in cost competitiveness by way of foreign assembly, which allows firms to retain higher production and employment levels in the United States than might otherwise be possible.

In addition to the use of foreign assembly plants to reduce labor costs, production-sharing operations may be designed to penetrate foreign markets where high tariffs or other trade barriers restrict direct export of finished goods. Production sharing may also take advantage of a certain unique foreign production technology, labor skills, raw materials, or specialized components. Table 4.5 provides examples of production sharing for the United States.

U.S. trade policy includes an **offshore-assembly provision (OAP)** that provides favorable treatment to products assembled abroad from U.S.–manufactured components. Under OAP, when a finished component originating in the United States (such as a semiconductor) is sent overseas and there is assembled with one or more other components to become a finished good (such as a television set), the cost of the U.S. component is not included in the dutiable value of the imported assembled article into which it has been incorporated. U.S. import duties thus apply only to the *value added in the foreign assembly process*, provided that U.S.–made components are used by overseas companies in their assembly operations. Manufactured goods entering the United States under OAP have included motor vehicles, office machines, television sets, aluminum cans, and semiconductors.

The U.S. OAP pertains not only to U.S. firms, but to foreign companies as well. For example, a U.S. computer company could produce components in the United States, send them to Taiwan for assembly, and ship computers back to the United States under favorable OAP. Alternatively, a Japanese photocopier firm desiring to export to the United States could purchase U.S.–manufactured components, assemble them in Malaysia, and ship photocopiers to the United States under favorable OAP.

Suppose that the United States imports television sets from South Korea at a price of $300 per set. If the tariff rate on such televisions is 10 percent, a duty of $30 would be paid on each television entering the United States, and the price to the U.S. consumer would be $330.[4] Now, suppose that U.S. components are used in the television sets assembled by the Koreans and that these components have a value of $200. Under OAP, the 10 percent U.S. tariff rate is levied on the value of the imported set *minus* the value of the U.S. components used in manufacturing the set. When the set enters the United States, its dutiable value is thus $300 − $200 = $100, and the duty is 0.1 × $100 = $10. The price to the U.S. consumer after the tariff has been levied is $300 + $10 = $310. With the OAP system, the consumer is better off because the effective tariff rate is only 3.3 percent ($10/$300) instead of the 10 percent shown in the tariff schedule.

The OAP provides potential advantages for the United States. By reducing import tariffs on foreign-assembled sets embodying U.S. components, OAP

[4]This assumes that the United States is a "small" country, as discussed later in this chapter.

TABLE 4.5

U.S. Production Sharing: Use of U.S. Components and Materials in Foreign Assembly Operations

Country	Products
Mexico	Apparel, autos and parts, wiring harnesses, internal combustion engines
Dominican Republic	Medical goods, apparel
Honduras	Apparel
El Salvador	Apparel
Malaysia	Semiconductors
Hong Kong	Semiconductors
Philippines	Semiconductors
South Korea	Semiconductors

Source: U.S. International Trade Commission.

provides incentives for Korean manufacturers desiring to export to the United States to purchase components from U.S. sources; this generates sales and jobs in the U.S. component industries. However, television-assembly workers in the United States object to OAP, which they claim exports jobs that rightfully belong to U.S. workers; it is in their interest to lobby for the abolition of OAP.

Postponing Import Duties

Import duties may have unintended side effects for some businesses. For example, duties may discourage a company from importing goods in amounts large enough to take advantage of quantity discount pricing. Before imported goods are released by the U.S. Customs Service, import duties must be paid, or a bond must be posted to guarantee their payment. Up-front payment of these duties may impose financial hardships on importers.

Consider a U.S. assembler who uses imported components. By purchasing its annual requirement of components at one time and shipping it in bulk, the firm could reduce the cost of the imported components. Paying the import duty on the entire year's supply of components at one time, however, might be too expensive for the importer. U.S. trade laws mitigate the effects of import duties by allowing U.S. importers to postpone and prorate over time their duty obligations through bonded warehouses and foreign trade zones.

Bonded Warehouse

According to U.S. tariff law, dutiable imports can be brought into a customs territory and left in a **bonded warehouse**, duty-free. These storage facilities are operated under the lock and key of the U.S. Customs Service. Owners of storage facilities must be bonded to ensure that they will satisfy all customs duty obligations.

Imported goods can be stored, repacked, or further processed in the bonded warehouse. As long as the products are kept in the bonded warehouse, the duty obligation is postponed. The goods may later be sold duty-free overseas or withdrawn for domestic sale upon payment of import duties. When goods are processed in a bonded warehouse with additional domestic materials and enter the domestic market at a later date, only the imported portion of the finished good is subject to customs duties.

Bonded warehouses are sometimes used for reexportation. Imported goods are stored in the bonded warehouse until suitable foreign markets can be found. If these goods are not stored in a bonded warehouse, the importer must pay duty on them when they enter the country. The importer can then claim a refund of 99 percent of the duties paid, referred to as a *drawback*, after they have been reexported. By using a bonded warehouse, however, a business can avoid the delay and costs associated with customs clearance and drawback application connected with reexport.

Foreign-Trade Zone

Because of inspection and surveillance by the U.S. Customs Service, storage in bonded warehouses is generally more costly than in ordinary storage facilities. As a less expensive alternative, the U.S. government permits importers to use a **foreign-trade zone (FTZ)**. FTZs enlarge the benefits of a bonded warehouse by eliminating the restrictive aspects of customs surveillance and by offering more suitable manufacturing facilities.

An FTZ is a site within the United States where foreign merchandise can be imported *without* formal U.S. customs entry (payment of customs duties) or government excise taxes. FTZs are intended to stimulate international trade, attract industry, and create jobs by providing an area that gives users tariff and tax breaks. Merchandise in the zone can be stored, used in manufacturing or assembling a final product, or handled in several other ways.

In 1970, there were 17 FTZs in the United States; as of 2004, there were more than 240 FTZs housing more than 2,500 firms. Many are situated at seaports, but some are located at inland distribution points. Despite their growing importance, FTZs account for only about 2 percent of the merchandise exports and imports of the United States. Among the businesses that enjoy FTZ status are Caterpillar, Chrysler, Eli Lilly and Co., General Electric, and International Business Machines (IBM).

By offering cost savings to U.S. importers and exporters, FTZs encourage international competitiveness. Companies importing merchandise into an FTZ enhance their cash flow because they do not pay customs duties or federal excise taxes until the goods are shipped out of the zone to U.S. markets. If a good is shipped from an FTZ to a foreign country, no U.S. import duty is imposed on the good. For example, in an FTZ located in Seattle, optical equipment is assembled using lenses from Japan, prisms from Germany, plastic castings from the United Kingdom, precision mechanisms from Switzerland, and control instruments from France. In an FTZ located in Kansas City, Kansas, pool tables and related equipment are produced using frames from the United States, slate from Italy, balls from Belgium, rubber from Japan, and cue sticks from Taiwan. U.S. Customs Service officials monitor the FTZs by performing audits and spot inspections.

Besides seeing FTZs as a mechanism to reduce costs on imported components through deferral of duty payment, manufacturers have sought FTZ status to obtain relief from "inverted" tariff schedules—those that place higher duty rates on imported inputs than on the industry's final product. Manufacturers in the FTZ can reduce their tariff liability on components or raw materials with higher duty rates by zone processing or assembly into finished goods that enter the U.S. market at a lower duty rate.

In short, the principal financial advantages of an FTZ include (1) improved cash flow through payment of duties at shipment out of the warehouse or factory instead of on receipt at the facility; (2) no payment of tariffs on scrap, waste, or obsolete materials; (3) the option of paying the tariff on the imported materials or on the final product shipped from the zone, whichever is less; (4) no tariff duty on the value of the labor, overhead, and profit incurred in zone processing in the United States; and (5) no tariff owed on exported merchandise.

Tariff Welfare Effects: Consumer Surplus and Producer Surplus

To analyze the effect of trade policies on national welfare, it is useful to separate the effects on consumers from those on producers. For each group, a measure of welfare is needed; these measures are known as consumer surplus and producer surplus.

Consumer surplus refers to the difference between the amount that buyers would be willing and able to pay for a good and the actual amount they do pay. To illustrate, assume that the price of a Pepsi is $.50. Being especially thirsty, suppose you would have been willing to pay up to $.75 for a Pepsi. Your consumer surplus on this purchase is $.25 ($.75 – $.50 = $.25). For all Pepsis bought, consumer surplus is merely the sum of the surplus for each unit.

Consumer surplus can also be depicted graphically. Let us first remember that (1) the height of the market demand curve indicates the maximum price that buyers are willing and able to pay for each successive unit of the good, and (2) in a competitive market, buyers pay a single price (the equilibrium price) for all units purchased. Referring now to Figure 4.2(a) on page 112, assume the market price of gasoline is $2 per gallon. If buyers purchase 4 gallons at this price, they spend $8, represented by area ACED. For those 4 gallons, buyers would have been willing and able to spend $12, as shown by area ABCED. The difference between what buyers actually spend and the amount they were willing and able to spend is consumer surplus; in this case, it equals $4 and is denoted by area ABC.

The size of consumer surplus is affected by the market price. A decrease in the market price will lead to an increase in the quantity purchased and a larger consumer surplus. Conversely, a higher market price will reduce the amount purchased and shrink the consumer surplus.

Let us now consider the other side of the market: producers. **Producer surplus** is the revenue producers receive over and above the minimum amount required to induce them to supply the good. This minimum amount has to cover the producer's total variable costs. Recall that total variable cost equals the sum of the marginal cost of producing each successive unit of output.

In Figure 4.2(b), producer surplus is represented by the area above the supply curve of gasoline and below the good's market price. Recall that the height of the market supply curve

FIGURE 4.2

Consumer Surplus and Producer Surplus

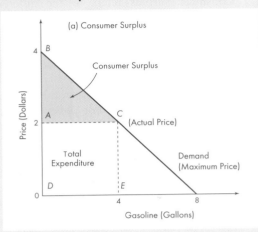

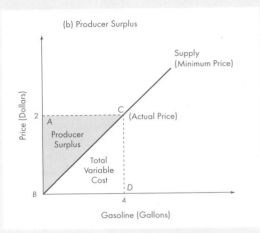

Consumer surplus is the difference between the maximum amount buyers are willing to pay for a given quantity of a good and the amount actually paid. Graphically, consumer surplus is represented by the area under the demand curve and above the good's market price. Producer surplus is the revenue producers receive over and above the minimum necessary for production. Graphically, producer surplus is represented by the area above the supply curve and below the good's market price.

indicates the lowest price at which producers will be willing to supply gasoline; this minimum price increases with the level of output because of rising marginal costs. Suppose that the market price of gasoline is $2 per gallon, and 4 gallons are supplied. Producers receive revenues totaling $8, represented by area $ACDB$. The minimum revenue they must receive to produce 4 gallons equals total variable cost, which equals $4 and is depicted by area BCD. Producer surplus is the difference, $4 ($8 − $4 = $4), and is depicted by area ABC.

If the market price of gasoline rises, more gasoline will be supplied, and producer surplus will rise. It is equally true that if the market price of gasoline falls, producer surplus will fall.

In the following sections, we will use the concepts of consumer surplus and producer surplus to analyze the effects of import tariffs on the nation's welfare.

Tariff Welfare Effects: Small-Nation Model

To measure the effects of a tariff on a nation's welfare, consider the case of a nation whose imports constitute a very small portion of the world market supply. This **small nation** would be a *price taker*, facing a constant world price level for its import commodity. This is not a rare case; many nations are not important enough to influence the terms at which they trade.

In Figure 4.3, the small nation before trade produces at market equilibrium point E, as determined by the intersection of its domestic supply and demand schedules. At equilibrium price $9,500, the quantity supplied is 50 units, and the quantity demanded is 50 units. Now suppose that the economy is opened to foreign trade and that the world auto price is $8,000, less than the domestic price.

FIGURE 4.3

Tariff Trade and Welfare Effects: Small-Nation Model

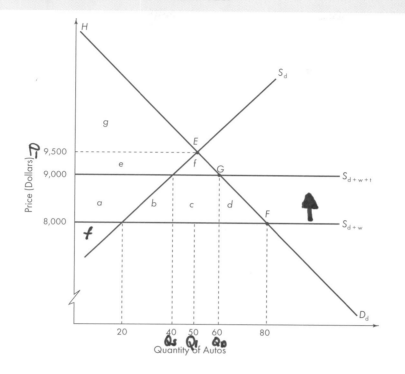

For a small nation, a tariff placed on an imported product is shifted totally to the domestic consumer via a higher product price. Consumer surplus falls as a result of the price increase. The small nation's welfare decreases by an amount equal to the protective effect and consumption effect, the so-called deadweight losses due to a tariff.

Because the world market will supply an unlimited number of autos at price $8,000, the world supply schedule would appear as a horizontal (perfectly elastic) line. Line S_{d+w} shows the supply of autos available to the small-nation consumers from domestic and foreign sources combined. This overall supply schedule is the one that would prevail in free trade.

Free-trade equilibrium is located at point F in the figure. Here the number of autos demanded is 80 units, whereas the number produced domestically is 20 units. The excess domestic auto demand is fulfilled by imports of 60 autos. Compared with the situation before trade occurred, free trade results in a fall in the domestic auto price from $9,500 to $8,000. Consumers are better off because they can import more autos at a lower price. However, domestic producers now sell fewer autos at a lower price than they did before trade.

Under free trade, the domestic auto industry is being damaged by foreign competition. Industry sales and revenues are falling, and workers are losing their jobs. Suppose management and labor unite and convince the government to levy a protective

Calculating the Welfare Effects of a Tariff

Figure 4.3 presents the welfare effects of a tariff in dollar terms. For example, the dollar value of the consumption effect (area *d*) equals $10,000. It is easy to carry out the calculation of triangular area *d*. Recall from geometry that the area of a triangle equals (base × height)/2. The height of the triangle ($1,000) equals the price increase in autos due to the tariff; the base (20 autos) equals the reduction in domestic consumption due to the tariff. The consumption effect is thus (20 × $1,000)/2 = $10,000.

Similarly, the dollar value of the protective effect (area *b*) equals $10,000. The height of the triangle equals the increase in price due to the tariff ($1,000); the triangle's base (20 autos) equals the increase in domestic auto production due to the tariff. The protection effect is thus (20 × $1,000)/2 = $10,000.

The calculation of all such "triangular" welfare effects of tariffs (and other protectionist devices) is based on the same formula. The reader will find this formula useful for calculating the welfare effects of trade barriers in response to the study questions at the end of chapters.

tariff on auto imports. Assume the small nation imposes a tariff of $1,000 on auto imports. Because this small nation is not important enough to influence world market conditions, the world supply price of autos remains constant, unaffected by the tariff. This means that the small nation's terms of trade remains unchanged. The introduction of the tariff *raises the home price of imports by the full amount of the duty, and the increase falls entirely on the domestic consumer.* The overall supply shifts upward by the amount of the tariff, from S_{d+w} to S_{d+w+t}.

The protective tariff results in a new equilibrium quantity at point *G*, where the domestic auto price is $9,000. Domestic production increases by 20 units, whereas domestic consumption falls by 20 units. Imports decrease from their pretariff level of 60 units to 20 units. This reduction can be attributed to falling domestic consumption and rising domestic production. The effects of the tariff are to impede imports and protect domestic producers. But what are the tariff's effects on the *national welfare*?

Figure 4.3 shows that before the tariff was levied, *consumer surplus* equaled areas *a* + *b* + *c* + *d* + *e* + *f* + *g*. With the tariff, consumer surplus falls to areas *e* + *f* + *g*, an overall loss in consumer surplus equal to areas *a* + *b* + *c* + *d*. This change

affects the nation's welfare in a number of ways. The welfare effects of a tariff include a revenue effect, a redistribution effect, a protective effect, and a consumption effect. As might be expected, the tariff provides the government with additional tax revenue and benefits domestic auto producers; at the same time, however, it wastes resources and harms the domestic consumer.

The tariff's **revenue effect** represents the government's collections of duty. Found by multiplying the number of imports (20 units) times the tariff ($1,000), government revenue equals area *c*, or $20,000. This represents the portion of the loss of consumer surplus, in monetary terms, that is transferred to the government. For the nation as a whole, the revenue effect does *not* result in an overall welfare loss; consumer surplus is merely shifted from the private to the public sector.

The **redistributive effect** is the transfer of consumer surplus, in monetary terms, to the domestic producers of the import-competing product. This is represented by area *a*, which equals $30,000. Under the tariff, domestic home consumers will buy from domestic firms 40 autos at a price of $9,000, for a total expenditure of $360,000. At the free-trade price of $8,000, the same 40 autos would have yielded $320,000. The imposition of the tariff thus results in home producers' receiving additional revenues totaling areas $a + b$, or $40,000 (the difference between $360,000 and $320,000). As the tariff encourages domestic production to rise from 20 to 40 units, however, producers must pay part of the increased revenue as higher costs of producing the increased output, depicted by area b, or $10,000. The remaining revenue, $30,000, area a, is a net gain in producer income. The redistributive effect, therefore, is a transfer of income from consumers to producers. Like the revenue effect, it does *not* result in an overall loss of welfare for the economy.

Area b, totaling $10,000, is referred to as the **protective effect** of the tariff. It illustrates the loss to the domestic economy resulting from wasted resources used to produce additional autos at increasing unit costs. As the tariff-induced domestic output expands, resources that are less adaptable to auto production are eventually used, increasing unit production costs. This means that resources are used less efficiently than they would have been with free trade, in which case autos would have been purchased from low-cost foreign producers. A tariff's protective effect thus arises because less efficient domestic production is substituted for more efficient foreign production. Referring to Figure 4.3, as domestic output increases from 20 to 40 units, the domestic cost of producing autos rises, as shown by supply schedule S_d. But the same increase in autos could have been obtained at a unit cost of $8,000 before the tariff was levied. Area b, which depicts the protective effect, represents a loss to the economy.

Most of the consumer surplus lost because of the tariff has been accounted for: c went to the government as revenue; a was transferred to home suppliers as income; and b was lost by the economy because of inefficient domestic production. The **consumption effect**, represented by area d, which equals $10,000, is the residual not accounted for elsewhere. It arises from the decrease in consumption resulting from the tariff's artificially increasing the price of autos from $8,000 to $9,000. A loss of welfare occurs because of the increased price and lower consumption. Like the protective effect, the consumption effect represents a real cost to society, not a transfer to other sectors of the economy.

Together, these two effects equal the **deadweight loss** of the tariff (areas $b + d$ in the figure).

As long as it is assumed that a nation accounts for a negligible portion of international trade, its levying an import tariff necessarily lowers its national welfare. This is because there is no favorable welfare effect resulting from the tariff that would offset the deadweight loss of consumer surplus. If a nation could impose a tariff that would improve its terms of trade vis-à-vis its trading partners, it would enjoy a larger share of the gains from trade. This would tend to increase its national welfare, offsetting the deadweight loss of consumer surplus. Because it is so insignificant relative to the world market, however, a small nation is unable to influence the terms of trade. Levying an import tariff, therefore, *reduces* a small nation's welfare.

Tariff Welfare Effects: Large-Nation Model

Now consider the case of an importing nation that is large enough so that changes in the quantity of its imports, by means of tariff policy, influence the world price of the product. This **large-nation** case could apply to the United States, which is a large importer of autos, steel, oil, and consumer electronics, and to other economic giants such as Japan and the European Union.

If the United States imposes a tariff on automobile imports, prices increase for American consumers. The result is a decrease in the quantity demanded, which may be significant enough to force Japanese firms to reduce the prices of their exports. Because Japanese firms can produce and export smaller amounts at a lower marginal cost, they are likely to prefer to reduce their price to the United States to limit the decrease in their sales to the United States. The tariff incidence is thus shared between U.S. consumers, who pay a higher price than under free trade for each auto imported, and Japanese firms, which realize a lower price than under free trade for each auto exported. The difference between these two prices is the tariff duty. U.S. welfare rises when the United States can shift some of the tariff to Japanese firms via export price reductions. The *terms of trade* improves for the United States at the expense of Japan.

Table 4.6 illustrates the extent to which U.S. import tariffs can reduce world prices of imported goods. For example, an 11 percent increase in the U.S. tariff on ball-bearing imports would increase the price to the American consumer by an estimated 10.2 percent. This leads to a decrease in the quantity of ball bearings demanded in the United States and a 0.8 percent decrease in the world price.

What are the economic effects of an import tariff for a large country? Referring to Figure 4.4, line S_d represents the domestic supply schedule, and line D_d depicts the home demand schedule. Autarky equilibrium occurs at point E. With free trade, the importing nation faces a total supply schedule of S_{d+w}. This schedule shows the number of autos that both domestic and foreign producers together offer domestic consumers. The total supply schedule is upward sloping rather than horizontal because the foreign supply price is not a fixed constant. The price depends on the quantity purchased by an importing country when it is a large buyer of the product. With free trade, our country achieves market equilibrium at point F. The price of autos falls to $8,000, domestic consumption rises to 110 units, and domestic production falls to 30 units. Auto imports totaling 80 units satisfy the excess domestic demand.

Suppose that the importing nation imposes a specific tariff of $1,000 on imported autos. By increasing the selling cost, the tariff results in a shift in the total supply schedule from S_{d+w} to S_{d+w+t}. Market equilibrium shifts from point F to point G, while product price rises from $8,000 to $8,800. The tariff-levying nation's consumer surplus falls by an amount equal to areas $a + b + c + d$. Area a, totaling $32,000, represents the *redistributive effect*; this amount is transferred from domestic consumers to domestic producers. Areas $d + b$ depict the tariff's deadweight loss, the deterioration in national welfare because of reduced consumption (*consumption effect* = $8,000) and an inefficient use of resources (*protective effect* = $8,000).

As in the small-nation example, a tariff's *revenue effect* equals the import tariff multiplied by the quantity of autos imported. This yields areas $c + e$, or $40,000. Notice, however, that the tariff revenue accruing to the government now comes from foreign producers as well as domestic consumers. This differs from the small-nation case, in which the supply schedule is horizontal and the tariff's burden falls entirely on domestic consumers.

The tariff of $1,000 is added to the free-trade import price of $8,000. Although the price in the protected market will exceed the foreign supply price by the amount of the duty, it will *not* exceed the free-trade foreign supply price by this amount.

TABLE 4.6

Effects of Increases in U.S. Tariffs on the World Price of Imported Goods

Product	Tariff (or Equivalent)	Increase in U.S. Price	Decrease in World Price
Ball bearings	11.0%	10.2%	0.8%
Chemicals	9.0	6.5	2.5
Jewelry	9.0	5.4	3.6
Orange juice	30.0	21.7	8.3
Glassware	11.0	7.3	3.7
Luggage	16.5	11.0	5.5
Resins	12.0	5.4	6.6
Footwear	20.0	16.1	3.9
Lumber	6.5	4.1	2.4

Source: G. Hufbauer and K. Elliot, *Measuring the Costs of Protection in the United States* (Washington, DC: Institute for International Economics, 1994), pp. 28–29.

FIGURE 4.4

Tariff Trade and Welfare Effects: Large-Nation Model

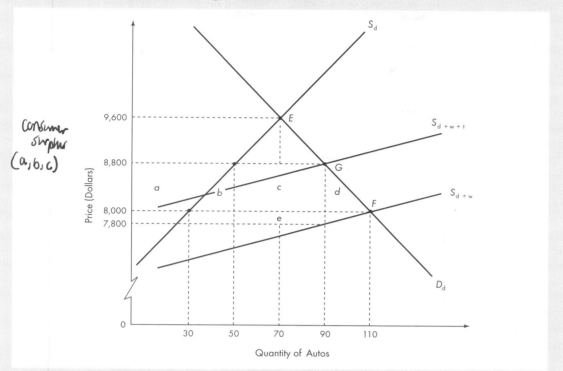

Consumer surplus (a, b, c)

producer surplus (b, d)

For a large nation, a tariff on an imported product may be partially shifted to the domestic consumer via a higher product price and partially absorbed by the foreign exporter via a lower export price. The extent by which a tariff is absorbed by the foreign exporter constitutes a welfare gain for the home country. This gain offsets some (all) of the deadweight welfare losses due to the tariff's consumption effect and protective effect.

Compared with the free-trade foreign supply price, $8,000, the domestic consumers pay only an additional $800 per imported auto. This is the portion of the tariff shifted forward to the consumer. At the same time, the foreign supply price of autos falls by $200. This means that foreign producers earn smaller revenues, $7,800, for each auto exported. Because foreign production takes place under increasing-cost conditions, the reduction of imports from abroad triggers a decline in foreign production, and unit costs decline. The reduction in the foreign supply price, $200, repre-

sents that portion of the tariff borne by the foreign producer. The levying of the tariff raises the domestic price of the import by only part of the duty as foreign producers lower their prices in an attempt to maintain sales in the tariff-levying nation. The importing nation finds that its terms of trade has improved if the price it pays for auto imports decreases while the price it charges for its exports remains the same.

Thus, the *revenue effect* of an import tariff in the large-nation case includes two components. The first is the amount of tariff revenue shifted from domestic consumers to the tariff-levying government; in Figure 4.4, this equals the level of imports (40 units) multiplied by the portion of the import tariff borne by domestic consumers ($800). Area *c* depicts the **domestic revenue effect**, which equals $32,000. The second element is the tariff revenue extracted from foreign producers in the form of a lower supply price. Found by multiplying auto imports (40 units) by the portion of the tariff falling on foreign producers ($200), the **terms-of-trade effect** is shown as area *e*, which equals $8,000. Note that the terms-of-trade effect represents a redistribution of income from the foreign nation to the tariff-levying nation because of the new terms of trade. The tariff's revenue effect thus includes the domestic revenue effect and the terms-of-trade effect.

A nation that is a major importer of a product is in a favorable trade situation. It can use its tariff policy to improve the terms at which it trades, and therefore its national welfare. But remember that the negative welfare effect of a tariff is the deadweight loss of consumer surplus that results from the protection and consumption effects. Referring to Figure 4.4, to decide if a tariff-levying nation can improve its national welfare, we must compare the impact of the deadweight loss (areas $b + d$) with the benefits of a more favorable terms of trade (area *e*). The conclusions regarding the welfare effects of a tariff are as follows:

1. If $e > (b + d)$, national welfare is increased.
2. If $e = (b + d)$, national welfare remains constant.
3. If $e < (b + d)$, national welfare is diminished.

In the preceding example, the domestic economy's welfare would have declined by an amount equal to $8,000. This is because the deadweight welfare losses, totaling $16,000, more than offset the $8,000 gain in welfare attributable to the terms-of-trade effect.

We have seen that a large nation can improve its terms of trade by imposing a tariff on imports. However, a tariff causes the volume of imports to decrease, which lessens the nation's welfare by reducing its consumption of low-cost imports. There is thus a gain due to improved terms of trade and a loss due to reduced import volume. A nation optimizes its economic welfare by imposing a tariff rate at which the positive difference between the gain of improving terms of trade and the loss of declining import volume is maximized; an **optimum tariff** refers to such a tariff rate.

A likely candidate for a nation imposing an optimum tariff would be the United States; it is a large importer, compared with world demand, of autos, electronics, and other products. Note, however, that an optimum tariff is only beneficial to the importing nation. Because any benefit accruing to the importing nation through a lower import price implies a loss to the foreign exporting nation, imposing an optimum tariff is a **beggar-thy-neighbor policy** that could invite retaliation. After all, if the United States were to impose an optimal tariff of 25 percent on its imports, why should Japan and the European Union not levy tariffs of 40 or 50 percent on their imports? When all countries impose optimal tariffs, it is likely that everyone's economic welfare will decrease as impediments to free trade become great. The possibility of foreign retaliation may be a sufficient deterrent for any nation considering whether to impose higher tariffs.

A classic case of a tariff-induced trade war was the implementation of the Smoot–Hawley tariff by the U.S. government in 1930. The tariff was initially intended to provide relief to U.S. farmers. However, senators and members of Congress from industrial states used the technique of vote trading to obtain increased tariffs on manufactured goods. The result was a policy that increased tariffs on more than a thousand products, with an average nominal duty on protected goods of 53 percent! Viewing the Smoot–Hawley tariff as an attempt to force unemployment on its workers, 12 nations promptly increased their duties against the United States. U.S. farm exports fell to one-third of their former level, and between 1930 and 1933 total U.S. exports fell by almost 60 percent. Although the Great Depression accounted for much of that decline, the adverse psychological impact of the Smoot–Hawley tariff on business activity cannot be ignored.

How a Tariff Burdens Exporters

The benefits and costs of protecting domestic producers from foreign competition, as discussed earlier in this chapter, are based on the direct effects of an import tariff. Import-competing businesses and workers can benefit from tariffs through increases in output, profits, jobs, and compensation. A tariff imposes costs on domestic consumers in the form of higher prices of protected products and reductions in consumer surplus. There is also a net welfare loss for the economy because not all of the loss of consumer surplus is transferred as gains to domestic producers and the government (the protective effect and consumption effect).

A tariff carries additional burdens. In protecting import-competing producers, a tariff leads indirectly to a reduction in domestic exports. The net result of protectionism is to move the economy toward greater self-sufficiency, with lower imports and exports. For domestic workers, the protection of jobs in import-competing industries comes at the expense of jobs in other sectors of the economy, including exports. Although a tariff is intended to help domestic producers, the economy-wide implications of a tariff are adverse for the export sector. The welfare losses due to restrictions in output and employment in the economy's export industry may offset the welfare gains enjoyed by import-competing producers.

Because a tariff is a tax on imports, the burden of a tariff falls initially on importers, who must pay duties to the domestic government. However, importers generally try to shift increased costs to buyers through price increases. There are at least three ways in which the resulting higher prices of imports injure domestic exporters.

First, exporters often purchase imported inputs subject to tariffs that *increase the cost of inputs*. Because exporters tend to sell in competitive markets where they have little ability to dictate the prices they receive, they generally cannot pass on a tariff-induced increase in cost to their buyers. Higher export costs thus lead to higher prices and reduced overseas sales.

Consider the hypothetical case of Caterpillar, a U.S. exporter of tractors. In Figure 4.5 on page 120, suppose the firm realizes constant long-run costs, suggesting that marginal cost equals average cost at each level of output. Let the production cost of a tractor equal $100,000, denoted by $MC_0 = AC_0$. Caterpillar maximizes profits by producing 100 tractors, the point at which marginal revenue equals marginal cost, and selling them at a price of $110,000 per unit. The firm's revenue thus totals $11 million ($100 \times \$110,000$) while its costs total $10 million ($100 \times \$100,000$); as a result, the firm realizes profits of $1 million. Suppose now that the U.S. government levies a tariff on steel imports, while foreign nations allow steel to be imported duty-free. If the production of tractors uses imported steel, and competitively priced domestic steel is not available, the tariff leads to an increase in Caterpillar's costs to, say, $105,000 per tractor, as denoted by $MC_1 = AC_1$. Again the firm maximizes profits by operating where marginal revenue equals marginal cost. However, Caterpillar must charge a higher price, $112,000; the firm's sales thus decrease to 90 tractors and profits decrease to $630,000. The import tariff applied to steel represents a tax on Caterpillar that reduces its international competitiveness. Protecting domestic steel producers from import competition can thus lessen the export competitiveness of domestic steel-using producers.

Tariffs also *raise the cost of living* by increasing the price of imports. Workers thus have the incentive to demand correspondingly higher wages, resulting in higher production costs. Tariffs lead to expanding output for import-competing companies that in turn bid for workers, causing money wages to rise. As these higher wages pass through the economy, export industries ultimately face higher wages and production costs, which lessen their competitive position in international markets.

Finally, import tariffs have *international repercussions* that lead to reductions in domestic exports. Tariffs cause the quantity of imports to decrease, which in turn decreases other nations' export revenues and ability to import. The decline

FIGURE 4.5

How an Import Tariff Burdens Domestic Exporters

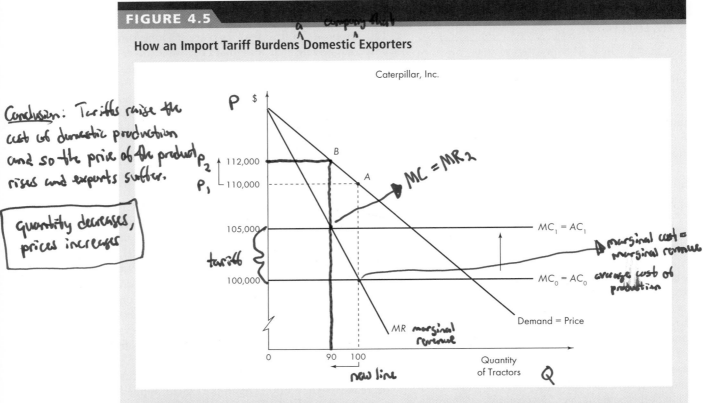

Caterpillar, Inc.

Handwritten annotations:
- *a company that (above title)*
- *Conclusion: Tariffs raise the cost of domestic production and so the price of the product rises and exports suffer.*
- *Quantity decreases, prices increase*
- *MC = MR 2*
- *marginal cost = marginal revenue*
- *average cost of production*
- *tariff*
- *MR marginal revenue*
- *new line*

A tariff placed on imported steel increases the costs of a steel-using manufacturer. This leads to a higher price charged by the manufacturer and a loss of international competitiveness.

in foreign export revenues results in a smaller demand for a nation's exports and leads to falling output and employment in its export industries.

If domestic export companies are damaged by import tariffs, why don't they protest such policies more vigorously? One problem is that tariff-induced increases in costs for export companies are subtle and invisible. Many exporters may not be aware of their existence. Also, the tariff-induced cost increases may be of such magnitude that some potential export companies are incapable of developing and have no tangible basis for political resistance.

Steel-Using Industries Oppose Restrictions on Steel Imports

In 2002, John Jenson, chairman of the Consuming Industries Trade Action Coalition, testified before the U.S. Senate Finance Committee regarding restrictions on steel imports.[5] He indicated that he voiced concerns of millions of American workers in steel-consuming industries regarding restrictions on steel imports.

[5]U.S. Senate Finance Committee, *Testimony of John Jenson*, February 13, 2002.

According to Jenson, restrictions on steel imports would be harmful to U.S. steel-using industries that employ 12.8 million workers compared to less than 200,000 workers employed by American steel producers. In our global economy, steel users must compete with efficient foreign manufacturers of all types of consumer and industrial installations, machines, and conveyances—everything from automobiles and earth movers to nuts and bolts. Forcing U.S. manufacturers to pay considerably more for steel inputs than their foreign competitors would deal U.S. manufacturers a triple blow: (1) increase raw material costs; (2) threaten access to steel products not manufactured in the United States; and (3) increase competition from abroad for the products they make. It would simply send our business offshore, devastating U.S. steel-using businesses, most of them small businesses.

Jenson's statement highlighted the main reasons for the opposition of steel-using industries to restrictions on steel imports:

- Import restraints do not address the most serious problem facing certain U.S. steel producers; that is, high and relatively inflexible costs such as wages and retirement benefits. If the United States restricts steel imports, it will not provide any lasting relief to U.S. steel mills because it won't solve the real problem.
- The U.S. market needs imports. The total production of steel in the United States, even at peak capacity, is not enough to satisfy domestic demand. Further, American steel-using manufacturers need imported steel meeting specifications that U.S. producers cannot or do not supply. Imports are necessary in many instances to allow U.S. manufacturers to compete globally.
- Import restrictions would jeopardize tens of thousands of Americans who work for steel-using manufacturers and U.S. exporters. Every state would lose more jobs than trade restrictions would save—even steel-intensive states like Indiana and West Virginia.

Jenson concluded that steel is an important industry to the U.S. economy. It is not the only industry, however, and the costs of saving the steel industry should not outweigh the benefits.

Tariff Examples

The previous section analyzed the welfare effects of import tariffs from a theoretical perspective. Now let us turn to some examples of import tariffs and examine estimates of their costs and benefits to the nation.

Bush's Steel Tariffs Buy Time for Troubled Industry

In spite of opposition from domestic steel-using industries, in 2002 President George W. Bush imposed tariffs ranging from 8 percent to 30 percent on a variety of imported steel products, as seen in Table 4.7 on page 122. Let us consider his policy.

ECONOMIC *Applications*

Visit EconDebate Online for a debate on this topic

In 1950, U.S. steelmakers dominated the world market. Accounting for half of global steel output, they produced almost 20 times as much steel as Japan and more steel than all of Europe combined. However, the market dominance of U.S. steelmakers gradually declined as they became complacent and insensitive to changing market conditions. By the 1960s, foreign steelmakers had made significant inroads into the American market, turning the United States into a net importer of steel. Since that time, sales and profits of U.S. steel mills have declined, and thousands of American steelworkers have lost their jobs.

Big U.S. integrated steel companies have lugged around outdated technology, high fixed costs, and enormous capacity. They also face tough competition from minimills that convert scrap directly into finished steel products. Minimills use modern technology to produce steel with about a 20 percent cost advantage over the integrated mills. Another problem facing big U.S. steelmakers is *legacy costs*, including pension and health-care benefits, which are owed to hundreds of thousands of both current and retired employees and add more than $9 to the cost of producing a ton of steel.

TABLE 4.7

President Bush's Steel Trade Remedy Program of 2002–2003

Products	Tariff Rates	
	Year 1	Year 2
Semifinished slab		
Plate, hot-rolled sheet, cold-rolled sheet, coated sheet	30%	24%
Tin mill products	30%	24%
Hot-rolled bar	30%	24%
Cold-finished bar	30%	24%
Rebar	15%	12%
Welded tubular products	15%	12%
Carbon and alloy flanges	13%	10%
Stainless steel bar	15%	12%
Stainless steel rod	15%	12%
Stainless steel wire	8%	7%

Source: President of the United States, *Message to Congress* (House Doc. 107-185), March 6, 2002.

Since the 1960s, big integrated U.S. steelmakers have argued that they need import restraints because unfairly traded (dumped and subsidized) imports deprive them of a chance to modernize as quickly as foreign rivals have. In response to pressure from U.S. steelmakers, in 2001 President Bush requested the U.S. International Trade Commission (USITC) to launch an investigation to determine whether the steel industry was seriously injured or threatened with serious injury from imports. After reviewing the facts, the USITC decided in 2002 that U.S. steelmakers in 16 out of 33 product categories were injured by imports, making those products eligible for trade restraints. The USITC especially noted excess steel in the world market producing the lowest prices in 20 years and the 30 bankruptcies of American steel companies.

The Bush remedy was a program in which 30 percent tariffs were initially imposed on imported steel that competes with the main products of most of the big integrated mills. The tariffs were scheduled to decrease to 24 percent the second year and to 18 percent the third year, and were then to expire. Other steel products faced tariffs from 15 percent to 8 percent. In return for granting steelmakers protection from imports, President Bush insisted that they bring their labor costs down and upgrade equipment.

Critics of the steel tariffs argued that the big integrated companies suffered from a lack of competitiveness due to previous poor investment decisions, diversion of funds into nonsteel businesses, and a reduction of investment during previous periods of import protection. They also noted that protecting steel would place a heavy burden on American steel-using industries such as automobiles and earth-moving equipment. Although the tariffs would temporarily save roughly 6,000 jobs, the cost to U.S. consumers and steel-using firms of saving these jobs was between $800,000 and $1.1 million per job. Moreover, the steel tariffs would cost as many as 13 jobs in steel-using industries for every 1 steel job protected.[6]

[6]Robert W. Crandall, *The Futility of Steel Trade Protection*, Criterion Economics, 2002. See also U.S. International Trade Commission, *Steel-Consuming Industries: Competitive Conditions with Respect to Steel Safeguard Measures*, September 2003.

The Bush tariffs did provide some relief to U.S. steelmakers from imports. Also, some cost-cutting occurred among steelmakers during 2002–2003: Producers merged and labor contracts were renegotiated, though often at considerable cost to the approximately 150,000 workers still employed in an industry that is just a shadow of its former self. However, the tariffs aroused heavy opposition among a large number of U.S. companies that use steel to make everything from auto parts to tin cans and washing machines. In numerous lobbying trips to Washington, chief executives of these firms noted that the tariffs drove up their costs and imperiled more jobs across the manufacturing belt than they saved in the steel industry. Indeed, President Bush found himself in a difficult political situation given the opposing interests of steel producers and steel users.

Citing an improving economy and cost-cutting efforts by domestic steel companies, President Bush removed the steel tariffs in December 2003. He noted that his tariffs provided domestic steelmakers time to restructure and regain competitiveness. However, his removal of the tariffs was primarily in response to the World Trade Organization's ruling that the tariffs were illegal (see Chapter 6). The World Trade Organization said the United States erred in seeking protectionism nearly four years after the industry suffered from a surge of imports during the meltdown of Asian economies. This decision gave the European Union and several other steel-exporting countries the authority to impose retaliatory tariffs of up to 30 percent on more than 2 billion dollars' worth of U.S. exports unless Bush eliminate his steel tariffs. Bowing to this pressure, Bush removed the tariffs. His action infuriated domestic steelmakers, who felt that they needed more time to regain competitiveness.

Lamb Tariffs Fleece U.S. Consumers

In 1999, the U.S. government imposed stiff tariffs on imports of lamb from Australia and New Zealand to protect high-cost U.S. producers and provide stability to the domestic market.[7] U.S. sheep producers have long been dependent on government. For more than half a century, until Congress enacted farm-policy reforms in 1995, they received subsidies for wool. Having lost that handout, burdened with inefficiencies and high costs, and facing domestic competition from pork, beef, and chicken, sheep producers attempted to reduce foreign competition by filing for import barriers.

Almost all U.S. lamb imports come from Australia and New Zealand, major agricultural producers with a comparative advantage. New Zealand has less than 4 million people but as many as 60 million sheep, compared with about 7 million sheep in the United States. New Zealand's farmers have invested substantial resources in effective marketing and new technology, making them highly efficient producers. New Zealand also wiped out domestic agricultural subsidies in the free-market reforms of the 1980s and is on track to eliminate all import tariffs by 2006.

Rather than copy this example, the American sheep producers requested temporary import relief to allow them time to become competitive in the future. The U.S. government at first appeared to be considering only modest amounts of protectionism. Australia and New Zealand even offered financial assistance to the U.S. producers. However, the government relented to the demands of the sheep industry and its advocates in Congress and enacted stiff import barriers. On top of existing tariffs, the government imposed a 9 percent tariff on all imports in the first year (declining to 6 percent and then 3 percent in years two and three), and a whopping 40 percent tariff on imports above the levels of 1998 (dropping to 32 percent and 24 percent).

The American Sheep Industry Association's president declared that the policy will restore stability to the market. However, the decision outraged farmers in Australia and New Zealand. Moreover, consumer groups in the United States noted that whenever sheep producers speak of bringing stability to the market, you know that consumers are getting fleeced.

Harley-Davidson Revs Up Sales with Tariffs

There have been approximately 150 manufacturers of motorcycles in the United States since the

---

[7]This example is drawn from Douglas A. Irwin, "Lamb Tariffs Fleece U.S. Consumers, *The Wall Street Journal*, July 12, 1999, p. A28.

Effects of Eliminating Import Tariffs

Eliminating Import Tariffs: Gains and Losses

Import-Competing Industry	Millions of Dollars			
	Consumer Gain	Producer Loss	Domestic Tax Loss	Job Loss (in Thousands)
Rubber footwear	$272.2	$44.1	$28.5	2.4
Women's footwear	325.1	54.6	38.0	3.5
Ceramic tile	90.0	10.0	11.6	0.4
Luggage	186.3	36.4	21.0	1.8
Women's handbags	134.4	25.7	15.5	1.6
Glasswear	185.8	77.2	14.8	2.5
Resins	93.1	45.1	5.8	1.1
Bicycles	38.1	10.0	4.0	0.6
Ball bearings	50.3	3.9	6.9	0.1
Canned tuna	61.3	35.0	3.2	0.8
Cedar shingles	25.3	11.5	6.1	0.1

Source: U.S. International Trade Commission, *The Economic Effects of Significant U.S. Import Restraints, Phase 1: Manufacturing* (Washington, DC: U.S. Government Printing Office, October 1989), Tables ES-1 and ES-2.

What would be the effects if the United States unilaterally removed tariffs on imported products? On the positive side, tariff elimination lowers the price of the affected imports and may lower the price of the competing U.S. good, resulting in economic gains to the U.S. consumer. On the negative side, the lower price to import-competing producers, as a result of eliminating the tariff, results in profit reductions; workers become displaced from the domestic industry that loses protection; and the U.S. government loses tax revenue as the result of eliminating the tariff. The table gives estimates of the short-run effects that would occur in the first year after tariff removals.

first commercially produced motorcycle was manufactured in 1901. By the 1980s, there were one U.S.–owned firm, Harley-Davidson Motor Co., and two Japanese-owned firms, Kawasaki and Honda, operating in the United States. Harley specializes in the production of heavyweight motorcycles (1,000 and 1,300 cc).

In the early 1970s, Harley had 100 percent of the U.S. market for heavyweight motorcycles; by the early 1980s, its market share was less than 15 percent. During this decade, Harley continually lost ground to Japanese competitors such as Suzuki, Yamaha, Honda, and Kawasaki. Being

used to tough competition, these Japanese firms were able to undercut Harley by $1,500 to $2,000 per motorcycle. Industry analysts maintained that Harley was plagued by inefficient production methods and poor management and that its per-unit costs were higher than those of the U.S. plants of Honda and Kawasaki.

During this period, Harley was the victim of a Honda–Yamaha struggle for domination of the motorcycle market. In the early 1980s, both Japanese motorcycle manufacturers flooded the U.S. market with a variety of new competitive models. Bloated Japanese inventories, stashed in

U.S. dealerships and warehouses, estimated to be a year-and-a-half supply of new motorcycles, led to heavy price cuts and intense product promotion.

By 1982, Harley was rapidly approaching bankruptcy and layoffs were mounting. Harley turned to the U.S. government for import relief. The government concluded that rising motorcycle imports from Japan were a substantial cause of a threat of serious injury to Harley and that temporary protectionism was justified to permit Harley to recover from its injuries and provide it time to complete a comprehensive program to fully compete with the Japanese.

In 1983, the U.S. government implemented a 5-year tariff program for heavyweight motorcycles (700 cc engines and larger). During the first year, the import tariff was raised from 4.4 percent to 49.4 percent; during the second year, the tariff was reduced to 39.4 percent; in the next three years, the tariff was cut by 15 percent, 5 percent, and 5 percent. After the fifth year, the tariff was to revert to 4.4 percent. The tariff hikes did not apply to motorcycle imports from Italy, Germany, and the United Kingdom, which accounted for less than 20 percent of U.S. imports of heavyweight motorcycles in 1982. The 5-year tariff program was intended to allow Harley sufficient time to eliminate its excess inventories and to benefit from improved economies of scale obtained from increased sales and production.

But the substantial tariff looked much better on paper than it worked out in reality. Stung, Japanese motorcycle manufacturers reacted promptly to circumvent the tariff policy. They quickly downsized their 750-cc motorcycle engines to 699 cc, thus evading the tariff that applied to motorcycle imports having engines of 700 cc or more. The press dubbed these downsized models "tariff busters." The downsized engine wiped out approximately half of the tariff's value to Harley. Also, Kawasaki and Honda quickly increased production of heavyweight motorcycles in their U.S. plants. That left only Suzuki and Yamaha motorcycles, with engines over 1,000 cc, subject to the tariff. These manufacturers were permitted to ship 7,000 to 10,000 of these heavyweight motorcycles to the United States before they had to start paying the extra import duty.

Although the outcome of the tariff was disappointing to Harley, its economic performance improved throughout the 1980s. By 1987, Harley enjoyed record profits of almost $18 million. It also enjoyed a 40 percent market share in the super-heavyweight motorcycle class, 11 percentage points ahead of its closest rival, Honda, and 17 points above its 1983 low of 23 percent. In March 1987, Harley announced that it no longer needed special tariffs to compete with the Japanese motorcycle firms. Harley indicated that, given temporary relief from predatory import practices, it had become competitive in world markets.[8]

Tariffs and the Poor

Empirical studies often maintain that the welfare costs of tariffs can be high. Tariffs also affect the distribution of income within a society. A legitimate concern of government officials is whether the welfare costs of tariffs are shared uniformly by all people in a country, or whether some income groups absorb a disproportionate share of the costs.

Several studies have considered the income-distribution effects of import tariffs. They conclude that tariffs tend to be inequitable because they impose the most severe costs on *low-income families*. Tariffs, for example, are often applied to products at the lower end of the price and quality range. Basic products such as shoes and clothing are subject to tariffs, and these items constitute large shares of the budgets of low-income families. Tariffs thus can be likened to sales taxes on the products protected, and, as typically occurs with sales taxes, their effects are *regressive*. Simply put, U.S. tariff policy is tough on the poor: Young single mothers purchasing cheap clothes and shoes at Wal-Mart often pay tariffs rates 5 to 10 times higher than rich families pay when purchasing at elite stores such as Nordstrom.[9]

[8]Daniel Klein, "Taking America for a Ride: The Politics of Motorcycle Tariffs," *Cato Institute Policy Analysis*, No. 32, January 1984. See also U.S. International Trade Commission, *Heavyweight Motorcycles, and Engines and Power Train Subassemblies Therefor* (Washington, DC: U.S. Government Printing Office, February 1983), and Peter Reid, *Well Made in America* (New York: McGraw-Hill, 1989).

[9]Edward Gresser, "Toughest on the Poor: America's Flawed Tariff System," *Foreign Affairs*, November–December 2002, pp. 19–23, and Susan Hickok, "The Consumer Cost of U.S. Trade Restraints," Federal Reserve Bank of New York, *Quarterly Review*, Summer 1985, pp. 10–11.

the poor tend to suffer b/c of tarrifs

International trade agreements have eliminated most U.S. tariffs on high-technology products like airplanes, semiconductors, computers, medical equipment, and medicines. The agreements have also reduced rates to generally less than 5 percent on mid-range manufactured products like autos, TV sets, pianos, felt-tip pens, and many luxury consumer goods. Moreover, tariffs on natural resources like oil, metal ores, and farm products like chocolate and coffee that are not grown in the United States are generally close to zero. However, inexpensive clothes, luggage, shoes, watches, and silverware have been excluded from most tariff reforms, and thus tariffs remain relatively high. Clothing tariffs, for example, are usually in the 10 percent to 32 percent range.

Tariffs vary from one consumer good to the next. They are much higher on cheap goods than on luxuries. This disparity occurs because elite firms such as Ralph Lauren, Coach, or Oakley, selling brand name and image, find small price advantages relatively unimportant. Because they have not lobbied the U.S. government for high tariffs, rates on luxury goods such as silk lingerie, silver-handled cutlery, leaded-glass beer mugs, and snakeskin handbags are very low. But producers of cheap water glasses, stainless steel cutlery, nylon lingerie, and plastic purses benefit by adding a few percentage points to their competitors' prices. So on the cheapest goods, tariffs are even higher than the overall averages for consumer goods suggest, as seen in Table 4.8. Simply put, U.S. tariffs are highest on the goods important to the poor. The U.S. tariffs system is not uniquely toughest on the poor. The tariffs of most U.S. trade partners operate in a similar fashion.

Besides bearing down hard on the poor, U.S. tariff policy affects different countries in different ways. It especially burdens countries that specialize in the cheapest goods, noticeably very poor countries in Asia and the Middle East. For example, average tariffs on European exports to the United States—mainly autos, computers, power equipment, and chemicals—today barely exceed 1 percent. Developing countries such as Malaysia, which specializes in information-technology goods, face tariff rates just as low. So do oil exporters such as Saudi Arabia and Nigeria.

TABLE 4.8

U.S. Tariffs Are High on Cheap Goods, Low on Luxuries

Product	Tariff Rate
Women's Underwear	
Man-made fiber	16.2%
Cotton	11.3
Silk	2.4
Men's Knitted Shirts	
Synthetic fiber	32.5
Cotton	20.0
Silk	1.9
Drinking Glasses	
30¢ or less	30.4
$5 or more	5.0
Leaded glass	3.0
Forks	
Stainless steel, under 25¢	14.5
Gold or silver plated	0.0
Handbags	
Plastic-sided	16.8
Leather, under $20	10.0
Reptile leather	5.3

Source: U.S. International Trade Commission, *Tariff Schedules of the United States* (Washington, DC: U.S. Government Printing Office, 2004); http://www.usitc.gov/taffairs.htm.

However, Asian countries like Cambodia and Bangladesh are hit hardest by U.S. tariffs; their cheap consumer goods often face tariff rates of 15 percent or more, some 10 times the world average.

Arguments for Trade Restrictions

The **free-trade argument** is, in principle, persuasive. It states that if each nation produces what it does best and permits trade, over the long run all will enjoy lower prices and higher levels of output, income, and consumption than could be achieved in isolation. In a dynamic world, comparative advantage is constantly changing owing to shifts in technologies, input productivities, and wages, as well as tastes and preferences. A free market compels adjustment to take place. Either the efficiency of an industry must improve, or else resources will flow from low-productivity uses to those with high productivity. Tariffs and other trade barriers are viewed as tools that prevent the economy from undergoing adjustment, resulting in economic stagnation.

Although the free-trade argument tends to dominate in the classroom, virtually all nations have imposed restrictions on the international flow of goods, services, and capital. Often, proponents of protectionism say that free trade is fine in theory, but that it does not apply in the real world. Modern trade theory assumes perfectly competitive markets whose characteristics do not reflect real-world market conditions. Moreover, even though protectionists may concede that economic losses occur with tariffs and other restrictions, they often argue that noneconomic benefits such as national security more than offset the economic losses. In seeking protection from imports, domestic industries and labor unions attempt to secure their economic welfare. Over the years, a number of arguments have been advanced to pressure the president and Congress to enact restrictive measures.

Job Protection

The issue of jobs has been a dominant factor in motivating government officials to levy trade restrictions on imported goods. During periods of economic recession, workers are especially eager to point out that cheap foreign goods undercut domestic production, resulting in a loss of domestic jobs to foreign labor. Alleged job losses to foreign competition historically have been a major force behind the desire of most U.S. labor leaders to reject free-trade policies.

This view, however, has a serious omission: It fails to acknowledge the dual nature of international trade. Changes in a nation's imports of goods and services are closely related to changes in its exports. Nations export goods because they desire to import products from other nations. When the United States imports goods from abroad, foreigners gain purchasing power that will eventually be spent on U.S. goods, services, or financial assets. U.S. export industries then enjoy gains in sales and

employment, whereas the opposite occurs in U.S. import-competing industries. Rather than promoting overall unemployment, imports tend to generate job opportunities in some industries as part of the process by which they decrease employment in other industries. However, the job gains due to open trade policies tend to be less visible to the public than the readily observable job losses stemming from foreign competition. The more conspicuous losses have led many U.S. business and labor leaders to combine forces in their opposition to free trade.

ECONOMIC *Applications*

Visit EconNews Online
International Trade

Trade restraints raise employment in the protected industry (such as steel) by increasing the price (or reducing the supply) of competing import goods. Industries that are primary suppliers of inputs to the protected industry also gain jobs. However, industries that purchase the protected product (such as auto manufacturers) face higher costs. These costs are then passed on to the consumer through higher prices, resulting in decreased sales. Thus employment falls in these related industries.

Economists at the Federal Reserve Bank of Dallas have examined the effects on U.S. employment of trade restrictions on textiles and apparel, steel, and automobiles. They conclude that trade protection has little or no positive effect on the level of employment in the long run. Trade restraints tend to provide job gains for only a few industries, while they result in job losses spread across many industries.[10]

A striking fact about protection to preserve jobs is that each job often ends up costing domestic consumers more than the worker's salary! As seen in Table 4.9 on page 128, the consumer cost of protecting each job preserved in the auto industry in the United States is estimated to be $105,000 a year; this is far above the salary a production employee in that industry would receive. The fact that costs to consumers for each production job saved are so high underpins the argument that an alternative approach should be used to

[10]Linda Hunter, "U.S. Trade Protection: Effects on the Industrial and Regional Composition of Employment," Federal Reserve Bank of Dallas, *Economic Review*, January 1990, pp. 1–13.

TABLE 4.9

Saving Jobs: Consumer Costs

Industry	Annual Cost to Consumers	
	Total (Millions of Dollars)	Per Job Saved (Dollars)
Specialty steel	$ 520	$1,000,000
Nonrubber footwear	700	55,000
Color TVs	420	42,000
Bolts, nuts, screws	110	550,000
Mushrooms	35	117,000
Automobiles	5,800	105,000
Textiles and apparel	27,000	42,000
Carbon steel	6,800	750,000
Motorcycles	104	150,000

Source: Gary Hufbauer et al., *Trade Protection in the United States: 31 Case Studies* (Washington, DC: Institute for International Economics, 1986), Tables 1.1 and 1.2.

help workers, and that workers departing from an industry facing foreign competition should be liberally compensated (subsidized) for moving to new industries or taking early retirement.

Protection Against Cheap Foreign Labor

One of the most common arguments used to justify the protectionist umbrella of trade restrictions is that tariffs are needed to defend domestic jobs against cheap foreign labor. As indicated in Table 4.10, production workers in Germany, Switzerland, and the United States have been paid much higher wages, in terms of the U.S. dollar, than workers in countries such as Sri Lanka and Mexico. So it could be argued that low wages abroad make it difficult for U.S. producers to compete with producers using cheap foreign labor and that unless U.S. producers are protected from imports, domestic output and employment levels will decrease.

Indeed, there is a widely held view that competition from goods produced in low-wage countries is unfair and harmful to American workers. Moreover, it is thought that companies that produce goods in foreign countries to take advantage

TABLE 4.10

Hourly Compensation Costs in U.S. Dollars for Production Workers in Manufacturing, 2002

Country	Hourly Compensation (Dollars per Hour)
Germany	$25.08
Switzerland	24.11
United States	21.33
Japan	18.83
New Zealand	8.89
Taiwan	5.41
Portugal	4.75
Brazil	2.57
Mexico	2.38
Sri Lanka	0.42

Source: U.S. Department of Labor, Bureau of Labor Statistics, *Foreign Labor Statistics: Hourly Compensation Costs in U.S. Dollars*, September 2003, at http://www.bls.gov.

of cheap labor should not be allowed to dictate the wages paid to American workers. A solution: Impose a tariff or tax on goods brought into the United States equal to the wage differential between foreign workers and U.S. workers in the same industry. That way, competition would be confined to who makes the best product, not who works for the least amount of money. Therefore, if Calvin Klein wants to manufacture sweatshirts in Pakistan, his firm would be charged a tariff or tax equal to the difference between the earnings of a Pakistani worker and a U.S. apparel worker.

Although this viewpoint may have widespread appeal, it fails to recognize the links among efficiency, wages, and production costs. Even if domestic wages are higher than those abroad, if domestic labor is more productive than foreign labor, domestic labor costs may still be competitive. Total labor costs reflect not only the wage rate but

also output per labor hour. If the productive superiority of domestic labor more than offsets the higher domestic wage rate, the home nation's labor costs will actually be less than they are abroad.

Figure 4.6 shows wages, labor productivity (output per worker), and unit labor costs in manufacturing, relative to the United States, for several nations: India, Philippines, Malaysia, Mexico, and Korea. We see that in 1990, wages in these nations were only fractions of U.S. wages; however, labor productivity levels in these nations were also fractions of U.S. labor productivity. Even if wage rates in, say, Malaysia are lower than in the United States, Malaysia still could have higher unit labor costs if its productivity is lower than U.S. productivity. The

---

FIGURE 4.6

Productivity, Wages, and Unit Labor Costs, Relative to the United States: Total Manufacturing, 1990

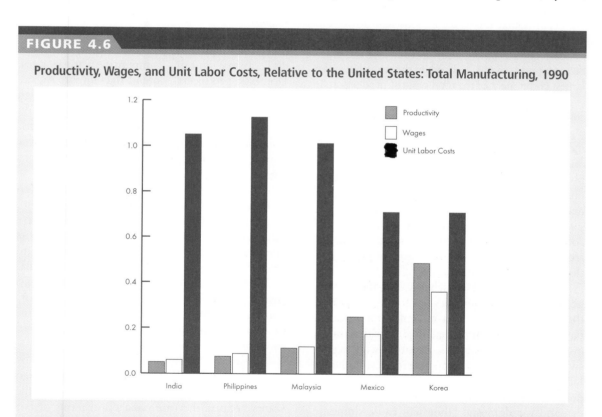

Low wages by themselves do not guarantee low production costs. To the degree that low wages reflect low labor productivity, any cost advantage of employing low-wage workers is neutralized.

Source: Stephen Golub, "Comparative and Absolute Advantage in the Asia–Pacific Region," *Pacific Basin Working Paper Series,* Federal Reserve Bank of San Francisco, October 1995.

figure also shows labor cost per unit of output (the ratio of wages to productivity) relative to the United States in 1990. For the five nations, we see that international differences in unit labor costs, relative to the United States, were invariably much smaller than differences in wages suggest. For example, Mexican wages in manufacturing were about 23 percent that of the United States, while Mexico's unit labor costs in manufacturing were about 75 percent that of the United States. In fact, unit labor cost in India and the Philippines were higher than those of the United States—the productivity gap exceeded the wage gap. These data show that low wages, by themselves, do not guarantee low production costs.

Another limitation of the cheap-foreign-labor argument is that low-wage nations tend to have a competitive advantage only in the production of goods requiring much labor and little of the other factor inputs—that is, only when the wage bill is the largest component of the total costs of production. It is true that a high-wage nation may have a relative cost disadvantage compared with its low-wage trading partner in the production of labor-intensive commodities. But this does not mean that foreign producers can undersell the home country across the board in all lines of production, causing the overall domestic standard of living to decline. Foreign nations should use the revenues from their export sales to purchase the products in which the home country has a competitive advantage—products requiring a large share of the factors of production that are abundant domestically.

Recall that the Heckscher–Ohlin theory suggests that as economies become integrated through trade, there is a tendency for resource payments to become equal in different nations, given competitive markets. A nation with expensive labor will tend to import products embodying large amounts of labor. As imports rise and domestic output falls, the resulting decrease in demand for domestic labor will cause domestic wages to fall to the foreign level.

In automobile manufacturing, for example, there has been sufficient international competition to warrant such a process. This was seen in the 1980s, when high unemployment in the U.S. auto industry permitted General Motors and Ford to scale down the compensation levels of their employees as a means of offsetting their cost disadvantages against the Japanese. The adverse implications of resource-price equalization for the wages of U.S. workers could explain why the United Auto Workers (UAW) supports protectionism. By shielding U.S. wage levels from market pressures created by foreign competition, protectionism would result in the U.S. government's validating the high wages and benefits of UAW members.

Fairness in Trade: A Level Playing Field

Fairness in trade is another reason given for protectionism. Business firms and workers often argue that foreign governments play by a different set of rules than the home government, giving foreign firms unfair competitive advantages. Domestic producers contend that import restrictions should be enacted to offset these foreign advantages, thus creating a **level playing field** on which all producers can compete on equal terms.

U.S. companies often allege that foreign firms are not subject to the same government regulations regarding pollution control and worker safety as U.S. companies; this is especially true in many developing nations (such as Mexico and South Korea), where environmental laws and enforcement have been lax. Moreover, foreign firms may not pay as much in corporate taxes and may not have to comply with employment regulations such as affirmative action, minimum wages, and overtime pay. Also, foreign governments may erect high trade barriers that effectively close their markets to imports, or they may subsidize their producers so as to enhance their competitiveness in world markets.

These fair-trade arguments are often voiced by organized lobbies that are losing sales to foreign competitors. They may sound appealing to the voters because they are couched in terms of fair play and equal treatment. However, there are several arguments against levying restrictions on imports from nations that have high trade restrictions or that place lower regulatory burdens on their producers.

First, there is a benefit to the domestic economy from trade even if foreign nations impose trade restrictions. Although foreign restrictions that lessen our exports may decrease our welfare, retaliating by levying our own import barriers—which protect inefficient domestic producers—decreases our welfare even more.

Second, the argument does not recognize the potential impact on global trade. If each nation were to increase trade restrictions whenever foreign restrictions were higher than domestic restrictions, there would occur a worldwide escalation in restrictions; this would lead to a lower volume of trade, falling levels of production and employment, and a decline in welfare. There may be a case for threatening to levy trade restrictions unless foreign nations reduce their restrictions; but if negotiations fail and domestic restrictions are employed, the result is undesirable. Other countries' trade practices are seldom an adequate justification for domestic trade restrictions.

Maintenance of the Domestic Standard of Living

Advocates of trade barriers often contend that tariffs are useful in maintaining a high level of income and employment for the home nation. It is argued that by reducing the level of imports, tariffs encourage home spending, which stimulates domestic economic activity. As a result, the home nation's level of employment and income will be enhanced.

Although this argument appears appealing on the surface, it merits several qualifications. It is apparent that all nations together cannot levy tariffs to bolster domestic living standards. This is because tariffs result in a redistribution of the gains from trade among nations. To the degree that one nation imposes a tariff that improves its income and employment, it does so at the expense of its trading partner's living standard. Nations adversely affected by trade barriers are likely to impose retaliatory tariffs, resulting in a lower level of welfare for all nations. It is little wonder that tariff restrictions designed to enhance a nation's standard of living at the expense of its trading partner are referred to as *beggar-thy-neighbor policies*.

Equalization of Production Costs

Proponents of a **scientific tariff** seek to eliminate what they consider to be unfair competition from abroad. Owing to such factors as lower wage costs, tax concessions, or government subsidies, foreign sellers may enjoy cost advantages over domestic firms. To offset any such advantage, tariffs equivalent to the cost differential should be imposed. Such provisions were actually part of the U.S. Tariff Acts of 1922 and 1930.

In practice, the scientific tariff suffers from a number of problems. Because within a given industry costs differ from business to business, how can costs actually be compared? Suppose that all U.S. steelmakers were extended protection from all foreign steelmakers. This would require the costs of the most efficient foreign producer to be set equal to the highest costs of the least efficient U.S. company. Given today's cost conditions, prices would certainly rise in the United States. This would benefit the more efficient U.S. companies, which would enjoy economic profits, but the U.S. consumer would be subsidizing inefficient production. Because the scientific tariff approximates a prohibitive tariff, it completely contradicts the notion of comparative advantage and wipes out the basis for trade and gains from trade.

Infant-Industry Argument

One of the more commonly accepted cases for tariff protection is the **infant-industry argument**. This argument does not deny the validity of the case for free trade. However, it contends that for free trade to be meaningful, trading nations should temporarily shield their newly developing industries from foreign competition. Otherwise, mature foreign businesses, which are at the time more efficient, can drive the young domestic businesses out of the market. Only after the young companies have had time to become efficient producers should the tariff barriers be lifted and free trade take place.

Although there is some truth in the infant-industry argument, it must be qualified in several respects. First, once a protective tariff is imposed, it is very difficult to remove, even after industrial maturity has been achieved. Special-interest groups can often convince policy makers that further protection is justified. Second, it is very difficult to determine which industries will be capable of realizing comparative-advantage potential and thus merit protection. Third, the infant-industry argument generally is not valid for mature, industrialized nations such as the United States, Germany, and Japan. Finally, there may be other ways of insulating a developing industry from cutthroat competition. Rather than adopt a protective tariff, the government could grant a subsidy to the industry. A subsidy has the advantage of not distorting domestic consumption and relative prices; its drawback is that instead of generating revenue, as an import tariff does, a subsidy spends revenue.

Noneconomic Arguments

Noneconomic considerations also enter into the arguments for protectionism. One such consideration is *national security*. The national-security argument contends that a country may be put in jeopardy in the event of an international crisis or war if it is heavily dependent on foreign suppliers. Even though domestic producers are not as efficient, tariff protection should be granted to ensure their continued existence. A good application of this argument involves the major oil-importing nations, which saw several Arab nations impose oil boycotts on the West to win support for the Arab position against Israel during the 1973 Middle East conflict. The problem, however, is stipulating what constitutes an essential industry. If the term is defined broadly, many industries may be able to win import protection, and the argument loses its meaning.

Another noneconomic argument is based on *cultural and sociological considerations*. New England may desire to preserve small-scale fishing; West Virginia may argue for tariffs on handblown glassware, on the grounds that these skills enrich the fabric of life; certain products such as narcotics may be considered socially undesirable, and restrictions or prohibitions may be placed on their importation. These arguments constitute legiti-

mate reasons and cannot be ignored. All the economist can do is point out the economic consequences and costs of protection and identify alternative ways of accomplishing the same objective.

In Canada, many nationalists maintain that Canadian culture is too fragile to survive without government protection. The big threat: U.S. cultural imperialism. To keep the Yanks in check, Canada has long maintained some restrictions on sales of U.S. publications and textbooks. By the 1990s, the envelope of Canada's cultural protectionism was expanding. The most blatant example was a 1994 law that levied an 80 percent tax on Canadian ads in Canadian editions of U.S. magazines—in effect, an effort to kill off the U.S. intruders. Without protections for the Canadian media, the cultural nationalists feared that U.S. magazines such as *Sports Illustrated*, *Time*, and *Business Week* could soon deprive Canadians of the ability to read about themselves in *Maclean's* and *Canadian Business*. Although U.S. protests of the tax ultimately led to its abolishment, the Canadian government continued to examine other methods of preserving the culture of its people.

It is important to note that most of the arguments justifying tariffs are based on the assumption that the national welfare, as well as the individual's welfare, will be enhanced. The strategic importance of tariffs for the welfare of import-competing producers is one of the main reasons that reciprocal tariff liberalization has been so gradual. It is no wonder that import-competing producers make such strong and politically effective arguments that increased foreign competition will undermine the welfare of the nation as a whole as well as their own. Although a liberalization of tariff barriers may be detrimental to a particular group, we must be careful to differentiate between the individual's welfare and the national welfare. If tariff reductions result in greater welfare gains from trade and if the adversely affected party can be compensated for the loss it has faced, the overall national welfare will increase. However, proving that the gains more than offset the losses in practice is very difficult.

The Political Economy of Protectionism

Recent history indicates that increasing dependence on international trade yields uneven impacts across domestic sectors. The United States has enjoyed comparative advantages in such products as agricultural commodities, industrial machinery, chemicals, and scientific instruments. However, some of its industries have lost their comparative advantage and suffered from international trade—among them apparel and textiles, motor vehicles, electronic goods, basic iron and steel, and footwear. Formulating international trade policy in this environment is difficult. Free trade can yield substantial benefits for the overall economy through increased productivity and lower prices, but specific groups may benefit if government provides them some relief from import competition. Government officials must consider these opposing interests when setting the course for international trade policy.

Considerable attention has been devoted to what motivates government officials when formulating trade policy. As voters, we do not have the opportunity to go to the polls and vote for a trade bill. Instead, formation of trade policy rests in the hands of elected officials and their appointees. It is generally assumed that elected officials form policies to maximize votes and thus remain in office. The result is a bias in the political system that favors protectionism.

The **protection-biased sector** of the economy generally consists of import-competing companies, the labor unions representing workers in that industry, and the suppliers to the companies in the industry. Seekers of protectionism are often established firms in an aging industry that have lost their comparative advantage. High costs may be due to lack of modern technology, inefficient management procedures, outmoded work rules, or high payments to domestic workers. The **free-trade-biased sector** generally comprises exporting companies, their workers, and their suppliers. It also consists of consumers, including wholesalers and retail merchants of imported goods.

Government officials understand that they will likely lose the political support of, say, the UAW if they vote against increases in tariffs on auto imports. They also understand that their vote on this trade issue will not be the key factor underlying the political support provided by many other citizens. Their support can be retained by appealing to them on other issues while voting to increase the tariff on auto imports to maintain UAW support.

U.S. protection policy is thus dominated by special-interest groups that represent producers. Consumers generally are not organized, and their losses due to protectionism are widely dispersed, whereas the gains from protection are concentrated among well-organized producers and labor unions in the affected sectors. Those harmed by a protectionist policy absorb individually a small and difficult-to-identify cost. Many consumers, though they will pay a higher price for the protected product, will not associate the higher price with the protectionist policy and thus are unlikely to be concerned about trade policy. Special-interest groups, however, are highly concerned about protecting their industries against import competition. They provide support for government officials who share their views and lobby against the election of those who do not. Clearly, government officials seeking reelection will be sensitive to the special-interest groups representing producers.

The political bias favoring domestic producers is seen in the tariff escalation effect, discussed earlier in this chapter. Recall that the tariff structures of industrial nations often result in lower import tariffs on intermediate goods and higher tariffs on finished goods. For example, U.S. imports of cotton yarn have traditionally faced low tariffs, while higher tariffs have been applied to cotton fabric imports. The higher tariff on cotton fabrics appears to be the result of ineffective lobbying efforts of diffused consumers, who lose to organized U.S. fabric producers lobbying for protectionism. But for cotton yarn, the protectionist outcome is less clear. Purchasers of cotton yarn are U.S. manufacturers who want low tariffs on imported inputs. These companies form trade associations and can pressure Congress for low tariffs as effectively as

Petition of the Candle Makers

Free-trade advocate Frederic Bastiat presented the French Chamber of Deputies with a devastating satire of protectionists' arguments in 1845. His petition asked that a law be passed requiring people to shut all windows, doors, and so forth so that the candle industry would be protected from the "unfair" competition of the sun. He argued that this would be a great benefit to the candle industry, creating many new jobs and enriching suppliers. Consider the following excerpts from his satire:

We are subjected to the intolerable competition of a foreign rival, who enjoys, it would seem, such superior facilities for the production of light, that he is flooding the domestic market with it at an incredibly low price. From the moment he appears, our sales cease, all consumers turn to him, and a branch of French industry whose ramifications are innumerable is at once reduced to complete stagnation. This rival is no other than the sun.

We ask you to be so good as to pass a law requiring the closing of all windows, dormers, skylights, shutters, curtains, and blinds—in short, all openings, holes, chinks, and fissures through which the light of

the sun is wont to enter houses, to the detriment of our industries.

By shutting out as much as possible all access to natural light, you create the necessity for artificial light. Is there in France an industry which will not, through some connection with this important object, be benefited by it? If more tallow be consumed, there will arise a necessity for an increase of cattle and sheep. If more oil be consumed, it will cause an increase in the cultivation of the olive tree. Navigation will profit as thousands of vessels would be employed in the whale fisheries. There is, in short, no market which would not be greatly developed by the granting of our petitions.

Although it is undoubtedly true that the French candle industry would benefit from a lack of sunlight, consumers would obviously not be happy about being forced to pay for light that they could get for free were there no government intervention.

Source: Frederic Bastiat, *Economic Sophisms*, edited and translated by Arthur Goddard (New York: D. Van Nostrand, 1964).

U.S. cotton suppliers, who lobby for high tariffs. Protection applied to imported intermediate goods, such as cotton yarn, is thus less likely.

Not only does the interest of the domestic producer tend to outweigh that of the domestic consumer in trade policy deliberations, but import-competing producers tend to exert stronger influence on legislators than do export producers. A problem faced by export producers is that their gains from international trade are often in addition to their prosperity in the domestic market; producers that are efficient enough to sell overseas are often safe from foreign competition in the domestic market. Most deliberations on trade policy emphasize protecting imports, and the indirect damage done by import barriers to export producers tends to be spread over many

export industries. But import-competing producers can gather evidence of immediate damage caused by foreign competition, including falling levels of sales, profits, and employment. Legislators tend to be influenced by the more clearly identified arguments of the import-competing industry and see that a greater number of votes are at stake among their constituents than among the constituents of the export producers.

A Supply and Demand View of Protectionism

The political economy of import protection can be analyzed in terms of supply and demand. Protectionism is supplied by the domestic government, while domestic companies and workers are the source of demand. The supply of protection depends on (1) the costs to society, (2) the political importance of the import-competing industry, (3) adjustment costs, and (4) public sympathy.

Enlightened government officials realize that although protectionism provides benefits to the domestic industry, society as a whole pays costs. These costs include the losses of consumer surplus because of higher prices and the resulting deadweight losses as import volume is reduced, lost economies of scale as opportunities for further trade are foregone, and the loss of incentive for technological development provided by import competition. The higher the costs of protection to society, the less likely it is that government officials will shield an industry from import competition.

The supply of protectionism is also influenced by the *political importance* of the import-competing industry. An industry that enjoys strong representation in the legislature is in a favorable position to win import protection. It is more difficult for politicians to disagree with 1 million autoworkers than with 20,000 copper workers. The national security argument for protection is a variant on the consideration of the political importance of the industry. Thus, for example, the U.S. coal and oil industries were successful in obtaining a national-security clause in U.S. trade law permitting protection if imports threaten to impair domestic security.

The supply of protection also tends to increase when domestic businesses and workers face large costs of adjusting to rising import competition (for example, unemployment or wage concessions). This protection is seen as a method of delaying the full burden of *adjustment*.

Finally, as *public sympathy* for a group of domestic businesses or workers increases (for example, if workers are paid low wages and have few alternative work skills), a greater amount of protection against foreign-produced goods tends to be supplied.

On the demand side, factors that underlie the domestic industry's demand for protectionism are (1) comparative disadvantage, (2) import penetration, (3) concentration, and (4) export dependence.

The demand for protection rises as the domestic industry's *comparative disadvantage* intensifies. This is seen in the U.S. steel industry, which has vigorously pursued protection against low-cost Japanese and South Korean steel manufacturers in recent decades.

Higher levels of *import penetration*, suggesting increasing competitive pressures for domestic producers, also trigger increased demands for protection. A significant change in the nature of the support for protectionism occurred in the late 1960s, when the AFL–CIO abandoned its long-held belief in the desirability of open markets and supported protectionism. The shift in the union's position was due primarily to the rapid rise in import-penetration ratios that occurred during the 1960s in such industries as electrical consumer goods and footwear.

Another factor that may affect the demand for protection is *concentration* of domestic production. The U.S. auto industry, for example, is dominated by the Big Three. Support for import protection can be financed by these firms without fear that a large share of the benefits of protectionism will accrue to nonparticipating firms. Conversely, an industry that comprises many small producers (for example, meat packing) realizes that a substantial share of the gains from protectionism may accrue to producers who do not contribute their fair share to the costs of winning protectionist legislation. The demand for protection thus tends to be stronger the more concentrated the domestic industry.

Finally, the demand for protection may be influenced by the degree of *export dependence*. One would expect that companies whose foreign sales constitute a substantial portion of total sales (for example, Boeing) would not be greatly concerned about import protection. Their main fear is that the imposition of domestic trade barriers might invite retaliation overseas, which would ruin their export markets.

Summary

1. Even though the free-trade argument has strong theoretical justifications, trade restrictions are widespread throughout the world. Trade barriers consist of tariff restrictions and nontariff trade barriers.

2. There are several types of tariffs. A specific tariff represents a fixed amount of money per unit of the imported commodity. An ad valorem tariff is stated as a fixed percentage of the value of an imported commodity. A compound tariff combines a specific tariff with an ad valorem tariff.

3. Concerning ad valorem tariffs, several procedures exist for the valuation of imports. The free-on-board (FOB) measure indicates a commodity's price as it leaves the exporting nation. The cost-insurance-freight (CIF) measure shows the product's value as it arrives at the port of entry.

4. The effective tariff rate tends to differ from the nominal tariff rate when the domestic import-competing industry uses imported resources whose tariffs differ from those on the final commodity. Developing nations have traditionally argued that many advanced nations escalate the tariff structures on industrial commodities to yield an effective rate of protection several times the nominal rate.

5. U.S. trade laws mitigate the effects of import duties by allowing U.S. importers to postpone and prorate over time their duty obligations by means of bonded warehouses and foreign-trade zones.

6. The welfare effects of a tariff can be measured by its protective effect, consumption effect, redistributive effect, revenue effect, and terms-of-trade effect.

7. If a nation is small compared with the rest of the world, its welfare necessarily falls by the total amount of the protective effect plus the consumption effect if it levies a tariff on imports. If the importing nation is large relative to the world, the imposition of an import tariff may improve its international terms of trade by an amount that more than offsets the welfare losses associated with the consumption effect and the protective effect.

8. Because a tariff is a tax on imports, the burden of a tariff falls initially on importers, who must pay duties to the domestic government. However, importers generally try to shift increased costs to buyers through price increases. Domestic exporters, who purchase imported inputs subject to tariffs, thus face higher costs and a reduction in competitiveness.

9. Although tariffs may improve one nation's economic position, any gains generally come at the expense of other nations. Should tariff retaliations occur, the volume of international trade decreases, and world welfare suffers. Tariff liberalization is intended to promote freer markets so that the world can benefit from expanded trade volumes and international specialization of inputs.

10. Tariffs are sometimes justified on the grounds that they protect domestic employment and wages, help create a level playing field for international trade, equate the cost of imported products with the cost of domestic import-competing products, allow domestic industries to be insulated temporarily from foreign competition until they can grow and develop, or protect industries necessary for national security.

Key Concepts and Terms

- Ad valorem tariff *(page 102)*
- Beggar-thy-neighbor policy *(page 118)*
- Bonded warehouse *(page 110)*
- Compound tariff *(page 103)*
- Consumer surplus *(page 111)*
- Consumption effect *(page 115)*

- Cost-insurance-freight (CIF) valuation *(page 104)*
- Customs valuation *(page 104)*
- Deadweight loss *(page 115)*
- Domestic revenue effect *(page 118)*
- Effective tariff rate *(page 105)*
- Foreign-trade zone (FTZ) *(page 110)*
- Free-on-board (FOB) valuation *(page 104)*
- Free-trade argument *(page 126)*

- Free-trade-biased sector *(page 133)*
- Infant-industry argument *(page 131)*
- Large nation *(page 115)*
- Level playing field *(page 130)*
- Nominal tariff rate *(page 105)*
- Offshore-assembly provision (OAP) *(page 109)*
- Optimum tariff *(page 118)*
- Producer surplus *(page 111)*
- Production sharing *(page 108)*

- Protection-biased sector *(page 133)*
- Protective effect *(page 115)*
- Protective tariff *(page 102)*
- Redistributive effect *(page 114)*
- Revenue effect *(page 114)*
- Revenue tariff *(page 102)*
- Scientific tariff *(page 131)*
- Small nation *(page 112)*
- Specific tariff *(page 102)*
- Tariff *(page 102)*
- Tariff escalation *(page 107)*
- Terms-of-trade effect *(page 118)*

Study Questions

1. Describe a specific tariff, an ad valorem tariff, and a compound tariff. What are the advantages and disadvantages of each?
2. What are the methods that customs appraisers use to determine the values of commodity imports?
3. Under what conditions does a nominal tariff applied to an import product overstate or understate the actual, or effective, protection afforded by the nominal tariff?
4. Less-developed nations sometimes argue that the industrialized nations' tariff structures discourage the less-developed nations from undergoing industrialization. Explain.
5. Distinguish between consumer surplus and producer surplus. How do these concepts relate to a country's economic welfare?
6. When a nation imposes a tariff on the importation of a commodity, economic inefficiencies develop that detract from the national welfare. Explain.
7. What factors influence the size of the revenue, protective, consumption, and redistributive effects of a tariff?

8. A nation that imposes tariffs on imported goods may find its welfare improving should the tariff result in a favorable shift in the terms of trade. Explain.
9. Which of the arguments for tariffs do you feel are most relevant in today's world?
10. Although tariffs may improve the welfare of a single nation, the world's welfare may decline. Under what conditions would this be true?
11. What impact does the imposition of a tariff normally have on a nation's terms of trade and volume of trade?
12. Suppose that the production of $1 million worth of steel in Canada requires $100,000 worth of taconite. Canada's nominal tariff rates for importing these goods are 20 percent for steel and 10 percent for taconite. Given this information, calculate the effective rate of protection for Canada's steel industry.
13. Would a tariff imposed on U.S. oil imports promote energy development and conservation for the United States?
14. What is meant by the terms *bonded warehouse* and *foreign-trade zone*? How does

each of these help importers mitigate the effects of domestic import duties?

15. **Xtra!** For a tutorial of this question, go to http://carbaughxtra.swlearning.com
Assume the nation of Australia is "small," unable to influence world price. Its demand and supply schedules for TV sets are shown in Table 4.11. Using graph paper, plot the demand and supply schedules on the same graph.

a. Determine Australia's market equilibrium for TV sets.
   (1) What are the equilibrium price and quantity?
   (2) Calculate the value of Australian consumer surplus and producer surplus.

b. Under free-trade conditions, suppose Australia imports TV sets at a price of $100 each. Determine the free-trade equilibrium, and illustrate graphically.
   (1) How many TV sets will be produced, consumed, and imported?
   (2) Calculate the dollar value of Australian consumer surplus and producer surplus.

c. To protect its producers from foreign competition, suppose the Australian government levies a specific tariff of $100 on imported TV sets.
   (1) Determine and show graphically the effects of the tariff on the price of TV sets in Australia, the quantity of TV sets supplied by Australian producers, the quantity of TV sets demanded by Australian consumers, and the volume of trade.
   (2) Calculate the reduction in Australian consumer surplus due to the tariff-induced increase in the price of TV sets.
   (3) Calculate the value of the tariff's consumption, protective, redistributive, and revenue effects.
   (4) What is the amount of deadweight welfare loss imposed on the Australian economy by the tariff?

16. **Xtra!** For a tutorial of this question, go to http://carbaughxtra.swlearning.com
Assume that the United States, as a steel-importing nation, is large enough so that changes in the quantity of its imports influence the world price of steel. The U.S. supply and demand schedules for steel are illustrated in Table 4.12, along with the overall amount of steel supplied to U.S. consumers by domestic and foreign producers.

Using graph paper, plot the supply and demand schedules on the same graph.

a. With free trade, the equilibrium price of steel is $ _____ per ton. At this price, _____ tons are purchased by U.S. buyers, _____ tons are supplied by U.S. producers, and _____ tons are imported.

b. To protect its producers from foreign competition, suppose the U.S. government levies a specific tariff of $250 per ton on steel imports.

TABLE 4.11

Demand and Supply: TV Sets (Australia)

Price of TVs	Quantity Demanded	Quantity Supplied
$500	0	50
400	10	40
300	20	30
200	30	20
100	40	10
0	50	0

TABLE 4.12

Supply and Demand: Tons of Steel (United States)

Price/Ton	Quantity Supplied (Domestic)	Quantity Supplied (Domestic + Imports)	Quantity Demanded
$100	0	0	15
200	0	4	14
300	1	8	13
400	2	12	12
500	3	16	11
600	4	20	10
700	5	24	9

(1) Show graphically the effect of the tariff on the overall supply schedule of steel.

(2) With the tariff, the domestic price of steel rises to \$ _____ per ton. At this price, U.S. buyers purchase _____ tons, U.S. producers supply _____ tons, and _____ tons are imported.

(3) Calculate the reduction in U.S. consumer surplus due to the tariff-induced price of steel, as well as the consumption, protective, redistribution, and domestic revenue effects. The deadweight welfare loss of the tariff equals \$ _____ .

(4) By reducing the volume of imports with the tariff, the United States forces the price of imported steel down to \$ _____ . The U.S. terms of trade thus (improves/worsens), which leads to (an increase/a decrease) in U.S. welfare. Calculate the terms-of-trade effect.

(5) What impact does the tariff have on the overall welfare of the United States?

netlink▶

4.1 The U.S. International Trade Commission Web site contains information about U.S. tariffs, as well as many documents that address contemporary issues in international economics. Examine the searchable version of the "Harmonized Tariff Schedule of the United States" or various publications on international economics by setting your browser to this URL:

http://www.usitc.gov/webpubs.htm

4.2 The Web site of the U.S. Department of Commerce/Bureau of Industry and Security provides information on U.S. export controls, including restrictions on exports of nuclear weapons and financial services encryption products. Set your browser to this URL:

http://www.bxa.doc.gov

4.3 U.S. embassy staffs prepare the *Country Commercial Guides* once a year.

They report the business and economic situation of foreign countries and the political climate as it affects U.S. business. To get information on topics such as marketing, trade regulation, investment climate, and business travel, set your browser to this URL:

http://www.export.gov/comm_svc/index.html

4.4 Reports issued by the Office of the United States Trade Representative (USTR) and related entities on the National Trade Estimate Report on Foreign Trade Barriers can be found at this Web site:

http://www.ustr.gov/

4.5 The Sectoral and Trade Barriers Database of selected countries prepared by the European Union can be accessed by setting the browser to this URL:

http://mkaccdb.eu.int

To access NetLink Exercises and the Virtual Scavenger Hunt, visit the Carbaugh Web site at http://carbaugh.swlearning.com.

Xtra!
CARBAUGH

Log onto the Carbaugh Xtra! Web site (http://carbaughxtra.swlearning.com) for additional learning resources such as practice quizzes, help with graphing, and current events applications.

chapter 5

Nontariff Trade Barriers

This chapter considers policies other than tariffs that restrict international trade. Referred to as **nontariff trade barriers** (NTBs), such measures have been on the rise since the 1960s and have become the most widely discussed topics at recent rounds of international trade negotiations. Indeed, the post–World War II success in international negotiations for the reduction of tariffs has made remaining NTBs even more visible.

NTBs encompass a variety of measures. Some have unimportant trade consequences; for example, labeling and packaging requirements can restrict trade, but generally only marginally. Other NTBs significantly affect trade patterns; examples include import quotas, voluntary export restraints, subsidies, and domestic content requirements. These NTBs are intended to reduce imports and thus benefit domestic producers.

Import Quota

An **import quota** is a physical restriction on the quantity of goods that may be imported during a specific time period; the quota generally limits imports to a level below that which would occur under free-trade conditions. For example, a quota might state that no more than 1 million kilograms of cheese or 20 million kilograms of wheat can be imported during some specific time period. Table 5.1 gives examples of import quotas that have been used by the United States.

A common practice to administer an import quota is for the government to require an **import license**. Each license specifies the volume of imports allowed, and the total volume allowed should not exceed the quota. These licenses require the importer to spend time filling out forms and waiting for official permission. Licenses can be sold to importing companies at a competitive price, or simply a fee. Instead, government may just give away licenses to preferred importers. However, this allocation method provides incentives for political lobbying and bribery.

Import quotas on manufactured goods have been outlawed by the World Trade Organization. Where import quotas have been used by advanced countries such as Japan and the United States is to protect agricultural producers. However, recent trade negotiations have called for countries to convert their quotas to equivalent tariffs.

TABLE 5.1

Examples of U.S. Import Quotas

Imported Article	Quota Quantity (Yearly)
Condensed milk (Australia)	91,625 kg
Condensed milk (Denmark)	605,092 kg
Evaporated milk (Germany)	9,997 kg
Evaporated milk (Netherlands)	548,393 kg
Blue-mold cheese (Argentina)	2,000 kg
Blue-mold cheese (Chile)	80,000 kg
Cheddar cheese (New Zealand)	8,200,000 kg
Italian cheese (Poland)	1,325,000 kg
Italian cheese (Romania)	500,000 kg
Swiss cheese (Switzerland)	1,850,000 kg

kg = kilograms.

Source: U.S. International Trade Commission, *Tariff Schedules of the United States* (Washington, DC: U.S, Government Printing Office, 2000).

One way of administering import limitations is through a **global quota**. This technique permits a specified number of goods to be imported each year, but does not specify where the product is shipped from or who is permitted to import. When the specified amount has been imported (the quota is filled), additional imports of the product are prevented for the remainder of the year.

In practice, the global quota becomes unwieldy because of the rush of both domestic importers and foreign exporters to get their goods shipped into the country before the quota is filled. Those who import early in the year get their goods; those who import late in the year may not. Moreover, goods shipped from distant locations tend to be discriminated against because of the longer transportation time. Smaller merchants without good trade connections may also be at a disadvantage relative to large merchants. Global quotas are thus plagued by accusations of favoritism against merchants fortunate enough to be the first to capture a large portion of the business.

To avoid the problems of a global quota system, import quotas are usually allocated to specific countries; this type of quota is known as a **selective quota**. For example, a country might impose a global quota of 30 million apples per year, of which 14 million must come from the United States, 10 million from Mexico, and 6 million from Canada. Customs officials in the importing nation monitor the quantity of a particular good that enters the country from each source; once the quota for that source has been filled, no more goods are permitted to be imported.

Selective quotas suffer from many of the same problems as global quotas. Consider the case of Kmart, which ordered more than a million dollars' worth of wool sweaters from China in the 1980s. Before the sweaters arrived in the United States, the Chinese quota was filled for the year; Kmart could not bring them into the country until the following year. By that time, the sweaters were out of style and had to be sold at discounted prices. The firm estimated that it recovered only 60 cents on the dollar on these sweater sales.

Another feature of quotas is that their use may lead to domestic monopoly of production and higher prices. Because a domestic firm realizes that foreign producers cannot surpass their quotas, it may raise its prices. Tariffs do not necessarily lead to monopoly power, because no limit is established on the amount of goods that can be imported into the nation.

Trade and Welfare Effects

Like a tariff, an import quota affects an economy's welfare. Figure 5.1 on page 142 represents the case of cheese, involving the United States in trade with the European Union. Suppose the United States is a "small" country in terms of the world cheese market. Assume that $S_{U.S.}$ and $D_{U.S.}$ denote the supply and demand schedules of cheese for the United States. S_{EU} denotes the supply schedule of the European Union. Under free trade, the price of European Union cheese and U.S. cheese equals $2.50 per pound. At this price, U.S. firms produce 1 pound, U.S. consumers purchase 8 pounds, and imports from the European Union total 7 pounds.

Suppose the United States limits its cheese imports to a fixed quantity of 3 pounds by imposing an import quota. Above the free-trade price, the total U.S. supply of cheese now equals U.S. production plus the quota. In Figure 5.1, this is illustrated

physical limitation on imports

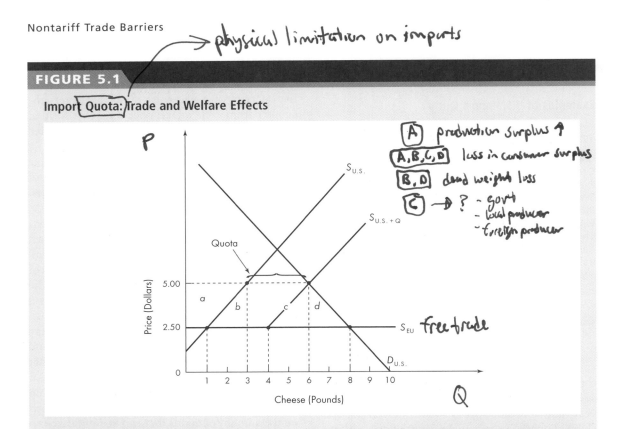

FIGURE 5.1

Import Quota: Trade and Welfare Effects

A — production surplus ↑
A,B,C,D — loss in consumer surplus
B,D — dead weight loss
C → $? - govt
           - local producer
           - foreign producer

S_{EU} free trade

By restricting available supplies of an imported product, a quota leads to higher import prices. This price umbrella allows domestic producers of the import-competing good to raise prices. The result is a decrease in consumer surplus. Of this amount, the welfare loss to the importing nation consists of the protective effect, the consumption effect, and that portion of the revenue effect that is captured by the foreign exporter.

by a shift in the supply curve from $S_{U.S.}$ to $S_{U.S.+Q}$. The reduction in imports from 7 pounds to 3 pounds raises the equilibrium price to $5; this leads to an increase in the quantity supplied by U.S. firms from 1 pound to 3 pounds and a decrease in U.S. quantity demanded from 8 pounds to 6 pounds.

Import quotas can be analyzed in terms of the same welfare effects identified for tariffs in the preceding chapter. Because the quota in our example results in a price increase to $5 per pound, U.S. consumer surplus falls by an amount equal to area $a + b + c + d$ ($17.50). Area a ($5) represents the *redistributive effect*, area b ($2.50) represents the *protective effect*, and area d ($2.50) represents the *consumption effect*. The *deadweight*

loss of welfare to the economy resulting from the quota is depicted by the protective effect plus the consumption effect.

But what about the quota's *revenue effect*, denoted by area c ($7.50)? This amount arises from the fact that U.S. consumers must pay an additional $2.50 for each of the 3 pounds of cheese imported under the quota, as a result of the quota-induced scarcity of cheese. The revenue effect represents "windfall profit," also known as "quota rent." Where does this windfall profit go?

To determine the distribution of the quota's revenue effect, it is useful to think of a series of exchanges as seen in the following example. Suppose that European exporting companies sell cheese to grocery stores (importing companies) in the United States, who sell it to U.S. consumers:[1]

European → U.S. grocery → U.S.
exporting stores consumers
companies (importing companies)

The distribution of the quota's revenue effect will be determined by the prices that prevail in the exchanges between these groups. Who obtains this windfall profit will depend upon the competitive relationships between the exporting companies and importing companies concerned.

One outcome occurs when European exporting companies are able to collude and in effect become a monopoly seller. If grocers in the United States behave as competitive buyers, they will bid against one another to buy European cheese. The delivered price of cheese will be driven up from $2.50 to $5 per pound. European exporting companies thus capture the windfall profit of the quota. The windfall profit captured by European exporters becomes a welfare loss for the U.S. economy, in addition to the deadweight losses resulting from the protective effect and consumption effect.

Instead, suppose that U.S. grocers organize as a single importing company (for example, Safeway grocery stores) and become a monopoly buyer. Also assume that European exporting companies operate as competitive sellers. Therefore, U.S. importing companies can purchase cheese at the prevailing world price of $2.50 per pound, reselling it to U.S. consumers at a price of $5 per pound. In this case, the quota's revenue effect accrues to the importing companies. Because these companies are American, this accrual does not represent an overall welfare loss for the U.S. economy.

Alternatively, the U.S. government may collect the quota's revenue effect from the importing companies. Suppose the government sells import licenses to U.S. grocers. By charging for permission to import, the government receives some or all of the quota's windfall profit. If import licenses are auctioned off to the highest bidder in a competitive market, the government will capture all of the

windfall profit that would have accrued to importing companies under the quota. This point will be discussed further in the next section of this text.

Allocating Quota Licenses

Because an import quota restricts the quantity of imports, usually below the free-trade quantity, not all domestic importers can obtain the same number of imports that they could under free trade. Governments thus allocate the limited supply of imports among domestic importers.

In oil and dairy products, the U.S. government has issued import licenses on the basis of their historical share of the import market. But this method discriminates against importers seeking to import goods for the first time. In other cases, the U.S. government has allocated import quotas on a pro rata basis, whereby U.S. importers receive a fraction of their demand equal to the ratio of the import quota to the total quantity demanded collectively by U.S. importers.

The U.S. government has also considered using another method of allocating licenses among domestic importers: the auctioning of import licenses to the highest bidder in a competitive market. This technique has been used in Australia and New Zealand.

Consider a hypothetical quota on U.S. imports of textiles. The quota pushes the price of textiles in the United States above the world price, making the United States an unusually profitable market. Windfall profits can be captured by U.S. importers (for example, Sears, Wal-Mart) if they buy textiles at the lower world price and sell them to U.S. buyers at the higher price made possible because of the quota. Given these windfall profits, U.S. importers would likely be willing to pay for the rights to import textiles. By auctioning import licenses to the highest bidder in a competitive market, the government could capture the windfall profits (the revenue effect shown as area c in Figure 5.1). Competition among importers to obtain the licenses would drive up the auction price to a level at which no windfall profits would remain, thus transferring the entire revenue effect to the government. The auctioning of import licenses would turn a quota into something akin to a tariff, which

[1]This example assumes that European exporting companies purchase cheese from European producers who operate in a competitive market. Because each producer is thus too small to affect the market price, it cannot capture any windfall profit arising under an import quota.

generates tax revenue for the government. In practice, few nations have used auctions to allocate rights to import products under quotas.

Sugar Import Quotas

The U.S. sugar industry provides an example of the impact of an import quota on a nation's welfare. Traditionally, U.S. sugar growers have received government subsidies in the form of price supports. Under this system, domestic sugar producers are provided a higher price than the free-market price; the difference between these two prices is the deficiency payment of the U.S. government. If the market price of sugar falls (or rises), the government's deficiency payment rises (or falls). To keep the market price of sugar close to the support price, and thus minimize its deficiency payments, the government has relied on import tariffs and quotas.

The price-support program ran into trouble when a glut of sugar in the world market sent the commercial price of sugar plunging to 6 cents a pound in 1982, compared with 41 cents a pound in 1980. This price was well below the 17-cents-a-pound support price of the federal government. Unless the government took action to prop up the commercial price paid to U.S. growers, the cost to the government of maintaining the support price of sugar would amount to an extra $800 million.

One way of boosting the U.S. commercial price of sugar was to raise the tariff on sugar imports. But, according to U.S. tariff codes, import duties could not exceed 50 percent of the world price of sugar. Although import duties were raised to their legal maximum, the import duty system was deemed inadequate to protect U.S. growers from cheap foreign sugar as world prices fell throughout 1982. However, the government did impose quotas on imported sugar as a means of boosting domestic prices.

In 1982, the United States announced an import quota system that fixed nation-by-nation import allocations for 24 countries. Each nation's quota was based on its average sugar exports to the United States between 1975 and 1981, excluding the highest and lowest years. The total amount any nation could export to the United States was adjusted on a quarterly basis in light of changing market conditions. The quota for the first year of the system was 2.98 million tons, well below the 4.4 to 5.4 million tons that had entered the United States each year from 1976 to 1981. By reducing sugar supplies, the quota was intended to force up the commercial price of sugar in the United States. The quota program thus transferred the cost of sugar support from the U.S. taxpayer to the U.S. sugar consumer.

Figure 5.2 illustrates the effects of the sugar quota during 1983, as estimated by the Federal Trade Commission. Note that the United States is assumed to be a "small" country with regard to the world sugar market. The world price of sugar, including transportation charges to the United States, was 15 cents a pound during 1983, denoted by curve S_W. In addition, the U.S. duty on sugar that year was 2.8 cents per pound. Therefore, the domestic market price was 17.8 cents, denoted by schedule S_{W+T}. At this price, the United States imported 5.06 million tons of sugar (9.356 − 4.296 = 5.06).

Under the quota program, U.S. sugar imports were cut from 5.06 million tons to 2.98 million tons. The quota-induced scarcity of sugar drove the domestic price up from 17.8 cents per pound to 21.8 cents per pound. This price increase reduced the cost of maintaining sugar price supports for the U.S. government. It also led to a decrease in U.S. consumer surplus equal to area $a + b + c + d$ ($735.2 million). Of this loss, the *redistributive effect* (area a) and the *protective effect* (area b) totaled $483.6 million, while the *consumption effect* (area d) equaled $13.2 million. The quota's *revenue effect* (area c) equaled $238.4 million. Because the sugar quota was administered by the exporting countries and U.S. importers operated as competitive buyers, the lion's share of the revenue effect was captured by foreign exporters.

Quotas Versus Tariffs

Previous analysis suggests that the revenue effect of import quotas differs from that of import tariffs. These two commercial policies can also differ in the impact they have on the volume of trade. The following example illustrates how, during periods of growing demand, an import quota restricts the volume of imports by a greater amount than does an equivalent import tariff.

FIGURE 5.2

The Effects of a Quota on Sugar Imports

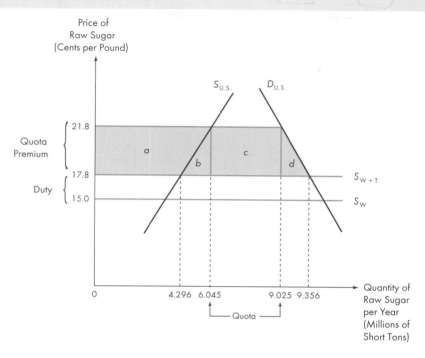

By forcing up the market price of sugar, an import quota reduces the costs to the U.S. government of maintaining price supports for domestic sugar producers. The higher market price of sugar, however, leads to decreases in welfare for U.S. consumers.

Figure 5.3 on page 146 represents a hypothetical trade situation of the United States in autos. The U.S. supply and demand schedules for autos are given by $S_{U.S._0}$ and $D_{U.S._0}$, and S_{J_0} represents the Japanese auto supply schedule. Suppose the U.S. government has the option of levying a tariff or a quota on auto imports to protect U.S. companies from foreign competition.

In Figure 5.3(a), a tariff of $1,000 would raise the price of Japanese autos from $6,000 to $7,000; auto imports would fall from 7 million units to 3 million units. In Figure 5.3(b), an import quota of 3 million units would put the United States in a trade position identical to that which occurs under the tariff: The quota-induced scarcity of autos results a rise in the price from $6,000 to $7,000. So far, it appears that the tariff and the quota are equivalent with respect to their restrictive impact on the volume of trade.

Now suppose the U.S. demand for autos rises from $D_{U.S._0}$ to $D_{U.S._1}$. Figure 5.3(a) shows that, despite the increased demand, the price of auto imports remains at $7,000. This is because the U.S. price cannot differ from the Japanese price by an amount exceeding the tariff duty. Auto imports rise from 3 million units to 5 million

demand ↑ ──→ more market friendly ──→ limits market

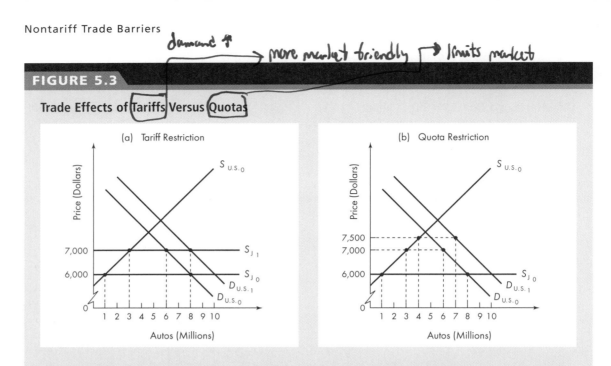

FIGURE 5.3

Trade Effects of Tariffs Versus Quotas

In a growing market, an import tariff is a less restrictive trade barrier than an equivalent import quota. With an import tariff, the adjustment that occurs in response to an increase in domestic demand is an increase in the amount of the product that is imported. With an import quota, an increase in demand induces an increase in product price. The price increase leads to a rise in production and a fall in consumption of the import-competing good, while the level of imports remains constant.

units. Under an import tariff, then, domestic adjustment takes the form of an increase in the quantity of autos imported rather than a rise in auto prices.

In Figure 5.3(b), an identical increase in demand induces a rise in domestic auto prices. Under the quota, there is no limit on the extent to which the U.S. price can rise above the Japanese price. Given an increase in domestic auto prices, U.S. companies are able to expand production. The domestic price will rise until the increased production plus the fixed level of imports are commensurate with the domestic demand. Figure 5.3(b) shows that an increase in demand from $D_{U.S._0}$ to $D_{U.S._1}$ forces auto prices up from $7,000 to $7,500. At the new price, domestic production equals 4 million units, and domestic consumption equals 7 million units. Imports total 3 million units, the same amount as under the quota before the increase in domestic demand. Adjustment

thus occurs in domestic *prices* rather than in the quantity of autos imported.

During periods of growing demand, then, an import quota is a more restrictive trade barrier than an equivalent import tariff. Under a quota, the government arbitrarily limits the quantity of imports. Under a tariff, the domestic price can rise above the world price only by the amount of the tariff; domestic consumers can still buy unlimited quantities of the import if they are willing and able to pay that amount. Even if the domestic industry's comparative disadvantage grows more severe, the quota prohibits consumers from switching to the imported good. Thus, a quota assures the domestic industry a ceiling on imports regardless of changing market conditions.[2]

[2]You might test your understanding of the approach used here by working out the details of two other hypothetical situations: (a) a reduction in the domestic supply of autos caused by rising production costs and (b) a reduction in domestic demand due to economic recession.

Simply put, a quota is a more restrictive barrier to imports than a tariff. A tariff increases the domestic price, but it may not limit the number of goods that can be imported into a country. Importers who are efficient enough to pay the tariff duty still get the product. Moreover, a tariff may offset by the price reductions of a foreign producer who can cut costs or slash profit margins. Tariffs thus allow for some degree of competition. However, by imposing an absolute limit on the imported good, a quota is more restrictive than a tariff and suppresses competition. Simply put, the degree of protection provided by a tariff is determined by the market mechanism, but a quota forecloses the market mechanism. As a result, member countries of the World Trade Organization have decided to phase out import quotas and replace them with tariffs—a process known as *tariffication*.

Tariff-Rate Quota: A Two-Tier Tariff

Another restriction used to insulate a domestic industry from foreign competition is the **tariff-rate quota**. The U.S. government has imposed this restriction on imports such as steel, brooms, cattle, fish, sugar, and milk, and other agricultural products.

As its name suggests, a tariff-rate quota displays both tariff-like and quota-like characteristics. This device allows a specified number of goods to be imported at one tariff rate (the *within-quota rate*), whereas any imports above this level face a higher tariff rate (the *over-quota rate*). A tariff-rate quota thus has three components: (1) a quota that defines the maximum volume of imports charged the within-quota tariff; (2) a within-quota tariff; and (3) an over-quota tariff. Simply put, a tariff-rate quota is a *two-tier tariff*. Tariff-rate quotas are applied for each trade year and if not filled during a particular year, the market access under the quota is lost. Table 5.2 provides examples of tariff-rate quotas applied to U.S. imports.

The tariff-rate quota appears to differ little from the import quota discussed earlier in this chapter. The distinction is that under an import quota it is legally impossible to import more than a specified amount. Under a tariff-rate quota, however, imports can exceed this specified amount, but a higher, over-quota tariff is applied on the excess.

In principle, a tariff-rate quota provides more access to imports than an import quota. In practice, many over-quota tariffs are prohibitively high and effectively exclude imports in excess of the quota. It is possible to design a tariff-rate quota so that it reproduces the trade-volume limit of an import quota.

Concerning the administration of tariff-rate quotas, **license on demand allocation** is the most common technique for the quotas that are enforced. Under this system, licenses are required to import at the within-quota tariff. Before the quota period begins, potential importers are invited to apply for

TABLE 5.2

Examples of U.S. Tariff-Rate Quotas

Product	Within-Quota Tariff Rate	Import-Quota Threshold	Over-Quota Tariff Rate
Peanuts	9.35 cents/kg	30,393 tons	187.9 percent ad valorem
Beef	4.4 cents/kg	634,621 tons	31.1 percent ad valorem
Milk	3.2 cents/L	5.7 million L	88.5 cents/L
Blue cheese	10.0 cents/kg	2.6 million kg	$2.60/kg
Cotton	4.4 cents/kg	2.1 million kg	36 cents/kg

Source: U.S. International Trade Commission, *Harmonized Tariff Schedule of the United States* (Washington, DC: U.S. Government Printing Office, 2003).

import licenses. If the demand for licenses is less than the quota, the system operates like a first-come, first-served system. Usually, if demand exceeds the quota, the import volume requested is reduced proportionally among all applicants. Other techniques for allocating quota licenses are first-come, first-served; historical market share; and auctions.

When the World Trade Organization (WTO) was established in 1995 (see Chapter 6), member countries changed their systems of import protection for those agricultural products helped by government farm programs. The WTO requires members to convert to tariffs all nontariff trade barriers (import quotas, variable levies, discretionary licensing, outright import bans) applicable to imports from other members. It thus put all nontariff barriers on a common standard—tariffs—that any exporter could readily measure and understand. Members are allowed to adopt tariff-rate quotas as a transitional instrument during this conversion period. At the writing of this text, the duration of this conversion period has not been defined. Thus, tariff-rate quotas will likely be around for some time to come.

For nonagricultural products, tariff-rate quotas have been used as temporary protection against surging imports into a country. In 2002, for example, the U.S. government imposed tariff-rate quotas on steel imports for a 3-year period, subject to annual review. Tariff-rate quotas have also been used to protect U.S. producers of brooms, stainless steel flatware, and fish. The welfare effects of a tariff-rate quota are discussed in "Exploring Further 5.1," at the end of this chapter.

Orderly Marketing Agreements

An **orderly marketing agreement (OMA)** is a market-sharing pact negotiated by trading partners. Its main purpose is to moderate the intensity of international competition, allowing less efficient domestic producers to participate in markets that would otherwise have been lost to foreign producers that sell a superior product at a lower price. OMAs involve trade negotiations between import-

ing and exporting nations, generally for a variety of labor-intensive manufactured goods. For example, most of the world's steelmakers agreed in 2002 to cut incrementally as much as 97.5 tons of steel capacity by 2010. The purpose of the accord was to eliminate excess world production and thus support higher steel prices.

A typical OMA consists of voluntary quotas applied to exports. These controls are known as **voluntary export restraints (VERs)**; they are sometimes supplemented by backup import controls to ensure that the restraints are effective. For example, Japan may impose limits on steel exports to Europe, or Taiwan may agree to cutbacks on shoe exports to the United States.

Because OMAs are reached through negotiations, on the surface they appear to be less one-sided than unilateral protectionist devices such as import tariffs and quotas. In practice, the distinction between negotiated versus unilateral trade curbs becomes blurred. Trade negotiations are often carried out with the realization that the importing nations may adopt more stringent protectionist devices should the negotiators be unable to reach an acceptable settlement. An exporting nation's motivation to negotiate OMAs may thus stem from its desire to avoid a more costly alternative—that is, a full-fledged trade war. OMAs have covered trade in such commodities as television sets, steel, textiles, autos, and ships, as seen in Table 5.3.

Recent rounds of trade negotiations have restricted the use of OMAs. Under the provisions of the Uruguay Round of 1986–1993 (see Chapter 6), nations cannot enact new OMAs in response to escape-clause claims of injury by domestic firms and workers. Moreover, existing OMAs were phased out in 1998, except for the Japan–European Union auto agreement, which ran until its scheduled close in 1999.

Export Quota Effects

A typical OMA involves limitations on export sales administered by one or more exporting nations or industries. What are the trade and welfare effects of **export quotas**?

Figure 5.4 on page 150 illustrates these effects in the case of trade in autos among the United

TABLE 5.3

Orderly Marketing Agreements

Manufactured Good	Principal Nations	Accord Provisions
Specialty steel	United States, European Union, Sweden, Japan, Canada	Japan negotiates export quota in U.S. market; United States imposes import quota on others.
TV sets	Japan, Benelux, Britain	Japan voluntarily limits exports to Britain and Benelux.
Ships	Japan, European Union	Japan enters into agreement with European Union to curb price competition.
Garments and textiles	41 exporting and importing nations	Export and import quotas; annual growth rates.
Autos	Japan, United States	Japan voluntarily restrains exports to the United States.

Source: *Annual Report of the President of the United States on the Trade Agreements Program* (Washington, DC: U.S. Government Printing Office, various issues).

States, Japan, and Germany. Assume that $S_{U.S.}$ and $D_{U.S.}$ depict the supply and demand schedules of autos for the United States. S_J denotes the supply schedule of Japan, assumed to be the world's low-cost producer, and S_G denotes the supply schedule of Germany.

Referring to Figure 5.4(a), the price of autos to the U.S. consumer is $20,000 under free trade. At that price, U.S. firms produce 1 auto, and U.S. consumers purchase 7 autos, with imports from Japan totaling 6 autos. Note that German autos are too costly to be exported to the United States at the free-trade price.

Suppose that Japan, responding to protectionist sentiment in the United States, decides to restrain auto shipments to the United States rather than face possible mandatory restrictions on its exports. Assume that the Japanese government imposes an export quota on its auto firms of 2 units, down from the free-trade level of 6 units. Above the free-trade price, the total U.S. supply of autos now equals U.S. production plus the export quota; the auto supply curve thus shifts from $S_{U.S.}$ to $S_{U.S.+Q}$ in Figure 5.4(a). The reduction in imports from 6 autos to 2 autos raises the equilibrium price to $30,000. This leads to an increase in the quanti-

ty supplied by U.S. firms from 1 auto to 3 autos and a decrease in the U.S. quantity demanded from 7 autos to 5 autos.

The export quota's price increase causes consumer surplus to fall by area $a + b + c + d + e + f + g + h + i + j + k + l$, an amount totaling $60,000. Area $a + h$ ($20,000) represents the transfer to U.S. auto companies as *profits*. The export quota results in a deadweight welfare loss for the U.S. economy equal to the *protective effect*, denoted by area $b + c + i$ ($10,000), and the *consumption effect*, denoted by area $f + g + l$ ($10,000). The export quota's *revenue effect* equals area $d + e + j + k$ ($20,000), found by multiplying the quota-induced increase in the Japanese price times the volume of autos shipped to the United States.

Remember that under an import quota, the disposition of the revenue effect is indeterminate: It will be shared between foreign exporters and domestic importers, depending on the relative concentration of bargaining power. But under an export quota, it is the foreign exporter who is able to capture the larger share of the quota revenue. In our example of the auto export quota, the Japanese exporters, in compliance with their government, self-regulate shipments to the United

FIGURE 5.4

Trade and Welfare Effects of a Voluntary Export Quota

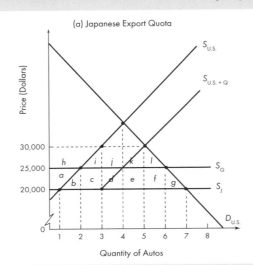

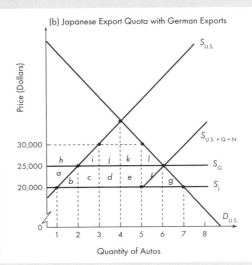

By reducing available supplies of a product, an export quota (levied by the foreign nation) leads to higher prices in the importing nation. The price increase induces a decrease in consumer surplus. Of this amount, the welfare loss to the importing nation equals the protective effect, the consumption effect, and the portion of the revenue effect that is captured by the foreign exporter. To the extent that nonrestrained countries augment shipments to the importing nation, the welfare loss of an export quota decreases.

States. This supply-side restriction, resulting from Japanese firms' behaving like a monopoly, leads to a scarcity of autos in the United States. Japanese automakers then are able to raise the price of their exports, capturing the quota revenue. For this reason, it is not surprising that exporters might prefer to negotiate a voluntary restraint pact in lieu of facing other protectionist measures levied by the importing country. As for the export quota's impact on the U.S. economy, the expropriation of revenue by the Japanese represents a welfare loss in addition to the deadweight losses of production and consumption.

Another characteristic of a voluntary export agreement is that it typically applies only to the most important exporting nation(s). This is in contrast to a tariff or import quota, which generally applies to imports from all sources. When volun-

tary limits are imposed on the chief exporter, the exports of the **nonrestrained suppliers** may be stimulated. Nonrestrained suppliers may seek to increase profits by making up part of the cutback in the restrained nation's shipments. They may also want to achieve the maximum level of shipments against which to base any export quotas that might be imposed on them in the future. For example, Japan was singled out by the United States for restrictions in textiles during the 1950s and in color television sets during the 1970s. Other nations quickly increased shipments to the United States to fill in the gaps created by the Japanese restraints. Hong Kong textiles replaced most Japanese textiles, and TV sets from Taiwan and Korea supplanted Japanese sets.

Referring to Figure 5.4(b), let us start again at the free-trade price of $20,000, with U.S. imports from Japan totaling 6 autos. Assume that Japan agrees to reduce its shipments to 2 units. However, suppose Germany, a nonrestrained supplier, exports 2 autos to the United States in response to the Japanese cutback. Above the free-trade price, the total U.S. supply of autos now equals U.S. production plus the Japanese export quota plus the nonrestrained exports coming from Germany. In Figure 5.4(b), this is illustrated by a shift in the supply curve from $S_{U.S.}$ to $S_{U.S.+Q+N}$. The reduction in imports from 6 autos to 4 autos raises equilibrium price to $25,000. The resulting deadweight losses of production and consumption inefficiencies equal area $b + g$ ($5,000), less than the deadweight losses under Japan's export quota in the absence of nonrestrained supply. Assuming that Japan administers the export restraint program, Japanese companies would be able to raise the price of their auto exports from $20,000 to $25,000 and earn profits equal to area $c + d$ ($10,000). Area $e + f$ ($10,000) represents a **trade-diversion effect**, which reflects inefficiency losses due to the shifting of 2 units from Japan, the world's low-cost producer, to Germany, a higher-cost source. Such trade diversion results in a loss of welfare to the world because resources are not being used in their most productive manner. The overall welfare of the United States thus decreases by area $b + c + d + e + f + g$ under the export-quota policy.

When increases in the nonrestrained supply offset part of the cutback in shipments that occurs under an export quota, the overall inefficiency loss for the importing nation (deadweight losses plus revenue expropriated by foreign producers) is *less* than that which would have occurred in the absence of nonrestrained exports. In the preceding example, this reduction amounts to area $i + j + k + l$ ($15,000). The next section will consider the effects of voluntary export quotas on the U.S. auto industry.

Japanese Auto Restraints Put Brakes on U.S. Motorists

In 1981, as domestic auto sales fell, protectionist sentiment gained momentum in the U.S. Congress, and legislation was introduced calling for import quotas. This momentum was a major factor in the administration's desire to negotiate a voluntary restraint pact with the Japanese. Japan's acceptance of this agreement was apparently based on its view that voluntary limits on its auto shipments would derail any protectionist momentum in Congress for more stringent measures.

The restraint program called for self-imposed export quotas on Japanese auto shipments to the United States for three years, beginning in 1981. First-year shipments were to be held to 1.68 million units, 7.7 percent below the 1.82 million units exported in 1980. In subsequent years, auto shipments were to be held to the same number plus 16.5 percent of any increase in domestic U.S. auto sales recorded in 1981. As it turned out, falling U.S. sales caused Japanese auto exports to be limited to 1.68 million units in 1982 and 1983. Still facing a weak auto industry, the United States was able to negotiate an export restraint pact with Japan for 1984, during which Japanese firms would limit auto shipments to the United States to 1.85 million units. In 1984, the United States released Japan from its formal commitment to the export agreement, but the Japanese government thought it imprudent to permit its automakers to export freely to the United States. The Japanese government has imposed its own export quotas on its auto manufacturers since the termination of the export agreement.

The purpose of the export agreement was to help U.S. automakers by diverting U.S. customers from Japanese to U.S. showrooms. As domestic sales increased, so would jobs for American autoworkers. It was assumed that Japan's export quota would assist the U.S. auto industry as it went through a transition period of reallocating production toward smaller, more fuel-efficient autos and adjusting production to become more cost-competitive. The restraint program would provide U.S. auto companies temporary relief from foreign competition so they could restore profitability and reduce unemployment.

Not all Japanese auto manufacturers were equally affected by the export quota. By requiring Japanese auto companies to form an export cartel against the U.S. consumer, the quota allowed the large, established firms (Toyota, Nissan, and Honda) to increase prices on autos sold in the United States. To derive more revenues from a limited number of autos, Japanese firms shipped autos to the United States with fancier trim, bigger engines, and more amenities such as air-conditioners and deluxe stereos as standard equipment. Product enrichment also helped the Japanese broaden their hold on the U.S. market and enhance the image of their autos. As a result, the large Japanese manufacturers earned record profits in the United States.

The export quota was unpopular, however, with smaller Japanese automakers, including Suzuki and Isuzu. Under the restraint program, as administered by the Japanese government, each company's export quota was based on the number of autos sold in the United States three years prior to initiation of the quota. Smaller producers claimed that the quota forced them to freeze their U.S. dealer networks and abandon plans to introduce new models. Table 5.4 depicts the estimated welfare effects for the United States of the Japanese export quota.

TABLE 5.4

Effects of Japanese Export Quota in Autos*

Effect	Amount
Price of Japanese autos sold in the United States (increase)	$1,300
Price of U.S. autos sold in the United States (increase)	$660
Cost to U.S. consumers (increase)	$15.7 million
Number of Japanese autos sold in the United States (decrease)	1 million units
Japanese share of U.S. auto market (decrease)	9.6%
Sales of U.S.–produced autos (increase)	618,000 units
U.S. auto industry jobs (increase)	44,000

*These estimates apply to 1984, the fourth year of the export quota.

Source: U.S. International Trade Commission, *A Review of Recent Developments in the U.S. Automobile Industry Including an Assessment of the Japanese Voluntary Restraint Agreements* (Washington, DC: U.S. Government Printing Office, 1985).

Domestic Content Requirements

Today, many products, such as autos and aircraft, embody worldwide production. Domestic manufacturers of these products purchase resources or perform assembly functions outside the home country, a practice known as *outsourcing* or *production sharing*. For example, General Motors has obtained engines from its subsidiaries in Mexico, Chrysler has purchased ball joints from Japanese producers, and Ford has acquired cylinder heads from European companies. Firms have used outsourcing to take advantage of lower production costs overseas, including lower wage rates. Domestic workers often challenge this practice, maintaining that outsourcing means that cheap foreign labor takes away their jobs and imposes downward pressure on the wages of those workers who are able to keep their jobs.

To limit the practice of outsourcing, organized labor has lobbied for the use of **domestic content requirements**. These requirements stipulate the minimum percentage of a product's total value that must be produced domestically if the product is to quality for zero tariff rates. The effect of content requirements is to pressure both domestic and foreign firms who sell products in the home country to use domestic inputs (workers) in the production of those products. The demand for domestic inputs thus increases, contributing to higher input prices. Manufacturers generally lobby against domestic content requirements, because they prevent manufacturers from obtaining inputs at the lowest cost, thus contributing to higher product prices and loss of competitiveness.

Worldwide, local content requirements have received most attention in the automobile industry. Developing countries have often used content requirements to foster domestic automobile production, as shown in Table 5.5.

Figure 5.5 illustrates possible welfare effects of an Australian content requirement on automobiles. Assume that D_A denotes the Australian demand schedule for Toyota automobiles while S_J depicts the supply price of Toyotas exported to Australia,

TABLE 5.5

Domestic Content Requirements Applied to Automobiles in Selected Countries

Country	Minimum Domestic Content Required (Percent) to Qualify for Zero Duty Rates
Argentina	76%
Mexico	62
Brazil	60
Uruguay	60
Vietnam	60
Chinese Taipei	40
Venezuela	30
Colombia	30

Source: U.S. Department of Commerce, International Trade Administration, Office of Automotive Affairs, *Vehicle Import Requirements,* December 2003, at http://www.ita.doc.gov/auto/impreq. html.

$24,000. With free trade, Australia imports 500 Toyotas. Japanese resource owners involved in manufacturing this vehicle realize incomes totaling $12 million, denoted by area $c + d$.

Suppose the Australian government imposes a domestic content requirement on autos. This policy causes Toyota to establish a factory in Australia to produce vehicles replacing the Toyotas previously imported by Australia. Assume that the transplant factory combines Japanese management with Australian resources (labor and materials) in vehicle production. Also assume that high Australian resource prices (wages) cause the transplant's supply price to be $33,000, denoted by S_T. Under the content requirement, Australian consumers demand 300 vehicles. Because production has shifted from Japan to Australia, Japanese resource owners lose $12 million of income. Australian resource owners gain $9.9 million of income (area

FIGURE 5.5

Welfare Effects of a Domestic Content Requirement

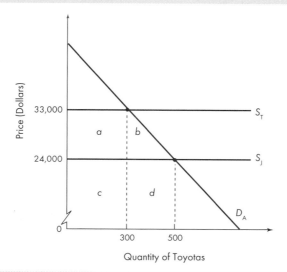

A domestic content requirement leads to rising production costs and prices to the extent that manufacturers are "forced" to locate production facilities in a high-cost nation. Although the content requirement helps preserve domestic jobs, it imposes welfare losses on domestic consumers.

How "Foreign" Is Your Car?

Did you know that U.S. buyers of cars and light trucks can learn how American or foreign their new vehicle is? On cars and trucks weighing 8,500 pounds or less, the law requires content labels telling buyers where the parts of the vehicle were made. Content is measured by the dollar value of components, not the labor cost of assembling vehicles. The percentages of North American (U.S. and Canadian) and foreign parts must be listed as an average for each car line. Manufacturers are free to design the label, which can be included on the price sticker or fuel economy sticker or can be separate. Below are some examples of the domestic and foreign content of vehicles sold in the United States for the 2004 model year. The data were collected from automobile stickers at dealers' lots.

Vehicle	Assembly	North American Parts Content (percent)	Foreign Parts Content (percent)
Ford Taurus	United States	95%	5%
Ford Focus	United States	80	20
Ford Crown Victoria	Canada	95	5
Lincoln Navigator	United States	90	5
GMC Yukon	United States	65	35
Pontiac Vibe AWD	United States	64	36
Cadillac Deville	United States	86	14
DaimlerChrysler Durango	United States	77	23
Chevrolet Suburban	Mexico	65	35
Chevrolet Tahoe	United States	65	35

$a + c$) minus the income paid to Japanese managers and the return to Toyota's capital investment (factory) in Australia.

However, the income gains of Australian resource owners inflict costs on Australian consumers. Because the content requirement causes the price of Toyotas to increase by $9,000, Australian consumer surplus decreases by area $a + b$ ($3,600,000). Of this amount, area b ($900,000) is a deadweight welfare loss for Australia. Area a ($2,700,000) is the consumer cost of employing higher-priced Australian resources instead of lower-priced Japanese resources; this amount represents a redistribution of welfare from Australian consumers to Australian resource owners. Similar to other import restrictions, content requirements lead to the subsidizing by domestic consumers of the domestic producer.

Subsidies

National governments sometimes grant **subsidies** to their producers to help improve their trade position. By providing domestic firms a cost advantage, a subsidy allows them to market their products at prices lower than warranted by their actual cost or profit considerations. Governmental subsidies assume a variety of forms, including outright cash disbursements, tax concessions, insurance arrangements, and loans at below-market interest rates. Table 5.6 provides examples of governmental subsidies for several nations.

TABLE 5.6

Examples of Governmental Subsidies

Country	Subsidy Policy
Australia	Export market development grants extended to Australian exporters to seek out and develop overseas markets
Canada	Rail transportation subsidies granted to Canadian exporters of wheat, barley, oats, and alfalfa
European Union	Export subsidies provided to many agricultural products such as wheat, beef, poultry, fruits, and dairy products; financial assistance extended to Airbus
Japan	Financial assistance extended to Japanese aerospace producers, including loans at low interest rates and assistance with R&D costs
United States	Export subsidies provided to U.S. producers of agricultural and manufactured goods through the Commodity Credit Corporation and the Export Import Bank

Source: Office of the U.S. Trade Representative, *Foreign Trade Barriers* (Washington, DC: U.S. Government Printing Office, various issues).

For purposes of our discussion, two types of subsidies can be distinguished: a **domestic subsidy**, which is sometimes granted to producers of import-competing goods, and an **export subsidy**, which goes to producers of goods that are to be sold overseas. In both cases, the government adds an amount to the price the purchaser pays rather than subtracting from it. The net price actually received by the producer equals the price paid by the purchaser plus the subsidy. The subsidized producer is thus able to supply a greater quantity at each consumer's price. Let us use Figure 5.6 on page 156 to analyze the effects of these two types of subsidies.

Domestic Subsidy

Figure 5.6(a) illustrates the trade and welfare effects of a production subsidy granted to import-competing manufacturers. Assume that the initial supply and demand schedules of the United States for steel are depicted by curves $S_{U.S._0}$ and $D_{U.S._0}$, so that the market equilibrium price is $430 per ton. Assume also that, because the United States is a small buyer of steel, changes in its purchases do not affect the world price of $400 per ton. Given a free-trade price of $400 per ton, the United States consumes 14 tons of steel, produces 2 tons, and imports 12 tons.

To partially insulate domestic producers from foreign competition, suppose the U.S. government grants them a production subsidy of $25 per ton of steel. The cost advantage made possible by the subsidy results in a shift in the U.S. supply schedule from $S_{U.S._0}$ to $S_{U.S._1}$. Domestic production expands from 2 to 7 million tons, and imports fall from 12 to 7 million tons. These changes represent the subsidy's trade effect.

The subsidy also affects the national welfare of the United States. According to Figure 5.6(a), the subsidy permits U.S. output to rise to 7 million tons. Note that, at this output, the net price to the steelmaker is $425—the sum of the price paid by the consumer ($400) plus the subsidy ($25). To the U.S. government, the total cost of protecting its steelmakers equals the amount of the subsidy ($25) times the amount of output to which it is applied (7 million tons), or $175 million.

Where does this subsidy revenue go? Part of it is redistributed to the more efficient U.S. producers in the form of *producer surplus*. This amount is denoted by area a ($112.5 million) in the figure. There is also a *protective effect*, whereby more costly domestic output is allowed to be sold in the market as a result of the subsidy. This is denoted by area b ($62.5 million) in the figure. To the

FIGURE 5.6

Trade and Welfare Effects of Subsidies

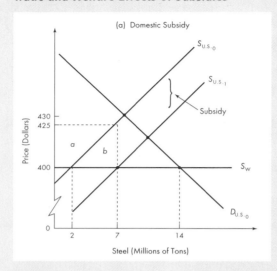

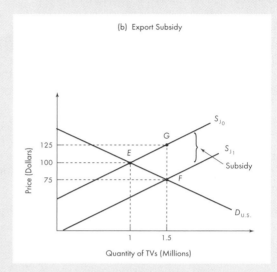

A government subsidy granted to import-competing producers leads to increased domestic production and reduced imports. The subsidy revenue accruing to the producer is absorbed by producer surplus and high-cost production (protective effect). A government subsidy granted to exporters results in an export revenue effect and a terms-of-trade effect.

United States as a whole, the protective effect represents a deadweight loss of welfare.

To encourage production by its import-competing manufacturers, a government might levy tariffs or quotas on imports. But tariffs and quotas involve larger sacrifices in national welfare than would occur under an equivalent subsidy. Unlike subsidies, tariffs and quotas distort choices for domestic consumers (resulting in a decrease in the domestic demand for imports), in addition to permitting less efficient home production to occur. The result is the familiar consumption effect of protection, whereby a deadweight loss of consumer surplus is borne by the home nation. This welfare loss is absent in the subsidy case. Thus, a subsidy tends to yield the same result for domestic producers as does an equivalent tariff or quota, but at a *lower* cost in terms of national welfare.

Subsidies are not free goods, however, for they must be financed by someone. The direct cost of the subsidy is a burden that must be financed out of tax revenues paid by the public. Moreover, when a subsidy is given to an industry, it is often in return for accepting government conditions on key matters (such as wage and salary levels). Thus a subsidy may not be as superior to other types of commercial policies as this analysis suggests.

Export Subsidy

Besides attempting to protect import-competing industries, many national governments grant subsidies, including special tax exemptions and the provision of capital at favored rates, to increase the volume of exports. By providing a cost advantage to domestic producers, such subsidies are intended to encourage a nation's exports by reducing the price paid by foreigners. Foreign consumers are favored over domestic consumers to the extent that the foreign price of a subsidized export is less than the product's domestic price.

The granting of an export subsidy yields two direct effects for the home economy: a *terms-of-trade* effect and an **export-revenue effect**. Because subsidies tend to reduce the foreign price of home-nation exports, the home nation's terms of trade is worsened. But lower foreign prices generally stimulate export volume. Should the foreign demand for exports be relatively elastic, so that a given percentage drop in foreign price is more than offset by the rise in export volume, the home nation's export revenues will increase.

Figure 5.6(b) illustrates the case of an export subsidy applied to television sets in trade between Japan and the United States. Under free trade, market equilibrium exists at point E, where Japan exports 1 million television sets to the United States at a price of $100 per unit. Suppose the Japanese government, to encourage export sales, grants to its exporters a subsidy of $50 per set. The Japanese supply schedule shifts from S_{J_0} to S_{J_1}, and market equilibrium moves to point F. The terms of trade thus turns against Japan because its export price falls from $100 to $75 per television set exported. Whether Japan's export revenue rises depends on how U.S. buyers respond to the price decrease. If the percentage increase in the number of television sets sold to U.S. buyers more than offsets the percentage decrease in price, Japan's export revenue will rise. This is the case in Figure 5.6(b), which shows Japan's export revenue rising from $100 million to $112.5 million as the result of the decline in the price of its export good.

Although export subsidies may benefit industries and workers in a subsidized industry by increasing sales and employment, the benefits may be offset by certain costs that fall on the society as a whole. Consumers in the exporting nation suffer as the international terms of trade moves against them. This situation comes about because, given a fall in export prices, a greater number of exports must be exchanged for a given dollar amount in imports. Domestic consumers also find they must pay higher prices than foreigners for the goods they

help subsidize. Furthermore, to the extent that taxes are required to finance the export subsidy, domestic consumers find themselves poorer. In the previous example, the total cost of the subsidy to Japanese taxpayers is $75 million ($50 subsidy times 1.5 million television sets).

Dumping

The case for protecting import-competing producers from foreign competition is bolstered by the antidumping argument. **Dumping** is recognized as a form of international price discrimination. It occurs when foreign buyers are charged lower prices than domestic buyers for an identical product, after allowing for transportation costs and tariff duties. Selling in foreign markets at a price below the cost of production is also considered dumping.

Forms of Dumping

Commercial dumping is generally viewed as sporadic, predatory, or persistent in nature. Each type is practiced under different circumstances.

Sporadic dumping (distress dumping) occurs when a firm disposes of excess inventories on foreign markets by selling abroad at lower prices than at home. This form of dumping may be the result of misfortune or poor planning by foreign producers. Unforeseen changes in supply and demand conditions can result in excess inventories and thus in dumping. Although sporadic dumping may be beneficial to importing consumers, it can be quite disruptive to import-competing producers, who face falling sales and short-run losses. Temporary tariff duties can be levied to protect home producers, but because sporadic dumping has minor effects on international trade, governments are reluctant to grant tariff protection under these circumstances.

Predatory dumping occurs when a producer temporarily reduces the prices charged abroad to drive foreign competitors out of business. When the producer succeeds in acquiring a monopoly position, prices are then raised commensurate with its market power. The new price level must be sufficiently high to offset any losses that occurred during the period of cutthroat pricing. The firm would presumably be confident in its ability to prevent the entry of potential competitors long enough for it to enjoy economic profits. To be successful, predatory dumping would have to be practiced on a massive basis to provide consumers with sufficient opportunity for bargain shopping. Home governments are generally concerned about predatory pricing for monopolizing purposes and may retaliate with antidumping duties that eliminate the price differential. Although predatory dumping is a theoretical possibility, economists have not found empirical evidence that supports its existence.

Persistent dumping, as its name suggests, goes on indefinitely. In an effort to maximize economic profits, a producer may consistently sell abroad at lower prices than at home. The rationale underlying persistent dumping is explained in the next section.

International Price Discrimination

Consider the case of a domestic seller that enjoys market power as a result of barriers that restrict competition at home. Suppose this firm sells in foreign markets that are highly competitive. This means that the domestic consumer response to a change in price is less than that abroad; the home demand is less elastic than the foreign demand. A profit-maximizing firm would benefit from international price discrimination, charging a *higher* price at home, where competition is weak and demand is less elastic, and a *lower* price for the same product in foreign markets to meet competition. The practice of identifying separate groups of buyers of a product and charging different prices to these groups results in increased revenues and profits for the firm as compared to what would occur in the absence of price discrimination.

Figure 5.7 illustrates the demand and cost conditions of South Korean Steel Inc. (SKS), which sells steel to buyers in South Korea (less elastic market) and in Canada (more elastic market); the total steel market consists of these two submarkets. Let D_{SK} be the South Korean steel demand and D_C be the Canadian demand, with the corresponding marginal revenue schedules represented

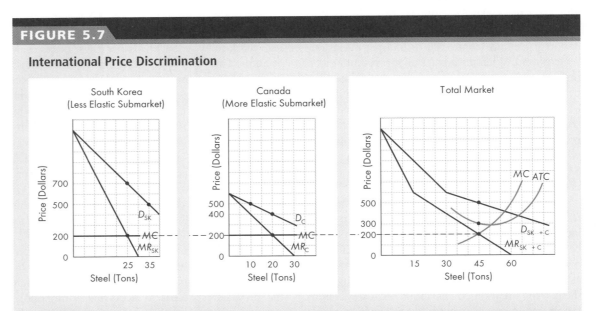

FIGURE 5.7

International Price Discrimination

A price-discriminating firm maximizes profits by equating marginal revenue, in each submarket, with marginal cost. The firm will charge a higher price in the less-elastic-demand (less competitive) market and a lower price in the more-elastic-demand (more competitive) market. Successful dumping leads to additional revenue and profits for the firm compared to what would be realized in the absence of dumping.

by MR_{SK} and MR_C, respectively. D_{SK+C} denotes the market demand schedule, found by adding horizontally the demand schedules of the two submarkets; similarly, MR_{SK+C} depicts the market marginal revenue schedule. The marginal cost and average total cost schedules of SKS are denoted respectively by MC and ATC.

SKS maximizes total profits by producing and selling 45 tons of steel, at which marginal revenue equals marginal cost. At this output level, $ATC = \$300$ per ton, and total cost equals $13,500 ($300 $\times$ 45 tons). The firm faces the problem of how to distribute the total output of 45 tons, and thus set price, in the two submarkets in which it sells. Should the firm sell steel to South Korean and Canadian buyers at a uniform (single) price, or should the firm practice differential pricing?

As a *nondiscriminating* seller, SKS sells 45 tons of steel to South Korean and Canadian buyers at the single price of $500 per ton, the maximum price permitted by demand schedule D_{SK+C} at the $MR = MC$ output level. To see how many tons of steel are sold in each submarket, construct a horizontal line in Figure 5.7 at the price of $500. The optimal output in each submarket occurs where the horizontal line intersects the demand schedules of the two nations. SKS thus sells 35 tons of steel to South Korean buyers at a price of $500 per ton and receives revenues totaling $17,500. The firm sells 10 tons of steel to Canadian buyers at a price of $500 per ton and realizes revenues of $5,000. Sales revenues in both submarkets combined equal $22,500. With total costs of $13,500, SKS realizes profits of $9,000.

Although SKS realizes profits as a nondiscriminating seller, its profits are not optimal. By engaging in price discrimination, the firm can increase its total revenues without increasing its costs, and thus increase its profits. The firm accomplishes this by charging *higher* prices to South Korean buyers, who have less elastic demand schedules, and *lower* prices to Canadian buyers, who have more elastic demand schedules.

As a price-discriminating seller, SKS again faces the problem of how to distribute the total output of 45 tons of steel, and thus set price, in the two submarkets in which it sells. To accomplish this, the firm follows the familiar $MR = MC$ principle,

whereby the marginal revenue of each submarket equals the marginal cost at the profit-maximizing output. This can be shown in Figure 5.7 by first constructing a horizontal line from $200, the point where $MC = MR_{SK+C}$. The optimal output and price in each submarket is then found where this horizontal line intersects the MR schedules of the submarkets. SKS thus sells 25 tons of steel to South Korean buyers at a price of $700 per ton and receives revenues totaling $17,500. The firm sells 20 tons of steel to Canadian buyers at a price of $400 per ton and collects revenues of $8,000. The combined revenues of the two submarkets equal $25,500, a sum $3,000 greater than in the absence of price discrimination. With total costs of $13,500, the firm realizes profits of $12,000, compared to $9,000 under a single pricing policy. As a price-discriminating seller, SKS thus enjoys higher revenues and profits.

Notice that the firm took advantage of its ability to price-discriminate, charging different prices in the two submarkets: $700 per ton to South Korean steel buyers and $400 per ton to Canadian buyers. For international price discrimination to be successful, certain conditions must hold. First, to ensure that at any price the demand schedules in the two submarkets have different demand elasticities, the submarkets' demand conditions must differ. Domestic buyers, for example, may have income levels or tastes and preferences that differ from those of buyers abroad. Second, the firm must be able to separate the two submarkets, preventing any significant resale of commodities from the lower-priced to the higher-priced market. This is because any resale by consumers will tend to neutralize the effect of differential prices and will narrow the discriminatory price structure to the point at which it approaches a single price to all consumers. Because of high transportation costs and governmental trade restrictions, markets are often easier to separate internationally than nationally.

Antidumping Regulations

Despite the benefits that dumping may offer to importing consumers, governments have often levied penalty duties against commodities they believe are being dumped into their markets from abroad. U.S. antidumping law is designed to prevent price discrimination and below-cost sales that injure U.S. industries. Under U.S. law, an **antidumping duty** is levied when the U.S. Department of Commerce determines a class or kind of foreign merchandise is being sold at *less than fair value (LTFV)* and the U.S. International Trade Commission (ITC) determines that LTFV imports are causing or threatening material injury (such as unemployment and lost sales and profits) to a U.S. industry. Such antidumping duties are imposed in addition to the normal tariff in order to neutralize the effects of price discrimination or below-cost sales.

The **margin of dumping** is calculated as the amount by which the foreign market value exceeds the U.S. price. Foreign market value is defined in one of two ways. According to the **priced-based definition**, dumping occurs whenever a foreign company sells a product in the U.S. market at a price below that for which the same product sells in the home market. When a home-nation price of the good is not available (for example, if the good is produced only for export and is not sold domestically), an effort is made to determine the price of the good in a third market.

In cases where the price-based definition cannot be applied, a **cost-based definition** of foreign market value is permitted. Under this approach, the Commerce Department "constructs" a foreign market value equal to the sum of (1) the cost of manufacturing the merchandise, (2) general expenses, (3) profit on home-market sales, and (4) the cost of packaging the merchandise for shipment to the United States. The amount for general expenses must equal at least 10 percent of the cost of manufacturing, and the amount for profit must equal at least 8 percent of the manufacturing cost plus general expenses.

Antidumping cases begin with a complaint filed concurrently with the Commerce Department and the International Trade Commission. The complaint comes from within an import-competing industry (for example, from a firm or labor union) and consists of evidence of the existence of dumping and data that demonstrate material injury or threat of injury.

The Commerce Department first makes a preliminary determination as to whether or not dumping has occurred, including an estimate of the size of the dumping margin. If the preliminary investigation finds evidence of dumping, U.S. importers must immediately pay a special tariff (equal to the estimated dumping margin) on all imports of the product in question. The Commerce Department then makes its final determination as to whether or not dumping has taken place, as well as the size of the dumping margin. If the Commerce Department rules that dumping did not occur, special tariffs previously collected are rebated to U.S. importers. Otherwise, the International Trade Commission determines whether or not material injury has occurred as the result of the dumping.

If the International Trade Commission rules that import-competing firms were not injured by the dumping, the special tariffs are rebated to U.S. importers. But if both the International Trade Commission and the Commerce Department rule in favor of the dumping petition, a permanent tariff is imposed that equals the size of the dumping margin calculated by the Commerce Department in its final investigation. Let us consider some cases involving dumping.

Smith Corona Finds Antidumping Victories Are Hollow

Although antidumping duties are intended to protect domestic producers from unfairly priced imports, they can be an inconclusive weapon. Consider the case of Smith Corona, Inc., which won several antidumping cases from the 1970s to the 1990s but had little to show for it.

Trouble erupted for Smith Corona in the 1970s when it encountered ferocious competition from Brother Industries Ltd. of Japan, which flooded the U.S. market with its portable typewriters. Responding to Smith Corona's dumping complaint, in 1980 the U.S. government imposed antidumping duties of 49 percent on Brother portables. Smith Corona's antidumping victory proved to be hollow, however, because Brother realized that the antidumping ruling applied only to typewriters without a memory or calculating function. Through

Swimming Upstream: The Case of Vietnamese Catfish

Trade Conflicts

In 2003, the U.S. government was strongly criticized for assaulting catfish imports from Vietnam. According to Senator John McCain and other critics, this policy was an example of how wealthy countries preach the gospel of free trade when it comes to finding markets for their manufactured goods, but become highly protectionist when their farmers face competition. Let us consider this trade dispute.

After pursuing pro-capitalistic reforms, Vietnam became one of globalization's success stories of the 1990s. The nation transformed itself from being a rice importer to the world's second largest rice exporter and also an exporter of coffee. Vietnam's rural poverty rate declined from 70 percent to 30 percent. The normalization of communication between the governments of Vietnam and the United States resulted in American trade missions intended on increasing free enterprise in Vietnam.

On one of these trade missions, delegates saw much promise in Vietnamese catfish, with the country's Mekong Delta and cheap labor providing a competitive advantage. Within several years, some half-million Vietnamese were earning income from catfish trade. Vietnam captured 20 percent of the frozen catfish-fillet market in the United States, forcing down prices. To the alarm of catfish farmers in Mississippi, the hub of the U.S. catfish industry, even local restaurants were serving Vietnamese catfish.

Before long, Vietnamese farmers faced a nasty trade war waged by Mississippi's catfish farmers involving product labeling and antidumping tariffs. Although these farmers are usually not large agribusinesses, they were strong enough to persuade the U.S. government to close the catfish market to the very Vietnamese farmers whose enterprise it had originally encouraged. The government declared that out of 2,000 types of cat-

fish, only the American-born family could be called "catfish." So the Vietnamese could market their fish in America only by using Vietnamese words such as "tra" and "basa." Mississippi catfish farmers issued warnings of a "slippery catfish wannabe," saying such fish were "probably not even sporting real whiskers" and "floating around in Third World rivers nibbling on who knows what." This disinformation campaign resulted in decreased sales of Vietnamese catfish in the United States.

Not satisfied with its labeling success, the Mississippi catfish farmers initiated an antidumping case against Vietnamese catfish. In this case, the U.S. Department of Commerce did not have strong evidence that the imported fish were being sold in America more cheaply than in Vietnam, or below their cost of production. But rather than leaving Mississippi catfish farmers to the forces of international competition, the department declared Vietnam a "nonmarket" economy. This designation implied that Vietnamese farmers must not be covering all the costs they would in a market economy such as the United States, and thus were dumping catfish into the American market. Thus, tariffs ranging from 37 percent to 64 percent were imposed by the department on Vietnamese catfish. The U.S. International Trade Commission made the tariffs permanent by stating that the American catfish industry was injured by unfair competition due to dumping by Vietnam. According to critics, this nonmarket designation should not have been used because the U.S. government was encouraging Vietnam to become a market economy.

Source: "Harvesting Poverty: The Great Catfish War," *The New York Times*, July 22, 2003, p. 18, and The World Bank, *Global Economic Prospects*, 2004, Washington, DC, p. 85.

the tactic of *product evolution*, Brother evaded the duties by upgrading its typewriter to include a tiny computer memory. It took until 1990 for Smith Corona to get this loophole plugged by the federal

court of appeals in Washington, DC. By that time, Brother had found a more permanent method of circumventing antidumping duties: It began assembling portable typewriters in the United States from components manufactured in Malaysia and Japan. These typewriters were no longer "imported," and thus the 1980s duties did not apply.

Then competition shifted to another product, the personal word processor. By 1990, Smith Corona complained that Brother and other Japanese manufacturers were dumping word processors in the United States. This led the U.S. government to impose import duties of almost 60 percent on Japanese word processors in 1991. But that victory was also hollow, because it applied only to word processors manufactured in Japan; the Japanese firms assembled their word processors in the United States.

Undeterred, Smith Corona filed another complaint, invoking a provision in U.S. trade law that was designed to deter foreign firms from evading antidumping duties by importing components and assembling them in the United States. But the provision assumed that imported components would come from domestic (Japanese) factories, so it did not cover components produced in third countries. Recognizing this loophole, Brother demonstrated that its imported components came from third countries, and therefore its word processors were not subject to antidumping duties. All in all, obtaining relief from foreign dumped goods was a difficult process for Smith Corona!

Canadians Press Washington Apple Producers for Level Playing Field

Not only have foreign producers dumped products in the United States, but U.S. firms have sometimes dumped goods abroad.

In 1989, the Canadian government ruled that U.S. Delicious apples, primarily those grown in Washington, had been dumped on the Canadian market, causing injury to 4,500 commercial apple growers. As a result of the ruling, a 42-pound box of Washington apples could not be sold in Canada for less than $11.87, the "normal value" (analogous to the U.S. concept of "fair value") established by the Canadian government for regular-storage apples. Canadian importers purchasing U.S. apples at below-normal value had to pay an antidumping duty to the Canadian govern-

ment so that the total purchase price equaled the established value. The antidumping order was for the five years 1989 to 1994.

The Canadian apple growers' complaint alleged that extensive tree plants in the United States during the late 1970s and early 1980s resulted in excess apple production. In 1987 and 1988, Washington growers experienced a record harvest and inventories that exceeded storage facilities. The growers dramatically cut prices in order to market their crop, leading to a collapse of the North American price of Delicious apples.

When Washington apple growers failed to provide timely information, the Canadian government estimated the normal value of a box of U.S. apples using the best information available. As seen in Table 5.7, the normal value for a box of apples in the crop-year 1987–1988 was $11.87. During this period, the U.S. export price to Canada was about $9 a box. Based on a comparison of the export price and the normal value of apples, the weighted-average dumping margin was determined to be 32.5 percent.

The Canadian government determined that the influx of low-priced Washington apples into

TABLE 5.7

Normal Value and the Margin of Dumping: Delicious Apples, Regular Storage, 1987–1988*

U.S. FOB per Packed Box (42 pounds)	Normal Value (in Dollars)
Growing and harvesting costs	$ 5.50
Packing, marketing, and storing costs	5.49
Total costs	10.99
Profit (8% margin)	.88
Total normal value	$11.87

Margin of Dumping	Percentage
Range	0–63.44%
Weighted-average margin	32.53

*The weighted-average dumping margin for controlled-atmosphere-storage apples was 23.86 percent.

Source: *Statement of Reasons: Final Determination of Dumping Respecting Delicious Apples Originating in or Exported from the United States of America,* Revenue Canada, Customs and Excise Division, December 1988.

the Canadian market displaced Canadian apples and resulted in losses to Canadian apple growers of $1 to $6.40 (Canadian dollars) per box during the 1987–1988 growing season. The Canadian government ruled that the dumped apples injured Canadian growers, and thus imposed antidumping duties on Washington apples.

Is the Antidumping Law Unfair?

U.S. antidumping law attempts to address the issue of unfairness to producers of import-competing goods. Because it is hard to define unfairness, it is not surprising that antidumping law is subject to criticism.

Should Average Variable Cost Be the Yardstick for Defining Dumping?

Under current rules, dumping can occur when a foreign producer sells goods in the United States at less than fair value. Fair value is equated with average total cost plus an 8 percent allowance for profit. However, many economists argue that fair value should be based on *average variable cost* rather than average total cost, especially when the domestic economy realizes temporary downturn in demand.

Consider the case of a radio producer under the following assumptions: (1) The producer's physical capacity is 150 units of output over the given time period; and (2) The domestic market's demand for radios is price-inelastic, whereas foreign demand is price-elastic. Refer to Table 5.8. Suppose that the producer charges a uniform price (no dumping) of $300 per unit to both domestic and foreign consumers. With domestic demand inelastic, domestic sales total 100 units. But with elastic demand conditions abroad, suppose the producer cannot market any radios at the prevailing price. Sales revenues would equal $30,000, with variable costs plus fixed costs totaling $30,000. Without dumping, the firm would find itself with excess capacity of 50 radios. Moreover, the firm would just break even on its domestic market operations.

Suppose this producer decides to dump radios abroad at lower prices than at home. As long as all variable costs are covered, any price that contributes to fixed costs will permit larger profits (smaller losses) than those realized with idle plant capacity at hand. According to Table 5.8, by charging $300 to home consumers, the firm can sell 100 units. Suppose that by charging a price of $250 per unit, the firm is able to sell an additional 50 units abroad. The total sales revenue of $42,500 would not only cover variable costs plus fixed costs, but would permit a profit of $2,500.

With dumping, the firm is able to increase profits even though it is selling abroad at a price less than average total cost (average total cost = $40,000/150 = $267). Firms facing excess productive capacity

---

TABLE 5.8

Dumping and Excess Capacity

	No Dumping	Dumping
Home sales	100 units @ $300	100 units @ $300
Export sales	0 units @ $300	50 units @ $250
Sales revenue	$30,000	$42,500
Less variable costs of $200 per unit	– 20,000	– 30,000
	$10,000	$12,500
Less total fixed costs of $10,000	– 10,000	– 10,000
Profit	$0	$2,500

may thus have the incentive to stimulate sales by cutting prices charged to foreigners—perhaps to levels that just cover average variable cost. Of course, domestic prices must be sufficiently high to keep the firm operating profitably over the relevant time period.

Put simply, many economists argue that antidumping law, which uses average total cost as a yardstick to determine fair value, is unfair. They note that economic theory suggests that under competitive conditions, firms price their goods at average variable costs, which are below average total costs. Therefore, the antidumping laws punish firms that are simply behaving in a manner typical of competitive markets. Moreover, the law is unfair because U.S. firms selling at home are not subject to the same rules. Indeed, it is quite possible for a foreign firm that is selling at a loss both at home and in the United States to be found guilty of dumping, when U.S. firms are also making losses and selling in the domestic market at exactly the same price.

Should the Antidumping Law Reflect Currency Fluctuations?

Another criticism of antidumping law is that it does not account for currency fluctuations. Consider the price-based definition of dumping: selling at lower prices in the foreign market. Because foreign producers often must set their prices for foreign customers in terms of a foreign currency, fluctuations in exchange rates can cause them to "dump" according to the legal definition. For example, suppose the Japanese yen appreciates against the U.S. dollar, which means that it takes fewer yen to buy a dollar. But if Japanese steel exporters are meeting competition in the United States and setting their prices in dollars, the appreciation of the yen will cause the price of their exports in terms of the yen to decrease, making it appear that they are dumping in the United States. Under the U.S. antidumping law, American firms are not required to meet the standard imposed on foreign firms selling in the United States. Does the antidumping law redress unfairness—or create it?

Other Nontariff Trade Barriers

Other NTBs consist of governmental codes of conduct applied to imports. Even though such provisions are often well disguised, they remain important sources of commercial policy. Let's consider three such barriers: government procurement policies, social regulations, and sea transport and freight regulations.

Government Procurement Policies

Because government agencies are large buyers of goods and services, they are attractive customers for foreign suppliers. If governments purchased goods and services only from the lowest-cost suppliers, the pattern of trade would not differ significantly from that which occurs in a competitive market. Most governments, however, favor domestic suppliers over foreign ones in the procurement of materials and products. This is evidenced by the fact that the ratio of imports to total purchases in the public sector is much smaller than in the private sector.

Governments often extend preferences to domestic suppliers in the form of **buy-national policies**. The U.S. government, through explicit laws, openly discriminates against foreign suppliers in its purchasing decisions. Although most other governments do not have formally legislated preferences for domestic suppliers, they often discriminate against foreign suppliers through hidden administrative rules and practices. Such governments utilize closed bidding systems that restrict the number of companies allowed to bid on sales, or they may publicize government contracts in such a way as to make it difficult for foreign suppliers to make a bid.

To stimulate domestic employment during the Great Depression, in 1933 the U.S. government passed the Buy American Act. This act requires federal agencies to purchase materials and products from U.S. suppliers if their prices are not "unreasonably" higher than those of foreign competitors. A product, to qualify as domestic, must have at least a 50 percent domestic component content and must be manufactured in the United States. As it stands today, U.S. suppliers of civilian agencies are given a 6 percent preference margin. This means that a U.S. supplier receives the government contract as long as the U.S. low bid is no more than 6 percent higher than the competing foreign bid. This preference margin rises to 12 percent if the low domestic bidder is situated in a labor-surplus area, and to 50 percent if the purchase is made by the Department of Defense. These preferences are waived when it is determined that the U.S.–produced good is not available in sufficient quantities or is not of satisfactory quality.

By discriminating against low-cost foreign suppliers in favor of domestic suppliers, buy-national policies are a barrier to free trade. Domestic suppliers are given the leeway to use less efficient production methods and to pay resource prices higher than those permitted under free trade. This yields a higher cost for government projects and deadweight welfare losses for the nation in the form of the protective effect and consumption effect.

The buy-American restrictions of the U.S. government have been liberalized with the adoption of the Tokyo Round of Multilateral Trade Negotiations in 1979. However, the pact does not apply to the purchase of materials and products by state and local government agencies. More than 30 states currently have buy-American laws, ranging from explicit prohibitions on purchases of foreign products to loose policy guidelines favoring U.S. products. Advocates of state buy-American laws usually maintain that the laws provide direct local economic benefit in the form of jobs; moreover, the threat of foreign retaliation is minimal at the state level.

Social Regulations

Since the 1950s, nations have assumed an ever-increasing role in regulating the quality of life for society. **Social regulation** attempts to correct a variety of undesirable side effects in an economy that relate to health, safety, and the environment—effects that markets, left to themselves, often ignore. Social regulation applies to a partic-

ular issue, say environmental quality, and affects the behavior of firms in many industries such as automobiles, steel, and chemicals.

CAFÉ Standards

Although social regulations may advance health, safety, and environmental goals, they can also serve as barriers to international trade. Consider the case of fuel economy standards imposed by the U.S. government on automobile manufacturers.

Originally enacted in 1975, **corporate average fuel economy (CAFÉ) standards** represent the foundation of U.S. energy conservation policy. Applying to all passenger vehicles sold in the United States, the standards are based on the average fuel efficiency of all vehicles sold by all manufacturers. Since 1990, the CAFÉ requirement for passenger cars has been 27.5 miles a gallon. Manufacturers whose average fuel economy falls below this standard are subject to fines.

During the 1980s, CAFÉ requirements were used not only to promote fuel conservation but also to protect jobs of U.S. autoworkers. The easiest way for U.S. car manufacturers to improve the average fuel efficiency of their fleets would have been to import smaller, more fuel-efficient vehicles from their subsidiaries in Asia and Europe. However, this would have decreased employment in an already depressed industry. The U.S. government thus enacted *separate but identical* standards for domestic and imported passenger cars. Therefore, General Motors, Ford, and DaimlerChrysler, which manufactured vehicles in the United States and also sold imported cars, would be required to fulfill CAFÉ targets for *both* categories of vehicles. U.S. firms thus could not fulfill CAFÉ standards by averaging the fuel economy of their imports with their less fuel-efficient, domestically produced vehicles. By calculating domestic and imported fleets separately, the U.S. government attempted to force domestic firms not only to manufacture more efficient vehicles but also to produce them in the United States! In short, government regulations sometimes place effective import barriers on foreign commodities, whether they are intended to do so or not, thus aggravating foreign competitors.

Hormones in Beef Production

The European Union's ban on hormone-treated meat is another case where social regulations can lead to a beef. Growth-promoting hormones are used widely by livestock producers to speed up growth rates and produce leaner livestock more in line with consumer preferences for diets with reduced fat and cholesterol. However, critics of hormones maintain that they can cause cancer for consumers of meat.

In 1989, the European Union enacted its ban on production and importation of beef derived from animals treated with growth-promoting hormones. The European Union justified the ban as needed to protect the health and safety of consumers.

The ban was immediately challenged by U.S. producers, who used the hormones in about 90 percent of their beef production. According to the United States, there was no scientific basis for the ban that restricted beef imports on the basis of health concerns. Instead, the ban was merely an attempt to protect the relatively high-cost European beef industry from foreign competition. U.S. producers noted that when the ban was imposed, European producers had accumulated large, costly-to-store beef surpluses that resulted in enormous political pressure to limit imports of beef. The European Union's emphasis on health concerns was thus a smokescreen for protecting an industry with comparative disadvantage, according to the United States.

The trade dispute eventually went to the World Trade Organization (WTO) (see Chapter 6), which ruled that the European Union's ban on hormone-treated beef was illegal and resulted in lost annual U.S. exports of beef to the European Union in the amount of $117 million. Nonetheless, the European Union, citing consumer preference, refused to lift its ban. Therefore, the WTO authorized the United States to impose tariffs high enough to prohibit $117 million of European exports to the United States. The United States exercised its right and slapped 100 percent tariffs on a list of European products that included tomatoes, roquefort cheese, prepared mustard, goose liver, citrus fruit, pasta, hams, and other products. The U.S. hit list focused on products from Denmark, France, Germany, and Italy—the biggest supporters of the European Union's ban

on hormone-treated beef. By effectively doubling the prices of the targeted products, the 100 percent tariffs pressured the Europeans to liberalize their imports of beef products.

Sea Transport and Freight Restrictions

During the 1990s, U.S. shipping companies serving Japanese ports complained of a highly restrictive system of port services. They contended that Japan's association of stevedore companies (companies that unload cargo from ships) used a system of prior consultations to control competition, allocate harbor work among themselves, and frustrate the implementation of any cost-cutting by shipping companies.

In particular, shipping companies contended that they were forced to negotiate with the Japanese stevedore-company association on everything from arrival times to choice of stevedores and warehouses. Because port services were controlled by the stevedore-company association, foreign carriers could not negotiate with individual stevedore companies about prices and schedules. Moreover, U.S. carriers maintained that the Japanese government approved these restrictive practices by refusing to license new entrants into the port service business and by supporting the requirement that foreign carriers negotiate with Japan's stevedore-company association.

A midnight trip to Tokyo Bay illustrates the frustration of U.S. shipping companies. The lights are dimmed and the wharf is quiet, even though the *Sealand Commerce* has just docked. At 1 A.M., lights turn on, cranes swing alive, and trucks appear to unload the ship's containers, which carry paper plates, computers, and pet food from the United States. At 4 A.M., however, the lights shut off and the work ceases. Longshoremen won't return until 8:30 A.M. and will take three more hours off later in the day. They have unloaded only 169 of 488 containers that they must handle before the ship sails for Oakland. At this rate, the job will take until past noon; but at least it isn't Sunday, when docks close altogether.

When the *Sealand Commerce* reaches Oakland, however, U.S. dockworkers will unload and load 24 hours a day, taking 30 percent less time for about half the price. To enter Tokyo Bay, the ship had to clear every detail of its visit with Japan's stevedore-company association; to enter the U.S. port, it will merely notify port authorities and the Coast Guard. According to U.S. exporters, this unequal treatment on waterfronts is a trade barrier because it makes U.S. exports more expensive in Japan.

In 1997, the United States and Japan found themselves on the brink of a trade war after the U.S. government decided to direct its Coast Guard and Customs service to bar Japanese-flagged ships from unloading at U.S. ports. The U.S. government demanded that foreign shipping companies be allowed to negotiate directly with Japanese stevedore companies to unload their ships, thus giving carriers a way around the restrictive practices of Japan's stevedore-company association. After consultation between the two governments, an agreement was reached to liberalize port services in Japan. As a result, the United States rescinded its ban against Japanese ships.

Summary

1. With the decline in import tariffs in the past two decades, nontariff trade barriers have gained in importance as a measure of protection. Nontariff trade barriers include such practices as (a) import quotas, (b) orderly marketing agreements, (c) domestic content requirements, (d) subsidies, (e) antidumping regulations, (f) discriminatory government procurement practices, (g) social regulations, and (h) sea transport and freight restrictions.

2. An import quota is a government-imposed limit on the quantity of a product that can be imported. Quotas are imposed on a global (worldwide) basis or a selective (individual country) basis. Although quotas have many of the same economic effects as tariffs, they tend to be more restrictive. A quota's revenue effect generally accrues to domestic importers or foreign exporters, depending on the degree of market power they possess. If government desired to capture the revenue effect, it could auction import quota licenses to the highest bidder in a competitive market.

3. A tariff-rate quota is a two-tier tariff placed on an imported product. It permits a limited number of goods to be imported at a lower tariff rate, whereas any imports beyond this limit face a higher tariff. Of the revenue generated by a tariff-rate quota, some accrues to the domestic government as tariff revenue and the remainder is captured by producers as windfall profits.

4. Orderly marketing agreements are market-sharing pacts negotiated by trading nations. They generally involve quotas on exports and imports. Proponents of orderly marketing agreements contend that they are less disruptive of international trade than unilaterally determined tariffs and quotas.

5. Because an export quota is administered by the government of the exporting nation (supply-side restriction), its revenue effect tends to be captured by sellers of the exporting nation. For the importing nation, the quota's revenue effect is a welfare loss in addition to the protective and consumption effects.

6. Domestic content requirements try to limit the practice of foreign sourcing and encourage the development of domestic industry. They typically stipulate the minimum percentage of a product's value that must be produced in the home country for that product to be sold there. Domestic content protection tends to impose welfare losses on the domestic economy in the form of higher production costs and higher-priced goods.

7. Government subsidies are sometimes granted as a form of protection to domestic exporters and import-competing companies. They may take the form of direct cash bounties, tax concessions, credit extended at low interest rates, or special insurance arrangements. Direct production subsidies for import-competing producers tend to involve a smaller loss in economic

welfare than do equivalent tariffs and quotas. The imposition of export subsidies results in a terms-of-trade effect and an export-revenue effect.

8. International dumping occurs when a firm sells its product abroad at a price that is (a) less than average total cost or (b) less than that charged to domestic buyers of the same product. Dumping can be sporadic, predatory, or per-

sistent in nature. Idle productive capacity may be the reason behind dumping. Governments often impose stiff penalties against foreign commodities that are believed to be dumped in the home economy.

9. Government rules and regulations in areas such as safety and technical standards and marketing requirements can have significant impacts on world trade patterns.

Key Concepts and Terms

- Antidumping duty *(page 160)*
- Buy-national policies *(page 164)*
- Corporate average fuel economy (CAFÉ) standards *(page 165)*
- Cost-based definition of dumping *(page 160)*
- Domestic content requirements *(page 152)*
- Domestic subsidy *(page 155)*
- Dumping *(page 157)*
- Export quotas *(page 148)*
- Export-revenue effect *(page 157)*

- Export subsidy *(page 155)*
- Global quota *(page 141)*
- Import license *(page 140)*
- Import quota *(page 140)*
- License on demand allocation *(page 147)*
- Margin of dumping *(page 160)*
- Nonrestrained suppliers *(page 150)*
- Nontariff trade barriers (NTBs) *(page 140)*
- Orderly marketing agreement (OMA) *(page 148)*
- Persistent dumping *(page 158)*

- Predatory dumping *(page 157)*
- Price-based definition of dumping *(page 160)*
- Selective quota *(page 141)*
- Social regulation *(page 165)*
- Sporadic dumping *(page 157)*
- Subsidies *(page 154)*
- Tariff-rate quota *(page 147)*
- Trade-diversion effect *(page 151)*
- Voluntary export restraints (VERs) *(page 148)*

Study Questions

1. In the past two decades, nontariff trade barriers have gained in importance as protectionist devices. What are the major nontariff trade barriers?
2. How does the revenue effect of an import quota differ from that of a tariff?
3. What are the major forms of subsidies that governments grant to domestic producers?
4. What is meant by voluntary export restraints, and how do they differ from other protective barriers?

5. Should U.S. antidumping laws be stated in terms of full production costs or marginal costs?
6. Which is a more restrictive trade barrier—an import tariff or an equivalent import quota?
7. Differentiate among sporadic, persistent, and predatory dumping.
8. A subsidy may provide import-competing producers the same degree of protection as tariffs or quotas but at a lower cost in terms of national welfare. Explain.

9. Rather than generating tax revenue as do tariffs, subsidies require tax revenue. Therefore, they are not an effective protective device for the home economy. Do you agree?

10. In 1980, the U.S. auto industry proposed that import quotas be imposed on foreign-produced cars sold in the United States. What would be the likely benefits and costs of such a policy?

11. Why did the U.S. government in 1982 provide import quotas as an aid to domestic sugar producers?

12. Which tends to result in a greater welfare loss for the home economy: (a) an import quota levied by the home government or (b) a voluntary export quota imposed by the foreign government?

13. What would be the likely effects of export restraints imposed by Japan on its auto shipments to the United States?

14. Why might U.S. steel-using firms lobby against the imposition of quotas on foreign steel sold in the United States?

15. Concerning international dumping, distinguish between the price-based and cost-based definitions of foreign market value.

16. **Xtra!** **For a tutorial of this question, go to http://carbaughxtra.swlearning.com**
Table 5.9 illustrates the demand and supply schedules for television sets in Venezuela, a "small" nation that is unable to affect world prices. On graph paper, sketch Venezuela's demand and supply schedules of television sets.

a. Suppose Venezuela imports TV sets at a price of $150 each. Under free trade, how many sets does Venezuela produce, consume, and import? Determine Venezuela's consumer surplus and producer surplus.

b. Assume that Venezuela imposes a quota that limits imports to 300 TV sets. Determine the quota-induced price increase and the resulting decrease in consumer surplus. Calculate the quota's redistributive effect, consumption effect, protective effect, and revenue effect. Assuming that Venezuelan import companies organize as buyers and bargain favorably with competitive foreign exporters, what is the overall welfare loss to Venezuela as a result of the quota? Suppose that foreign exporters organize as a monopoly seller. What is the overall welfare loss to Venezuela as a result of the quota?

c. Suppose that, instead of a quota, Venezuela grants its import-competing producers a subsidy of $100 per TV set. In your diagram, draw the subsidy-adjusted supply schedule for Venezuelan producers. Does the subsidy result in a rise in the price of TV sets above the free-trade level? Determine Venezuela's production, consumption, and imports of TV sets under the subsidy. What is the total cost of the subsidy to the Venezuelan government? Of this amount, how much is transferred to Venezuelan producers in the form of producer surplus, and how much is absorbed by higher production costs due to inefficient domestic production? Determine the overall welfare loss to Venezuela under the subsidy.

17. **Xtra!** **For a tutorial of this question, go to http://carbaughxtra.swlearning.com**
Table 5.10 on page 170 illustrates the demand and supply schedules for computers in Ecuador, a "small" nation that is unable to affect world prices. On graph paper, sketch Ecuador's demand and supply schedules of computers.

a. Assume that Hong Kong and Taiwan can supply computers to Ecuador at a per-unit price of $300 and $500, respectively. With

TABLE 5.9

Venezuelan Supply of and Demand for Television Sets

Price per TV Set	Quantity Demanded	Quantity Supplied
$100	900	0
200	700	200
300	500	400
400	300	600
500	100	800

TABLE 5.10

Computer Supply and Demand: Ecuador

Price of Computer	Quantity Demanded	Quantity Supplied
$ 0	100	—
200	90	0
400	80	10
600	70	20
800	60	30
1,000	50	40
1,200	40	50
1,400	30	60
1,600	20	70
1,800	10	80
2,000	0	90

free trade, how many computers does Ecuador import? From which nation does it import?

b. Suppose Ecuador and Hong Kong negotiate a voluntary export agreement in which Hong Kong imposes on its exporters a quota that limits shipments to Ecuador to 40 computers. Assume Taiwan does not take advantage of the situation by exporting computers to Ecuador. Determine the quota-induced price increase and the reduction in consumer surplus for Ecuador. Determine the quota's redistributive effect, protective effect, consumption effect, and revenue effect. Because the export quota is administered by Hong Kong, its exporters will capture the quota's revenue effect. Determine the overall welfare loss to Ecuador as a result of the quota.

c. Again assume that Hong Kong imposes an export quota on its producers that restricts shipments to Ecuador to 40 computers, but now suppose that Taiwan, a nonrestrained exporter, ships an additional 20 computers to Ecuador. Ecuador thus imports 60 com-

puters. Determine the overall welfare loss to Ecuador as a result of the quota.

d. In general, when increases in nonrestrained supply offset part of the cutback in shipments that occur under an export quota, will the overall welfare loss for the importing country be greater or smaller than that which occurs in the absence of nonrestrained supply? Determine this amount in example of Ecuador.

18. **Xtra!** For a tutorial of this question, go to
    CARBAUGH http://carbaughxtra.swlearning.com

Figure 5.8 illustrates the practice of international dumping by British Toys, Inc. (BTI). Figure 5.8(a) shows the domestic demand and marginal revenue schedules faced by BTI in the United Kingdom, and Figure 5.8(b) shows the demand and marginal revenue schedules faced by BTI in Canada. Figure 5.8(c) shows the combined demand and marginal revenue schedules for the two markets, as well as BTI's average total cost and marginal cost schedules.

a. In the absence of international dumping, BTI would charge a uniform price to U.K. and Canadian customers (ignoring transportation costs). Determine the firm's profit-maximizing output and price, as well as total profit. How much profit accrues to BTI on its U.K. sales and on its Canadian sales?

b. Suppose now that BTI engages in international dumping. Determine the price that BTI charges its U.K. buyers and the profits that accrue on U.K. sales. Also determine the price that BTI charges its Canadian buyers and the profits that accrue on Canadian sales. Does the practice of international dumping yield higher profits than the uniform pricing strategy? If so, by how much?

19. Why is a tariff-rate quota viewed as a compromise between the interests of the domestic consumer and those of the domestic producer? How does the revenue effect of a tariff-rate quota differ from that of an import tariff?

FIGURE 5.8

International Dumping Schedules

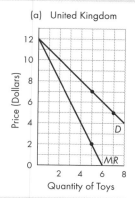

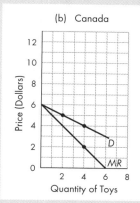

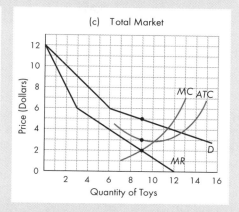

Tariff-Rate Quota Welfare Effects

The welfare effects of tariff-rate quotas have been briefly discussed in this chapter. Let us further examine these welfare effects.

Figure 5.9 illustrates the welfare effects of a hypothetical tariff-rate quota on sugar. Assume that the U.S. demand and supply schedules for sugar are given by $D_{U.S.}$ and $S_{U.S.}$, and the equilibrium (autarky) price of sugar is $540 per ton. Assuming free trade, suppose the United States faces a constant world price of sugar equal to $400 per ton. At the free-trade price, U.S. production equals 5 tons, U.S. consumption equals 40 tons, and imports equal 35 tons.

To protect its producers from foreign competition, suppose the United States enacts a tariff-rate import quota of 5 tons. Imports within this limit face a 10 percent tariff, but a 20 percent tariff applies to imports in excess of the limit.

Because the United States initially imports an amount exceeding the limit as defined by the tariff-rate quota, both the within-quota rate and the over-quota rate apply. This two-tier tariff causes the price of sugar sold in the United States to rise from $400 to $480 per ton. Domestic production increases to 15 tons, domestic consumption falls to 30 tons, and imports fall to 15 tons. Increased sales allow the profits of U.S. sugar producers to rise by an amount equal to area e ($800). The dead-weight losses to the U.S. economy, in terms of production and consumption inefficiencies, equal areas f ($400) and g ($400), respectively.

An interesting feature of the tariff-rate quota is the revenue it generates. Some of it accrues to the domestic government as tariff revenue, but the remainder is captured by business as windfall profits—a gain to business resulting from sudden or unexpected government policy.

In this example, after enactment of the tariff quota, imports total 15 tons of sugar. The U.S. government collects area a ($200), found by multiplying the within-quota duty of $40 times 5 tons. Area b + c ($800), found by multiplying the remaining 10 tons of imported sugar times the over-quota duty of $80, also accrues to the government.

Area d ($200) in the figure represents windfall profits. Under the tariff-rate quota, the domestic price of the first 5 tons of sugar imported is $440, reflecting the foreign supply price of $400 plus the import duty of $40. Suppose U.S. import companies can obtain foreign sugar at $440 per ton. By reselling the 5 tons to U.S. consumers at $480 per ton, the price of over-quota sugar, U.S. importers would capture area d as windfall profits. But this opportunity will not last long, because foreign sugar suppliers will want to capture the windfall gain. To the extent that they can restrict sugar exports to the United States, foreign producers could force up the price of sugar and expropriate profits from U.S. importing companies. Foreign producers conceivably could capture the entire area d by raising their supply price to $480 per ton. The portion of the windfall profit captured by foreign sugar producers represents a welfare loss to the U.S. economy.

FIGURE 5.9

Tariff-Rate Quota: Trade and Welfare Effects

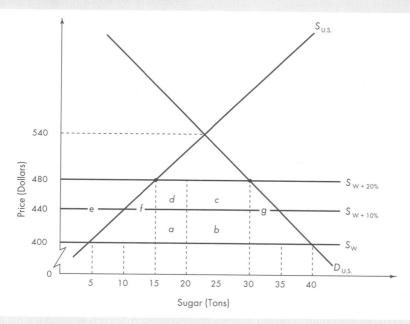

The imposition of a tariff-rate quota leads to higher product prices and a decrease in consumer surplus for domestic buyers. Of the tariff-rate quota's revenue effect, a portion accrues to the domestic government, while the remainder accrues to domestic importers or foreign exporters as windfall profits.

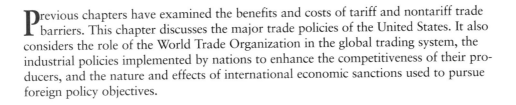

chapter 6

Trade Regulations and Industrial Policies

Previous chapters have examined the benefits and costs of tariff and nontariff trade barriers. This chapter discusses the major trade policies of the United States. It also considers the role of the World Trade Organization in the global trading system, the industrial policies implemented by nations to enhance the competitiveness of their producers, and the nature and effects of international economic sanctions used to pursue foreign policy objectives.

U.S. Tariff Policies Before 1930

As Table 6.1 makes clear, U.S. tariff history has been marked by fluctuations. The dominant motive behind the early tariff laws of the United States was to provide the government an important source of tax revenue. This *revenue objective* was the main reason Congress passed the first tariff law in 1789 and followed it up with 12 more tariff laws by 1812. But as the U.S. economy diversified and developed alternative sources of tax revenue, justification for the revenue argument was weakened. The tariffs collected by the federal government today are about 1 percent of total federal revenues, a negligible amount.

As the revenue argument weakened, the *protective argument* for tariffs developed strength. In 1791, Alexander Hamilton presented to Congress his famous "Report on Manufacturers," which proposed that the young industries of the United States be granted import protection until they could grow and prosper—the *infant-industry* argument. Although Hamilton's writings did not initially have a legislative impact, by the 1820s protectionist sentiments in the United States were well established. During the 1920s, the average level of tariffs on U.S. imports was three to four times the 8 percent levels of 1789.

The surging protectionist movement reached its high point in 1828 with the passage of the so-called Tariff of Abominations. This measure increased duties to an average level of 45 percent, the highest in the years prior to the Civil War, and provoked the South, which wanted low duties for its imported manufactured goods. The South's opposition to this tariff led to the passage of the Compromise Tariff of 1833, providing

TABLE 6.1

U.S. Tariff History: Average Tariff Rates

Tariff Laws and Dates	Average Tariff Rate* (%)
McKinley Law, 1890	48.4%
Wilson Law, 1894	41.3
Dingley Law, 1897	46.5
Payne–Aldrich Law, 1909	40.8
Underwood Law, 1913	27.0
Fordney–McCumber Law, 1922	38.5
Smoot–Hawley Law, 1930	53.0
1930–1949	33.9
1950–1969	11.9
1970–1989	6.4
1990–1999	5.2
2003	4.4

*Ratio of duties collected to FOB value on dutiable imports.

Source: U.S. Census Bureau, *Statistical Abstract of the United States* (Washington, DC: U.S. Government Printing Office, various issues). See also World Trade Organization, *Annual Report*, various issues.

for a downsizing of the tariff protection afforded U.S. manufacturers. During the 1840s and 1850s, the U.S. government found that it faced an excess of tax receipts over expenditures. Therefore, the government passed the Walker Tariffs, which cut duties to an average level of 23 percent in order to eliminate the budget surplus. Further tariff cuts took place in 1857, bringing the average tariff levels to their lowest level since 1816, around 16 percent.

During the Civil War era, tariffs were again raised with the passage of the Morill Tariffs of 1861, 1862, and 1864. These measures were primarily intended as a means of paying for the Civil War. By 1970, protection climbed back to the heights of the 1840s; however, this time the tariff levels would not be reduced. During the latter part of the 1800s, U.S. policy makers were impressed by the arguments of American labor and business leaders who complained that *cheap foreign labor* was causing goods to flow into the United States. The enactment of the McKinley and Dingley Tariffs largely rested upon this argument. By 1897, tariffs on protected imports averaged 46 percent.

Although the Payne–Aldrich Tariff of 1909 marked the turning point against rising protection-

ism, it was the enactment of the Underwood Tariff of 1913 that reduced duties to 27 percent on average. Trade liberalization might have remained on a more permanent basis had it not been for the outbreak of World War I. Protectionist pressures built up during the war years and maintained momentum after the war's conclusion. During the early 1920s, the *scientific tariff concept* was influential, and in 1922 the Fordney–McCumber Tariff contained, among other provisions, one that allowed the president to increase tariff levels if foreign production costs were below those of the United States. Average tariff rates climbed to 38 percent under the Fordney–McCumber law.

Smoot–Hawley Act

The high point of U.S. protectionism occurred with the passage of the **Smoot–Hawley Act** in 1930, under which U.S. average tariffs were raised to 53 percent on protected imports. As the Smoot–Hawley bill moved through the U.S. Congress, formal protests from foreign nations flooded Washington, eventually adding up to a document of some 200 pages. Nevertheless, both the House of Representatives and the Senate approved the bill. Although about a thousand U.S. economists beseeched President Herbert Hoover to veto the legislation, he did not do so, and the tariff was signed into law on June 17, 1930. Simply put, the Smoot–Hawley Act tried to divert national demand away from imports and toward domestically produced goods.

The legislation provoked retaliation by 25 trading partners of the United States. Spain implemented the Wais tariff in reaction to U.S. tariffs on cork, oranges, and grapes. Switzerland boycotted U.S. exports to protest new tariffs on watches and shoes. Canada increased its tariffs threefold in reaction to U.S. tariffs on timber, logs, and many food products. Italy retaliated against tariffs on olive oil and hats with tariffs on U.S. automobiles. Mexico, Cuba, Australia, and New Zealand also participated in tariff wars. Other beggar-thy-neighbor policies, such as foreign-exchange controls and currency depreciations, were also implemented. The effort by several nations to run a trade surplus by reducing imports led to a breakdown of the international trading system. Within two years after the Smoot–Hawley Act, U.S. exports decreased by nearly two-thirds. Figure 6.1 shows the decline of world trade as the global economy fell into the Great Depression.

How did President Hoover fall into such a protectionist trap? The president felt compelled to honor the 1928 Republican platform calling for tariffs to aid the weakening farm economy. The stock market crash of 1929 and the imminent Great Depression further led to a crisis atmosphere. Republicans had been sympathetic to protectionism for decades. Now they viewed import tariffs as a method of fulfilling demands that government should initiate positive steps to combat domestic unemployment.

President Hoover felt bound to tradition and to the platform of the Republican party. Henry

Ford spent an evening with Hoover requesting a presidential veto of what he referred to as "economic stupidity." Other auto executives sided with Ford. However, tariff legislation had never before been vetoed by a president, and Hoover was not about to set a precedent. Hoover remarked that "with returning normal conditions, our foreign trade will continue to expand."

By 1932, U.S. trade with other nations had collapsed. Presidential challenger Franklin Roosevelt denounced the trade legislation as ruinous. Hoover responded that Roosevelt would have U.S. workers compete with peasant labor overseas. Following Hoover's defeat in the presidential election of 1932, the Democrats dismantled the Smoot–Hawley legislation. But they used caution, relying on reciprocal trade agreements instead of across-the-board tariff concessions by the United States. Sam Rayburn, the Speaker of the House of Representatives, insisted that any party member who wanted to be a member of the House Ways and Means Committee had to support trade reciprocity instead of protectionism. The Smoot–Hawley approach was discredited, and the United States pursued trade liberalization via reciprocal trade agreements.

Reciprocal Trade Agreements Act

The combined impact on U.S. exports of the Great Depression and the foreign retaliatory tariffs imposed in reaction to the Smoot–Hawley Act resulted in a reversal of U.S. trade policy. In 1934, Congress passed the **Reciprocal Trade Agreements Act**, which set the stage for a wave of *trade liberalization*. Specifically aimed at tariff reduction, the act contained two features: (1) negotiating authority and (2) generalized reductions.

Under this law, the president was given the unprecedented authority to negotiate bilateral tariff-reduction agreements with foreign governments (for example, between the United States and Sweden). Without congressional approval, the president could lower tariffs by up to 50 percent of the existing level. Enactment of any tariff reductions was dependent on the willingness of other nations to reciprocally lower their tariffs on U.S.

FIGURE 6.1

Smoot–Hawley Protectionism and World Trade, 1929–1933 (Millions of Dollars)

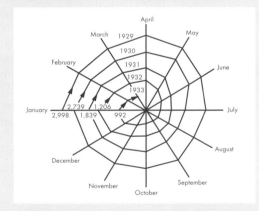

The figure shows the pattern of world trade from 1929 to 1933. Following the Smoot–Hawley Tariff Act of 1930, which raised U.S. tariffs to an average level of 53 percent, other nations retaliated by increasing their own import restrictions, and the volume of world trade decreased as the global economy fell into the Great Depression.

Source: Data taken from League of Nations, *Monthly Bulletin of Statistics*, February, 1934. See also Charles Kindleberger, *The World in Depression* (Berkeley, CA: University of California Press, 1973), p. 170.

goods. From 1934 to 1947, the United States entered into 32 bilateral tariff agreements, and over this period the average level of tariffs on protected products fell to about half of the 1934 levels.

The Reciprocal Trade Agreements Act also provided for generalized tariff reductions through the **most-favored-nation (MFN) clause**. This clause is an agreement between two nations to apply tariffs to each other at rates as low as those applied to any other nation. For example, if the United States extends MFN treatment to Brazil and then grants a low tariff on imports of machinery from France, the United States is obligated to provide the identical low-tariff treatment on imports of machinery from Brazil. Brazil thus receives the same treatment as the initially most-favored nation, France. The advantage to Brazil of MFN status is that it can investigate all of the tariff policies of the United States concerning imported machinery to see if treatment to some nation is more favorable than that granted to it; if any more favorable terms are found, Brazil can call for equal treatment. In 1998, the U.S. government replaced the term *most-favored nation* with **normal trade relations**, which will be used throughout the rest of this textbook.

According to the provisions of the World Trade Organization (see next section), there are two exceptions to the normal trade relations clause: (1) Industrial nations can grant preferential tariffs to imports from developing nations that are not granted to imports from other industrial nations; and (2) Nations belonging to a regional trading arrangement (for example, the North American Free Trade Agreement) can eliminate tariffs applied to imports of goods coming from other members while maintaining tariffs on imports from nonmembers.

Granting normal trade relation status or imposing differential tariffs has been used as an instrument of foreign policy. For example, a nation may punish unfriendly nations with high import tariffs on their goods and reward friendly nations with low tariffs. The United States has granted normal trade relation status to most of the nations with which it trades. As of 2002, the United States did not grant normal trade relation status to the following countries: Afghanistan, Cuba, Laos, North Korea, and Vietnam. U.S. tariffs on imports from these countries are often three or four (or more) times as high as those on comparable imports from nations receiving normal trade relation status, as seen in Table 6.2.

TABLE 6.2

U.S. Tariffs on Imports from Nations Granted, and Not Granted, Normal Trade Relation Status: Selected Examples

	Tariff (Percent)	
Product	With Normal Trade Relation Status	Without Normal Trade Relation Status
Hams	1.2 cents/kg	7.2 cents /kg
Sour cream	3.2 cents/liter	15 cents/liter
Butter	12.3 cents/liter	30.9 cents/liter
Fish	3% ad valorem	25% ad valorem
Saws	4% ad valorem	30% ad valorem
Cauliflower	10% ad valorem	50% ad valorem
Coffee	10% ad valorem	20% ad valorem
Woven fabrics	15.7% ad valorem	81% ad valorem
Babies' shirts	20.2% ad valorem	90% ad valorem
Gold necklaces	5% ad valorem	80% ad valorem

Source: U.S. International Trade Commission, *Harmonized Tariff Schedule of the United States* (Washington, DC: U.S. Government Printing Office, 2003).

General Agreement on Tariffs and Trade

Partly in response to trade disruptions during the Great Depression, the United States and some of its allies sought to impose order on trade flows after World War II. The first major postwar step toward liberalization of world trade was the **General Agreement on Tariffs and Trade (GATT)**, signed in 1947. GATT was crafted as an agreement among contracting parties, the member nations, to decrease trade barriers and to place all nations on an equal footing in trading relationships. GATT was never intended to become an organization; instead, it was a set of bilateral agreements among countries around the world to reduce trade barriers.

In 1995, GATT was transformed into the **World Trade Organization (WTO)**. The WTO embodies the main provisions of GATT, but its role was expanded to include a mechanism intended to improve GATT's process for resolving trade disputes among member nations. Let us first discuss the operation of the original GATT system.

The GATT System

GATT was based on several principles designed to foster more liberalized trade. One was *nondiscrimination*, embodying the principles of normal trade relations and *national treatment*. Under the normal trade relations principle, all member nations are bound to grant to each other treatment as favorable as they give to any nation with regard to trade matters. This allows comparative advantage to be the main determinant of trade patterns, which promotes global efficiency. There have been exceptions to the normal trade relations principle; for example, regional trade blocs (European Union, North American Free Trade Agreement) have been allowed. Under the national-treatment principle, member nations must treat other nations' industries no less favorably than they do their own domestic industries, once foreign goods have entered the domestic market; thus, in principle, domestic regulations and taxes cannot be biased against foreign products.

The GATT principle of nondiscrimination made trade liberalization a *public good*: What was produced by one nation in negotiation with another was available to all. This gave rise to the coordination problem shared by all public goods: that of getting each party to participate rather than sit back and let others do the liberalizing, thus free-riding on their efforts. A weakness of GATT trade negotiations from the 1940s to the 1970s was the limited number of nations that were actively negotiating participants; many nations—especially the developing nations—remained on the sidelines as free riders on others' liberalizations: They maintained protectionist policies to support domestic producers while realizing benefits from trade liberalization abroad.

Another aspect of GATT was its role in the settlement of trade disputes. Historically, trade disputes consisted of matters strictly between the disputants; no third party was available to which they might appeal for a favorable remedy. As a result, conflicts often remained unresolved for years, and when they were settled the stronger country generally won at the expense of the weaker country. GATT improved the dispute-resolution process by formulating complaint procedures and providing a conciliation panel to which a victimized country could express its grievance. GATT's dispute-settlement process, however, did not include the authority to enforce the conciliation panel's recommendations—a weakness that inspired the formation of the World Trade Organization.

GATT also obligated its members to use tariffs rather than quotas to protect their domestic industry. GATT's presumption was that quotas were inherently more trade distorting than tariffs because they allowed the user to discriminate between suppliers, were not predictable and transparent to the exporter, and imposed a maximum ceiling on imports. Here, too, there were exceptions to GATT's prohibition of quotas. Member nations could use quotas to safeguard their balance of payments, promote economic development, and allow the operation of domestic agricultural-support programs. Voluntary export-restraint agreements, which used quotas, also fell outside the quota restrictions of GATT because the agreements were voluntary.

Multilateral Trade Negotiations

GATT has also sponsored a series of negotiations, or rounds, to reduce tariffs and nontariff trade barriers, as summarized in Table 6.3. The first round of GATT negotiations, completed in 1947, achieved tariff reductions averaging 21 percent. However, tariff reductions were much smaller in the GATT rounds of the late 1940s and 1950s. During this period, protectionist pressures intensified in the United States as the war-damaged industries of Japan and Europe were reconstructed. Moreover, GATT negotiations emphasized *bilateral* bargaining (for example, between Canada and France) for tariff cuts on particular products, carried out concurrently by all of the participating nations. The process was slow and tedious, and nations often were unwilling to consider tariff cuts on many goods. A new approach to trade negotiations was thus considered desirable.

During the period 1964–1967, GATT members participated in the so-called **Kennedy Round** of trade negotiations, named after U.S. President John F. Kennedy, who issued an initiative calling for the negotiations. A *multilateral* meeting of GATT participants occurred at which the form of negotiations shifted from a product-by-product format to an across-the-board format. Tariffs were negotiated on broad categories of goods, and a given rate reduction applied to the entire group—a more streamlined approach. The Kennedy Round cut tariffs on manufactured goods by an average of 35 percent, to an average ad valorem level of 10.3 percent.

The GATT rounds from the 1940s to the 1960s focused almost entirely on tariff reduction. As average tariff rates in industrial nations decreased during the postwar period, the importance of nontariff barriers increased. In response to these changes, negotiators shifted emphasis to the issue of nontariff distortions in international trade.

At the **Tokyo Round** of 1973 to 1979, signatory nations agreed to tariff cuts that took the across-the-board form initiated in the Kennedy Round. The average tariff on manufactured goods of the nine major industrial countries was cut from 7.0 percent to 4.7 percent, a 40 percent decrease. Tariff reductions on finished products were deeper than those on raw materials, thus tending to decrease the extent of tariff escalation. After the Tokyo Round, tariffs were so low that they were not a significant barrier to trade in industrial countries. A second accomplishment of the Tokyo Round was the agreement to remove or

TABLE 6.3

GATT Negotiating Rounds

Negotiating Round and Coverage	Dates	Number of Participants	Tariff Cut Achieved (Percent)
Addressed Tariffs			
Geneva	1947	23	21%
Annecy	1949	13	2
Torquay	1951	38	3
Geneva	1956	26	4
Dillon Round	1960–1961	26	2
Kennedy Round	1964–1967	62	35
Addressed Tariff and Nontariff Barriers			
Tokyo Round	1973–1979	99	33
Uruguay Round	1986–1993	125	34
Doha Round	2002–	148	—

lessen many nontariff barriers. Codes of conduct were established in six areas: customs valuation, import licensing, government procurement, technical barriers to trade (such as product standards), antidumping procedures, and countervailing duties.

In spite of the trade liberalization efforts of the Tokyo Round, during the 1980s, world leaders felt that the GATT system was weakening. GATT members had increasingly used bilateral arrangements, such as voluntary export restraints, and other trade-distorting actions, such as subsidies, that stemmed from protectionist domestic policies. World leaders also felt that GATT needed to encompass additional areas, such as trade in intellectual property, services, and agriculture. They also wanted GATT to give increasing attention to the developing countries, who had felt bypassed by previous GATT rounds of trade negotiations.

These concerns led to the **Uruguay Round** from 1986 to 1993. As seen in Table 6.4, the Uruguay Round achieved across-the-board tariff cuts for industrial countries averaging 40 percent. Tariffs were eliminated entirely in several sectors, including steel, medical equipment, construction equipment,

pharmaceuticals, and paper. Also, many nations agreed for the first time to bind, or cap, a significant portion of their tariffs, giving up the possibility of future rate increases above the bound levels. Significant progress was also made by the Uruguay Round in decreasing or eliminating nontariff barriers. The government-procurement code opened a wider range of markets for signatory nations. The Uruguay Round tightened up on antidumping activity and made extensive efforts to eliminate quotas on agricultural products and required nations to rely instead on tariffs. In the apparel and textile sector, various bilateral quotas were to be phased out by 2005. The safeguards agreement prohibited the use of voluntary export restraints. Moreover, the Uruguay Round called for the transformation of GATT into a permanent international institution, the World Trade Organization, responsible for governing the conduct of trade relations among its members (see next section).

Although completion of the Uruguay Round was a notable achievement, many serious trade problems remained. The pact did not explicitly address the interface of trade policies with environmental and labor standards or the trade effects of

TABLE 6.4

Uruguay Round Tariff Reductions on Industrial Products by Selected Countries

Country	Average Tariff Rate (Percent)	
	Pre–Uruguay Round	Post–Uruguay Round
Industrial Countries		
Australia	20.1%	12.2%
Canada	9.0	4.8
European Union	5.7	3.6
Japan	3.9	1.7
United States	5.4	3.5
Developing Countries		
Argentina	38.2	30.9
Brazil	40.7	27.0
Chile	34.9	24.9
Colombia	44.3	35.3
India	71.4	32.4

Source: "Uruguay Round Outcome Strengthens Framework for Trade Relations," *IMF Survey,* November 14, 1994, p. 355.

domestic policies, such as competition and investment policy. Moreover, there was the tendency for the global economy to become segregated into three major trading blocs: the European Union; the North American Free Trade Area; and a bloc that included Southeast Asian countries, Japan, and possibly Australia. Although regional trading blocs promote free trade among member countries, potentially they can lead to additional bilateral deals and interbloc trade disputes.

World Trade Organization

On January 1, 1995, the day on which the Uruguay Round took effect, GATT was transformed into the World Trade Organization. This transformation turned GATT from a trade accord into a membership organization, responsible for governing the conduct of trade relations among its members. GATT obligations remain at the core of the WTO. However, the WTO agreement requires that its members adhere not only to GATT rules, but also to the broad range of trade pacts that have been negotiated under GATT auspices in recent decades. This undertaking ends the free ride of many GATT members (especially developing countries) that benefited from, but refused to join, new agreements negotiated in GATT since the 1970s.

How different is the WTO from the old GATT? The WTO is a full-fledged international organization, headquartered in Geneva, Switzerland; the old GATT was basically a provisional treaty serviced by an ad hoc secretariat. The WTO has a far wider scope than the old GATT, bringing into the multilateral trading system, for the first time, trade in services, intellectual property, and investment. The WTO also administers a unified package of agreements to which all members are committed; in contrast, the GATT framework included many side agreements (for example, antidumping measures and subsidies) whose membership was limited to a few nations. Moreover, the WTO reverses policies of protection in certain "sensitive" areas (for example, agriculture and textiles) that were more or less tolerated in the old GATT. The WTO is not a government; individual nations remain free to set their own appropriate levels of environment, labor, health, and safety protections.

Through various councils and committees, the WTO administers the many agreements contained in the Uruguay Round, plus agreements on government procurement and civil aircraft. It oversees the implementation of the tariff cuts and reduction of nontariff measures agreed to in the negotiations. It is also a watchdog of international trade, regularly examining the trade regimes of individual members. In its various bodies, members flag proposed or draft measures by others that can cause trade conflicts. Members are also required to update various trade measures and statistics, which are maintained by the WTO in a large database.

Settling Trade Disputes

A major objective of the WTO was strengthening the GATT mechanism for settling trade disputes. The old GATT dispute mechanism suffered from long delays, the ability of accused parties to block decisions of GATT panels that went against them, and inadequate enforcement. The dispute-settlement mechanism of the WTO addresses each of these weaknesses. It guarantees the formation of a dispute panel once a case is brought and sets time limits for each stage of the process. The decision of the panel may be taken to a newly created appellate body, but the accused party can no longer block the final decision. The dispute-settlement issue was especially important to the United States because this nation was the most frequent user of the GATT dispute mechanism.

The first case settled by the WTO involved a dispute between the United States and several other countries.[1] In 1994, the U.S. government adopted a regulation imposing certain conditions on the quality of the gasoline sold in the United States. The aim of this resolution, established by the Environmental Protection Agency (EPA) under the Clean Air Act, was to improve air quality by reducing pollution caused by gasoline emissions. The regulation set different pollution standards for domestic and imported gasolines. It was challenged before the WTO by Venezuela and later by Brazil.

[1] Drawn from World Trade Organization, *Solving Trade Disputes*, Geneva, Switzerland, 1999.

According to Venezuelan officials, there was a violation of the WTO's principle of national treatment, which suggests that once imported gasoline is on the U.S. market it cannot receive treatment less favorable than domestically produced gasoline. Venezuela argued that its gasoline was being submitted to controls and standards much more rigorous than those imposed on gasoline produced in the United States.

The United States argued that this discrimination was justified under WTO rules. The United States maintained that clean air is an exhaustible resource and that it was justified under WTO rules to preserve it. It also claimed that its pollution regulations were necessary to protect human health, which is also allowed by the WTO. The major condition is that these provisions should not be protectionism in disguise.

Venezuela refuted that argument. Venezuela was in no way questioning the right of the United States to impose high environmental standards. But it said that if the United States wanted clean gasoline then it should have submitted both the domestic and imported gasolines to the same high standards.

The new regulations put in place by the United States had an important impact for Venezuela and for its gasoline producers. Venezuela maintained that producing the gasoline according to the EPA's double standard was much more expensive than if Venezuela had followed the same specifications as American producers. Moreover, the U.S. market was critically important for Venezuela because two-thirds of Venezuela's gasoline exports were sold to the United States.

When Venezuela realized that the discriminatory aspects of the American gasoline regime would not be modified by the United States, it brought the case to the WTO. Brazil also complained about the discriminatory aspect of U.S. regulation. The two complaints were heard by a WTO panel, which ruled in 1996 that the United States unjustly discriminated against imported gasoline. When the United States appealed this ruling, a WTO appellate board confirmed the findings of the panel. The United States agreed to cease its discriminatory actions against imported gasoline by revising its environmental laws. Venezuela and Brazil were satisfied by the action of the United States.

Does the WTO Reduce National Sovereignty?

Do WTO rules or dispute settlements reduce the sovereignty of the United States or other countries? The United States benefits from WTO dispute settlement by having a set of rules to hold other countries accountable for their trade actions. At the same time, the U.S. government was careful to structure the WTO dispute-settlement rules to preserve the rights of Americans. Nevertheless, critics on both the left and right, such as Ralph Nader and Patrick Buchanan, contend that by participating in the WTO the United States has seriously undermined its sovereignty.

However proponents note that the findings of a WTO dispute-settlement panel cannot force the United States to change its laws. Only the United States determines exactly how it will respond to the recommendations of a WTO panel, if at all. If a U.S. measure is found to be in violation of a WTO provision, the United States may on its own decide to change the law; compensate a foreign country by lowering our trade barriers of equivalent amount in another sector; or do nothing and possibly undergo retaliation by the affected country in the form of increased barriers to U.S. exports of an equivalent amount. But the United States retains full sovereignty in its decision of whether or not to implement a panel recommendation. Simply put, WTO agreements do not preclude the United States from establishing and maintaining its own laws or limit the ability of the United States to set its environmental, labor, health, and safety standards at the level it considers appropriate. However, the WTO does not allow a nation to use trade restrictions to enforce its own environmental, labor, health, and safety standards when they have selective and discriminatory effects against foreign producers.

Most trade-dispute rulings of the WTO are resolved amicably, without resorting to retaliatory trade barriers. However, retaliation is sometimes used. For example, in 1999 the United States won its hormone-treated beef and banana cases in which the WTO ruled that the European Union unfairly restricted imports of these products. The WTO thus authorized the U.S. government to raise tariffs on European exports to the United States. After a prolonged struggle, the banana dispute was resolved, but the European Union has steadfastly refused to revise its policy on hormone-treated beef. The chance that the European Union will accept U.S. hormone-treated beef appears dim.

Economists generally agree that the real issue raised by the WTO is not whether it decreases national sovereignty, but whether the specific obligations that it imposes on a nation are greater or less than the benefits the nation receives from applying the same requirements to others (along with itself). According to this standard, the benefits of the United States of joining the WTO greatly exceed the costs. By granting the United States the status of normal trade relations with all 148 members, the agreement improves U.S. access to foreign markets. Moreover, it reduces the ability of other nations to impose restrictions to limit access to their markets. If the United States withdrew from the WTO, it would lose the ability to use the WTO mechanism to induce other nations to decrease their own trade barriers, and thus would harm U.S. exporting firms and their workers. Simply put, economists generally contend that the WTO puts some constraints on the decision making of the private and public sectors. But the costs of these constraints are outweighed by the economic benefits that citizens derive from freer trade.

Should Retaliatory Tariffs Be Used for WTO Enforcement?

However, critics contend that the WTO's dispute-settlement system based on tariff retaliation places smaller countries, without much market power, at a disadvantage. Suppose that Ecuador, a small country, receives WTO authorization to retaliate against unfair trade practices of the United States, a large country. With competitive conditions, if Ecuador applies a higher tariff to imports from the United States, its national welfare will decrease, as explained in Chapter 4. Therefore, Ecuador may be reluctant to impose a retaliatory tariff even though it has the approval of the WTO.

However, for countries large enough to affect prices in world markets, the issue is less clear. This is because a retaliatory tariff may improve a large country's terms of trade, thus enhancing its national welfare. If the United States raises a tariff barrier, it reduces the demand for the product on world markets. The decreased demand makes imports less expensive for the United States so that to pay for these imports, the United States can export less. The terms of trade (ratio of export prices to import prices) thus improves for the United States. This offsets at least some of the welfare reductions that take place through less efficiency due to increasing the tariff.

Simply put, although a small country could decide to impose retaliatory tariffs to teach a larger trading partner a lesson, it will find such behavior relatively more costly to initiate than its larger trading partner because it cannot obtain favorable movements in its terms of trade. The limited market power of small countries thus makes them less likely to induce compliance to WTO rulings through retaliation. However, the problems smaller nations face in retaliating are the opposite of the special benefits they gain in obtaining WTO tariff concessions without being required to make reciprocal concessions.

Some maintain that the WTO's current dispute-settlement system should be modified. For example, free traders object to retaliatory tariffs on the grounds that the WTO's purpose is to reduce trade barriers. Instead, they propose that offending countries should be assessed monetary fines. A system of fines has the advantage of avoiding additional trade protection and not placing smaller countries at a disadvantage. However, this system encounters the problem of deciding how to place a monetary value on violations. Also, fines might be difficult to collect because the offending country's government would have to initiate specific budgetary authorization. Moreover, the notion of accepting an obligation to allow foreigners to levy monetary fines on a nation such as the United States would likely be criticized as taxation without representation, and the

WTO would be attacked as undermining national sovereignty.

U.S. export subsidies provide an example of retaliatory tariffs authorized by the WTO. From 1984 to 2004, the U.S. tax code provided a tax benefit that enabled American exporters to exempt between 15 percent and 30 percent of their export income from U.S. taxes. In 1998, the European Union lodged a complaint with the WTO, arguing that the U.S. tax benefit was an export subsidy in violation of WTO agreements. This led to the WTO's ruling in 2003 that the tax benefit was illegal and that the European Union could immediately impose $4 billion in punitive duties on U.S. exports to Europe. Although the European Union gave the U.S. government time to eliminate its export subsidy program, inertia resulted in continuation of the program. Therefore, the Europeans began implementing retaliatory tariffs in 2004. A 5 percent penalty tariff was levied on U.S. exports such as jewelry and refrigerators, toys, and paper. The penalty climbed by 1 percentage point for each month that U.S. lawmakers failed to bring U.S. tax laws in line with the WTO ruling. This marked the first time that the United States came under WTO penalties for failure to adhere to its rulings. Although some in Congress resisted surrendering to the WTO on anything, the pressure provided by the tariffs convinced Congress to repeal the export subsidies.

Does the WTO Harm the Environment?

In recent years, the debate has intensified on the links between trade and the environment, and the role the WTO should play in promoting environment-friendly trade. A central concern of those who have raised the profile of this issue in the WTO is that there are circumstances where trade and the pursuit of trade liberalization may have harmful environmental effects. Indeed, these concerns were voiced when thousands of environmentalists descended on the World Trade Organization summit in Seattle in 1999. They protested the WTO's influence on everything from marine destruction to global warming. Let us consider the opposing views on the links between trade and the environment.[2]

Harming the Environment

Two main arguments are forwarded as to how trade liberalization may harm the environment. First, trade liberalization leads to a "race to the bottom" in environmental standards. If some countries have low environmental standards, industry is likely to shift production of environment-intensive or highly polluting products to such pollution havens. Trade liberalization can make the shift of smokestack industries across borders to pollution havens even more attractive. If these industries then create pollution with global adverse effects, trade liberalization can, indirectly, promote environmental degradation. Worse, trade-induced competitive pressure may force countries to lower their environmental standards, thus encouraging trade in products creating global pollution.

Why would developing nations adopt less stringent environmental policies than industrial nations? Poorer nations may place a higher priority on the benefits of production (more jobs and income) relative to the benefits of environmental quality than wealthy nations. Moreover, developing nations may have greater environmental capacities to reduce pollutants by natural processes (such as Latin America's rain-forest capacity to reduce carbon dioxide in the air) than do industrial nations that suffer from the effects of past pollution. Developing nations can thus tolerate higher levels of emissions without increasing pollution levels. Finally, the introduction of a polluting industry into a sparsely populated developing nation will likely have less impact on the capacity of the environment to reduce pollution by natural processes than it would have in a densely populated industrial nation.

A second concern of environmentalists about the role of trade relates to social preferences. Some practices may simply be unacceptable for certain people or societies, so they oppose trade

---

[2]World Trade Organization, *Annual Report*, Geneva, Switzerland, 1998, pp. 54–55, and "Greens Target WTO's Plan for Lumber," *The Wall Street Journal*, November 24, 1999, pp. A2 and A4.

in products that encourage such practices. These can include killing dolphins in the process of catching tuna and using leghold traps for catching animals for their furs. During the 1990s, relations between environmentalists and the WTO clashed when the WTO ruled against a U.S. ban on imports of shrimp from countries using nets that trap turtles, after complaints by India, Malaysia, Pakistan, and Thailand. Also, the United States was found guilty of violating world trade law when it banned imports of Mexican tuna caught in ways that drown dolphins. Indeed, critics maintained that the free-trade policies of the WTO contradicted the goal of environmental quality.

To most economists, any measure that liberalizes trade enhances productivity and growth, puts downward pressure on inflation by increasing competition, and creates jobs. In Japan, tariffs are so high on imported finished-wood products that U.S. firms don't have much market there. High local prices limit domestic demand in Japan. But if tariffs were abolished, demand for lumber products from the United States could surge, creating additional logging jobs in the United States and additional import-related jobs in Japan.

But environmentalists view the tariff elimination differently. Their main concern is that a non-tariff market, which would result in lower prices, will stimulate so much demand that logging will intensify in the world's remaining ancient forests, which they say serve as habitat for complex ecosystems that otherwise cannot survive intact in forests that have been cut into fragments. Such old forests still exist across much of Alaska, Canada, and Russia's Siberian region. Environmentalists note that in Pennsylvania, New York, and other states in the Northeast, the forests have been so chopped up that many large predators have been driven from the land, leaving virtually no check on the deer population. Therefore, deer are in a state of overpopulation.

However, trade liberalization proponents play down the adverse impacts, arguing that reduced tariffs would boost world economies by decreasing the cost of housing, paper, and other products made from wood, while actually helping forest conditions. For example, timber officials in the United States say they could go into a country like Indonesia and persuade local firms to adopt more conservation-minded techniques.

Improving the Environment

On the other hand, it is argued that trade liberalization may improve the quality of the environment rather than promote degradation. First, trade stimulates economic growth, and growing prosperity is one of the key factors in societies' demand for a cleaner environment. As people get richer, they want a cleaner environment—and they acquire the means to pay for it. Granted, trade can increase the cost of the wrong environmental policies. If farmers freely pollute rivers, for instance, higher agricultural exports will increase pollution. But the solution to this is not to shut off exports: It is to impose tougher environmental laws that make polluters pay.

Second, trade and growth can encourage the development and dissemination of environment-friendly production techniques as the demand for cleaner products grows and trade increases the size of markets. International companies may also contribute to a cleaner environment by using the most modern and environmentally clean technology in all their operations. This is less costly than using differentiated technology based on the location of production and helps companies to maintain a good reputation.

Although there is no dispute that in theory intensified competition could give rise to pollution havens, the empirical evidence suggests that it has not happened on a significant scale. The main reason is that the costs imposed by environmental regulation are small relative to other cost considerations, so this factor is unlikely to be at the basis of relocation decisions. The U.S. Census Bureau finds that even the most polluting industries spend no more than 2 percent of their revenues on abating pollution. Other factors such as labor costs, transportation costs, and the adequacy of infrastructure are much more important. For all the talk of a race to the bottom, there is no evidence for a race to the bottom—a competitive lowering of environmental standards.

WTO Rulings Outrage Environmentalists

The protection of dolphins and sea turtles, which are playful and harmless, has received much sympathy in the United States. However, protecting these creatures has threatened the methods used to catch tuna and shrimp. Let's see how the environmentalists' goal of protecting dolphins and sea turtles clashed with the free-trade goal of the WTO.

For many years, fisheries in the Eastern Tropical Pacific have found tuna by looking for dolphins—surface-swimming dolphins that travel above schools of tuna. A net drawn around the dolphins catches the tuna and the dolphins. However, as the nets draw tight underwater, the dolphins, being mammals, drown.

To environmentalists, saving the dolphins is a matter of environmental and moral consciousness. As a result, the United States passed the Marine Mammals Protection Act of 1972. The act outlawed the setting of nets on dolphins by U.S. tuna fisheries anywhere in the world; it also outlawed this method for foreign fisheries in U.S. waters, out to a 200-mile limit. However, the law did not apply to foreigners catching tuna outside U.S. waters.

Across the border in Mexico, saving dolphins meant losing business and jobs for tuna fisheries. They maintained that they had to catch enough tuna to justify a fishing expedition. To do so required them to use the most efficient methods of fishing, even if they were unsafe for dolphins. Mexican fisheries were thus unwilling to refrain from setting nets on dolphins.

To convince Mexico to use dolphin-safe methods of catching tuna, the U.S. government pressured three major tuna retailing firms in the United States (Bumble Bee, Chicken of the Sea, and StarKist) to refuse to purchase tuna from fisheries using dolphin-unsafe methods. These tuna retailers responded with "dolphin-safe" tuna labels to steer concerned shoppers to tuna caught without setting nets on dolphins. But the force of the marketplace, said environmentalists, wasn't enough. They insisted on the force of law.

In 1991, the U.S. government slapped an embargo on tuna imports from Mexico and four other countries. Mexico immediately complained to the WTO (then known as GATT). The U.S. embargo, Mexico argued, violated the WTO agreement against restricting trade through dis-

Is the Kyoto Protocol a Lot of "Hot Air"?

As we have learned, global warming is a highly controversial issue. Although the earth does undergo periodic warming and cooling trends, environmentalists are concerned that the current warming trend seems to have progressed much more quickly than previous warming trends. They hypothesize that the increased warming rate is due to a larger amount of carbon dioxide that has been emitted into the atmosphere in the past 200 years. Combustion of fossil fuels, such as coal and oil, paired with deforestation are the main reasons for so much carbon dioxide in the atmosphere. Environmentalists estimate that as a result of the increase in the combustion of fossil fuels, carbon dioxide levels in the atmosphere will double in the next 25 years, causing the earth's temperature to increase by 2 to 4 degrees. One of the most feared consequences of a global warming is a rise in sea level that could flood low-lying areas and damage the economy of coastal nations.

In 1997, representatives from almost 180 nations met in Kyoto, Japan, to discuss a global strategy for a reduction in the emission of greenhouse gases. The intent of the treaty was that although the costs of unabated climate change may be difficult to quantify, it is necessary to provide a meaningful incentive for countries to lower their emissions of carbon dioxide and other greenhouse gases. The logic was that the effort must be global in nature, as otherwise individual nations would not have the proper motivation for lowering their consumption of fossil fuels.

criminatory action. Application of the embargo was against the free-trade principles of the WTO, according to Mexico. But the United States denied that the tuna embargo discriminated against Mexico. Even though the United States was embargoing certain countries, and not embargoing others, the United States was embargoing on objective criteria that applied to all countries, according to the United States.

In 1991, the WTO decided in favor of Mexico and upheld its prohibition of policies that exclude imports according to how they are produced. The WTO ruled that the United States, by levying an embargo only against Mexico and four other countries, was in the breach of the rule of nondiscrimination. The embargo, said the WTO, hurt not only the tuna industry but the ultimate beneficiary of free trade, the consumer, as well. Simply put, WTO does not allow a nation to use trade restrictions to enforce its own environmental laws when they have selective and discriminatory effects on foreign producers.

Another case involves sea turtles, an endangered specie. Nations such as Thailand, Malaysia, India, and Pakistan have often caught shrimp with nets that trap and kill an estimated 150,000 sea turtles each year. The U.S. Endangered Species Act, passed in 1989, mandated that shrimpers in U.S. waters include devices in their nets to exclude turtles; it also placed embargoes on imports of shrimp from nations that do not protect sea turtles from deadly entrapment in nets. Four Asian nations, who were unwilling to equip their nets, filed a complaint with the WTO in 1997 that claimed that the U.S. Endangered Species Act was an illegal trade barrier. Ruling in favor of these nations, the WTO said that the United States could not use trade policy to force other nations to adopt environmental policies to protect endangered species. Following this decision, the United States reached agreements with these nations to use turtle-excluding nets, and the United States provided financial and technical assistance in how to use them.

Indeed, environmentalists have been outraged by some decisions of the WTO. They maintain that too often the WTO is blindly for free trade at any cost.

The representatives agreed to a 5.2 percent average reduction from 1990 global pollution levels by the year 2012, subject to ratification by their governments. Because the United States has been the largest contributor of global emissions, the treaty would commit the United States to a target of reducing greenhouse gases by 7 percent below 1990 levels.

Although 84 countries had signed the Kyoto Protocol by 2001, the treaty takes effect only after ratification by countries that produced 55 percent of the included industrialized nations' greenhouse gas emissions in 1990. The United States, the world's biggest polluter, rejected the treaty: It is responsible for about one-fourth of the world's greenhouse gasses—chiefly carbon dioxide from cars, power plants, and factories. The United States indicated that it favored a different approach to controlling emissions based on voluntary measures and market mechanisms. President George W. Bush noted that as the world proceeds on a path of ever-greater energy efficiency, and as low-cost fuels become depleted and thus more costly, increases in the global level of carbon dioxide will moderate. Therefore, global temperature forecasts of environmentalists are exaggerated. Moreover, it is not certain that meeting the targets of the Kyoto Protocol would reduce greenhouse emissions by an amount necessary to prevent further global warming.

Of particular concern to the United States was sharply higher prices for energy and electricity that would occur because of the Kyoto Protocol. As the United States reduced emissions to meet the target of the treaty, gasoline prices would rise by an esti-mated 65 cents per gallon, and industrial gas and electricity prices would double. The United States would lose more than 2.4 million jobs in energy-intensive industries such as autos, steel, paper, and chemicals, and family income would fall by an average of $2,700. Put simply, the Kyoto Protocol would impose a heavy burden on every U.S. household and industry, including agriculture.

Also, the Kyoto Protocol would give develop-ing countries a competitive advantage over the United States and other industrial countries. This is because none of the developing countries, including those with large and growing emissions such as India and China, are required to limit their emissions. As a result, energy and energy-related costs would become much higher in the United States than in countries that do not adhere to the same emission limits. This would increase the costs of companies in the United States relative to their foreign competitors, thus promoting competitive disadvantage.

Moreover, even if the United States sharply reduced its emissions unilaterally without an inter-national agreement limiting emissions abroad, emissions from developing countries will grow as they realize increases in population and economic growth. As countries like India and China bring dozens of new coal-fired power plants on line each year, their emissions of carbon dioxide will grow greater and greater. By not holding developing countries accountable for their emissions, the goals of the Kyoto Protocol may not be achieved.

The Doha Round of Trade Negotiations

Although the WTO attempts to foster trade liberal-ization, achieving it can be difficult. Let us see why.

In 1998, members of the WTO accepted President Bill Clinton's invitation to come to Seattle, Washington, and kick off a new round of trade negotiations for a new century. The participants attempted to establish an agenda for negotiations that included trade in agriculture, intellectual prop-erty rights, labor and environmental matters, and help for the lesser-developed countries. However,

the Seattle meetings marked the debut of the devel-oping nations as highly organized and assertive par-ticipants pursuing their own trade agendas. Believing that they had been taken to the cleaners in previous rounds of trade negotiations, the develop-ing nations were determined not to allow that to occur again. Disagreements among developing countries and industrial countries were a major fac-tor that resulted in a breakdown of the meetings. The meeting became known as "The Battle in Seattle" because of the rioting and disruption that took place in the streets during the meeting.

Although trade liberalization proponents were discouraged by the collapse of the Seattle meeting, they continued to press for another round of trade talks. The result was a WTO sum-mit meeting of 2001, which took place in Doha, Qatar. The meeting resulted in trade ministers' agreeing to launch a new round of talks that could keep the global economy on track toward freer trade and investment.

The rhetoric of the Doha summit was elabo-rate: Doha would decrease trade-distorting farm support, cut tariffs on farm goods, and eliminate agricultural-export subsidies; it would slash industrial tariffs, especially in areas that poor countries cared about, such as textiles; it would free up trade in services; and it would negotiate global rules in four new areas—in competition, investment, transparency in government procure-ment, and trade facilitation. Table 6.5 summa-rizes the major provisions of the Doha summit.

The Doha round was formally called the "Doha development agenda." This is because the majority of the WTO's 148 members rank as medium-to-low income, developing countries. These nations have the highest trade barriers and the most difficulty meeting existing obligations of the WTO. The developing countries would benefit significantly from liberalization of remaining trade barriers in the United States, Japan, and Europe, as well as reform of their own trade restrictions. By characterizing the talks in this manner, however, officials created the impression that the negotia-tions were solely about what the developed coun-tries should do for developing ones, and not what developing countries needed to do to promote their own economic development. The emphasis

TABLE 6.5

Likely Winners and Losers from a Successful Completion of the Doha Agenda

The agreement of 148 countries in Doha, Qatar, to start a new round of global trade negotiations is still years away. Here's an early look at the potential impact.

Trade Issue	Winners	Losers
Public health trumps patents	AIDS patients in Africa	Drug companies of the United States and Europe
Agricultural subsidies to be phased out	Farmers in developing countries	European and Japanese farmers
U.S. refuses to import more textiles from developing countries	U.S. textile companies	Pakistani textile producers
U.S. antidumping laws up for negotiation	Foreign steelmakers	U.S. steelmakers

on development inspired many developing countries to justify their demands for new concessions by arguing that they had paid too much in previous trade talks and had gotten nothing in return; now it was payback time.

In 2003, WTO participants convened in Cancun, Mexico, to consider principles for taking the Doha agenda forward. From the start, countries disowned major portions of the agenda. The European Union, for example, denied it had ever promised to get rid of export subsidies. Led by India, many poor countries denied that they ever signed up for talks on new rules regarding intellectual property and competition policy. Other poor countries spent more time complaining about their grievances over earlier trade rounds than they did in negotiating the new one. Several rich countries showed little interest in compromise. Japan, for example, appeared content simply to reject any cuts in rice tariffs. This kind of posturing resulted in self-imposed deadlines being missed and all tough political decisions regarding opening economies to trade being put off.

Agriculture cropped up as an especially "hot potato" for trade negotiators. Although average tariffs on manufactured goods have decreased from 40 percent to 4 percent over the past 50 years, agri-

cultural tariffs have remained at about 40 percent. Australia and Argentina, with comparative advantages in many agricultural products, want free trade in farming. However, it is the European Union and Japan, with many small, highly subsidized and massively inefficient farmers, that find every step to freer farm trade distasteful. Even the United States, which publically advocates freer trade in agriculture, provides considerable protection for farmers. The developing countries demanded that rich countries, as the most dominant subsidizers of agricultural products, should slash subsidies and free farm trade. However, Europe, Japan, and the United States were unwilling to roll back their agricultural subsidies.

Another sticking point of the Cancun meetings was Europe's obsession with trade and the environment. Although Europeans say that they simply want to clarify the existing environmental rules of the WTO, the United States fears that Europe may press for more stringent rules that impose harsh costs on the U.S. economy. Moreover, developing countries worry that the Europeans want to use environmental issues as a back door to protectionism. If Europe is obliged to lower agricultural trade barriers, it will simply keep out food products by finding some "green" objection to them.

The failure of the Cancun meetings did not necessarily mean that the Doha trade round is dead. The Uruguay Round took eight years before it succeeded in 1993. However, achieving a final agreement on these contentious issues will be difficult. But if a multilateral agreement cannot be reached under the auspices of the WTO, the alternative is regional and bilateral agreements that are easier to achieve, but offer far less scope. Following the Cancun meetings, the United States, China, Japan, and India hinted that they would likely engage more aggressively in negotiating regional trade agreements, a topic that will be further discussed in Chapter 8 of this text.

Trade Promotion Authority (Fast-Track Authority)

If international trade agreements were subject to congressional amendments, achieving such pacts would be arduous, if not hopeless. The provisions that had been negotiated by the president would soon be modified by a deluge of congressional amendments, which would quickly meet the disapproval of the trading partner, or partners, that had accepted the original terms.

To prevent this scenario, the mechanism of **trade promotion authority** (also known as **fast-track authority**) was devised in 1974. Under this provision, the president must formally notify Congress of his or her intent to enter trade negotiations with another country. This notification starts a clock in which Congress has 60 legislative days to permit or deny "fast-track" authority. If fast-track authority is approved, the president has a limited time period in which to complete the trade negotiations; extensions of this time period are permissible with congressional approval. Once the negotiations are completed, their outcome is subject only to a straight up-or-down vote (without amendment) in both houses of the Congress within 90 legislative days of submission. In return, the president agrees to consult actively with Congress and the private sector throughout the negotiation of the trade agreement.

Fast-track authority was instrumental in negotiating and implementing major trade agreements such as the Uruguay Round Agreements Act of 1994 and the North American Free Trade Agreement of 1993. Most analysts contend that the implementation of future trade agreements will require fast-track authority for the president. Efforts to renew fast-track authority have faced stiff opposition, largely due to congressional concerns about delegating too much discretionary authority to the president and disagreements over the goals of U.S. trade negotiations. In particular, labor unions and environmentalists have sought to ensure that trade agreements will address their concerns. They believe that high labor and environmental standards in the United States put American producers at a competitive disadvantage and that increased trade with countries with lax standards may lead to pressure to lower U.S. standards. If other countries are to trade with the United States, shouldn't they have similar labor and environmental standards?

Supporters of fast-track authority have generally argued that, although labor and environmental standards are important, they do not belong in a trade agreement. Instead, these issues should be negotiated through secondary agreements that accompany a trade agreement. However, labor leaders and environmentalists contend that past secondary agreements have lacked enforcement provisions and thus have done little to improve the quality of life abroad.

The Escape Clause (Safeguards)

In addition to the WTO's addressing unfair trade practices, the United States itself has adopted a series of **trade remedy laws** designed to produce a fair trading environment for all parties engaging in international business. These laws include the escape clause, countervailing duties, antidumping duties, and unfair trading practices. Table 6.6 summarizes the provisions of the U.S. trade remedy laws, which are discussed in the following sections.

The **escape clause** is intended to provide **safeguards** (relief) to U.S. firms and workers desiring protection from surges in imports. In an escape-clause case, it makes no difference whether the

TABLE 6.6

Trade Remedy Law Provisions

Statute	Focus	Criteria for Action	Response
Fair trade (escape clause)	Increasing imports	Increasing imports are substantial cause of injury	Duties, quotas, tariff-rate quotas, orderly marketing arrangements, adjustment assistance
Subsidized imports (countervailing duty)	Manufacturing production, or export subsidies	Material injury or threat of material injury	Duties
Dumped imports (antidumping duty)	Imports sold below cost of production or below foreign market price	Material injury or threat of material injury	Duties
Unfair trade (Section 301)	Foreign practices violating a trade agreement or injurious to U.S. trade	Unjustifiable, unreasonable, or discriminatory practices, burdensome to U.S. commerce	All appropriate and feasible action

imports are fairly or unfairly traded. All that matters is whether imports are a substantial cause of serious injury (or threat thereof) to the domestic industry. The escape clause allows the president to terminate or make modifications in trade concessions granted foreign nations and to levy restrictions on surging imports. Safeguards provided by the escape clause are temporary: Trade restrictions can be enacted for a 3-year period and are to be phased down over this period in the transition to open markets. The idea is to give the domestic industry time to adjust, after which competition will be allowed to resume.

An escape-clause action is initiated by a petition from an American industry or the president of the United States to the U.S. International Trade Commission (USITC), which investigates and recommends a response to the president. An affirmative decision by the USITC is reported to the president, who determines what remedy, if any, is in the national interest. Table 6.7 on page 192 provides examples of safeguards granted to U.S. businesses under the escape clause.

Countervailing Duties

As consumers, we tend to appreciate the low prices of foreign subsidized steel. But foreign export subsidies are resented by import-competing producers, who must charge higher prices because they do not receive such subsidies. From their point of view, the export subsidies give foreign producers an unfair competitive advantage.

As viewed by the World Trade Organization, export subsidies constitute unfair competition. Importing countries can retaliate by levying a **countervailing duty**. The size of the duty is limited to the amount of the foreign export subsidy. Its purpose is to increase the price of the imported good to its fair market value.

Upon receipt of a petition by a U.S. industry or firm, the U.S. Department of Commerce conducts a preliminary investigation as to whether or not an export subsidy was given to a foreign supplier. If the preliminary investigation finds a reasonable indication of an export subsidy, U.S. importers must immediately pay a special tariff

TABLE 6.7

Safeguard Relief Granted Under the Escape Clause: Selected Examples

Product	Type of Relief
Porcelain-on-steel cooking ware	Additional duties imposed for 4 years of 20 cents, 20 cents, 15 cents, and 10 cents per pound in the first, second, third, and fourth years, respectively
Prepared or preserved mushrooms	Additional duties imposed for 3 years of 20%, 15%, and 10% ad valorem in the first, second, and third years, respectively
High-carbon ferrochromium	Temporary duty increase
Color TV receivers	Orderly marketing agreements with Taiwan and Korea
Footwear	Orderly marketing agreements with Taiwan and Korea

Source: *Annual Report of the President of the United States on the Trade Agreements Program* (Washington, DC: U.S. Government Printing Office, various issues).

(equal to the estimated subsidy margin) on all imports of the product in question. The Commerce Department then conducts a final investigation to determine whether an export subsidy was in fact granted, as well as the amount of the subsidy. If it determines that there was no export subsidy, the special tariff is rebated to the U.S. importers. Otherwise, the case is investigated by the U.S. International Trade Commission, which determines if the import-competing industry suffered material injury as a result of the subsidy.[3] If both the Commerce Department and the International Trade Commission rule in favor of the subsidy petition, a permanent countervailing duty is imposed that equals the size of the subsidy margin calculated by the Commerce Department in its final investigation. Once the foreign nation stops subsidizing exports of that product, the countervailing duty is removed.

[3]For those nations that are signatories to the WTO Subsidy Code, the International Trade Commission must determine that their export subsidies have injured U.S. producers before countervailing duties are imposed. The export subsidies of nonsignatory nations are subject to countervailing duties immediately following the Commerce Department's determination of their occurrence; the International Trade Commission does not have to make an injury determination.

Lumber Quotas Hammer Home Buyers

Let us consider a countervailing-duty case involving the U.S. lumber industry. During the 1980s and 1990s, the United States and Canada quarreled over softwood lumber. The stakes were enormous: Canadian firms exported more than $7 billion worth of lumber annually to U.S. customers. This dollar value of U.S. lumber imports from Canada almost equaled that of its steel imports from the rest of the world!

The lumber dispute followed a repetitive pattern. First, some U.S. lumber producers accused their Canadian rivals of receiving government subsidies. In particular, they alleged that the Canadians paid unfairly low tree-cutting fees to harvest timber from lands owned by the Canadian government. In the United States, companies bid years in advance for the right to cut trees in government forests. Because the tree-cutting fees are fixed, the companies must forecast their prices accurately in order to ensure profitability. By contrast, Canadian regulations permit provincial governments to reduce their tree-cutting fees when lumber prices decline so as to keep their sawmills profitable. U.S. sawmill operators maintain that this practice subsidizes the Canadian lumber mills. However, the Canadians responded that their timber-pricing policies were not market-distorting, and they generally won on the technical merits. Despite losing those battles, the American lumber lobby usually ended up winning the war: Their relentless political pressure forced Canada to accept some form of trade restraint just to ensure commercial peace.

For example, in 1996, the Coalition for Fair Lumber Imports, a group of U.S. sawmill companies, filed a countervailing-duty petition with the U.S. government charging that domestic producers were hurt by subsidized lumber exports from Canada. The complaint ultimately led to the Softwood Lumber Agreement of 1996, which established a tariff-rate quota to protect U.S. producers. Up to 14.7 billion board feet of Canadian softwood lumber exports from Canada to the United States could enter duty free. The next 0.65 billion board feet of exports was subject to a tariff of $50 per thousand board feet. The Canadian government also agreed to raise the tree-cutting fees it charged provincial producers. As a result of the trade agreement, lumber imports to the United States fell about 14 percent.

Proponents of the accord maintained that it created a "level playing field" in which American lumber companies and Canadian lumber companies could compete. However, critics argued that the trade pact failed to take into account the interests of American lumber users in the lumber-dealing, homebuilding, and home-furnishing industries. It also overlooked the interests of American buyers of new homes and home furnishings according to the critics.

In the United States, a coalition of lumber users—including Home Depot, the National Association of Home Builders, and the National Lumber and Building Material Dealers Association—banded together to protest the lumber quotas. They noted that the trade restrictions increased the price of lumber between 20 percent and 35 percent, or $50–$80 per thousand board feet. Therefore, the cost of the average new home increased between $800 and $1,300 because of the restrictions. Moreover, every $1,000 increase

in housing prices means that an additional 300,000 families are unable to buy a home. The lumber quotas thus served as a tax that kept the dream of home ownership out of reach for many lower-income Americans.

Critics acknowledged that barriers against Canadian lumber imports would benefit some U.S. lumber producers and their workers. But in 2000, there were only 217,000 American jobs in logging and sawmills. That figure compared to 510,000 jobs in lumber-using manufacturing industries; 744,000 jobs in the wholesale and retail lumber trade; and more than 4.7 million jobs in homebuilding. Lumber-using workers thus outnumbered lumber-producing workers by more than 25 to 1.[4] Simply put, critics maintained that workers in the lumber-using industries stood to lose far more than workers in the lumber-producing industries would gain.

Following the imposition of quotas on lumber imports, trade tensions continued to fester between the United States and Canada. In 2002, the U.S. government determined that Canada continued to subsidize its lumber industry by charging low fees to log public lands, thus allowing its producers to sell their lumber in the United States at below-market prices. As a result, the U.S. government set a 19 percent duty to punish Canada for the subsidies and a second tariff averaging 9 percent for dumping. The Canadians were outraged by the policy, contending that their lumber is cheaper because of productive efficiency rather than unfair trade practices.

Antidumping Duties

The objective of U.S. antidumping policy is to offset two unfair trading practices by foreign nations: (1) export sales in the United States at prices below the average total cost of production; and (2) price discrimination, in which foreign firms sell in the United States at a price less than that charged in the exporter's home market. Both

---

[4]Brink Lindsey, Mark Groombridge, and Prakash Loungani, *Nailing the Homeowner: The Economic Impact of Trade Protection of the Softwood Lumber Industry*, CATO Institute, July 6, 2000, pp. 5–8.

U.S. Steel Companies Lose an Unfair Trade Case and Still Win

For years, the U.S. steel industry has dominated at the complaint department of the U.S. International Trade Commission (USITC). During the 1980s and 1990s, it accounted for almost half of the nation's unfair-trade complaints, even though steel constituted less than 5 percent of U.S. imports. Year after year, the steel industry swamped the USITC with petitions alleging that foreign steel was being subsidized or dumped into the U.S. market. However, the steel industry was not very successful in its petitions against cheap imports. During the 1990s, for example, it lost more than half its cases.

To the steel industry, however, winning isn't everything. Filing and arguing its cases is part of the competitive strategy of the Big Steel consortium—U.S. Steel, Bethlehem, AK Steel, LTV Corp., Inland Steel Industries Inc., and National Steel. The consortium knows that it can use the trade laws to influence the supply of steel in the marketplace and thus limit foreign competition. Whenever the market gets weak, for whatever reason, the consortium files an unfair trade case.

Here's how the strategy works. The market gets soft, and the consortium files trade cases alleging foreign subsidization or dumping, and then imports from the target companies decrease. The case proceeds for a year or so, allowing domestic steelmakers to increase market share and raise prices. Even if the USITC rules against the case, the market gets time to recover.

Once a case is filed, it takes months to proceed through a 4-stage legal process, and time benefits domestic steelmakers. U.S. steelmakers usually win the first round, in which the industry has to show the USITC a "reasonable indication"

of harm from imports. Armed with that finding, the U.S. Department of Commerce can set preliminary duties on the imports. Importers must post a financial bond to cover those duties. Then, the Commerce Department determines the final duties, based on the extent of foreign subsidization or dumping, and the case goes back to the USITC for a final determination of injury. If the U.S. companies lose, the duty is never collected, and the bond is lifted. If they win, however, the importer may be liable for the full amount.

During this process, U.S. importers have the right to continue importing. They might continue to import if they feel strongly that the U.S. steelmakers will lose the case. However, the USITC is a political body, with some of its presidentially appointed commissioners free-traders and others more protectionist. Because U.S. importers realize that they run a big risk if they are wrong, the response is usually to stop importing when a case is filed.

In 1997, Trinidad was hit with a complaint on steel wire rod, which is used to make wire. Wire-rod producers in Trinidad cut their U.S. shipments by 40 percent after the preliminary ruling, even though Trinidad's steelmakers eventually won the case.

Put simply, just by filing unfair trade cases, the U.S. steel industry may win. Whatever they spend on legal fees, they may recoup many times over in extra revenue. That's the great thing about filing: Even if you lose, you win.

Source: "U.S. Steelmakers Win Even When They Lose an Unfair-Trade Case," *The Wall Street Journal*, March 27, 1998, pp. A1, A6.

---

practices can inflict economic hardship on U.S. import-competing producers; by reducing the price of the foreign export in the U.S. market, they encourage U.S. consumers to buy a smaller quantity of the domestically produced good.

Antidumping investigations are initiated upon a written request by the import-competing industry that includes evidence of (1) dumping; (2) material injury, such as lost sales, profits, or jobs; and (3) a

link between the dumped imports and the alleged injury. Antidumping investigations commonly involve requests that foreign exporters and domestic importers fill out detailed questionnaires. Parties that elect not to complete questionnaires can be put at a disadvantage with respect to case decisions; findings are made on the best information available, which may simply be information supplied by the domestic industry in support of the dumping allegation.

If investigators determine that dumping is occurring and is causing material injury to the domestic industry, then the U.S. response is to impose an antidumping duty (tariff) on dumped imports equal to the margin of dumping. The effect of the duty is to offset the extent to which the dumped goods' prices fall below average total cost, or below the price at which they are sold in the exporter's home market.

An antidumping case can be terminated prior to conclusion of the investigation if the exporter of the product to the United States agrees to cease dumping, to stop exporting the product to the United States, to increase the price to eliminate the dumping, or to negotiate some other agreement that will decrease the quantity of imports. Indeed, the mere threat of an antidumping investigation may induce foreign companies to increase their export prices and thus to stop any dumping they were practicing.

The major targets of U.S. antidumping action have included Japan, China, Taiwan, South Korea, Canada, Brazil, Italy, and Germany. Antidumping duties have been applied to a wide range of U.S. imports, such as paper clips, fresh garlic, cellular phones, cement, forklift trucks, stainless steel, wire rod, and cement. Canada and Mexico have been the most frequent initiators of antidumping orders against the United States.

Remedies Against Dumped and Subsidized Imports

Recall that the direct effect of dumping and subsidizing imports is to lower import prices, an effect that provides benefits and costs for the importing country. There are benefits to consumers if imports are finished goods and to consuming industries that use imports as intermediate inputs into their own production (*downstream* industry). Conversely, there are costs to the import-competing industry, its workers, and other domestic industries selling intermediate inputs to production of the import-competing industry (*upstream* industry). Dumping at prices below fair market value and subsidizing exports are considered unfair trade practices under international trade law; they can be neutralized by the imposi-

tion of antidumping or countervailing duties on dumped or subsidized imports.

Figure 6.2 on page 196 illustrates the effects of unfair trade practices on Canada, a nation too small to influence the foreign price of steel; for simplicity, the figure assumes that Canada's steel, iron ore, and auto companies operate in competitive markets. In Figure 6.2(a), S_C and D_C represent the Canadian supply and demand for steel. Suppose that South Korea, which has a comparative advantage in steel, supplies steel to Canada at the fair-trade price of $600 per ton. At this price, Canadian production equals 200 tons, Canadian consumption equals 300 tons, and imports equal 100 tons.

Now suppose that as a result of South Korean dumping and subsidizing practices, Canada imports steel at a price of $500 per ton; the margin of dumping and subsidization thus equals $100 ($600 − $500 = $100). The unfair trade practice reduces Canadian production from 200 tons to 100 tons, increases Canadian consumption from 300 tons to 400 tons, and increases Canadian imports from 100 tons to 300 tons. Falling prices and quantities, in turn, lead to falling investment and employment in the Canadian steel industry. Although the producer surplus of Canadian steelmakers decreases by area *a* due to unfair trade, Canadian buyers find their consumer surplus rising by area *a + b + c + d*. The Canadian steel market as a whole benefits from unfair trade because the gains to its consumers exceed the losses to its producers by area *b + c + d*!

Unfair trade also affects Canada's upstream and downstream industries. If the Canadian iron-ore industry (upstream) supplies mainly to Canadian steelmakers, the demand for Canadian iron ore will decrease as their customers' output falls due to competition from cheaper imported steel. As illustrated in Figure 6.2(b), without unfair trade, the quantity of iron ore demanded by Canadian steelmakers is Q_0 tons at a price of P_0 per ton. Because of unfair trade in the steel industry, the demand for iron ore decreases from D_C to $D_{C'}$; production thus falls as do revenues and employment in this industry. In autos (downstream), production will increase as manufacturing costs decrease because of the availability of cheaper imported steel. As illustrated in Figure 6.2(c),

FIGURE 6.2

Effects of Dumped and Subsidized Imports and Their Remedies

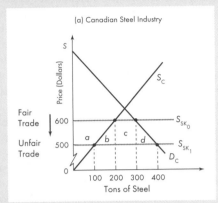
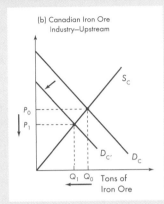
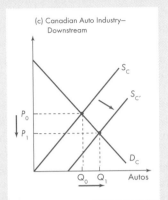

Dumped or subsidized imports provide benefits to consumers if imports are finished goods and to consuming industries that use the imports as intermediate inputs into their own production; they inflict costs on the import-competing domestic industry, its workers, and other domestic industries selling intermediate inputs to the import-competing industry. An antidumping or countervailing duty inflicts costs on consumers if imports are finished goods and on consuming industries that use the imports as intermediate inputs into their own production; benefits are provided to the import-competing domestic industry, its workers, and other domestic industries selling intermediate inputs to the protected industry.

Canadian auto production increases from Q_0 units to Q_1 units, as the supply curve shifts downward from S_C to $S_{C'}$, with accompanying positive effects on revenues and employment; the decrease in production costs also improves the Canadian auto industry's competitiveness in international markets.

Suppose that unfair trade in steel results in the imposition by the Canadian government of an antidumping duty or countervailing duty on imported steel equal to the margin of dumping or subsidization ($100). The effect of an exactly offsetting duty in the steel industry is a regaining of the initial prices and quantities in Canada's steel, iron-ore, and auto industries, as seen in Figure 6.2. The duty raises the import price of unfairly traded steel in Canada, leading to increased steel production by Canadian steelmakers; this results in increased demand, and therefore higher prices, for Canadian iron ore, but also implies increased production costs, higher prices, and lower sales for

Canadian automakers. With the import duty, the decrease in consumer surplus more than offsets the increase in producer surplus in the Canadian steel market.

The U.S. International Trade Commission estimated the economic effects of antidumping duties and countervailing duties for U.S. petitioning industries and their upstream suppliers and downstream consumers for the year 1991. The study concluded that these duties typically benefited successful petitioning industries by raising prices and improving output and employment. However, the costs to the rest of the economy were far greater. The study estimated that the U.S. economy would have experienced a net welfare gain of $1.59 billion in the year 1991 had U.S. antidumping duties and countervailing duties *not* been in effect. In other words, these duties imposed costs on consumers, downstream industries, and the economy as a whole at least $1.59 billion greater than the benefits enjoyed by the successful petitioning industries and their employees.[5] Remember, however, that the purpose of antidumping and countervailing duty laws is not to protect consumers, but rather to discourage unfairly traded imports that cause harm to competing domestic industries and workers.

Section 301: Unfair Trading Practices

Section 301 of the Trade Act of 1974 gives the United States trade representative (USTR) authority, subject to the approval of the president, and means to respond to unfair trading practices by foreign nations. Included among these unfair practices are foreign-trade restrictions that hinder U.S. exports and foreign subsidies that hinder U.S. exports to third-country markets. The USTR responds when he or she determines that such practices result in "unreasonable" or "discriminatory" burdens on U.S. exporters. The legislation was primarily a congressional response to dissatisfaction with GATT's ineffectiveness in resolving trade disputes. Table 6.8 provides examples of Section 301 cases.

Section 301 investigations are usually initiated on the basis of petitions by adversely affected U.S.

companies and labor unions; they also can be initiated by the president. If, after investigation, it is determined that a foreign nation is engaging in unfair trading practices, the USTR is empowered to (1) impose tariffs or other import restrictions on products and services and (2) deny the foreign country the benefits of trade-agreement concessions.

Although the ultimate sanction available to the United States is retaliatory import restrictions, the purpose of Section 301 is to obtain successful resolution of conflicts. In a large majority of cases, Section 301 has been used to convince foreign nations to modify or eliminate what the United States has considered to be unfair trading practices; only in a small minority of cases has the United States retaliated against foreign producers by means of tariffs or quotas. However, foreign nations have often likened Section 301 to a "crowbar" approach for resolving trade disputes, which invites retaliatory trade restrictions. At least two reasons have been advanced for the limitations of this approach to opening foreign markets to U.S. exports: (1) Nationalism unites the people of a foreign nation against U.S. threats of trade restrictions; (2) The foreign nation reorients its economy toward trading partners other than the United States.

Europe Slips in Banana Dispute

An example of a Section 301 case is the banana dispute between the United States and Europe. In

[5]U.S. International Trade Commission, *The Economic Effects of Antidumping and Countervailing Duty Orders and Suspension Agreements* (Washington, DC: International Trade Commission, June 1995), Chapter 10.

TABLE 6.8

Section 301 Investigations of Unfair Trading Practices: Selected Examples

U.S. Petitioner	Product	Unfair Trading Practice
Heilman Brewing Co.	Beer	Canadian import restrictions
Amtech Co.	Electronics	Norwegian government procurement code
Great Western Sugar Co.	Sugar	European Union subsidies
National Soybean Producers Association	Soybeans	Brazilian subsidies
Association of American Vintners	Wine	South Korean import restrictions

Source: U.S. International Trade Commission, *Operation of the Trade Agreements Program* (Washington, DC: U.S. Government Printing Office, various issues).

1993, the European Union (EU) implemented a single EU-wide regime on banana imports. The regime gave preferential entry to bananas from EU's former colonies, including parts of the Caribbean, Africa, and Asia. They also restricted entry from other countries, including several in Latin America where U.S. companies predominate.

The EU implemented the banana regime as part of its move toward a single, unified market that was inaugurated in 1992. Before the regime, individual countries imported bananas under an assortment of national practices. For example, Spain imported bananas exclusively from the Canary Islands; other EU countries imposed a 20 percent tariff on banana imports; and Germany allowed tariff-free entry. The banana regime was also justified on the grounds that European nations were obligated by treaty to protect their former colonies' banana industries from foreign competition.

The banana regime entered into force in 1993 and resulted in a maze of import quotas, licenses, and preferential tariffs that favored bananas from former European colonies. Under the banana regime, a modest tariff was applied to EU banana imports from its former colonies while substantial tariff and nontariff restrictions were applied to imports from other suppliers in Latin America. The root of the problem of the banana regime was that producers in the former Caribbean colonies of the EU were too small to compete on equal terms with the vast plantations of Latin America. Moreover, the entire economies of some Caribbean states depended on banana trade. In seeking to safeguard these fragile economies, the banana regime was on moral high ground, according to the EU.

Because the amount of bananas Europe allowed in was far less than the amount consumers wanted to purchase, the price of bananas in Europe was inflated to about twice the U.S. level. In 1999, a pound of bananas sold for about 50 cents in the United States but went for about a dollar in Europe. Therefore, bananas were lucrative for holders of the licenses that allowed selling under Europe's higher prices.

According to the United States, the EU's banana regime resulted in unfair treatment for American companies. U.S. trade officials maintained that Chiquita Brands International and Dole Food Co., which handle and distribute bananas of Latin American nations, lost half of their business because of EU's banana regime. Put simply, the United States contended that the EU must adopt a single trade policy for bananas that applies the same set of criteria for all suppliers of the world.

As a result, the United States, Mexico, Ecuador, Honduras, and Guatemala brought this issue to the World Trade Organization and successfully argued their case. The WTO ruled that the EU's banana regime discriminated against U.S. and Latin American distribution companies and banana exports from Latin American countries. Also, the WTO found that the banana regime caused $191 million in lost U.S. exports on an annual basis. This decision resulted in the United States' applying 100 percent tariffs on a list of selected European products equivalent in value to the loss in U.S. exports caused by the EU's banana regime. After a prolonged struggle, the banana dispute was resolved.

Protection of Intellectual Property Rights

In the 1800s, Charles Dickens criticized U.S. publishers for printing unauthorized versions of his works without paying him one penny. But U.S. copyright protection did not apply to foreign (British) authors, so Dickens's popular fiction could be pirated without punishment. In recent years, it is U.S. companies whose profit expectations have been frustrated. Publishers in South Korea run off copies of bootlegged U.S. textbooks without providing royalty payments. U.S. research laboratories find themselves in legal tangles with Japanese electronics manufacturers concerning patent infringement.

Certain industries and products are well-known targets of pirates, counterfeiters, and other infringers of **intellectual property rights (IPRs)**. Counterfeiting has been widespread in industries such as automobile parts, jewelry, sporting goods, and watches. Piracy of audio and videotapes, computer software, and printed materials has been widespread throughout the world. Industries in which product life cycles are shorter than the time necessary to obtain and enforce a patent are also subject to thievery; examples are photographic equipment and telecommunications. Table 6.9 provides examples of IPR violations in China.

Intellectual property is an invention, idea, product, or process that has been registered with the government and that awards the inventor (or author) exclusive rights to use the invention for a given time period. Governments use several techniques to protect intellectual property. *Copyrights* are awarded to protect works of original authorship (for example, music compositions, textbooks); most nations issue copyright protection for the remainder of the author's life plus 50 years. *Trademarks* are awarded to manufacturers and provide exclusive rights to a distinguishing name or symbol (for example, "Coca-Cola"). *Patents* secure to an inventor for a term, usually 15 years or more, the exclusive right to make, use, or sell the invention.

In spite of efforts to protect IPRs, competing firms sometimes infringe on the rights of others by making a cheaper imitation of the original product. In 1986, the courts ruled that Kodak had infringed on Polaroid's patents for instant cameras and awarded Polaroid more than $900 million in damages. Another infringement would occur if a company manufactured an instant camera similar to Polaroid's and labeled and marketed it as a Polaroid camera; this is an example of a counterfeit product.

The lack of effective international procedures for protecting IPRs becomes a problem when the expense of copying an innovation (including the cost of penalties if caught) is less than the cost of purchasing or leasing the technology. Suppose that Warner-Lambert Drug Co. develops a product that cures the common cold, called "Cold-Free," and that the firm plans to export it to Taiwan. If

TABLE 6.9

Intellectual Property Right Violations in China

Affected Firm	Violation in China
Epson	Copying machines and ink cartridges are counterfeited.
Microsoft	Counterfeiting of Windows and Windows NT, with packaging virtually indistinguishable from the real product and sold in authorized outlets.
Yamaha	Five of every six JYM150-A motorcycles and ZY125 scooters bearing Yamaha's name are fake in China. Some state-owned factories manufacture copies 4 months following the introduction of a new model.
Gillette	Up to one-fourth of its Parker pens, Duracell batteries, and Gillette razors sold in China are pirated.
Anheuser-Busch	Some 640 million bottles of fake Budweiser beer are sold annually in China.
Nike	Replicas of its T-shirts and sport shoes are widely sold throughout China.
Bestfoods	Bogus versions of Knorr bouillon and Skippy Peanut Butter lead to tens of millions of dollars in forgone sales each year.
Procter & Gamble	About 15 percent of the detergents and soaps bearing its Tide, Vidal Sassoon, Safeguard, and Head and Shoulders brands are bogus, costing $150 million annually in forgone sales.
DaimlerChrysler	Fake windshields, oil filters, brake disks, and shock absorbers for Mercedes cars are manufactured and sold in China.

Source: "Will China Follow WTO Rules?" *Business Week*, June 5, 2000, pp. 42–48.

Cold-Free is not protected by a patent in Taiwan, either because Taiwan does not recognize IPRs or Warner-Lambert has not filed for protection, cheaper copies of Cold-Free could legally be developed and marketed. Also, if Warner-Lambert's trademark is not protected, counterfeit cold remedies that are indistinguishable from Cold-Free could be legally sold in Taiwan. These copies would result in reduced sales and profits for Warner-Lambert. Moreover, if "Cold-Free" is a trademark that consumers strongly associate with Warner-Lambert, a counterfeit product of noticeably inferior quality could adversely affect Warner-Lambert's reputation and thus detract from the sales of both Cold-Free and other Warner-Lambert products.

Although most nations have regulations protecting IPRs, there have been many problems associated with trade in products affected by IPRs. One problem is differing IPR regulations across nations. For example, the United States uses a first-to-invent rule when determining patent eligibility, whereas most other nations employ a first-to-file rule. Another problem is lack of enforcement of international IPR agreements. These problems stem largely from differing incentives to protect intellectual property, especially between nations that are innovating, technological exporters and those that are noninnovating, technological importers. Developing nations, lacking in research and development and patent innovation, sometimes pirate foreign technology and use it to produce goods at costs lower than could be achieved in the innovating country. Poorer developing nations often find it difficult to pay the higher prices that would prevail if innovated products (such as medical supplies) were provided patent protection. Thus, they have little incentive to provide patent protection to the products they need.

As long as the cost of pirating technology, including the probability and costs of being caught, is less than the profits captured by the firm doing the pirating, technology pirating tends to continue. Pirating, however, reduces the rate of profitability earned by firms in the innovating nations, which in turn deters them from investing in research and development. Over time, this leads to fewer products and welfare losses for the people of both nations.

The United States has faced many obstacles in trying to protect its intellectual property. Dozens of nations lack adequate legal structures to protect the patents of foreign firms. Others have consciously excluded certain products (such as chemicals) from protection to support their industries. Even in advanced countries, where legal safeguards exist, the fast pace of technological innovation often outruns the protection provided by the legal system.

Trade Adjustment Assistance

According to the free-trade argument, in a dynamic economy in which trade proceeds according to the comparative-advantage principle, resources flow from uses with lower productivity to those with higher productivity. The result is a more efficient allocation of the world's resources over time. In the short run, however, painful adjustments may occur as less efficient companies go out of business and workers lose their jobs. These displacement costs can be quite severe to affected parties.

Many industrial nations have enacted programs for giving **trade adjustment assistance** to those who incur short-run hardships because of displaced domestic production. The underlying rationale comes from the notion that if society in general enjoys welfare gains from the increased efficiency stemming from trade liberalization, some sort of compensation should be provided for those who are temporarily injured by import competition. As long as free trade generates significant gains to the nation, the winners can compensate the losers and still enjoy some of the gains from free trade.

The U.S. trade adjustment assistant program assists domestic workers displaced by foreign trade and increased imports. The program provides benefits such as extended income support beyond normal unemployment insurance benefits, services such as job training, and allowances for job search and relocation. To businesses and communities, the program offers technical aid in moving into new lines of production, market research assistance, and low-interest loans. The major beneficiaries of benefits of the program have been workers and firms in the apparel and textile industry, followed by the oil and gas, electronics, and metal and machinery industries.

Although the trade adjustment assistance program is considered a significant innovation in trade policy, critics maintain that it has suffered from an unstable source of funding. This has resulted in delayed approval of assistance requests. Also, trade adjustment assistance cannot resolve all the workers' challenges, especially those faced by lower-skilled workers. For example, many workers applying for training assistance do not have a high-school education, have been out of the educational system for 20 years or more, or have limited English skills. Therefore, training programs are unlikely to complete the match between these workers and the kinds of jobs available in a high-skilled economy. Critics also maintain that trade adjustment assistance has sometimes been used to financially sustain a losing concern rather than help it become more competitive by switching to superior technologies and developing new products.

Will Wage Insurance Make Free Trade More Acceptable to Workers?

Although the trade adjustment assistant program assists domestic workers displaced by foreign trade and increased imports, many workers feel threatened by international trade. Worker fears about globalization and union pressure on government officials hinder efforts to liberalize trade. That's why some economists advocate something called **wage insurance**.

The concept of wage insurance is simple. Trade, although a benefit to the economy overall, harms workers who produce things or provide services susceptible to import competition. Trade-related job losses are concentrated in manufacturing industries where import competition is strong, including automobile, steel, textile, apparel, computing, and electronics industries. Compensating the losers makes more sense than trying to protect them by denying the benefits of trade to all.

When trade or technology puts someone out of work, a worker often takes a new job that pays less. On average, a worker in a manufacturing industry hit by import competition who loses one job and gets another earns 13 percent less, according to the estimates of Professor Lori Kletzer of the University of California at Santa Cruz.[6] About a third earn as much or more, and they don't need help. But about a quarter take jobs that pay 30 percent less, or worse. Because the rest of us benefit—by getting cheaper goods, more efficient services, and a more productive economy—we can afford to make up some of the difference.

Rather than protecting workers by restricting imports, which results in losses for the overall economy, why not provide wage insurance? A proposal developed by Professor Kletzer and Robert Litan of the Brookings Institution would give eligible workers half the difference between their old wage and their new one, up to $10,000 a year, for two years following a layoff. Maintaining that what matters is the type of job lost and the type of job regained, not why the job was lost, economists Kletzer and Litan would offer wage insurance to any displaced worker who had more than two years on the job. The money would begin flowing only after a worker took a new job. In contrast, the trade adjustment assistance program basically offers extra unemployment benefits to those out of work or in training.

But wage insurance is expensive. It would have cost almost $4 billion in 1997, when the jobless rate was 4.9 percent. A cheaper alternative would cover only workers over age 50 who earn less than $50,000 a year. The rationale: Older workers are the least likely to be successfully retrained for new jobs. Another possibility is to limit wage insurance to only those workers in industries most vulnerable to imports, such as steel and textiles.

Proponents of wage insurance contend that it encourages workers to find a new job quickly, as contrasted with unemployment insurance, which creates an incentive to delay looking for work.

---

[6]Lori Kletzer and Robert Litan, *A Prescription to Relieve Worker Anxiety*, International Economics Policy Briefs, Institute for International Economics, Washington, DC, February 2001. See also Trade Deficit Review Commission, *The U.S. Trade Deficit*, Washington, DC, 2000.

They also contend that wage insurance yields benefits for both younger workers and older workers. For younger workers, it makes it easier for them to acquire training and the new skills that will make them more employable over the course of their working lives. Wage insurance can enable older workers to reach retirement without having to sharply lower their standard of living or dip into retirement savings after a job loss. Simply put, proponents of wage insurance contend that, by reducing worker anxiety, wage insurance will reduce worker opposition to trade liberalization and globalization more broadly.

To win authority for fast-track power to negotiate future trade agreements with Latin America, in 2002 President George W. Bush bowed to congressional pressure and initiated a 5-year pilot program of wage insurance for trade-displaced workers. To receive income maintenance benefits, eligible workers must be over 50 years old, earn less than $50,000 a year, and be employed full-time at the firm from which they were separated. Workers can receive wage insurance for up to two years; total wage insurance is capped at $10,000 over this period. It remains to be seen whether this new income maintenance benefit will reduce world opposition to liberal trade agreements.

Industrial Policies of the United States

Besides enacting regulations intended to produce a fair trading environment for all parties engaging in international business, the United States has implemented *industrial policies* to enhance the competitiveness of domestic producers. As discussed in Chapter 3, such policies involve government channeling of resources into specific, targeted industries that it views as important for future economic growth. Among the methods used to channel resources are tax incentives, loan guarantees, and low-interest loans.

Today, almost all nations implement some kinds of industrial policies. Although industrial policies are generally associated with formal, explicit efforts of governments (as in Japan and France) to enhance the development of specific industries (such as steel or electronics), other traditionally free-enterprise nations (such as Germany and United States) also have less formal, implicit industrial policies.

What has been the U.S. approach to industrial policy? The U.S. government has attempted to provide a favorable climate for business, given the social, environmental, and safety constraints imposed by modern society. Rather than formulating a coordinated industrial policy to affect particular industries, the U.S. government has generally emphasized macroeconomic policies (such as fiscal and monetary policies) aimed at such objectives as economic stability, growth, and the broad allocation of the gross domestic product.

There is no doubt, however, that the U.S. government uses a number of measures to shape the structure of the economy that would be called "industrial policies" in other nations. The most notable of these measures is agricultural policy. In agriculture, a farmer who initiates a major innovation can be imitated by many other farmers, who capture the benefits without sharing the risks. To rectify this problem, the U.S. government is involved in research in agricultural techniques and in the dissemination of this information to farmers through its agricultural extension service, as well as the fostering of large-scale projects such as irrigation facilities. The U.S. government has also provided support for the shipping, shipbuilding, and energy industries, primarily on the grounds of national security.

U.S. government defense spending is often cited as an industrial policy. As the world's largest market for military goods, it is no wonder that the United States dominates their production. U.S. spending on military goods supports domestic manufacturers and permits them to achieve large economies of scale. U.S. defense spending has provided spillover benefits to civilian industries, especially commercial aircraft, computers, and electronics. Military research and development provides U.S. companies with expertise that they can apply elsewhere.

In manufacturing, the U.S. government has provided assistance to financially troubled industries. In automobiles, for example, the government provided a $1.5 billion loan guarantee in 1979 and 1980 to bail out Chrysler Corporation. It also negotiated voluntary export restrictions with the Japanese on autos in the 1980s to ease the burden of import competition. The steel and textile industries have also been major recipients of trade protection.

Export Promotion and Financing

Another element of U.S. industrial policy is export promotion. The U.S. government furnishes exporters with marketing information and technical assistance, in addition to trade missions that help expose new exporters to foreign customers. The government also promotes exports by sponsoring exhibits of U.S. goods at international trade fairs and establishing overseas trade centers that enable U.S. businesses to exhibit and sell machinery and equipment.

The United States also encourages exports by allowing its manufacturers to form export trade associations to facilitate the marketing of U.S. products abroad. Moreover, U.S. manufacturers and financial institutions are permitted to combine their resources into joint export trading companies to export their own products or to act as an export service for other producers. Sears, Rockwell, General Electric, Control Data, and General Motors are examples of firms that have formed export trading companies.

Moreover, the United States provides export subsidies to its producers in the form of low-cost credit. The maintenance of competitive credit terms for U.S. exporters is a function of the U.S. Export-Import Bank and the Commodity Credit Corporation. The **Export-Import Bank** (*Eximbank*) is an independent agency of the U.S. government established to encourage exports of U.S. businesses. The Eximbank provides:

- Guarantees of working capital loans for U.S. exporters to cover pre-export costs
- Export credit insurance that protects U.S. exporters or their lenders against commercial or political risks of nonpayment by foreign buyers
- Guarantees of commercial loans to creditworthy foreign buyers of U.S. goods and services
- Direct loans to these foreign buyers when private financing is unavailable

- Special programs to promote U.S. exports of environmentally beneficial goods and services
- Asset-based financing for large commercial aircraft and other appropriate exports
- Project financing to support U.S. exports to international infrastructure projects

In offering competitive interest rates in financing exports, Eximbank has sometimes been criticized because part of its funds are borrowed from the U.S. Treasury. Critics question whether U.S. tax revenues should subsidize exports to foreign countries at interest rates lower than could be obtained from private institutions. To this extent, it is true that tax funds distort trade and redistribute income toward exporters.

Table 6.10 on page 204 provides examples of direct loans and loan guarantees made by Eximbank. Major beneficiaries of Eximbank credit have included aircraft, telecommunications, power-generating equipment, and energy developments. Firms such as Boeing, McDonnell Douglas, and Westinghouse have enjoyed substantial benefits from these programs.

Officially supported lending for U.S. exports is also provided by the **Commodity Credit Corporation** (CCC), a government-owned corporation administered by the U.S. Department of Agriculture. The CCC makes available export credit financing for eligible agricultural commodities. The interest rates charged by the CCC are usually slightly below prevailing rates charged by private financial institutions.

Industrial Policies of Japan

Although the United States has generally not used explicit industrial policies to support specific industries, such policies have been used elsewhere. Consider the case of Japan.

Japan has become a technological leader in the post–World War II era. During the 1950s, Japan's exports consisted primarily of textiles and other low-tech products. By the 1960s and 1970s, its exports emphasized capital-intensive products such as autos, steel, and ships. By the 1980s and 1990s, Japan had become a major world competitor in high-tech goods, such as optical fibers and semiconductors.

TABLE 6.10

Examples of Loans Provided by Eximbank of the United States (in Millions of Dollars)

Foreign Borrower/U.S. Exporter	Purpose	Loan or Loan Guarantee
Banco Santander Noroeste of Brazil/General Electric	Locomotives	87.7
Government of Bulgaria/Westinghouse	Instruments	81.8
Air China/Boeing	Aircraft	69.8
Government of Croatia/Bechtel International	Highway construction	228.7
Government of Ghana/Wanan International	Electrical equipment	21.1
Government of Indonesia/IBM	Computer hardware	20.2
Japan Airlines/Boeing	Aircraft	212.3
Fevisa Industrial of Mexico/Pennsylvania Crusher Inc.	Glass manufacturing equipment	17.7
Delta Communications of Mexico/Motorola	Communications equipment	11.5

Source: Export-Import Bank of the United States, *Annual Report*, 2003; http://www.exim.gov.

Advocates of industrial policy assert that government assistance for emerging industries has helped transform the Japanese economy from low-tech to heavy industry to high-tech. They claim that protection from imports, R&D subsidies, and the like fostered the development of Japanese industry. Clearly, the Japanese government provided assistance to shipbuilding and steel during the 1950s, to autos and machine tools during the 1960s, and to high-tech industries beginning in the early 1970s. Japanese industrial policy has had two distinct phases: From the 1950s to the early 1970s, the Japanese government assumed strong control over the nation's resources and the direction of the economy's growth. Since the mid-1970s, the government's industrial policy has been more modest and subtle.

To implement its industrial policies in manufacturing, the Japanese government has created the **Ministry of Economy, Trade and Industry (METI).** METI attempts to facilitate the shifting of resources into high-tech industries by targeting specific industries for support. With the assistance of consultants from leading corporations, trade unions, banks, and universities, METI forms a consensus on the best policies to pursue. The next step of industrial policy is to increase domestic R&D, investment, and production. Targeted industries have received support in the form of trade protection, allocations of foreign exchange, R&D subsidies, loans at below-market interest rates, loans that must be repaid only if a firm becomes profitable, favorable tax treatment, and joint government–industry research projects intended to develop promising technologies.

Without government support, it is improbable that Japanese semiconductor, telecommunications equipment, fiber optics, and machine-tool industries would be as competitive as they are. Not all Japanese industrial policies have been successful, however, as seen in the cases of computers, aluminum, and petrochemicals. Even industries in which Japan is competitive in world markets, such as shipbuilding and steel, have witnessed prolonged periods of excess capacity. Moreover, some of Japan's biggest success stories (TVs, stereos, and VCRs) were not the industries most heavily targeted by the Japanese government.

The extent to which industrial policy has contributed to Japan's economic growth since World War II is unclear. Japan has benefited from a high domestic savings rate, an educated and motivated labor force, good labor–management relations, a shift of labor from low-productivity sectors (such as agriculture) to high-productivity manufacturing, entrepreneurs willing to assume risks, and the like. These factors have enhanced Japan's transformation from a low-tech nation to a high-tech nation. It is debatable how rapidly this transformation would have occurred in the absence of an industrial policy. Although Japan has the most visible industrial policy of the industrial nations, the importance of that policy to Japan's success should not be exaggerated.

Has Industrial Policy Helped Japan?

It is commonly argued that the Japanese government has provided assistance to high-growth or high-productivity growth industries to improve their international competitiveness. Moreover, the alleged success of Japanese targeting is often used as the justification for industrial policy in the United States. What is the evidence concerning Japanese industrial policy?

Contrary to the popular wisdom, recent research has found that a disproportionate amount of Japanese targeting has occurred in *low-growth* industries rather than high-growth industries. Moreover, evidence does not support the contention that industrial policy measures have fostered Japanese productivity.

Table 6.11 shows the relative levels of economic growth and government assistance granted to 13 Japanese industries from 1955 to 1990. Column 1 ranks these industries according to their growth rates. Electrical machinery, for example, was the fastest-growing industry, and textiles realized the slowest growth. Columns 2–5 show the usage of various industrial-policy tools. The industry that received the most government assistance in a category ranked first, and the industry that received the least ranked thirteenth. Mining, for example, received the most low-interest-rate loans, net subsidies, and tax breaks, but received the least amount of trade protection (tariffs and quotas).

The figures in the table do not provide strong support for Japan's industrial policy. In fact, it appears that the Japanese government targeted many laggard industries for assistance. For each of

---

TABLE 6.11

Relative Levels of Economic Growth Rates and Targeting of Japanese Industries, 1955–1990

Industry	Growth Rate	Low-Interest-Rate Loans	Net Subsidies*	Trade Protection	Tax Breaks
Electrical machinery	1	8	9	8	8
General machinery	2	12	4	11	8
Transportation equipment	3	7	11	4	8
Fabricated metal	4	10	6	12	7
Petroleum and coal	5	2	13	7	3
Precision instruments	6	13	10	6	8
Ceramics, stone, and glass	7	5	8	9	3
Pulp and paper	8	6	5	10	13
Chemicals	9	3	7	5	3
Basic metals	10	4	2	3	6
Processed food	11	9	12	1	12
Mining	12	1	1	13	1
Textiles	13	11	3	2	2

*Subsidies less indirect taxes.

Source: Richard Beason and David Weinstein, "Growth, Economies of Scale, and Targeting in Japan: 1955–1990," *Review of Economics and Statistics*, May 1996, p. 288.

the industrial-policy tools, the correlation between an industry's growth and the amount of government aid it received was negative. Therefore, the Japanese government provided more backing to losers than to winners.

Strategic Trade Policy

Beginning in the 1980s, a new argument for industrial policy gained prominence. The theory behind **strategic trade policy** is that government can assist domestic companies in capturing economic profits from foreign competitors.[7] Such assistance entails government support for certain "strategic" industries (such as high-technology) that are important to future domestic economic growth and that provide widespread benefits (externalities) to society.

The essential notion underlying strategic trade policy is *imperfect competition*. Many industries participating in trade, the argument goes, are dominated by a small number of large companies—large enough for each company to significantly influence market price. Such market power gives these companies the potential to attain long-run economic profits. According to the strategic-trade policy argument, government policy can alter the terms of competition to favor domestic companies over foreign companies and shift economic profits in imperfectly competitive markets from foreign to domestic companies.

A standard example is the aircraft industry. With high fixed costs of introducing a new aircraft and a significant learning curve in production that leads to decreasing unit production costs, this industry can support only a small number of manufacturers. It is also an industry that typically is closely associated with national prestige.

Assume that two competing manufacturers, Boeing (representing the United States) and Airbus (a consortium owned jointly by four European governments), are considering whether to con-

struct a new aircraft. If *either* firm manufactures the aircraft by itself, it will attain *profits* of $100 million. If *both* firms manufacture the aircraft, they will each suffer a *loss* of $5 million. Now assume the European governments decide to subsidize Airbus production in the amount of $10 million. Even if both companies manufacture the new aircraft, Airbus is now certain of making a $5 million profit. But the point is this: Boeing will *cancel* its new aircraft project. The European subsidy thus ensures not only that Airbus will manufacture the new aircraft but also that Boeing will suffer a loss if it joins in. The result is that Airbus achieves a profit of $110 million and can easily repay its subsidy to the European governments. If we assume that the two manufacturers produce entirely for export, the subsidy of $10 million results in a transfer of $100 million in profits from the United States to Europe. Table 6.12 summarizes these results. The welfare effects of strategic trade policy are discussed in "Exploring Further 6.1" at the end of this chapter.

Consider another example. Suppose the electronics industry has just two companies, one in Japan and one in the United States. In this industry, learning-by-doing reduces unit production costs indefinitely with the expansion of output. Suppose the Japanese government considers its electronics industry to be "strategic" and imposes trade barriers that close its domestic market to the U.S. competitor; assume the United States keeps its electronics market open. The Japanese manufacturer can expand its output and thus reduce its unit cost. Over a period of time, this competitive advantage permits it to drive the U.S. manufacturer out of business. The profits that the U.S. company had extracted from U.S. buyers are transferred to the Japanese.

Advocates of strategic trade policy recognize that the classical argument for free trade considered externalities at length. The difference, they maintain, is that the classical theory was based on *perfect competition* and thus could not appreciate the most likely source of the externality, whereas modern theories based on imperfect competition can. The externality in question is the ability of companies to capture the fruits of expensive innovation. Classical theory based on perfect competi-

[7]The argument for strategic trade policy was first presented in J. Brander and B. Spencer, "International R&D Rivalry and Industrial Strategy," *Review of Economic Studies* 50 (1983), pp. 707–722. See also P. Krugman, ed., *Strategic Trade Policy and the New International Economics* (Cambridge, MA: MIT Press, 1986).

TABLE 6.12

Effects of a European Subsidy Granted to Airbus

Hypothetical Payoff Matrix: Millions of Dollars

Without Subsidy

		Airbus	
		Produces	Does Not Produce
Boeing	Produces	Airbus − 5 Boeing − 5	Airbus 0 Boeing 100
Boeing	Does Not Produce	Airbus 100 Boeing 0	Airbus 0 Boeing 0

With European Subsidy

		Airbus	
		Produces	Does Not Produce
Boeing	Produces	Airbus 5 Boeing − 5	Airbus 0 Boeing 100
Boeing	Does Not Produce	Airbus 110 Boeing 0	Airbus 0 Boeing 0

Source: Paul Krugman, "Is Free Trade Passe?" *Economic Perspectives*, Fall 1987, pp. 131–144.

tion neglected this factor because large fixed costs are involved in innovation and research and development, and such costs ensure that the number of competitors in an industry will be small.

The strategic-trade policy concept has been criticized on several grounds. From a political perspective, there is danger that special-interest groups will dictate who will be the recipients of government support. Also, if a worldwide cycle of activist trade-policy retaliation and counter retaliation were to occur, all nations would be worse off. Moreover, governments lack the information to intervene intelligently in the marketplace. In our Boeing–Airbus example, the activist government must know how much profit would be achieved as a result of proceeding with the new aircraft, both with and without foreign competition. Minor miscalculations could result in an intervention that makes the home economy worse off, instead of better off. Finally, the mere existence of imperfect competition does not guarantee that there is a strategic opportunity to be pursued, even by an omniscient government. There must also be a continuing source of economic profits, with no potential competition to erase them. But continuing economic profits are probably less common than governments think.

The case of the European subsidization of aircraft during the 1970s provides an example of the benefits and costs encountered when applying the strategic-trade policy concept. During the 1970s, Airbus received a government subsidy of $1.5 billion. The subsidy was intended to help Airbus offset the 20 percent cost disadvantage it faced on the production of its A300 aircraft compared to that of its main competitor, the Boeing 767. Did the subsidy help the European nations involved in the Airbus consortium? The evidence suggests no. Airbus itself lost money on its A300 plane and continued to face cost disadvantages relative to Boeing. There were benefits to European airlines and passengers because the subsidy kept Airbus prices lower; however, the amount of Airbus's losses roughly matched this gain. Because the costs of the subsidy had to be financed by higher taxes, Europe was probably worse off with the subsidy. The United States also lost, because Boeing's profits were smaller and were not fully offset by lower prices accruing to U.S. aircraft users; but the European subsidy did not drive Boeing out of the market. The only obvious gainers were other nations, whose airlines and passengers enjoyed benefits from lower Airbus prices at no cost to themselves.[8]

[8]R. Baldwin and P. Krugman, "Industrial Policy and International Competition in Wide-Bodied Jet Aircraft," in R. Baldwin, ed., *Trade Policy Issues and Empirical Analysis* (Chicago: University of Chicago Press, 1988), pp. 45–77.

Economic Sanctions

Instead of promoting trade, governments may restrict trade for domestic and foreign-policy objectives. **Economic sanctions** are government-mandated limitations placed on customary trade or financial relations among nations. They have been used to protect the domestic economy, reduce nuclear proliferation, set compensation for property expropriated by foreign governments, combat international terrorism, preserve national security, and protect human rights. The nation initiating the economic sanctions, the *imposing nation*, hopes to impair the economic capabilities of the *target nation* to such an extent that the target nation will succumb to its objectives.

ECONOMIC *Applications*

Visit EconDebate Online for a debate on this topic

The imposing nation can levy several types of economic sanctions. *Trade sanctions* involve boycotts on imposing-nation exports. The United States has used its role as a major producer of grain, military hardware, and high-technology goods as a lever to win overseas compliance with its foreign-policy objectives. Trade sanctions may also include quotas on imposing-nation imports from the target nation. *Financial sanctions* can entail limitations on official lending or aid. During the late 1970s, the U.S. policy of freezing the financial assets of Iran was seen as a factor in the freeing of the U.S. hostages. Table 6.13 pro-vides examples of economic sanctions levied by the United States for foreign-policy objectives.

Figure 6.3 can be used to illustrate the goal of economic sanctions levied against a target country, say, Iraq. The figure shows the hypothetical production possibilities curve of Iraq for machines and oil. Prior to the imposition of sanctions, suppose that Iraq is able to operate at maximum efficiency as shown by point A along production possibilities curve PPC_0. Under the sanctions program, a refusal of the imposing nations to purchase Iraqi oil leads to idle wells, refineries, and workers in Iraq. Unused production capacity thus forces Iraq to move inside PPC_0. If imposing nations also impose export sanctions on productive inputs, and thus curtail equipment sales to Iraq, the output potential of Iraq would decrease. This is shown by an inward shift of Iraq's production possibilities curve to PPC_1. Economic inefficiencies and reduced production possibilities, caused by economic sanctions, are thus intended to inflict hardship on the people and government of Iraq. Over time, sanctions may cause a reduced growth rate for Iraq. Even if short-run welfare losses from sanctions are not large, they can appear in inefficiencies in the usage of labor and capital, deteriorating domestic expectations, and reductions in savings, investment, and employment. Thus, sanctions do reduce the Iraq's output potential.

TABLE 6.13

Selected Economic Sanctions of the United States

Year	Target Country	Objectives
1998	Pakistan	Discourage nuclear proliferation
1998	India	Discourage nuclear proliferation
1993	Haiti	Improve human rights
1992	Serbia	Terminate civil war in Bosnia–Herzegovina
1990	Iraq	Terminate Iraq's military takeover of Kuwait
1985	South Africa	Improve human rights
1981	Soviet Union	Terminate martial law in Poland
1981	Nicaragua	Cease support for El Salvador rebels
1979	Iran	Release U.S. hostages; settle expropriation claims
1961	Cuba	Improve national security

FIGURE 6.3

Effects of Economic Sanctions

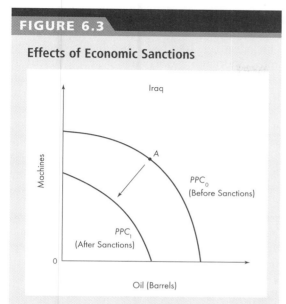

Economic sanctions placed against a target country have the effect of forcing it to operate inside its production possibilities curve. Economic sanctions can also result in an inward shift in the target nation's production possibilities curve.

Factors Influencing the Success of Sanctions

The historical record of economic sanctions provides some insight into the factors that govern their effectiveness. Among the most important determinants of the success of economic sanctions are (1) the number of nations imposing sanctions, (2) the degree to which the target nation has economic and political ties to the imposing nation(s), (3) the extent of political opposition in the target nation, and (4) cultural factors in the target nation.

Although unilateral sanctions may have some success in achieving intended results, it helps if sanctions are imposed by a large number of nations. Multilateral sanctions generally result in greater economic pressure on the target nation than unilateral measures. Multilateral measures also increase the probability of success by demonstrating that more than one nation disagrees with

the target nation's behavior, thus enhancing the political legitimacy of the effort. International ostracism can have a significant psychological impact on the people of a target nation. Failure to get strong multilateral cooperation, however, can result in sanctions' becoming counterproductive; disputes among the imposing nations over sanctions can be interpreted by the target nation as a sign of disarray and weakness.

Sanctions tend to be more effective if the target nation had substantial economic and political relationships with the imposing nation(s) before the sanctions were imposed. Then the potential costs to the target nation are very high if it does not comply with the wishes of the imposing nation(s). For example, the Western sanctions against South Africa during the 1980s helped convince the government to reform its apartheid system, in part because South Africa conducted four-fifths of its trade with six Western industrial nations and obtained almost all of its capital from the West.

Strength of political opposition within the target nation also affects the success of sanctions. When the target government faces substantial domestic opposition, economic sanctions can lead powerful business interests (such as companies with international ties) to pressure the government to conform to the imposing nation's wishes. Selected, moderate sanctions, with the threat of more severe measures to follow, inflict some economic hardship on domestic residents, while providing an incentive for them to lobby for compliance to forestall more severe sanctions; thus, the political advantage of levying graduated sanctions may outweigh the disadvantage of giving the target nation time to adjust its economy. If harsh, comprehensive sanctions are imposed immediately, domestic business interests have little incentive to pressure the target government to modify its policy; the economic damage has already been done.

When the people of the target nation have strong cultural ties to the imposing nation(s), they are likely to identify with the imposing nation's objectives, thus enhancing the effectiveness of sanctions. For example, South African whites have generally thought of themselves as part of the Western community. When economic sanctions were imposed on South Africa in the 1980s because of its apartheid practices, many liberal whites felt isolated and morally ostracized by the Western world; this encouraged them to lobby the South African government for political reforms.

Iraqi Sanctions

The Iraqi sanctions provide an example of the difficulties of pressuring a country to modify its behavior. In August 1990, the Iraqi military crossed into Kuwait and within six hours occupied the whole country. Iraqi President Saddam Hussein maintained that his forces had been invited into Kuwait by a revolutionary government that had overthrown the Kuwaiti emir and his government.

In response to Iraq's aggression, a United Nations resolution resulted in economic sanctions against Iraq. Sanctions were applied by virtually the entire international community, with only a few hard-line Iraqi allies refusing to cooperate. Under the sanctions program, imposing nations placed embargoes on their exports to Iraq, froze Iraqi bank accounts, terminated purchases of Iraqi oil, and suspended credit granted to Iraq. To enforce the sanctions, the United States supplied naval forces to prevent ships from leaving or arriving in Iraq or occupied Kuwait. The sanctions were intended to convince Iraq that its aggression was costly and that its welfare would be enhanced if it withdrew from Kuwait. If Saddam Hussein could not be convinced to leave Kuwait, it was hoped the sanctions would pressure the Iraqi people or military into removing him from office.

The sanctions were intended to have both short- and long-term consequences for Iraq. By blocking Iraqi imports of foodstuffs, the sanctions forced Iraq to adopt food rationing within several weeks of their initiation; although Iraq is self-sufficient in fruits and vegetables, shortages of flour, rice, sugar, and milk developed immediately following the imposition of sanctions. Over the longer term, the sanctions were intended to force Iraq to deindustrialize, interfering with its goal of becoming a regional economic power.

Despite the widespread application of sanctions against Iraq, it was widely felt that they would not bite hard enough to quickly destabilize the regime of Saddam Hussein. Over the short term, Iraq's ability to survive under the sanctions depended on how it rationed its existing stocks. One advantage Iraq had was a highly disciplined and authoritarian society and a people inured to shortages during its previous 8-year war with Iran; to enforce its rationing program, Saddam Hussein declared that black marketers would be executed. It was also widely believed that prior to the invasion of Kuwait, Saddam Hussein had spent some $3 billion from hidden funds to stockpile goods for domestic consumers. A plentiful agricultural harvest was also predicted for 1991.

Smuggled goods represented another potential source of supplies for Iraq. Although the United Nations pressured the governments of Jordan and Turkey, Iraq's neighbors, to comply with the sanctions, the potential rewards to smugglers increased as scarcities intensified and prices rose in Iraq. Reports indicated that families and tribes that straddled the Turkey–Iraq and Jordan–Iraq borders smuggled foodstuffs into Iraq. In addition, commodities flowed into Iraq from two of its traditional enemies, Iran and Syria. Such "leakages" detracted from the restrictive impact of the sanctions.

The sanctions also resulted in costs for the imposing nations. The closing down of the Iraqi and Kuwaiti oil trade removed some 5 million barrels of oil per day from the world marketplace, which led to price increases. From August to October 1990, oil prices jumped from $18 a barrel to $40 a barrel; oil prices subsequently decreased as other oil producers announced they would increase their production. In addition, nations dependent on Iraq for trade, especially neighboring countries, were hard hit by the embargoes. Turkey, for example, lost an estimated $2.7 billion as a result of the embargoes in 1990. Jordan's economy, much smaller and more dependent on Iraq's, faced a crisis even more severe. When the embargoes were initially imposed, most estimates suggested it would take up to two years before they would force Iraq to alter its policies. Therefore, the Bush administration concluded that sanctions would not succeed in a timely manner and a military strike against Iraq was necessary.

Following the ouster of the Iraqi army from Kuwait in 1990, the United Nations continued to impose sanctions against Iraq. The sanctions were to be kept in place until Iraq agreed to scrap its nuclear and biological weapons programs. However, Saddam Hussein dug his heels in and refused to make concessions. Therefore, the sanctions program continued throughout the 1990s into the 2000s.

Sanctions were devastating for Iraq. Analysts estimate that Iraq's economy shrunk more than two-thirds because of the sanctions. Moreover, that figure understates the extent of contraction. Every sector of the Iraqi economy depended to some degree on imports. The simplest textile mills could not operate without foreign-made parts; farmers needed imported pumps to run their irrigation systems; and the government could not repair war-damaged telephone, electricity, water, road, and sewage networks without material from abroad. As a result, factories and businesses shut down, forcing people out of work. Government employees remained on the job, but inflation reduced the purchasing power of their salaries to a pittance. Scientists, engineers, and academics abandoned their professions to drive taxis, sell liquor and cigarettes, and fish for a living. Crime and prostitution flourished. Moreover, the people of Iraq suffered from lack of food and medicine. Indeed, sanctions affected the lives of all Iraqis every moment of the day. The sanctions were lifted following the U.S.–Iraq war of 2002 when Saddam Hussein was ousted from office.

Summary

1. The trade policies of the United States have reflected the motivations of many groups, including government officials, labor leaders, and business management.

2. U.S. tariff history has been marked by ups and downs. Many of the traditional arguments for tariffs (revenue, jobs) have been incorporated into U.S. tariff legislation.

3. The Smoot–Hawley Act of 1930 raised U.S. tariffs to an all-time high, with disastrous results. Passage of the Reciprocal Trade Act of 1934 resulted in generalized tariff reductions by the United States, as well as the enactment of most-favored-nation provisions.

4. The purposes of the General Agreement on Tariffs and Trade (GATT) were to decrease trade barriers and place all nations on an equal footing in trading relationships. In 1995, GATT was transformed into the World Trade Organization, which embodies the main provisions of GATT and provides a mechanism intended to improve the process of resolving trade disputes among member nations. The Tokyo Round and Uruguay Round of multilateral trade negotiations went beyond tariff reductions to liberalize various nontariff trade barriers.

5. Trade remedy laws can help protect domestic firms from stiff foreign competition. These laws include the escape clause, provisions for antidumping and countervailing duties, and Section 301 of the 1974 Trade Act, which addresses unfair trading practices of foreign nations.

6. The escape clause provides temporary protection to U.S. producers who desire relief from foreign imports that are fairly traded.

7. Countervailing duties are intended to offset any unfair competitive advantage that foreign producers might gain over domestic producers because of foreign subsidies.

8. Economic theory suggests that if a nation is a net importer of a product subsidized or dumped by foreigners, the nation as a whole gains from the foreign subsidy or dumping. This is because the gains to domestic consumers of the subsidized or dumped good more than offset the losses to domestic producers of the import-competing goods.

9. U.S. antidumping duties are intended to neutralize two unfair trading practices: (1) export sales in the United States at prices below average total cost; and (2) international price discrimination, in which foreign firms sell in

the United States at a price lower than that charged in the exporter's home market.

10. Section 301 of the 1974 Trade Act allows the U.S. government to levy trade restrictions against nations that are practicing unfair competition, if trade disagreements cannot be successfully resolved.

11. Intellectual property includes copyrights, trademarks, and patents. Foreign counterfeiting of intellectual property has been a significant problem for many industrial nations.

12. Because foreign competition may displace import-competing businesses and workers, the United States and other nations have initiated programs of trade adjustment assistance involving government aid to adversely affected businesses, workers, and communities.

13. The United States has been reluctant to formulate an explicit industrial policy in which government picks winners and losers among products and firms. Instead, the U.S. government has generally taken a less activist approach in providing assistance to domestic producers (such as the Export-Import Bank and export trade associations).

14. According to the strategic-trade policy concept, government can assist firms in capturing economic profits from foreign competitors. The strategic-trade policy concept applies to firms in imperfectly competitive markets.

15. Economic sanctions consist of trade and financial restraints imposed on foreign nations. They have been used to preserve national security, protect human rights, and combat international terrorism.

Key Concepts and Terms

- Commodity Credit Corporation (CCC) *(page 203)*
- Countervailing duty *(page 191)*
- Economic sanctions *(page 208)*
- Escape clause *(page 190)*
- Export-Import Bank *(page 203)*
- Fast-track authority *(page 190)*
- General Agreement on Tariffs and Trade (GATT) *(page 178)*
- Intellectual property rights (IPRs) *(page 198)*
- Kennedy Round *(page 179)*
- Ministry of Economy, Trade and Industry (METI) *(page 204)*
- Most-favored-nation (MFN) clause *(page 177)*
- Normal trade relations *(page 177)*
- Reciprocal Trade Agreements Act *(page 176)*
- Safeguards *(page 190)*
- Section 301 *(page 197)*
- Smoot–Hawley Act *(page 175)*
- Strategic trade policy *(page 206)*
- Tokyo Round *(page 179)*
- Trade adjustment assistance *(page 200)*
- Trade promotion authority *(page 190)*
- Trade remedy laws *(page 190)*
- Uruguay Round *(page 180)*
- Wage Insurance *(page 201)*
- World Trade Organization (WTO) *(page 178)*

Study Questions

1. To what extent have the traditional arguments that justify protectionist barriers actually been incorporated into U.S. trade legislation?
2. At what stage in U.S. trade history did protectionism reach its high point?
3. What is meant by the most-favored-nation clause, and how does it relate to the tariff policies of the United States?
4. GATT and its successor, the World Trade Organization, have established a set of rules for the commercial conduct of trading nations. Explain.
5. What are trade remedy laws? How do they attempt to protect U.S. firms from unfairly (fairly) traded goods?
6. What is intellectual property? Why has intellectual property become a major issue in recent rounds of international trade negotiations?
7. How does the trade adjustment assistance program attempt to help domestic firms and workers who are displaced as a result of import competition?
8. Under the Tokyo Round of trade negotiations, what were the major policies adopted concerning nontariff trade barriers? What about the Uruguay Round?
9. Describe the industrial policies adopted by the U.S. government. How have these policies differed from those adopted by Japan?
10. If the United States is a net importer of a product that is being subsidized or dumped by Japan, not only do U.S. consumers gain, but they gain more than U.S. producers lose from the Japanese subsidies or dumping. Explain why this is true.
11. What is the purpose of strategic trade policy?
12. What is the purpose of economic sanctions? What problems do they pose for the nation initiating the sanctions? When are sanctions most successful in achieving their goals?
13. **Xtra!** For a tutorial of this question, go to http://carbaughxtra.swlearning.com

Assume that the nation of Spain is "small," unable to influence the Brazilian (world) price of steel. Spain's supply and demand schedules are illustrated in Table 6.14. Assume Brazil's price to be $400 per ton. Using graph paper, plot the demand and supply schedules of Spain and Brazil on the same graph.

a. With free trade, how many tons of steel will be produced, purchased, and imported by Spain? Calculate the dollar value of Spanish producer surplus and consumer surplus.
b. Suppose the Brazilian government grants its steel firms a production subsidy of $200 per ton. Plot Brazil's subsidy-adjusted supply schedule on your graph.
   (1) What is the new market price of steel? At this price, how much steel will Spain produce, purchase, and import?
   (2) The subsidy helps/hurts Spanish firms because their producer surplus rises/falls by $ _____ ; Spanish steel users realize a rise/fall in consumer surplus of $ _____ . The Spanish economy as a whole benefits/suffers from the subsidy by an amount totaling $ _____ .

TABLE 6.14

Steel Supply and Demand for Spain

Price	Quantity Supplied	Quantity Demanded
$ 0	0	12
200	2	10
400	4	8
600	6	6
800	8	4
1,000	10	2
1,200	12	0

6.1 The Export-Import Bank is a government-held corporation that encourages the sale of U.S. goods in foreign markets. For more information on its activities, set your browser to this URL:

http://www.exim.gov

6.2 The Canadian International Trade Tribunal considers cases of dumping. Examine some recent cases at its Web site by setting your browser to this URL:

http://www.citt.gc.ca

6.3 An in-depth look at R&D expenditures and the extent of government support in the United States can be found at the National Science Foundation's Web site:

http://www.nsf.gov/sbe/srs/fedfunds/start.htm

Compare that to R&D expenditures in Japan by visiting the Statistics Bureau & Statistics Center, Management and Coordination Agency of Japan, at the following Web site:

http://www.stat.go.jp/english/index.htm

6.4 Evaluation of industrial policy cases of Japan and Korea can be found in *The World Bank Research Observer*, Volume 15, Number 1, February 2000, issue at the following Web site:

http://www.worldbank.org/research/journals/wbro/obsfeb00/art3.htm

To access NetLink Exercises and the Virtual Scavenger Hunt, visit the Carbaugh Web site at http://carbaugh.swlearning.com.

 Log onto the Carbaugh Xtra! Web site (http://carbaughxtra.swlearning.com) for additional learning resources such as practice quizzes, help with graphing, and current events applications.

Welfare Effects of Strategic Trade Policy

The welfare effects of governmental subsidies in the commercial jetliner industry can be analyzed in terms of the theory of strategic trade policy. Analysts generally agree that commercial jetliners fit the requirements for strategic trade policy. The jetliner industry is highly concentrated, with Boeing and Airbus competing in what is essentially a duopoly market. Also, the commercial jetliner industry provides spillover benefits to a number of sectors of the economy.

To analyze the strategic trade implication of subsidies, we can consider an example in which Boeing and Airbus vie for monopoly profits in the Japanese market for commercial jetliners. Figure 6.4 on page 216 illustrates several possible outcomes. These outcomes depend on which producer first penetrates the Japanese market, how much government assistance is granted to producers, and the reaction of the producer's rival.

Suppose that Boeing is the first to develop and market commercial jetliners and thus becomes a monopoly seller in Japan. In our example, Boeing faces a constant marginal production cost of $130 million per jet, denoted by schedule MC_0.[9] As a monopoly, Boeing maximizes profit by selling that output at which marginal revenue equals marginal cost; 5 jets are sold at a price of $150 million. Boeing realizes a profit of $20 million per jet

[9]For production with constant marginal cost, average variable cost and marginal cost are identical. Marginal cost always lies below average total cost for such processes. The average total cost schedule is downsloping because of declining average fixed cost.

and a total profit of $100 million (minus the fixed costs of becoming established in Japan). Japanese airlines, who purchase jetliners, also realize consumer surplus of $50 million (the area under the demand schedule down to the price of $150 million) from the availability of the jets. World welfare thus rises by these two amounts, which total $150 million. Table 6.15 on page 217 summarizes these effects.

Suppose that Airbus is formed to produce commercial jetliners and that its marginal costs are identical to those of Boeing, $130 million per jet. To enhance international competitiveness, assume the governments of Europe grant a subsidy of $30 million on each jet produced by Airbus. The marginal costs of Airbus now equal $100 million ($130 million less the $30 million subsidy), as shown by MC_1. With the help of government, Airbus is in a position to export to Japan. If the subsidy policy convinces Boeing that it can no longer compete with Airbus, Boeing will exit the Japanese market and Airbus will become the monopoly seller of jetliners. The subsidy thus facilitates Airbus success in the Japanese market.

With the subsidy, Airbus maximizes profits by selling 10 jets, where marginal revenue equals marginal cost, at a price of $140 million per jet. Airbus realizes a profit of $40 million per jet and a total profit of $400 million on the 10 jets (minus fixed costs). European taxpayers lose the $300 million granted to Airbus as a subsidy ($30 million × 10 jets). However, Europe realizes overall gains equal

Welfare Effects of Strategic Trade Policy

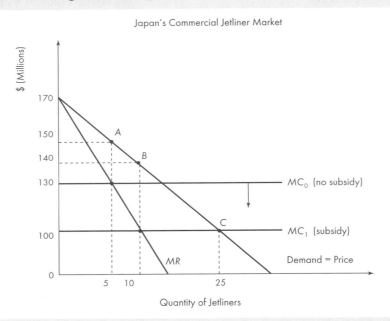

Japan's Commercial Jetliner Market

A subsidy granted by the governments of Europe to Airbus improves its competitiveness in the Japanese market; a sufficiently large European subsidy will convince Boeing to retreat from the Japanese market, assuming that no retaliatory subsidies are granted by the U.S. government. Although Airbus realizes increased export profits, European taxpayers pick up the tab for the subsidy. If these export profits exceed the subsidy's cost to European taxpayers, Europe achieves net gains. Airline companies in Japan realize consumer surplus gains resulting from lower-priced jetliners due to the subsidy.

to the amount by which its export profits (less fixed costs) exceed the taxpayer cost of the subsidy, or $100 million ($400 million – $300 million = $100 million). At the price of $140 million, Japanese airlines attain consumer surplus of $150 million from the availability of jetliners. The welfare gains to the world thus

total $250 million ($100 million + $150 million = $250 million).

This example assumes that if Europe provides a subsidy to Airbus, it will drive Boeing out of the Japanese market, thus capturing its profits. Suppose, however, that the United States retaliates and subsidizes Boeing. In this

TABLE 6.15

Welfare Effects of Strategic Trade Policy: Commercial Jetliners

Situation	Gains (Losses): Millions of Dollars			
	Boeing/ Airbus Profit*	− Subsidy Cost to U.S./ European Taxpayers' Welfare*	+ Consumer Surplus of Japanese Airlines	= World Welfare
a. Boeing is the first to penetrate the Japanese market, and thus becomes a monopoly seller.	$100	$0	$50	$150
b. European governments grant a subsidy to Airbus, which now monopolizes the Japanese market.	400	−300	150	250
c. U.S. and European governments grant offsetting subsidies to their producers; both nations compete in the Japanese market.	0	−750	875	125

*Minus fixed costs.

case, the welfare of the United States and Europe tends to decrease, while Japanese welfare increases.

To illustrate, assume that Boeing and Airbus initially have identical marginal production costs of $130 million and that the United States and Europe provide a per-unit subsidy of $30 million to their producers; the subsidy-adjusted marginal costs for Boeing and Airbus are now $100 million. With government support, neither firm will back down and exit the Japanese market. With competition and intense price-cutting, Boeing and Airbus will reduce their prices to $100 million, at which price 25 jets are sold and no profits are realized by either firm.[10] The total cost of

the subsidy to the U.S. and European governments is $750 million ($30 million × 25 jets). The United States and Europe are clearly worse off than in the case of no subsidies. Their taxpayers bear the burdens of the subsidy, but their firms do not realize the profits that come with increased market share. On the other hand, Japanese airlines realize consumer surplus of $875 million. To the extent that the gains to the Japanese airlines exceed the losses of Europe and the United States, the subsidy enhances world welfare.

[10]Because Boeing and Airbus compete with each other, each must accept a price no higher than marginal cost. Both firms lose the fixed costs of becoming established in Japan. Over time, one or both firms may go bankrupt.

chapter 7

Trade Policies for the Developing Nations

It is a commonly accepted practice to array all nations according to real income and then to draw a dividing line between the advanced and the developing ones. Included in the category of **advanced nations** are those of North America and Western Europe, plus Australia, New Zealand, and Japan. Most nations of the world are classified as developing, or less-developed, nations. The **developing nations** are most of those in Africa, Asia, Latin America, and the Middle East. Table 7.1 provides economic and social indicators for selected nations. In general, advanced nations are characterized by relatively high levels of gross domestic product per capita, longer life expectancies, and higher levels of adult literacy.

Although international trade can provide benefits to domestic producers and consumers, some economists maintain that the current international trading system hinders economic development in the developing nations. They believe that conventional international trade theory based on the principle of comparative advantage is irrelevant for these nations. This chapter examines the reasons some economists provide to explain their misgivings about the international trading system. The chapter also considers policies aimed at improving the economic conditions of the developing nations.

Developing-Nation Trade Characteristics

If we examine the characteristics of developing-nation trade, we find that developing nations are highly dependent on the advanced nations. A majority of developing-nation exports go to the advanced nations, and most developing-nation imports originate in the advanced nations. Trade among the developing nations is relatively minor, although it has increased in recent years.

Another characteristic is the composition of developing-nations' exports, with its emphasis on **primary products** (agricultural goods, raw materials, and fuels). Of the manufactured goods that are exported by the developing nations, many (such as textiles) are labor intensive and include only modest amounts of technology in their production. Table 7.2 on page 220 presents the structure of output for selected advanced nations and developing nations.

TABLE 7.1

Basic Economic and Social Indicators for Selected Nations, 2002

	Gross National Product per Capita*	Life Expectancy (Years)	Adult Illiteracy (Percent)
United States	$35,060	78	Under 5%
Switzerland	31,250	70	"
Japan	26,070	80	"
Sweden	25,080	79	"
Chile	9,180	75	5
Mexico	8,540	72	10
Malaysia	8,280	72	15
Algeria	5,330	70	36
Indonesia	2,990	65	21
Guinea	1,990	46	76
Chad	1,990	48	52
Mozambique	1,650	46	59

*At purchasing power parity.

Source: The World Bank Group, *Data by Country*, http://www.worldbank.org/data. Scroll to "Country at a Glance." See also the World Bank, *World Development Report, 2004.*

It is significant, however, that in the past three decades the dominance of primary products in developing-nation trade has greatly diminished. Many developing nations have been able to increase their exports of manufactured goods and services relative to primary products: China, India, Mexico, South Korea, Hong Kong, Bangladesh, Sri Lanka, Turkey, Morocco, Indonesia, Vietnam, and so on. These nations that have integrated into the world's industrial economy have realized higher significant poverty reduction.

How have developing countries been able to move into exports of manufactured products? Investments in people and in factories both played a role. Average educational levels and capital stock per worker rose sharply throughout the developing world. Also, improvements in transport and communications, in conjunction with developing-country reforms, allowed the production chain to be broken up into components, with developing countries playing a key role in global production sharing. Finally, the liberalization of trade barriers in developing countries after the mid-1980s

increased their competitiveness. This was especially true for manufactured goods and processed primary products. Simply put, developing countries are gaining ground in higher-technology exports. However, they have been frustrated about modest success in exporting these goods to advanced nations.

However, developing countries with total populations of around 2 billion people have not integrated strongly into the global industrial economy; many of these countries are in Africa and the former Soviet Union. Their exports usually consist of a narrow range of primary products. These countries have often been handicapped by poor infrastructure, inadequate education, rampant corruption, and high trade barriers. Also, transport costs to industrial-country markets are often higher than the tariffs on their goods, so that transport costs are even more of a barrier to integration than the trade policies of rich countries. For these developing countries, incomes have been falling and poverty has been rising in the past 20 years. It is important for them to diversify exports

TABLE 7.2

Structure of Output for Selected Advanced Nations and Developing Nations, 2002

	Value Added as a Percent of GDP		
Economy	Agriculture, Forestry, and Fishing	Industry	Services
Advanced Nations			
United States	2%	26%	72%
Japan	2	38	60
Canada	3	29	68
France	3	26	71
Italy	3	29	68
Developing Nations			
Albania	33	24	43
Chad	36	18	46
Pakistan	23	23	54
Tanzania	44	16	40
Mali	38	26	36

Source: The World Bank Group, *Data by Country*, http://www.worldbank.org/data. Scroll to "Country at a Glance Tables." See also The World Bank, *World Development Report, 2004.*

by breaking into global markets for manufactured goods and services where possible.

Tensions Between Developing Countries and Advanced Countries

In spite of the trade frustrations of developing countries, most scholars and policy makers today agree that the best strategy for a poor country to develop is to take advantage of international trade. In the past two decades, many developing countries saw the wisdom of this strategy and opened their markets to international trade and foreign investment. And yet, ironically, in spite of the support that scholars from advanced countries have given to this change, the advanced world has sometimes increased its own barriers to imports from these developing countries. Why is this so?

Think of the world economy as a ladder. On the bottom rungs are developing countries that produce mainly textiles and other low-tech goods.

Toward the top are the United States, Japan, and other industrial countries that manufacture sophisticated software, electronics, and pharmaceuticals. Up and down the middle rungs are all the other nations, producing everything from memory chips, to autos, to steel. From this perspective, economic development is simple: Everyone attempts to climb to the next rung. This works well if the topmost countries can create new industries and products, thus adding another rung to the ladder. Such invention permits older industries to move overseas while new jobs are generated at home. But if innovation stalls at the highest rung, then that's bad news for Americans who must compete with lower-wage workers in developing countries.

A predicament faced by developing countries is that in order to make progress, they must displace producers of the least advanced goods that are still being produced in the advanced countries. For example, if Zambia is going to produce textiles and apparel, it will compete against American and European producers of these goods. As producers in advanced countries suffer from import competition, they tend to seek trade protection in order to avoid it. However, this protection denies critical market access to developing countries, thwarting their attempts to grow. Thus, there is a bias against their catching up to the advanced countries.

Those who are protected in advanced countries from the competition with developing countries tend to include those who are already near the bottom of the advanced countries' income distributions. Many of these people work in labor-intensive industries and have limited skills and low wages. These are the people that income redistribution programs ought to aid, not hinder. To some extent, advanced countries face a trade-off between helping their own poor and helping the world's poor. But critics note that the world as a whole needs to treat all poor as its own and that a purpose of international institutions is to ensure that. For example, it is the responsibility of the World Trade Organization (WTO) to prevent advanced countries' trade policies from tilting too far in favor of their own people and against the world's. This is why recent meetings of the WTO have been filled with tensions between poor and rich countries.

However, providing developing countries greater access to the markets of advanced countries will not solve all the developing countries' problems. They face structural weaknesses in their economies, which are compounded by nonexistent or inadequate institutions and policies in the fields of law and order, sustainable macroeconomic management, and public services.

Trade Problems of the Developing Nations

The theory of comparative advantage maintains that all nations can enjoy the benefits of free trade if they specialize in production of those goods in which they have a comparative advantage and exchange some of these goods for goods produced by other nations. Policy makers in the United States and many other advanced nations maintain that the market-oriented structure of the international trading system furnishes a setting in which the benefits of comparative advantage can be realized. They claim that the existing international trading system has provided widespread benefits and that the trading interests of all nations are best served by pragmatic, incremental changes in the existing system. Advanced nations also maintain that to achieve trading success, they must administer their own domestic and international economic policies.

On the basis of their trading experience with the advanced nations, some developing nations have become dubious of the *distribution* of trade benefits between them and the advanced nations. They have argued that the protectionist trading policies of advanced nations hinder the industrialization of many developing nations. Accordingly, developing nations have sought a new international trading order with improved access to the markets of advanced nations. Among the problems that have plagued developing nations have been unstable export markets, worsening terms of trade, and limited access to markets of industrial countries.

Unstable Export Markets

One characteristic of many developing nations is that their exports are concentrated in only one or a few primary products. This situation is shown in Table 7.3 on page 222, which illustrates the dependence of selected developing nations on a single primary product. A poor harvest or a decrease in market demand for that product can significantly reduce export revenues and seriously disrupt domestic income and employment levels.

Many observers maintain that a key factor underlying the instability of primary-product prices and export receipts is the low price elasticity of the demand and supply schedules for products such as tin, copper, and coffee, as indicated in Table 7.4 on page 222. Recall that the price elasticity of demand (supply) refers to the percentage change in quantity demanded (supplied) resulting from a 1 percent change in price. To the extent that commodity demand and supply schedules are *relatively* inelastic, suggesting that the percentage change in price exceeds the percentage change in

ECONOMIC *Applications*

Visit EconNews Online
Developing Economies

TABLE 7.3

Developing-Nation Dependence on Primary Products, 2002

Country	Major Export Product	Major Export Product as a Percentage of Total Exports
Nigeria	Oil	96%
Saudi Arabia	Oil	86
Venezuela	Oil	86
Burundi	Coffee	79
Mauritania	Iron ore	56
Zambia	Copper	56
Ethiopia	Coffee	54
Chad	Cotton	40
Rwanda	Coffee	31

Source: The World Bank Group, *Data by Country*, http://www.world bank.org/data. Scroll to "Country at a Glance Tables."

TABLE 7.4

Long-Run Price Elasticities of Supply and Demand for Selected Commodities

Commodity	Supply Elasticity (Developing Countries)	Demand Elasticity (Industrialized Countries)
Coffee	0.3	0.2
Cocoa	0.3	0.3
Tea	0.2	0.1
Sugar	0.2	0.1
Wheat	0.6	0.5
Copper	0.1	0.4
Rubber	0.4	0.5

Source: Jere Behrman, "International Commodity Agreements: An Evaluation of the UNCTAD Integrated Commodity Program," in William Cline, ed., *Policy Alternatives for a New International Economic Order* (New York: Praeger, 1979), pp. 118–121.

quantity, a small shift in either schedule can induce a large change in price and export receipts.

Figure 7.1 illustrates the export market of Costa Rica, a producer of coffee. In Figure 7.1(a), once coffee has been planted, the quantity supplied is fixed for the following marketing period, irre-spective of how the price of coffee may fluctuate. Let the supply of coffee be perfectly inelastic (vertical), as shown in the figure. Because of changing preferences, suppose the world demand for coffee falls from D_0 to D_1. The decrease in demand causes the price of coffee to decline from $6 to $3 per pound; this price decrease is larger than would occur if Costa Rica's supply schedule were upward-sloping (that is, if it exhibited greater price elasticity). As a result of the price decline, Costa Rica's export receipts fall from $240 to $120. Conversely, an increase in the world demand for coffee would lead to higher prices and export receipts for Costa Rica. We conclude that export prices and earnings can be extremely volatile when supply is inelastic and there occurs a change in demand.

Not only do changes in demand induce wide fluctuations in price when supply is inelastic, but changes in supply induce wide fluctuations in price when demand is inelastic. The latter situation is illustrated in the two-period framework of Figure 7.1(b). Costa Rica's export supply schedule, S_0, is portrayed as perfectly inelastic, while the world demand schedule, D_0, is relatively price-inelastic. In equilibrium, the price of coffee equals $3 per pound, and Costa Rica's export receipts total $120.

In time period 1, suppose the world demand for coffee increases so that the demand schedule shifts from D_0 to D_1. This results in a substantial increase in price, from $3 to $5.25 per pound, and an increase in Costa Rica's export receipts from $120 to $210. Suppose that, because of the price increase, growers in Costa Rica plant additional coffee in the next time period, shifting the supply schedule from S_0 to S_1. With a relatively inelastic demand, the ensuing decrease in price will be substantial; the price of coffee falls from $5.25 to $1.50 per pound, and Costa Rica's export receipts fall to $90. Again we see that export prices and receipts can be very volatile when supply and demand conditions are price-inelastic.

Worsening Terms of Trade

How the gains from international trade are distributed among trading partners has been controversial, especially among developing nations whose exports

FIGURE 7.1

Export Price Instability for a Developing Country

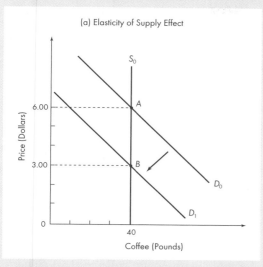

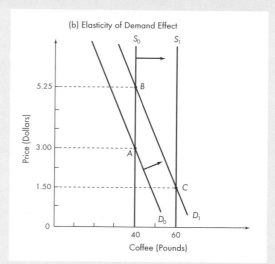

When the supply of a commodity is highly price-inelastic, decreases (or increases) in demand will generate wide variations in price. When the demand for a commodity is highly price-inelastic, increases (or decreases) in supply will generate wide variations in price.

are concentrated in primary products. These nations generally maintain that the benefits of international trade accrue disproportionately to the industrial nations.

Developing nations complain that their commodity terms of trade has deteriorated in the past century or so, suggesting that the prices of their exports relative to their imports have fallen. Worsening terms of trade has been used to justify the refusal of many developing nations to participate in trade-liberalization negotiations. It also has underlain the developing nations' demands for preferential treatment in trade relations with the advanced nations.

Observers maintain that the monopoly power of manufacturers in the industrial nations results in higher prices. Gains in productivity accrue to manufacturers in the form of higher earnings rather than price reductions. Observers further contend that the export prices of the primary

products of developing nations are determined in competitive markets. These prices fluctuate downward as well as upward. Gains in productivity are shared with foreign consumers in the form of lower prices. The developing nations maintain that market forces cause the prices they pay for imports to rise faster than the prices commanded by their exports, resulting in a deterioration in their commodity terms of trade. Moreover, as income rises there is a tendency for people to spend more on manufactured goods than primary goods, thus contributing to a worsening in the developing nations' terms of trade.

The developing nations' assertion of worsening commodity terms of trade was supported by a UN study in 1949.[1] The study concluded that from the period 1876–1880 to 1946–1947, the prices of

[1] United Nations Commission for Latin America, *The Economic Development of Latin America and Its Principal Problems*, 1950.

Does the Fair-Trade Movement Help Poor Coffee Farmers?

[Globalization]

Does "Fair Trade" Help Farmers in Poor Countries?

What fair-trade coffee costs wholesale roaster Dean's Beans in 2004. Prices for one-pound bulk bags of organic coffee.

Wholesale roaster (Dean's Beans)

Costs	
Price paid to coffee grower	$1.41
Administrative costs and shipping	0.39
Shrinkage during roasting	0.36
Operating and maintenance cost	2.50
Packaging and miscellaneous costs	0.14
	4.80
Price at which wholesale roaster sells to stores	5.00
Wholesale roaster profit	0.20
Retail store	
Price at which store sells to customer	8.49
Price at which store buys from wholesale roaster	5.00
Retail store profit, before expenses	3.49

Source: Data taken from "At Some Retailers, Fair Trade Carries a Very High Cost," *The Wall Street Journal*, June 8, 2004, pp. A1 and A10.

Nicaraguan coffee farmer Santiago Rivera has traveled far beyond his mountain home to publicize what is known as the "fair-trade" coffee movement. Have you heard of fair-trade coffee? You soon may. Started in Europe in the early 1990s and just making its way across the United States, the objective of the fair-trade coffee movement is to increase the incomes of poor farmers in developing countries by implementing a system where the farmers can sell their beans directly to roasters and retailers, bypassing the traditional practice of selling to middlemen in their own countries.

This arrangement permits farmers, who farm mainly in the mountainous regions of Latin America and other tropical regions where high-flavor, high-priced beans sold to gourmet stores are grown, to earn as much as $1.26 per pound for their beans, compared with the $.40 per pound they were getting from middlemen.

Under the fair-trade system, farmers organize in cooperatives of as many as 2,500 members, which set prices and arrange for export directly to brokerage firms and other distributors. Middlemen—known as "coyotes" in Nicaragua—previously handled this role. So far,

primary products compared with those of manufactured goods fell by 32 percent. However, because of inadequacies in data and the problems of constructing price indexes, the UN study was hardly conclusive. Other studies led to opposite conclusions about terms-of-trade movements. A 1983 study confirmed that the commodity terms of trade of developing nations deteriorated from 1870 to 1938, but much less so than had been maintained previously; by including data from the late 1940s up to 1970, the study found no evidence of deterioration.[2] Consistent with these findings, a 1984 study concluded that the terms of trade of developing nations actually improved somewhat from 1952 to 1970.[3]

[2] J. Sporas, *Equalizing Trade?* (Oxford: Clarendon Press, 1983).

[3] M. Michaely, *Trade Income Levels and Dependence* (Amsterdam: North-Holland, 1984).

It is difficult to conclude whether the developing nations as a whole have experienced a deterioration or an improvement in their terms of trade. Conclusions about terms-of-trade movements become clouded by the choice of the base year used in comparisons, by the problem of making allowances for changes in technology and productivity as well as for new products and product qualities, and by the methods used to value exports and imports and to weight the commodities used in the index.

Limited Market Access

In the past two decades, developing countries as a whole have improved their penetration of world markets. However, global protectionism has been a hindrance to their market access. This is especial-

500,000 of the developing world's 4 million coffee farmers have joined the fair-trade movement. However, the movement has led to incidents of violence in some places in Latin America, mostly involving middlemen who are being bypassed.

The fair-trade coffee movement is the latest example of how social activists are using free-market economics to foster social change. Organizers of the movement say they have signed up eight gourmet roasters and about 120 stores, including big chains like Safeway. Fair-trade coffee carries a logo identifying it as such.

Fair trade achieved much success in Europe, where fair-trade coffee sells in 35,000 stores and has sales of $250 million a year. In some countries like the Netherlands and Switzerland, fair-trade coffee accounts for as much as 5 percent of total coffee sales. Based on those achievements, organizers in Europe are expanding their fair-trade efforts to include other commodity items, including sugar, tea, chocolate, and bananas. But fair-trade activists admit that selling Americans on the idea of buying coffee with a social theme will be more challenging than it was in Europe. Americans, they note, tend to be less aware of social problems in the developing world than Europeans.

The fair-trade movement has yet to get the support of major U.S. coffee houses such as Maxwell and Folgers. Nevertheless, organizers are trying to nudge Seattle's two big coffee giants, Starbucks Coffee Co. and Seattle Coffee Co., into agreeing to purchase some of the fair-trade coffee. In Oakland, Mayor Jerry Brown is persuading his colleagues to give more thought to how they purchase coffee. "I would hope that the people sipping their cappuccinos would take a moment to reflect on the sweat and labor of those who provided it."

However, critics question the extent to which "fair-traded" coffee actually helps. They note that the biggest winners are not the farmers, but rather the retailers that sometimes charge huge markups on fair-traded coffee while promoting themselves as corporate citizens, as seen in the table. They get away with it because consumers generally are given little or no information about how much of a product's price goes to farmers.

Source: "A Global Effort for Poor Coffee Farmers," *The Wall Street Journal,* November 23, 1999, pp. A2 and A4.

ly true for agriculture and labor-intensive manufactured products such as clothing and textiles, as seen in Figure 7.2 on page 226. These products are important to the world's poor because they represent more than half of low-income countries' exports and about 70 percent of least-developed countries' export revenues.

Tariffs imposed by the industrial countries on imports from developing countries tend to be higher than those they levy on other industrial countries. Outside of agriculture, tariffs on imports from other industrial countries in 2002 averaged 1 percent, while those from developing countries faced tariff averages ranging from 2.1 percent (Latin America) to 8.1 percent (South Asia). The differences in tariff averages reflect in part the presence of major trading blocks such as the European Union and North American Free Trade Agreement, which have abolished tariffs for industrial-country trade partners. Also, because developing countries did not actively participate in multilateral trade liberalization agreements prior to the 1990s, their products tended to be omitted from the sharp reductions in tariffs made in those rounds. Simply put, average tariff rates in rich countries are low, but they maintain barriers in exactly the areas where developing countries have comparative advantage: agriculture and labor-intensive manufactured goods.

Developing countries also are plagued by tariff escalation, as discussed in Chapter 4. In industrial countries, tariffs escalate steeply, especially on agricultural products. Tariff escalation has the potential of decreasing demand for processed imports

FIGURE 7.2

Trade Barriers Limit Export Opportunities of Developing Countries. . . .

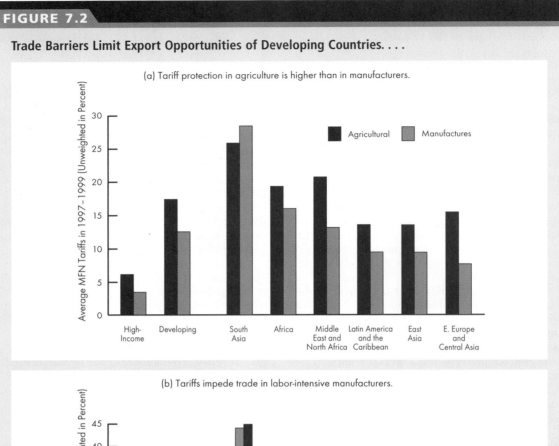

(a) Tariff protection in agriculture is higher than in manufacturers.

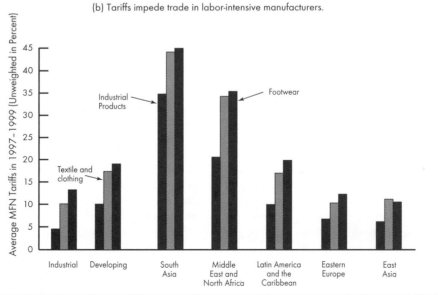

(b) Tariffs impede trade in labor-intensive manufacturers.

They face high tariff walls, especially in agricultural commodities and labor-intensive manufacturers.

Source: The World Bank, *Global Economic Prospects and Developing Countries*, 2002, p. 45.

from developing countries, thus restricting their diversification into higher value-added exports. Though less prevalent, tariff escalation also affects imports of industrial products, especially at the semiprocessed stage. Examples of such products, in which many developing countries have a comparative advantage, include textiles and clothing, leather and leather products, wood, paper, furniture, metals, and rubber products.

Global protectionism in agriculture is another problem for developing countries. In addition to using tariffs to protect their farmers from import-competing products, industrial countries support their farmers with sizable subsidies. Subsidies are often rationalized on the noneconomic benefits of agriculture, such as food security and maintenance of rural communities. By encouraging production of agricultural commodities, subsidies discourage agricultural imports, thus displacing developing-country exports in industrial-country markets. The case of U.S. subsidies to sugar producers illustrates the adverse effects of support on developing countries' exporters. Moreover, the unwanted surpluses of agricultural commodities that result from government support are often dumped into world markets with the aid of export subsidies. This depresses prices for many agricultural commodities and reduces the export revenues of developing countries.

Moreover, protectionist barriers have caused developing-country producers of textiles and clothing to forego sizable export earnings. For decades, industrial countries imposed quotas on imports of these products. Although the Uruguay Round Agreement on Textiles and Clothing called for an abolishment of the quotas over a 10-year period (1995–2005), market access in textiles and clothing will remain restricted because tariff barriers are high.

Finally, antidumping and countervailing duties have become popular substitutes for traditional trade barriers, which are gradually being reduced in the course of regional and multilateral trade liberalization. Developing countries have argued that industrial countries such as the United States have limited access to their markets through aggressive use of antidumping and countervailing duties. Such policies have resulted in significant reductions in export volumes and market shares, according to the developing countries.

Indeed, poor countries have leaned on the United States and Europe to reduce trade barriers. However, rich countries note that poor countries need to reduce their own tariffs, which are often higher than those of their rich counterparts. The average tariff rate of developing countries is more than 20 percent compared with less than 5 percent of developed countries, as seen in Table 7.5. Tariff escalation is also widely practiced by developing countries; their average tariff for fully processed agricultural and manufactured products is higher than on unprocessed products. Although trade among developing countries is a much smaller share of total trade, average tariffs in manufactured goods are about three times higher for trade among developing countries than

ECONOMIC *Applications*

Visit EconNews Online
International Trade

TABLE 7.5

Tariffs of Selected Developing Countries and Advanced Countries

Poor nations typically impose higher tariffs than rich nations. Average unweighted applied tariff rates for selected countries for all goods in 2002:

	Average Tariff Rate (Percent)
Developing Countries	
India	30.9%
Nigeria	23.4
Pakistan	20.6
Kenya	20.2
Mexico	15.6
China	15.3
Argentina	13.4
Brazil	12.9
Hong Kong	0.0
Advanced Countries	
Japan	5.1%
United States	4.4
Canada	4.2
European Union	3.9

Source: The World Bank, *Global Economic Prospects*, Washington, DC, 2004. See also World Trade Organization, *Annual Report, 2003*.

for exports to advanced countries. Critics thus note that developing countries themselves are part of their problem and they should liberalize trade.

However, this argument does not sit well with many poor nations. They say that quickly reducing tariffs could throw their already fragile economies into an even worse state. Just as is the case in rich nations that reduce tariffs, some workers inevitably will lose jobs as businesses switch to the lowest-cost centers. But unlike the United States and European countries, poor countries do not have social safety net and reeducation programs to cushion the blow. The message that the developing world receives is that it should do some market liberalization of its own. However, it is paradoxical that advanced nations want developing nations to lift their trade barriers, yet advanced nations like the United States and Canada had significant trade barriers during their developing stages.

As U.S. Subsidies and Food Aid Support American Farmers, Developing Growers Cry Foul

After the first major rainfall of the 2002 agricultural season in West Africa, cotton farmers hitched their plows to oxen and began turning over the dirt of their fields. But why? The price being offered to West Africa's cotton farmers was 10 percent lower than the previous year's—a meager amount, given that world cotton prices had declined to the most unprofitable level in 30 years. After the previous harvest, once the farming costs were paid, the typical West African farmer was left with less than $2,000 for the year to support two dozen family members and relatives. Indeed, West African farmers worried that the lower prices in 2002, along with higher pesticide and fertilizer costs, would mean that they would be unable to replenish their cattle herds or send their children to high school.

At the same time, cotton seedlings in the United States pushed up through thick black soil of Perthshire Farms, a 10,000-acre cotton plantation in the Mississippi Delta. Farmers climbed into the air-conditioned cabs of their $130,000 Caterpillar tractors and prepared to apply fertiliz-

er to the seedlings. There were no obvious indications in Mississippi that world cotton prices were depressed. Why? Because U.S. farmers receive governmental subsidies in abundance, while West African growers don't.

Since the September 11, 2001, terrorist attacks against the United States, such subsidies have fostered an acute controversy: They work directly against the U.S. policy to combat poverty as part of a broader campaign against terrorism. Fearing that poverty in the developing world may make it a breeding ground for instability and terrorism, the U.S. government aims to promote development aid and open trade. But this strategy is counteracted by subsidies to U.S. farmers, which help lower world prices of some vital cash crops that developing countries depend on.

Although subsidies shield farmers in America from declining world prices, they generally further reduce prices by encouraging continued production, and thus harm tillers in less-subsidized countries. Few places are these economics more apparent than in the discrepancy between the cotton farmers in Mississippi and West Africa. America is the world's largest exporter of cotton, and West Africa is the third largest, leaving both subject to market forces that slashed prices by 66 percent from 1995 to 2002.

Armed with almost $3.5 billion in subsidy checks, which constituted about half of their income, U.S. cotton farmers in 2002 harvested a record crop of about 10 billion pounds of cotton, aggravating a U.S. surplus and pushing prices below the breakeven price of most farmers around the world. However, West Africa's governments, hard-pressed to provide even the most basic education and health care to their people, can't keep up with subsidies of their own.

The reason Mississippi's farmers are so dependent on subsidies is that they are among the highest-cost cotton producers in the world. They could grow corn, soybeans, and wheat much more cheaply, but switching would render much of their investment worthless. For example, a cotton-picking machine costs about $300,000 and is useless for other crops.

Analysts estimate that if the U.S. subsidies were removed, the world price of cotton would rise and revenue to West African countries would increase by about $250 million. But in Mississippi, there is little sympathy for the removal of subsidies—cotton is king in Mississippi, and its growers don't want competition from West Africa's farmers. Simply put, American cotton farmers maintain that they cannot survive without subsidies. However, West Africa's growers feel that life is unfair when they must compete against American farmers as well as the U.S. government.

American food-aid policies are another source of controversy. It is true that U.S. food donated to the developing world has saved millions of lives made destitute by the failure of their farms. But growers in developing countries complain that the U.S. government purchases surplus grain from American farmers and sends it halfway around the world, instead of first purchasing what foreigners grow. By law, the United States is bound to send its own homegrown food for assistance, instead of spending cash on foreign produce, in all but the most exceptional cases. It is a policy that supports American farmers, processors, and shippers, as well as the world's hungry. The complaints of farmers in West Africa do not get much sympathy in the United States, where farmers oppose the U.S. government's spending taxpayer money to purchase foreign crops.

Nevertheless, developing countries refer to the food-aid policy of the European Union as a better method. Under this system, Europe donates cash to buy as much food as possible in a poor country rather than always sending food. Although such local purchases can add more bureaucracy to the process, they provide greater flexibility, making it easier to style food packages to local tastes and nutritional needs rather than being linked to what is available because of European surpluses. Local purchases can also be cheaper. Analysts estimate that transport and handling costs from America to hungry recipients in Africa add about $200 to each ton of grain. The greatest benefit, however, is the economic stimulus it provides by placing cash in the hands of farmers in the developing world.

In 2004, the World Trade Organization issued an interim ruling that declared America's subsidies to its cotton farmers illegal. It remains to be seen whether this ruling results in a dismantling of America's agricultural subsidies as well as the subsidies of other nations.

Aiding the Developing Countries

Dissatisfied with their economic performance and convinced that many of their problems are due to shortcomings of the existing international trading system, developing nations have pressed collective demands on the advanced nations for institutions and policies that improve the climate for economic development in the international trading system. Among the institutions and policies that have been created to support developing countries are the World Bank, International Monetary Fund, and the generalized system of preferences.

World Bank

During the 1940s, two international institutions were established to ease the transition from a wartime to a peacetime environment and to help prevent a recurrence of the turbulent economic conditions of the Great Depression era. The World Bank and the International Monetary Fund were established at the United Nations Monetary and Financial Conference held at Bretton Woods, New Hampshire, in July 1944. Developing nations view these institutions as sources of funds to promote economic development and financial stability.

The **World Bank** is an international organization that provides loans to developing countries aimed toward poverty reduction and economic development. It lends money to member governments and their agencies and to private firms in the member nations. The World Bank is not a "bank" in the common sense. It is one of the United Nations' specialized agencies, made up of 184 member countries. These countries are jointly responsible for how the institution is financed and how its money is spent.

The "World Bank Group" is the name that has come to be used for five closely associated institutions. The International Bank for Reconstruction and Development and the International Development Association provide low-cost loans and grants to developing countries. The International Finance Corporation provides equity, long-term loans, loan guarantees, and advisory services to developing countries that would otherwise have limited access to capital. The Multilateral Investment Guarantee Agency encourages foreign investment in developing countries by providing guarantees to foreign investors against losses caused by war, civil disturbance, and the like. Finally, the International Center for Settlement of Investment disputes encourages foreign investment by providing international facilities for conciliation and arbitration of investment disputes, thus helping foster an atmosphere of mutual confidence between developing countries and foreign investors.

The World Bank makes loans to developing members that cannot obtain money from other sources at reasonable terms. These loans are for specific development projects such as hospitals, schools, highways, and dams. The World Bank is involved in projects as diverse as raising AIDS awareness in Guinea, supporting education of girls in Bangladesh, improving health-care delivery in Mexico, and helping India rebuild after a devastating earthquake. The World Bank provides low-interest rate loans, and in some cases interest-free loans, to developing countries that have little or no capacity to borrow on market terms.

In recent years, the World Bank has financed debt-refinancing activities of some of the heavily indebted developing nations. The bank encourages private investment in member countries. In 2003, the World Bank lent about $18.5 billion to developing countries, as seen in Table 7.6. The World Bank receives its funds from contributions of wealthy developed countries.

Some 10,000 development professionals from nearly every country in the world work in the World Bank's Washington, DC, headquarters or in its 109 country offices. They provide many technical assistance services for members.

International Monetary Fund

Another source of aid to developing countries (as well as advanced countries) is the **International Monetary Fund (IMF)**, which is headquartered in Washington, DC. Consisting of 184 nations, the IMF can be thought of as a bank for the central

TABLE 7.6

World Bank Lending by Sector, 2003 (Millions of Dollars)

Developing-Country Sector

Agriculture, fishing, and forestry	$ 1,213.2
Law and justice and public administration	3,947.5
Information and communication	115.3
Education	2,348.7
Finance	1,455.3
Health and other social services	3,442.6
Industry and trade	796.7
Energy and mining	1,088.4
Transportation	2,727.3
Water, sanitation, and flood protection	1,378.3
	$18,513.2

Source: World Bank, *Annual Report, 2003,* http://www.worldbank.org.

banks of member nations. Over a given time period, some nations will face balance-of-payments surpluses, and others will face deficits. A nation with a deficit initially draws on its stock of foreign currencies, such as the dollar, that are accepted in payment by other nations. However, the deficit nation will sometimes have insufficient amounts of currency. That is when other nations, via the IMF, can provide assistance. By making available currencies to the IMF, the surplus nations channel funds to nations with temporary deficits. Over the long run, deficits must be corrected, and the IMF attempts to ensure that this adjustment will be as prompt and orderly as possible.

The funds of the IMF come from two major sources: quotas and loans. Quotas (or subscriptions), which are pooled funds of member nations, generate most of the IMF's funds. The size of a member's quota depends on its economic and financial importance in the world; nations with larger economic importance have larger quotas. The quotas are increased periodically as a means of boosting the IMF's resources. The IMF also obtains funds through loans from member nations. The IMF has lines of credit with major industrial nations as well as with Saudi Arabia.

All IMF loans are subject to some degree of *conditionality*. This means that to obtain a loan, a deficit nation must agree to implement economic and financial policies as stipulated by the IMF. These policies are intended to correct the member's balance-of-payments deficit and promote noninflationary economic growth. However, the conditionality attachment to IMF lending has often met strong resistance among deficit nations. The IMF has sometimes demanded that deficit nations undergo austerity programs including severe reductions in public spending, private consumption, and imports in order to live within their means.

Critics of the IMF note that its bailouts may contribute to the so-called *moral-hazard problem*, whereby nations realize the benefits of their decisions when things go well but are protected when things go poorly. If nations do not suffer the costs of bad decisions, won't they be encouraged to make other bad decisions in the future? A second area of concern is the contractionary effect of the IMF's restrictive monetary and fiscal policy conditions. Won't such conditions cause business and bank failures, induce a deeper recession, and limit government spending to help the poor? Many analysts feel the answer is yes.

Generalized System of Preferences

Given inadequate access to markets of industrial countries, developing countries have pressed industrial countries to reduce their tariff walls. To help developing nations strengthen their international competitiveness and expand their industrial base, many industrialized nations have extended nonreciprocal tariff preferences to exports of developing nations. Under this **generalized system of preferences (GSP)**, major industrial nations temporarily reduce tariffs on designated manufactured imports from developing nations below the levels applied to imports from other industrial nations. The GSP is not a uniform system, however, because it consists of many individual schemes that differ in the types of products covered and extent of tariff reduction. Simply put, the GSP attempts to promote economic development in developing countries through increased trade, rather than foreign aid.

Trade preferences granted by industrial countries are voluntary. They are not WTO obligations. Donor countries determine eligibility criteria, product coverage, the size of preference margins, and the duration of the preference. In practice, industrial-country governments rarely grant deep preferences in sectors where developing countries have a large export potential. Thus, developing countries often obtain only limited preferences in sectors where they have a comparative advantage. The main reason for limited preferences is that in some sectors there is strong domestic opposition to liberalization in industrial countries.

Since its origin in 1976, the U.S. GSP program has extended duty-free treatment to about 3,000 items. Criteria for eligibility include not aiding international terrorists and complying with international environmental, labor, and intellectual property laws. The U.S. program grants complete tariff-free and quota-free access to eligible products from eligible countries. Beneficiaries of the U.S. program include some 150 developing nations and their dependent territories. Like the GSP programs of other industrial nations, the U.S. program excludes certain import-sensitive products from preferential tariff treatment. Textiles and apparel, footwear, and many agricultural products are not eligible for the GSP. Also, a country's GSP eligibility for a given product may be removed if annual exports of that product reach $100 million or if there is significant damage to domestic industry. Table 7.7 on page 232 provides examples of imported products from developing countries that are generally eligible for GSP treatment by the United States.

Although the GSP program provides preferential access to industrial countries' markets, several factors erode its effectiveness in reducing trade barriers faced by poor countries. First, preferences mainly apply to products that already face relatively low tariffs. Too, tariff preferences can also be eroded by nontariff measures, such as antidumping duties and safeguards. Moreover, products and countries have been removed from GSP eligibility because of lobbying by domestic interest groups in importing countries. Finally, preferences do little to assist the majority of the world's poor. Most of these living on less than $1 per day live in countries like India and Pakistan, which receive limited preferences in products in which they have a comparative advantage. As a result, developing countries have been frustrated about limited access to the markets of industrial countries.

TABLE 7.7

Imports from Developing Countries that Are Generally Eligible for GSP Treatment by the United States, 2003

The following products receive duty-free access to the U.S. market:

Product	General U.S. Rate of Duty
Live goats	95 cents each
Turkeys	16.2 cents/kg
Milk and cream	6.8 cents/kg
Olives	9.5 cents/kg
Walnuts	28.7 cents/kg
Antifreeze	9.8% ad valorem
V-belts	5.1% ad valorem
Steel	3% ad valorem
Color televisions	5% ad valorem

Source: U.S. International Trade Commission, *The Year in Trade: Operation of the Trade Agreements Program, 2003* (Washington, DC: U.S. Government Printing Office).

Stabilizing Primary-Product Prices

Although developing countries have been gaining ground in exports of manufactured goods, agriculture and natural resource products remain a main source of employment. As we have learned, the export prices and revenues for these products can be quite volatile.

In an attempt to stabilize export prices and revenues of primary products, developing nations have attempted to implement **international commodity agreements (ICAs)**. ICAs are agreements between leading producing and consuming nations of commodities about matters such as stabilizing prices, assuring adequate supplies to consumers, and promoting the economic development of producers. Table 7.8 gives examples of ICAs. To promote stability in commodity markets, ICAs have relied on production and export controls, buffer stocks, and multilateral contracts.

Production and Export Controls

If an ICA accounts for a large share of total world output (or exports) of a commodity, its members

TABLE 7.8

International Commodity Agreements

Agreement	Membership	Principal Stabilization Tools
International Cocoa Organization	26 consuming nations 18 producing nations	Buffer stock, export quota
International Tin Agreement	16 consuming nations 4 producing nations	Buffer stock, export controls
International Coffee Organization	24 consuming nations 43 producing nations	Export quota
International Sugar Organization	8 consuming nations 26 producing nations	Buffer stock, export quota
International Wheat Agreement	41 consuming nations 10 producing nations	Multilateral contract

Source: United Nations Conference on Trade and Development, http://www.unctad.org/en/enhome.htm. See also *Annual Report of the President of the United States on the Trade Agreements Program* (Washington, DC: U.S. Government Printing Office, various issues).

may agree on **export controls** to stabilize export revenues. The idea behind such measures is to offset a decrease in the market demand for the primary commodity by assigning cutbacks in the market supply. If successful, the rise in price due to the curtailment in supply will be sufficient to compensate for the reduction in demand, so that total export earnings will remain at the original level.

Figure 7.3 illustrates the process by which export receipts can be maintained at target levels for members of the International Coffee Agreement. Assume initial market equilibrium at point E. With the equilibrium price at $1 per pound and sales of 60 million pounds, the association's export receipts total $60 million. Let this figure be the target that the association wishes to maintain.

Suppose the market demand for coffee decreases from D_0 to D_1 because of a global economic downturn. The association's export revenues would now fall below the target level. To prevent this from occurring, the coffee producers could artificially hold back the supply of coffee to S_1. Market equilibrium would be at point F, where 40 million pounds of coffee would be sold at a price of $1.50 per pound. Total export receipts would again be at $60 million, the association's target figure. This stabilization technique is contrary to what we might expect because it is based on efforts to increase prices during eras of worsening demand conditions.

In their efforts to stabilize export receipts, producers' associations have adopted export quotas to

ECONOMIC *Applications*

Visit EconData Online

FIGURE 7.3

Production and Export Controls

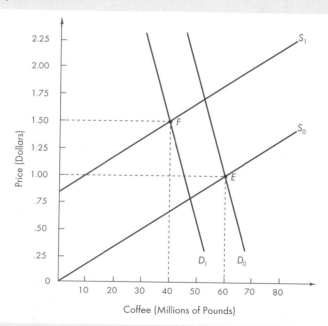

Production controls and export restrictions are used to offset decreases in market demand and increases in market supply so as to stabilize commodity prices. These restrictions, however, are often associated with cheating on the part of participating nations.

regulate market supply. Over the longer run, however, export quotas must be accompanied by **production controls** to be effective. If production is not controlled, expanding surpluses of the member nations will lead to a greater likelihood that prices will be cut and that the association will eventually fail.

Buffer Stocks

Another technique for limiting commodity price swings is the **buffer stock**, in which a producers' association (or international agency) is prepared to buy and sell a commodity in large amounts. The buffer stock consists of supplies of a commodity financed and held by the producers' association. The buffer stock manager buys from the market when supplies are abundant and prices are falling below acceptable levels, and sells from the buffer stock when supplies are tight and prices are high.

Figure 7.4 illustrates the hypothetical price-stabilization efforts of the International Tin Agreement. Assume that the association sets a price range, with a floor of $3.27 per pound and a ceiling of $4.02 per pound to guide the stabilization operations of the buffer-stock manager. Starting at equilibrium point A in Figure 7.4(a), suppose the buffer-stock manager sees the demand for tin rising from D_0 to D_1. To defend the ceiling price of $4.02, the manager must be prepared to sell 20,000 pounds of tin to offset the excess demand for tin at the ceiling price. Conversely, starting at equilibrium point E in Figure 7.4(b), suppose the supply of tin rises from S_0 to S_1. To defend the floor price of $3.27, the buffer-stock manager must purchase the 20,000-pound excess supply that exists at that price.

FIGURE 7.4

Buffer Stock: Price Ceiling and Price Support

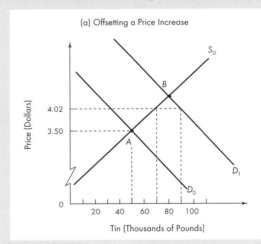

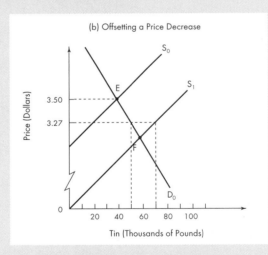

During periods of rising tin demand, the buffer-stock manager sells tin to prevent the price from rising above the ceiling level. Prolonged defense of the ceiling price, however, may result in depletion of the tin stockpile, undermining the effectiveness of this price-stabilization tool and lending to an upward revision of the ceiling price. During periods of abundant tin supplies, the manager purchases tin to prevent the price from falling below the floor level. Prolonged defense of the price floor, however, may exhaust the funds to purchase excess supplies of tin at the floor price and may lead to a downward revision of the floor price.

Proponents of buffer stocks contend that the scheme offers the primary producing nations several advantages. A well-run buffer stock can promote economic efficiency because primary producers can plan investment and expansion if they know that prices will not gyrate. It is also argued that soaring commodity prices invariably ratchet industrial prices upward, whereas commodity price decreases exert no comparable downward pressure. By stabilizing commodity prices, buffer stocks can moderate the price inflation of the industrialized nations. Buffer stocks in this context are viewed as a means of providing primary producers more stability than is allowed by the free market.

Setting up and administering a buffer-stock program is not without costs and problems. The basic difficulty in stabilizing prices with buffer stocks is agreeing on a target price that reflects long-term market trends. If the target price is set too low, the buffer stocks will become depleted as the stock manager sells the commodity on the open market in an attempt to hold market prices in line with the target price. If the target price is set too high, the stock manager must purchase large quantities of the commodity in an effort to support market prices. The costs of holding the stocks tend to be high, for they include transportation expenses, insurance, and labor costs. In their choice of price targets, buffer-stock officials have often made poor decisions. Rather than conduct massive stabilization operations, buffer-stock officials will periodically revise target prices should they fall out of line with long-term price trends.

Multilateral Contracts

Multilateral contracts are another method of stabilizing commodity prices. Such contracts generally stipulate a *minimum price* at which importers will purchase guaranteed quantities from the producing nations and a *maximum price* at which producing nations will sell guaranteed amounts to the importers. Such purchases and sales are designed to hold prices within a target range. Trading under a multilateral contract has often occurred among several exporters and several importing nations, as in the case of the International Sugar Agreement and the International Wheat Agreement.

One possible advantage of the multilateral contract as a price-stabilization device is that, in comparison with buffer stocks or export controls, it results in less distortion of the market mechanism and the allocation of resources. This result is because the typical multilateral contract does not involve output restraints and thus does not check the development of more efficient low-cost producers. If target prices are not set near the long-term equilibrium price, however, discrepancies will occur between supply and demand. Excess demand would indicate a ceiling too low, whereas excess supply would suggest a floor too high. Multilateral contracts also tend to furnish only limited market stability, given the relative ease of withdrawal and entry by participating members.

The OPEC Oil Cartel

Instead of forming international commodity agreements to stabilize export prices and revenues, some nations have formed cartels. Unlike commodity agreements, cartels involve unilateral attempts by exporting nations to increase the price of a product and export revenue by exerting their collective power. One of the most successful cartels in recent history has been the Organization of Petroleum Exporting Countries.

The **Organization of Petroleum Exporting Countries (OPEC)** is a group of nations that sells petroleum on the world market. The OPEC nations attempt to support prices higher than would exist under more competitive conditions to maximize member-nation profits. After operating in obscurity throughout the 1960s, OPEC was able to capture control of petroleum pricing in 1973 and 1974, when the price of oil rose from approximately $3 to $12 per barrel. Triggered by the Iranian revolution in 1979, oil prices doubled from early 1979 to early 1980. By 1981, the price of oil averaged almost $36 per barrel. OPEC's market power stemmed from a strong and inelastic demand for oil combined with its control of about half of world oil production and two-thirds of world oil reserves. Largely because of world recession and falling demand, oil prices fell to $11 per barrel in 1986, only to rebound thereafter.

Prior to OPEC, oil-producing nations behaved like individual competitive sellers. Each nation by itself was so unimportant relative to the overall market that changes in its export levels did not significantly affect international prices over a sustained period of time. By agreeing to restrict competition among themselves via production quotas, the oil-exporting nations found that they could exercise considerable control over world oil prices, as seen in the price hikes of the 1970s.

Maximizing Cartel Profits

A **cartel** attempts to support prices higher than they would be under more competitive conditions, thus increasing the profits of its members. Let us consider some of the difficulties encountered by a cartel in its quest for increased profits.

Assume that there are 10 suppliers of oil, of equal size, in the world oil market and that oil is a standardized product. As a result of previous price wars, each supplier charges a price equal to minimum average cost. Each supplier is afraid to raise its price because it fears that the others will not do so and all of its sales will be lost.

Rather than engage in cutthroat price competition, suppose these suppliers decide to collude and form a cartel. How will a cartel go about maximizing the collective profits of its members? The answer is, by behaving like a profit-maximizing monopolist: Restrict output and drive up price. Figure 7.5 illustrates the demand and cost conditions of the ten oil suppliers as a group [Figure 7.5(a)] and the group's average supplier [Figure 7.5(b)]. Before the cartel is organized, the market price of oil under competition is $20 per barrel. Because each supplier is able to achieve a price that just covers its minimum average cost, economic profit equals zero. Each supplier in the market produces 150 barrels per day. Total industry output equals 1,500 barrels per day (150 × 10 = 1,500).

FIGURE 7.5

Maximizing OPEC Profits

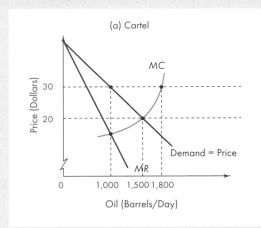

(a) Cartel

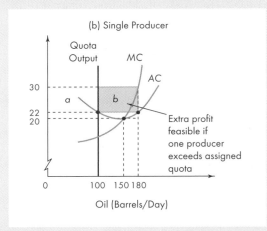

(b) Single Producer

As a cartel, OPEC can increase the price of oil from $20 to $30 per barrel by assigning production quotas for its members. The quotas decrease output from 1,500 to 1,000 barrels per day and permit producers that were pricing oil at average cost to realize a profit. Each producer has the incentive to increase output beyond its assigned quota, to the point at which the OPEC price equals marginal cost. But if all producers increase output in this manner, there will be a surplus of oil at the cartel price, forcing the price of oil back to $20 per barrel.

Suppose the oil suppliers form a cartel whose objective is to maximize the collective profits of its members. To accomplish this objective, the cartel must first establish the profit-maximizing level of output; this output is where marginal revenue equals marginal cost. The cartel then divides up the cartel output among its members by setting up production quotas for each supplier.

In Figure 7.5(a), the cartel will maximize group profits by restricting output from 1,500 barrels per day to 1,000 barrels per day. This means that each member of the cartel must decrease its output from 150 barrels to 100 barrels per day, as shown in Figure 7.5(b). This production quota results in a rise in the market price of a barrel of oil from $20 to $30. Each member realizes a profit of $8 per barrel ($30 − $22 = $8) and a total profit of $800 on the 100 barrels of oil produced (area a).

The next step is to ensure that no cartel member sells more than its quota. This is a difficult task, because each supplier has the incentive to sell more than its assigned quota at the cartel price. But if all cartel members sell more than their quotas, the cartel price will fall toward the competitive level, and profits will vanish. Cartels thus attempt to establish penalties for sellers that cheat on their assigned quotas.

In Figure 7.5(b), each cartel member realizes economic profits of $800 by selling at the assigned quota of 100 barrels per day. However, an *individual* supplier knows that it can increase its profits if it sells more than this amount at the cartel price. Each individual supplier has the incentive to increase output to the level at which the cartel price, $30, equals the supplier's marginal cost; this occurs at 180 barrels per day. At this output level, the supplier would realize economic profits of $1,440, represented by area $a + b$. By cheating on its agreed-upon production quota, the supplier is able to realize an increase in profits of $640 ($1,440 − $800 = $640), denoted by area b. Note that this increase in profits occurs if the price of oil does not decrease as the supplier expands output—that is, if the supplier's extra output is a negligible portion of the industry supply.

A single supplier may be able to get away with producing more than its quota without sig-

nificantly decreasing the market price of oil. But if each member of the cartel increases its output to 180 barrels per day to earn more profits, total output will be 1,800 barrels (180 × 10 = 1,800). To maintain the price at $30, however, industry output must be held to only 1,000 barrels per day. The excess output of 800 barrels puts downward pressure on price, which causes economic profits to decline. If economic profits fall back to zero (the competitive level), the cartel will likely break up.

Besides the problem of cheating, there are several other obstacles to forming a cartel:

Number of Sellers

Generally speaking, the larger the number of sellers, the more difficult it is to form a cartel. Coordination of price and output policies among three sellers that dominate the market is more easily achieved than when there are 10 sellers each having 10 percent of the market.

Cost and Demand Differences

When cartel members' costs and product demands differ, it is more difficult to agree on price. Such differences result in a different profit-maximizing price for each member, so there is no single price that can be agreed upon by all members.

Potential Competition

The increased profits that may occur under a cartel may attract new competitors. Their entry into the market triggers an increase in product supply, which leads to falling prices and profits. A successful cartel thus depends on its ability to block the market entry of new competitors.

Economic Downturn

Economic downturn is generally problematic for cartels. As market sales dwindle in a weakening economy, profits fall. Cartel members may conclude that they can escape serious decreases in profits by reducing prices, in expectation of gaining sales at the expense of other cartel members.

Substitute Goods

The price-making ability of a cartel is weakened when buyers can substitute other goods (coal and natural gas) for the good that it produces (oil).

Are International Labor Standards Needed to Prevent Social Dumping?

Trade Conflicts

A U.S. presidential task force composed of apparel industry representatives, unions, and human rights activists recently agreed to codes of conduct for labor practices by multinational corporations. In response to negative publicity, Nike, the athletic shoe and apparel company, hired former U.S. ambassador Andrew Young to conduct an independent investigation of its labor practices. Moreover, the Federation of International Football Associations announced it would not purchase soccer balls made with child labor. These events point to a growing concern about labor standards in the developing world.

High unemployment rates in Western Europe and stagnant wages of unskilled workers in the United States have contributed to a new ambivalence in the industrial countries about the benefits of trade with developing countries. Labor unions and human rights activists in industrial countries fear that industrial-country wages and benefits are being forced down by unfair competition from countries with much lower labor costs—so-called "social dumping." They also maintain that market access in the industrial countries should be conditioned on raising labor standards in developing countries to prevent a "race to the bottom" in wages and benefits. Trade sanctions imposed in response to violations of labor standards are sometimes referred to as a "social clause."

There are two main arguments for the international harmonization of labor standards. The economic argument suggests that low wages and labor standards in developing countries threaten the living standards of workers in developed countries. The moral argument asserts that low wages and labor standards violate the human rights of workers in the developing countries. Human rights activists believe that raising labor standards in developing countries will benefit workers in these countries and that some labor practices are morally intolerable, such as the exploitation of working children and discrimination based on gender.

Proponents of the international harmonization of labor standards will not usually admit openly to any protectionist intent. However, developing countries remain deeply suspicious that disguised protectionism motivates many of the calls for compliance with labor standards of industrial countries, especially if the latter are to be enforced with trade sanctions. Some unions and human rights groups in the United States continue to insist that conditions on wages and benefits should be attached to agreements on labor standards.

That fairness should be observed in international competition seems indisputable. What constitutes fairness is not so obvious. Does the abundance of cheap labor in China render it an unfair competitor in the production of goods requiring relatively large amounts of unskilled labor? If so, do the plentiful coconut trees in the Philippines render it an unfair competitor in the production of coconut oil?

Another question concerns the implementation of international labor standards. Most industrial-county labor standards are not feasible for many developing countries. Concerning child labor, for example, it is indeed disturbing that young children in developing countries toil under harsh conditions for low pay. But the earnings of these children may be important to their families'—and their own—survival. Moreover, setting strict standards in a developing country's regulated sector may consign children to even more degrading, less remunerative work in the unregulated sector. Moreover, if the goal is to enhance the welfare of developing countries, perhaps a more effective way would be to allow free international migration from low- to high-standard countries, an argument rarely made by proponents of harmonization of labor standards.

Nonobservance of international labor standards may impair, rather than enhance, overall competitiveness. To be sure, exploitative child labor and forced labor may suppress wage rates, but such practices also prevent those victimized from shifting readily into activities that best match their skills and goals, and thus reduce their productivity.

Source: Stephen Golub, "Are International Labor Standards Needed to Prevent Social Dumping?" *Finance and Development*, December 1997, pp. 20–23.

OPEC as a Cartel

OPEC has generally disavowed the term *cartel*. However, its organization is composed of a secretariat, a conference of ministers, a board of governors, and an economic commission. OPEC has repeatedly attempted to formulate plans for systematic production control among its members as a way of firming up oil prices. However, OPEC hardly controls prices. The group currently controls less than 40 percent of world supply, insufficient to establish an effective cartel. Moreover, OPEC's production agreements have not always lived up to expectations because too many member nations have violated the agreements by producing more than their assigned quotas. Since 1983, when production quotas were first assigned to members, OPEC's actual production levels have almost always been greater than its target levels, meaning that countries have been selling more oil

than they're supposed to—in other words, they've been cheating, as shown in Figure 7.6. Simply put, OPEC does not have any club with which to enforce its edicts.

The exception is Saudi Arabia, owner of the world's largest reserves and lowest production costs. The Saudis spend immense capital to maintain more production capacity than they use, allowing them to influence, or threaten to influence, prices over the short run.

In the future, it is likely that OPEC will struggle to achieve higher prices amid growing supply competition. The recovery of Iraq's exports, following two wars with the United States and its allies, may strain OPEC's efforts to support higher prices. By 2007, significant new supplies from West Africa, the Caspian, Russia, deepwater areas of the Atlantic basin, and elsewhere are expected to come on stream and, coupled with rising capacity within

FIGURE 7.6

OPEC Production and Quotas: Blowing the Tops off Oil Caps

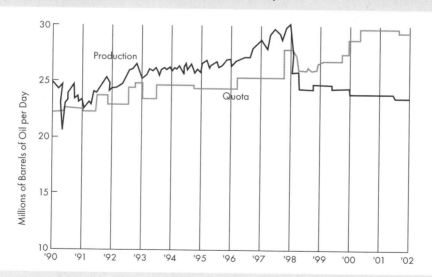

Since quotas were first assigned to members, OPEC's actual production levels have almost always been greater than its target levels. In other words, the cartel members have been cheating.

Source: *OPEC Fact Sheet,* http://www.eia.doe.gov.

OPEC, exert downward pressure on prices. In addition, the United States might initiate policies to increase the supply and/or decrease demand. However, achieving these measures involves difficult choices for Americans, such as:

- *Raising the fuel economy standards mandated by the federal government.* Analysts estimated that if the gas mileage of new cars had increased by only one mile per gallon each year since 1987, and the mileage of light trucks by a half-mile per gallon, the United States would be saving 1.3 million barrels of oil each day. However, increasing fuel economy standards would meet resistance from auto producers, who would see their production costs increasing because of this policy.

- *Increasing the federal excise tax on gasoline.* Although the resulting hike in the price of gasoline would provide an incentive for consumers to conserve, this would conflict with the preference of Americans for low-priced gasoline. Moreover, rising gasoline prices would especially harm low-income consumers with the least ability to pay.

- *Allowing oil companies to drill on federal land designated as wilderness in Alaska, where there is a good chance they might find oil.* Perhaps, but what happens when the wilderness is destroyed, never to return? Who pays for that?

- *Diversifying imports.* Although it could be expensive, the United States might forge closer ties with oil producers outside the Middle East to diminish dependence on the unstable region. However, this would require the United States to work even more closely with unsavory regimes in countries like Angola, Indonesia, and Vietnam. Also, OPEC oil is very cheap to get out of the ground. While it costs deepwater drillers like ExxonMobil or Conoco $6 to $8 to produce a barrel in the Gulf of Mexico or the North Sea, the Saudis and Kuwaitis spend a fraction of that—$1 a barrel or less. This cost advantage enhances OPEC's market power.

Economic Growth Strategies: Import Substitution Versus Export-Led Growth

Besides seeking economic assistance from advanced countries, developing countries have pursued two competing strategies for industrialization: (1) an inward-looking strategy (import substitution), in which industries are established largely to supply the domestic market, and foreign trade is assigned negligible importance; (2) an outward-looking strategy (export-led growth) of encouraging the development of industries in which the country enjoys comparative advantage, with heavy reliance on foreign nations as purchasers of the increased production of exportable goods.

Import Substitution

During the 1950s and 1960s, the industrialization strategy of **import substitution** became popular in developing nations such as Argentina, Brazil, and Mexico; some countries still use it today. Import substitution involves extensive use of trade barriers to protect domestic industries from import competition. The strategy is inward-oriented in that trade and industrial incentives favor production for the domestic market over the export market. For example, if fertilizer imports occur, import substitution calls for establishment of a domestic fertilizer industry to produce replacements for fertilizer imports. In the extreme, import-substitution policies could lead to complete self-sufficiency.

The rationale for import substitution arises from the developing countries' perspective on trade. Many developing countries feel that they cannot export manufactured goods because they cannot compete with established firms of the industrial countries, especially in view of the high trade barriers maintained by industrial countries. Given the need for economic growth and development, developing countries have no choice but to manufacture for themselves some of the goods they now import. The use of tariffs and quotas restricts imports, and the domestic market is reserved for domestic manufacturers. This rationale is often combined with the infant-industry argument: Protecting start-up industries will allow them to grow to a size where they can compete with the industries of the developed countries.

In one respect, import substitution appears logical: If a good is demanded and imported, why not produce it domestically? The economist's answer is that it may be more costly to produce it domestically and cheaper to import it; comparative advantage should decide which goods are imported and which are exported.

Encouraging economic development via import substitution has several advantages:

- The risks of establishing a home industry to replace imports are low because the home market for the manufactured good already exists.
- It is easier for a developing nation to protect its manufacturers against foreign competitors than to force industrial nations to reduce their trade restrictions on products exported by the developing nations.
- To avoid the import tariff walls of the developing country, foreigners have an incentive to locate manufacturing plants in the country, thus providing jobs for local workers.

In contrast to these advantages are several disadvantages:

- Because trade restrictions shelter domestic industries from international competition, they have no incentive to increase their efficiency.
- Given the small size of the domestic market in many developing countries, manufacturers cannot take advantage of economies of scale and thus have high unit costs.
- Because the resources employed in the protected industry would otherwise have been employed elsewhere, protection of import-competing industries automatically discriminates against all other industries, including potential exporting ones.
- Once investment is sunk in activities that were profitable only because of tariffs and quotas, any attempt to remove those restrictions is generally strongly resisted.
- Import substitution also breeds corruption. The more protected the economy, the greater the gains to be had from illicit activity such as smuggling.

Import-Substitution Laws Backfire on Brazil

Although import-substitution laws have often been used by developing nations in their industrialization efforts, they sometimes backfire. Let us consider the example of Brazil.

In 1991, Enrico Misasi was the president of the Brazilian unit of Italian computer-maker Olivetti Inc., but he did not have an Olivetti computer. The computer behind his desk was instead manufactured by two Brazilian firms; it cost three times more than an Olivetti, and its quality was inferior. Rather than manufacturing computers in Brazil, Olivetti Inc. was permitted to manufacture only typewriters and calculators.

This anomaly was the result of import-substitution policies practiced by Brazil until 1991. From the 1970s until 1991, importing a foreign personal computer—or a microchip, a fax machine, or dozens of other electronic goods—was prohibited. Not only were electronic imports prohibited, but foreign firms willing to invest in Brazilian manufacturing plants were also banned. Joint ventures were deterred by a law that kept foreign partners from owning more than 30 percent of a local business. These restrictions were intended to foster a home-grown electronics industry. Instead, even the law's proponents came to admit that the Brazilian electronics industry was uncompetitive and technologically outdated.

The costs of the import ban were clearly apparent by the early 1990s. Almost no Brazilian automobiles were equipped with electronic fuel injection or antiskid brake systems, both widespread throughout the world. Products such as Apple Computer's Macintosh computer were not permitted to be sold in Brazil. Brazil chose to allow Texas Instruments to shut down its Brazilian semiconductor plant, resulting in a loss of 250 jobs, rather than permit Texas Instruments to invest $133 million to modernize its product line. By adhering to its import-substitution policy, Brazil wound up a largely computer-unfriendly nation: By 1991, only

12 percent of small- and medium-sized Brazilian companies were at least partially computerized, and only 0.5 percent of Brazil's classrooms were equipped with computers. Many Brazilian companies postponed modernization because computers available overseas were not manufactured in Brazil and could not be imported. Some Brazilian companies resorted to smuggling in computers and other electrical equipment; those companies that adhered to the rules wound up with outdated and overpriced equipment.

Realizing that the import-substitution policy had backfired on its computer industry, in 1991 the Brazilian government scrapped a cornerstone of its nationalistic approach by lifting the electronics import ban—though continuing to protect domestic industry with high import duties. The government also permitted foreign joint-venture partners to raise their ownership shares from 30 percent to 49 percent and to transfer technology into the Brazilian economy.

Export-Led Growth

Another development strategy is **export-led growth,** or **export-oriented policy.** The strategy is outward-oriented because it links the domestic economy to the world economy. Instead of pursuing growth through the protection of domestic industries suffering comparative disadvantage, the strategy involves promoting growth through the export of manufactured goods. Trade controls are either nonexistent or very low, in the sense that any disincentives to export resulting from import barriers are counterbalanced by export subsidies. Industrialization is viewed as a natural outcome of development instead of being an objective pursued at the expense of the economy's efficiency. By the 1970s, many developing countries were abandoning their import-substitution strategies and shifting emphasis to export-led growth.

Export-oriented policies have a number of advantages: (1) They encourage industries in which developing countries are likely to have a comparative advantage, such as labor-intensive manufactured goods; (2) By providing a larger market in which to sell, they allow domestic manufacturers greater scope for exploiting economies of scale;

(3) By maintaining low restrictions on imported goods, they impose a competitive discipline on domestic firms that forces them to increase efficiency.

Figure 7.7 illustrates the relationship between openness to international trade and economic growth for developing countries. A sample of 72 countries was split into "globalizers" and "nonglobalizers." The globalizers were defined as the 24 countries that achieved the largest increases in their ratio of trade to gross domestic product from 1975 to 1995. During the 1960s and 1970s, the nonglobalizers experienced somewhat faster growth of real income per capita on average than the globalizers. During the 1980s, however, globalizers experienced much higher growth rates; real income per capita grew an average of 3.5 percent a year in these countries, compared with 0.8 percent for the nonglobalizers. The divergence was even greater during the 1990s, with 5.0 percent annual growth for the globalizers versus 1.4 percent for the rest. To put these differences into perspective, had the average globalizer and the average nonglobalizer each begun with an income per capita of $1,000 in 1980, by 2000 the globalizer's income per capita would have growth to $2,300, and the nonglobalizer's only to $1,240.

This supports the notion that the economic performance of nations implementing export-led growth policies has been superior to that of nations using import-substitution policies. Export-led growth policies introduce international competition to domestic markets, which encourages efficient firms and discourages inefficient ones. By creating a more competitive environment, they also promote higher productivity and hence faster economic growth. Conversely, import-substitution policies relying on trade protection switch demand to products produced domestically. Exporting is then discouraged by both the increased cost of imported inputs and the increased cost of domestic inputs relative to the price received by exporters.

Is Economic Growth Good for the Poor?

Although the evidence strongly suggests that trade is good for growth, is growth good for poor workers in developing countries? Critics argue

FIGURE 7.7

Openness and Economic Growth

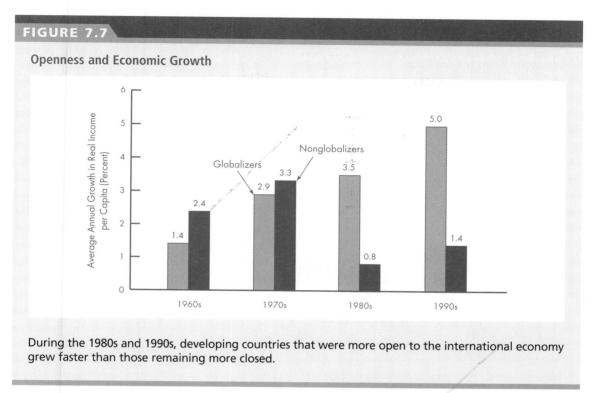

During the 1980s and 1990s, developing countries that were more open to the international economy grew faster than those remaining more closed.

Source: David Dollar and Aart Kraay, *Trade, Growth, and Poverty,* World Bank Development Research Group, 2001.

that growth tends to be bad for the poor if the growth in question has been promoted by trade or foreign investment. Investment inflows, they say, make economies less stable, exposing workers to the risk of financial crisis and to the attentions of industrial-country banks. Moreover, they contend that growth driven by trade provides Western multinational corporations a dominant role in third-world development. That is bad, because Western multinationals are not interested in development at all, only in making larger profits by ensuring that the poor stay poor. The proof of this, say critics, lies in the evidence that economic inequality increases even as developing countries, and industrial countries, increase their national income, and in the multinationals' use of sweatshops when producing goods. So if workers' welfare is your primary concern, the fact that trade promotes growth, even if true, misses the point.

However, there is strong evidence that growth aids the poor. Developing countries that have

achieved continuing growth, as in East Asia, have made significant progress in decreasing poverty. The countries where widespread poverty persists, or is worsening, are those where growth is weakest, notably in Africa. Although economic policy can affect the extent of poverty, in the long run growth is much more important.

There is intense debate over the extent to which the poor benefit from economic growth. Critics argue that the potential benefits of economic growth for the poor are undermined or even offset entirely by sharp increases in inequality that accompany growth. However, proponents contend that liberal economic policies such as open markets and monetary and fiscal stability raise incomes of the poor and everyone else in society proportionately. Researchers at the World Bank have investigated this topic. As seen in Figure 7.8 on page 244, they confirm that, in a sample of 92 industrial and developing countries

ECONOMIC *Applications*

Visit EconDebate Online for a debate on this topic

FIGURE 7.8

Growth Is Good for the Poor

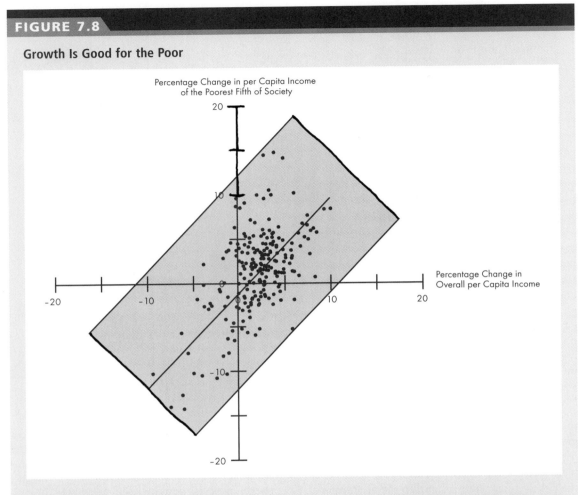

The figure shows a regression line based on a sample of 92 industrial and developing countries. Each point in the figure represents one country. The figure shows that average incomes of the poorest fifth of society rise proportionately with overall incomes. This suggests that economic growth benefits the poor as much as everyone else.

Source: David Dollar and Aart Kraay, *Growth Is Good for the Poor*, The World Bank, Washington, DC, 2001, p. 45.

across the world, the incomes of the poor have risen one for one with overall growth. This implies that growth generally does benefit the poor as much as everyone else, so that growth-enhancing policies should be at the center of successful poverty reduction strategies.

However, suppose it were true that income equality is increasing between the industrial and developing countries. Would this be a terrible indictment of globalization? Perhaps not. It would be disturbing if inequality throughout the world were increasing because incomes of the poorest were decreasing in absolute terms, instead of in relative terms. However, this is rare. Even in Africa, which is behaving poorly in relative terms, incomes have been increasing and broader indicators of development have been getting better. Perhaps it is too little, but something is better than nothing.

Can All Developing Countries Achieve Export-Led Growth?

Although exporting can promote growth for developing economies, it depends on the willingness and ability of industrial countries to go on absorbing large amounts of goods from developing countries. Pessimists argue that this process involves a fallacy of composition. If all developing countries tried to export simultaneously, the price of their exports would be driven down on world markets. Moreover, industrialized nations may become apprehensive of foreign competition, especially during eras of high unemployment, and thus impose tariffs to reduce competition from imports. Will liberalizing trade will be self-defeating if too many developing countries try to export simultaneously?

Although developing countries as a group are enormous in terms of geography and population, in economic terms they are small. Taken together, the exports of all the world's poor and middle-income countries equal only 5 percent of world output. This is an amount approximately equivalent to the national output of the United Kingdom. Even if growth in the global demand for imports were somehow capped, a concerted export drive by those parts of the developing world not already engaged in the effort would put no great strain on the global trading system.

Pessimists also tend to underestimate the scope for intraindustry specialization in trade, which gives developing countries a further set of new trade opportunities. The same goes for new trade among developing countries, as opposed to trade with the industrial countries. Often, as developing countries grow, they move away from labor-intensive manufactures to more sophisticated kinds of production. This makes room in the markets they previously served for goods from countries that are not yet so advanced. For example, in the 1970s, Japan withdrew from labor-intensive manufacturing, making way for exports from South Korea, Taiwan, and Singapore. In the 1980s and 1990s, South Korea, Taiwan, and Singapore did same, as China began moving

into those markets. As developing countries grow by exporting, their own demand for imports rises.

East Asian Economies

In spite of the sluggish economic performance of many developing countries, some have realized strong and sustained economic growth, as seen in Table 7.9. What accounts for this performance?

East Asia's Growth Strategy

The **East Asian tigers** are highly diverse in natural resources, populations, cultures, and economic policies. However, they have in common characteristics underlying their economic success: (1) high rates of investment and (2) high and increasing endowments of human capital due to universal primary and secondary education.

To foster competitiveness, East Asian governments have invested in their people and provided a favorable competitive climate for private enterprise. They have also kept their economies open to international trade. The East Asian economies have actively sought foreign technology, such as licenses, capital-good imports, and foreign training.

The East Asian economies have generally discouraged the organization of trade unions—

TABLE 7.9

East Asian Economies' Growth Rates, 1992–2002

Country	GDP Growth Average Annual Percent
China	9.0%
Singapore	6.1
South Korea	5.3
Malaysia	5.3
Philippines	3.7
Hong Kong, China	3.3
Thailand	2.5
Indonesia	2.5

Source: The World Bank Group, *Data by Country*, http://www.worldbank.org/data. Scroll to "Country at a Glance Tables." See also the World Bank, *World Development Report*, 2004.

whether by deliberate suppression (South Korea and Taiwan), by government paternalism (Singapore), or by a laissez-faire policy (Hong Kong). The outcome has been the prevention of minimum-wage legislation and the maintenance of free and competitive labor markets.

In the post–World War II era, trade policies in the East Asian economies (except Hong Kong) began with a period of import substitution. To develop their consumer-good industries, these countries levied high tariffs and quantitative restrictions on imported goods. They also subsidized some manufacturing industries such as textiles. Although these policies initially led to increased domestic production, as time passed they inflicted costs on the East Asian economies. Because import-substitution policies encouraged the importing of capital and intermediate goods and discouraged the exporting of manufactured goods, they led to large trade deficits for the East Asian economies. To obtain the foreign exchange necessary to finance these deficits, the East Asian economies shifted to a strategy of outward orientation and export promotion.

Export-push strategies were enacted in the East Asian economies by the late 1950s and 1960s. Singapore and Hong Kong set up trade regimes that were close to free trade. Japan, South Korea, and Taiwan initiated policies to promote exports while protecting domestic producers from import competition. Indonesia, Malaysia, and Thailand adopted a variety of policies to encourage exports while gradually reducing import restrictions. These measures contributed to an increase in the East Asian economies' share of world exports, with manufactured exports accounting for most of this growth.

The stunning success of the East Asian economies has created problems, however. The industrialize-at-all-costs emphasis has left many of the East Asian economies with major pollution problems. Whopping trade surpluses have triggered a growing wave of protectionist sentiment overseas, especially in the United States, which sees the East Asian economies depending heavily on the U.S. market for future export growth.

Flying-Geese Pattern of Growth

It is widely recognized that East Asian economies have followed a **flying-geese pattern of economic growth** in which countries gradually move up in technological development by following in the pattern of countries ahead of them in the development process. For example, Taiwan and Malaysia take over leadership in apparel and textiles from Japan as Japan moves into the higher-technology sectors of automotive, electronic, and other capital goods. A decade or so later, Taiwan and Malaysia are able to upgrade to automotive and electronics products, while the apparel and textile industries move to Thailand, Vietnam, and Indonesia.

To some degree, the flying-geese pattern is a result of market forces: Labor-abundant nations will become globally competitive in labor-intensive industries, such as footwear, and will graduate to more capital- or skill-intensive industries as savings and education deepen the availability of capital and skilled workers. However, as the East Asian economies have demonstrated, more than just markets are necessary for flying-geese development. Even basic labor-intensive products, such as electronics assembly, are increasingly determined by multinational enterprises and technologies created in industrial nations.

For East Asian economies, a strong export platform has underlain their flying-geese pattern of development. East Asian governments have utilized several versions of an export platform, such as bonded warehouses, free-trade zones, joint ventures, and strategic alliances with multinational enterprises. Governments supported these mechanisms with economic policies that aided the incentives for labor-intensive exports.

China: Awakening Giant

In the early 1970s, the People's Republic of China was an insignificant participant in the world market for goods. The value of its exports and imports was less than $15 billion, and it was only the 30th largest exporting country. China was also a negligible participant in world financial markets. By 2001, China had growth to the world's second largest economy, with a national output over half that of the United States and 60 percent larger than Japan's. What caused this transformation?

Modern China began in 1949, when a revolutionary communist movement captured control of the nation. Soon after the communist takeover, China instituted a Soviet model of central planning with emphasis on rapid economic growth, particularly industrial growth. The state took over urban manufacturing industry, collectivized agriculture, eliminated household farming, and established compulsory production quotas.

In the late 1950s, China departed from the Soviet model and shifted from large-scale, capital-intensive industry to small-scale, labor-intensive industry scattered across the countryside. Little attention was paid to linking individual reward to individual effort. Instead, a commitment to the success of the collective plans was relied on as the motivation for workers. This system proved to be an economic failure. Although manufacturing output rose following the reforms, product quality was low and production costs were high. Because China's agricultural output was insufficient to feed its people, China became a large importer of grains, vegetable oils, and cotton. As a result of this economic deterioration, plant managers, scientists, engineers, and scholars, who favored material incentives and reform, were denounced and sent to work in the fields.

By the 1970s, China could see its once-poor neighbors—Japan, Singapore, Taiwan, and South Korea—enjoying extraordinary growth and prosperity. This led to China's "marketizing" its economy through small, step-by-step changes to minimize economic disruption and political opposition. In agriculture and industry, reforms were made to increase the role of the producing unit, to increase individual incentives, and to reduce the role of state planners. Most goods were sold for market-determined—not state-controlled—prices. Greater competition was allowed both between new firms and between new firms and state firms; by 2000, nonstate firms manufactured about 75 percent of

China's industrial output. Moreover, China opened its economy to foreign investment and joint ventures. The Chinese government's monopoly over foreign trade was also disbanded; in its place, economic zones were established in which firms could keep foreign exchange earnings and hire and fire workers.

ECONOMIC *Applications*

Visit EconNews Online
International Trade

By 2000, China had made all of the easy economic adjustments in its transition toward capitalism: letting farmers sell their own produce and opening its doors to foreign investors and salespeople. Other reforms still needed addressing: (1) a massive restructuring of state-owned industries, which were losing money; (2) a cleanup of bankrupt state banks; (3) the creation of a social security system in a society that once guaranteed a job for life; and (4) establishment of a monetary system with a central bank free of Communist Party or government control. If China were to shut down money-losing enterprises, millions of workers would be laid off with no benefits; their addition to the 100 million-plus workers already adrift in China could be volatile. In addition, banks that lent the state companies cash would require cash infusions if bankruptcies increased in the state sector. Such loans could render a central bank monetary policy ineffective and could fuel inflation.

Although China has dismantled much of its centrally planned economy and has permitted free enterprise to replace it, political freedoms have not increased. Recall the Chinese government's use of military force to end a pro-democracy demonstration in Beijing's Tiananmen Square in 1989, which led to loss of life and demonstrated the Communist Party's determination to maintain its political power. China's evolution toward capitalism has thus consisted of expanded use of market forces under a communist political system. Today, China describes itself as a *socialist market economy.*

Concerning international trade, China has followed a pattern consistent with the principle of comparative advantage. On the export side, China has supplied a growing share of the world's demand for relatively inexpensive sporting goods, toys, footwear, garments, and textiles. These goods embody labor-intensive production methods and reflect China's abundance of labor. On the import side, China is a growing market for machinery, transportation equipment, and other capital goods that require higher levels of technologies than China can produce domestically. Most of China's economic expansion since 1978 has been driven by rapid growth in exports and investment spending. Table 7.10 illustrates China's direction of trade in 2002.

How will future trading patterns evolve for China? Among major developing nations, China is the most poorly endowed with land except for Singapore. Therefore, China's specialization in labor-intensive manufacturing relative to agriculture is expected to be the greatest. This will result in China's importing food and moving into manufacturing exports to feed and generate employment for an expanding population. Its high savings rate allows the buildup of capital necessary to make the transition. At the same time, China will likely lose market shares in primary products.

What manufactured goods China exports will also depend on the quality of the labor force. With more people educated up to the secondary-school level than to the tertiary level, and with low capital per worker, China is more likely to emphasize low-skilled manufactures and light industry. With its weaker higher-education base,

TABLE 7.10

Direction of China's Trade in 2002

Area	Exports (Billions of Dollars)	Imports (Billions of Dollars)
Industrial Countries	$177.5	$132.6
Japan	48.5	53.5
United States	70.1	27.3
Other	58.9	51.8
Developing Countries	147.5	147.3
Africa	6.0	5.4
Asia	110.7	112.1
Europe	11.1	12.2
Other	19.7	17.6
	$325.0	$279.9

Source: International Monetary Fund, *Direction of Trade Statistics Yearbook*, Washington, DC, December 2003.

China is unlikely to emerge as a major source of knowledge-based and complementary skilled-labor products.

China is a nation currently in transition from an agricultural economy to an industrial one. It surely will transition one day to a largely services economy and "outgrow" manufacturing, as did the United States in gaining its wealth, education, and human capital. But right now, China is following the footsteps of early twentieth-century America; that is, developing its industrial base.

China Enters the World Trade Organization

After 15 years of negotiations, China formally entered the WTO in December 2001. China made its accession to the WTO a priority for several reasons. First, it would represent international recognition of China's growing economic power. Also, it would give China access to the dispute-resolution process in the WTO, reducing the threat of unilaterally imposed restrictions on Chinese exports. Furthermore, it would make it easier for reformers in China to push for liberalization policies if they could argue that such steps are necessary to fulfill China's international obligations. Finally, Chinese leaders realized that WTO membership would induce the United States to grant China permanent normal trade relations, thus ending the annual trade status renewal process and subsequent congressional debate over U.S.–China relations.

U.S. trade officials insisted that China's entry into the WTO had to be based on meaningful terms that would require China to significantly reduce trade and investment barriers within a relatively short period of time. Many U.S. trade analysts viewed China's WTO accession process as an opportunity for gaining substantially greater access to China's market and to help reduce the large and increasing U.S.–China trade imbalance. Other analysts contended that it would advance the cause of human rights in China by enhancing the rule of law there for business activities, diminishing the central government's control over the economy and promoting the expansion of the private sector in China.

Does Foreign Direct Investment Hinder or Help Economic Development?

Foreign investment brings higher wages, and is a major source of technology transfer and managerial skills in host developing countries. This contributes to rising prosperity in the developing countries concerned, as well as enhancing demand for higher value-added exports from advanced economies. — OECD *Policy Brief,* No. 6, 1998

As investors search the globe for the highest return, they are often drawn to places endowed with bountiful natural resources but handicapped by weak or ineffective environmental laws. Many people and communities are harmed as the environment that sustains them is damaged or destroyed—villagers are displaced by large construction projects, for example, and indigenous peoples watch their homelands disappear as timber companies level old-growth forests. Foreign investment-fed growth also promotes western-style consumerism, boosting car ownership, paper use, and Big Mac consumption rates toward the untenable levels found in the United States—with grave potential consequences for the health of the natural world, the stability of the earth's climate, and the security of food supplies. — Hilary French, "Capital Flows and the Environment," *Foreign Policy in Focus,* August 1998

One of the requirements for economic development in a low-income economy is an increase in the nation's stock of capital. A developing nation may increase the amount of capital in the domestic economy by encouraging foreign direct investment. Foreign direct investment occurs when foreign firms either locate production plants in the domestic economy or acquire a substantial ownership position in a domestic firm. This topic will be discussed further in Chapter 9.

Many developing economies have attempted to restrict foreign direct investment because of nationalist sentiment and concerns about foreign economic and political influence. One reason for this sentiment is that many developing countries have operated as colonies of more developed economies. This colonial experience has often resulted in a legacy of concern that foreign direct investment may serve as a modern form of economic colonialism in which foreign companies might exploit the resources of the host country.

In recent years, however, restrictions on foreign direct investment in many developing economies have been substantially reduced as a result of international treaties, external pressure from the IMF or World Bank, or unilateral actions by governments that have come to believe that foreign direct investment will encourage economic growth in the host country. This has resulted in a rather dramatic expansion in the level of foreign direct investment in some developing economies.

Foreign direct investment may encourage economic growth in the short run by increasing aggregate demand in the host economy. In the long run, the increase in the stock of capital raises the productivity of labor and leads to higher incomes and further increases in aggregate demand. Another long-run impact, however, comes through the transfer of technological knowledge from industrial to developing economies. Many economists argue that this transfer of technology may be the primary benefit of foreign direct investment.

It is often argued, however, that it is necessary to restrict foreign direct investment in a given industry for national security purposes. This serves as a justification for prohibitions on investment in defense industries and in other industries that are deemed essential for national security. Most governments, for example, would be concerned if their weapons were produced by companies owned by firms in countries that might serve as future enemies.

Environmentalists are concerned that the growth of foreign direct investment in developing economies may lead to a deterioration in the global environment since investment is expanding more rapidly in countries that have relatively lax environmental standards. The absence of restrictive environmental standards, it is argued, is one of the reasons for the relatively high rate of return on capital investment in less-developed economies. Technology transfer from the developed economies, however, may also result in the adoption of more efficient and environmentally sound production techniques than would have been adopted in the absence of foreign investment.

Source: John Kane, *Does Foreign Direct Investment Hinder or Help Economic Development?* South-Western Policy Debate, 2004.

Among the agreements that China made when it acceded to the WTO are:

- Reduce its average tariff for industrial goods to 8.9 percent and to 15 percent for agriculture by 2010.
- Limit subsidies for agricultural production to 8.5 percent of the value of farm output and not maintain export subsidies on agricultural exports.
- Grant full trade and distribution rights to foreign enterprises in China. Price controls will not be used to provide protection to Chinese firms.
- Fully open the banking system to foreign financial institutions. Joint ventures in insurance and telecommunication will be permitted.
- Protect the intellectual property of foreigners according to internationally agreed-upon standards.

Besides affecting its domestic economy, China's accession to the WTO affects trade everywhere, as seen in Table 7.11. In particular, China's economic success will likely come at the expense of workers and companies throughout the developing world that offer cheap labor but not much else. In India, for example, which has some of the world's lowest wages, low-tech industries cannot compete with the Chinese in productivity. India's products will increasingly become less attractive to consumers as Chinese-made goods surge into the world economy.

Does the U.S. economy gain from China's accession to the WTO? Many sectors of the U.S. economy will likely benefit from China's accession to the WTO as Beijing removes certain trade barriers: agriculture, beverages, chemicals, plastics, electronic equipment, and the like. However, trade liberalization will foster efficiency gains for China because of further investment in China's economy, thereby expanding production. Also, China will benefit from increased imports of capital goods, which would improve its productivity. Therefore, some U.S. industries will lose ground to imports of Chinese goods: footwear, wearing apparel, wood products, and other light manufacturers.

TABLE 7.11

China's Entry into the WTO Will Affect Trade Everywhere

North America	North American farmers will get a new market for millions of tons of grain. Computer, telecom-gear, semiconductor producers will get tariff-free access to China.
Mexico	Shoe and garment manufacturers will be handicapped as quotas restricting Chinese exports to the United States are lifted.
European Union	Imports of Chinese dishes, shoes, and kitchen utensils will increase as Europe eliminates quotas.
Japan	Imports of various consumer goods will increase as more Japanese manufacturers shift production to China-based suppliers. Electronics, vehicle, and equipment exports will increase.
Southeast Asia	Malaysia, Indonesia, Thailand, and the Philippines will lose foreign investment to China. Pressure will increase to upgrade industries and workforces.
Taiwan	Its trade surplus with China will decline. More production will shift to China, enhancing competitiveness of Taiwanese tech companies.
South Korea	Exports of fabrics to China's expanding apparel industry could decrease, as could outflow of steel and industrial gear.

Source: "Asia's Future: China," *Business Week*, October 29, 2001, pp. 48–52.

Summary

1. Developing nations tend to be characterized by relatively low levels of gross domestic product per capita, shorter life expectancies, and lower levels of adult literacy. Many developing countries believe that the current international trading system, based on the principle of comparative advantage, is irrelevant for them.

2. Among the alleged problems facing the developing nations are (a) unstable export markets, (b) worsening terms of trade, and (c) limited market access.

3. Among the institutions and policies that have been created to support developing countries are the World Bank, International Monetary Fund, and the generalized system of preferences.

4. International commodity agreements have been formed to stabilize the prices and revenues of producers of primary products. The methods used to attain this stability are buffer stocks, export controls, and multilateral contracts. In practice, these methods have yielded modest success.

5. The OPEC oil cartel was established in 1960 in reaction to the control that the major international oil companies exercised over the posted price of oil. OPEC has used production quotas to support prices and earnings above what could be achieved in more competitive conditions.

6. Besides seeking financial assistance from advanced nations, developing nations have promoted internal industrialization through policies of import substitution and export promotion. Countries emphasizing export promotion have tended to realize higher rates of economic growth than countries emphasizing import-substitution policies.

7. The East Asian economies have realized remarkable economic growth in recent decades. The foundation of such growth has included high rates of investment, the increasing endowments of an educated workforce, and the use of export-promotion policies.

8. By the 1990s, China had become a high performing Asian economy. Although China has dismantled much of its centrally planned economy and permitted free enterprise to replace it, political freedoms have not increased. Today, China describes itself as a socialist market economy. Being heavily endowed with labor, China specializes in many labor-intensive products. In 2001, China became a member of the WTO.

Key Concepts and Terms

- Advanced nations (page 218)
- Buffer stock (page 234)
- Cartel (page 236)
- Developing nations (page 218)
- East Asian tigers (page 245)
- Export controls (page 233)
- Export-led growth (page 242)
- Export-oriented policy (page 242)
- Flying-geese pattern of economic growth (page 246)
- Generalized system of preferences (GSP) (page 231)
- Import substitution (page 240)
- International commodity agreements (ICAs) (page 232)
- International Monetary Fund (IMF) (page 230)
- Multilateral contract (page 235)
- Organization of Petroleum Exporting Countries (OPEC) (page 235)
- Primary products (page 218)
- Production controls (page 234)
- World Bank (page 229)

Study Questions

1. What are the major reasons for the skepticism of many developing nations regarding the comparative-advantage principle and free trade?
2. Stabilizing commodity prices has been a major objective of many primary-product nations. What are the major methods used to achieve price stabilization?
3. What are some examples of international commodity agreements? Why have many of them broken down over time?
4. Why are the less-developed nations concerned with commodity-price stabilization?
5. The average person probably never heard of the Organization of Petroleum Exporting Countries until 1973 or 1974, when oil prices skyrocketed. In fact, OPEC was founded in 1960. Why is it that OPEC did not achieve worldwide prominence until the 1970s? What factors contributed to OPEC's problems in the 1980s?
6. Why is cheating a typical problem for cartels?
7. The generalized system of preferences is intended to help developing nations gain access to world markets. Explain.
8. How are import-substitution and export-promotion policies used to aid in the industrialization of developing nations?
9. Describe the strategy that East Asia used from the 1970s to the 1990s to achieve high rates of economic growth. Can the Asian miracle continue in the new millennium?
10. How has China achieved the status of a high-performing Asian economy? Why has China's normal-trade-relation status been a source of controversy in the United States? What are the likely effects of China's entry into the WTO?

netlink

7.1 The United Nations Conference on Trade and Development (UNCTAD) helps developing nations compete successfully in world markets. A description of UNCTAD's operations and a discussion of the problems of developing countries can be found by setting your browser to this URL:

http://www.unctad.org

7.2 For information on individual developing nations, the CIA's annual *The World Factbook* provides comprehensive information on most countries and territories, including geography, natural resources, demographics, government, and economic statistics. The CIA's *Handbook of International Economic Statistics* also contains much useful information on countries and regions. Set your browser to this URL:

http://www.odci.gov/cia/publications/factbook/index.html

7.3 To get a glimpse of U.S. foreign policy and U.S. relations with the countries in the Asia–Pacific region, log onto the Web sites of the Bureau of East Asian and Pacific Affairs at this URL:

http://www.state.gov/p/eap

To access NetLink Exercises and the Virtual Scavenger Hunt, visit the Carbaugh Web site at http://carbaugh.swlearning.com.

 **Xtra!** Log onto the Carbaugh Xtra! Web site (**http://carbaughxtra.swlearning.com**) for additional learning resources such as practice quizzes, help with graphing, and current events applications.

chapter 8

Regional Trading Arrangements

Since World War II, advanced nations have significantly lowered their trade restrictions. Such trade liberalization has stemmed from two approaches. The first is a reciprocal reduction of trade barriers on a nondiscriminatory basis. Under the General Agreement on Tariffs and Trade—and its successor, the World Trade Organization— member nations acknowledge that tariff reductions agreed on by any two nations will be extended to all other members. Such an international approach encourages a gradual relaxation of tariffs throughout the world.

A second approach to trade liberalization occurs when a small group of nations, typically on a regional basis, forms a **regional trading arrangement**. Under this system, member nations agree to impose lower barriers to trade within the group than to trade with nonmember nations. Each member nation continues to determine its domestic policies, but the trade policy of each includes preferential treatment for group members. Regional trading arrangements (free-trade areas and customs unions) have been an exception to the principle of nondiscrimination embodied in the World Trade Organization. This chapter investigates the operation and effects of regional trading arrangements.

Regional Integration Versus Multilateralism

Recall that a major purpose of the WTO is to promote trade liberalization through worldwide agreements. However, getting a large number of countries to agree on reforms can be extremely difficult. By the early 2000s, the WTO was stumbling in its attempt to achieve a global trade agreement, and countries increasingly looked to more narrow, regional agreements as an alternative. Are regional trading arrangements building blocks or stumbling blocks to a multilateral trading system?

Trade liberalization under a regional trading arrangement is very different from the multilateral liberalization embodied in the WTO. Under regional trading arrangements, nations reduce trade barriers only for a small group of partner nations, thus discriminating against the rest of the world. Under the WTO, trade liberalization by any one nation is extended to all WTO members, about148 nations, on a nondiscriminatory basis.

Although regional trading blocs can complement the multilateral trading system, by their very nature regional trading blocs are discriminatory; they are a departure from the principle of normal trading relations, a cornerstone of the WTO system. Some analysts note that regional trading blocs that decrease the discretion of member nations to pursue trade liberalization with outsiders are likely to become stumbling blocks to multilateralism. For example, if Malaysia has already succeeded in finding a market in the United States, it would have only a limited interested in a free-trade pact with the United States. But its less successful rival, Argentina, would be eager to sign a regional free-trade agreement and thus capture Malaysia's share of the U.S. market—not by making a better or cheaper product, but by obtaining special treatment under U.S. trade law. Once Argentina gets its special privilege, what incentive would it have to go to WTO meetings and sign a multilateral free-trade agreement that would eliminate those special privileges?

Two other factors suggest that the members of a regional trading arrangement may not be greatly interested in worldwide liberalization. First, trade-bloc members may not realize additional economies of scale from global trade liberalization, which often provides only modest opening of foreign markets. Regional trade blocs, which often provide more extensive trade liberalization, may allow domestic firms sufficient production runs to exhaust scale economies. Second, trade-bloc members may want to invest their time and energy in establishing strong regional linkages rather than investing them in global negotiations.

On the other hand, when structured according to principles of openness and inclusiveness, regional blocs can be building blocks rather than stumbling blocks for global free trade and investment. There are several ways in which regional blocs can foster global market opening. First, regional agreements may achieve deeper economic integration among members than do multilateral accords, because of greater commonality of interests and simpler negotiating processes. Second, a self-reinforcing process is set in place by the establishment of a regional free-trade area: As the market encompassed by a free-trade area enlarges, it becomes increasingly attractive for nonmembers to join to receive the same trade preferences as member nations. Third, regional liberalization encourages partial adjustment of workers out of import-competing industries in which the nation's comparative disadvantage is strong and into exporting industries in which its comparative advantage is strong. As adjustment proceeds, the portion of the labor force that benefits from liberalized trade rises, and the portion that loses falls; this promotes political support for trade liberalization in a self-reinforcing process. For all of these reasons, when regional agreements are formed according to principles of openness, they may overlap and expand, thus promoting global free trade from the bottom up.

Let us next consider the various types of regional trading blocs and their economic effects.

Types of Regional Trading Arrangements

Since the mid-1950s, the term **economic integration** has become part of the vocabulary of economists. Economic integration is a process of eliminating restrictions on international trade, payments, and factor mobility. Economic integration thus results in the uniting of two or more national economies in a regional trading arrangement. Before proceeding, let us distinguish the types of regional trading arrangements.

A **free-trade area** is an association of trading nations whose members agree to remove all tariff and nontariff barriers among themselves. Each member, however, maintains its own set of trade restrictions against outsiders. An example of this stage of integration is the *North American Free Trade Agreement (NAFTA)*, consisting of Canada, Mexico, and the United States. The United States also has free-trade agreements with Israel and Chile. Another free-trade agreement occurred in 1999 when the European Union and Mexico reached a deal that will end all tariffs on their bilateral trade in industrial goods by 2007.

Like a free-trade association, a **customs union** is an agreement among two or more trading partners to remove all tariff and nontariff trade barriers among themselves. In addition, however, each member nation imposes identical trade restrictions against nonparticipants. The effect of the common external trade policy is to permit free trade within the customs union, whereas all trade restrictions imposed against outsiders are equalized. A well-known example is **Benelux** (Belgium, the Netherlands, and Luxembourg), formed in 1948.

A **common market** is a group of trading nations that permits (1) the free movement of goods and services among member nations, (2) the initiation of common external trade restrictions against nonmembers, and (3) the free movement of factors of production across national borders within the economic bloc. The common market thus represents a more complete stage of integration than a free-trade area or a customs union. The **European Union (EU)**[1] achieved the status of a common market in 1992.

Beyond these stages, economic integration could evolve to the stage of **economic union**, in which national, social, taxation, and fiscal policies are harmonized and administered by a supranational institution. Belgium and Luxembourg formed an economic union during the 1920s. The task of creating an economic union is much more ambitious than achieving the other forms of integration. This is because a free-trade area, customs union, or common market results primarily from the abolition of existing trade barriers, but an economic union requires an agreement to transfer economic sovereignty to a supranational authority. The ultimate degree of economic union would be the unification of national monetary policies and the acceptance of a common currency administered by a supranational monetary authority. The economic union would thus include the dimension of a **monetary union**.

The United States serves as an example of a monetary union. Fifty states are linked together in a complete monetary union with a common currency, implying completely fixed exchange rates among the 50 states. Also, the Federal Reserve serves as the single central bank for the nation; it issues currency and conducts the nation's monetary policy. Trade is free among the states, and both labor and capital move freely in pursuit of maximum returns. The federal government conducts the nation's fiscal policy and deals in matters concerning retirement and health programs, national defense, international affairs, and the like. Other programs, such as police protection and education, are conducted by state and local governments so that states can keep their identity within the union.

Impetus for Regionalism

Regional trading arrangements are pursued for a variety of reasons. A motivation of virtually every regional trading arrangement has been the prospect of enhanced economic growth. An expanded regional market can allow economies of large-scale production, foster specialization and learning-by-doing, and attract foreign investment. Regional initiatives can also foster a variety of noneconomic objectives, such as managing immigration flows and promoting regional security. Moreover, regionalism may enhance and solidify domestic economic reforms. East European nations, for example, have viewed their regional initiatives with the European Union as a means of locking in their domestic policy shifts toward privatization and market-oriented reform.

Smaller nations may seek safe-haven trading arrangements with larger nations when future access to the larger nations' markets appears uncertain. This was an apparent motivation for the formation of NAFTA. In North America, Mexico was motivated to join NAFTA partially by fear of changes in U.S. trade policy toward a more managed or strategic trade orientation. Canada's pursuit of a free-trade agreement was significantly motivated by a desire to discipline the use of countervailing duties and antidumping duties by the United States.

As new regional trading arrangements are formed, or existing ones are expanded or deepened, the opportunity cost of remaining outside an arrangement increases. Nonmember exporters could realize costly decreases in market share if their sales are diverted to companies of the member nations. This prospect may be sufficient to tip the political balance in favor of becoming a member of

---

[1]Founded in 1957, the European Community was a collective name for three organizations: the European Economic Community, the European Coal and Steel Community, and the European Atomic Energy Commission. In 1994, the European Community was replaced by the European Union following ratification of the Maastricht Treaty by the 12 member countries of the European Community. For simplicity, the name European Union is used throughout this chapter in discussing events that occurred before and after 1994.

a regional trading arrangement, as exporting interests of a nonmember nation outweigh its import-competing interests. The negotiations between the United States and Mexico to form a free-trade area appeared to have strongly influenced Canada's decision to join NAFTA, and thus not get left behind in the movement toward free trade in North America.

Effects of a Regional Trading Arrangement

What are the possible welfare implications of regional trading arrangements? We can delineate the theoretical benefits and costs of such devices from two perspectives. First are the **static effects of economic integration** on productive efficiency and consumer welfare. Second are the **dynamic effects of economic integration**, which relate to member nations' long-run rates of growth. Because a small change in the growth rate can lead to a substantial cumulative effect on national output, the dynamic effects of trade-policy changes can yield substantially larger magnitudes than those based on static models. Combined, these static and dynamic effects determine the overall welfare gains or losses associated with the formation of a regional trading arrangement.

Static Effects

The static welfare effects of lowering tariff barriers among members of a trade bloc are illustrated in the following example. Assume a world composed of three countries: Luxembourg, Germany, and the United States. Suppose that Luxembourg and Germany decide to form a customs union, and the United States is a nonmember. The decision to form a customs union requires that Luxembourg and Germany abolish all tariff restrictions between themselves while maintaining a common tariff policy against the United States.

Referring to Figure 8.1, assume the supply and demand schedules of Luxembourg to be S_L and D_L. Assume also that Luxembourg is very small relative to Germany and to the United States. This means that Luxembourg cannot influence foreign prices, so that foreign supply schedules of grain are perfectly elastic. Let Germany's supply price be $3.25

per bushel and that of the United States, $3 per bushel. Note that the United States is assumed to be the more efficient supplier.

Before the formation of the customs union, Luxembourg finds that under conditions of free trade, it purchases all of its import requirements from the United States. Germany does not participate in the market because its supply price exceeds that of the United States. In free-trade equilibrium, Luxembourg's consumption equals 23 bushels, production equals 1 bushel, and imports equal 22 bushels. If Luxembourg levies a tariff equal to 50 cents on each bushel imported from the United States (or Germany), then imports will fall from 22 bushels to 10 bushels.

Suppose that, as part of a trade liberalization agreement, Luxembourg and Germany form a customs union. Luxembourg's import tariff against Germany is dropped, but it is still maintained on imports from the nonmember United States. This means that Germany now becomes the low-price supplier. Luxembourg now purchases all of its imports, totaling 16 bushels, from Germany at $3.25 per bushel, while importing nothing from the United States.

The movement toward freer trade under a customs union affects world welfare in two opposing ways: a welfare-increasing **trade-creation effect** and a welfare-reducing **trade-diversion effect**. The overall consequence of a customs union on the welfare of its members, as well as on the world as a whole, depends on the relative strengths of these two opposing forces.

Trade creation occurs when some domestic production of one customs-union member is replaced by another member's lower-cost imports. The welfare of the member countries is increased by trade creation because it leads to increased production specialization according to the principle of comparative advantage. The trade-creation effect consists of a *consumption effect* and a *production effect*.

Before the formation of the customs union and under its own tariff umbrella, Luxembourg imports from the United States at a price of $3.50 per bushel. Luxembourg's entry into the customs union results in its dropping all tariffs against Germany. Facing a lower import price of $3.25, Luxembourg increases its consumption of grain by 3 bushels. The

FIGURE 8.1

Static Welfare Effects of a Customs Union

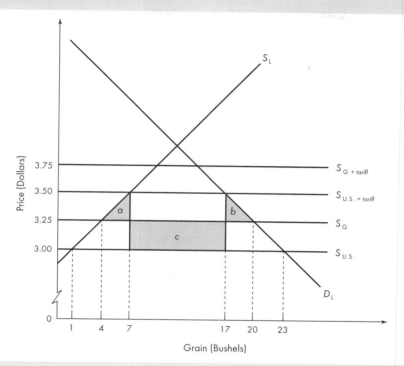

The formation of a customs union leads to a welfare-increasing trade-creation effect and a welfare-decreasing trade-diversion effect. The overall effect of the customs union on the welfare of its members, as well as on the world as a whole, depends on the relative strength of these two opposing forces.

welfare gain associated with this increase in consumption equals triangle *b* in Figure 8.1.

The formation of the customs union also yields a production effect that results in a more efficient use of world resources. Eliminating the tariff barrier against Germany means that Luxembourg producers must now compete against lower-cost, more efficient German producers. Inefficient domestic producers drop out of the market, resulting in a decline in home output of 3 bushels. The reduction in the cost of obtaining this output equals triangle *a* in the figure. This represents the favorable production effect. The overall trade-creation effect is given by the sum of triangles *a* + *b*.

Although a customs union may add to world welfare by way of trade creation, its trade-diversion effect generally implies a welfare loss. Trade diversion occurs when imports from a low-cost supplier outside the union are replaced by purchases from a higher-cost supplier within the union. This suggests that world production is reorganized less efficiently. In Figure 8.1, although the total volume of trade increases under the customs union, part of this trade (10 bushels) has been diverted from a low-cost supplier, the United States, to a high-cost supplier, Germany. The increase in the cost of obtaining these 10 bushels of imported grain equals area *c*. This is the welfare loss to Luxembourg, as well as to the

Did Britain Gain from Entering the European Union?
Trade Creation Versus Trade Diversion

In 1973, life in Britain changed. Prices of agricultural goods increased sharply. It cost families more to keep food on the table. It wasn't an accident. A government decision pushed prices up. Britain turned away cheaper produce from its former colony, Australia. Instead, it increased farm output and purchased rural commodities from its more expensive European neighbors. But why was that decision made? Was there gain to offset the pain?

Britain's trading relationship with Australia was bound by the tradition of empire. The former colony had supplied food to the plates of Mother England. In 1950, a third of Australia's exports wound up in Britain. But in 1973, that tradition was broken. Britain signed an agreement to join its neighbors and enter the European Union (formerly the European Community). Although the British generally believed that it was the right thing to do, they had to accept the economic consequences.

Those economics hit Australian farmers hard. Their traditional trade with Britain ended almost overnight. In joining the EU, Britain had to comply with its common agriculture policy, which set common barriers against agricultural producers outside the EU. Tariffs and quotas increased the price of non-EU produce to British consumers. Therefore, Australia's preferential access to the British market ended. It was shut out as Britain fell in line with other more costly European producers. Upon entering the EU, Britain's imports of Australian beef fell more than 75 percent, and the 800,000 tons of imported Australian wheat stopped almost instantly.

British consumers paid a high price for the change. Before joining the EU, British food bills were the cheapest in Europe. Australia's beef, wheat, and other agricultural goods were efficiently produced and comparatively cheap. When Britain joined the EU, however, more expensive goods from Europe pushed its food prices up 25 percent on average; that increased its overall rate of inflation by 3 to 4 percent. Simply put, Britain lost because trade was diverted from a low- to high-cost producer; it had to pay more for agricultural goods.

But there's another side to this story. Trade in manufactured goods from Europe increased significantly as Britain entered the EU and thus abolished tariffs and quotas placed on imports of these goods from European nations. This allowed lower-priced imports from European trading partners to replace higher-priced British output, thus increasing welfare.

Evaluating whether entering the EU was good or bad for the British became an empirical question. Did the welfare-expanding effect of trade creation in manufactured goods more than offset the welfare-contracting effect of trade diversion in agricultural products? Many empirical studies have been conducted on the effects of Britain's entrance into the EU. They generally support the conclusion that significant trade diversion occurred in agriculture and significant trade creation occurred in manufacturing. The overall effect between trade creation and trade diversion is still being debated.

Source: Richard Pomfret, *Unequal Trade: The Economics of Discriminatory International Trade Policies* (New York: Blackwell Publishers, 1988).

world as a whole. Our static analysis concludes that the formation of a customs union will increase the welfare of its members, as well as the rest of the world, if the positive trade-creation effect more than offsets the negative trade-diversion effect. Referring to the figure, this occurs if $a + b$ is greater than c.

This analysis illustrates that the success of a customs union depends on the factors contributing to trade creation and diversion. Several factors that bear on the relative size of these effects can be identified. One factor is the kinds of nations that tend to benefit from a customs union. Nations whose preunion economies are quite competitive are likely to benefit from trade creation because the formation of the union offers greater opportunity for specialization in production. Also, the larger the size and the greater the number of nations in the union, the greater the gains are likely to be, because there is a greater possibility that the world's low-cost producers will be union members. In the extreme case in which the union consists of the entire world, there can exist only trade creation, not trade diversion. In addition, the scope for trade diversion is smaller when the customs union's common external tariff is lower rather than higher. Because a lower tariff allows greater trade to take place with nonmember nations, there will be less replacement of cheaper imports from nonmember nations by relatively high-cost imports from partner nations.

Dynamic Effects

Not all welfare consequences of a regional trading arrangement are static in nature. There may also be dynamic gains that influence member-nation growth rates over the long run. These dynamic gains stem from the creation of larger markets by the movement to freer trade under customs unions. The benefits associated with a customs union's dynamic gains may more than offset any unfavorable static effects. Dynamic gains include *economies of scale, greater competition*, and a *stimulus of investment*.

Perhaps the most noticeable result of a customs union is market enlargement. Being able to penetrate freely the domestic markets of other member nations, producers can take advantage of economies of scale that would not have occurred in smaller markets limited by trade restrictions. Larger markets may permit efficiencies attributable to greater specialization of workers and machinery, the use of the most efficient equipment, and the more complete use of by-products. There is evidence that significant economies of scale have been achieved by the EU in such products as steel, automobiles, footwear, and copper refining.

The European refrigerator industry provides an example of the dynamic effects of integration. Prior to the formation of the EU, each of the major European nations that produced refrigerators

(Germany, Italy, and France) supported a small number of manufacturers that produced primarily for the domestic market. These manufacturers had production runs of fewer than 100,000 units per year, a level too low to permit the adoption of automated equipment. Short production runs translated into high per-unit cost. The EU's formation resulted in the opening of European markets and paved the way for the adoption of large-scale production methods, including automated press lines and spot welding. By the late 1960s, the typical Italian refrigerator plant manufactured 850,000 refrigerators annually. This volume was more than sufficient to meet the minimum efficient scale of operation, estimated to be 800,000 units per year. The late 1960s also saw German and French manufacturers averaging 570,000 units and 290,000 units per year, respectively.[2]

Broader markets may also promote greater competition among producers within a customs union. It is often felt that trade restrictions promote monopoly power, whereby a small number of companies dominate a domestic market. Such companies may prefer to lead a quiet life, forming agreements not to compete on the basis of price. But with the movement to more open markets under a customs union, the potential for successful collusion is lessened as the number of competitors expands. With freer trade, domestic producers must compete or face the possibility of financial bankruptcy. To survive in expanded and more competitive markets, producers must undertake investments in new equipment, technologies, and product lines. This will have the effect of holding down costs and permitting expanded levels of output. Capital investment may also rise if nonmember nations decide to establish subsidiary operations inside the customs unions to avoid external tariff barriers.

▌European Union

In the years immediately after World War II, the countries of Western Europe suffered balance-of-payments deficits in response to reconstruction

[2]Nicholas Owen, *Economies of Scale, Competitiveness, and Trade Patterns Within the European Community* (New York: Oxford University Press, 1983), pp. 119–139.

efforts. To shield its firms and workers from external competitive pressures, they initiated an elaborate network of tariff and exchange restrictions, quantitative controls, and state trading. In the 1950s, however, these trade barriers were generally viewed to be counterproductive. Therefore, Western Europe began to dismantle its trade barriers in response to successful tariff negotiations under the auspices of GATT.

It was against this background of trade liberalization that the European Union (EU), then known as the European Community, was created by the Treaty of Rome in 1957. The EU initially consisted of six nations: Belgium, France, Italy, Luxembourg, the Netherlands, and West Germany. By 1973, the United Kingdom, Ireland, and Denmark had joined the trade bloc. Greece joined the trade bloc 1981, followed by Spain and Portugal in 1987. In 1995, Austria, Finland, and Sweden were admitted into the EU. In 2004, 10 other Central and Eastern European countries joined the EU: Cyprus, the Czech Republic, Estonia, Hungary, Latvia, Lithuania, Malta, Poland, Slovakia, and Slovenia. This brought the membership of the EU up to 25 countries. Two others, Bulgaria and Romania, hope to join the EU by 2007. The EU views the enlargement process as an opportunity to promote stability in Europe and further the integration of the continent by peaceful means.

EU expansion will produce both winners and losers. Most studies agree that Germany, Italy, Austria, Sweden, and Finland, who have close trade and investment ties with Central and Eastern European nations, will be gainers. France, Spain, Portugal, Greece, and Ireland are likely to be losers, given the sizable funding they receive from EU programs—especially France's agricultural funds—as the money gets stretched over more countries. Clearly, the Central and Eastern European nations stand to the gain the most as their economies become integrated with other European economies.

Pursuing Economic Integration

According to the Treaty of Rome of 1957, the EU agreed in principle to follow the path of economic integration and eventually become an economic union. In pursuing this goal, members of the EU first dismantled tariffs and established a free-trade area by 1968. This liberalization of trade was accompanied by a fivefold increase in the value of industrial trade—higher than world trade, in general. The success of the free-trade area inspired the EU to continue its process of economic integration. In 1970, the EU became a full-fledged customs union when it adopted a common external tariff system for its members.

Several studies have been conducted on the overall impact of the EU on its members' welfare during the 1960s and 1970s. In terms of static welfare benefits, one study concluded that trade creation was pronounced in machinery, transportation equipment, chemicals, and fuels, whereas trade diversion was apparent in agricultural commodities and raw materials.[3] The broad conclusion can be drawn that trade creation in the manufactured-goods sector during the 1960s and 1970s was significant: 10 percent to 30 percent of total EU imports of manufactured goods. Moreover, trade creation exceeded trade diversion by a wide margin, estimated at 2 percent to 15 percent. In addition, analysts also noted that the EU realized dynamic benefits from integration in the form of additional competition and investment and also economies of scale. For instance, it has been determined that many firms in small nations, such as the Netherlands and Belgium, realized economies of scale by producing both for the domestic market and for export. However, after becoming members of the EU, sizable additional economies of scale were gained by individual firms, reducing the range of products manufactured and increasing the output of the remaining products.[4]

After forming a customs union, the EU made little progress toward becoming a common market until 1985. The hostile economic climate (recession and inflation) of the 1970s led EU members to shield their people from external forces rather than dismantle trade and investment restrictions. By the 1980s, however, EU members were increasingly frustrated with barriers that hindered transactions

[3]Mordechai E. Kreinin, *Trade Relations of the EEC: An Empirical Approach* (New York: Praeger, 1974), Chapter 3.

[4]Richard Harmsen and Michael Leidy, "Regional Trading Arrangements," in *International Trade Policies: The Uruguay Round and Beyond*, Volume II, International Monetary Fund, World Economic and Financial Surveys, 1994, p. 99.

within the bloc. European officials also feared that the EU's competitiveness was lagging behind that of Japan and the United States.

In 1985, the EU announced a detailed program for becoming a common market. This resulted in the elimination of remaining nontariff trade barriers to intra-EU transactions by 1992. Examples of these barriers included border controls and customs red tape, divergent standards and technical regulations, conflicting business laws, and protectionist procurement policies of governments. The elimination of these barriers resulted in the formation of a European common market and turned the trade bloc into the second largest economy in the world, almost as large as the U.S. economy.

While the EU was becoming a common market, its heads of government agreed to pursue much deeper levels of integration. Their goal was to begin a process of replacing their central banks with a European Central Bank and replacing their national currencies with a single European currency. The **Maastricht Treaty**, signed in 1991, set 2002 as the date at which this process would be complete. In 2002, a full-fledged **European Monetary Union (EMU)** emerged with a single currency, known as the **euro**.

When the Maastricht Treaty was signed, economic conditions in the various EU members differed substantially. The treaty specified that to be considered ready for monetary union, a country's economic performance would have to be similar to the performance of other members. Countries cannot, of course, pursue different rates of money growth, have different rates of economic growth, and different rates of inflation while having currencies that don't move up or down relative to each other. So the first thing the Europeans had to do was align their economic and monetary policies.

This effort, called *convergence*, has led to a high degree of uniformity in terms of price inflation, money supply growth, and other key economic factors. The specific **convergence criteria** as mandated by the Maastricht Treaty are as follows:

- **Price stability.** Inflation in each prospective member is supposed to be no more than 1.5 percent above the average of the inflation rates in the three countries with lowest inflation rates.

- **Low long-term interest rates.** Long-term interest rates are to be no more than 2 percent above the average interest rate in those countries.

- **Stable exchange rates.** The exchange rate is supposed to have been kept within the target bands of the monetary union with no devaluations for at least two years prior to joining the monetary union.

- **Sound public finances.** One fiscal criterion is that the budget deficit in a prospective member should be at most 3 percent of GDP; the other is that the outstanding amount of government debt should be no more than 60 percent of a year's GDP.

In 1999, 11 of the EU's 15 members fulfilled the economic tests as mandated by the Maastricht Treaty and became the founding members of the European Monetary Union (EMU). These countries included Belgium, Germany, Spain, France, Ireland, Italy, Luxembourg, the Netherlands, Austria, Portugal, and Finland. In 2001, Greece became the twelfth country to join the EMU.

Recall that in 2004, 10 countries joined the European Union: Cyprus, the Czech Republic, Estonia, Hungary, Latvia, Lithuania, Malta, Poland, Slovakia, and Slovenia. They are thus obligated to join the EMU and adopt the euro as their national currency. Membership in EMU is not automatic, however, because the accession countries must first satisfy the convergence criteria as mandated by the Maastricht Treaty. However, the candidates see the convergence criteria as a small price to pay for the exchange-rate stability and the low interest rates that come with full entry into the monetary union.

An important motivation for EMU was the momentum it provides for political union, a long-standing goal of many European policy makers. France and Germany took the initiative toward EMU. Monetary union was viewed as an important way to anchor Germany securely in Europe. Moreover, it provided the French a larger role in determining monetary policy for Europe, which they would achieve with a common central bank. Prior to EMU, Europe's monetary policy was mainly determined by the German Bundesbank.

The EMU Presents Different Faces to Portugal and Sweden

The year 1999 marked the advent of the historic EMU. European economies had to meet strict monetary and fiscal criteria before joining. Although Portugal and Sweden both met these criteria, only Portugal decided to exercise its option to become a member of the EMU. Consider the differing views of the two countries.[5]

In Lisbon, businessman Jorge Cruz Morais explains why Portugal supports the European Monetary Union. "We have to be in the first boat," he says. "If monetary union started without us, we'd fall off the map." In Stockholm, however, economist Roland Spant explains why Sweden shouldn't participate. "It is a giant step into the unknown," he says. "It's like jumping from the Empire State Building and inventing the parachute on the way down."

Situated at the opposite extremes of Europe, the countries of Portugal and Sweden were at the opposite ends of the debate over the EMU prior to its inception in 1999. Portugal wanted to be part of the common currency; Sweden wanted to stay out. Indeed, depending on whose eyes it was viewed through, EMU either meant Europe's boldest postwar move toward closer units or a major gamble with clear advantages but also significant risks.

It is easy to understand Portugal's preference for further European integration. Until its dictatorship disintegrated in the early 1970s, Portugal was long ostracized by Europe, and it looked for a place in the world. When Portugal joined the European Union in the 1980s, the move was not motivated only by economics: It was also an attempt to gain respectability. By the 1990s, Portugal feared that exclusion from the EMU would cause it to be an outsider once again. Another reason for membership was that prior to 1999, Portugal received a significant portion of funds paid to the European Union by member nations for infrastructure and other projects, far more than it paid in. Also, Portugal's exports to fulfill the strict monetary and fiscal criteria to qualify for the euro brought interest rates down sharply in the 1990s. This produced a boom rather than the pain felt in other European countries, and Portugal looked to EMU to lock in fiscal discipline.

On the downside, some business leaders felt that Portuguese industry was not fully prepared for the post-EMU onslaught of competition. Although Portugal had relatively low labor costs in 1997, they could boomerang into a big risk: A common currency could unleash a wave of demands by Portuguese workers for wages that would equal average European wages. However, the productivity of the average Portuguese was half that of the average German worker. Higher wages would thus result in relatively higher production costs for many Portuguese firms and a loss of competitiveness.

Although Sweden qualified for the common currency with flying colors, it decided not to join. The reason lay partly in Sweden's historic preference for neutrality with regard to the rest of Europe. Also, Sweden's decision to join the European Union in 1995 coincided with budgetary reductions that hurt the country's welfare state. Many Swedes thus associated the European Union with hardship and felt that monetary union could only make things worse by increasing pressure for tax harmonization, thus making it more difficult to finance welfare programs.

Moreover, Swedes maintained that by linking itself into a common currency, Sweden could no longer use a floating exchange to compensate for its high wage costs—and with a jobless rate of more than 12 percent, this might further increase unemployment. Finally, Swedish business leaders felt that such key domestic industries as mining, paper, and pulp were more sensitive to the dollar than to European currencies, so Sweden needed to retain monetary sovereignty to be able to react to events across the Atlantic ocean.

Most important, Swedes argued that Europe simply was not prepared for a monetary union. They contended that Europe, unlike the United States, was not a homogeneous market: Its economic structures and cycles were too different to justify tying the countries into a rigid arrangement. Put simply, it was not workable to have 15 governments and one central bank. If Italy has 6 percent inflation and Germany 1 percent, what should the European Central Bank do?

[5]Drawn from "A Tale of Two Nations Shows Europe's Union Has Differing Sides," *The Wall Street Journal*, July 29, 1997, pp. A1 and A2.

Indeed, both Portugal and Sweden had good reasons to join the EMU, and good reasons not to join. Their decisions involved balancing things that could not be measured as well as broad political goals. Later in this chapter, we will consider the economic costs and benefits of a common currency as applied to the European Monetary Union.

Agricultural Policy

Besides providing for free trade in industrial goods among its members, the EU has abolished restrictions on agricultural products traded internally. A **common agricultural policy** has replaced the agricultural-stabilization policies of individual member nations, which differed widely before the formation of the EU. A substantial element of the common agricultural policy has been the support of prices received by farmers for their produce. Schemes involving deficiency payments, output controls, and direct income payments have been used for this purpose. In addition, the common agricultural policy has supported EU farm prices through a system of **variable levies**, which applies tariffs to agricultural imports entering the EU. Exports of any surplus quantities of EU produce have been assured through the adoption of **export subsidies**.

One problem confronting the EU's price-support programs is that agricultural efficiencies differ among EU members. Consider the case of grains. German farmers, being high-cost producers, have sought high support prices to maintain their existence. The more efficient French farmers do not need as high a level of support prices as the Germans do to keep them in operation; nevertheless, French farmers have found it in their interest to lobby for high price supports. In recent years, high price supports have been applied to products such as beef, grains, and butter. The common agricultural policy has thus encouraged inefficient farm production by EU farmers and has restricted food imports from more efficient nonmember producers. Such trade diversion has been a welfare-decreasing effect of the EU.

Variable Levy

Figure 8.2 on page 264 illustrates the operation of a system of variable levies and export subsidies. Assume that S_{EU_0} and D_{EU_0} represent the EU's supply and demand schedules for wheat and that the world price of wheat equals $3.50 per bushel. Referring to Figure 8.2(a), assume that the EU wishes to guarantee its high-cost farmers a price of $4.50 per bushel. This price cannot be sustained as long as imported wheat is allowed to enter the EU at the free-market price of $3.50 per bushel. Suppose the EU, to validate the support price, initiates a variable levy. Given an import levy of $1 per bushel, EU farmers are permitted to produce 5 million bushels of wheat, as opposed to the 3 million bushels that would be produced under free trade. At the same time, the EU imports total 2 million bushels instead of 6 million bushels.

Suppose now that, owing to increased productivity overseas, the world price of wheat falls to $2.50 per bushel. Under a variable levy system, the levy is determined daily and equals the difference between the lowest price on the world market and the support price. The sliding-scale nature of the variable levy results in the EU's increasing its import tariff to $2 per bushel. The support price of wheat is sustained at $4.50, and EU production and imports remain unchanged. EU farmers are thus insulated from the consequences of variations in foreign supply. Should EU wheat production decrease, the import levy could be reduced to encourage imports. EU consumers would be protected against rising wheat prices.

The variable import levy tends to be more restrictive than a fixed tariff. It discourages foreign producers from absorbing part of the tariff and cutting prices to maintain export sales. This would only trigger higher variable levies. For the same reason, variable levies discourage foreign producers from subsidizing their exports in order to penetrate domestic markets

The completion of the Uruguay Round of trade negotiations in 1994 brought rules to bear on the use of variable levies. It required that all nontariff barriers, including variable levies, be converted to equivalent tariffs. However, the method of conversion used by the EU essentially maintained the variable levy system, except for one difference. The actual tariff applied on agricultural imports can vary, like the previous variable levy, depending on world prices. However, there is now an upper limit applied to how high the tariff can rise.

FIGURE 8.2

Variable Levies and Export Subsidies

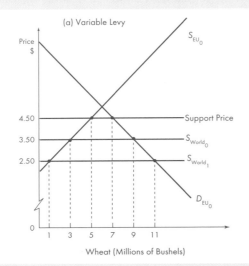
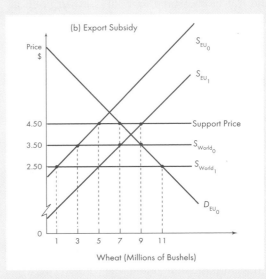

The common agricultural policy of the EU has used variable levies to protect EU farmers from low-cost foreign competition. During periods of falling world prices, the sliding-scale nature of the variable levy results in automatic increases in the EU's import tariff. Export subsidies have also been used by the EU to make its agricultural products more competitive in world markets.

Export Subsidy

The EU has also used a system of export subsidies to ensure that any surplus agricultural output will be sold overseas. The high price supports of the common agricultural policy have given EU farmers the incentive to increase production, often in surplus quantities. But the world price of agricultural commodities has generally been below the EU price. The EU pays its producers export subsidies so they can sell surplus produce abroad at the low price but still receive the higher, international support price.

In Figure 8.2(b), let the world price of wheat be $3.50 per bushel. Suppose that improving technologies result in a shift in the EU supply schedule from S_{EU_0} to S_{EU_1}. At the internal support price, $4.50, EU production exceeds EU consumption by 2 million bushels. To facilitate the export of this surplus output, the EU provides its producers an export subsidy of $1 per bushel. EU

wheat would be exported at a price of $3.50, and EU producers would receive a price (including the subsidy) of $4.50. The EU export subsidies are also characterized by a sliding scale. Should the world price of wheat fall to $2.50, the $4.50 support price would be maintained through the imposition of a $2 export subsidy.

The EU's policy of assuring a high level of income for its farmers has been costly. High support prices for products including milk, butter, cheese, and meat have led to high internal production and low consumption. The result has often been huge surpluses that must be purchased by the EU to defend the support price. To reduce these costs, the EU has sold surplus produce in world markets at prices well below the cost of acquisition. These subsidized sales have met with resistance from farmers in other countries.

Virtually every industrial country subsidizes its agricultural products. As seen in Table 8.1, gov-

TABLE 8.1

Government Support for Agriculture, 2001

Country	Producer-Subsidy Equivalents* as a Percent of Farm Prices
Australia	4%
Canada	17
European Union	35
Iceland	59
Japan	59
South Korea	64
Switzerland	69
New Zealand	1
United States	21

*The producer-subsidy equivalent represents the total assistance to farmers in the form of market price support, direct payments, and transfers that indirectly benefit farmers.

Source: Organization of Economic Cooperation and Development (OECD), *Agricultural Policies in OECD Countries : Monitoring and Evaluation, 2003.* See also World Trade Organization, *Annual Report,* 2003.

ernment programs accounted for 35 percent of the value of agricultural products in the EU in 2001. This amount is even higher in certain countries such as Japan, but it is much lower in others, including the United States, Australia, and New Zealand. Countries with relatively low agricultural subsidies have criticized the high-subsidy countries as being too protectionist.

Government Procurement Policies

Another sensitive issue confronting the EU has been government procurement policies. Governments are major purchasers of goods and services, ranging from off-the-shelf items such as paper and pencils to major projects such as nuclear power facilities and defense systems. Government procurement has been used by EU nations to support national and regional firms and industries for several reasons: (1) national security (for example, aerospace); (2) compensation for local communities near environmentally damaging public industries (such as nuclear fuels); (3) support for emerging high-tech industries (for example, lasers); and (4) politics (as in assistance to highly visible industries, such as automobiles).

Although there may be sound justifications for purchasing locally, by the 1980s it was widely recognized that EU public procurement policies served as formidable barriers to foreign competitors; individual EU nations permitted only a minor fraction, often about 2 percent, of government contracts to be awarded to foreign suppliers. By downplaying intra-EU competition, governments paid more than they should for the products they needed and, in so doing, supported suboptimal producers within the community.

When the EU became a common market in 1992, it removed discrimination in government procurement by permitting all EU competitors to bid for public contracts. The criteria for awarding public contracts are specified as either the lowest price or the most economically advantageous tender that includes such factors as product quality, delivery dates, and reliability of supplies.

It was believed that savings from a more competitive government procurement policy would come from three sources: (1) EU governments would be able to purchase from the cheapest foreign suppliers (static trade effect). (2) Increased competition would occur as domestic suppliers decreased prices to compete with foreign competitors that had previously been shut out of the home market (competition effect). (3) Industries would be restructured over the long run, permitting the surviving companies to achieve economies of scale (restructuring effect).

These three sources of savings are illustrated in Figure 8.3 on page 266, which represents public procurement of computers. Suppose a liberalized procurement policy permits the British government to buy computers from the cheapest EU supplier, assumed to be Germany. The result is a reduction in average costs from $AC_{U.K.}$ to AC_G. At the same time, increased competition results in falling prices and decreased profit margins. At an output of 10,000 computers, unit prices are reduced from $10,000 to $7,000, and profit margins from $Profit_0$ to $Profit_1$. What's more, exploitation of economies of scale gives rise to further decreases in unit costs and prices, as output expands from 10,000 to 25,000 computers along cost schedule AC_G.

It is estimated that liberalizing government procurement markets has generated savings of 0.5 percent of EU gross domestic product. In the process,

FIGURE 8.3

Opening Up of Government Procurement

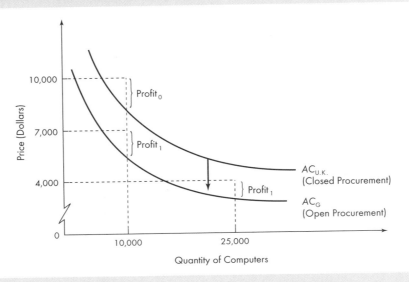

Procurement liberalization allows the U.K. government to import computers from Germany, the low-cost EU producer. Cost savings result from the trade effect, the competition effect, and the restructuring (economies-of-scale) effect.

some 350,000 additional jobs have been created. The price savings from open competition (trade and competition effects) are estimated at 40 to 50 percent for pharmaceuticals in Germany and the United Kingdom; 60 to 70 percent for telecommunications equipment in Germany and Belgium; and about 10 percent for automobiles in the United Kingdom and Italy. In sectors where companies were too small to compete internationally, additional savings arose from mergers that resulted in a smaller number of EU companies able to exploit economies of scale. Examples included electric locomotives, turbine generators, and boilers, where decreases in units of costs of 12 to 20 percent were possible.[6]

[6]European Union, *Public Procurement: Regional and Social Aspects* (Brussels: Commission of the European Communities, July 1989). See also Keith Hartley, "Public Purchasing," in D. Gowland and S. James, eds., *Economic Policy After 1992* (Brookfield, VT: Dartmouth Publishing Co, 1991), pp. 114–125.

Economic Costs and Benefits of a Common Currency: The European Monetary Union

As we have learned, the formation of the EMU in 1999 resulted in the creation of a single currency (the euro) and a European Central Bank. Switching to a new currency is extremely difficult. Just imagine the task if each of the 50 U.S. states had its own currency and its own central bank, and then had to agree with the other 49 states on a single currency and a single financial system. That's exactly what the Europeans have done.

The European Central Bank is located in Frankfurt, Germany, and is responsible for the monetary policy and exchange-rate policy of the EMU. The European Central Bank alone controls the supply of euros, sets the short-term euro interest rate,

Euro Facts

The year 2000 was a momentous one in Europe because it marked the introduction of euro notes and coins into the member economies of the European Monetary Union. What are the characteristics of the euro?

The sign for the new single currency looks likes an *E* with two horizontal parallel lines across it. It was inspired by the Greek letter epsilon, in reference to the cradle of European civilization and to the first letter of the word "Europe." The parallel lines represent the stability of the euro.

What do euro notes look like? Referring to the above euro note, the designs of euro notes are symbolic and closely related to the historical phases that make up Europe's architectural heritage. Windows and gateways dominate the front side of each banknote as symbols of the spirit of openness and cooperation in the EU. The reverse side of each banknote features a bridge from a particular age, a metaphor for communication among the people of Europe and between Europe and the rest of the world.

Like U.S. currency, euro notes and coins come in a variety of denominations. There are 7 euro notes

and 8 euro coins. The denominations of the notes range from 500 to 5 euro, and the coins range from 2 euro to 1 euro cent. Vending machines and other coin- or note-operated automatic machines in the participating member countries have been adapted for use with euro notes and coins.

According to the schedule for the changeover to the euro, in 2002 euro notes and coins replaced notes and coins in national currencies, which were withdrawn from circulation. Since then, the national currency is no longer valid for everyday use, but people can exchange their old banknotes for euro banknotes at the national central banks. Also, as of 2002 old national currency units can no longer be used in written form such as checks, contracts, and pay slips.

Why did it take from 1999, when the euro was adopted, to 2002 for the actual introduction of the euro notes and coins? Mainly because it took that long to print and mint them. After all, we are talking about 14.5 billion banknotes and 50 billion coins.

and maintains permanently fixed exchange rates for the member countries. With a common central bank, the central bank of each participating nation performs operations similar to those of the 12 regional Federal Reserve Banks in the United States.

For Americans, the benefits of a common currency are easy to understand. Americans know they can walk into a McDonald's or Burger King anywhere in the United States and

Visit EconDebate Online for a debate on this topic

purchase hamburgers with the dollar bills in their purses and wallets. The same was not true in European countries prior to the formation of the EMU. Because each was a distinct nation with its own currency, a French person could not buy something at a German store without first exchanging his French francs for German marks. This would be like someone from St. Louis having to exchange her Missouri currency for Illinois currency each time she visits Chicago. To make matters worse, because marks and francs floated against each other within a range, the number of marks the French traveler receives today would probably differ from the number he would have received yesterday or tomorrow. On top of exchange-rate uncertainty, the traveler also had to pay a fee to exchange the currency, making a trip across the border a costly proposition indeed. Although the costs to individuals can be limited because of the small quantities of money involved, firms can incur much larger costs. By replacing the various European currencies with a single currency, the euro, the EMU can avoid such costs. Simply put, the euro will lower the costs of goods and services, facilitate a comparison of prices within the EU, and thus promote more uniform prices.

Optimum Currency Area

Much of the analysis of the benefits and costs of a common currency is based on the theory of optimum currency areas.[7] An **optimum currency area**

[7]The theory of "optimum currency areas" was first analyzed by Robert Mundell, who won the 1999 Nobel Prize in Economics. See Robert Mundell, "A Theory of Optimum Currency Areas," *American Economic Review*, Vol. 51, September 1961, pp. 717–725.

is a region in which it is economically preferable to have a single official currency rather than multiple official currencies. For example, the United States can be considered an optimal currency area. It is inconceivable that the current volume of commerce among the 50 states would occur as efficiently in a monetary environment of 50 different currencies. Table 8.2 highlights some of the advantages and disadvantages of forming a common currency area.

According to the theory of optimum currency areas, there are gains to be had from sharing a currency across countries' boundaries. These gains include more uniform prices, lower transaction costs, greater certainty for investors, and enhanced competition. Also, a single monetary policy, run by an independent central bank, should promote price stability.

However, a single policy can also entail costs, especially if interest-rate changes affect different economies in different ways. Also, the broader benefits of a single currency must be compared against the loss of two policy instruments: an independent monetary policy and the option of changing the exchange rate. Losing these is particularly acute if a country or region is likely to suffer from economic disturbances (recession) that affect it differently from the rest of the single-currency area, because it will no longer be able to respond by adopting a more expansionary monetary policy or adjusting its currency.

Optimum currency theory then considers various reactions to economic shocks, noting three. The first is the mobility of labor: Workers in the affected country must be able and willing to move

---

TABLE 8.2

Advantages and Disadvantages of Adopting a Common Currency

Advantages	Disadvantages
The risks associated with exchange fluctuations are eliminated within a common currency area.	Absence of individual domestic monetary policy to counter macroeconomic shocks.
Costs of currency conversion are lessened.	Inability of an individual country to use inflation to reduce public debt in real terms.
The economies are insulated from monetary disturbances and speculation.	The transition from individual currencies to a single currency could lead to speculative attacks.
Political pressures for trade protection are reduced.	

freely to other countries. The second is the flexibility of prices and wages: The country must be able to adjust these in response to a disturbance. The third is some automatic mechanism for transferring fiscal resources to the affected country.

The theory of optimal currency areas concludes that for a currency area to have the best chance of success, countries involved should have similar business cycles and similar economic structures. Also, the single monetary policy should affect all the participating countries in the same manner. Moreover, there should be no legal, cultural, or linguistic barriers to labor mobility across borders; there should be wage flexibility; and there should be some system of stabilizing transfers.

Europe as a Suboptimal Currency Area

Although Europe may not be an ideal currency area, forming a monetary union has some advantages. A monetary union may improve economic efficiency through lowering transaction costs of exchanging one currency for another. Tourists are familiar with the time and expense of changing one currency into another while traveling in Europe. Eliminating the transaction costs would benefit both consumers and businesses. A single currency would also facilitate genuine comparison of prices within Europe. Another advantage is the elimination of exchange-rate risk; businesses would more readily trade and invest in other European countries if they did not have to consider what the future exchange rate would be. EMU would also stimulate competition and would facilitate the broadening and deepening of European financial markets.

The overall magnitudes of these gains appear to be relatively small. The European Commission estimates that savings in transaction costs will be about 0.4 percent of the EU's gross domestic product.[8] Even though small, the efficiency gains are greater the more a country trades with other countries in the monetary union. For example, the Netherlands, whose trade with Germany has typ-

ically exceeded 20 percent of its total trade, would benefit considerably by a monetary union with Germany. In contrast, only about 2 percent of the total trade of the Netherlands has typically been with Spain, making the benefits of monetary union with Spain much smaller.

A main disadvantage of EMU is that each participating European country loses the use of monetary policy and the exchange rate as a tool in adjusting to economic disturbances. If one country experiences a recession, it can no longer relax monetary policy or allow its currency to depreciate to stimulate its economy. The use of fiscal policy, too, may be limited by the need to keep budget deficits under control under EMU. Economic revival depends on wage flexibility and perhaps the ability and willingness of labor to move to new locations. Because wage rigidity in Europe is considerable and labor mobility is low, recovering from a recession could be difficult, leading to political pressure for an easing of the single monetary policy, or increased government debt of the country in recession.

Are the members of the EU an optimum currency area? In other words, do the microeconomic gains of greater efficiency outweigh the macroeconomic costs of the loss of the exchange rate as an adjustment tool? Several economists have suggested that the costs exceed the gains for the countries as a whole, and thus monetary union is not a good idea for all countries.[9] For a smaller set of countries, however, the gains may exceed the costs, and monetary union makes sense. Trade among the smaller set of countries is much higher than trade with all countries, so that the efficiency gains are higher.

Challenges for EMU

The economic effect of EMU on Europe and on the United States will depend mostly on the policy decisions that are made in Europe in the years ahead. The actual move to a single currency, by itself, will likely have only a relatively small effect.

Perhaps the most important monetary policy challenge for EMU is the ability of the European Central Bank to focus on price stability over the long term. Some are concerned that, over time, monetary policy may become too expansionary,

[8]Commission of the European Communities, Directorate-General for Economic and Financial Affairs, "One Market, One Money: An Evaluation of the Potential Benefits and Costs of Forming an Economic and Monetary Union," *European Economy*, No. 44, October 1990, p. 11.

[9]Paul DeGrauwe, *The Economics of Monetary Integration* (New York: Oxford University Press, 1994), pp. 89–94.

given the large number of countries voting on monetary policy, and the fact that strong anti-inflationary actions are not well ingrained in countries such as Portugal, Spain, and Italy.

The operation of monetary policy may also present some challenges. If there is wide difference in economic growth rates among EMU countries, it may be difficult to decide on appropriate short-term interest rates. Tightening monetary policy to reduce inflationary pressures may be appropriate for some countries, while loosening monetary policy to stimulate activity may be appropriate for other countries. Therefore, determining monetary policy for the eurozone as a whole, which the European Central Bank is required to do, may be difficult at times.

Although fiscal policy remains the province of national governments, avoidance of excessive budget deficits is important for the success of EMU. Because large budget deficits can lead to high interest rates and lower economic activity, budgetary restraint is desirable by itself. Most countries had considerable difficulty in reducing budget deficits and debts to meet the convergence criteria of EMU. Cutting government expenditures, especially on well-established social programs, was (and is) politically difficult. In the face of aging populations in most countries, pressures on budgets may grow even stronger.

Finally, the need for structural reform in European countries presents a challenge for EMU countries. Labor-market flexibility is probably the most important structural issue. Real (inflationary adjusted) wage flexibility in Europe is estimated to be half that of the United States. Moreover, labor mobility is quite low in Europe, not only between countries, but also within them. Incentives to work and to acquire new skills are inadequate. Regulations that limit employers' ability to dismiss workers make them unwilling to hire and train new workers. Also, high taxes and generous unemployment benefits provided by European governments contribute to sluggish economies.

Analysts note that structural reforms are necessary for several reasons. First, they would lower the EU's persistently high structural unemployment rate. Second, firms would provide needed flexibility in adjusting to recessions, especially those that affected one or a few countries in the eurozone. If prices and wages were flexible downward, for example, a decline in demand would be followed by lower prices, tending to raise demand. Increased labor mobility would be particularly useful in adjusting to recessions.

EMU and the United States

Is EMU good for the United States? At present, the U.S. dollar is by far the most widely used currency in international trade and finance. Many internationally-traded goods, such as oil, are priced, and paid for, in dollars. Bank loans and securities often are denominated in dollars. The dollar's international role is based on the strength of the U.S. economy and financial markets and also the large size of U.S. international trade and investment flows.

Many analysts agree that EMU, if successful, will eventually lead to decline in the dollar's role as an international payments and reserve currency. However, this decline would likely occur slowly, not suddenly, for several reasons. First, the dollar is the predominant currency in Asia and Latin America; it is unlikely the euro will replace the dollar in those areas any time in the near future. Second, the dollar serves as a safe haven at times of political and economic uncertainty. Simply put, European financial markets are unlikely to be transformed overnight; the U.S. financial market will probably remain the most liquid in the world for a long period of time.

Over the years, the U.S. government, which has a strong interest in a prosperous and stable Europe, has supported European efforts at economic integration. The policy on EMU has generally been that if it is good for Europe, it will be good for the United States. It will be good for Europe if the conditions for sustained economic growth, particularly monetary policy credibility, sustainable fiscal deficits, and structural reforms, are achieved by European governments. If these concerns are addressed, EMU will likely stimulate economic growth and competitiveness in Europe, which should benefit the United States. Because U.S. trade with the eurozone is small relative to the size of the U.S. economy, the effect of EMU on bilateral trade flows is expected to be fairly low.

North American Free Trade Agreement (NAFTA)

The success of Europe in forming the European Union has inspired the United States to launch several regional free-trade agreements. During the 1980s, for example, the United States entered into discussions for a free-trade agreement with Canada, which became effective in 1989. This paved the way for Mexico, Canada, and the United States to form the **North American Free Trade Agreement (NAFTA)**, which went into effect in 1994.

NAFTA's visionaries in the United States made a revolutionary gamble. Mexico's authoritarian political system, repressed economy, and resulting poverty were creating problems that could not be contained at the border in perpetuity. Mexican instability would eventually spill over the Rio Grande. The choice was easy: Either help Mexico develop as part of an integrated North America, or watch the economic gap widen and the risks for the United States increase.

The establishment of NAFTA was expected to provide each member nation better access to the others' markets, technology, labor, and expertise. In many respects, there were remarkable fits between the nations: The United States would benefit from Mexico's pool of cheap and increasingly skilled labor, while Mexico would benefit from U.S. investment and expertise. However, negotiating the free-trade agreement was difficult because it required meshing two large advanced industrial economies (United States and Canada) with that of a sizable developing nation (Mexico). The huge living-standard gap between Mexico, with its lower wage scale, and the United States and Canada was a politically sensitive issue. One of the main concerns about NAFTA is whether Canada and the United States as developed countries have little to gain from trade liberalization with Mexico, a developing country. Table 8.3 highlights some of the likely gains and losses of integrating the Mexican and U.S. economies.

NAFTA's Benefits and Costs for Mexico and Canada

NAFTA's benefits to Mexico have been proportionately much greater than for the United States and Canada, because Mexico integrated with economies many times larger than its own. Eliminating trade barriers has led to increases in the production of goods and services for which Mexico has a comparative advantage. Mexico's gains have come at the expense of other low-wage countries, such as Korea and Taiwan. Generally, Mexico has produced more goods that benefit from a low-wage, low-skilled workforce, such as tomatoes, avocados, fruits, vegetables, processed foods, sugar, tuna, and glass;

TABLE 8.3

Winners and Losers in the United States Under Free Trade with Mexico

U.S. Winners	U.S. Losers
Higher-skill, higher-tech businesses and their workers benefit from free trade.	Labor-intensive, lower-wage, import-competing businesses lose from reduced tariffs on competing imports.
Labor-intensive businesses that relocate to Mexico benefit by reducing production costs.	Workers in import-competing businesses lose if their businesses close or relocate.
Domestic businesses that use imports as components in the production process save on production costs.	
Consumers in the United States benefit from less expensive products due to increased competition with free trade.	

labor-intensive manufactured exports, such as appliances and economy automobiles, have also increased. Rising investment spending in Mexico has helped increase wage incomes and employment, national output, and foreign-exchange earnings; it also has facilitated the transfer of technology.

Although agriculture represents only 4 to 5 percent of Mexico's GDP, it supports about a quarter of the country's population. Most Mexican agricultural workers are subsistence farmers who plant grains and oilseeds in small plots, which have supported them for generations. Mexican producers of rice, beef, pork, and poultry claim that they have been devastated by U.S. competition in the Mexican market resulting from NAFTA. They claim that they cannot compete against imports from the United States, where easy credit, better transportation, better technology, and major subsidies give U.S. farmers an unfair advantage.

For Canada, initial concerns about NAFTA were less to do with the flight of low-skilled manufacturing jobs, because trade with Mexico was much smaller than it was for the United States. Instead, the main concern was that closer integration with the U.S. economy would threaten Canada's European-style social welfare model, either by causing certain practices and policies (such as universal health care or a generous minimum wage) to be considered as uncompetitive, or else by imposing downward pressure on the country's base of personal and corporate taxes, thus starving government programs of resources. However, Canada's social-welfare model currently stands intact, and in sharp contrast to the United States. As long as most Canadians are willing to pay the higher taxes necessary to finance generous governmental services, NAFTA poses no threat to the Canadian way of life.

Canada's benefits from NAFTA have been mostly in the form of safeguards: maintenance of its status in international trade, no loss of its current free-trade preferences in the U.S. market, and equal access to Mexico's market. Canada also desired to become part of any process that would eventually broaden market access to Central and South America. Although Canada hoped to benefit from trade with Mexico over time, most researchers have estimated relatively small gains thus far because of the small amount of existing Canada–Mexico trade.

Another benefit of NAFTA for Canada and Mexico is economies of large-scale production. To illustrate, Figure 8.4 represents the Canadian auto market, in which Canada is assumed to be a net exporter to the United States. Assume that prior to the elimination of U.S. trade restrictions, the U.S. demand for Canadian autos is $D_{U.S._0}$. Also assume that the Canadian auto demand is D_C. The overall demand schedule is thus denoted by $D_C + D_{U.S._0}$. Economies of scale are denoted in the downward-sloping cost schedule AC. For simplicity, assume that Canadian manufacturers price their automobiles at average cost. In the absence of a free-trade agreement, the total number of autos demanded is 100 units, and the price received by Canadian manufacturers is $10,000 per unit.

Under bilateral free trade with the United States, Canadian auto companies encounter a danger and an opportunity. The danger is that competing U.S. manufacturers may undercut Canadian companies that maintain prices at $10,000. But bilateral free trade also provides the Canadian companies an opportunity. The elimination of U.S. trade restrictions results in a shift in the export demand schedule faced by Canadian manufacturers from $D_{U.S._0}$ to $D_{U.S._1}$; thus, the overall demand schedule is now $D_C + D_{U.S._1}$. The total number of autos supplied by Canadian manufacturers increases to 120 units, and the resulting cost reductions permit the price charged by Canadian manufacturers to decrease to $8,000. Economies of large-scale production thus permit Canadian firms to adopt more competitive price policies.

For Canadian consumers, the $2,000 price reduction results in an increase in consumer surplus equal to area *a*, located under demand schedule D_C. Note that the gain to the Canadian consumer does *not* come at the expense of the Canadian manufacturer! The Canadian manufacturer can afford to sell autos at a lower price without any decrease in unit profits because economies of scale lead to reductions in unit costs. Economies of large-scale production therefore can provide benefits for *both* the producer *and* the consumer.

FIGURE 8.4

Economies of Scale in Canadian Auto Manufacturing: Benefits to Canada of Abolishing U.S. Trade Restrictions

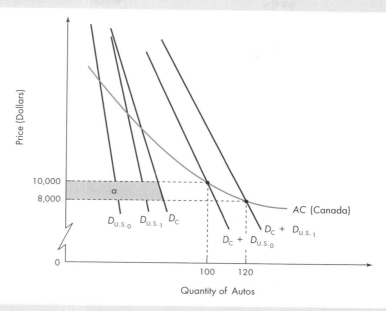

With bilateral free trade, competing U.S. automakers may undercut Canadian manufacturers who maintain prices at $10,000. But longer production runs for Canadian manufacturers, made possible by the opening of the U.S. auto market, can result in cost reductions with economies of scale.

Although NAFTA has succeeded in stimulating increased trade and foreign investment, NAFTA alone has not been enough to modernize Mexico or guarantee prosperity. This has been a disappointment to many Mexicans. However, trade and investment can do only so much. Since the beginnings of NAFTA, the government of Mexico has struggled to deal with the problems of corruption, poor education, red tape, crumbling infrastructure, lack of credit, and a tiny tax base. These factors greatly influence a country's economic development. For Mexico to become an economically advanced nation, it needs a better educational system, cheaper electricity, better roads, and investment incentives for generating growth—things that NAFTA cannot provide.

What NAFTA can provide is additional wealth so government can allocate the gains to things that are necessary. If a government doesn't allocate new wealth correctly, the advantages of free trade quickly erode.

NAFTA's Benefits and Costs for the United States

NAFTA proponents maintain that the agreement has benefited the U.S. economy overall by expanding trade opportunities, reducing prices, increasing competition, and enhancing the ability of U.S. firms to attain economies of large-scale production. The United States has produced more goods that benefit from large amounts of physical capital and a highly skilled workforce, including chemicals, plastics, cement, sophisticated electronics and communications gear, machine tools, and household appliances. U.S. insurance companies have also benefited from fewer restrictions on foreign insurers operating in Mexico. U.S. companies, particularly larger ones, have realized better access to cheaper labor and parts. Moreover, the United States has benefited from a more reliable source of petroleum, less illegal Mexican immigration, and enhanced Mexican political stability as a result of the nation's increasing wealth. In spite of these benefits, the overall economic gains for the United States are estimated to be modest, because the U.S. economy is 25 times the size of the Mexican economy and many U.S.–Mexican trade barriers were dismantled prior to the implementation of NAFTA.

But even ardent proponents of NAFTA acknowledge that it has inflicted pain on some segments of the U.S. economy. On the business side, the losers have been industries such as citrus growing and sugar that rely on trade barriers to limit imports of low-priced Mexican goods. Other losers are unskilled workers, such as those in the apparel industry, whose jobs are most vulnerable to competition from low-paid workers abroad.

U.S. labor unions have been especially concerned that Mexico's low wage scale encourages U.S. companies to locate in Mexico, resulting in job losses in the United States. Cities such as Muskegon, Michigan, which has thousands of workers cranking out such basic auto parts as piston rings, are especially vulnerable to low-wage Mexican competition. Indeed, the hourly manufacturing compensation for Mexican workers has been a small fraction of that paid to U.S. and Canadian workers, as seen in Table 8.4. Although studies have shown that wages are not necessarily the driving factor in business-location decisions, the huge disparity between U.S. and Mexican wages cannot be ignored.

Another concern is Mexico's environmental regulations, criticized as being less stringent than those of the United States. U.S. labor and environmental activists fear that polluting Mexican plants might cause plants in the United States, which are cleaner but more expensive to operate, to close down. Environmentalists also fear that increased Mexican growth will bring increased air and water pollution. However, NAFTA advocates counter that a more prosperous Mexico would be more able and more willing to enforce its environmental regulations; more economic openness is also associated with production closer to state-of-the-art technology, which tends to be cleaner.

Proponents of NAFTA view it as an opportunity to create an enlarged productive base for the

TABLE 8.4

Hourly Manufacturing Compensation Costs for Production Workers (in U.S. Dollars)

Year	United States	Canada	Mexico
1989	$14.32	$14.77	$1.43
1991	15.58	17.16	1.84
1993	16.51	16.43	2.40
1995	17.20	16.03	1.51*
1997	17.74	16.68	1.53
1999	19.11	15.65	2.09
2001	20.60	15.80	2.33
2002	21.33	16.02	2.38

*From 1994 to 1995, the Mexican peso depreciated against the U.S. dollar from 3.3 pesos per dollar to 6.4 pesos per dollar, thus reducing Mexican labor compensation expressed in dollars.

Source: U.S. Department of Labor, Bureau of Labor Statistics, *Foreign Labor Statistics: Hourly Compensation Costs in U.S. Dollars*, 2003, at http://www.bls.gov/bls/newsrels.htm.

entire region through a new allocation of productive factors that would permit each nation to contribute to a larger pie. However, an increase in U.S. and Canadian trade with Mexico resulting from the reduction of trade barriers under NAFTA would partly displace U.S. and Canadian trade with other nations, including those in Central and South America, the Caribbean, and Asia. Some of this displacement would be expected to result in a loss of welfare associated with trade diversion—the shift from a lower-cost supplier to a higher-cost supplier. But because the displacement was expected to be small, it was projected to have a minor negative effect on the U.S. and Canadian economies.

In order to make the NAFTA treaty more agreeable to a skeptical U.S. Congress, the president negotiated side agreements with Mexico and Canada. Concerning the environment, an agency was established in Canada to investigate environmental abuses in any of the three countries. Fines or trade sanctions can be levied on countries that fail to enforce their own environmental laws. As for labor, an agency was established in the United States to investigate labor abuses if two of the three countries agree. Fines or trade sanctions can be imposed if countries fail to enforce minimum-wage standards, child-labor laws, or worker-safety rules.

On balance and to date, the effects of NAFTA on the U.S. economy have been relatively small. These effects have included increases in overall U.S. income and increases in U.S. trade with Mexico, but little impact on overall levels of unemployment, although with some displacement of workers from sector to sector. For particular industries or products with a greater exposure to intra-NAFTA trade, effects have generally been greater, including displacement effects on individual workers.

What are the effects of NAFTA concerning trade creation and trade diversion? As seen in Table 8.5, over the period 1994 to 1998, the flow of U.S. imports from Canada was estimated to have increased by $1.074 billion because of NAFTA, with $690 billion of that trade expansion representing trade creation and $384 billion representing trade diversion—imports that previously came into the United States from other lower-cost countries but now come from Canada, the higher-cost producer. Overall, the table suggests that NAFTA resulted in greater trade creation than trade diversion for the United States, thus improving its welfare. However, NAFTA is estimated to have a significant excess of trade diversion over trade creation in the cases of Canadian imports from Mexico and Mexican imports from Canada. If these estimates are accurate, outside-world producers of the products involved (e.g., automobile engines, data processing equipment, paper, and paperboard) would not appreciate the effects of NAFTA.

It is in politics, not economics, that NAFTA has had its biggest impact. The trade agreement has come to symbolize a close embrace between the United States and Mexico. Given the history of hostility between the two countries, this embrace

TABLE 8.5

Trade Effects of NAFTA: Trade Creation and Trade Diversion (Thousands of Dollars)

Trade Flow	Trade Expansion	Trade Creation	Trade Diversion
U.S. imports from Canada	$1,074,186	$689,997	$384,189
U.S. imports from Mexico	334,912	284,774	50,138
Canadian imports from the United States	63,656	38,444	25,212
Canadian imports from Mexico	167,264	3,321	163,943
Mexican imports from the United States	77,687	50,036	27,651
Mexican imports from Canada	28,001	902	27,099

Source: David Karemera and Kalu Ohah, "An Industrial Analysis of Trade Creation and Trade Diversion of NAFTA," *Journal of Economic Integration*, September 1998, pp. 419–420.

is remarkable. Its cause was the realization by U.S. officials that their chance of curbing the flow of illegal immigrants would be far greater were their southern neighbors wealthy instead of poor. Put simply, the United States bought itself an ally with NAFTA.

Supreme Court Justices Let Mexican Trucks Roll In

Achieving a global market isn't as easy as it looks. Consider the conflict between free traders, who desire the efficiency of a deregulated trucking system, and social activists who are concerned about highway safety.

The safety of the trucking system is of concern to Americans and Canadians. The United States and Canada have laws on their books limiting the number of consecutive hours a trucker can be on the road. We periodically test our drivers for drug or alcohol use. We inspect every vehicle. We have a computerized database to check the validity of licenses and the prior violations of anyone licensed to operate a tractor-trailer. We require thorough training for every U.S. trucker on the road. In contrast, Mexico has no roadside inspection program or drug testing for drivers. It does not require logbooks or have weighing stations for trucks. It does not have a requirement for labeling of hazardous or toxic cargo, or a system to verify drivers' licenses.

According to the NAFTA agreement, the United States, Mexico, and Canada agreed to open their roads to each other's rigs. However, in 1995 President Bill Clinton, in violation of our treaty obligations, unilaterally imposed restrictions on Mexican trucks, confining them to stateside areas within 20 miles of the Mexican border. Mexican goods traveling farther than this arbitrary zone must first be loaded onto American trucks. Therefore, Mexico imposed a border ban against U.S. truckers: U.S. rigs can cross the Mexican border but cannot leave a commercial zone that extends no more than 20 miles. Like Mexican drivers on the other side, they drop loads at transfer points, from which Mexican trucks and drivers complete the delivery.

In Mexico, as in the United States, there are two trucking businesses: long-haul companies that use newer, better-maintained vehicles, and short-haulers with more aged fleets who need to travel just short distances. For example, Mexican products rolling into the United States arrive at a Mexican border depot on long-haul trucks. They are loaded onto short-haulers that go back and forth over the border between depots on each side. Finally, an American long-haul trucker takes the cargo from the American border depot to its United States destination. This requires 3 to 5 trucks to cross one line. Indeed, analysts note that the movement of goods across the border is immensely inefficient.

A main purpose of the NAFTA agreement is to cut transportation costs. By allowing Mexican long-haul trucks to transport goods directly into the United States and likewise for U.S. long-haul trucks into Mexico, the need for storage and warehousing would decline. The reduction in short-haul truckers would cut costs to shippers, and, because they normally do not backhaul, would reduce traffic and congestion on the border by lowering the number of empty trucks.

In 2001, a NAFTA arbitration panel ruled that the United States was in violation of its treaty obligations, noting that it discriminated against Mexican truckers. However, the U.S. government refused to modify its standards on the grounds that 37 percent of Mexican trucks inspected at the border are removed from the road for safety violations, compared with about 24 percent of American trucks inspected nationwide.

In 2004, the Supreme Court, dealing the Teamsters union a defeat, ruled that Mexican trucks have unrestricted access to American highways. Mexican trucks, of course, have to meet the same safety, environmental, and insurance standards as their American competitors. This decision ended a dispute that had festered since the beginnings of NAFTA.

The short-term effect of implementing the Supreme Court's ruling will likely be gradual as Mexican firms contend with several stumbling blocks including a lack of prearranged back hauls, higher insurance and capital costs, and expensive border-processing delays. In the long run, Mexican drivers and trucks will continue to dominate the crossings at the border, but the pattern of operation will change. The use of shuttle truckers is likely to decrease as they lose part of their market share to

Mexican long-haul carriers. The most common trips for these carriers will likely be from the Mexican interior to warehouse facilities in the United States or to nearby cities in the border states. Operating beyond the border states at a profit would almost always necessitate an arranged back haul. In contrast, relatively few U.S. firms are anticipated to apply for operating authority in Mexico. Most are expected to operate through their Mexican partners or subsidiaries.

Is NAFTA an Optimum Currency Area?

The increasing convergence of the NAFTA countries has stimulated a debate on the issues of adopting a common currency and forming an American monetary union among Canada, Mexico, and the United States. Of central relevance to the economic suitability of such a monetary union is the concept of the optimum currency area, as discussed in this chapter.

According to the theory of optimum currency areas, the greater the linkages between countries, the more suitable it is for them to adopt a single official currency. One such linkage is the degree of economic integration among the three NAFTA members. As expected, trade within NAFTA is quite substantial. Canada and Mexico rank as the first and second, respectively, largest trading partners of the United States in terms of trade turnover (imports plus exports). Likewise, the United States is the largest trading partner of Canada and Mexico.

Another linkage is the similarity of economic structures among the three NAFTA members. Canada's advanced industrial economy resembles that of the United States. In the past decade, Canada's average real income per capita, inflation rate, and interest rate were very close to those of the United States. Mexico, however, is a growing economy that is aspiring to maintain economic and financial stability with a much lower average real income per capita and significantly higher inflation and interest rates compared with those of Canada and the United States. Moreover, the value of the peso relative to the U.S. dollar has been quite volatile, although the peso has been more stable against the Canadian dollar. Other problems endured by Mexico are high levels of external debt, balance of payments deficits, and weak financial markets.

Some analysts are skeptical whether Mexico's adopting the U.S. dollar as its official currency would be beneficial. If Mexico adopted the dollar, its central bank would be unable to use monetary policy to impact production and employment in the face of economic shocks, which might further weaken its economy. However, adopting the dollar offers Mexico several advantages, including achievement of long-term credibility in Mexican financial markets, long-term monetary stability and reduced interest rates, and increased discipline and confidence as a result of reducing inflation to the levels of the United States. Put simply, most observers feel that the case for Mexican participation in a North American optimum currency area is questionable on economic grounds. However, the Mexican government has shown interest in dollarizing its economy in an attempt to develop stronger political ties to the United States.

Canadians have generally expressed dissatisfaction concerning the adoption of the U.S. dollar as their official currency. In particular, Canadians are concerned about the loss of national sovereignty that such a policy would entail. They also note that there is no added benefit of credibility to monetary and fiscal discipline, since Canada, like the United States, is already committed to achieving low inflation, low interest rates, and a low level of debt relative to gross domestic product. Put simply, the case for Canadian participation in any North American currency area is less strong on political grounds than economically. At the writing of this text, the likelihood of a North American currency area in the near term appeared to be dim.

Free Trade Area of the Americas

"Never in America has there been a matter requiring more good judgment or more vigilance, or demanding a clearer and more thorough examination." So said Jose Marti, Cuba's independence hero of the first effort by the United States to unite the two halves of the Americas in 1889. By the early 2000s, the region's governments were still stumbling on toward that goal, but hardly in step.

Attempting to widen the scope of North American economic integration, in 1994 the United States convened the Summit of the Americas, which was attended by 34 nations in North and South America; this included all of the nations in the hemisphere except Cuba. The cornerstone of the conference was a call for the creation of a **Free Trade Area of the Americas (FTAA)**. The idea dates back to the 1820s, when Henry Clay, speaker of the House and secretary of state, sought to strengthen U.S. ties with the new Latin republics.

If established, an FTAA will represent the largest trading bloc in the world. It would create a market of more than 850 million consumers with a combined income of more than $14 trillion. It also would level the playing field for U.S. exporters who, at the turn of the century, faced trade barriers more than three times higher those of the United States. The United States tangibly demonstrated its commitment to this objective by entering into a free-trade agreement with Chile in 2003, thus providing momentum for negotiations with other nations in Latin America.

Over the past two decades, Latin America has embraced progressively more open trade policies, intraregionally and with the world, as part of its overall economic platform. The larger economies of Latin America, once known for their collective indebtedness, are considered among the more promising emerging markets for trade and investment opportunities now in the 2000s. Three economic-policy shifts in Latin America paved the way for this new perspective: (1) reduced roles for government in managing the economies, with greater reliance placed on markets, private ownership, and deregulation; (2) use of conventional and generally restrictive macroeconomic policies to promote economic growth and stability; and (3) the movement away from protectionism, often by way of unilateral reductions in tariffs and other trade barriers.

However, there are obstacles that need to be addressed in order for the FTAA to become a reality. One challenge involves the FTAA's allowance for other trade agreements in the hemisphere. Countries in the hemisphere are members of 21 free-trade agreements as well as four customs unions that span the region. Although these agreements can become a "spaghetti bowl" of conflicting arrangements, an FTAA presents an opportunity to simplify these arrangements under a single agreement. Table 8.6 identifies the major regional trade agreements that exist throughout the Americas.

Another concern is that smaller partners in the hemisphere should be given special assistance.

TABLE 8.6

Major Western Hemisphere Regional Trade Agreements

Agreement	Members	Year Effective
Free Trade Area of the Americas	34 countries	Negotiating
North American Free Trade Agreement (NAFTA)	Canada, Mexico, United States	1994
Southern Cone Common Market (MERCOSUR)	Argentina, Brazil, Paraguay, Uruguay	1991
Caribbean Community and Common Market	Antigua, Bahamas, Barbados, Barbuda, Belize, Dominica, Grenada, Guyana, Haiti, Jamaica, Montserrat, St. Kitts, Nevis, St. Lucia, St. Vincent, Surinam, Trinidad, and Tobago	1973
Andean Community	Bolivia, Colombia, Ecuador, Peru, Venezuela	1969
Central American Common Market	Costa Rica, El Salvador, Guatemala, Honduras, Nicaragua	1961

The U.S.–Chile Free-Trade Agreement

[Free Trade]

In addition to complicated multilateral trade negotiations involving the World Trade Organization, the United States has pursued simpler bilateral agreements that are expected to be less politically sensitive and thus more likely to win congressional approval. This occurred in 2003, when the United States and Chile signed a bilateral free-trade agreement, concluding a 14-round negotiation process than began in 2000. The free-trade agreement took effect on January 1, 2004.

With the implementation of the U.S.–Chile free-trade agreement, Chile joined a select group of only five other countries that have a free-trade agreement with the United States: Canada, Mexico, Jordan, Israel, and Singapore. Market access is a major portion of the agreement. When the agreement went into effect in 2004, 87 percent of U.S.–Chilean bilateral trade in consumer and industrial products became duty-free immediately, with the rest receiving reduced tariff treatment over time. Some 75 percent of U.S. farm exports will enter Chile duty-free by 2008, and duties on all goods will be fully phased out by 2016. The agreement also phases out export subsidies on agricultural products and increases market access for a broad range of services including banking and insurance.

Proponents of the U.S.–Chile free-trade agreement maintained that it offered both economic and political benefits, with Chile seen as a crucial foothold in South America, a region historically linked closely with Europe and Asia. From an economic perspective, U.S. businesses considered Chile a main target for expanding exports and repeatedly emphasized the need to decrease the higher tariffs they faced relative to Canada and other countries that already had free-trade agreements with Chile. Lower-cost U.S. imports from Chile also provided benefits to individual and business consumers. U.S. investors also saw Chile's political and economic stability as attractive for foreign investment. From a trade-strategy perspective, it was argued that a free-trade agreement with Chile would support U.S. initiatives with the Free Trade Area of the Americas, currently under negotiation, by fostering greater Chilean support for U.S. issues and helping define key negotiating parameters (labor and environment provisions) that could be precedent setting. Finally, Chile was seen as an opportunity for the United States to encourage economic and trade reform in Latin America, for which Chile had become a regional model.

Chile also saw a logic in forming a free-trade agreement with the United States because export promotion has been a foundation of its growth and development strategy. Guaranteed Chilean access to the large U.S. market provides opportunities for increased and more diversified trade. Chile also envisioned increased foreign investment as a benefit of the free-trade agreement.

However, opposition to a bilateral free-trade agreement was strong for both economic and political reasons. Some economists, even those who support free trade, noted that bilateral and regional agreements are poor substitutes for multilateral arrangements. Although both Chile and the United States saw their welfare increasing through trade creation, critics noted that the agreement would likely also cause trade diversion, which would negatively affect both those inside and outside of the agreement. There was also strong opposition by interest groups, especially import-competing industries that absorb the brunt of the adjustment costs of the agreement. Other groups protesting globalization in general noted that the agreement did not adequately address the adverse effects on labor and the environment. At the writing of this text, the U.S.–Chile free-trade agreement is in its infancy. It remains to be seen whether or not the agreement will live up to the expectations of its advocates.

Source: Drawn from J. Hornbeck, *The U.S.–Chile Free-Trade Agreement*, Congressional Research Service, Washington, DC, September 2003.

Skeptics note that an FTAA should not merely reflect the interests of the hemisphere's two largest economies, the United States and Brazil.

Yet another challenge revolves around agricultural issues. Agricultural makes up, on average, 7 percent of Latin America's GDP and a significantly larger share of its exports. In FTAA negotiations, the United States has refused to lower subsidies and tariffs that protect U.S. farmers, arguing that those protections should be negotiated in global trade agreements, not regional ones, because the European Union is the biggest subsidizer of agriculture. But Brazil contends that its farmers cannot compete in U.S. markets, so it demands that subsidies and tariffs be on the bargaining table. However, farmers in the United States fear that a flood of cheap agricultural products from Brazil and other Latin American nations would occur if trade barriers are removed, which would wipe them out. Other difficult negotiating issues for the FTAA involve honoring intellectual property rights and opening of government contracts to foreign bidders.

These differences have kept the region's governments from uniting the two halves of the Americas. To keep the region on the road to forming an FTAA, in 2003 the governments put together a less ambitious compromise. Out went the wide-ranging accord they had spent years negotiating. Instead, they will seek a flexible, 34-country agreement, comprising only a few common standards and some tariff cuts.

The FTAA is perhaps the most ambitious economic initiative in the Western Hemisphere's history and one that would have a tremendous effect on the lives of its inhabitants. Many roadblocks and detours will likely have to be faced before it is completed.

Asia–Pacific Economic Cooperation

Since 1989, the United States has been a member of **Asia–Pacific Economic Cooperation (APEC)**, which also includes Australia, Brunei, Canada, Chile, China, Indonesia, Japan, Malaysia, Mexico, New Zealand, Papua New Guinea, the Philippines, Singapore, South Korea, Taiwan, and Thailand. In 1993, leaders of the APEC countries put forth their vision of an Asia–Pacific economic community in which barriers to trade and investment in the region would be eliminated by the year 2020. All countries would begin to liberalize at a common date, but the pace of implementation would take into account the differing levels of economic development among APEC economies: The industrialized countries would achieve free trade and investment no later than 2010, and the developing economies no later than 2020. It remains to be seen whether the APEC goal of economic integration will be achieved.

Transition Economies

Trade preferences have also been extended to commercial and financial practices involving nations making the transition from a centrally planned economy to a market economy; such economies are known as the **transition economies**. Prior to the economic reforms in Eastern European nations in the 1990s, these nations were classified as nonmarket economies; the Western nations, including the United States, were classified as market economies. Table 8.7 shows the gross national income per capita for the transition economies as of 2002. Let us consider the major features of these economic systems.

In a **market economy**, the commercial decisions of independent buyers and sellers acting in their own interest govern both domestic and international trade. Market-determined prices value alternatives and allocate scarce resources. This means that prices play rationing and signaling roles that make the availability of goods consistent with buyer preferences and purchasing power.

In a **nonmarket economy** (one that is centrally planned), there is less regard for market considerations. State planning and control govern foreign and sometimes domestic trade. The central plan often controls the prices and output of goods bought and sold, with small recognition given to considerations of cost and efficiency. The state fixes prices to ration arbitrary quantities among buyers, and these prices are largely insulated from foreign-trade influences. Given these different pricing mechanisms, trade between market economies and centrally planned economies can be difficult. Because market-determined prices underlie the basis for trade according to the theory of comparative advantage, the theory has little to say about how nonmarket economies carry out their international trade policies.

TABLE 8.7

GNP per Capita* for the Transition Economies, 2002

Former Republics of the Soviet Union		Central and Eastern European Countries	
Estonia	11,120	Slovenia	17,690
Lithuania	9,880	Czech Republic	14,400
Latvia	8,940	Hungary	12,810
Russia	7,820	Slovakia	12,190
Kazakstan	5,480	Poland	10,130
Belarus	5,330	Croatia	9,760
Ukraine	4,650	Romania	6,290
Armenia	3,060	Boznia-Herzegovina	5,800
Azerbaijan	2,920	Yugoslavia, Fed. Republic	5,600
Uzbekistan	1,590	Albania	4,040
Moldova	1,560		
Kyrgyz Republic	1,520		
Tajikistan	900		

*At purchasing power parity.

Source: The World Bank Group, http://www.worldbank.org/data. Scroll to "Data by Country" and then to "ICT at a Glance Tables."

The nonmarket nations of Eastern Europe and Asia historically have experienced only modest trade flows with the Western world. By the 1970s and 1980s, however, the nonmarket nations were increasingly looking to Western markets. In terms of the volume and composition of East–West trade, Western Europe has accounted for the largest share, whereas the U.S. share has been minor. Political considerations largely explain the small amount of U.S. trade with the East. The United States historically has placed controls on strategic exports of technology and goods to communist countries; it has also imposed restrictions on the credit terms extended to them.

Industrial Cooperation

Until recently, East–West trade was relatively simple: Exports to and imports from Eastern European countries were settled in hard currency or credit. But with the expansion of East–West trade has come *countertrade*, which establishes a greater degree of interdependence between the private corporations of Western economies and the state enterprises of the Eastern European countries.

Countertrade refers to all international trade in which goods are exchanged for goods— a kind of barter. If swapping goods for goods sounds less efficient than using cash or credit, that's because it is. During tough economic times, however, shortages of hard currency and tight credit can hinder East–West trade. Instead of facing the possibility of reduced foreign sales, Western producers have viewed countertrade as the next best alternative.

Many Western nations conduct countertrade with the Eastern European countries, as shown in Table 8.8 on page 282. In the United States, General Motors, Sears, and General Electric have established trading companies that conduct countertrade. A simple form of countertrade occurs when an Eastern European country agrees to pay for the delivery of plant, machinery, or equipment with the goods produced by the plant. For example, Germany has sold Russia steel pipe in exchange for deliveries of natural gas; Austria has supplied Poland with technological expertise and equipment in exchange for diesel engines and truck

ECONOMIC *Applications*

Visit EconNews Online
Transitional Economies

TABLE 8.8

Examples of Eastern European Countertrade Agreements with the West

Western Country (Supplier)	Type of Eastern European Import	Type of Eastern European Export
Germany	Polyethylene plant	Polyethylene
Italy	Detergent plant	Organic chemicals
United States	Fertilizer plant	Ammonia
Japan	Forestry handling equipment	Timber products
United Kingdom	Methanol plant	Methanol
France	Pulp paper plant	Wood pulp
Austria	Large-diameter pipe	Natural gas

Source: U.S. Department of Commerce, International Trade Administration.

components. With the opening of the economies of the former Soviet Union, the role of countertrade has diminished in recent years.

Industrial cooperation has also resulted in *coproduction agreements*, by which Western companies establish production facilities in an Eastern European country. Because most Eastern European countries do not allow foreign ownership of such operations, an agreement is made whereby ownership is held by Eastern European nationals. Coproduction agreements are widely used in the areas of machine building, chemical products, electrical and electronic devices, and pharmaceutical goods.

Industrial cooperation may assume several other forms. Western companies have often made *joint R&D agreements* with Eastern European countries, particularly in industrial processes and technical areas. The findings of such activities are patented jointly, and license royalties are shared between the partners. Also popular are *contract manufacturing agreements*: Western nations supply materials and design specifications to Eastern European enterprises, which produce the goods and ship them back to the Western nations.

The motivations for industrial cooperation vary. For a Western company, such agreements get around the hard-currency scarcities of the Eastern European countries and permit access to the markets of Eastern Europe. Western companies can also tap additional supplies of raw materials and intermediate goods, or possibly maximize revenues by selling obsolete equipment. The Eastern European partner typically views industrial cooperation as a means of obtaining new technologies and expanding industrial capacity with small sacrifices of hard currency.

The Transition Toward a Market-Oriented Economy

In 1989, the world began to witness unprecedented developments in Eastern Europe, as many countries moved toward democracy and economic reform. Countries such as Hungary, Poland, Czechoslovakia, and the Soviet Union discarded their centrally controlled state economies and moved toward systems in which private ownership of property predominated and most resources were allocated through markets. These transitions reflected the failure of central planning systems to provide either political freedom or a decent standard of living.

In 1990, for example, per capita real income in the Soviet Union was less than one-tenth of per capita real income in the United States. Another example is the case of the two Germanys. Starting from the same point at the end of World War II and sharing a common culture, East Germany and West Germany followed two different paths. East Germany became an industrial wasteland with run-down, outmoded factories, and a polluted environment, while West Germany achieved one of the highest living standards in the world.

The fundamental motivation for change in Eastern Europe was the failure of the economies there to generate a high standard of living for their people. The economic policies pursued in these countries failed because they were unable to provide adequate incentives for producers to supply efficiently the goods and services that consumers wanted to purchase. Widespread use of price controls, reliance on inefficient public enterprises, extensive barriers to competition with the rest of the world, and government regulation of production and investment all obstructed the normal operation of markets. The lack of enforceable property rights severely restricted incentives for entrepreneurs.

In Eastern Europe, central plans decided production levels. As a result, there was no reason to expect that the output produced would meet the wants or needs of the people. Shortages and surpluses occurred frequently, but managers had little motivation to modify their output as long as quotas were realized. Government investment choices led to underproduction of consumer goods and widespread rationing. Incentives to innovate were almost completely absent, except in the defense sector; but the European countries were unable to transfer their high levels of defense technology into improvements for consumers. Inefficient state-owned enterprises were common, and public funds were channeled into favored industries irrespective of the economic consequences.

Over time, the weaknesses of the political and economic systems of Eastern Europe and the contrasting success of the market-oriented systems became obvious. This created pressure that led to the collapse of Eastern Europe's communist governments.

As the economies of the communist countries deteriorated, piecemeal reforms occurred. Many Eastern European countries attempted to combine economic decentralization with partial price decontrol; however, the removal of price controls has often led to destabilizing bouts of inflation. It was hoped that with reduced central control, state-owned enterprises would operate as if they were part of well-functioning markets. Although national planning objectives were still stipulated, individual firms could establish their own goals and be responsible for production decisions. The system of price controls became more flexible and some small-scale enterprise was allowed. These piecemeal reforms, however, were doomed to failure. Private property rights were generally absent, which limited profit incentives and discouraged entrepreneurship, and state-owned monopolies were maintained. Apparently, widespread economic reforms were needed to revitalize the Eastern European economies.

Economists generally agree that Eastern Europe's transition toward a healthy market economy requires major restructuring of their economies: Sound fiscal and monetary policies must be established, domestic price controls must be removed, economies must be opened to international market forces, private property rights must be established along with a legal system to protect these rights, domestic competition must be promoted, and government's involvement in the economy must be reduced.

Although there is general agreement on what the former communist economies need to do, much debate exists about the sequence and timing of specific reforms. Advocates of *shock therapy* (the "big bang" approach) maintain that the economies in transition should proceed immediately on all fronts. That is, they should privatize, abandon price controls, liberalize trade, develop market institutions, and so on as quickly as possible. Although the initial economic pain may be severe, it will subside as the transition to a market economy leads to rising living standards. Poland and East Germany, starting from different circumstances, are undergoing rapid transformations to a market economy. Although the output and employment costs of the transition have been greater than initially expected, the measures are seen as a basis for a significant improvement in living standards over the longer term.

Advocates of a *gradualist* approach fear that the big-bang approach will cause too great a shock to the economic system and that organizations cannot change so quickly; the initial economic disruptions might create excessive burdens for the people and even lead to a return to the former communist system. Gradualists maintain that the best approach is to build up market institutions, gradually decontrol prices, and privatize only the most efficient government enterprises at first. Hungary, the Czech Republic, and Russia are examples of former communist countries that have adopted more gradual economic reforms. Table 8.9 shows the 2003 Index of Economic Freedom for selected transition economies as well as Hong Kong, Singapore, and the United States. The higher the score factor, the greater the level of government interference in the economy and the less economic freedom.

Russia and the World Trade Organization

Since 1995, Russia has been negotiating terms for accession to the World Trade Organization. Progress toward accession has been uneven over the years, with negotiations to date consisting of detailed examinations of Russia's trade policies and its legal and administrative framework for trade. However, the negotiations gained momentum following the September 11, 2001, terrorist attacks against the United States, when Russia and the United States became more closely allied in their efforts to eliminate terrorism.

Russia's WTO accession negotiations have been slow for several reasons. Still in transition from a nonmarket to a market economy since the breakup of the Soviet Union, Russia faces the ongoing challenges of restructuring its economy, privatizing government-owned industries, and implementing market-oriented economic reforms. Reaching political consensus on reforms—particularly on reforms that would open the Russian economy to more efficient foreign competitors—often has proved difficult and time-consuming. A 1998 economic crisis, precipitated by a loss of the financial markets' confidence in Russia, was a significant setback that forced Russian policy makers to make domestic economic-crisis management their priority. Also, rising world oil prices beginning in 2000 (oil is Russia's major export) generated a windfall budget surplus and slowed the impetus in Russia

TABLE 8.9

Economies in Transition: 2003 Index of Economic Freedom*

Economy	Composite Index	
Hong Kong	1.45	Less Government Interference
Singapore	1.50	
United States	1.80	
Bahrain	2.00	
Lithuania	2.35	
Latvia	2.45	
Czech Republic	2.50	
Hungary	2.65	
Poland	2.90	
Bulgaria	3.35	
Ukrane	3.65	
Romania	3.70	
Russia	3.70	
Turkmenistan	4.15	
Uzbekistan	4.25	More Government Interference

*Based on 10 broad economic factors in 161 economies: trade, taxation, government intervention, monetary policy, foreign investment, banking, wages and prices, property rights, regulation, black market.

Source: The Heritage Foundation, *2003 Index of Economic Freedom Rankings*, at http://www.heritage.org/index.

for domestic economic reforms and integration into the global economy.

The goal of WTO membership has been the cornerstone of Russian economic policies to integrate Russia into the global economy following decades of Soviet self-imposed isolation. Although the WTO does not require that its members enact specific legislation, its members have requested that Russia develop new laws and regulations in line with international standards, improve enforcement of regulations already compliant with WTO rules, and agree to terms that will open Russian markets to foreign competition before Russia's accession application is approved. Issues that must be addressed include Russian agricultural subsidies, the Russian customs system, foreign investment regulations, market access in Russia's service sectors, Russian technical barriers to trade, and Russia's need to improve its administration and enforcement of intellectual property rights.

Accession to the WTO generally enjoys broad political support in Russia. Russian officials estimate that Russian trade gains could total as much as $18 billion over 5 years following WTO accession as a result of reduced tariff and nontariff trade barriers of Russia's trading partners. However, critics fear that an open-trade regime could have an adverse impact on many Russian industries that are not globally competitive, such as autos, steel, and agriculture.

Summary

1. Trade liberalization has assumed two main forms. One involves the reciprocal reduction of trade barriers on a nondiscriminatory basis, as seen in the operation of the World Trade Organization. The other approach involves the establishment by a group of nations of regional trading arrangements among themselves. The European Union and the North American Free Trade Agreement are examples of regional trading arrangements.

2. The term *economic integration* refers to the process of eliminating restrictions on international trade, payments, and factor input mobility. The stages of economic integration are (a) free-trade area, (b) customs union, (c) common market, (d) economic union, and (e) monetary union.

3. The welfare implications of economic integration can be analyzed from two perspectives. First are the static welfare effects, resulting from trade creation and trade diversion. Second are the dynamic welfare effects that stem from greater competition, economies of scale, and the stimulus to investment spending that economic integration makes possible.

4. From a static perspective, the formation of a customs union yields net welfare gains if the consumption and production benefits of trade creation more than offset the loss in world efficiency owing to trade diversion.

5. Several factors influence the extent of trade creation and trade diversion: (a) the degree of competitiveness that member-nation economies have prior to formation of the customs union, (b) the number and size its members, and (c) the size of its external tariff against nonmembers.

6. The European Union was originally founded in 1957 by the Treaty of Rome. Today it consists of 25 members. By 1992, the EU had essentially reached the common-market stage of integration. Empirical evidence suggests that the EU has realized welfare benefits in trade creation that have outweighed the losses from trade diversion. One of the stumbling blocks confronting the EU has been its common agricultural policy, which has required large government subsidies to support European farmers. The Maastricht Treaty of 1991 called for the formation of a monetary union for eligible EU members, which was initiated in 1999.

7. The formation of the European Monetary Union in 1999 resulted in the creation of a single currency (the euro) and a European Central Bank. With a common central bank, the central bank of each participating nation

performs operations similar to those of the 12 regional Federal Reserve Banks in the United States.

8. Much of the analysis of the benefits and costs of Europe's common currency is based on the theory of optimum currency areas. According to this theory, the gains to be had from sharing a currency across countries' boundaries include more uniform prices, lower transactions costs, greater certainty for investors, and enhanced competition. These gains must be compared against the loss of an independent monetary policy and the option of changing the exchange rate.

9. In 1989, the United States and Canada successfully negotiated a free-trade agreement under which free trade between the two nations would be phased in over a 10-year period. This agreement was followed by negotiation of the North American Free Trade Agreement (NAFTA) by the United States, Mexico, and Canada.

10. By the 1990s, nations of Eastern Europe and the former Soviet Union were making the transition from centrally planned economies to market economies. These transitions reflected the failure of central planning systems to provide either political freedom or a decent standard of living.

11. It is widely agreed that the transition of economies of Eastern Europe and the former Soviet Union into healthy market economies will require major restructuring: (a) establishing sound fiscal and monetary policies; (b) removing price controls; (c) opening economies to competitive market forces; (d) establishing private property rights and a legal system to protect those rights; and (e) reducing government's involvement in the economy.

Key Concepts and Terms

- Asia–Pacific Economic Cooperation (APEC) *(page 280)*
- Benelux *(page 255)*
- Common agricultural policy *(page 263)*
- Common market *(page 255)*
- Convergence criteria *(page 261)*
- Countertrade *(page 281)*
- Customs union *(page 254)*
- Dynamic effects of economic integration *(page 256)*
- Economic integration *(page 254)*
- Economic union *(page 255)*

- Euro *(page 261)*
- European Monetary Union (EMU) *(page 261)*
- European Union (EU) *(page 255)*
- Export subsidies *(page 263)*
- Free-trade area *(page 254)*
- Free Trade Area of the Americas (FTAA) *(page 278)*
- Maastricht Treaty *(page 261)*
- Market economy *(page 280)*
- Monetary union *(page 255)*
- Nonmarket economy *(page 280)*

- North American Free Trade Agreement (NAFTA) *(page 271)*
- Optimum currency area *(page 268)*
- Regional trading arrangement *(page 253)*
- Static effects of economic integration *(page 256)*
- Trade-creation effect *(page 256)*
- Trade-diversion effect *(page 256)*
- Transition economies *(page 280)*
- Variable levies *(page 263)*

Study Questions

1. How can trade liberalization exist on a nondiscriminatory basis versus a discriminatory basis? What are some actual examples of each?
2. What is meant by the term *economic integration*? What are the various stages that economic integration can take?
3. How do the static welfare effects of trade creation and trade diversion relate to a nation's decision to form a customs union? Of what importance to this decision are the dynamic welfare effects?
4. Why has the so-called common agricultural policy been a controversial issue for the European Union?
5. What are the welfare effects of trade creation and trade diversion for the European Union, as determined by empirical studies?
6. **Xtra!** **For a tutorial of this question, go to**
   CARBAUGH **http://carbaughxtra.swlearning.com**
   Table 8.10 depicts the supply and demand schedules of gloves for Portugal, a small nation that is unable to affect the world price. On graph paper, draw the supply and demand schedules of gloves for Portugal.
   a. Assume that Germany and France can supply gloves to Portugal at a price of $2 and $3, respectively. With free trade, which nation exports gloves to Portugal? How many gloves does Portugal produce, consume, and import?
   b. Suppose Portugal levies a 100 percent nondiscriminatory tariff on its glove imports. Which nation exports gloves to

   Portugal? How many gloves will Portugal produce, consume, and import?
   c. Suppose Portugal forms a customs union with France. Determine the trade-creation effect and the trade-diversion effect of the customs union. What is the customs union's overall effect on the welfare of Portugal?
   d. Suppose instead that Portugal forms a customs union with Germany. Is this a trade-diverting or trade-creating customs union? By how much does the customs union increase or decrease the welfare of Portugal?

TABLE 8.10

Supply and Demand for Gloves: Portugal

Price ($)	Quantity Supplied	Quantity Demanded
0	0	18
1	2	16
2	4	14
3	6	12
4	8	10
5	10	8
6	12	6
7	14	4
8	16	2
9	18	0

netlink

8.1 The home page of the proposed Free Trade Area of the Americas, a plan to integrate the economies of North and South America, can be found by setting your browser to this URL:

http://www.alca-ftaa.org

8.2 The Asia–Pacific Economic Cooperation is a regional organization of 18 countries that promotes free trade and economic coordination. Visit its Web site by setting your browser to this URL:

http://www.apecsec.org.sg

8.3 Information about the European Union can be found by visiting its home page, along with that of the Government & Social Science Information Service, administered by the University of

California, Berkeley. To find these two sites, set your browser to these URLs:

http://europa.eu.int/

and

http://www.lib.berkeley.edu/doemoff/gov_eugde.html

8.4 To get information on NAFTA, log onto the Web page of the North American Integration and Development (NAID) Center at the University of California at Los Angeles:

http://naid.sppsr.ucla.edu

8.5 The Association of Southeast Asian Nations (ASEAN) was established on August 8, 1967, to promote economic growth, social progress, and cultural development. Visit its Web site at this URL:

http://www.aseansec.org

To access NetLink Exercises and the Virtual Scavenger Hunt, visit the Carbaugh Web site at http://carbaugh.swlearning.com.

Xtra! Log onto the Carbaugh Xtra! Web site (http://carbaughxtra.swlearning.com) for additional learning resources such as practice quizzes, help with graphing, and current events applications.

chapter 9

International Factor Movements and Multinational Enterprises

Our attention so far has been on international flows of goods and services. However, some of the most dramatic changes in the world economy have been due to international flows of factors of production, including labor and capital. In the 1800s, European capital and labor (along with African and Asian labor) flowed to the United States and fostered its economic development. In the 1960s, the United States sent large amounts of investment capital to Canada and Western Europe; in the 1980s and 1990s, investment flowed from Japan to the United States. Today, workers from southern Europe find employment in northern European factories, while Mexican workers migrate to the United States. The tearing down of the Berlin Wall in 1990 triggered a massive exodus of workers from East Germany to West Germany.

The economic forces underlying international movements in factors of production are virtually identical to those underlying international flows of goods and services. Productive factors move, when they are permitted to, from nations where they are abundant (low productivity) to nations where they are scarce (high productivity). Productive factors flow in response to differences in returns (such as wages and yields on capital) as long as these are large enough to more than outweigh the cost of moving from one country to another.

A nation in which labor is scarce can either import labor-intensive products or import labor itself; the same applies to capital. Thus, *international trade in goods and services and flows of productive factors are substitutes for each other*. One cannot conduct a satisfactory study of international trade without also analyzing the international mobility of labor and capital.

This chapter considers the role of international capital flows (investment) as a substitute for trade in capital-intensive products. Special attention is given to the multinational enterprise that carries on the international reallocation of capital. The chapter also analyzes the international mobility of labor as a substitute for trade in labor-intensive products.

The Multinational Enterprise

Although the term *enterprise* can be precisely defined, there is no universal agreement on the exact definition of a **multinational enterprise** (**MNE**). But a close look at some representative MNEs suggests that these businesses have a number of identifiable features. Operating in many host countries, MNEs often conduct research and development (R&D) activities in addition to manufacturing, mining, extraction, and business-service operations. The MNE cuts across national borders and is often directed from a company planning center that is distant from the host country. Both stock ownership and company management are typically multinational in character. A typical MNE has a high ratio of foreign sales to total sales, often 25 percent or more. Regardless of the lack of agreement as to what constitutes an MNE, there is no doubt that the multinational phenomenon is massive in size. Table 9.1 provides a glimpse of some of the world's largest corporations.

MNEs may diversify their operations along vertical, horizontal, and conglomerate lines within the host and source countries. **Vertical integration** often occurs when the parent MNE decides to establish foreign subsidiaries to produce intermediate goods or inputs that go into the production of the finished good. For industries such as oil refining and steel, such *backward integration* may include the extraction and processing of raw materials. Most manufacturers tend to extend operations backward only to the production of component parts. The major international oil companies represent a classic case of backward vertical integration on a worldwide basis. Oil-production subsidiaries are located in areas such as the Middle East, whereas the refining and marketing operations occur in the industrial nations of the West. MNEs may also practice *forward integration* in the direction of the final consumer market. Automobile manufacturers, for example, may establish foreign subsidiaries to market the finished goods of the parent company. In practice, most vertical foreign investment is backward. MNEs often wish to integrate their operations vertically to benefit from economies of scale and international specialization.

Horizontal integration occurs when a parent company producing a commodity in the source country sets up a subsidiary to produce the identical product in the host country. These subsidiaries are independent units in productive capacity and are established to produce and market the parent

---

TABLE 9.1

The World's Largest Corporations, 2003

Firm	Headquarters	Revenues ($ Billions)
Wal-Mart Stores	United States	$243.5
General Motors	United States	186.8
ExxonMobil	United States	182.5
Royal Dutch Shell	Netherlands	179.4
BP	United Kingdom	178.7
Ford Motor	United States	163.9
DaimlerChrysler	United States	141.4
Toyota Motor	Japan	131.8
General Electric	United States	131.7
Mitsubishi	Japan	109.4

Source: "The 2003 Global 500," *Fortune*, at http://www.fortune.com.

company's product in overseas markets. Coca-Cola and Pepsi-Cola, for example, are bottled not only in the United States but also throughout much of the world. MNEs sometimes locate production facilities overseas to avoid stiff foreign tariff barriers, which would place their products at a competitive disadvantage. Parent companies also like to locate close to their customers because differences in national preferences may require special designs for their products.

Besides making horizontal and vertical foreign investments, MNEs may diversify into nonrelated markets, in what is known as **conglomerate integration**. For example, in the 1980s, U.S. oil companies stepped up their nonenergy acquisitions in response to anticipated declines of future investment opportunities in oil and gas. ExxonMobil acquired a foreign copper-mining subsidiary in Chile, and Tenneco bought a French company producing automotive exhaust systems.

To carry out their worldwide operations, MNEs rely on **foreign direct investment**—acquisition of a controlling interest in an overseas company or facility. Foreign direct investment typically occurs when (1) the parent company obtains sufficient common stock in a foreign company to assume voting control (the U.S. Department of Commerce defines a company as directly foreign owned when a "foreign person" holds a 10 percent interest in the company); (2) the parent company acquires or constructs new plants and equipment overseas; (3) the parent company shifts funds abroad to finance an expansion of its foreign subsidiary; or (4) earnings of the parent company's foreign subsidiary are reinvested in plant expansion.

Table 9.2 summarizes the position of the United States with respect to foreign direct investment in 2002. Data are provided concerning U.S. direct investment abroad and foreign direct investment in the United States. In recent years, the majority of U.S. foreign direct investment has flowed to Europe and Canada, especially in the manufacturing sector. Most foreign direct investment in the United States has come from Europe, Japan, and Canada—areas that have invested heavily in U.S. manufacturing, petroleum, and wholesale trade facilities.

TABLE 9.2

Direct Investment Position of the United States on an Historical Cost Basis, 2002*

Country	U.S. Direct Investment Abroad		Foreign Direct Investment in the United States	
	Amount (Billions of Dollars)	Percentage	Amount (Billions of Dollars)	Percentage
Canada	$ 152.5	10.0%	$ 92.0	6.8%
Europe	796.9	52.4	1,006.5	74.9
Latin America	272.4	17.9	52.3	3.9
Africa	15.1	1.0	2.3	0.1
Middle East	14.2	1.0	6.8	0.5
Asia and Pacific	269.9	17.7	188.0	14.0
	$1,521.0	100.0%	$1,347.9	100.0%

*Historical-cost valuation is based on the time the investment occurred, with no adjustment for price changes.

Source: U.S. Department of Commerce, *U.S. Direct Investment Position Abroad and Foreign Direct Investment Position in the United States on a Historical-Cost Basis,* at http://www.bea.doc.gov/. See also U.S. Department of Commerce, *Survey of Current Business* (Washington, DC: U.S. Government Printing Office, December 2003).

Motives for Foreign Direct Investment

The case for opening markets to foreign direct investment is as compelling as it is for trade. More open economies enjoy higher rates of private investment, which is a major determinant of economic growth and job creation. Foreign direct investment is actively court-ed by countries, not least because it generates spillovers such as improved management and better technology. As is true with firms that trade, firms and sectors where foreign direct investment is intense tend to have higher average labor productiv-ity and pay higher wages. Outward investment allows firms to remain competitive and thus sup-ports employment at home. Investment abroad stim-ulates exports of machinery and other capital goods.

ECONOMIC *Applications*

Visit EconDebate Online for a debate on this topic

New MNEs do not pop up haphazardly in for-eign nations; they develop as a result of conscious planning by corporate managers. Both economic theory and empirical studies support the notion that foreign direct investment is conducted in anticipa-tion of *future profits*. It is generally assumed that investment flows from regions of low anticipated profit to those of high anticipated profit, after allowing for risk. Although expected profits may ultimately explain the process of foreign direct investment, corporate management may emphasize a variety of other factors when asked about their investment motives. These factors include market-demand conditions, trade restrictions, investment regulations, labor costs, and transportation costs. All these factors have a bearing on cost and revenue conditions and hence on the level of profit.

Demand Factors

The quest for profits encourages MNEs to search for new markets and sources of demand. Some MNEs set up overseas subsidiaries to tap foreign markets that cannot be maintained adequately by export products. This sometimes occurs in response to dis-satisfaction over distribution techniques abroad. Consequently, a business may set up a foreign mar-keting division and, later, manufacturing facilities. This incentive may be particularly strong when it is realized that local taste and design differences exist. A close familiarity with local conditions is of utmost importance to a successful marketing program.

The location of foreign manufacturing facilities may be influenced by the fact that some parent companies find their productive capacity already sufficient to meet domestic demands. If they wish to enjoy growth rates that exceed the expansion of domestic demand, they must either export or estab-lish foreign production operations. General Motors (GM), for example, has felt that the markets of such countries as Britain, France, and Brazil are strong enough to permit the survival of GM manufactur-ing subsidiaries. But Boeing Aircraft has centralized its manufacturing operations in the United States and exports abroad because an efficient production plant for jet planes is a large investment relative to the size of most foreign markets.

Market competition may also influence a firm's decision to set up foreign facilities. Corporate strate-gies may be defensive in nature if they are directed at preserving market shares from actual or potential competition. The most certain method of prevent-ing foreign competition from becoming a strong force is to acquire foreign businesses. For the United States, the 1960s and early 1970s witnessed a tremendous surge in acquisition of foreign business-es. Approximately half of the foreign subsidiaries operated by U.S. MNEs were originally acquired through purchase of already existing concerns dur-ing this era. Once again, General Motors exempli-fies this practice, purchasing and setting up auto producers around the globe. GM has been success-ful in gaining control of many larger foreign-model firms, including Monarch (GM Canada) and Opel (GM Germany). It did not acquire smaller-model firms such as Toyota, Datsun, and Volkswagen, all of which have become significant competitors for General Motors.

Cost Factors

MNEs often seek to increase profit levels through reductions in production costs. Such cost-reducing foreign direct investments may take a number of forms. The pursuit of essential raw materials may underlie a company's intent to go multinational. This is particularly true of the extractive industries and certain agricultural commodities. United Fruit, for example, has established banana-producing facilities in Honduras to take advantage of the natural trade advantages afforded by the weather and growing conditions. Similar types of natural trade advantages explain why Anaconda has set up mining operations in Bolivia and why Shell produces and refines oil in Indonesia. Natural supply advantages such as resource endowments or climatic conditions may indeed influence a company's decision to invest abroad.

Production costs include factors other than material inputs, notably labor. *Labor costs* tend to differ among national economies. MNEs may be able to hold costs down by locating part or all of their productive facilities abroad. Many U.S. electronics firms, for instance, have had their products produced or at least assembled abroad to take advantage of cheap foreign labor. (The mere fact that the United States may pay higher wages than those prevailing abroad does not necessarily indicate higher costs. High wages may result from U.S. workers' being more productive than their foreign counterparts. Only when high U.S. wages are not offset by superior U.S. labor productivity will foreign labor become relatively more attractive.)

MNE location can also be affected by transportation costs, especially in industries where transportation costs are a high fraction of product value. When the cost of transporting raw materials used by an MNE is significantly higher than the cost of shipping its finished products to markets, the MNE will generally locate production facilities closer to its raw material sources than to its markets; lumber, basic chemicals, aluminum, and steel are among the products that fit this description. Conversely, when the cost of transporting finished products is significantly higher than the cost of transporting the raw materials that are used in their manufacture, MNEs locate production facilities close to their markets. Beverage manufacturers, such as Coca-Cola and Pepsi-Cola, transport syrup concentrate to plants all over the world, which add water to the syrup, bottle it, and sell it to consumers. When transportation costs are a minor fraction of product value, MNEs tend to locate where the availability and cost of labor and other inputs provide them

the lowest manufacturing cost. MNEs producing electronic components, garments, and shoes offer examples of such locational mobility.

Government policies may also lead to foreign direct investment. Some nations seeking to lure foreign manufacturers to set up employment-generating facilities in their countries may grant subsidies, such as preferential tax treatment or free factory buildings, to MNEs. More commonly, direct investment may be a way of circumventing import tariff barriers. The very high tariffs that Brazil levies on auto imports means that foreign auto producers wishing to sell in the Brazilian market must locate production facilities in that country. Another example is the response of U.S. business to the formation of the European Union, which imposed common external tariffs against outsiders while reducing trade barriers among member nations. U.S. companies were induced to circumvent these barriers by setting up subsidiaries in the member nations. Another example is Japanese businesses that apparently located additional auto-assembly plants in the United States in the 1980s and 1990s to defuse mounting protectionist pressures.

Supplying Products to Foreign Buyers: Whether to Produce Domestically or Abroad

Once a firm knows that foreign demand for its goods exists, it must ascertain the least-cost method of supplying these goods abroad. Suppose Anheuser-Busch (A-B) of the United States wants to sell its Budweiser beer in Canada. A-B can do this in one of three ways: (1) brew Bud in the United States and export it to Canada (direct exporting); (2) establish its own production subsidiary in Canada (foreign direct investment); or (3) license the rights to a Canadian brewery to produce and market Bud in Canada. The method A-B chooses depends on the extent of economies of scale, transportation and distribution costs, and international trade barriers. These considerations are discussed in the following sections.

Direct Exporting Versus Foreign Direct Investment/Licensing

Let us consider A-B's decision to supply Bud to Canada via direct exports versus foreign direct investment or licensing. We will first analyze the influence of economies of scale on A-B's decision. One would expect economies of scale to encourage A-B to export Bud to Canada when the quantity of beer demanded in Canada is relatively small, and to encourage Canadian production, via either licensing agreements or foreign direct investment, when a relatively large quantity of beer is demanded in Canada.

To illustrate this principle, assume that A-B, a Canadian brewery, and a Canadian subsidiary of A-B all have identical production functions exhibiting economies of scale and that the firms pay the same price for their inputs. As illustrated in Figure 9.1, their average cost schedules are identical and are denoted by AC.

Suppose U.S. consumers demand 200 cases per year of Bud at the going price. Producing this output permits A-B to realize economies of scale and a cost

of $8 per case. Suppose that Canadians demand a smaller quantity of Bud, say 100 cases. Because this quantity is too small to permit efficient production in Canada, the Canadian brewery or A-B's production subsidiary realizes a higher cost of $11 per case. A-B thus minimizes cost by increasing its U.S. production to meet the additional Canadian demand. By brewing 300 cases, A-B achieves a longer production run and the resulting economies of scale so that costs fall to $6 per case. Canadian consumers are thus supplied 100 cases of Bud via direct export. As long as the cost of transporting Bud from the United States to Canada is less than $5 a case, A-B increases its profit by exporting beer to Canada.

If the quantity of Bud demanded by Canadians is 300 cases or more, it may be more profitable for A-B to locate production in Canada, either by licensing production technology to a Canadian brewery or by investing in a production subsidiary. Referring to Figure 9.1, suppose Canadians demand 400 cases of Bud whereas Bud sales in the United States remain at 200 cases. With economies of scale exhausted at 300 cases, the larger Canadian demand does not permit A-B to brew Bud at a cost

FIGURE 9.1

The Choice Between Direct Exporting and Foreign Direct Investment/Licensing

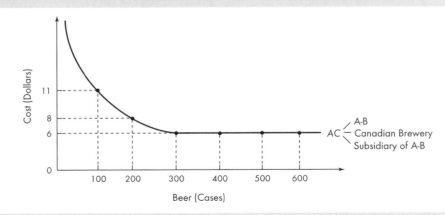

When the Canadian market's size is large enough to permit efficient production in Canada, a U.S. firm increases profits by establishing a Canadian production subsidiary or licensing the rights to a Canadian firm to produce and market its product in Canada. The U.S. firm increases profits by exporting its product to Canada when the Canadian market is too small to permit efficient production.

lower than $6 per case. By increasing output from 100 to 400 cases, however, the Canadian brewery or production subsidiary of A-B could match A-B's efficiency because they realize the least possible cost of $6 per case. Given equal production costs, A-B minimizes total cost by avoiding the additional costs of transporting beer to Canada. A-B thus increases profits by either licensing its beer technology to a Canadian brewer or investing in a production subsidiary in Canada.

Similar to transportation costs, trade restrictions can neutralize production-cost advantages. If Canada has high import tariffs, production-cost advantages in the United States may be offset, so that foreign direct investment or licensing is the only feasible way of penetrating the Canadian market.

Foreign Direct Investment Versus Licensing

Once a firm chooses foreign production as a method of supplying goods abroad, it must decide whether it

is more efficient to establish a foreign production subsidiary or license the technology to a foreign firm to produce its goods. In the United Kingdom, there are KFC establishments that are owned and run by local residents. The parent U.S. organization merely provides its name and operating procedures in return for royalty fees paid by the local establishments. Although licensing is widely used in practice, it presupposes that local firms are capable of adapting their operations to the production process or technology of the parent organization.

Figure 9.2 portrays the hypothetical cost conditions confronting A-B as it contemplates whether to license Bud production technology to a Canadian brewery or invest in a Canadian production subsidiary. Curve $AVC_{Subsidiary}$ represents the average variable cost (such as labor and materials) of A-B's production subsidiary, and AVC_{Canada} represents the average variable cost of a Canadian brewery. The establishment of a foreign production subsidiary also entails fixed costs denoted by curve $AFC_{Subsidiary}$. These include

FIGURE 9.2

The Choice Between Foreign Direct Investment and Licensing

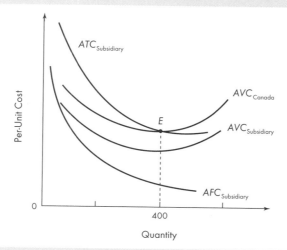

The decision to establish foreign operations through direct investment or licensing depends on (1) the extent to which capital is used in the production process, (2) the size of the foreign market, and (3) the amount of fixed cost a business must bear when establishing an overseas facility.

expenses of coordinating the subsidiary with the parent organization and the sunk costs of assessing the market potential of the foreign country. The total unit costs that A-B faces when establishing a foreign subsidiary are given by $ATC_{Subsidiary}$.

Comparing $ATC_{Subsidiary}$ with AVC_{Canada}, for a relatively small market of less than 400 cases of beer, the Canadian brewery has an absolute cost advantage. Licensing Bud production technology to a Canadian brewery in this case is more profitable for A-B. But if the Canadian market for Bud exceeds 400 cases, A-B's production subsidiary has an absolute cost advantage; A-B increases profits by supplying beer to Canadians via foreign direct investment.

Several factors influence the output level at which A-B's production subsidiary begins to realize an absolute cost advantage vis-à-vis the Canadian brewery (400 cases in Figure 9.2). To the extent that production is capital-intensive and A-B's production subsidiary can acquire capital at a lower cost than that paid by the Canadian brewery, the variable cost advantage of the subsidiary is greater. This neutralizes the influence of a fixed-cost disadvantage for the subsidiary at a lower level of output. The amount of the production subsidiary's fixed costs also has a bearing on this minimum output level. Smaller fixed costs lower the subsidiary's average total costs, again resulting in a smaller output at which the subsidiary first begins to have an absolute cost advantage.

As noted, international business decisions are influenced by such factors as production costs, fixed costs of locating overseas, the relative importance of labor and capital in the production process, and the size of the foreign market. Another factor is the element of risk and uncertainty. When determining where to locate production operations, management is concerned with possibilities such as currency fluctuations and subsidiary expropriations.

International Trade Theory and Multinational Enterprise

Perhaps the main explanation of the development of MNEs lies in the strategies of corporate management. The reasons for engaging in international business can be outlined in terms of the comparative-advantage principle. Corporate managers see advantages they can exploit in the forms of access to factor inputs, new technologies and products, and managerial know-how. Organizations establish overseas subsidiaries largely because profit prospects are best enhanced by foreign production.

From a trade-theory perspective, the multinational-enterprise analysis is fundamentally in agreement with the predictions of the comparative-advantage principle. Both approaches contend that a given commodity will be produced in the low-cost country. The major difference between the multinational-enterprise analysis and the conventional trade model is that the former stresses the international movement of factor inputs, whereas the latter is based on the movement of merchandise among nations.

International trade theory suggests that the aggregate welfare of both the source and host countries is enhanced when MNEs make foreign direct investments for their own benefit. The presumption is that if businesses can earn a higher return on overseas investments than on those at home, resources are transferred from lower to higher productive uses, and on balance the world allocation of resources will improve. Thus, *analysis of MNEs is essentially the same as conventional trade theory, which rests on the movement of products among nations.*

Despite the basic agreement between conventional trade theory and the multinational-enterprise analysis, there are some notable differences. The conventional model presupposes that goods are exchanged between independent organizations on international markets at competitively determined prices. But MNEs are generally vertically integrated companies whose subsidiaries manufacture intermediate goods as well as finished goods. In an MNE, sales become *intrafirm* when goods are transferred from subsidiary to subsidiary. Although such sales are part of international trade, their value may be determined by factors other than a competitive pricing system.

Japanese Transplants in the U.S. Automobile Industry

During the 1980s, the growth of Japanese direct investment in the U.S. auto industry was widely publicized. From 1980 to 1990, Japanese automakers invested more than $5 billion in U.S.–based assembly facilities, known as **transplants**. Eight Japanese-affiliated auto manufacturers and more than a hundred Japanese parts suppliers operated or constructed facilities in the United States. By 1990, Japanese transplants built more than 15 percent of the passenger cars produced in the United States. Table 9.3 provides examples of Japanese transplant automakers in the United States.

Establishing transplants in the United States provided a number of benefits to Japanese automakers, including opportunities to:

- Silence critics who insist that autos sold in the United States must be built there.
- Avoid export restraints imposed by the Japanese government and potential import barriers of the United States.
- Gain access to an expanding market at a time when the Japanese market was nearing saturation.
- Provide a hedge against fluctuations in the yen–dollar exchange rate.

The rapid growth of Japanese investment in the U.S. auto industry led to concerns over the future of U.S.–owned auto-manufacturing and parts-supplier industries. Proponents of foreign direct investment maintained that it would foster improvement in the overall competitive position of the domestic auto-assembly and parts industries. They also argued that foreign investment generates jobs and provides consumers with a wider product choice at lower prices than would otherwise be available.

However, the United Auto Workers (UAW) union maintained that this foreign investment would result in job losses in the auto-assembly and parts-supplier industries. They and other critics argued that Japanese transplants would decrease the market share for U.S. automakers and parts suppliers and contribute to excess capacity at both automakers and parts-suppliers levels.

One factor that influences the number of workers hired is a company's *job classifications*, which stipulate the scope of work each employee performs. As the number of job classifications increases, the scope of work decreases, along with the flexibility of using available employees; this can lead to falling worker productivity and rising production costs.

Japanese-affiliated auto companies have traditionally used significantly fewer job classifications than traditional U.S. auto companies. Japanese transplants use work teams, and each team member is trained to do all the operations performed by the team. A typical Japanese-affiliated assembly

TABLE 9.3

Japanese Auto Plants in the United States

Plant Name/Parent Company	Location
Honda of America, Inc. (Honda)	Marysville, Ohio
	East Liberty, Ohio
Nissan Motor Manufacturing Corp. (Nissan)	Smyrna, Tennessee
New United Motor Manufacturing, Inc. (Toyota/General Motors)	Fremont, California
Toyota Motor Manufacturing, USA, Inc. (Toyota)	Georgetown, Kentucky
Mazda Motor Manufacturing, USA, Inc. (Mazda)	Flat Rock, Michigan
Diamond-Star Motors Corp. (Mitsubishi/Chrysler)	Normal, Illinois
Ford Motor Co. (Nissan/Ford)	Avon Lake, Ohio

plant has three to four job classifications: one team leader, one production technician, and one or two maintenance technicians. Often, jobs are rotated among team members. In contrast, traditional U.S. auto plants have enacted more than 90 different job classifications, and employees generally perform only those operations specifically permitted for their classification. These trends have contributed to the superior labor productivity of Japanese transplants compared to the U.S. Big Three. Although powerful forces within the U.S. Big Three have resisted change, international competition has forced U.S. automakers to slowly dismantle U.S. management and production methods and remake them along Japanese lines.

For policy makers, the broader issue is whether the Japanese transplants have lived up to expectations. When the Japanese initiated investment in U.S. auto-manufacturing facilities in the 1980s, many Americans viewed them as models for a revitalized U.S. auto industry and new customers for U.S. auto-parts suppliers. Transplants were seen as a way of providing jobs for U.S. autoworkers whose jobs were dwindling as imports increased. When the transplant factories were announced, Americans anticipated that transplant production would be based primarily on American parts, material, and labor; transplant production would displace imports in the U.S. market while transferring new management techniques and technology to the United States.

Certainly, the transplant factories boosted the economies in the regions where they located. There is also no doubt that the transplants helped to transfer Japanese quality control, just-in-time delivery, and other production techniques to the United States. However, the original expectations of the transplants were only partially fulfilled. Skeptics contended that Japanese manufacturing operations were twice as likely to import parts for assembly in the United States as the average foreign company, and were four times as likely to import parts as the average U.S. company. Extensive use of imported parts by Japanese transplants would contribute to a U.S. automotive trade deficit with Japan and would result in fewer jobs for U.S. autoworkers.

How productive and profitable are Japanese transplants relative to the U.S. Big Three auto manufacturers? Table 9.4 provides the estimated labor hours per vehicle and profit per vehicle for North American auto manufacturers in 2002.

International Joint Ventures

Another area of multinational enterprise involvement is **international joint ventures**. A joint venture is a business organization established by two or more companies that combines their skills and assets. It may have a limited objective (research or

---

TABLE 9.4

Assembly Labor Productivity and Profit per Vehicle of North American Auto Manufacturers, 2002

Manufacturer	Labor Hours per Vehicle*	North American Operations Profit per Vehicle
Nissan	16.83	$2,069
Mitsubishi	21.33	—
Toyota	21.83	1,214
Honda	22.27	1,581
General Motors	24.44	701
Ford	26.14	−114
DaimlerChrysler	28.04	226

*The labor productivity figures of Nissan, Honda, and Toyota reflect partial reporting of assembly plants located in North America.

Source: J. D. Harbour and Associates, *The Harbour Report 2003*, Troy MI, pp. 30, 150.

production) and be short-lived. It may also be multinational in character, involving cooperation among several domestic and foreign companies. Joint ventures differ from mergers in that they involve the creation of a *new* business firm, rather than the union of two existing companies. Table 9.5 provides examples of recent joint ventures between U.S. and foreign companies.

There are three types of international joint ventures. The first is a joint venture formed by two businesses that conduct business in a third country. For example, a U.S. oil firm and a British oil firm may form a joint venture for oil exploration in the Middle East. Next is the formation of a joint venture with local private interests. Honeywell Information Systems of Japan was formed by Honeywell, Inc., of the United States and Mitsubishi Office Machinery Company of Japan to sell information-systems equipment to the Japanese. The third type of joint venture includes participation by local government. Bechtel of the United States, Messerschmitt-Boelkow-Blom of West Germany, and National Iranian Oil (representing the government of Iran) formed Iran Oil Investment Company for oil extraction in Iran.

Several reasons have been advanced to justify the creation of joint ventures. Some functions, such as R&D, can involve costs too large for any one company to absorb by itself. Many of the world's largest copper deposits have been owned and mined jointly by the largest copper companies on the grounds that joint financing is required to raise enough capital. The exploitation of oil deposits is often done by a consortium of several oil companies. Exploratory drilling projects typically involve several companies united in a joint venture, and several refining companies traditionally own long-distance crude-oil pipelines. Oil refineries in foreign countries may be co-owned by several large U.S. and foreign oil companies.

Another factor that encourages the formation of international joint ventures is the restrictions some governments place on foreign ownership of local businesses. Governments in developing nations often close their borders to foreign companies unless they are willing to take on local partners. Mexico, India, and Peru require that their own national companies represent a major interest in any foreign company conducting business within their borders. The foreign investor is forced to either accept local equity participation or forgo operation in the country. Such government policies are defended on the grounds that joint ventures result in the transfer of managerial techniques and know-how to the developing nation. Joint ventures may also prevent the possibility of excessive political influence on the part of foreign investors. Finally, joint ventures help minimize dividend transfers abroad and thus strengthen the developing nation's balance of payments.

TABLE 9.5

Joint Ventures Between U.S. and Foreign Companies

Joint Venture	Partner	Foreign Partner	Products
CAMMI	General Motors	Suzuki (Japan)	Subcompact cars
AutoAlliance	Ford	Mazda (Japan)	Subcompact cars
New United Motor Manufacturing	General Motors	Toyota (Japan)	Subcompact cars
Siecor	Corning Glass Works	Siemens (Germany)	Optical cable
Himont	Hercules	Montedison (Italy)	Polypropylene resin
International Aero Engines	United Technologies	Rolls-Royce (Britain)	Aircraft engines

International joint ventures are also viewed as a means of forestalling protectionism against imports. Apparently motivated by fear that rising protectionism would restrict their access to U.S. markets, Japanese manufacturers (Toyota Motor Enterprise) increasingly formed joint ventures with U.S. enterprises in the 1980s. Such ventures typically resulted in U.S. workers' assembling Japanese components, with the finished goods sold to U.S. consumers. Not only did this process permit Japanese production to enter the U.S. market, but it also blurred the distinction between U.S. and Japanese production. Just who is us? And who is them? The rationale for protecting domestic output and jobs from foreign competition is thus lessened.

There are, however, disadvantages to forming an international joint venture. A joint venture is a cumbersome organization compared with a single organization. Control is divided, creating problems of "two masters." Success or failure depends on how well companies can work together despite having different objectives, corporate cultures, and ways of doing things. The action of corporate chemistry is difficult to predict, but it is critical, because joint-venture agreements usually provide both partners an ongoing role in management. When joint-venture ownership is divided equally, as often occurs, deadlocks in decision making can take place. If balance is to be preserved between different economic interests, negotiation must establish a hierarchical command. Even when negotiated balance is achieved, it can be upset by changing corporate goals or personnel.

Welfare Effects

International joint ventures can yield both welfare-increasing effects and welfare-decreasing effects for the domestic economy. Joint ventures lead to *welfare gains* when (1) the newly established business adds to preexisting productive capacity and fosters additional competition, (2) the newly established business is able to enter new markets that neither parent could have entered individually, or (3) the business yields cost reductions that would have been unavailable if each parent performed the same function separately. However, the formation of a joint venture may also result in *welfare losses*. For instance, it may give rise to increased market power, suggesting greater ability to influence market output and price. This is especially likely to occur when the joint venture is formed in markets in which the parents conduct business. Under such circumstances, the parents, through their representatives in the joint venture, agree on prices and output in the very market that they themselves operate. Such coordination of activities limits competition, reinforces upward pressure on prices, and lowers the level of domestic welfare.

Let's consider an example that contrasts two situations: (1) Two competing companies sell autos in the domestic market. (2) The two competitors form a joint venture that operates as a single seller (a monopoly) in the domestic market. We would expect to see a higher price and smaller quantity when the joint venture behaves as a monopoly. This will always occur as long as the marginal cost curve for the joint venture is identical to the horizontal sum of the marginal cost curves of the individual competitors. The result of this *market-power effect* is a deadweight welfare loss for the domestic economy—a reduction in consumer surplus that is not offset by a corresponding gain to producers. If, however, the formation of the joint venture entails *productivity gains* that neither parent could realize prior to its formation, domestic welfare may increase. This is because a smaller amount of the domestic economy's resources is now required to produce any given output. Whether domestic welfare rises or falls because of the joint venture depends on the magnitudes of these two opposing forces.

Figure 9.3 illustrates the welfare effects of two parent companies' forming a joint venture in the market in which they operate.[1] Assume that Sony Auto Company of Japan and American Auto Company of the United States are the only two firms producing autos for sale in the U.S. market. Suppose each company realizes constant long-run costs, suggesting that average total cost equals marginal cost at each level of output. Let the cost schedules of each company prior to the formation

---

[1]See Robert Carbaugh and Darwin Wassink, "International Joint Ventures and the U.S. Auto Industry," *The International Trade Journal,* Fall 1986.

FIGURE 9.3

Welfare Effects of an International Joint Venture

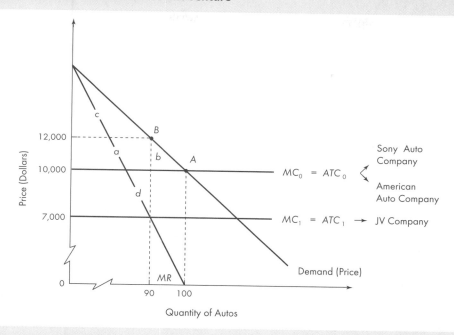

An international joint venture can yield a welfare-decreasing market-power effect and a welfare-increasing cost-reduction effect. The source of the cost-reduction effect may be lower resource prices or improvements in technology and productivity. The joint venture leads to improvements in national welfare if its cost-reduction effect is due to improvements in technology and productivity and if it more than offsets the market-power effect.

of the joint venture be $MC_0 = ATC_0$, which equals $10,000. $MC_0 = ATC_0$ thus becomes the long-run market supply schedule of autos.

Assume that Sony Auto Company and American Auto Company initially operate as competitors, charging a price equal to marginal cost. In Figure 9.3, market equilibrium exists at point A, where 100 autos are sold at a price of $10,000 per unit. Consumer surplus totals area $a + b + c$. Producer surplus does not exist, given the horizontal supply schedule of autos (recall that producer surplus equals the sum of the differences between the market price and each of the minimum prices indicated on the supply schedule for quantities between zero and the market output).

Now suppose that the two competitors announce the formation of a joint venture known as JV Company, which manufactures autos for sale in the United States. The autos sold by JV replace the autos sold by the two parents in the United States.

Suppose the formation of JV Company entails new production efficiencies that result in cost reductions. Let JV's new cost schedule, $MC_1 = ATC_1$, be located at $7,000. As a monopoly, JV maximizes profit by equating marginal revenue with marginal cost. Market equilibrium exists at point B, where 90 autos are sold at a price of $12,000 per unit. The price increase leads to a reduction in consumer surplus equal to area $a + b$.

Do U.S. Multinationals Exploit Foreign Workers?

Average Annual Wage Paid by Foreign Affiliates of U.S. Multinationals and Average Annual Domestic Manufacturing Wage by Host Country, 1994[*] (Thousands of Dollars)

	All Countries	High-Income	Middle-Income	Low-Income
Average wage paid by affiliates	$15.1	$32.4	$9.5	$3.4
Average domestic manufacturing wage	9.9	22.6	5.4	1.7
Ratio	1.5	1.4	1.8	2.0

*Calculations exclude wages of the multinationals' expatriate employees.

Source: Edward Graham, *Fighting the Wrong Enemy*, Institute for International Economics, Washington, DC, 2000, p. 94.

Do U.S. multinational businesses exploit workers in developing countries? According to critics, maximizing profits is the only thing that matters to multinationals: They search the globe for the cheapest labor when deciding where to locate factories. The only gain from this behavior, critics argue, accrues to the owners of the businesses who have shifted operations from low-wage factories in industrialized countries to poverty-wage factories in developing countries. Simply put, workers in developing countries are underpaid, according to critics.

Indeed, multinationals are in business for profits. But this does not seem to be troublesome for many workers in developing countries who compete to work for them. People who go to work for a foreign-owned business do so because they prefer it to the alternative, whatever that may be. In their own view, the new jobs make them better off.

Of this amount, area *a* is transferred to JV as producer surplus. Area *b* represents the loss of consumer surplus that is *not* transferred to JV and that becomes a deadweight welfare loss for the U.S. economy (the consumption effect).

Against this deadweight welfare loss lies the efficiency effect of JV Company: a decrease in unit costs from $10,000 to $7,000 per auto. JV can produce its profit-maximizing output, 90 autos, at a cost reduction equal to area *d* as compared with the costs that would exist if the parent companies produced the same output. Area *d* thus represents additional producer surplus, which is a welfare gain for the U.S. economy. Our analysis concludes that, for the United States, the formation of JV Company is desirable if area *d* exceeds area *b*.

It has been assumed that JV Company achieves cost reductions that are unavailable to either parent as a stand-alone company. Whether the cost reductions benefit the overall U.S. economy depends on their source. If they result from *productivity* improvements (for example, new work rules leading to higher output per worker), a welfare gain exists for the economy, because fewer resources are required to produce a given number of autos and the excess can be shifted to other industries. However, the cost reductions stemming from JV Company's formation may be *monetary* in nature. Being a newly formed company, JV may be able to negotiate wage concessions from domestic workers that could not be achieved by American Auto Company. Such a cost reduction represents a transfer of dollars from domestic workers to JV profits and does not constitute an overall welfare gain for the economy.

However, assume that the critics are right, and that these workers are being exploited. One remedy would be to admonish multinationals from operating in developing countries at all. But if multinationals stopped hiring workers in developing countries, the workers would, in their own estimation, become worse off. Another course is to entice multinationals to pay workers in developing countries wages that are as high as the wages paid to workers in industrial countries. However, this would discourage direct investment in developing countries. Why? Workers in developing countries are paid less than workers in industrial countries because they are generally less productive: They often work with less advanced machinery and there is inadequate surrounding infrastructure, which reduces productivity. These workers are attractive to multinationals, in spite of their lower productivity, because they are cheap. If you were to wipe out that offsetting advantage, you would make them unemployable. Put simply, bucking under pressure to extend U.S. or European pay scales to developing countries could mean shutting down local factories—hurting people, not helping them.

Productivity aside, should "responsible" multinationals pay their developing-country employees more than other local workers? To hire workers, they may not have to provide a premium over local wages if they can offer other advantages, such as a modern factory in which to work rather than a sweatshop. By participating in the local labor market and adding to the total demand for labor, the multinationals would most likely be increasing wages for all workers, not just those they employ.

However, the evidence suggests that multinationals do pay a wage premium, which apparently reflects the desire to recruit relatively skilled workers. The table shows that the wages paid by multinationals to poor-country workers are about double the local manufacturing wage; wages paid by multinationals to workers in middle-income countries are about 1.8 times the local manufacturing wage. In short, do U.S. multinationals underpay workers in developing countries? By U.S. standards, they do. But U.S. standards are irrelevant in developing countries: Very few workers are paid at U.S. levels in these countries. The key point is that, by local standards, these workers typically fare quite well.

Multinational Enterprises as a Source of Conflict

The advocates of MNEs often point out the benefits these enterprises can provide for the nations they affect, including both the source country where the parent organization is located and the host country where subsidiary firms are established. Benefits allegedly exist in the forms of additional levels of investment and capital, creation of new jobs, and development of technologies and production processes. But critics contend that MNEs often create trade restraints, conflict with national economic and political objectives, and have adverse effects on a nation's balance of payments. These arguments perhaps explain why some nations frown on direct investment, while others welcome it. This section examines some of the more controversial issues involving multinationals. The frame of reference is the U.S. MNE, although the same issues apply no matter where the parent organization is based.

Employment

One of the most hotly debated issues surrounding the MNE is its effects on employment in both the host and source countries. MNEs often contend that their foreign direct investment yields favorable benefits to the labor force of the recipient nation. Setting up a new multinational automobile manufacturing plant in Canada creates more jobs for Canadian workers. But the MNE's effect on jobs varies from business to business. One source of controversy arises when the direct investment spending of foreign-based MNEs is used to purchase already existing local businesses rather than to establish new ones. In this case, the investment spending may not result in additional production capacity and may not have noticeable effects on employment in the host country. Another problem arises when MNEs bring in foreign managers and other top executives to run the subsidiary in the host country. In the U.S. oil companies locating in Saudi Arabia, the Saudis are increasingly demanding that their own people be employed in higher-level positions.

As for the source country, the issues of runaway jobs and cheap foreign labor are of vital concern to home workers. Because labor unions are confined to individual countries, the multinational nature of these businesses permits them to escape much of the collective-bargaining influence of domestic unions. It is also pointed out that MNEs can seek out those countries where labor has minimal market power.

ECONOMIC *Applications*

Visit EconDebate Online for a debate on this topic

The ultimate impact that MNEs have on employment in the host and source countries seems to depend in part on the time scale. In the short run, the source country will likely experience an employment decline when production is shifted overseas. But other industries in the source country may find foreign sales rising over time. This is because foreign labor consumes as well as produces and tends to purchase more as employment and income increase as a result of increased investment. Perhaps the main source of controversy stems from the fact that the MNEs are involved in rapid changes in technology and in the transmission of productive enterprise to host countries. Although such efforts may promote global welfare in the long run, the potential short-run adjustment problems facing source-country labor cannot be ignored.

Technology Transfer

Besides promoting runaway jobs, multinationals can foster the transfer of technology (knowledge and skills applied to how goods are produced) to other nations. Such a process is known as **technology transfer**.

Technology has been likened to a contagious disease: It spreads out farther and more quickly if there are more personal contacts. Foreign trade is viewed as a channel through which people in different nations make contacts and through which people in one nation get to know about the products of other nations. Foreign direct investment is an even more effective method of technology transfer. When foreign firms having technological advantages establish local production subsidiaries, the personal contacts between these subsidiaries and local firms are more frequent and closer than when firms are located abroad.

International trade and foreign direct investment also facilitate technology transfer via the so-called *demonstration effect*: As a firm shows how its products operate, this sends important information to other firms that such products exist and are usable. Technology diffusion is also aided by the *competition effect*: When a foreign firm manufacturers a superior product that is popular among consumers, other firms are threatened. To survive, they have to innovate and improve the quality of their products.

Although technology transfer may increase the productivity and competitiveness of recipient nations, donor nations may react against it because it is detrimental to their economic base. Donor nations contend that the establishment of production operations abroad by multinational enterprises decreases their export potential and leads to job losses for their workers. By sharing technical knowledge with foreign nations, a donor nation may eventually lose its international competitiveness, thus causing a decrease in its rate of economic growth.

Consider the case of U.S. technology transfer to China in the mid-1990s. After decades of mutual hostility, the United States hoped that by the 1990s China would open itself to the outside world and engage in free trade, so that foreign nations could trade with China according to the principle of comparative advantage. Instead, China used its leverage as a large buyer of foreign products to pressure multinational enterprises to localize production and transfer technology to China to help it become competitive. With multinational enterprises willing to outbid each other to woo Chinese bureaucrats, China was in a favorable position to reap the benefits of technology diffusion.

For example, Microsoft Corporation, under threat of having its software banned, codeveloped a Chinese version of Windows 95 with a local partner and agreed to aid efforts to develop a Chinese software industry. Another example was General Motors. To beat out Ford Motor for the right to become a partner in manufacturing sedans in Shanghai, General Motors agreed to bring in dozens of parts joint ventures and to design much of the car in China. It also agreed to establish five research institutes to teach Chinese engineers to turn technological theory in fields such as power trains and fuel-injection systems into commercial applications.

U.S. multinationals argued that transferring technology to China was largely risk-free because a competitive challenge from China was decades away. However, the acceleration of technology transfer in the mid-1990s became increasingly unpopular with U.S. labor unions, which feared that their members were losing jobs to lower-paid Chinese workers. U.S. government officials also feared that technology transfer was helping create a competitor of extreme proportions. Let us consider two U.S. companies that have engaged in technology transfer to China, General Electric Company and Boeing.

General Electric's Trade-Off for Entry into Chinese Market: Short-Term Sales for Long-Term Competition

For decades, General Electric had an effective strategy for being competitive in the Chinese market for power-generating equipment: Sell the best equipment at the lowest price. By the early 2000s, however, the formula was altered. Besides offering high-quality gas-fired turbines at a competitive price, GE had to agree to share with the Chinese sophisticated technology for producing the turbines. To be considered for turbine contracts worth several billion dollars, GE, Mitsubishi, Siemens, and other competitors were obligated to form joint ventures with state-owned Chinese power companies. GE was also required to transfer to its new partners technology and advanced manufacturing specifications for its gas-fired turbine, which GE had spent more than $500 million to develop. GE officials noted that the Chinese

desire having complete access to its technology, while GE desires protecting the technology in which it made a large financial investment.

The vast size of China's electricity market convinced GE executives that this market was worth pursuing in spite of technology demands. The U.S. market for gas-fired turbines was weak because of past spending sprees to increase capacity by power companies and utilities. On the other hand, China was expected to spend more than $10 billion a year constructing electricity plants in the near future. GE officials thus faced the trade-off of short-term sales in China for long-term competition from Chinese manufacturers. In the end, GE won an order for 13 of its gas-fired turbines, and as part of the agreement also had to share technology with its Chinese partners.

Before the gas-fired turbine venture with GE, Chinese manufacturers had mastered only the technology required for making much less efficient steam-powered turbines. That technology was obtained in part through previous joint ventures with firms such as Westinghouse Electric Company. However, the Chinese demanded the technology behind the more efficient gas-fired turbines.

GE officials noted that Chinese competition was not imminent in highly advanced products like gas-fired turbines. In the past, even after acquiring expertise from foreign corporations, Chinese firms lacked the skill necessary to fully exploit the technology and become competitive in world markets. Moreover, by the time Chinese companies mastered the technology they initially obtained from GE, GE had developed more advanced technologies. Nonetheless, Chinese officials looked ahead to new rounds of power-generating equipment bidding by GE and its competitors, when Chinese officials hoped to obtain even more lucrative technology-sharing deals.[2]

Boeing Workers Contest Technology Transfer to China

Sharing the manufacture of a product with foreign workers is a popular but controversial practice in today's global economy. Does it lead to job losses

[2]"China's Price for Market Entry: Give Us Your Technology, Too," *The Wall Street Journal*, February 26, 2004, pp. A–1 and A–6.

for domestic workers? Consider the case of commercial jet manufacturing.

In the mid-1990s, Boeing's domestic sales of jetliners weakened because of a post–Cold War decrease in U.S. defense spending and cost-cutting by U.S. airlines in a mature travel market. Boeing increasingly looked to growing foreign markets, especially China, as a source of potential sales.

Being a major buyer in a sluggish market, China used its leverage to insist that if foreign producers wanted to sell jetliners to China, they would have to subcontract a portion of the planes' production to Chinese manufacturers. Such technological transfers would help China learn the art of jet-plane manufacturing and eventually result in China's becoming a builder of jetliners. China succeeded in pressuring Boeing and Airbus to locate factories that produce airliner doors, tail fins, and a myriad of other parts in China.

The three Western airline producers bid to help China develop the hundred-seat jet, even though the winner would have only about a 20 percent stake in the venture. Each firm wanted to ensure that the design of the jet fit into its own lineup of larger jets, which cost $45 million to $185 million each.

The possibility of Boeing's helping China develop a jetliner threatened Boeing machinists, who saw the potential of their jobs being lost to the Chinese. The workers went on strike, demanding, among other things, that the firm cease or slow the granting of production contracts to China in exchange for orders of U.S. planes. The workers also pressed the Clinton Administration to halt U.S. exports of jetliner manufacturing and technology to China; they complained that the United States was moving toward becoming a seller of jetliner technology rather than a manufacturer of jets.

Boeing justified production sharing on the grounds that curtailment of subcontracting to China would cost its machinists more jobs than would be saved. Without any Boeing subcontracting, the contract would likely be awarded to Airbus, which indicated that it would subcontract production to China; more jobs would thus be lost by Boeing workers than would occur with Boeing's subcontracting some production to China. Boeing emphasized that its strategy was to

share what it must, but only what it must, to maintain its 60 percent share of China's jetliner market.

After a lengthy strike, the machinists and Boeing agreed to a new contract. Boeing pledged to consult with the machinists' union on plans for subcontracting work. The firm also agreed to help its workers whose jobs were lost as a result of subcontracting, retraining them for other positions in the company as they became available. As it happens, Boeing lost out to Airbus in the contest to become China's partner in building the hundred-seat jet. Some observers noted that Boeing may have been better off for having lost this contest, because China's Western partner stood to become embroiled in a long and costly development effort.

National Sovereignty

Another controversial issue involving the conduct of MNEs is their effect on the economic and political policies of the host and source governments. There is a suspicion in many nations that the presence of MNEs in a given country results in a loss of its national sovereignty. For example, MNEs may resist government attempts to redistribute national income through taxation. By using accounting techniques that shift profits overseas, an MNE may be able to evade taxes of a host country. An MNE could accomplish this by raising prices on goods from its subsidiaries in nations with modest tax rates to reduce profits on its operations in a high-tax nation where most of its business actually takes place.

The political influence of MNEs is also questioned by many, as illustrated by the case of Chile. For years, U.S. businesses had pursued direct investments in Chile, largely in copper mining. When Salvador Allende was in the process of winning the presidency, he was opposed by U.S. businesses fearing that their Chilean operations would be expropriated by the host government. International Telephone and Telegraph tried to prevent the election of Allende and attempted to promote civil disturbances that would lead to his fall from power. Another case of MNEs' meddling in host-country affairs is that of United Brands (now Chiquita), the MNE engaged in food-product sales. In 1974, the company paid a $1.25 million bribe to the president of Honduras in return for an export-tax reduction applied to bananas. When the payoff was revealed, the president was removed from office.

There are other areas of controversy. Suppose a Canadian subsidiary of a U.S.-based MNE conducts trade with a country subject to U.S. trade embargoes. Should U.S. policy makers outlaw such activities? The Canadian subsidiary may be pressured by the parent organization to comply with U.S. foreign policy. During international crises, MNEs may move funds rapidly from one financial center to another to avoid losses (make profits) from changes in exchange rates. This conduct makes it difficult for national governments to stabilize their economies.

In a world where national economies are interdependent and factors of production are mobile, the possible loss of national sovereignty is often viewed as a necessary cost whenever direct investment results in foreign control of production facilities. Whether the welfare gains accruing from the international division of labor and specialization outweigh the potential diminution of national independence involves value judgments by policy makers and interested citizens.

Balance of Payments

The United States offers a good example of how an MNE can affect a nation's balance of payments. In brief, the *balance of payments* is an account of the value of goods and services, capital movements (including foreign direct investment), and other items that flow into or out of a country. Items that make a positive contribution to a nation's payments position include exports of goods and services and capital inflows (foreign investment entering the home country), whereas the opposite flows would weaken the payments position. At first glance, we might conclude that when U.S. MNEs make foreign direct investments, these payments represent an outflow of capital from the United States and hence a negative factor on the U.S. payments position. Although this view may be true in the short run, it ignores the positive effects on trade flows and earnings that direct investment provides in the long run.

When a U.S. MNE sets up a subsidiary overseas, it generally purchases U.S. capital equipment and materials needed to run the subsidiary. Once in operation, the subsidiary tends to purchase additional capital equipment and other material inputs from the United States. Both of these factors stimulate U.S. exports, strengthening its payments position.

ECONOMIC *Applications*
Visit EconData Online

Another long-run impact that U.S. foreign direct investment has on its balance of payments is the return inflow of income generated by overseas operations. Such income includes earnings of overseas affiliates, interest and dividends, and fees and royalties. These items generate inflows of revenues for the economy and strengthen the balance-of-payments position.

Taxation

One of the most controversial issues involving MNEs for U.S. policy makers is the taxation of income stemming from foreign direct investment. Labor unions and other groups often contend that U.S. tax laws provide a disincentive to invest at home that results from tax concessions offered by the U.S. government on foreign direct investment. These concessions include *foreign tax credits* and *tax deferrals.*

According to U.S. tax law, an MNE headquartered in the United States is permitted credits against its U.S. income-tax liabilities in an amount equal to the income taxes it pays to foreign governments. Assuming that a Canadian subsidiary earns $100,000 taxable income and that Canada's income-tax rate is 25 percent, the company would pay the Canadian government $25,000. But if that income were applied to the parent organization in the United States, the tax owed to the U.S. government would be $48,000, given an income-tax rate of 48 percent. Under the tax credit system, the parent organization would pay the U.S. government only $23,000 ($48,000 − $25,000 = $23,000). The rationale of the foreign tax credit is that MNEs headquartered in the United States should not be subject to double taxation, whereby the same income would be subject to comparable taxes in two countries. The foreign tax credit is designed to prevent the combined tax rates of the foreign host and domestic source governments from exceeding the higher of the two national rates. In this example, should Canada's income-tax rate be 48 percent, the parent organization would not pay any taxes in the United States on the income of its Canadian subsidiary.

U.S.–based MNEs also enjoy a tax-deferral advantage. Under U.S. tax laws, the parent organization has the option of deferring U.S. taxes paid on the income of its foreign subsidiary as long as that income is retained overseas rather than repatriated to the United States. This system amounts to an interest-free loan extended by the U.S. government to the parent for as long as the income is maintained abroad. Retained earnings of an overseas subsidiary can be reinvested abroad without being subject to U.S. taxes. No similar provisions apply to domestic investments. Such discriminatory tax treatment encourages foreign direct investment over domestic investment.

Transfer Pricing

Another device that MNEs utilize in their effort to decrease their overall tax burden is **transfer pricing**. Using this technique, an MNE reports most of its profits in a low-tax country, even though the profits were earned in a high-tax country. For example, if corporate profit taxes are higher in the parent country than in the host country, and if the parent firm is exporting to its subsidiary in the host country, the MNE can lower its overall tax burden by *underpricing* its exports to its host-country subsidiary, thus shifting profits from the parent to the subsidiary, as illustrated in Figure 9.4. Profits are thus transferred from the branch in the high-tax country to the branch in the low-tax country. Conversely, if the host-country subsidiary is exporting to the parent and the parent country has high tax levels, it would be in the interest of the subsidiary to *overprice* its exports, thus decreasing taxable profits in the parent country. The result is lower overall taxes for the MNE in question.

Russian oil companies provide an example of transfer pricing. For years they have sold oil at low prices to foreign trading subsidiaries, which export the fuel at much higher world prices and then book the profits. The result is that profits are recorded in the sector that sells them rather than the one that produces them. This is one way that the Russian companies avoid paying higher federal taxes on their income.

Both foreign governments and the U.S. government are interested in the part that transfer prices play in the realization of corporate profits. Abuses in pricing across national borders are illegal if they can be proved. According to U.S. Internal Revenue Service (IRS) regulations, enterprises dealing with their own subsidiaries are required to set prices "at arms length," just as they would for unrelated customers. However, proving that the prices that one subsidiary charges another are far from market prices is very difficult.

There's no question that transfer-pricing abuses can be enormous. It is estimated that foreign-based multinationals dodge more than $20 billion in U.S. taxes each year, while U.S. multinationals account for an additional $5 billion in lost U.S. taxes on profits dubiously allocated to foreign tax havens. In its biggest known tax-abuse victory, the IRS argued that Toyota of Japan had systematically over-charged its U.S. subsidiary for years on most of the automobiles, trucks, and parts sold in the United States. What would have been taxable profits from the United States were shifted back to Japan. Although Toyota denied improprieties, it agreed to a $1 billion settlement with the IRS, paid in part with tax rebates from the Japanese government.

U.S. Production Sharing with Mexico

The ships sail east from South Korea and Japan to the Mexican port of Guaymas. There, rolls of steel are transferred to trains and shipped to Ford Motor's assembly plant in Hermosillo, Sonora. Ford stamps and assembles the steel into Mercury auto bodies, puts in Japanese engines, and transports the autos to the United States. Manufacturers such as Ford not only have changed the methods by which autos are produced but also have brought industry to Mexico's north, turning cow towns like Hermosillo into manufacturing centers.

Mexico's north, once a desert buffer between the capital, Mexico City, and the United States,

FIGURE 9.4

Transfer Pricing

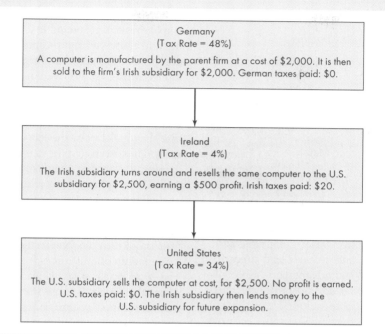

Germany
(Tax Rate = 48%)

A computer is manufactured by the parent firm at a cost of $2,000. It is then sold to the firm's Irish subsidiary for $2,000. German taxes paid: $0.

Ireland
(Tax Rate = 4%)

The Irish subsidiary turns around and resells the same computer to the U.S. subsidiary for $2,500, earning a $500 profit. Irish taxes paid: $20.

United States
(Tax Rate = 34%)

The U.S. subsidiary sells the computer at cost, for $2,500. No profit is earned. U.S. taxes paid: $0. The Irish subsidiary then lends money to the U.S. subsidiary for future expansion.

This hypothetical example illustrates how MNEs can shift profits to countries with low corporate tax rates and thus get away with a smaller total tax bite. The MNE is headquartered in Germany (high-tax country) and has subsidiaries in Ireland (low-tax country) and in the United States. The bottom line is that the MNE pays no taxes either in Germany or in the United States.

has been the recipient of direct investment by foreign companies that have set up manufacturing facilities from the beaches south of San Diego to the Gulf Coast dunes beyond Brownsville, Texas. Mexico's **maquiladoras**, or industrial parks, typically host an assemblage of U.S.–owned companies that combine U.S. parts and supplies and Mexican assembly to manufacture goods that are exported to the United States. The mix of maquiladora products has traditionally been dominated by electronics (such as television sets) and automobiles. The largest concentration of maquiladora plants is in the border cities, including Ciudad Juárez, Tijuana, and Mexicali. Table 9.6 on page 310 provides examples of companies that have located production facilities in Mexico.

Today, more than 1,300 maquiladoras operate in Mexico, employing more than half a million workers. The maquiladoras' managers point out that their workers are among the most highly skilled in Mexico and that they have trained large numbers of Mexican technicians, engineers, accountants, and middle managers.

The maquiladoras are engaged primarily in labor-intensive assembly operations that combine Mexican labor with U.S. capital and technology. Maquilas (firms) benefit from relatively low wages in Mexico and proximity to the United States. Proximity not only reduces transportation costs,

TABLE 9.6

Companies with Production Facilities in Mexico: Selected Examples

Company	Product
Unisys	Electronics
Borg-Warner	Auto parts
Motorola	Electronics
Honda	Auto parts
General Instruments	Electronics
Lasating	Ceramics
Calmar Inc.	Plastics
Carrier	Metal
Emerson Electric	Electronics
Mattel	Toys

compared with more distant low-wage countries (such as Taiwan), but also eases communication, facilitates supervision, and reduces lead times for delivery. Mexico's regional advantage is especially strong for such products as motor-vehicle parts that may require quick turnaround and benefit from good rail and highway connections between parts factories in the central United States, Mexican assembly plants in the Rio Grande Valley, and final auto-assembly plants in the central United States. Mexico's attractiveness as an assembly location relative to that of other countries is reinforced by higher relative wage costs in such competing nations as Singapore, Taiwan, and South Korea.

The maquiladoras have drawn a considerable amount of capital to Mexico's northern border region, providing jobs and earning much-needed foreign exchange. But they have generated much controversy in both Mexico and the United States. Opposition in the United States has come mainly from labor unions that maintain that maquiladora investment by U.S. companies results in "runaway jobs." Proponents of the maquiladoras counter that northern Mexico is actually competing with other countries for labor-intensive factories and that jobs "lost" to the maquilas would eventually have been lost to other low-wage countries. Without the maquilas, many small and medium-sized U.S. companies would be driven out of business by foreign low-wage competitors in South Korea, Taiwan, and

elsewhere. Having their unskilled jobs performed just across the border allows these companies to maintain the jobs of their skilled workers in the United States. They also contend that when U.S. jobs migrate to the border, a large amount of employment is generated in U.S. border communities and elsewhere in the United States because border production requires large quantities of U.S. inputs. Moreover, if it were not for the maquiladoras, additional Mexicans would likely be living in the United States as illegal immigrants.

In Mexico, critics of the maquiladoras contend that they make poor models for Mexican development. They assert that the maquilas exploit Mexican workers by paying them subsistence-level wages. Also, U.S. employers have relied on the most vulnerable and cheapest workers—young women and girls, who represent two-thirds of the maquiladora labor force. It is also maintained that a negligible fraction of the components used in the assembly of maquiladora output comes from Mexican suppliers. The work itself is low-skilled, so workers receive minimal training. Because the maquiladoras do not transfer technology, there is little linkage between the maquiladoras and the rest of the Mexican economy, and few secondary benefits are generated. Maquiladoras tend to make Mexico more dependent on the rest of the world because important economic decisions are made outside of Mexico.

NAFTA, which went into force in 1994, has increased the competitiveness of production-sharing operations located in Mexico compared with those in East Asia and elsewhere. Producers within NAFTA have an incentive to purchase parts from fellow NAFTA beneficiaries to meet the NAFTA rules-of-origin requirements. Furthermore, U.S. and Canadian firms wishing to establish production-sharing facilities abroad are drawn to Mexico because products made in Mexico have preferential access to both NAFTA markets.

International Labor Mobility: Migration

Historically, the United States has been a favorite target for international **migration**. Because of its vast inflow of migrants, the United States has been described as the melting pot of the world. Table 9.7 indicates the volume of immigration to the United States from the 1820s to 2001. Western Europe was a major source of immigrants during this era, with Germany, Italy, and the United Kingdom among the largest contributors. In recent years, large numbers of Mexicans have migrated to the United States, as well as people from Asia. Migrants have been motivated by better economic opportunities and by noneconomic factors such as politics, war, and religion.

Although international labor movements can enhance the world economy's efficiency, they are often restricted by government controls. The United States, like most countries, limits immigration. Following waves of immigration at the turn of the century, the Immigration Act of 1924 was enacted. Besides restricting the overall flow of immigrants to the United States, the act implemented a quota that limited the number of immigrants from each foreign country. Because the quotas were based on the number of U.S. citizens who had previously emigrated from those countries, the allocation system favored emigrants from northern Europe relative to southern Europe. In the late 1960s, the quota formula was

modified, which led to increasing numbers of Asian immigrants to the United States.

Effects of Migration

Figure 9.5 on page 312 illustrates the economics of labor migration. Suppose the world consists of two countries, the United States and Mexico, that are initially in isolation. The horizontal axes denote the total quantity of labor in the United States and Mexico, and the vertical axes depict the wages paid to labor. For each country, the demand schedule for labor is designated by the value of the marginal product (VMP) of labor.[3] Also assume a fixed labor supply of 7 workers in the United States, denoted by $S_{U.S._0}$, and 7 workers in Mexico, denoted by S_{M_0}.

The equilibrium wage in each country is determined at the point of intersection of the supply and demand schedules for labor. In Figure 9.5(a), the U.S. equilibrium wage is $9, and total labor income is $63; this amount is represented by the area $a + b$. The remaining area under the labor demand schedule is area c, which equals $24.50; this represents the share of the nation's income accruing to owners of capital.[4] In Figure 9.5(b), the equilibrium wage for Mexico is $3; labor income totals $21, represented by area $f + g$; capital owners enjoy incomes equaling area $h + i + j$, or $24.50.

Suppose labor can move freely between Mexico and the United States and assume that migration is costless and occurs solely in response

TABLE 9.7

U.S. Immigration, 1820–2001

Period	Number (Thousands)
1820–1840	751
1841–1860	4,311
1861–1880	5,127
1881–1900	8,935
1901–1920	14,531
1921–1940	4,635
1941–1960	3,550
1961–1980	7,815
1981–1990	7,338
1991–2000	9,095
2001	1,004

Source: Data taken from U.S. Immigration and Naturalization Service, *Statistical Yearbook*, annual, at http://www.ins.usdoj.gov/graphics/index.htm. See also U.S. Department of Commerce, Bureau of the Census, *Statistical Abstracts of the United States* (Washington, DC: U.S. Government Printing Office) at http://www.census.gov/statab/www.

[3]The value of the marginal product of labor (VMP) refers to the amount of money producers receive from selling the quantity that was produced by the last worker hired; in other words, VMP = product price × the marginal product of labor. The VMP curve is the labor demand schedule. This follows from an application of the rule that a business hiring under competitive conditions finds it most profitable to hire labor up to the point at which the price of labor (wage rate) equals its VMP. The location of the VMP curve depends on the marginal productivity of labor and the price of the product that it produces. Under pure competition, price is constant. Therefore, it is because of diminishing marginal productivity that the labor demand schedule is downward-sloping.

[4]How do we know that area c represents the income accruing to U.S. owners of capital? Our analysis assumes two productive factors, labor and capital. The total income (value of output) that results from using a given quantity of labor with a fixed amount of capital equals the area under the VMP curve of labor for that particular quantity of labor. Labor's share of that area is calculated by multiplying the wage rate times the quantity of labor hired. The remaining area under the VMP curve is the income accruing to the owners of capital.

FIGURE 9.5

Effects of Labor Migration from Mexico to the United States

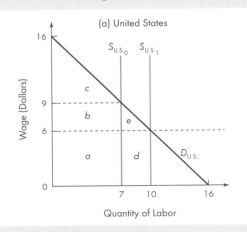
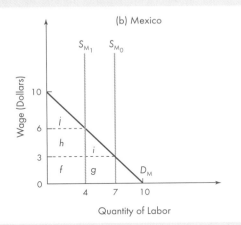

Prior to migration, the wage rate in the United States exceeds that of Mexico. Responding to the wage differential, Mexican workers immigrate to the United States; this leads to a reduction in the Mexican labor supply and an increase in the U.S. labor supply. Wage rates continue to fall in the United States and rise in Mexico until they eventually are equalized. The labor migration hurts native U.S. workers but helps U.S. owners of capital; the opposite occurs in Mexico. Because migrant workers flow from uses of lower productivity to higher productivity, world output expands.

to wage differentials. Because U.S. wage rates are relatively high, there is an incentive for Mexican workers to migrate to the United States and compete in the U.S. labor market; this process will continue until the wage differential is eliminated. Suppose three workers migrate from Mexico to the United States. In the United States, the new labor supply schedule becomes $S_{U.S._1}$; the excess supply of labor at the $9 wage rate causes the wage rate to fall to $6. In Mexico, the labor emigration results in a new labor supply schedule at S_{M_1}; the excess demand for labor at wage rate $3 causes the wage rate to rise to $6. The effect of **labor mobility** is thus to equalize wage rates in the two countries.[5]

[5]Wage-rate equalization assumes unrestricted labor mobility in which workers are concerned only about their incomes. It also assumes that migration is costless for labor. In reality, there are economic and psychological costs of migrating to another country. Such costs may result in only a small number of persons' finding the wage gains in the immigrating country high enough to compensate them for their migration costs. Thus, complete wage equalization may not occur.

Our next job is to assess how labor migration in response to wage differentials affects the world economy's efficiency. Does world output expand or contract with open migration? For the United States, migration increases the labor supply from $S_{U.S._0}$ to $S_{U.S._1}$. This leads to an expansion of output; the value of the additional output is denoted by area $d + e$ ($22.50). For Mexico, the decrease in labor supply from S_{M_0} to S_{M_1} results in a contraction in output; the value of the lost output is represented by area $g + i$ ($13.50). The result is a net gain of $9 in world output as a result of labor migration. This is because the *VMP* of labor in the United States exceeds that of Mexico throughout the relevant range. Workers are attracted to the United States by the higher wages paid. These higher wages signal to Mexican labor the higher value of worker productivity, thus attracting workers to those areas where they will be most efficient. As workers are used more productively, world output expands.

Does U.S. Immigration Policy Harm Domestic Workers?

The net gains from current immigration are small, so it is unlikely that these gains can play a crucial role in the policy debate. Economic research teaches a very valuable lesson: The economic impact of immigration is essentially distributional. Current immigration redistributes wealth from unskilled workers, whose wages are lowered by immigrants, to skilled workers and owners of companies that buy immigrants' services, and from taxpayers who bear the burden of paying for the social services used by immigrants to consumers who use the goods and services produced by immigrants.

—George Borjas, "The New Economics of Immigration," *The Atlantic Online*, November 1996

Highly skilled immigrants, who also create jobs for Americans, are not the only ones contributing to our economic boom. Even the less-skilled immigrants contribute to our economy and our lives by working in jobs most Americans do not want, such as cleaning offices, cooking in restaurants, and ringing up purchases in the grocery store. They, in turn, contribute by buying homes, clothes, and groceries. The wonderful cultural diversity brought to the United States by immigrants has become secondary to their willingness to work hard and become part of today's America.

—Bronwyn Lance, "The Economic Impact of Immigrants," May 2000, http://www.worldandihome school.com/public_articles/2000/may/wis17530.asp

Most U.S. residents today are the descendants of immigrants who arrived in the United States during the past 150 years. Concerns about the effect of immigration on domestic workers, however, have resulted in the passage of several laws designed to restrict immigration. Unions, in particular, have argued for a more restrictive immigration policy on the grounds that immigration lowers the wage and employment levels for domestic residents.

There were no substantial restrictions on immigration into the United States until the passage of the Quota Law of 1921. This law set quotas on the number of immigrants based upon the country of origin. The Quota Law primarily restricted immigration from eastern and southern Europe. The Immigration and Nationality Act Amendments of 1965 eliminated the country-specific quota system and instead established a limit on the maximum number of immigrants allowed into the United States. Under this act, preferential treatment is given to those who immigrate for the purpose of family reunification. Those possessing exceptional skills are also given priority. No limit, however, is placed upon the number of political refugees allowed to immigrate into to the United States. Not all immigrants, of course, enter the country through legal channels. Individuals often enter on student or tourist visas and begin working in violation of their visa status. Other individuals enter the country illegally without a valid U.S. visa. The Immigration Reform and Control Act of 1986 addresses the issue of illegal immigration by imposing substantial fines on employers that hire illegal immigrants.

The Illegal Immigration Reform and Immigrant Responsibility Act of 1996 provided several new restrictions to immigration. Host families can only accept immigrants if the host family receives an income that is at least 125 percent of the poverty level. This act also requires that the Immigration and Naturalization Service maintain stricter records of entry and exit by nonresident aliens.

Migration also affects the *distribution of income*. As we will see, the gains in world income resulting from labor mobility are not distributed equally among all nations and factors of production. The United States as a whole benefits from immigration; its overall income gain is the sum of the losses by native U.S. workers, gains by Mexican immigrants now living in the United States, and gains by U.S. owners of capital. Mexico experiences overall income losses as a result of its labor emigration; however, workers remaining in Mexico gain relative to Mexican owners of capital. As previously suggested, the Mexican immigrants gain from their relocation to the United States.

For the United States, the gain in income as a result of immigration is denoted by area $d + e$

($22.50) in Figure 9.5(a). Of this amount, Mexican immigrants capture area d ($18), while area e ($4.50) is the extra income accruing to U.S. owners of capital thanks to the availability of additional labor to use with the capital. However, immigration forces wage rates down from $9 to $6. The earnings of the native U.S. workers fall by area b ($21); this amount is transferred to U.S. owners of capital.

As for Mexico, its labor emigration results in a decrease in income equal to $g + i$ ($13.50); this represents a transfer from Mexico to the United States. The remaining workers in Mexico gain area h ($12) as a result of higher wages. However, Mexican capital owners lose because less labor is available for use with their capital.

Although immigration may lower wage rates for some native U.S. workers, it should also be noted that these lower wage rates benefit U.S. producers. Lower wage rates also result in lower equilibrium product prices, thereby benefiting consumers. From society's perspective, the gains from immigration to producers and consumers should be weighed against the losses to low-wage workers.

We can conclude that the effect of labor mobility is to increase overall world income and to redistribute income from labor to capital in the United States and from capital to labor in Mexico. Migration has an impact on the distribution of income similar to an increase in exports of labor-intensive goods from Mexico to the United States.

Immigration as an Issue

The preceding example makes it clear why domestic labor groups in capital-abundant nations often prefer restrictions on immigration; open immigration tends to reduce their wages. When migrant workers are unskilled, as is typically the case, the negative effect on wages mainly affects unskilled domestic workers. Conversely, domestic manufacturers will tend to favor unrestricted immigration as a source of cheap labor.

Another controversy about immigrants is whether they are a drain on government resources. Nations that provide generous welfare payments to the economically disadvantaged may fear they will induce an influx of nonproductive people who will not produce as did the immigrants of Figure 9.5, but will enjoy welfare benefits at the expense of domestic residents and working immigrants. However, fiscal relief may not be far away. The children of immigrants will soon enter the labor force and begin paying taxes, thus supporting not only their kids' education, but also their parents' retirement. In a matter of two generations, most immigrant families tend to assimilate to the point that their fiscal burdens are indistinguishable from those of other natives. When it's all added up, most long-run calculations show that immigrants make a net positive contribution to public coffers.

Developing nations have sometimes feared open immigration policies because they can result in a **brain drain**—emigration of highly educated and skilled people from developing nations to industrial nations, thus limiting the growth potential of the developing nations. The brain drain has been encouraged by national immigration laws, as in the United States and other industrial nations, that permit the immigration of skilled persons while restricting that of unskilled workers.

In the previous labor-migration example, we implicitly assumed that the Mexican workers' migration decision was more or less permanent. In practice, much labor migration is temporary, especially in the European Union. That is, a country such as France will allow the immigration of foreign workers on a temporary basis when needed; these workers are known as **guest workers**. During periods of business recession, France will refuse to issue work permits when foreign workers are no longer needed. Such a practice tends to insulate the French economy from labor shortages during business expansions and labor surpluses during business recessions. However, the labor-adjustment problem is shifted to the labor-emigrating countries.

There is also the problem of illegal migration. In the United States, this has become a political hot potato, with millions of illegal immigrants finding employment in the so-called underground economy, often at below-minimum wages. Some 3 to 15 million illegal immigrants are estimated to be in the United States, many of them from Mexico. For the United States, and especially the southwestern states, immigration of Mexican workers has provided a cheap supply of agricultural and less-skilled workers. For Mexico, it has been a major source of foreign exchange and a safety cushion against domestic unemployment. Illegal immigration also affects the distribution of income for U.S. natives because it tends to reduce the income of low-skilled U.S. workers.

On the other hand, immigrants not only diversify an economy, but they may also contribute to economic growth. It is because immigrants are often different from natives that the economy as a whole profits. In many instances, immigrants both cause prices to fall, which benefits all consumers, and enable the economy to domestically produce a wider variety of goods than natives could alone. If immigrants weren't different from natives, they would only augment the population and the scale of the economy, but not have an effect on the overall growth rate of per capita income. According to the National Research Council, the overall effect of immigration on the U.S. gross domestic product is between $1 billion and $10 billion a year.[6] Although these amounts may seem negligible in an $8 trillion economy (about one-eighth of 1 percent at most), they are still a gain—and not the drain many believe immigration to be.

As we learned from Figure 9.5, immigrants increase the supply of labor in the economy. This results in a lower market wage for all workers if *all workers are the same*. But all workers are not the same. Some natives will compete with immigrants for positions because they possess similar skills; others will work alongside immigrants, complementing the immigrants' skills with their own. This skill distinction means that not all native workers will receive a lower wage. Those who compete with (are substitutes for) immigrants will

receive a lower wage than they would without immigration, while those who complement immigrants will receive a higher wage. Most analyses of various countries have found that a 10 percent increase in the immigrant share of the population reduces native wages by 1 percent at most. This finding suggests that most immigrants are not substituting for native labor—skilled or unskilled—but are, instead, complementing it.[7]

Advocates of increased immigration note that children do not begin working the minute they are born. It requires substantial expenditures in the form of food, clothing, shelter, education, and other child-rearing costs to produce an adult worker. These investments in human capital formation are quite substantial. Immigrant workers, unlike newborn children, are able to begin engaging in productive activities upon their arrival in the country. The cost of much of their human capital formation was borne by the country from which they emigrated. Because most immigrants arrive at a stage in their life in which they are relatively productive, higher immigration rates generally result in an increase in the proportion of the population that is working. As the proportion of the population that is working rises, per capita income also rises.

Concern over the future of social security is also used to support relaxed immigration restrictions. Declining birthrates in the United States, combined with rising life spans, result in a steady increase in the ratio of retired to working individuals over the next few decades. An increase in the number of younger immigrants could help to alleviate this problem.

[6]See National Research Council Panel on the Demographic and Economic Impacts of Immigration, *The New Americans: Economic, Demographic, and Fiscal Effects of Immigration* (Washington DC: National Academy Press, 1997).

[7]R.M Friedberg and J. Hunt, "The Impact of Immigrants on Host Country Wages, Employment and Growth," *Journal of Economic Perspectives*, Spring 1995, pp. 23–44.

Summary

1. Today the world economy is characterized by the international movement of factor inputs. The multinational enterprise plays a central part in this process.

2. There is no single agreed-upon definition of what constitutes an MNE. Some of the most identifiable characteristics of multinationals are the following: (a) Stock ownership and management are multinational in character; (b) Company headquarters may be far removed from the country where a particular activity occurs; and (c) Foreign sales represent a high proportion of total sales.

3. MNEs have diversified their operations along vertical, horizontal, and conglomerate lines.

4. Among the major factors that influence decisions to undertake foreign direct investment are (a) market demand, (b) trade restrictions, (c) investment regulations, and (d) labor productivity and costs.

5. In planning to set up overseas operations, a business must decide whether to construct (or purchase) plants abroad or extend licenses to foreign businesses to produce its goods.

6. The theory of multinational enterprise essentially agrees with the predictions of the comparative-advantage principle. However, conventional trade theory assumes that commodities are traded between independent, competitive businesses, whereas MNEs are often vertically integrated businesses, with substantial intrafirm sales. Thus, MNEs may use transfer pricing to maximize overall company profits rather than the profits of any single subsidiary.

7. In recent years, companies have increasingly linked up with former rivals in a vast array of joint ventures. International joint ventures can yield welfare-increasing effects as well as market-power effects.

8. Some of the more controversial issues involving MNEs are (a) employment, (b) technology transfer, (c) national sovereignty, (d) balance of payments, and (e) taxation.

9. There are major differences between the theory of multinational enterprise and conventional trade theory. The conventional model assumes that commodities are traded between independent, competitive businesses. However, MNEs are often vertically integrated businesses with substantial intrafirm sales. Also, MNEs may use transfer pricing to maximize overall company profits instead of the profits of any single subsidiary.

10. Mexico's maquiladoras are assemblages of foreign-owned companies that use foreign parts and Mexican assembly to produce goods that are exported to the United States. Maquiladora products have traditionally emphasized electronics and automobiles.

11. International labor migration occurs for economic and noneconomic reasons. Migration increases output and decreases wages in the country of immigration, as it decreases output and increases wages in the country of emigration. For the world as a whole, migration leads to net increases in output.

Key Concepts and Terms

- Brain drain *(page 314)*
- Conglomerate integration *(page 291)*
- Foreign direct investment *(page 291)*
- Guest workers *(page 314)*
- Horizontal integration *(page 290)*
- International joint ventures *(page 298)*
- Labor mobility *(page 312)*
- Maquiladoras *(page 309)*
- Migration *(page 310)*
- Multinational enterprise (MNE) *(page 290)*
- Technology transfer *(page 304)*
- Transfer pricing *(page 308)*
- Transplants *(page 297)*
- Vertical integration *(page 290)*

Study Questions

1. Multinational enterprises may diversify their operations along vertical, horizontal, and conglomerate lines within the host and source countries. Distinguish among these diversification approaches.
2. What are the major foreign industries in which U.S. businesses have chosen to place direct investments? What are the major industries in the United States in which foreigners place direct investments?
3. Why is it that the rate of return on U.S. direct investments in the developing nations often exceeds the rate of return on its investments in industrial nations?
4. What are the most important motives behind an enterprise's decision to undertake foreign direct investment?
5. What is meant by the term *multinational enterprise*?
6. Under what conditions would a business wish to enter foreign markets by extending licenses or franchises to local businesses to produce its goods?
7. What are the major issues involving multinational enterprises as a source of conflict for source and host countries?
8. Is the theory of multinational enterprise essentially consistent or inconsistent with the traditional model of comparative advantage?
9. What are some examples of welfare gains and welfare losses that can result from the formation of international joint ventures among competing businesses?
10. What effects does labor migration have on the country of immigration? The country of emigration? The world as a whole?
11. **Xtra!** **For a tutorial of this question, go to** **http://carbaughxtra.swlearning.com**
Table 9.8 illustrates the revenue conditions facing ABC, Inc., and XYZ, Inc., which operate as competitors in the U.S. calculator market. Each firm realizes constant long-run costs ($MC = AC$) of $4 per unit. On graph paper, plot the enterprise demand, marginal revenue, and $MC = AC$ schedules. On the basis of this information, answer the following questions.

TABLE 9.8

Price and Marginal Revenue: Calculators

Quantity	Price ($)	Marginal Revenue ($)
0	9	—
1	8	8
2	7	6
3	6	4
4	5	2
5	4	0
6	3	-2
7	2	-4

a. With ABC and XYZ behaving as competitors, the equilibrium price is $_____ and output is _____. At the equilibrium price, U.S. households attain $_____ of consumer surplus, while company profits total $_____.
b. Suppose the two organizations jointly form a new one, JV, Inc., whose calculators replace the output sold by the parent companies in the U.S. market. Assuming that JV operates as a monopoly and that its costs ($MC = AC$) equal $4 per unit, the company's output would be _____ at a price of $_____, and total profit would be $_____. Compared to the market equilibrium position achieved by ABC and XYZ as competitors, JV as a monopoly leads to a deadweight loss of consumer surplus equal to $_____.
c. Assume now that the formation of JV yields technological advances that result in a per-unit cost of only $2; sketch the new $MC = AC$ schedule in the figure. Realizing that JV results in a deadweight loss of consumer surplus, as described in part b, the net effect of the formation of JV on U.S. welfare is a gain/loss of $_____. If JV's cost reduction was due to wage concessions of JV's U.S. employees, the net welfare gain/ loss for the United States would equal $_____. If JV's cost reductions

resulted from changes in work rules leading to higher worker productivity, the net welfare gain/loss for the United States would equal $_____.

12. **Xtra!** For a tutorial of this question, go to http://carbaughxtra.swlearning.com Table 9.9 illustrates the hypothetical demand and supply schedules of labor in the United States. Assume that labor and capital are the only two factors of production. On graph paper, plot these schedules.

a. Without immigration, suppose the labor force in the United States is denoted by schedule S_0. The equilibrium wage rate is $_____; payments to native U.S. workers total $_____, while payments to U.S. capital owners equal $_____.

b. Suppose immigration from Hong Kong results in an overall increase in the U.S. labor force to S_1. Wages would rise/fall to $_____, payments to native U.S. workers would total $_____, and payments to Hong Kong immigrants would total $_____. U.S. owners of capital would receive payments of $_____.

c. Which U.S. factor of production would gain from expanded immigration? Which U.S. factor of production would likely resist policies permitting Hong Kong workers to freely migrate to the United States?

TABLE 9.9

Demand and Supply of Labor

Wage ($)	Quantity Demanded	Quantity Supplied$_0$	Quantity Supplied$_1$
8	0	2	4
6	2	2	4
4	4	2	4
2	6	2	4
0	8	2	4

International Monetary Relations

chapter 10

The Balance of Payments

When trade occurs between the United States and other nations, many types of financial transactions are recorded on a summary called the balance of payments. In this chapter, we examine the monetary aspects of international trade by considering the nature and significance of a nation's balance of payments.

The **balance of payments** is a record of the economic transactions between the residents of one country and the rest of the world. Nations keep record of their balance of payments over the course of a 1-year period; the United States and some other nations also keep such a record on a quarterly basis.

An *international transaction* is an exchange of goods, services, or assets between residents of one country and those of another. But what is meant by the term *resident*? Residents include businesses, individuals, and government agencies that make the country in question their legal domicile. Although a corporation is considered to be a resident of the country in which it is incorporated, its overseas branch or subsidiary is not. Military personnel, government diplomats, tourists, and workers who emigrate temporarily are considered residents of the country in which they hold citizenship.

Double-Entry Accounting

The arrangement of international transactions into a balance-of-payments account requires that each transaction be entered as a credit or a debit. A **credit transaction** is one that results in a *receipt* of a payment from foreigners. A **debit transaction** is one that leads to a *payment* to foreigners. This distinction is clarified when we assume that transactions take place between U.S. residents and foreigners and that all payments are financed in dollars.

From the U.S. perspective, the following transactions are credits (+), leading to the receipt of dollars from foreigners:

- Merchandise exports
- Transportation and travel receipts
- Income received from investments abroad
- Gifts received from foreign residents

- Aid received from foreign governments
- Investments in the United States by overseas residents

Conversely, the following transactions are debits (–) from the U.S. viewpoint because they involve payments to foreigners:

- Merchandise imports
- Transportation and travel expenditures
- Income paid on investments of foreigners
- Gifts to foreign residents
- Aid given by the U.S. government
- Overseas investment by U.S. residents

Although we speak in terms of credit transactions and debit transactions, every international transaction involves an exchange of assets and so has both a credit and a debit side. Each credit entry is balanced by a debit entry, and vice versa, so that the recording of any international transaction leads to two offsetting entries. In other words, the balance-of-payments accounts utilize a **double-entry accounting** system. The following two examples illustrate the double-entry technique.

Example 1

IBM sells $25 million worth of computers to a German importer. Payment is made by a bill of exchange, which increases the balances of New York banks at their Bonn correspondents' bank. Because the export involves a transfer of U.S. assets abroad for which payment is to be received, it is entered in the U.S. balance of payments as a credit transaction. IBM's receipt of payment held in the German bank is classified as a short-term financial movement because the financial claims of the United States against the German bank have increased. The entries on the U.S. balance of payments would appear as follows:

	Credits (+)	Debits (–)
Merchandise exports	$25 million	
Short-term financial movement		$25 million

Example 2

A U.S. resident who owns bonds issued by a Japanese company receives interest payments of $10,000. With payment, the balances owned by New York banks at their Tokyo affiliate are increased. The impact of this transaction on the U.S. balance of payments would be as follows:

	Credits (+)	Debits (–)
Service exports	$10,000	
Short-term financial movement		$10,000

These examples illustrate how every international transaction has two equal sides, a credit and a debit. If we add up all the credits as pluses and all the debits as minuses, the net result is zero; that is, the total credits must always equal the total debits. This means that the *total* balance-of-payments account must always be in balance. There is no such thing as an overall balance-of-payments surplus or deficit.

Even though the entire balance of payments must numerically balance by definition, it does *not* necessarily follow that any single subaccount or subaccounts of the statement must balance. For instance, total merchandise exports may or may not be in balance with total merchandise imports. When reference is made to a balance-of-payments surplus or deficit, it is particular subaccounts of the balance of payments that are referred to, not the overall value. A *surplus* occurs when the balance on a subaccount (subaccounts) is positive; a *deficit* occurs when the balance is negative.

Balance-of-Payments Structure

Let us now consider the structure of the balance of payments by examining its various subaccounts.

Current Account

The **current account** of the balance of payments refers to the monetary value of international flows associated with transactions in goods and services, investment income, and unilateral transfers. Each of these flows will be described in turn.

Merchandise trade includes all of the goods the United States exports or imports: agricultural products, machinery, autos, petroleum, electronics, textiles, and the like. The dollar

Visit EconData Online

International Payments Process

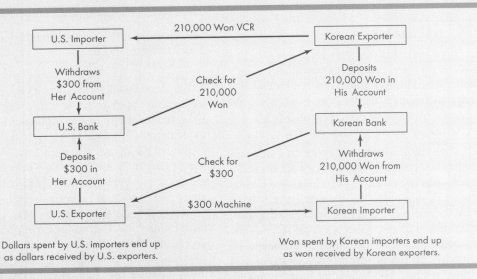

Dollars spent by U.S. importers end up
as dollars received by U.S. exporters.

Won spent by Korean importers end up
as won received by Korean exporters.

When residents in different countries contemplate selling or buying products, they must consider how payments will occur. Assume that you, as a resident of the United States, buy a VCR directly from a producer in South Korea. How, when, and where will the South Korean producer obtain his won so that he can spend the money in South Korea?

Initially, you would write a check for $300, which your U.S. bank would convert to 210,000 won (assuming an exchange rate of 700 won per dollar). When the South Korean producer receives your payment in won, he deposits the funds in his bank. The bank in South Korea thus holds a check from a U.S. bank that promises to pay a stipulated amount of won.

Assume that at the same time you paid for your VCR, a buyer in South Korea paid a U.S. producer $300 for machinery. The flowchart illustrates the path of both transactions.

When trade is in balance, money of different countries does not actually change hands across the oceans. In this example, the value of South Korea's exports to the United States equals the value of South Korea's imports from the United States; the won that South Korean importers use to purchase dollars to pay for U.S. goods are equal to the won that South Korean exporters receive in payment for the products they ship to the United States. The dollars that would flow, in effect, from U.S. importers to U.S. exporters exhibit a similar equality.

In theory, importers in a country pay the exporters in that same country in the national currency. In reality, however, importers and exporters in a given country do not deal directly with one another; to facilitate payments, banks carry out these transactions.

value of merchandise exports is recorded as a plus (credit), and the dollar value of merchandise imports is recorded as a minus (debit). Combining the exports and imports of goods gives the **merchandise trade balance**. When this balance is negative, the

result is a merchandise trade deficit; a positive balance implies a merchandise trade surplus.

Exports and imports of *services* include a variety of items. When U.S. ships carry foreign products or foreign tourists spend money at U.S. restaurants and motels, valuable services are being provided by U.S. residents, who must be compensated. Such services are considered exports and are recorded as credit items on the goods and services account. Conversely, when foreign ships carry U.S. products or when U.S. tourists spend money at hotels and restaurants abroad, then foreign residents are providing services that require compensation. Because U.S. residents are, in effect, importing these services, the services are recorded as debit items. Insurance and banking services are explained in the same way. Services also include items such as transfers of goods under military programs, construction services, legal services, technical services, and the like.

To get a broader understanding of the international transactions of a country, we must add services to the merchandise trade account. This total gives the **goods and services balance**. When this balance is positive, the result is a surplus on goods and services transactions; a negative balance implies a deficit. Just what does a surplus or deficit balance appearing on the U.S. goods and services account mean? If the goods and services account shows a surplus, the United States has transferred more resources (goods and services) to foreigners than it has received from them over the period of one year. Besides measuring the value of the *net transfer of resources*, the goods and services balance also furnishes information about the status of a nation's gross domestic product (GDP). This is because the balance on the goods and services account is defined essentially the same way as the *net export of goods and services*, which is part of a nation's GDP.

Recall from your macroeconomics course that GDP is equal to the value of the goods and services produced in an economy over a period of time. In an economy with trade, GDP is equal to the sum of four different types of spending in the economy: consumption, gross investment, government spending, and net exports of goods and services. In effect, net exports represent the value of goods and services that are produced domestically but not included in domestic consumption.

For a nation's GDP, then, the balance on the goods and services account can be interpreted as follows. A positive balance on the account shows an excess of exports over imports, and this difference must be added to the GDP. When the account is in deficit, the excess of imports over exports must be subtracted from the GDP. If a nation's exports of goods and services equal its imports, the account will have a net imbalance of zero and will not affect the status of the GDP. Therefore, depending on the relative value of exports and imports, the balance on the goods and services account contributes to the level of a nation's national product.

Broadening our balance-of-payments summary further, we must include *income receipts and payments*. This item consists of the net earnings (dividends and interest) on U.S. investments abroad—that is, earnings on U.S. investments abroad less payments on foreign assets in the United States. It also includes compensation of employees.

Finally, our balance-of-payments summary is expanded to include **unilateral transfers**. These items include transfers of goods and services (gifts in kind) or financial assets (money gifts) between the United States and the rest of the world. *Private transfer payments* refer to gifts made by individuals and nongovernmental institutions to foreigners. These might include a remittance from an immigrant living in the United States to relatives back home, a birthday present sent to a friend overseas, or a contribution by a U.S. resident to a relief fund for underdeveloped nations. *Governmental transfers* refer to gifts or grants made by one government to foreign residents or foreign governments. The U.S. government makes transfers in the form of money and capital goods to underdeveloped nations, military aid to foreign governments, and remittances such as retirement pensions to foreign workers who have moved back home. In some cases, U.S. governmental transfers represent payments associated with foreign assistance programs that can be used by foreign governments to finance trade with the United States. It should be noted that many U.S. transfer (foreign aid) programs are tied to the purchase of U.S. exports (such as military equipment or farm exports) and thus represent a subsidy to U.S. exporters. When investment income and unilateral transfers are combined with the balance on goods and services, we arrive at the current account balance. This is the broadest measure of a nation's balance of payments regularly quoted in the newspapers and in national television and radio news reports.

Capital and Financial Account

Capital and financial transactions in the balance of payments include all international purchases or sales of assets. The term *assets* is broadly defined to include items such as titles to real estate, corporate stocks and bonds, government securities, and ordinary commercial bank deposits. The **capital and financial account**[1] includes both private-sector and official (central bank) transactions.

Capital transactions consist of capital transfers and the acquisition and disposal of certain nonfinancial assets. The major types of capital transfers are debt forgiveness and migrants' goods and financial assets accompanying them as they leave or enter the country. The acquisition and disposal of certain nonfinancial assets include the sales and purchases of rights to natural resources, patents, copyrights, trademarks, franchises, and leases. Though conceptually important, capital transactions are generally very small in U.S. accounts and thus will not be emphasized in this chapter.

The vast majority of transactions appearing in the capital and financial account come from financial transactions. The following are examples of private-sector financial transactions:

Direct Investment

Direct investment occurs when residents of one country acquire a controlling interest (stock ownership of 10 percent or more) in a business enterprise in another country.

Securities

Securities are private-sector purchases of short- and long-term debt securities, such as Treasury bills, Treasury notes, Treasury bonds, and securities of private enterprises.

[1]Since 1999, U.S. international transactions have been classified into three groups—the current account, the capital account, and the financial account. The transactions were formerly classified into the current account and capital account. See "Upcoming Changes in the Classification of Current and Capital Transactions in the U.S. International Accounts," *Survey of Current Business*, February 1999. This article can also be found at http://www.bea.doc.gov/bea/ai/ 0299bop2/maintext.htm.

Bank Claims and Liabilities

Bank claims consist of loans, overseas deposits, acceptances, foreign commercial paper, claims on affiliated banks abroad, and foreign government obligations. Bank liabilities include demand deposits and NOW (negotiable order of withdrawal) accounts, passbook savings deposits, certificates of deposit, and liabilities to affiliated banks abroad.

Capital and financial transactions are recorded in the balance-of-payments statement by applying a plus sign (credit) to capital and financial inflows and a minus sign (debit) to capital and financial outflows. For the United States, a *financial inflow* might occur under the following circumstances: (1) U.S. liabilities to foreigners rise (for example, a French resident purchases securities of IBM); (2) U.S. claims on foreigners decrease (Citibank receives repayment for a loan it made to a Mexican enterprise); (3) foreign-held assets in the United States rise (Toyota builds an auto-assembly plant in the United States); (4) U.S. assets overseas decrease (Coca-Cola sells one of its Japanese bottling plants to a Japanese buyer). A *financial outflow* would imply the opposite.

The following rule may be helpful in appreciating the fundamental difference between credit and debit transactions that make up the capital and financial account. Any transaction that leads to the home country's receiving payments from foreigners can be regarded as a credit item. A capital (financial) inflow can be likened to the *export* of goods and services. Conversely, any transaction that leads to foreigner's receiving payment from the home country is considered a debit item. A capital (financial) outflow is similar in effect to the *import* of goods and services.

Besides including private-sector transactions, the capital and financial account includes **official settlements transactions** of the home country's central bank. Official settlements transactions refer to the movement of financial assets among official holders (for example, the U.S. Federal Reserve and the Bank of England). These financial assets fall into two categories: official reserve assets (U.S. government assets abroad) and liabilities to foreign official agencies (foreign official assets in the United States).

Table 10.1 summarizes the **official reserve assets** position of the United States as of 2003. One such asset is the stock of gold reserves held by the U.S. government. Next are convertible currencies, such as the Japanese yen, that are readily acceptable as payment for international transactions and can be easily exchanged for one another. Another reserve asset is the special drawing right (SDR), described in Chapter 17. Last is the reserve position that the United States maintains in the International Monetary Fund. Central banks often buy or sell international reserve assets in private-sector markets to affect their currencies' exchange rates, as will be discussed in Chapter 17.

Official settlements transactions also include liabilities to foreign official holders. These liabilities refer to foreign official holdings with U.S. commercial banks and official holdings of U.S. Treasury securities. Foreign governments often wish to hold such assets because of the interest earnings they provide. Table 10.2 illustrates the U.S. liabilities to foreign official holders as of 2003.

Statistical Discrepancy: Errors and Omissions

The data-collection process that underlies the published balance-of-payments figures is far from perfect. The cost of collecting balance-of-payments statistics is high, and a perfectly accurate collection system would be prohibitively costly. Government statisticians thus base their figures partly on information collected and partly on estimates. Probably the most reliable information consists of merchandise trade data, which are collected mainly from customs records. Capital and financial account information is derived from reports by financial institutions indicating changes in their liabilities and claims to foreigners; these data are not matched with specific current account transactions. Because statisticians do not have a system whereby they can simultaneously record the credit side and debit side of each transaction, such information for any particular transaction tends to come from different sources. Large numbers of transactions fail to get recorded.

When statisticians sum the credits and debits, it is not surprising when the two totals do not match. Because total debits must equal total credits in principle, statisticians insert a *residual* to make them equal. This correcting entry is known as **statistical discrepancy**, or errors and omissions. In the balance-of-payments statement, statistical discrepancy is treated as part of the capital and financial account

TABLE 10.1

U.S. Reserve Assets, 2003

Type	Amount (Billions of Dollars)
Gold stock*	$11.0
Special drawing rights	12.1
Reserve positions in the International Monetary Fund	23.6
Convertible foreign currencies	37.4
Total	$84.1

*Gold is valued at $42.22/fine troy ounce.

Source: *Federal Reserve Bulletin,* May 2004, p. A-44.

TABLE 10.2

Selected U.S. Liabilities to Foreign Official Institutions, 2003

	Amount (Billions of Dollars)
BY TYPE	
Liabilities reported by U.S. banks*	$ 168.1
U.S. Treasury bills and certificates	214.2
U.S. Treasury bonds and notes	514.9
Other U.S. securities	293.5
Total	$1,190.7
BY AREA	
Europe	$ 277.1
Canada	10.4
Latin America/Caribbean	73.0
Asia	800.8
Africa	15.7
Other	13.7
Total	$1,190.7

*Includes demand deposits, time deposits, bank acceptances, commercial paper, negotiable time certificates of deposit, and borrowings under repurchase agreements.

Source: *Federal Reserve Bulletin,* May 2004, p. A-45.

because short-term financial transactions are generally the most frequent source of error.

U.S. Balance of Payments

For the United States, the method the U.S. Department of Commerce uses in presenting balance-of-payments statistics is shown in Table 10.3. This format groups specific transactions together along functional lines to provide analysts with information about the impact of international transactions on the domestic economy. The *partial balances* published on a regular basis include the merchandise trade balance, the balance on goods and services, the current account balance, and information about capital and financial transactions.

The *merchandise trade balance*, commonly referred to as the **trade balance** by the news media, is derived by computing the net exports (imports)

in the merchandise accounts. Owing to its narrow focus on traded goods, the merchandise trade balance offers limited policy insight. The popularity of the merchandise trade balance is due largely to its availability on a monthly basis. Merchandise trade data can rapidly be gathered and reported, whereas measuring trade in services requires time-consuming questionnaires.

As seen in Table 10.3, the United States had a merchandise trade deficit of $549.4 billion in 2003, resulting from the difference between U.S. merchandise exports ($713.8 billion) and U.S. merchandise imports ($1,263.2 billion). The United States was thus a net importer of merchandise. Table 10.4 shows that the United States has consistently faced merchandise trade deficits in recent decades. This situation contrasts with the 1950s and 1960s, when merchandise trade surpluses were common for the United States.

TABLE 10.3

U.S. Balance of Payments, 2003 (Billions of Dollars)

Current Account		Capital and Financial Account	
Merchandise trade balance	−549.4	Capital account transactions, net	−3.1
Exports	713.8	Financial account transactions, net	579.0
Imports	−1,263.2	Statistical discrepancy	−34.1
Services balance	59.2	Balance on capital and financial account	541.8
Travel and transportation, net	−9.3		
Military transactions, net	−10.9		
Royalties and license fees, net	28.0		
Other services, net	51.4		
Goods and services balance	−490.2		
Income balance	16.6		
Investment income, net	21.9		
Compensation of employees, net	−5.3		
Unilateral transfers balance	−68.2		
U.S. government grants	−21.8		
U.S. government pensions	−5.3		
Private remittances	−41.1		
Current account balance	−541.8		

Source: U.S. Department of Commerce, *Survey of Current Business,* May 2004. See also Bureau of Economic Analysis, *U.S. International Transactions Accounts Data,* at http://www.bea.doc.gov.

TABLE 10.4

U.S. Balance of Payments, 1970–2003 (in Billions of Dollars)

Year	Merchandise Trade Balance	Services Balance	Goods and Services Balance	Income Balance	Unilateral Transfers Balance	Current Account Balance
1980	−25.5	6.1	−19.4	30.1	−8.3	2.4
1982	−36.5	12.3	−24.2	29.8	−17.1	−11.5
1984	−112.5	3.3	−109.2	30.0	−20.6	−99.8
1986	−145.1	6.3	−138.8	11.8	−24.2	−151.2
1988	−127.0	12.2	−114.8	11.6	−25.0	−128.2
1990	−109.0	30.2	−78.8	20.7	−33.7	−91.8
1992	−96.1	55.7	−40.4	4.5	−32.0	−67.9
1994	−166.1	59.9	−106.2	−9.2	−35.8	−151.2
1996	−191.3	87.0	−104.3	17.2	−42.1	−129.2
1998	−246.9	82.6	−164.3	−12.1	−44.1	−220.5
2000	−452.2	76.5	−375.7	−14.9	−54.1	−444.7
2002	−482.9	64.9	−418.0	−4.0	−58.9	−480.9
2003	−549.4	59.2	−490.2	16.6	−68.2	−541.8

Source: U.S. Department of Commerce, *Survey of Current Business,* various issues.

Trade deficits generally are not popular with domestic residents and policy makers because they tend to exert adverse consequences on the home nation's terms of trade and employment levels, as well as on the stability of the international money markets. For the United States, economists' concerns over persistent trade deficits have often focused on their possible effects on the terms at which the United States trades with other nations. With a trade deficit, the value of the dollar may fall in international currency markets as dollar outpayments exceed dollar inpayments. Foreign currencies would become more expensive in terms of dollars, so that imports would become more costly to U.S. residents. A trade deficit that induces a decrease in the dollar's international value imposes a real cost on U.S. residents in the form of higher import costs.

Another often-publicized consequence of a trade deficit is its adverse impact on employment levels in certain domestic industries, such as steel or autos. A worsening trade balance may injure domestic labor, not only by the number of jobs lost to foreign workers who produce our imports but also by the employment losses due to deteriorating export sales. It is no wonder that home-nation unions often raise the most vocal arguments about the evils of trade deficits for the domestic economy. Keep in mind, however, that a nation's trade deficit, which leads to decreased employment in some industries, is offset by capital and financial account inflows that generate employment in other industries. Rather than determining total domestic employment, a trade deficit influences the distribution of employment among domestic industries.

Discussion of U.S. competitiveness in merchandise trade often gives the impression that the United States has consistently performed poorly relative to other industrial nations. However, the merchandise trade deficit is a narrow concept, because goods are only part of what the world trades. Another part of trade is services. A better indication of the nation's international payments position is the *goods and services balance.* Table 10.3 shows that in 2003, the United States generated a surplus of $59.2 billion on service transactions. Combining this surplus with the merchandise trade deficit of $549.4 billion yields a deficit on the goods and services balance of $490.2 billion. This means that the United States transferred fewer resources (goods and services) to other nations than it received from them during 2003.

In recent decades, the United States has generated a surplus in its services account, as seen in Table 10.4. The United States has been competitive in services categories such as transportation, construction, engineering, brokers' commissions, and certain health-care services. The United States also has traditionally registered large net receipts from transactions involving proprietary rights—fees, royalties, and other receipts derived mostly from long-established relationships between U.S.–based parent companies and their affiliates abroad.

Adjusting the balance on goods and services for income receipts and payments and net unilateral transfers gives the balance on current account. As Table 10.3 shows, the United States had a *current account* deficit of $541.8 billion in 2003. This means that an excess of imports over exports—of goods, services, income flows, and unilateral transfers—resulted in decreasing net foreign investment for the United States. However, we should *not* become unduly preoccupied with the current account balance, for it ignores capital and financial account transactions. If foreigners purchase more U.S. assets in the United States (such as land, buildings, and bonds), then the United States can afford to import more goods and services from abroad. To look at one aspect of a nation's international payment position without considering the others is misleading.

Taken as a whole, U.S. international transactions always balance. This means that any force leading to an increase or decrease in one balance-of-payments account sets in motion a process leading to exactly offsetting changes in the balances of other accounts. As seen in Table 10.3, the United States had a current account deficit in 2003 of $541.8 billion. Offsetting this deficit was a combined surplus of $541.8 billion in the remaining capital and financial accounts, as follows: (1) capital account transactions, net, $–3.1 billion outflow; (2) financial transactions, net, $579 billion inflow; (3) statistical discrepancy, 34.1 billion outflow.

What Does a Current Account Deficit (Surplus) Mean?

Concerning the balance of payments, the current account and the capital and financial account are not unrelated; they are essentially reflections of one another. Because the balance of payments is a double-entry accounting system, total debits will always equal total credits. It follows that if the current account registers a *deficit* (debits outweigh credits), the capital and financial account must register a *surplus*, or net capital/financial *inflow* (credits outweigh debits). Conversely, if the current account registers a *surplus*, the capital and financial account must register a *deficit*, or net capital/financial *outflow*.

To better understand this notion, assume that in a particular year your spending is greater than your income. How will you finance your "deficit"? The answer is by borrowing or by selling some of your assets. You might liquidate some real assets (for example, sell your personal computer) or perhaps some financial assets (sell a U.S. government security that you own). In like manner, when a nation experiences a current account deficit, its expenditures for foreign goods and services are greater than the income received from the international sales of its own goods and services, after making allowances for investment income flows and gifts to and from foreigners. The nation must somehow finance its current account deficit. But how? The answer lies in selling assets and borrowing. In other words, a nation's current account deficit (debits outweigh credits) is financed essentially by a net financial inflow (credits outweigh debits) in its capital and financial account.

Net Foreign Investment and the Current Account Balance

The current account balance is synonymous with **net foreign investment** in national income accounting. A *current account surplus* means an excess of exports over imports of goods, services, investment income, and unilateral transfers. This permits a net receipt of financial claims for home-nation residents. These funds can be used by the home nation to build up its financial assets or to reduce its liabilities to the rest of the world, improving its net foreign investment position (its net worth vis-à-vis the rest of the world). The home nation thus becomes a net *supplier* of funds (lender) to the rest of the world. Conversely, a *current account deficit* implies an excess of imports over exports of goods, services, investment income, and unilateral transfers. This leads to an increase in net foreign claims upon the home nation. The home nation becomes a net *demander* of funds from abroad, the demand being met through borrowing from other nations or liquidating foreign assets. The result is a worsening of the home nation's net foreign investment position.

The current account balance thus represents the bottom line on a nation's income statement. If it is positive, the nation is spending less than its total income and accumulating asset claims on the rest of the world. If it is negative, domestic expenditure exceeds income and the nation borrows from the rest of the world.

The net borrowing of an economy can be expressed as the sum of the net borrowing by each of its sectors: government and the private sector, including business and households. Net borrowing by government equals its budget deficit: the excess of outlays (G) over taxes (T). Private-sector net borrowing equals the excess of private investment (I) over private saving (S). The net borrowing of the nation is given by the following identity:

$$(G - T) + (I - S) = \text{Current}$$

(G − T)	+	(I	−	S)	=	Current
Government deficit		Private investment		Private saving		account deficit

An important aspect of this identity is that the current account deficit is a macroeconomic phenomenon: It reflects imbalances between government outlays and taxes as well as imbalances between private investment and saving. Any effective policy to decrease the current account deficit must ultimately reduce these discrepancies. Reducing the current account deficit requires either decreases in the government's budget deficit or increases in private saving relative to investment, or both. However, these options are difficult to achieve. Decreasing budget deficits may require unpopular tax hikes or government program cutbacks.

Efforts to reduce investment spending would be opposed because investment is a key determinant of the nation's productivity and standard of living. Finally, incentives to stimulate saving, such as tax breaks, may be opposed on the grounds that they favor the rich rather than the poor.

Decreasing a current account deficit is not entirely in the hands of the home nation. For the world as a whole, the sum of all nations' current account balances must equal zero. Thus, a reduction in one nation's current account deficit must go hand in hand with a decrease in the current account surplus of the rest of the world. Complementary policy in foreign nations, especially those with large current account surpluses, can help in successful transition.

Impact of Financial Flows on the Current Account

In the preceding section, we described a country's capital and financial flows as responsive to developments in the current account. However, the process can, and often does, work the other way around, with capital and financial flows initiating changes in the current account. For example, if foreigners want to purchase U.S. financial instruments exceeding the amount of foreign financial obligations that Americans want to hold, they must pay for the excess with shipments of foreign goods and services. Therefore, a financial inflow to the United States is associated with a U.S. current account deficit.

Let us elaborate on how a U.S. current account deficit can be caused by a net financial inflow to the United States. Suppose domestic saving falls short of desired domestic investment. Therefore, U.S. interest rates rise relative to interest rates abroad, which attracts an inflow of foreign saving to help support U.S. investment. The United States thus becomes a net importer of foreign saving, using the borrowed purchasing power to acquire foreign goods and services, and resulting in a like-sized net inflow of goods and services—a current account deficit. But how does a financial inflow cause a current account deficit for the United States? When foreigners start purchasing more of our assets than we are purchasing of theirs, the dollar becomes more costly in the foreign-exchange market (see

Chapter 11). This causes U.S. goods to become more expensive to foreigners, resulting in declining exports; also, foreign goods become cheaper to Americans, resulting in increasing imports. The result is a rise in the current account deficit, or a decline in the current account surplus.

Economists believe that, in the 1980s, a massive financial inflow caused a current account deficit for the United States. The financial inflow was the result of an increase in the U.S. interest rate relative to interest rates abroad. The higher interest rate, in turn, was mainly due to the combined effects of the U.S. federal government's growing budget deficit and a decline in the private saving rate.

Is a Current Account Deficit a Problem?

Contrary to commonly held views, a current account deficit has little to do with foreign trade practices or any inherent inability of a country to sell its goods on the world market. Instead, it is because of underlying macroeconomic conditions at home requiring more imports to meet current domestic demand for goods and services than can be paid for by export sales. In effect, the domestic economy spends more than it produces, and this excess of demand is met by a net inflow of foreign goods and services leading to the current account deficit. This tendency is minimized during periods of recession but expands significantly with the rising income associated with economic recovery and expansion.

When a nation realizes a current account deficit, it becomes a net borrower of funds from the rest of the world. Is this a problem? Not necessarily. The benefit of a current account deficit is the ability to push current spending beyond current production. However, the cost is the debt service that must be paid on the associated borrowing from the rest of the world.

Is it good or bad for a country to get into debt? The answer obviously depends on what the country does with the money. What matters for future incomes and living standards is whether the deficit is being used to finance more consumption or more investment. If used exclusively to finance an increase in domestic investment, the burden could be slight. We know that investment spending increases the nation's stock of capital and expands the economy's capacity to produce goods and services. The value of this extra output may be sufficient to both pay foreign creditors and also augment domestic spending. In this case, because future consumption need not fall below what it otherwise would have been, there would be no true economic burden. If, on the other hand, foreign borrowing is used to finance or increase domestic consumption (private or public), there is no boost given to future productive capacity. Therefore, to meet debt service expense, future consumption must be reduced below what it otherwise would have been. Such a reduction represents the burden of borrowing. This is not necessarily bad; it all depends on how one values current versus future consumption.

During the 1980s, when the United States realized current account deficits, the rate of domestic saving decreased relative to the rate of investment. In fact, the decline of the overall saving rate was mainly the result of a decrease of its public saving component, caused by large and persistent federal budget deficits in this period—budget deficits are in effect negative savings that subtract from the pool of savings. This indicated that the United States used foreign borrowing to increase current consumption, not productivity-enhancing public investment. The U.S. current account deficits of the 1980s were thus greeted by concern by many economists.

In the 1990s, however, U.S. current account deficits were driven by increases in domestic investment. This investment boom contributed to expanding employment and output. It could not, however, have been financed by national saving alone. Foreign lending provided the additional capital needed to finance the boom. In the absence of foreign lending, U.S. interest rates would have been higher, and investment would inevitably have been constrained by the supply of domestic saving. Therefore, the accumulation of capital and the growth of output and employment would all have been smaller had the United States not been able to run a current account deficit in the 1990s. Rather than choking off growth and

Do Current Account Deficits Cost Americans Jobs?

The sizable U.S. current account deficits that have occurred in recent years have prompted concerns that American jobs are in jeopardy. Increasing competition in the domestic market from low-cost Asian imports could put pressure on U.S. firms to lay off workers. Exporters such as Ford, whose sales decline as a strong dollar raises the price of its autos in foreign markets, could also move to restrict employment. Finally, jobs in export-oriented firms such as Boeing were hurt by the 1997–1998 recession in Asia, which weakened the demand for U.S. goods. Adding to concerns about the employment effects of the current account deficit is the fear that increasing numbers of U.S. firms will shut down domestic operations and shift production to other countries, largely to take advantage of lower labor costs.

Nevertheless, although export and import trends raise concerns about U.S. job losses, employment statistics do not bear out the relationship between a rising current account deficit and lower employment. During the 1990s, the unemployment rate declined steadily, reaching a 25-year low in 1998, while the current account deficit mounted. Are the concerns over U.S. job losses from international trade misplaced?

According to economists at the Federal Reserve Bank of New York, the U.S. current account deficit is not a threat to employment for the economy as a whole. A high current account deficit may indeed hurt employment in particular firms and industries as workers are displaced by increased imports or by the relocation of production abroad. At the economy-wide level, however, the current account deficit is matched by an equal inflow of foreign funds, which finances employment-sustaining investment spending that would not otherwise occur. When viewed as the net inflow of foreign investment, the current account deficit produces jobs for the economy as a whole—both from the direct effects of higher employment in investment-oriented industries and from the indirect effects of higher investment spending on economy-wide employment. Viewing the current account deficit as a net inflow of foreign investment thus helps to dispel misconceptions about the adverse consequences of economic globalization on the domestic job market.

Source: Matthew Higgins and Thomas Klitgaard, "Viewing the Current Account Deficit as a Capital Inflow," *Current Issues and Economics and Finance*, Federal Reserve Bank of New York, December 1999, pp. 1–6.

employment, the large current account deficit allowed faster long-run growth in the U.S. economy, which improved economic welfare.

Business Cycles, Economic Growth, and the Current Account

How is the current account related to a country's business cycle and long-run economic growth? Concerning the business cycle, *rapid* growth of production and employment is commonly associated with large or growing trade and current account *deficits*, whereas *slow* output and employment growth is associated with large or growing *surpluses*. For example, the U.S. current account

improved during the recessions of 1973–1975, 1980, and 1990–1991, but declined during the cyclical upswings of 1970–1972, 1983–1990, and 1993–2000. This reflects both a decline in demand for imports during recessions and the usual cyclical movements of saving and investment.

During a recession, both saving and investment tend to fall. Saving falls as households try to maintain their consumption patterns in the face of a temporary fall in income; investment declines because capacity utilization declines and profits fall. However, because investment is highly sensitive to the need for extra capacity, it tends to drop more sharply than saving during recessions. The current account balance thus tends to rise. Consistent with this, but viewed from a different angle, the trade balance typically improves during a recession, because imports tend to fall with overall consumption and investment demand. The opposite occurs during periods of boom, when sharp increases in investment demand typically outweigh increases in saving, producing a decline of the current account. Of course, factors other than income influence saving and investment, so that the tendency of a country's current account deficit to decline in recessions is not ironclad.

The relationship just described between the current account and economic performance typically holds not only on a short-term or cyclical basis, but also on a long-term basis. Often, countries enjoying *rapid* economic growth possess long-run current account *deficits*, whereas those with *weaker* economic growth have long-run current account *surpluses*. This relationship likely derives from the fact that rapid economic growth and strong investment often go hand in hand. Where the driving force is the discovery of new natural resources, technological progress, or the implementation of economic reform, periods of rapid economic growth are likely to be periods in which new investment is unusually profitable. However, investment must be financed with saving, and if a country's national saving is not sufficient to finance all new profitable investment projects, the country will rely on foreign saving to finance the difference. It thus experiences a net financial inflow and a corresponding current account deficit. As long as the new investments are profitable, they will generate the extra earnings needed to repay the claims contracted to undertake them. Thus, when current account deficits reflect strong, profitable investment programs, they work to raise the rate of output and employment growth, not to destroy jobs and production.

Historically, countries at relatively early stages of rapid economic development—such as the United States in the 1800s and Argentina, Australia, and Canada in the early 1900s—have enjoyed an excess of investment over saving, running large current account deficits for long periods. The same general pattern has held in more recent times: Faster-growing developing countries

have generally run larger current account deficits than the slower-growing mature economies.

The link between trade, current account deficits, and economic growth is also confirmed by comparing the U.S. trade balance with those of other major industrial countries from 1992–1997. Figure 10.1 shows a negative correlation between output growth and the trade balance, and between employment growth and the trade balance, respectively. During this period, the United States enjoyed the fastest output and employment growth—and the largest trade deficit—among the countries shown. Conversely, Japan had the largest trade surplus, but the second-slowest rate of growth. Trade surpluses were also the norm in Europe, where growth of output and employment was disappointing.

Can the United States Continue to Run Current Account Deficits Year After Year?

In the past two decades, the United States has run continuous deficits in its current account. Can the United States run deficits indefinitely? Because the current account deficit arises mainly because foreigners desire to purchase American assets, there is no economic reason why it cannot continue indefinitely. As long as the investment opportunities are large enough to provide foreign investors with competitive rates of return, they will be happy to continue supplying funds to the United States. Simply put, there is no reason why the process cannot continue indefinitely: There are no automatic forces that will cause either a current account deficit or a current account surplus to reverse.

U.S. history illustrates this point. From 1820 to 1875, the United States ran current account deficits almost continuously. At this time, the United States was a relatively poor (by European standards) but rapidly growing country. Foreign investment helped foster that growth. This situation changed after World War I. The United States was richer, and investment opportunities were more limited. Thus, current account surpluses were present almost continuously between 1920 and 1970. During the last 25 years, the situation

FIGURE 10.1

Economic Growth, Employment Growth, and Trade Balances of Major Industrial Countries, 1992–1997

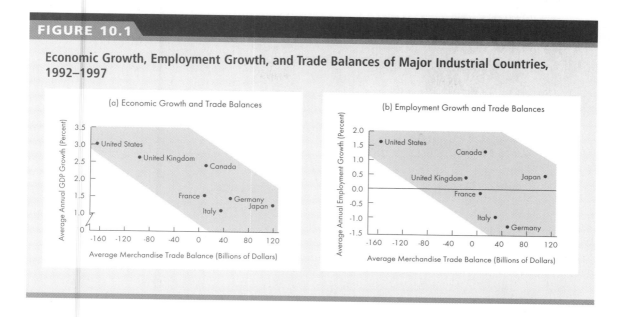

(a) Economic Growth and Trade Balances

(b) Employment Growth and Trade Balances

has again reversed. The current account deficits of the United States are underlaid by its system of secure property rights, a stable political and monetary environment, and a rapidly growing labor force (compared with Japan and Europe), which make the United States an attractive place to invest. Moreover, the U.S. saving rate is low compared to its major trading partners. The U.S. current account deficit reflects this combination of factors, and it is likely to continue as long as they are present.

At the turn of the century, America's current account deficit was high and rising. By 2003, the U.S. current account deficit was just over 5 percent of GDP, the highest in the country's history, as seen in Figure 10.2 on page 334. Even in the late 1800s, after the Civil War, America's deficit was generally below 3 percent of GDP. During the budget deficits of President Ronald Reagan in the 1980s, the current account deficit peaked at 3.4 percent of GDP. Because of relatively good prospects for growth in the United States compared to the rest of the world, international capital was flowing to the United States in search of the safety and acceptable returns offered there. However, capital was not flowing to emerging markets as in the

1990s. Europe faced high unemployment and sluggish growth, and Japan faced economic contraction and continuing financial problems. Not surprisingly in this setting, capital flowed into the United States because of the relatively superior past performance and expectations for future growth in the U.S. economy. Simply put, the U.S. current account deficit reflected a surplus of good investment opportunities in the United States and a deficit of growth prospects elsewhere in the world. However, many economists feel that economies become overextended and hit trouble when their current account deficits reach 4 to 5 percent of GDP.

However, some maintain that because of spreading globalization, the pool of savings offered to the United States by world financial markets is deeper and more liquid than ever. This allows foreign investors to continue furnishing America with the money it needs without demanding higher interest rates in return. Presumably, a current account deficit of 5 percent or more of GDP would not have been readily fundable several decades ago. The ability to move that much of world saving to the United

ECONOMIC Applications

Visit EconNews Online
International Finance

FIGURE 10.2

U.S. Current Account Balance as a Percent of GDP

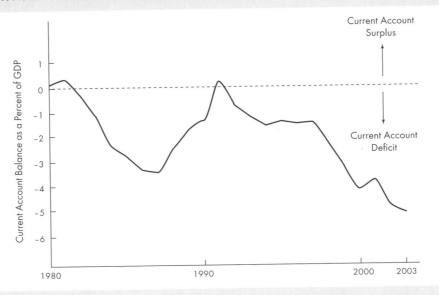

For most years since 1980, the United States has realized current account deficits. In the early 2000s, these deficits were rising rapidly. In effect, the United States had to borrow annually from foreigners to spend more than it produces.

States in response to relative rates of return would have been hindered by a far lower degree of international financial integration. In recent years, however, the increasing integration of financial markets has created an expanding class of foreigners who are willing and able to invest in America.

The consequence of a current account deficit is a growing foreign ownership of the capital stock of the United States and a rising fraction of U.S. income that must be diverted overseas in the form of interest and dividends to foreigners. A possibly serious problem could emerge if foreigners lose confidence in the ability of the United States to generate the resources necessary to repay the funds borrowed from abroad. As a result, suppose that foreigners decide to reduce the fraction of their saving they send to the United States. The initial effect could be both a sudden and large decline in the value of the dollar as the supply of dollars increases on the foreign-exchange market and a sudden and large increase in U.S. interest rates as an important source of saving was withdrawn from financial markets. Large increases in interest rates could cause problems for the U.S. economy as they reduce the market value of debt securities, cause prices on the stock market to decline, and raise questions about the solvency of various debtors. Simply put, whether the United States can sustain its current account deficit over the foreseeable future depends on whether foreigners are willing to increase their investments in U.S. assets. The current account deficit puts the economic fortunes of the United States partially in the hands of foreign investors.

Although the appropriate level of the U.S. current account deficit is difficult to assess, at least two principles are relevant should it prove necessary to reduce the deficit. First, the United States has an interest in policies that stimulate foreign growth, because it is better to reduce the current account deficit through faster growth abroad than through slower growth at home. A recession at home would obviously be a highly undesirable means of reducing the deficit.

Second, any reductions in the deficit are better achieved through increased national saving than through reduced domestic investment. If there are attractive investment opportunities in the United States, we are better off borrowing from abroad to finance these opportunities than forgoing them. On the other hand, incomes in this country would be even higher in the future if these investments were financed through higher national saving. Increases in national saving allow interest rates to remain lower than they would otherwise be. Lower interest rates would lead to higher domestic investment, which, in turn, would boost demand for equipment and construction. For any given level of investment, increased saving would also result in higher net exports, which would again raise employment in these sectors.

However, shrinking the U.S. current account deficit can be difficult. The economies of foreign nations may not be strong enough to absorb additional American exports, and Americans may be reluctant to curb their appetite for foreign goods. Also, the U.S. government has shown a bias toward deficit spending. Turning around a deficit is associated with a sizable fall in the exchange rate and a decrease in output in the adjusting country, topics that will be discussed in subsequent chapters.

Balance of International Indebtedness

A main feature of the U.S. balance of payments is that it measures the economic transactions of the United States over a period of one year or one quarter. But at any particular moment, a nation will have a fixed stock of assets and liabilities against the rest of the world. The statement that summarizes this situation is known as the **balance of international indebtedness**. It is a record of the international position of the United States at a particular time (year-end data).

The U.S. balance of international indebtedness indicates the international investment position of the United States, reflecting the value of U.S. investments abroad as opposed to foreign investments in the United States. The United States is considered a **net creditor** to the rest of the world when U.S. claims on foreigners exceed foreign claims on the United States at a particular time. When the reverse occurs, the United States assumes a **net debtor** position.

The terms *net creditor* and *net debtor* in themselves are not particularly meaningful. We need additional information about the specific types of claims and liabilities involved. The balance of international indebtedness therefore looks at the short- and long-term investment positions of both the private and government sectors of the economy. Table 10.5 on page 336 gives examples of the U.S. balance of international indebtedness.

Of what use is the balance of international indebtedness? Perhaps of greatest significance is that it breaks down international investment holdings into several categories so that policy implications can be drawn from each separate category about the *liquidity status* of the nation. For the short-term investment position, the strategic factor is the amount of short-term liabilities (bank deposits and government securities) held by foreigners. This is because these holdings potentially can be withdrawn at very short notice, resulting in a disruption of domestic financial markets. The balance of official monetary holdings is also significant. Assume that this balance is negative from the U.S. viewpoint. Should foreign monetary authorities decide to liquidate their holdings of U.S. government securities and have them converted into official reserve assets, the financial strength of the dollar would be reduced. As for a nation's long-term investment position, it is of less importance for the U.S. liquidity position because long-term

TABLE 10.5

International Investment Position of the United States at Year-End (in Billions of Dollars)

	1995	2000	2002
Type of Investment*			
U.S. Assets Abroad			
U.S. government assets	257.2	213.6	244.3
U.S. private assets	3,148.6	5,953.6	5,944.9
Total	3,405.8	6,167.2	6,189.2
Foreign Assets in the United States			
Foreign official assets	671.7	922.4	1,132.5
Other foreign assets	3,234.2	7,087.5	7,443.9
Total	3,905.9	8,009.9	8,576.4
Net International Investment Position	−500.1	−1,842.7	−2,387.2

*At current cost.

Source: U.S. Department of Commerce, Bureau of Economic Analysis, *The International Investment Position of the United States at Year-End*, at http://www.bea.gov. See also U.S. Department of Commerce, *Survey of Current Business*, various June and July issues.

investments generally respond to basic economic trends and are not subject to erratic withdrawals.

United States as a Debtor Nation

In the early stages of its industrial development, the United States was a net international debtor. Relying heavily on foreign funds, the United States built up its industries by mortgaging part of its wealth to foreigners. After World War I, the United States became a net international creditor. The U.S. international investment position evolved steadily from a net-creditor position of $6 billion in 1919 to a position of $337 billion in 1983. By 1987, however, the United States had become a net international debtor, in the amount of $23 billion, for the first time since World War I; since then, the United States has continued to be a net international debtor, as seen in Table 10.5.

How did this turnabout occur so rapidly? The reason was that foreign investors placed more funds in the United States than U.S. residents invested abroad. The United States was considered attractive to investors from other countries because of its rapid economic recovery from the recession of the early 1980s, its political stability, and its relatively high interest rates. U.S. investments overseas fell because of a sluggish loan demand in Europe, a desire by commercial banks to reduce their overseas exposure as a reaction to the debt-repayment problems of Latin American countries, and decreases in credit demand by oil-importing developing nations as the result of declining oil prices. Of the foreign investment funds in the United States, less than one-fourth went to direct ownership of U.S. real estate and business. Most of the funds were in financial assets such as bank deposits, stocks, and bonds.

For the typical U.S. resident, the transition from net creditor to net debtor went unnoticed. However, the net-debtor status of the United States raised an issue of propriety. To many observers, it seemed inappropriate for the United States, one of the richest nations in the world, to be borrowing on a massive scale from the rest of the world.

Summary

1. The balance of payments is a record of a nation's economic transactions with all other nations for a given year. A credit transaction is one that results in a receipt of payments from foreigners, whereas a debit transaction leads to a payment abroad. Owing to double-entry bookkeeping, a nation's balance of payments will always balance.

2. From a functional viewpoint, the balance of payments identifies economic transactions as (a) current account transactions and (b) capital and financial account transactions.

3. The balance on goods and services is important to policy makers because it indicates the net transfer of real resources overseas. It also measures the extent to which a nation's exports and imports are part of its gross national product.

4. The capital and financial account of the balance of payments shows the international movement of loans, investments, and the like. Capital and financial inflows (outflows) are analogous to exports (imports) of goods and services because they result in the receipt (payment) of funds from (to) other nations.

5. Official reserves consist of a nation's financial assets: (a) monetary gold holdings, (b) convertible currencies, (c) special drawing rights, and (d) drawing positions on the International Monetary Fund.

6. The current method employed by the Department of Commerce in presenting the U.S. international payments position makes use of a functional format emphasizing the following *partial* balances: (a) merchandise trade balance, (b) balance on goods and services, and (c) current account balance.

7. Because the balance of payments is a double-entry accounting system, total debits will always equal total credits. It follows that if the current account registers a deficit (surplus), the capital and financial account must register a surplus (deficit), or net capital/financial inflow (outflow). If a country realizes a deficit (surplus) in its current account, it becomes a net demander (supplier) of funds from (to) the rest of the world.

8. Concerning the business cycle, rapid growth of production and employment is commonly associated with large or growing trade and current account deficits, whereas slow output and employment growth is associated with large or growing current account surpluses.

9. The international investment position of the United States at a particular time is measured by the balance of international indebtedness. Unlike the balance of payments, which is a flow concept (over a period of time), the balance of international indebtedness is a stock concept (at a single point in time).

Key Concepts and Terms

- Balance of international indebtedness *(page 335)*
- Balance of payments *(page 320)*
- Capital and financial account *(page 324)*
- Credit transaction *(page 320)*
- Current account *(page 321)*
- Debit transaction *(page 320)*
- Double-entry accounting *(page 321)*
- Goods and services balance *(page 323)*
- Merchandise trade balance *(page 322)*
- Net creditor *(page 335)*
- Net debtor *(page 335)*
- Net foreign investment *(page 328)*
- Official reserve assets *(page 325)*
- Official settlements transactions *(page 324)*
- Statistical discrepancy *(page 325)*
- Trade balance *(page 326)*
- Unilateral transfers *(page 323)*

Study Questions

1. What is meant by the balance of payments?
2. What economic transactions give rise to the receipt of dollars from foreigners? What transactions give rise to payments to foreigners?
3. Why does the balance-of-payments statement "balance"?
4. From a functional viewpoint, a nation's balance of payments can be grouped into several categories. What are these categories?
5. What financial assets are categorized as official reserve assets for the United States?
6. What is the meaning of a surplus (deficit) on the (a) merchandise trade balance, (b) goods and services balance, and (c) current account balance?
7. Why has the goods and services balance sometimes shown a surplus while the merchandise trade balance shows a deficit?
8. What does the balance of international indebtedness measure? How does this statement differ from the balance of payments?
9. Indicate whether each of the following items represents a debit or a credit on the U.S. balance of payments:
   a. A U.S. importer purchases a shipload of French wine.
   b. A Japanese automobile firm builds an assembly plant in Kentucky.
   c. A British manufacturer exports machinery to Taiwan on a U.S. vessel.
   d. A U.S. college student spends a year studying in Switzerland.
   e. U.S. charities donate food to people in drought-plagued Africa.
   f. Japanese investors collect interest income on their holdings of U.S. government securities.
   g. A German resident sends money to her relatives in the United States.
   h. Lloyds of London sells an insurance policy to a U.S. business firm.
   i. A Swiss resident receives dividends on her IBM stock.
10. **Xtra!** For a tutorial of this question, go to
    CARBAUGH **http://carbaughxtra.swlearning.com**
    Table 10.6 summarizes hypothetical transactions, in billions of U.S. dollars, that took place during a given year.

TABLE 10.6

International Transactions of the United States (Billions of Dollars)

Travel and transportation receipts, net	$ 25
Merchandise imports	450
Unilateral transfers, net	–20
Allocation of SDRs	15
Receipts on U.S. investments abroad	20
Statistical discrepancy	40
Compensation of employees	–5
Changes in U.S. assets abroad, net	–150
Merchandise exports	375
Other services, net	35
Payments on foreign investments in the United States	–10

   a. Calculate the U.S. merchandise trade, services, goods and services, income, unilateral transfers, and current account balances.
   b. Which of these balances pertains to the net foreign investment position of the United States? How would you describe that position?
11. Given the hypothetical items shown in Table 10.7, determine the international investment position of the United States. Is the United States a net-creditor nation or a net-debtor nation?

TABLE 10.7

International Investment Position of the United States (Billions of Dollars)

Foreign official assets in the United States	$ 25
Other foreign assets in the United States	225
U.S. government assets abroad	150
U.S. private assets abroad	75

netlink

10.1 The Bureau of Economic Analysis compiles information on the U.S. balance of payments, U.S. exports and imports, and the international investment position of the United States. Set your browser to this URL:

http://www.bea.doc.gov

You can go directly to the *Survey of Current Business* and other BEA publications pages by setting your browser to this URL:

http://www.bea.doc.gov/bea/pubs.htm

10.2 Summary statistics on international aspects of the economy can be found at the White House Briefing Room. Set your browser to this URL:

http: //www.whitehouse.gov/news/fsbr. html

To go directly to the Council of Economic Advisers Publications page that includes the *Economic Report of the President*, log onto this URL:

http://www.whitehouse.gov/cea/pubs.html

To access NetLink Exercises and the Virtual Scavenger Hunt, visit the Carbaugh Web site at http://carbaugh.swlearning.com.

Xtra! Log onto the Carbaugh Xtra! Web site (http://carbaughxtra.swlearning.com) for additional learning resources such as practice quizzes, help with graphing, and current events applications.

chapter 11

Foreign Exchange

Among the factors that make international economics a distinct subject is the existence of different national monetary units of account. In the United States, prices and money are measured in terms of the dollar. The peso represents Mexico's unit of account, whereas the franc and yen signify the units of account of Switzerland and Japan, respectively.

A typical international transaction requires two distinct purchases. First, the foreign currency is bought; second, the foreign currency is used to facilitate the international transaction. For example, before French importers can purchase commodities from, say, U.S. exporters, they must first purchase dollars to meet their international obligation. Some institutional arrangements are required that provide an efficient mechanism whereby monetary claims can be settled with a minimum of inconvenience to both parties. Such a mechanism exists in the form of the foreign-exchange market.[1] In this chapter, we will examine the nature and operation of this market.

Foreign-Exchange Market

The **foreign-exchange market** refers to the organizational setting within which individuals, businesses, governments, and banks buy and sell foreign currencies and other debt instruments.[2] Only a small fraction of daily transactions in foreign exchange actually involve trading of currency. Most foreign-exchange transactions involve the transfer of bank deposits. Major U.S. banks, such as Citibank, maintain inventories of foreign exchange in the form of foreign-denominated deposits held in branch or correspondent banks in foreign cities. Americans can obtain this foreign exchange from hometown banks that, in turn, purchase it from Citibank.

The foreign-exchange market is by far the largest and most liquid market in the world. The estimated worldwide amount of foreign-exchange transactions is around $1.5 trillion a day. Individual trades of $200 million to $500 million are not uncommon.

[1] This chapter considers the foreign-exchange market in the absence of government restrictions. In practice, foreign-exchange markets for many currencies are controlled by governments; therefore, the range of foreign-exchange activities discussed in this chapter are not all possible.

[2] This section draws from Sam Cross, *The Foreign Exchange Market in the United States*, Federal Reserve Bank of New York, 1998.

Quoted prices change as often as 20 times a minute. It has been estimated that the world's most active exchange rates can change up to 18,000 times during a single day.

Not all currencies are traded on foreign-exchange markets. Currencies that are not traded are avoided for reasons ranging from political instability to economic uncertainty. Sometimes a country's currency is not exchanged for the simple reason that the country produces very few products of interest to other countries.

Unlike stock or commodity exchanges, the foreign-exchange market is not an organized structure. It has no centralized meeting place and no formal requirements for participation. Nor is the foreign-exchange market limited to any one country. For any currency, such as the U.S. dollar, the foreign-exchange market consists of all locations where dollars are exchanged for other national currencies. Three of the largest foreign-exchange markets in the world are located in London, New York, and Tokyo. A dozen or so other market centers also exist around the world, such as Paris and Zurich. Because foreign-exchange dealers are in constant telephone and computer contact, the market is very competitive; in effect, it functions no differently than if it were a centralized market.

The foreign-exchange market opens on Monday morning in Hong Kong, which is still Sunday evening in New York. As the day progresses, markets open in Tokyo, Frankfurt, London, New York, Chicago, San Francisco, and elsewhere. As the West Coast markets of the United States close, Hong Kong is only one hour away from opening for Tuesday business. Indeed, the foreign-exchange market is a round-the-clock operation.

A typical foreign-exchange market functions at three levels: (1) in transactions between commercial banks and their commercial customers, who are the ultimate demanders and suppliers of foreign exchange; (2) in the domestic interbank market conducted through brokers; and (3) in active trading in foreign exchange with banks overseas.

Exporters, importers, investors, and tourists buy and sell foreign exchange from and to commercial banks rather than each other. As an example, consider the import of German autos by a U.S. dealer. The dealer is billed for each car it imports at the rate of 50,000 euros per car. The U.S. dealer cannot write a check for this amount because it does not have a checking account denominated in euros. Instead, the dealer goes to the foreign-exchange department of, say, Chase Manhattan Bank to arrange payment. If the exchange rate is 1.1 euros = \$1, the auto dealer writes a check to Chase Manhattan Bank for \$45,454.55 (50,000/1.1 = 45,454.55) per car. Chase Manhattan will then pay the German manufacturer 50,000 euros per car in Germany. Chase Manhattan is able to do this because it has a checking deposit in euros at its branch in Bonn.

ECONOMIC *Applications*

Visit EconData Online

The major banks who trade foreign exchange generally do not deal directly with one another but instead use the services of *foreign-exchange brokers*. The purpose of a broker is to permit the trading banks to maintain desired foreign-exchange balances. If at a particular moment a bank does not have the proper foreign-exchange balances, it can turn to a broker to buy additional foreign currency or sell the surplus. Brokers thus provide a wholesale, interbank market in which trading banks can buy and sell foreign exchange. Brokers are paid a commission for their services by the selling bank.

The third tier of the foreign-exchange market consists of the transactions between the trading banks and their overseas branches or foreign correspondents. Although several dozen U.S. banks trade in foreign exchange, it is the major New York banks that usually carry out transactions with foreign banks. The other, inland trading banks meet their foreign-exchange needs by maintaining correspondent relationships with the New York banks. Trading with foreign banks permits the matching of supply and demand of foreign exchange in the New York market. These international transactions are carried out primarily by telephone and computers.

Prior to 2000, companies that needed hard currency on a daily basis to meet foreign payrolls or to convert sales in foreign currencies into U.S. dollars traditionally dealt with traders at major banks such as Citicorp, JP Morgan, and Chase Manhattan. This required corporate customers to work the phones, talking to traders at several banks at once to get the right quotation. However, there was little head-to-head competition among the banks, and corporate clients were looking for alternatives. All of this changed when start-up Currenex, Inc., built an online marketplace where banks could compete to offer foreign-currency exchange service to companies. The concept was embraced by major banks as well as corporate clients such as Home Depot. Being online makes the currency trading process more transparent. Corporate clients can see multiple quotes instantly and shop for the best deal.

Types of Foreign-Exchange Transactions

When conducting purchases and sales of foreign currencies, banks promise to pay a stipulated amount of currency to another bank or customer on an agreed-upon date. Banks typically engage in three types of foreign-exchange transactions: spot, forward, and swap.

A **spot transaction** is an outright purchase and sale of foreign currency for cash settlement not more than two business days after the date the transaction is recorded as a spot deal. The 2-day period is known as *immediate delivery*. By convention, the settlement date is the second business day after the date on which the transaction is agreed to by the two traders. The 2-day period provides ample time for the two parties to confirm the agreement and arrange the clearing and necessary debiting and crediting of bank accounts in various international locations.

In many cases, a business or financial institution knows it will be receiving or paying an amount of foreign currency on a specific date in the future. For example, in August a U.S. importer may arrange for a special Christmas-season shipment of Japanese radios to arrive in October. The agreement with the Japanese manufacturer may call for payment in yen on October 20. To guard against the possibility of the yen's becoming more expensive in terms of the dollar, the importer might contract with a bank to buy yen at a stipulated price, but not actually receive them until October 20 when they are needed. When the contract matures, the U.S. importer pays for the yen

with a known amount of dollars. This is known as a **forward transaction**.

Forward transactions differ from spot transactions in that their maturity date is more than two business days in the future. A forward-exchange contract's maturity date can be a few months or even years in the future. The exchange rate is fixed when the contract is initially made. No money necessarily changes hands until the transaction actually takes place, although dealers may require some customers to provide collateral in advance.

Trading foreign currencies among banks also involves swap transactions. A **currency swap** is the conversion of one currency to another currency at one point in time, with an agreement to reconvert it back to the original currency at a specified time in the future. The rates of both exchanges are agreed to in advance. Swaps provide an efficient mechanism through which banks can meet their foreign-exchange needs over a period of time. Banks are able to use a currency for a period in exchange for another currency that is not needed during that time.

For example, Chase Manhattan Bank may have excess balances of dollars but needs pounds to meet the requirements of its corporate clients. At the same time, Royal Bank of Scotland may have excess balances of pounds and insufficient amounts of dollars. The banks could negotiate a swap agreement in which Chase Manhattan Bank agrees to exchange dollars for pounds today and pounds for dollars in the future. The key aspect is that the two banks arrange the swap as a single transaction in which they agree to pay and receive stipulated amounts of currencies at specified rates.

Figure 11.1 illustrates the distribution of foreign-exchange transactions by U.S. banking institutions, by transaction type. As of 2001, currency swaps accounted for the largest share of foreign-exchange transactions. Also, the average daily amount of foreign-exchange transactions was $254 billion in 2001. The U.S. dollar was by far the most important currency traded in foreign-exchange markets, being involved in more than 90 percent of all transactions. The euro was the second most actively traded currency and was one of the currencies in 39 percent of all trades. Other leading currencies were the Japanese yen, Canadian dollar, and Swiss franc.

FIGURE 11.1

Distribution of Foreign-Exchange Transactions by U.S. Banks

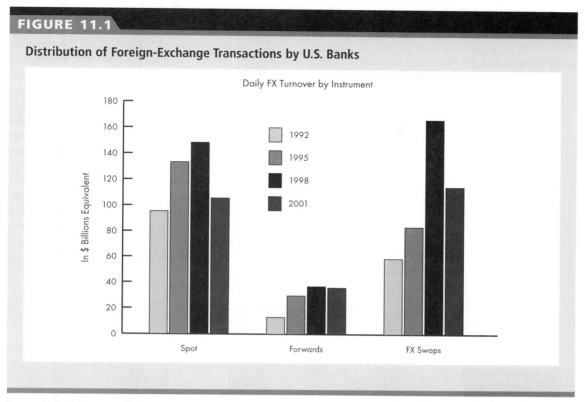

Daily FX Turnover by Instrument

Source: Federal Reserve Bank of New York, *2001 Triennial Central Bank Survey of Foreign Exchange and Derivatives Market Activity*, p. 3.

Interbank Trading

In the foreign-exchange market, currencies are actively traded around the clock and throughout the world. Banks are linked by telecommunications equipment that permits instantaneous communication. A relatively small number of money center banks carry out most of the foreign-exchange transactions in the United States. Virtually all the big New York banks have active currency-trading operations, as do their counterparts in London, Tokyo, Hong Kong, Frankfurt, and other financial centers. Large banks in cities such as Los Angeles, Chicago, San Francisco, and Detroit also have active currency-trading operations. For most U.S. banks, currency transactions are not a large part of their business; these banks have ties to correspondent banks in New York and elsewhere to conduct currency transactions.

All these banks are prepared to purchase or sell foreign currencies for their customers. Bank purchases from and sales to consumers are classified as *retail transactions* when the amount involved is less than 1 million currency units. *Wholesale transactions*, involving more than 1 million currency units, generally occur between banks or with large corporate customers. Bank transactions with each other constitute the **interbank market**. It is in this market that most foreign-exchange trading occurs.

Foreign-exchange departments of major commercial banks typically serve as profit centers. A bank's foreign-exchange dealers are in constant contact with other dealers to buy and sell currencies. In most large banks, dealers specialize in one or more foreign currencies. The chief dealer establishes the overall trading policy and direction of trading, trying to service the foreign-exchange needs of the bank's customers and make a profit for the bank.

Currency trading is conducted on a 24-hour basis, and exchange rates may fluctuate at any moment. Bank dealers must be light sleepers, ready to react to a nighttime phone call that indicates exchange rates are moving sharply in foreign markets. Banks often allow senior dealers to conduct exchange trading at home in response to such developments.

With the latest electronic equipment, currency exchanges are negotiated on computer terminals; a push of a button confirms a trade. Dealers use electronic trading boards that permit them to instantly register transactions and verify their bank's positions. Besides trading currencies during daytime hours, major banks have established night-trading desks to capitalize on foreign-exchange fluctuations during the evening and to accommodate corporate requests for currency trades. In the interbank market, currencies are traded in amounts involving at least 1 million units of a specific foreign currency. Table 11.1 lists leading banks that trade in the foreign-exchange market.

How do banks such as Bank of America or Citibank earn profits in foreign-exchange transactions? Banks that regularly deal in the interbank market quote both a bid and an offer rate to other banks. The **bid rate** refers to the price that the bank is willing to pay for a unit of foreign currency; the **offer rate** is the price at which the bank is willing to sell a unit of foreign currency. The difference between the bid and the offer rate is the **spread** that varies by the size of the transaction and the liquidity of the currencies being traded. At any given time, a bank's bid quote for a foreign currency will be less than its offer quote. The spread is intended to cover the bank's costs of implementing the exchange of currencies. The large trading banks are prepared to "make a market" in a currency by providing bid and offer rates on request.

Foreign-exchange dealers who simultaneously purchase and sell foreign currency earn the spread as profit. For example, Citibank might quote bid and offer rates for the Swiss franc at $.5851/.5854. The bid rate is $.5851 per franc. At this price, Citibank would be prepared to buy 1 million francs for $585,100. The offer rate is $.5854 per franc. Citibank would be willing to sell 1 million francs for $585,400. If Citibank is able to simultaneously buy and sell 1 million francs, it will earn $300 on the transaction. This profit equals the spread ($.0003) multiplied by the amount of the transaction (1 million francs).

Besides earning profits from a currency's bid/offer spread, foreign-exchange dealers attempt to profit by anticipating correctly the future direction of currency movements. Suppose a Citibank dealer expects the Japanese yen to *appreciate* (strengthen) against the U.S. dollar. The dealer will likely *raise* both bid and offer rates, attempting to persuade other dealers to sell yen to Citibank and dissuade other dealers from purchasing yen from Citibank. The bank dealer thus purchases more yen than are sold. If the yen appreciates against the dollar as predicted, the Citibank dealer can sell the yen at a higher rate and earn a profit. Conversely, should the Citibank dealer anticipate that the yen is about to *depreciate* (weaken) against the dollar, the dealer will *lower* the bid and offer rates. Such action encourages sales and discourages purchases; the dealer thus sells more yen than are bought. If the yen depreciates as expected, the dealer can purchase yen back at a lower price to make a profit.

If exchange rates move in the desired direction, foreign-exchange traders earn profits. However, losses accrue if exchange rates move in the oppo-

TABLE 11.1

Top 10 Banks by Share of Foreign-Exchange Market*

Bank	Share of Foreign-Exchange Market
UBS	11.5%
Citigroup	9.9
Deutsche Bank	9.8
JP MorganChase	6.8
Goldman Sachs	5.6
Credit Suisse First Boston	4.2
HSBC	3.9
Morgan Stanley	3.9
Barclays Capital	3.8
ABN Amro	3.6

*Ranked by *Euromoney* survey of over 3,000 users of foreign exchange. This survey is updated annually.

Source: *Euromoney*, May 2003.

site, unexpected direction. To limit possible losses on exchange-market transactions, banks impose financial restrictions on their dealers' trading volume. Dealers are subject to *position limits* that stipulate the amount of buying and selling that can be conducted in a given currency. Although banks maintain formal restrictions, they have sometimes absorbed substantial losses from unauthorized trading activity beyond position limits. Because foreign-exchange departments are considered by bank management to be profit centers, dealers feel pressure to generate an acceptable rate of return on the bank's funds invested in this operation.

Reading Foreign-Exchange Quotations

Most daily newspapers publish foreign-exchange rates for major currencies. The **exchange rate** is the price of one currency in terms of another—for example, the number of dollars required to purchase 1 British pound (£). In shorthand notation, ER = $ /£, where ER is the exchange rate. For example, if ER = 2, then purchasing £1 will require $2 (2/1 = 2). It is also possible to define the exchange rate as the number of units of foreign currency required to purchase 1 unit of domestic currency, or ER′ = £/$. In our example, ER′ = 0.5 (1/2 = 0.5), which implies that it requires £0.5 to buy $1. Of course, ER′ is the reciprocal of ER (ER′ = 1/ER).

Table 11.2 on page 346 shows the exchange rates listed for March 9, 2004, in *The Wall Street Journal*. In columns 2 and 3 (*U.S. dollar equivalent*) of the upper portion of Table 11.2, the selling prices of foreign currencies are listed in dollars. The columns state how many dollars are required to purchase one unit of a given foreign currency. For example, the quote for the Argentinian peso for Tuesday was .3439. This means that $.3439 was required to purchase 1 peso. Columns 4 and 5 (*Currency per U.S. dollar*) show the foreign-exchange rates from the opposite perspective, telling how many units of a foreign currency are required to buy a U.S. dollar. Again referring to Tuesday, it would take 2.91 Argentinian pesos to purchase 1 U.S. dollar.

The term *mid-range rate* in the table's heading refers to the price at which a New York bank will sell

foreign exchange, in amounts of $1 million and more, to another bank. The table heading also states at what time during the day the quotation was made because currency prices fluctuate throughout the day in response to changing supply and demand conditions. *The Wall Street Journal* customarily quotes the rates at the close of trading, 4 P.M. Eastern time. Next-day readers of the newspaper are thus offered the most recent currency prices. Retail foreign-exchange transactions, in amounts under $1 million, carry an additional service charge and are thus made at a different exchange rate.

An exchange rate determined by free-market forces can and does change frequently. When the dollar price of pounds increases, for example, from $2 = £1 to $2.10 = £1, the dollar has *depreciated* relative to the pound. Currency **depreciation** means that it takes more units of a nation's currency to purchase a unit of some foreign currency. Conversely, when the dollar price of pounds decreases, say, from $2 = £1 to $1.90 = £1, the value of the dollar has *appreciated* relative to the pound. Currency **appreciation** means that it takes fewer units of a nation's currency to purchase a unit of some foreign currency.

In the upper portion of Table 11.2, look at columns 2 and 3 (*U.S. dollar equivalent*). Going forward in time from Monday (March 8) to Tuesday (March 9), we see that the dollar cost of an Argentine peso increased from $.3411 to $.3439; the dollar thus depreciated against the peso. This means that the peso appreciated against the dollar. To verify this conclusion, refer to columns 4 and 5 of the table (*Currency per U.S. dollar*). Going forward in time from Monday to Tuesday, we see that the peso cost of the dollar decreased from 2.9317 pesos = $1 to 2.9078 pesos = $1. In similar fashion, we see that from Monday to Tuesday the dollar appreciated against Europe's euro from $1.2408 = 1 to $1.2314 = 1; the euro thus depreciated against the dollar, from .8059 = $1 to .8121 = $1.

Most tables of exchange-rate quotations express currency values relative to the U.S. dollar, regardless of the country where the quote is provided. Yet there are many instances in which the U.S. dollar is not part of a foreign-exchange transaction. In such cases, the people involved need to obtain an exchange quote

TABLE 11.2

Foreign-Exchange Quotations

Exchange Rates

March 9, 2004

The foreign exchange mid-range rates below apply to trading among banks in amounts of $1 million and more, as quoted at 4 p.m. Eastern time by Reuters and other sources. Retail transactions provide fewer units of foreign currency per dollar.

Country	U.S. $ EQUIVALENT		CURRENCY PER U.S. $	
	Tue	Mon	Tue	Mon
Argentina (Peso)-y	.3439	.3411	2.9078	2.9317
Australia (Dollar)	.7576	.7586	1.3200	1.3182
Bahrain (Dinar)	2.6526	2.6525	.3770	.3770
Brazil (Real)	.3465	.3474	2.8860	2.8785
Canada (Dollar)	.7554	.7583	1.3238	1.3187
1-month forward	.7545	.7574	1.3254	1.3203
3-months forward	.7531	.7561	1.3278	1.3226
6-months forward	.7513	.7542	1.3310	1.3259
Chile (Peso)	.001677	.001685	596.30	593.47
China (Renminbi)	.1208	.1208	8.2781	8.2781
Colombia (Peso)	.0003729	.0003730	2681.68	2680.97
Czech. Rep. (Koruna)				
Commercial rate	.03738	.03764	26.752	26.568
Denmark (Krone)	.1652	.1665	6.0533	6.0060
Ecuador (US Dollar)	1.0000	1.0000	1.0000	1.0000
Egypt (Pound)-y	.1616	.1616	6.1897	6.1897
Hong Kong (Dollar)	.1284	.1284	7.7882	7.7882
Hungary (Forint)	.004854	.004892	206.02	204.42
India (Rupee)	.02213	.02213	45.188	45.188
Indonesia (Rupiah)	.0001170	.0001165	8547	8584
Israel (Shekel)	.2223	.2222	4.4984	4.5005
Japan (Yen)	.008982	.008996	111.33	111.16
1-month forward	.008991	.009005	111.22	111.05
3-months forward	.009007	.009021	111.02	110.85
6-months forward	.009034	.009048	110.69	110.52
Jordan (Dinar)	1.4113	1.4113	.7086	.7086
Kuwait (Dinar)	3.3928	3.3937	.2947	.2947

Country	U.S. $ EQUIVALENT		CURRENCY PER U.S. $	
Lebanon (Pound)	.0006605	.0006605	1514.00	1514.00
Malaysia (Ringgit)-b	.2632	.2632	3.7994	3.7994
Malta (Lira)	2.8830	2.9056	.3469	.3442
Mexico (Peso)				
Floating rate	.0913	.0912	10.9505	10.9673
New Zealand (Dollar)	.6758	.6747	1.4797	1.4821
Norway (Krone)	.1432	.1433	6.9832	6.9784
Pakistan (Rupee)	.01748	.01748	57.208	57.208
Peru (new Sol)	.2885	.2884	3.4662	3.4674
Philippines (Peso)	.01777	.01777	56.275	56.275
Poland (Zloty)	.2597	.2586	3.8506	3.8670
Russia (Ruble)-a	.03503	.03503	28.547	28.547
Saudi Arabia (Riyal)	.2667	.2666	3.7495	3.7509
Singapore (Dollar)	.5855	.5863	1.7079	1.7056
Slovak Rep. (Koruna)	.03037	.03060	32.927	32.680
South Africa (Rand)	.1527	.1525	6.5488	6.5574
South Korea (Won)	.0008532	.0008522	1172.06	1173.43
Sweden (Krona)	.1344	.1356	7.4405	7.3746
Switzerland (Franc)	.7797	.7849	1.2825	1.2740
1-month forward	.7803	.7855	1.2816	1.2731
3-months forward	.7814	.7865	1.2798	1.2715
6-months forward	.7831	.7883	1.2770	1.2686
Taiwan (Dollar)	.03009	.03003	33.234	33.300
Thailand (Baht)	.02540	.02543	39.370	39.324
Turkey (Lira)	.00000076	.00000076	1315789	1315789
U.K. (Pound)	1.8250	1.8491	.5479	.5408
1-month forward	1.8200	1.8438	.5495	.5424
3-months forward	1.8107	1.8345	.5523	.5451
6-months forward	1.7953	1.8194	.5570	.5496
United Arab (Dirham)	.2722	.2723	3.6738	3.6724
Uruguay (Peso)				
Financial	.03390	.03390	29.499	29.499
Venezuela (Bolivar)	.000521	.000521	1919.39	1919.39
SDR	1.4740	1.4739	.6784	.6785
Euro	1.2314	1.2408	.8121	.8059

Special Drawing Rights (SDR) are based on exchange rates for the U.S., British, and Japanese currencies. Source: International Monetary Fund.

a-Russian Central Bank rate. b-Government rate. y-Floating rate.

Key Currency Cross Rates

Late New York Trading Tuesday, March 9, 2004

	Dollar	Euro	Pound	SFranc	Peso	Yen	CdnDlr
Canada	1.3238	1.6301	2.4159	1.0322	.12089	.01189	...
Japan	111.33	137.10	203.18	86.807	10.167	...	84.102
Mexico	10.9505	13.4845	19.985	8.5381	...	.09836	8.2720
Switzerland	1.2825	1.5793	2.3406	...	.11712	.01152	.9688
U.K.	.54790	.6747	...	.4272	.05004	.00492	.41392
Euro	.81210	...	1.4821	.63318	.07416	.00729	.61345
U.S.	...	1.2314	1.8250	.77970	.09132	.00898	.75540

between two nondollar currencies. As an example, if a British importer needs francs to purchase Swiss watches, the exchange rate of interest is the Swiss franc relative to the British pound. The exchange rate between any two currencies (such as the franc and the pound) can be derived from the rates of these two currencies in terms of a third currency (the dollar). The resulting rate is called the **cross exchange rate**.

Referring to the New York foreign-exchange market quotations in the upper portion of Table 11.2, we see that, as of Tuesday, the dollar value of the U.K. pound is $1.8250 and the dollar value of the Swiss franc is $0.7797. We can then calculate the value of the U.K. pound relative to the Swiss franc as follows:

$$\frac{\$ \text{ value of U.K. pound}}{\$ \text{ value of Swiss franc}} = \frac{\$1.8250}{\$0.7797} = 2.3406$$

Thus, each U.K. pound buys about 2.34 Swiss francs; this is the cross exchange rate between the pound and the franc. In similar fashion, cross exchange rates can be calculated between any other two nondollar currencies in Table 11.2.

The lower portion of Table 11.2 gives the cross exchange rates for several leading currencies. Here, to find the value of the U.K. pound relative to the Swiss franc, we simply locate the intersection of the pound column and the Switzerland row. The cross rate is given as 2.3406. In like manner, the cross exchange rates of other key currencies can be read directly from the table.

Forward and Futures Markets

Foreign exchange can be bought and sold for delivery immediately (the **spot market**) or for future delivery (the **forward market**). Forward contracts are normally made by those who will receive or make payment in foreign exchange in the weeks or months ahead. As seen in Table 11.2, the New York foreign-exchange market is a spot market for most currencies of the world. Regular forward markets, however, exist only for the more widely traded currencies. Exporters and importers, whose foreign-exchange receipts and payments are in the future, are the primary participants in the forward market. The forward quotations for currencies such as the British pound, Canadian dollar, Japanese yen, and Swiss franc are for delivery 1 month, 3 months, or 6 months from the date indicated in the table's caption (March 9, 2004).

Trading in foreign exchange can also be done in the **futures market**. In this market, contracting parties agree to future exchanges of currencies and set

applicable exchange rates in advance. The futures market is distinguished from the forward market in that only a limited number of leading currencies are traded; moreover, trading takes place in standardized contract amounts and in a specific geographic location. Table 11.3 on page 348 summarizes the major differences between the forward market and the futures market.

One such futures market is the **International Monetary Market (IMM)** of the Chicago Mercantile Exchange. Founded in 1972, the IMM is an extension of the commodity futures markets in which specific quantities of wheat, corn, and other commodities are bought and sold for future delivery at specific dates. The IMM provides trading facilities for the purchase and sale for future delivery of financial instruments (such as foreign currencies) and precious metals (such as gold). The IMM is especially popular with smaller banks and companies. Also, the IMM is one of the few places where individuals can speculate on changes in exchange rates.

Foreign-exchange trading on the IMM is limited to major currencies. Contracts are set for delivery on the third Wednesday of March, June, September, and December. Price quotations are in terms of U.S. dollars per unit of foreign currency, but futures contracts are for a fixed amount (for example, 62,500 British pounds).

Here is how to read the IMM's futures prices as listed in Table 11.4 on page 348.[3] The *size of each contract* is shown on the same line as the currency's name and country. For example, a contract for yen covers the right to purchase 12.5 million yen. Moving to the right of the size of the contract, we see the expression *$ per yen (.00)*, which shows the number of cents required to purchase one yen. The first column of the table shows the **maturity months** of the contract; using March as an example, the remaining columns yield the following information:

Open refers to the price at which yen was first sold when the IMM opened on the morning of March 9, 2004. Depending on overnight events in the world, the opening price may not be identical

[3]This section is adapted from R. Wurman and others, *The Wall Street Journal: Guide to Understanding Money and Markets* (New York: Simon and Schuster, Inc., 1990).

TABLE 11.3

Forward Contract Versus Futures Contract

	Forward Contract	Futures Contract
Issuer	Commercial bank	International Monetary Market (IMM) of the Chicago Mercantile Exchange and other foreign exchanges such as the Tokyo International Financial Futures Exchange
Trading	"Over the counter" by telephone	On the IMM's market floor
Contract size	Tailored to the needs of the exporter/importer/investor; no set size	Standardized in round lots
Date of delivery	Negotiable	Only on particular dates
Contract costs	Based on the bid/offer spread	Brokerage fees for sell and buy orders
Settlement	On expiration date only, at prearranged price	Profits or losses paid daily at close of trading

TABLE 11.4

Foreign Currency Futures, March 9, 2004: Selected Examples

	Open	High	Low	Settle	Change	Lifetime High	Lifetime Low	Open Interest
JAPAN YEN (CME)—12.5 million yen; $ per yen (0.00)								
Mar	.8986	.9080	.8960	.8991	+.0008	.9518	.8240	109,762
June	.9016	.9100	.8985	.9016	+.0008	.9542	.8496	49,665
Est vol 30,075 vol Mon 79,934; open int 159,521, +2,601								
CANADIAN DOLLAR (CME)—100,000 dlrs.; $ per Can $								
Mar	.7579	.7587	.7536	.7552	-.0013	.7863	.6150	45,456
June	.7555	.7566	.7513	.7531	-.0013	.7850	.6201	21,771
Sept	.7540	.7550	.7498	.7518	-.0013	.7815	.6505	2,145
Dec	.7486	.7540	.7486	.7505	-.0013	.7800	.6940	1,501
Mar05	.7520	.7525	.7485	.7492	-.0013	.7775	.7291	160
Est vol 17,930; vol Mon 36,833; open int 71,070, +4,753								
MEXICAN PESO (CME)—500,000 new Mex. peso; $ per MP								
Mar	.09087	.09125	.09087	.09115	.00010	.09330	.08600	32,287
June	.09000	.09020	.08975	.09007	.00012	.09125	.08495	16,549
Sept	.08890	.08890	.08890	.08892	.00012	.08935	.08600	276
Est vol 18,548; vol Mon 22,586; open int 49,840, +3,593								

Source: *The Wall Street Journal*, March 10, 2004, p. C14.

to the closing price from the previous trading day. Because prices are expressed in terms of cents per yen, the .8986 implies that yen opened for sale at .8986 cents per yen. Multiply this price by the size of a contract and you've calculated the full value of one contract at the open of trading for that day: .8986 cents × 12.5 million = $112,325.

The *high*, *low*, and *settle* columns indicate the contract's highest, lowest, and closing prices for the day. Viewed together, these figures provide an indication of how volatile the market for the yen was during the day. After opening at .8986 cents per yen, yen for March delivery never sold for more than .9080 cents per yen and never for less than .8960 cents per yen; trading finally settled, or ended, at .8991 cents per yen. Multiplying the size of the yen contract times the yen's settlement price gives the full value of a yen contract at the closing of the trading day: .8991 cents × 12.5 million = $112,388.

Change compares today's closing price with the closing price as listed in the previous day's paper. A plus (+) sign means prices ended higher; a minus (−) means prices ended lower. In the yen's case, the yen for March delivery settled .0008 cents higher than it did the previous trading day.

Lifetime high and *low* show the volatility that has occurred in the trading of this particular contract—an indication of risk and reward.

Open interest refers to the total number of contracts outstanding; that is, those that have not been canceled by offsetting trades. It shows how much interest there is in trading a particular contract. The months closest to March 9 generally attract the most trading activity.

The last line of Table 11.4 gives information concerning the estimated volume of trading on the current day, the actual volume on the previous trading day, the current number of contracts (open interest) across all maturity dates for this currency, and the change in the number of contracts since the previous trading day.

Foreign-Currency Options

During the 1980s, a new feature of the foreign-exchange market was developed: the option market. An **option** is simply an agreement between a holder (buyer) and a writer (seller) that gives the holder the *right*, but not the obligation, to buy or sell financial instruments at any time through a specified date. Although the holder is not obligated to buy or sell currency, the writer is obligated to fulfill a transaction. Having a throwaway feature, options are a unique type of financial contract in that you only use the contract if you want to. By contrast, forward contracts *obligate* a person to carry out a transaction at a specified price, even if the market has changed and the person would rather not.

Foreign-currency options provide an options holder the right to buy or sell a fixed amount of foreign currency at a prearranged price, within a few days or a couple of years. The options holder can choose the exchange rate she wants to guarantee, as well as the length of the contract. Foreign-currency options have been used by companies seeking to hedge against exchange-rate risk as well as by speculators in foreign currencies.

There are two types of foreign currency options. A **call option** gives the holder the right to *buy* foreign currency at a specified price, whereas a **put option** gives the holder the right to *sell* foreign currency at a specified price. The price at which the option can be exercised (that is, the price at which the foreign currency is bought or sold) is called the **strike price**. The holder of a foreign-currency option has the right to exercise the contract but may choose not to do so if it turns out to be unprofitable. The writer of the options contract (for example, Bank of America, Citibank, Merrill Lynch International Bank) must deliver the foreign currency if called on by a call-holder or must buy foreign currency if it is put to them by a put-holder. For this obligation, the writer of the options contract receives a *premium*, or fee (the option price). Financial institutions have been willing to write foreign-currency options because they generate substantial premium income (the fee income on a $5 million deal can run $100,000 or more). However, writing currency options is a risky business because the writer takes chances on tricky pricing. Foreign-currency options are traded in a variety of currencies in Europe and the United

States. *The Wall Street Journal* publishes daily listings of foreign currency options contracts, as seen in Table 11.5. The table shows quotes for calls and puts as well as the strike price on the option. It is left for more advanced textbooks to discuss the mechanics of trading foreign-currency options.

To see how exporters can use foreign-currency options to cope with exchange-rate risk, consider the case of Boeing, which submits a bid for the sale of jet planes to an airline company in Japan. Boeing must deal not only with the uncertainty of winning the bid but also with exchange-rate risk. If Boeing wins the bid, it will receive yen in the future. But what if the yen depreciates in the interim, from, say, 115 yen = $1 to 120 yen = $1? Boeing's yen holdings would convert into fewer dollars, thus eroding the profitability of the jet sale. Because Boeing wants to sell yen in exchange for dollars, it can offset this exchange-market risk by purchasing put options that give the company the right to sell yen for dollars at a specified price. Having obtained a put option, if Boeing wins the bid it has limited the exchange-rate risk. On the other hand, if the bid is lost, Boeing's losses are limited to the cost of the option. Foreign-currency options thus provide a worst-case rate of exchange for companies conducting international business. The maximum amount the company can lose by

covering its exchange-rate risk is the amount of the option price.

Exchange-Rate Determination

What determines the equilibrium exchange rate in a free market? Let us consider the exchange rate from the perspective of the United States—in dollars per unit of foreign currency. Like other prices, the exchange rate in a free market is determined by both supply and demand conditions.

Demand for Foreign Exchange

A nation's *demand for foreign exchange* is derived from, or corresponds to, the *debit* items on its balance of payments. For example, the U.S. demand for pounds may stem from its desire to import British goods and services, to make investments in Britain, or to make transfer payments to residents in Britain.

Like most demand schedules, the U.S. demand for pounds varies inversely with its price; that is, fewer pounds are demanded at higher prices than at lower prices. This relationship is depicted by line D_0 in Figure 11.2. As the dollar depreciates against the pound (the dollar price of the pound rises), British goods and services become more expensive to U.S. importers. This is because more dollars are required to purchase each pound needed to finance the import purchases. The higher exchange rate reduces the number of imports bought, lowering the number of pounds demanded by U.S. residents. In like manner, an appreciation of the U.S. dollar relative to the pound would be expected to induce larger import purchases and more pounds demanded by U.S. residents.

Supply of Foreign Exchange

The *supply of foreign exchange* refers to the amount of foreign exchange that will be offered to the market at various exchange rates, all other factors held constant. The supply of pounds, for example, is generated by the desire of British residents and businesses to import U.S. goods and services, to lend funds and make investments in the United States, to repay debts owed to U.S. lenders, and to extend transfer payments to U.S. residents.

TABLE 11.5

Futures Options Prices of the Euro, March 9, 2004: Chicago Mercantile Exchange

Euro (CME)

125,000 euros; cents per euro

Strike Price	Calls-Settle			Puts-Settle		
	Mar	Apr	May	Mar	Apr	May
9825	6.37	......	......	0.00	0.00	......
9850	3.87	3.27	......	0.00	0.02	0.05
9875	1.37	0.08	1.00	0.00	0.12	0.25
9900	0.00	0.02	0.05	1.12	......	......
9925	0.00	......	......	3.62	......	......
9950	0.00	......	......	6.12	......	......

Est vol 348,562
Mn vol 266,075 calls 153,340 puts
Op int Mon 4,611,989 calls 5,075,525 puts

Source: *The Wall Street Journal*, March 10, 2004, p. C14.

FIGURE 11.2

Exchange-Rate Determination

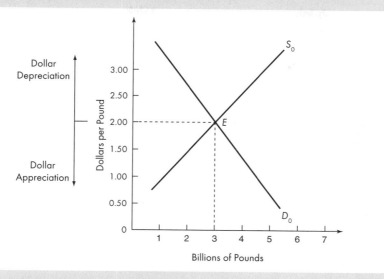

The equilibrium exchange rate is established at the point of intersection of the supply and demand schedules of foreign exchange. The demand for foreign exchange corresponds to the debit items on a nation's balance-of-payments statement; the supply of foreign exchange corresponds to the credit items.

In each of these cases, the British offer pounds in the foreign-exchange market to obtain the dollars they need to make payments to U.S. residents. Note that the supply of pounds results from transactions that appear on the *credit* side of the U.S. balance of payments; thus, one can make a connection between the balance of payments and the foreign-exchange market.

The supply of pounds is denoted by schedule S_0 in Figure 11.2. The schedule represents the number of pounds offered by the British to obtain dollars with which to buy U.S. goods, services, and assets. It is depicted in the figure as a positive function of the U.S. exchange rate. As the dollar depreciates against the pound (dollar price of the pound rises), the British will be inclined to buy more U.S. goods. The reason, of course, is that at higher and higher dollar prices of pounds, the British can get more U.S. dollars and hence more U.S. goods per

British pound. U.S. goods thus become cheaper to the British, who are induced to purchase additional quantities. As a result, more pounds are offered in the foreign-exchange market to buy dollars with which to pay U.S. exporters.

Equilibrium Rate of Exchange

As long as monetary authorities do not attempt to stabilize exchange rates or moderate their movements, the *equilibrium exchange rate* is determined by the market forces of supply and demand. In Figure 11.2, exchange-market equilibrium occurs at point E, where S_0 and D_0 intersect. Three billion pounds will be traded at a price of $2 per pound. The foreign-exchange market is precisely cleared, leaving neither an excess supply nor an excess demand for pounds.

Given the supply and demand schedules of Figure 11.2, there is no reason for the exchange rate

Globalization

Weak Dollar Is Bonanza for European Tourists

Jackie Murphy held up a white pair of jogging shoes for her husband, Edward, to examine in a Nike store aisle piled high with boxes of shoes. She smiled when she saw the price tag.

"They're only $55!" said Murphy, a tourist from London, England. "Do you like them? Try them on."

Although Murphy is an experienced shopper—it is one of her favorite pastimes back home—she was shocked at her purchasing power on a vacation to Orlando in 2004. The power came primarily from a currency exchange rate that had the British pound approaching twice the value of the U.S. dollar. "The exchange rate is fantastic," said Edward Murphy, who sells electronics in London. "We couldn't have timed it better to come over on our vacation." In 2004, the dollar reached a record low against the euro and an 11-year low against the pound.

Many European and Canadian visitors followed the Murphy example, in part because of the inexpensive U.S. dollar. The American tourist industry was delighted about this situation. Because of the cheaper dollar, tourists could afford to stay longer, stay at nicer and more expensive hotels, take more tours, eat at more restaurants, and shop with bargain-basement enthusiasm. Adding to the bonanza for Europeans, air fares to and from the United States declined.

For example, the cheap dollar encouraged 15-year-old Molly Sanders of Liverpool, England, to purchase six heavy-metal T-shirts during a visit to Orlando, and her parents decided they could afford a road trip to Miami. The family booked hotel reservations and purchased theme-park tickets in the United States rather than in Britain. By obtaining the tickets in dollars instead of pounds, they saved about $21 each day they went to the parks.

The exchange rate also led the British travel firm Virgin Holidays to renegotiate prices with the U.S. car rental companies and hotels that it uses. The new prices permitted the firm in 2004 to offer a package of airfare to Orlando, seven night' accommodations, and rental car for 399 pounds, or 130 pounds less than what it previously offered. At the prevailing exchange rate, the discounted price was equal to $718, for about $234 in savings.

Source: "Coming to America: Exchange Rate Attracts Foreign Visitors," *Yakima Herald Republic*, March 18, 2004, p. 6-A.

to deviate from the equilibrium level. But in practice, it is unlikely that the equilibrium exchange rate will remain very long at the existing level. This is because the forces that underlie the location of the supply and demand schedules tend to change over time, causing shifts in the schedules. Should the *demand* for pounds shift *rightward* (an increase in demand), the dollar will *depreciate* against the pound; *leftward* shifts in the demand for pounds (a decrease in demand) cause the dollar to *appreciate*. Conversely, a *rightward* shift in the *supply* of pounds (increase in supply) causes the dollar to *appreciate* against the pound; a *leftward* shift in the supply of pounds (decrease in supply) results in a *depreciation* of the dollar. What causes shifts in these schedules? This topic will be considered in Chapter 12.

Is a Strong Dollar Always Good and a Weak Dollar Always Bad?

Is a strong (appreciating) dollar always good and a weak (depreciating) dollar always bad? A strengthening or weakening dollar can affect many parties, among them consumers, tourists, investors, exporters, and importers. Table 11.6 summarizes these effects.

Consider also the effects of the fluctuating dollar on U.S. firms during the 1990s.[4] In 1995, the U.S. dollar's exchange value depreciated, especially against the Japanese yen. This meant that more dollars were needed to purchase the yen; as a result,

[4]"U.S. Importers Take on the Dollar's Fall," *The Wall Street Journal*, April 17, 1995, p. A2, and "Strong Dollar Creates Winners and Losers," *The Wall Street Journal*, February 6, 1997, p. A2.

TABLE 11.6

Advantages and Disadvantages of a Strengthening and Weakening Dollar

Strengthening (Appreciating) Dollar

Advantages	Disadvantages
1. U.S. consumers see lower prices on foreign goods.	1. U.S. exporting firms find it harder to compete in foreign markets.
2. Lower prices on foreign goods help keep U.S. inflation low.	2. U.S. firms in import-competing markets find it harder to compete with lower-priced foreign goods.
3. U.S. consumers benefit when they travel to foreign countries.	3. Foreign tourists find it more expensive to visit the United States.

Weakening (Depreciating) Dollar

Advantages	Disadvantages
1. U.S. exporting firms find it easier to sell goods in foreign markets.	1. U.S. consumers face higher prices on foreign goods.
2. Firms in the United States have less competitive pressure to keep prices low.	2. Higher prices on foreign goods contribute to higher inflation in the United States.
3. More foreign tourists can afford to visit the United States.	3. U.S. consumers find traveling abroad more costly.

goods imported by U.S. companies became more expensive. How did U.S. importers adjust to the dollar depreciation? Consider the following cases:

High Sierra Sport Co., a Leather-Goods Manufacturer in Illinois

As the dollar's exchange value plunged, faxes poured in from its Asian suppliers informing it of price hikes; one indicated nylon prices were going up, the next indicated zipper costs were increasing. When the firm decided to launch two new lines of handbags, Taiwanese and Korean suppliers warned it of pending increases in fabric prices. High Sierra's solution: Raise the prices of leather goods rather than absorb the higher cost of imported inputs.

Trek Bicycle Inc., a Bike Manufacturer in Wisconsin

This company manufactured bikes and also imported bikes made to its design from Taiwanese

manufacturers. In both cases, from 30 percent to 50 percent of the bike components came from Japanese suppliers. Trek paid its Taiwanese bike suppliers in dollars, but these firms had to purchase Japanese components with yen. As the dollar started depreciating, Trek was initially protected because the Taiwanese were absorbing the currency variance. As negotiations for the next year's models proceeded, however, the prices of Taiwanese bikes went up. To reduce the foreign content of its bikes, Trek announced plans to build a second Wisconsin factory.

During 1996–2002, the dollar was appreciating on the foreign-exchange markets. This resulted in U.S. Treasury Secretary Robert Rubin declaring, "A strong dollar is in America's interest." The question is, which America was he talking about? As seen in the next two examples, not all Americans benefited from the rising dollar.

Computer Network Technology Inc., a Producer of Network Systems in Minnesota

The dollar's climb in 1997 resulted in rising costs of its network systems to Japan. The systems produced by European firms thus became more competitive in the Japanese market. As a result, Computer Network Technology's sales fell and its earnings dropped by $100,000.

Sony Computer Entertainment, a U.S.–Based Unit of Sony Corp

As the dollar steadily soared against the yen, many U.S.–based subsidiaries of Japanese companies questioned whether they should pack up and head home. For example, Sony Computer Entertainment Inc., seeking to capitalize on the appreciation of the dollar against the yen, announced that it would halt production of its PlayStation home-video game in the United States and shift it back to Japan.

Indexes of the Foreign-Exchange Value of the Dollar: Nominal and Real Exchange Rates

Since 1973, the value of the U.S. dollar in terms of foreign currencies has changed daily. In this environment of market-determined exchange rates, measuring the international value of the dollar is a confusing task. Financial pages of newspapers may be headlining a *depreciation* of the dollar relative to some currencies, while at the same time reporting its *appreciation* relative to others. Such events may leave the general public confused as to the actual value of the dollar.

Suppose the U.S. dollar appreciates 10 percent relative to the yen and depreciates 5 percent against the pound. The change in the dollar's exchange value is some weighted average of the changes in these two bilateral exchange rates. Throughout the day, the value of the dollar may change relative to the values of any number of currencies under market-determined exchange rates. Direct comparison of the dollar's exchange rate over time thus requires a *weighted average* of all the bilateral changes. This

average is referred to as the dollar's **exchange-rate index**; it is also known as the **effective exchange rate** or the **trade-weighted dollar**.

The exchange-rate index is a weighted average of the exchange rates between the domestic currency and the nation's most important trading partners, with weights given by relative importance of the nation's trade with each of these trade partners. One popular index of exchange rates is the so-called "major currency index," which is constructed by the U.S. Federal Reserve Board of Governors. This index reflects the impact of changes in the dollar's exchange rate on U.S. exports and imports with seven major trading partners of the United States. The base period of the index is March 1973.

Table 11.7 illustrates the **nominal exchange-rate index** of the U.S. dollar. This is the average value of the dollar, not adjusted for changes in prices levels of the United States and its trading partners. An *increase* in the nominal exchange-rate index (from year to year) indicates a dollar *appreciation* relative to the currencies of the other nations in the index and a *loss* of competitiveness for the United States. Conversely, a *decrease* in the nominal exchange rate implies a dollar *depreciation* relative to the other currencies in the index and an *improvement* in U.S. international competitiveness. Simply put, the nominal exchange-rate index is based on **nominal exchange rates**—those published in *The Wall Street Journal*— which do not reflect changes in price levels in trading partners.

However, a problem arises when interpreting changes in the nominal exchange-rate index when prices are not constant. When prices of goods and services are changing in either the United States or a partner country (or both), one does not know the change in the relative price of foreign goods and services by simply looking at changes in the nominal exchange rate and failing to consider the new level of prices within both countries. For example, if the dollar appreciated against the peso by 5 percent, we would expect that, other things constant, U.S. goods would be 5 percent less competitive against Mexican goods in world markets than was previously the case. However, suppose that, at the same time that the dollar appreciated, U.S. goods prices increased more rapidly than Mexican goods prices.

TABLE 11.7

Exchange Rate Indexes of the U.S. Dollar (March 1973 = 100)*

Year	Nominal Exchange-Rate Index	Real Exchange-Rate Index
1973 (March)	100.0	100.0
1980	87.4	91.3
1982	116.6	109.0
1984	138.3	117.7
1986	112.0	99.2
1988	92.7	83.5
1990	89.1	84.7
1992	86.6	81.8
1994	91.3	84.0
1996	87.4	85.3
1998	95.8	97.7
2000	98.3	103.1
2002	102.9	110.9
2003	88.6	94.6

*The "major currency index" includes the following nations and their trade weights with the United States: Canada, 30.3 percent; Euro area, 28.7 percent; Japan, 25.6 percent; United Kingdom, 8.0 percent; Switzerland, 3.2 percent; Australia, 2.6 percent; Sweden, 1.6 percent.

Source: "New Summary Measures of the Foreign-Exchange Value of the Dollar, *Federal Reserve Bulletin*, October 1998, pp. 811–818. See also *Federal Reserve Bulletin*, various issues.

In this situation, the decrease in U.S. competitiveness against Mexican goods would be more than 5 percent, and the nominal 5 percent exchange rate change would be misleading. Put simply, overall international competitiveness of U.S. manufactured goods depends not on the behavior of nominal exchange rates, but on movements in nominal exchange rates relative to prices.

As a result, economists calculate the **real exchange rate**, which embodies the changes in prices in the countries in the calculation. Simply put, the real exchange rate is the nominal exchange rate adjusted for relative price levels. To calculate the real exchange rate, we use the following formula:

$$\text{Real exchange rate} = \text{Nominal exchange rate} \times \frac{\text{Foreign country's price level}}{\text{(Home country's price level)}}$$

where both the nominal exchange rate and real exchange rate are measured in units of domestic currency per unit of foreign currency.

To illustrate, suppose that in 2002 the nominal exchange rate for the United States and Europe is 90 cents per euro; by 2004, the nominal exchange rate falls to 80 cents per euro. This is an 11 percent appreciation of the dollar against the euro [(90 − 80)/90 = .11)], leading one to expect a substantial drop in competitiveness of U.S. goods relative to European goods. To calculate the real exchange rate, we must look at prices. Let us assume that the base year is 2002, at which consumer prices are set equal to 100. By 2004, however, U.S. consumer prices increase to a level of 108 while European consumer prices increase to a level of 102. The real exchange rate would then be calculated as follows:

$$\text{Real exchange rate}_{2004} = (80 \text{ cents} \times 102/108)$$
$$= 75.6 \text{ cents per euro}$$

In this example, the real exchange rate indicates that U.S. goods are *less* competitive on international markets than would be suggested by the nominal exchange rate. This result occurs because the dollar appreciates in nominal terms *and* U.S. prices increase *more* rapidly than European prices. In real terms, the dollar appreciates not by 11 percent (as with the nominal exchange rate) but by 16 percent [(75.6 − 90)/90 = .16]. Simply put, for variations in the exchange rate to have an effect on the composition of U.S. output, output growth, employment, and trade, there must be a change in the real exchange rate. That is, the change in the nominal exchange rate must alter the amount of goods and services that the dollar buys in foreign countries. Real exchange rates offer such a comparison and, therefore, provide a better gauge of international competitiveness than nominal exchange rates.

In addition to constructing a nominal exchange rate index, economists construct a real exchange rate index for a broad sample of U.S. trading partners. Table 11.7 also shows the **real exchange rate index** of the U.S. dollar. This is the average value of the dollar based on real exchange rates. The index is constructed so that an appreciation of the dollar corresponds to higher index values. The importance that monetary authorities attach to the real exchange-rate index stems from economic theory, which states that a rise in the real exchange rate will tend to reduce the international competitiveness of U.S. firms; conversely, a fall in the real exchange rate tends to increase the international competitiveness of U.S. firms.[5]

Arbitrage

We have seen how the supply and demand for foreign exchange can set the market exchange rate. This analysis was from the perspective of the U.S. (New York) foreign-exchange market. But what about the relationship between the exchange rate in the U.S. market and that in other nations? When restrictions do not modify the ability of the foreign-exchange market to operate efficiently, normal market forces result in a consistent relationship among the market exchange rates of all currencies.

That is to say, if £1 = $2 in New York, then $1 = £0.5 in London. The prices for the same currency in different world locations will be identical.

The factor underlying the consistency of the exchange rates is called **exchange arbitrage**. Exchange arbitrage refers to the *simultaneous* purchase and sale of a currency in different foreign-exchange markets in order to profit from exchange-rate differentials in the two locations. This process brings about an identical price for the same currency in different locations and thus results in one market.

Suppose that the dollar/pound exchange rate is £1 = $2 in New York but £1 = $2.01 in London. Foreign-exchange traders would find it profitable to purchase pounds in New York at $2 per pound and immediately resell them in London for $2.01. A profit of 1 cent would be made on each pound sold, less the cost of the bank transfer and the interest charge on the money tied up during the arbitrage process. This return may appear to be insignificant, but on a $1 million arbitrage transaction it would generate a profit of approximately $5,000—not bad for a few minutes' work! As the demand for pounds increases in New York, the dollar price of a pound will rise above $2; as the supply of pounds increases in London, the dollar price of the pound will fall below $2.01. This arbitrage process will continue until the exchange rate between the dollar and the pound in New York is approximately the same as it is in London. Arbitrage between the two currencies thus unifies the foreign-exchange markets.

The preceding example illustrates **two-point arbitrage**, in which two currencies are traded between two financial centers. A more intricate form of arbitrage, involving three currencies and three financial centers, is known as **three-point arbitrage**, or triangular arbitrage. Three-point arbitrage involves switching funds among three currencies in order to profit from exchange-rate inconsistencies, as seen in the following example.

Consider three currencies—the U.S. dollar, the Swiss franc, and the British pound, all of which are traded in New York, Geneva, and London. Assume that the rates of exchange that prevail in all three financial centers are as follows: (1) £1 = $1.50; (2) £1 = 4 francs; (3) 1 franc = $0.50. Because the same exchange rates (prices) prevail in all three

[5]For discussions of the nominal and real exchange-rate indexes see "New Summary Measures of the Foreign-Exchange Value of the Dollar," *Federal Reserve Bulletin*, October 1998, pp. 811–818, and "Real Exchange Rate Indexes for the Canadian Dollar," *Bank of Canada Review*, Autumn, 1999, pp. 19–28.

financial centers, two-point arbitrage is not profitable. However, these quoted exchange rates are mutually inconsistent. Thus, an arbitrager with $1.5 million could make a profit as follows:

1. Sell $1.5 million for £1 million.
2. Simultaneously, sell £1 million for 4 million francs.
3. At the same time, sell 4 million francs for $2 million.

The arbitrager has just made a risk-free profit of $500,000 ($2 million – $1.5 million) before transaction costs!

These transactions tend to cause shifts in all three exchange rates that bring them into proper alignment and eliminate the profitability of arbitrage. From a practical standpoint, opportunities for such profitable currency arbitrage have decreased in recent years, given the large number of currency traders—aided by sophisticated computer information systems—who monitor currency quotes in all financial markets. The result of this activity is that currency exchange rates tend to be consistent throughout the world, with only minimal deviations due to transaction costs.

The Forward Market

Foreign-exchange markets, as we have seen, may be spot or forward. In the *spot market*, currencies are bought and sold for immediate delivery (generally, two business days after the conclusion of the deal). In the *forward market*, currencies are bought and sold now for future delivery, typically 1 month, 3 months, or 6 months from the date of the transaction. The exchange rate is agreed on at the time of the contract, but payment is not made until the future delivery actually takes place. Only the most widely traded currencies are included in the regular forward market, but individual forward contracts can be negotiated for most national currencies.

The Forward Rate

The rate of exchange used in the settlement of forward transactions is called the **forward rate**. This rate is quoted in the same way as the spot rate: the price of one currency in terms of another currency. Table 11.8 provides examples of forward rates as of March 9, 2004. Thus, under the Tuesday quotations, the selling price of 1-month forward U.K. pounds is $1.8200 per pound; the selling price of 3-month forward pounds is $1.8107 per pound, and for 6-month forward pounds it is $1.7953 per pound.

It is customary for a currency's forward rate to be stated in relation to its spot rate. When a foreign currency is worth more in the forward market than in the spot market, it is said to be at a **premium**; conversely, when the currency is worth less in the forward market than in the spot market, it is said to be at a **discount**. The per annum percentage premium (discount) in forward quotations is computed by the following formula:

$$\text{Premium (discount)} = \frac{\text{Forward rate} - \text{Spot rate}}{\text{Spot rate}} \times \frac{12}{\text{No. of months forward}}$$

TABLE 11.8

Forward Exchange Rates: Selected Examples

EXCHANGE RATES
Tuesday, March 9, 2004

The New York foreign-exchange mid-range rates below apply to trading among banks in amounts of $1 million and more, as quoted at 4 P.M. Eastern time by Reuters and other sources. Retail transactions provide fewer units of foreign currency per dollar.

Country	U.S. $ equiv.		Currency per U.S.$	
	Tue	Mon	Tue	Mon
Canada (Dollar)	.7554	.7583	1.3238	1.3187
1-month forward	.7545	.7574	1.3254	1.3203
3-months forward	.7531	.7561	1.3278	1.3226
6-months forward	.7513	.7542	1.3310	1.3259
Japan (Yen)	.008982	.008996	111.33	111.16
1-month forward	.008991	.009005	111.22	111.05
3-months forward	.009007	.009021	111.02	110.85
6-months forward	.009034	.009048	110.69	110.52
Switzerland (Franc)	.7797	.7849	1.2825	1.2740
1-month forward	.7803	.7855	1.2816	1.2731
3-months forward	.7814	.7865	1.2798	1.2715
6-months forward	.7831	.7883	1.2770	1.2686
U.K. (Pound)	1.8250	1.8491	.5479	.5408
1-month forward	1.8200	1.8438	.5495	.5424
3-months forward	1.8107	1.8345	.5523	.5451
6- months forward	1.7953	1.8194	.5570	.5496

Source: Data taken from *The Wall Street Journal*, March 10, 2004, p. C14.

If the result is a negative forward premium, it means that the currency is at a forward discount.

According to Table 11.8, on Tuesday the 1-month forward Swiss franc was selling at $0.7803, whereas the spot price of the franc was $0.7797. Because the forward price of the franc exceeded the spot price, the franc was at a 1-month forward premium of 0.06 cents, or at a 0.92 percent forward premium per annum against the dollar:

$$\text{Premium} = \frac{\$0.7803 - \$0.7797}{\$0.7797} \times \frac{12}{1} = .0092$$

Similarly, the franc was at a 3-month premium of 0.17 cents, or at a 0.87 percent forward premium per annum against the dollar:

$$\text{Premium} = \frac{\$0.7814 - \$0.7797}{\$0.7797} \times \frac{12}{3} = 0.0087$$

As for the British pound, the 6-month forward pound was at a discount of 3.25 percent per annum against the dollar:

$$\text{Discount} = \frac{\$1.7953 - \$1.8250}{\$1.8250} \times \frac{12}{6} = -0.0325$$

Forward Rate Differs from the Spot Rate

What determines the forward rate? Why might it be at a premium or discount compared to the spot rate? The reason is that forward rates are strictly a mathematical calculation based on interest-rate differentials between countries. When a country's interest rates are *higher* than those of the United States, its currency tends to be at a forward *discount* in terms of the dollar; when a country's interest rates are *lower* than those of the United States, its currency tends to be at a forward *premium*.

To illustrate, suppose that the interest rate is 8 percent in New York and 3 percent in Zurich. Also assume that both the spot and forward exchange rates equal $.50 per franc. In this situation, a Swiss investor will obviously send his funds to New York. However, other investors will realize this opportunity and move their funds to New York as well. In the process, investors will sell francs on the spot market and buy them on the forward market; the francs purchased on the forward market eventually will return to Switzerland when the investment is liquidated. This will decrease the franc on the spot market to say, $.49 per franc, or by 2 percent. However, on the forward market, the franc will increase to $.515 per franc, or by 3 percent. Therefore, the franc will move to a 5 percent forward premium and the funds will not move between financial centers. The interest rate differential in favor of New York, 5 percent, will be exactly offset by the 5 percent forward premium on the franc. We conclude that when a country's interest rates are *lower* than those of the United States, its currency tends to be at a forward *premium*. This topic will be further examined later in this chapter.

Forward Market Functions

The forward market can be used to protect international traders and investors from the risks involved in fluctuations of the spot rate. The process of avoiding or covering a foreign-exchange risk is known as **hedging**. People who expect to make or receive payments in a foreign currency at a future date are concerned that if the spot rate changes, they will have to make a greater payment or will receive less in terms of the domestic currency than expected. This could wipe out anticipated profit levels.

In 1997, many Asian companies lost large sums when Asian currencies sharply depreciated against the U.S. dollar. For example, Siam Cement PCL, a chemicals giant in Thailand, was forced to absorb an extraordinary loss of $517 million in the third quarter of 1997. The company had $4.2 billion in foreign borrowing, and none of it was hedged. The foreign-exchange loss wiped out all of the profits that Siam Cement had chalked up between 1994 and 1996! Prior to 1997, few Asian economies bothered to hedge their foreign-exchange risks because most Asian currencies were tied to the dollar. The ties were broken, however, as a result of the Asian financial crises of 1997, and this caught many Asian managers by surprise; they were unprepared for the adverse effects of volatile currencies.

How can firms and investors insulate themselves from volatile currency values? They can deal in the forward market, as shown in the following examples.

Case 1:

U.S. importer hedges against a dollar depreciation.
Assume Sears Roebuck and Co. owes 1 million francs to a Swiss watch manufacturer in three month's time. During this period, Sears is in an exposed or *uncovered* position. Sears bears the risk that the dollar price of the franc might rise in three months (the dollar might depreciate against the franc), say, from $0.60 to $0.70 per franc; if so, purchasing 1 million francs would require an extra $100,000.

To cover itself against this risk, Sears could immediately buy 1 million francs in the spot market, but this would immobilize its funds for three months. Alternatively, Sears could contract to purchase 1 million francs in the forward market, at today's forward rate, for delivery in three months. In three months, Sears would purchase francs with dollars, at the contracted price and use the francs to pay the Swiss exporter. Sears has thus hedged against the possibility that francs will be more expensive than anticipated in three months. Note that hedging in the forward market does not require Sears to tie up its own funds when it purchases the forward contract. However, the contract is an obligation that can affect the company's credit. Sears' bank will want to be sure that it has an adequate balance or credit line so that it will be able to pay the necessary amount in three months.

Case 2:

U.S. exporter hedges against a dollar appreciation.
Assume that Microsoft Corporation anticipates receiving 1 million francs in three months from its exports of computer software to a Swiss retailer. During this period, Microsoft is in an *uncovered* position. If the dollar price of the franc falls (the dollar appreciates against the franc), say, from $0.50 to $0.40 per franc, Microsoft's receipts will be worth $100,000 less when the 1 million francs are converted into dollars.

To avoid this foreign-exchange risk, Microsoft can contract to sell its expected franc receipts in the forward market at today's forward rate. By locking into a set forward-exchange rate, Microsoft is guaranteed that the value of its franc receipts will be maintained in terms of the dollar, even if the value of the franc should happen to fall.

The forward market thus eliminates the uncertainty of fluctuating spot rates from international transactions. Exporters can hedge against the possibility that the domestic currency will appreciate against the foreign currency, and importers can hedge against the possibility that the domestic currency will depreciate against the foreign currency. Hedging is not limited to exporters and importers. It applies to anyone who is obligated to make a foreign-currency payment or who will enjoy foreign-currency receipts at a future time. International investors, for example, also make use of the forward market for hedging purposes.

As our examples indicate, importers and exporters participate in the forward market to avoid the risk of fluctuations in foreign-exchange rates. Because they make forward transactions mainly through commercial banks, the foreign-exchange risk is transferred to those banks. Commercial banks can minimize foreign-exchange risk by matching forward purchases from exporters with forward sales to importers. However, because the supply of and demand for forward currency transactions by exporters and importers usually do not coincide, the banks may assume some of the risk.

Suppose that on a given day, a commercial bank's forward purchases do not match its forward sales for a given currency. The bank may then seek out other banks in the market that have offsetting positions. Thus, if Chase Manhattan Bank has an excess of 50-million euro forward purchases over forward sales during the day, it will attempt to find another bank (or banks) that has an excess of forward sales over purchases. These banks can then enter forward contracts among themselves to eliminate any residual exchange risk that might exist.

How Markel Rides Foreign-Exchange Fluctuations

To corporate giants such as General Electric and Ford Motor Company, currency fluctuations are a fact of life of global production. But for tiny companies such as Markel Corporation, swings in the world currency market have major implications for its bottom line.[6]

[6]Drawn from "Ship Those Boxes: Check the Euro," *The Wall Street Journal*, February 7, 2003, p. C1.

Markel Corporation is a family-owned tubing maker located in Plymouth Meeting, Pennsylvania. Its tubing and insulated lead wire are used in the appliance, automotive, and water-purification industries. About 40 percent of Markel's $26 million in sales in 2003 were exported, mostly to Europe.

To shield itself from fluctuations in exchange rates, Markel uses a 4-part business model: Charge customers relatively stable prices in their own currencies to establish overseas market share; use forward currency markets to foster revenue stability over the next few months; cut costs and improve efficiency to make it through the times when currency trading turns unprofitable; and roll the dice and hope things turn out favorably.

Markel's executives believe that their strategy of setting their prices in foreign currencies, mainly the euro, has helped the firm attain 70 percent of the world market in high-performance, Teflon-based cable-control liners, tubes that allow car accelerator or shift mechanisms to move smoothly. But it also implies that Markel signs contracts that result in the delivery of heaps of euros months or even years down the road, when the value of those euros in dollars may be much less than it was at signing.

To reduce the uncertainty over the period of a few months, Markel purchases forward contracts through PNC Financial Services Group in Pittsburgh. Markel promises the bank, say, 50,000 euros in three months, and the bank guarantees a certain number of dollars no matter what happens to the exchange rate. When Markel's chief financial officer thinks the dollar is about to appreciate against the euro, she might hedge her entire expected euro revenue stream with a forward contract. When she thinks the dollar is going to depreciate, she will hedge perhaps half and take a chance that she will make more dollars by remaining exposed to currency fluctuations.

However, she doesn't always guess right. In April 2003, for example, Markel had to provide PNC with 50,000 euros from a contract the company purchased three months earlier. The bank paid $1.05 per euro, or $52,500. Had Markel waited, it could have sold at the going rate, $1.08, and made an additional $1,500.

To make matters worse, Markel reached an export deal with a German manufacturer in 1998 and set the sales price assuming the euro would be at $1.18 by 2003—about the level it was traded at when introduced officially in 1999. But the euro's exchange value sharply declined, bottoming out at 82 cents in 2000. That meant each euro Markel received for its products was worth far less in dollars than the company had anticipated. During 2000–2002, Markel realized more than $650,000 in currency losses, and the company posted overall losses. This resulted in pay cuts for Markel employees and efforts to cut costs by improving efficiency.

Markel rode out its losses and by 2003 good times were beginning to return. Most of Markel's currency deals were written assuming that the euro would be valued between 90 cents and 95 cents. But when the euro soared to $1.08, aided by an imminent war with Iraq, nervous U.S. financial markets, and concerns about the U.S. trade deficit, Markel began to realize currency windfalls. Company executives estimated that if the euro remained between $1.05 and $1.07, and the British pound stayed at about $1.60, Markel would realize $400,000 to $500,000 in currency gains in 2003: not enough to offset the currency losses of the three previous years, but at least a step in the right direction.

However, the risk of currency fluctuations goes both ways. Markel demands multiyear contracts for its imported raw materials that are denominated in dollars. This means that its Japanese supplier bears the risk of swings in exchange rates: It will take home fewer yen as the dollar depreciates.

Does Foreign-Currency Hedging Pay Off?

As a firm that realizes more than half of its sales in profits in foreign currencies, Minnesota Mining & Manufacturing Co. (3M) is very sensitive to fluctuations in exchange rates. As the dollar appreciates against other currencies, 3M's profits decline; as the dollar depreciates, its profits increase. Indeed, when currency markets go wild, like they did during 1997–1998 when Asian currencies and the Russian ruble crashed relative to the dollar, deciding whether or not to hedge is a crucial business decision. Yet 3M didn't use hedges, such as the for-

Exchange-Rate Risk: The Hazard of Investing Abroad

Return on a 3-Month German Investment

	Deutsche Mark Return[*]	Percentage Change in $/DM Exchange Rate	Dollar Return
May 27–August 26	2.4%	16.6%	19.0%
September 30–December 30	2.3	–12.5	–10.2

[*]In 2002, the euro replaced the deutsche mark as the currency of Germany.

Exchange-rate fluctuations can substantially change the returns on assets denominated in a foreign currency. A real-world demonstration follows.

Throughout 1992, short-term interest rates in Germany were significantly higher than those in the United States; however, an American choosing between a dollar-denominated and deutsche mark–denominated certificate of deposit (CD) with similar liquidities and default risks would not necessarily have earned a higher return on the German CD.

On May 27, 1992, an American saver with $10,000 to invest had the choice between a 3-month CD with an annual interest rate of 3.85 percent from an American bank and a 3-month CD with an annual interest rate of 9.65 percent (approximately 2.4 percent for 3 months) from a German bank. After 3 months, the U.S. CD was worth $10,096 and the German CD was worth $11,900 after exchanging the marks for dollars. As the table shows, the substantially larger value of the German CD was due primarily to a 16.6 percent appreciation of the mark against the dollar from May 27 to August 26.

Now consider the choice facing our investor on September 30, 1992: a 3-month U.S. CD offering an annual interest rate of 3.09 percent, and a comparable German investment offering an annual interest rate of 9.1 percent (approximately 2.3 percent for 3 months). After 3 months, the U.S. CD was worth $10,077. If the investor purchased the German CD, however, she would have had only $8,964 at the end of the 3 months—$1,036 less than the purchase price. This loss resulted from the 12.5 percent appreciation of the dollar against the mark between September and December 1992. With hindsight, the American saver would have preferred the U.S. CD to the German CD, even though the German interest rate was higher.

These examples provide a clear message. Even though interest rates play a key role in determining the relative attractiveness of assets denominated in domestic and foreign currencies, the effects of exchange-rate changes can swamp the effects of interest-rate differentials. Such large differences in returns illustrate why many investors choose to hedge against exchange-rate changes.

Source: Patricia S. Pollard, "Exchange-Rate Risk: The Hazard of Investing Abroad," *International Economic Conditions*, Federal Reserve Bank of St. Louis, February 1993, p. 1.

ward market or currency options market, to guard against currency fluctuations.[7]

In 1998, the producer of Scotch Tape and Post-it notes announced that the appreciating dollar had cost the firm $330 million in profits and $1.8 billion in revenue during the previous three years. Indeed, 3M's no-hedging policy had investors nervous. Was 3M unwise in not hedging its currency risk? Not according to many analysts and other big firms that chose to hedge very little, if at all. Firms ranging from ExxonMobil to Deere

[7]"Perils of the Hedge Highwire," *Business Week*, October 26, 1998, pp. 74–76.

to Kodak have maintained that currency fluctuations improve profits as often as they hurt them. In other words, although an appreciation of the dollar would detract from their profits, a dollar depreciation would add to them. As a result, hedging isn't necessary, as the ups and down of currencies even out over the long run.

The standard argument for hedging is increased stability of cash flows and earnings. Surveys of corporate America's largest companies have found that one-third of them do some kind of foreign-currency hedging. For example, drug giant Merck and Co. hedges some of its foreign cash flows using the currency options market to sell the currencies for dollars at fixed rates. Merck maintains that it can protect against adverse currency moves by exercising its options, or enjoy favorable moves by not exercising them. Either way, the firm aims to guarantee that cash flow from foreign sales remains stable so that it can sustain research spending in years when a strong dollar trims foreign earnings. According to Merck's chief financial officer, the firm pays money for insurance to dampen volatility from unknown events.

Yet many well-established companies see no need to pay for protection against currency risk. Instead, they often choose to cover the risks out of their own deep pockets. According to 3M officials, if you consider the cost of hedging over the entire cycle, the drain on your earnings is very high for purchasing that insurance. Indeed, foreign-currency hedging eats into profits. A simple forward contract that locks in an exchange rate costs up to half a percentage point per year of the revenue being hedged. Other techniques such as currency options are more costly. What's more, fluctuations in a firm's business can detract from the effectiveness of foreign-currency hedging.

Indeed, many companies have decided hedging is not worth the trouble. For example, in late 1993 Eastman Kodak concluded that the benefits of extensive use of foreign-currency hedging did not justify the costs because the ups and downs of currencies would even out over the long run. As a result, the firm switched from hedging its overall receipts and payments to hedging only a few specific contracts. Moreover, IBM had reduced the impact of currency fluctuations without hedging by locating plants in many countries where it does business, so its costs are in the same currency as its revenues.

Interest Arbitrage

Investors make their financial decisions by comparing the rates of return of foreign investment with those of domestic investment. If rates of return from foreign investment are larger, they will desire to shift their funds abroad. **Interest arbitrage** refers to the process of moving funds into foreign currencies to take advantage of higher investment yields abroad. But investors assume a risk when they have foreign investments: When the investment's proceeds are converted back into the home currency, their value may fall because of a change in the exchange rate. Investors can eliminate this exchange risk by obtaining "cover" in the forward market.

Uncovered Interest Arbitrage

Uncovered interest arbitrage occurs when an investor does not obtain exchange-market cover to protect investment proceeds from foreign-currency fluctuations. Although this practice is rarely used, it is a good pedagogical starting point.

Suppose the interest rate on 3-month Treasury bills is 6 percent (per annum) in New York and 10 percent (per annum) in London, and that the current spot rate is $2 per pound. A U.S. investor would seek to profit from this opportunity by exchanging dollars for pounds at the rate of $2 per pound and using these pounds to purchase 3-month British Treasury bills in London. The investor would earn 4 percent more per year, or 1 percent more for the 3 months, than if the same dollars had been used to buy 3-month Treasury bills in New York. These results are summarized in Table 11.9.

However, it is *not* necessarily true that our U.S. investor realizes an extra 1 percent rate of return (per 3 months) by moving funds to London. This amount will be realized only if the exchange value of the pound remains constant over the investment period. If the pound *depreci-*

TABLE 11.9

Uncovered Interest Arbitrage: An Example

	Rate per Year	Rate per 3 Months
U.K. 3-month Treasury bill interest rate	10%	2.5%
U.S. 3-month Treasury bill interest rate	6%	1.5%
Uncovered interest differential favoring the United Kingdom	4%	1.0%

ates against the dollar, the investor makes *less*; if the pound *appreciates* against the dollar, the investor makes *more*!

Suppose our investor earns an extra 1 percent by purchasing 3-month British Treasury bills rather than U.S. Treasury bills. Over the same period, suppose the dollar price of the pound falls from $2.00 to $1.99 (the pound *depreciates* against the dollar). When the proceeds are converted back into dollars, the investor *loses* 0.5 percent—($2 – $1.99)/$2 = .005. The investor thus earns only 0.5 percent more (1 percent – 0.5 percent) than if the funds had been placed in U.S. Treasury bills. The reader can verify that if the dollar price of the pound fell from $2 to $1.98 over the investment period, the U.S. investor would earn nothing extra by investing in British Treasury bills.

Alternatively, suppose that over the 3-month period the pound rises from $2 to $2.02, a 1 percent *appreciation* against the dollar. This time, in addition to the extra 1 percent return on British Treasury bills, our investor realizes a return of 1 percent from the appreciation of the pound. The reason? When she bought pounds to finance her purchase of British Treasury bills, she paid $2 per pound; when she converted her investment proceeds back into dollars, she received $2.02 per pound—($2.02 – $2)/$2 = .01. Because the pound's appreciation adds to her investment's profitability, she earns 2 percent more than if she had purchased U.S. Treasury bills.

In summary, a U.S. investor's extra rate of return on an investment in the United Kingdom, as compared to the United States, equals the interest-rate differential adjusted for any change in the value of the pound, as follows:

Extra return = (U.K. interest rate – U.S. interest rate) – % depreciation of the pound

or

Extra return = (U.K. interest rate – U.S. interest rate) + % appreciation of the pound

Covered Interest Arbitrage

Investing funds in a foreign financial center involves an exchange-rate risk. Because investors typically desire to avoid this risk, interest arbitrage is usually *covered*.

Covered interest arbitrage involves two basic steps. First, an investor exchanges domestic currency for foreign currency, at the current spot rate, and uses the foreign currency to finance a foreign investment. At the same time, the investor contracts in the forward market to sell the amount of the foreign currency that will be received as the proceeds from the investment, with a delivery date to coincide with the maturity of the investment. It pays for the investor to make the foreign investment if the positive interest-rate differential in favor of the foreign investment more than offsets the cost of obtaining the forward cover.

Suppose the interest rate on 3-month Treasury bills is 12 percent (per annum) in London and 8 percent (per annum) in New York; the interest differential in favor of London is 4 percent per annum, or 1 percent for the 3 months. Suppose also that the current spot rate for the pound is $2, while the 3-month forward pound sells for $1.99. This means that the 3-month forward pound is at a 0.5 percent *discount*—($1.99 – $2)/$2 = –.005.

By purchasing 3-month Treasury bills in London, a U.S. investor could earn 1 percent more for the 3 months than if he bought 3-month Treasury bills in New York. To eliminate the uncertainty over how many dollars will be received when the pounds are reconverted into dollars, the investor sells enough pounds on the 3-month forward market to coincide with the anticipated proceeds of the investment. The cost of the forward cover equals the difference between the spot rate and the contracted 3-month forward rate; this difference is the discount on the forward pound, or 0.5 percent. Subtracting this 0.5 percent from the interest-rate differential of 1 percent, the investor is able to realize a net rate of return that is 0.5 percent higher than if he had bought U.S. Treasury bills. These results are summarized in Table 11.10.

This investment opportunity will not last long, because the net profit margin will soon disappear. As U.S. investors purchase spot pounds, the spot rate will rise. Concurrently, the sale of forward pounds will push the forward rate downward. The result is a *widening* of the discount on the forward pounds, which means that the cost of covering the exchange-rate risk increases. This arbitraging process will continue until the forward discount on the pound widens to 1 percent, at which point the extra profitability of the foreign investment vanishes. The discount on the pound now equals the interest-rate differential between New York and London:

Pound forward discount = U.K. interest rate − U.S. interest rate

In short, the theory of foreign exchange suggests that the forward discount or premium on one currency against another reflects the difference in the short-term interest rates between the two nations. The currency of the higher-interest-rate nation should be at a forward *discount* while the currency of the lower-interest-rate nation should be at a forward *premium*.

International differences in interest rates do exert a major influence on the relationship between the spot and forward rates. But on any particular day, one would hardly expect the spread on short-term interest rates between financial centers to precisely equal the discount or premium on foreign exchange, for several reasons. First, changes in interest-rate differentials do not always induce an immediate investor response necessary to eliminate the investment profits. Second, investors sometimes transfer funds on an uncovered basis; such transfers do not have an effect on the forward rate. Third, factors such as governmental exchange controls and speculation may weaken the connection between the interest-rate differential and the spot and forward rates.

Foreign-Exchange Market Speculation

Besides being used for the financing of commercial transactions and investments, the foreign-exchange market is also used for exchange-rate speculation. **Speculation** is the attempt to profit by trading on expectations about prices in the future. Some speculators are traders acting for financial institutions or firms; others are individuals. In either case, speculators buy currencies that they expect to go up in value and sell currencies that they expect to go down in value.

Note the difference between arbitrage and speculation. With arbitrage, a currency trader

TABLE 11.10

Covered Interest Arbitrage: An Example

	Rate per Year	Rate per 3 Months
U.K. 3-month Treasury bill interest rate	12%	3%
U.S. 3-month Treasury bill interest rate	8%	2%
Uncovered interest-rate differential favoring the United Kingdom	4%	1%
Forward discount on the 3-month pound		−0.5%
Covered interest-rate differential favoring the United Kingdom		0.5%

How to Play the Falling Dollar

When the dollar is expected to depreciate, U.S. investors may look to foreign markets for big returns. Why? A declining dollar makes foreign-denominated financial instruments valued at more in dollar terms. However, those in the business emphasize that trading currency is "speculation," not investing. If the dollar rebounds, any foreign-denominated investment would provide lower returns. Simply put, big losses can easily occur if your bet is wrong.

The most direct way to play an anticipated drop in the dollar would be to stroll down to Bank of America and purchase $10,000 of euros, put the bills in your safe deposit box, and reconvert the currency to dollars in, say, six months. However, it's not an especially efficient way to do the job because of transaction costs.

Another way is to purchase bonds denominated in a foreign currency. A U.S. investor who anticipates that the yen's exchange value will significantly appreciate in the near future might purchase bonds issued by the Japanese government or corporations and expressed in yen. These bonds can be purchased from brokerage firms such as Charles Schwab and J.P. Morgan Chase & Co. The bonds are paid for in yen, which are purchased by converting dollars into yen at the prevailing spot rate. If the yen goes up, the speculator gets not only the accrued interest from the bond but also its appreciated value in dollars. The catch is that, in all likelihood, others have the same expectations. The overall demand for the bonds may be sufficient to force up the bond price, resulting in a lower interest rate. For the investor to win, the yen's appreciation must exceed the loss of interest income. In many cases, the exchange-rate changes are not large enough to make such investments worthwhile. Besides investing in a particular foreign bond, one can invest in a foreign-bond mutual fund, provided by brokerage firms like Merrill Lynch. Although you can own a foreign-bond fund

with as little as $2,500, you generally must pony up $100,000 or more to own bonds directly.

Rather than investing in foreign bonds, some investors choose to purchase stocks of foreign corporations, denominated in foreign currencies. The investor in this case is trying to predict the trend of not only the foreign currency but also its stock market. The investor must be highly knowledgeable about both financial and economic affairs in the foreign country. Instead of purchasing individual stocks, an investor could put money in a foreign-stock mutual fund.

For investors who expect that the spot rate of a foreign currency will soon rise, the answer lies in a savings account denominated in a foreign currency. For example, a U.S. investor may contact a major Citibank or a U.S. branch of a foreign bank and take out an interest-bearing certificate of deposit expressed in a foreign currency. An advantage of such a savings account is that the investor is guaranteed a fixed interest rate. An investor who has guessed correctly also enjoys the gains stemming from the foreign currency's appreciation. However, the investor must be aware of the possibility that governments might tax or shut off such deposits or interfere with the investor's freedom to hold another nation's currency.

Finally, you can play the falling dollar by putting your money into a variety of currency derivatives, all of which are risky. For example, you can trade futures contracts at the Chicago Mercantile Exchange. Or trade currency directly by opening an account at a firm that specializes in that businesses, such as Saxo Bank (Danish) or CMC (British). The minimum lot is often $10,000, and you can leverage up to 95 percent. Thus, for a $100,000 trade, the typical size, you'd have to put only $5,000 down. Additional information on the techniques of currency speculation is found in "Exploring Further 11.1."

simultaneously buys a currency at a low price and sells that currency at a high price, thus making a riskless profit. A speculator's goal is to buy a currency at one moment (such as today) and sell that currency at a higher price in the future (such as tomorrow). Speculation thus implies the deliberate assumption of exchange risk: If the price of the currency falls between today and tomorrow, the speculator loses money. An exchange-market speculator deliberately assumes foreign-exchange risk on the expectation of profiting from future changes in the spot exchange rate. Such activity can exert either a stabilizing or a destabilizing influence on the foreign-exchange market.

Stabilizing speculation goes against market forces by *moderating* or *reversing* a rise or fall in a currency's exchange rate. For example, it would occur when a speculator buys foreign currency with domestic currency when the domestic price of the foreign currency falls, or depreciates. The hope is that the domestic price of the foreign currency will soon increase, leading to a profit. Such purchases increase the demand for the foreign currency, which moderates its depreciation. Stabilizing speculation performs a useful function for bankers and businesspeople, who desire stable exchange rates.

Destabilizing speculation goes with market forces by *reinforcing* fluctuations in a currency's exchange rate. For example, it would occur when a speculator sells a foreign currency when it depreciates, on the expectation that it will depreciate further in the future. Such sales depress the foreign currency's value. Destabilizing speculation can disrupt international transactions in several ways. Because of the uncertainty of financing exports and imports, the cost of hedging may become so high that international trade is impeded. What is more, unstable exchange rates may disrupt international investment activity. This is because the cost of obtaining forward cover for international capital transactions may rise significantly as foreign-exchange risk intensifies.

To lessen the amount of destabilizing speculation, some government officials propose government regulation of foreign-currency markets. If foreign-currency markets are to be regulated by government, however, will such intervention be superior to the outcome that occurs in an unregulated market? Will government be able to identify better than markets what the "correct" exchange rate is? Many analysts contend that government would make even bigger mistakes. Moreover, markets are better than government in admitting their mistakes and reversing out of them. That is because, unlike governments, markets have no pride. Destabilizing speculation will be further discussed in Chapter 15.

Summary

1. The foreign-exchange market provides the institutional framework within which individuals, businesses, and financial institutions purchase and sell foreign exchange. Two of the world's largest foreign-exchange markets are located in New York and London.

2. The exchange rate is the price of one unit of foreign currency in terms of the domestic currency. From a U.S. viewpoint, the exchange rate might refer to the number of dollars necessary to buy a Swiss franc. A dollar depreciation (appreciation) is an increase (decrease) in the number of dollars required to buy a unit of foreign exchange.

3. In the foreign-exchange market, currencies are traded around the clock and throughout the world. Most foreign-exchange trading is in the interbank market. Banks typically engage in three types of foreign-exchange transactions: spot, forward, and swap.

4. *The Wall Street Journal's* foreign-exchange quotations include those of the New York foreign-exchange market and the International Monetary Market located in Chicago. Both spot quotations and forward quotations are provided.

5. The equilibrium rate of exchange in a free market is determined by the intersection of the supply and demand schedules of foreign exchange. These schedules are derived from the credit and debit items in a nation's balance of payments.

6. Exchange arbitrage permits the rates of exchange in different parts of the world to be kept the same. This is achieved by selling a currency when its price is high and purchasing when the price is low.

7. Foreign traders and investors often deal in the forward market for protection from possible exchange-rate fluctuations. However, speculators also buy and sell currencies in the futures markets in anticipation of sizable profits. In general, interest arbitrage determines the relationship between the spot rate and the forward rate.

8. Speculation in the foreign-exchange markets may be either stabilizing or destabilizing in nature.

Key Concepts and Terms

- Appreciation *(page 345)*
- Bid rate *(page 344)*
- Call option *(page 349)*
- Covered interest arbitrage *(page 363)*
- Cross exchange rate *(page 346)*
- Currency swap *(page 342)*
- Depreciation *(page 345)*
- Destabilizing speculation *(page 366)*
- Discount *(page 357)*
- Effective exchange rate *(page 354)*
- Exchange arbitrage *(page 356)*
- Exchange rate *(page 345)*
- Exchange-rate index *(page 354)*
- Foreign-currency options *(page 349)*
- Foreign-exchange market *(page 340)*
- Forward market *(page 347)*
- Forward rate *(page 357)*
- Forward transaction *(page 342)*
- Futures market *(page 347)*
- Hedging *(page 358)*
- Interbank market *(page 343)*
- Interest arbitrage *(page 362)*
- International Monetary Market (IMM) *(page 347)*
- Long position *(page 371)*
- Maturity months *(page 347)*
- Nominal exchange rate *(page 354)*
- Nominal exchange-rate index *(page 354)*
- Offer rate *(page 344)*
- Option *(page 349)*
- Premium *(page 357)*
- Put option *(page 349)*
- Real exchange rate *(page 355)*
- Real exchange-rate index *(page 356)*
- Short position *(page 371)*
- Speculation *(page 364)*
- Spot market *(page 347)*
- Spot transaction *(page 342)*
- Spread *(page 344)*
- Stabilizing speculation *(page 366)*
- Strike price *(page 349)*
- Three-point arbitrage *(page 356)*
- Trade-weighted dollar *(page 354)*
- Two-point arbitrage *(page 356)*
- Uncovered interest arbitrage *(page 362)*

Study Questions

1. What is meant by the foreign-exchange market? Where is it located?
2. What is meant by the forward market? How does this differ from the spot market?
3. The supply and demand for foreign exchange are considered to be derived schedules. Explain.
4. Explain why exchange-rate quotations stated in different financial centers tend to be consistent with one another.
5. Who are the participants in the forward-exchange market? What advantages does this market afford these participants?
6. What explains the relationship between the spot rate and the forward rate?
7. What is the strategy of speculating in the forward market? In what other ways can one speculate on exchange-rate changes?
8. Distinguish between stabilizing speculation and destabilizing speculation.

9. If the exchange rate changes from $1.70 = £1 to $1.68 = £1, what does this mean for the dollar? For the pound? What if the exchange rate changes from $1.70 = £1 to $1.72 = £1?

10. Suppose $1.69 = £1 in New York and $1.71 = £1 in London. How can foreign-exchange arbitragers profit from these exchange rates? Explain how foreign-exchange arbitrage results in the same dollar/pound exchange rate in New York and London.

11. **Xtra!** **For a tutorial of this question, go to** **CARBAUGH** **http://carbaughxtra.swlearning.com** Table 11.11 shows supply and demand schedules for the British pound. Assume that exchange rates are flexible.
    a. The equilibrium exchange rate equals _____ . At this exchange rate, how many pounds will be purchased, and at what cost in terms of dollars?
    b. Suppose the exchange rate is $2 per pound. At this exchange rate, there is an excess (supply/demand) of pounds. This imbalance causes (an increase/a decrease) in the dollar price of the pound, which leads to (a/an) _____ in the quantity of pounds supplied and (a/an) _____ in the quantity of pounds demanded.
    c. Suppose the exchange rate is $1 per pound. At this exchange rate, there is an excess (supply/demand) for pounds. This imbalance causes (an increase/ a decrease) in the price of the pound, which leads to

(a/an) _____ in the quantity of pounds supplied and (a/an) _____ in the quantity of pounds demanded.

12. Suppose the spot rate of the pound today is $1.70 and the 3-month forward rate is $1.75.
    a. How can a U.S. importer who has to pay 20,000 pounds in 3 months hedge her foreign-exchange risk?
    b. What occurs if the U.S. importer does not hedge and the spot rate of the pound in 3 months is $1.80?

13. Suppose the interest rate (on an annual basis) on 3-month Treasury bills is 10 percent in London and 6 percent in New York, and the spot rate of the pound is $2.
    a. How can a U.S. investor profit from uncovered interest arbitrage?
    b. If the price of the 3-month forward pound is $1.99, will a U.S. investor benefit from covered interest arbitrage? If so, by how much?

14. Table 11.12 gives hypothetical dollar/franc exchange values for Wednesday, May 5, 2003.
    a. Fill in the last two columns of the table with the reciprocal price of the dollar in terms of the franc.
    b. On Wednesday, the spot price of the two currencies was _____ dollars per franc, or _____ francs per dollar.
    c. From Tuesday to Wednesday, in the spot market the dollar (appreciated/depreciated) against the franc; the franc (appreciated/depreciated) against the dollar.
    d. In Wednesday's spot market, the cost of buying 100 francs was _____ dollars; the cost of buying 100 dollars was _____ francs.
    e. On Wednesday, the 30-day forward franc was at a (premium/discount) of _____ dollars, which equaled _____ percent on an annual basis. What about the 90-day forward franc?

15. Assume a speculator anticipates that the spot rate of the franc in three months will be lower than today's 3-month forward rate of the franc, $0.50 = 1 franc.

TABLE 11.11

Supply and Demand of British Pounds

Quantity of Pounds Supplied	Dollars per Pound	Quantity of Pounds Demanded
50	$2.50	10
40	2.00	20
30	1.50	30
20	1.00	40
10	.50	50

TABLE 11.12

Dollar/Franc Exchange Values

	U.S. $ Equivalent		Currency per U.S.$	
	Wed.	Tues.	Wed.	Tues.
Switzerland (franc)	.5851	.5846		
30-day forward	.5853	.5848		
90- day forward	.5854	.5849		
180- day forward	.5851	.5847		

a. How can this speculator use $1 million to speculate in the forward market?

b. What occurs if the franc's spot rate in 3 months is $0.40? $0.60? $0.50?

16. You are given the following spot exchange rates: $1 = 3 francs, $1 = 4 schillings, and 1 franc = 2 schillings. Ignoring transaction costs, how much profit could a person make via three-point arbitrage?

netlink▸

11.1 The Web site of the Wells Fargo Bank provides an overview of exchange rates and international trade in its International Services section. Set your browser to this URL:

http://www.wellsfargo.com/inatl/inatl.jhtml

11.2 L.P. Bloomberg, a well-known financial-services firm, provides currency information at its Web site, including its currency calculator, key cross-country rates, and currency by region. Go to

Market Data after setting your browser to this URL:

http://www.bloomberg.com

11.3 Olsen and Associates is a leading developer of online forecasting technology for business and finance. OANDA, its Internet subsidiary, offers a currency converter that will tell you current and historical exchange rates for 192 currencies. Set your browser to this URL:

http://www.oanda.com

To access NetLink Exercises and the Virtual Scavenger Hunt, visit the Carbaugh Web site at http://carbaugh.swlearning.com.

Xtra!

CARBAUGH

Log onto the Carbaugh Xtra! Web site (http://carbaughxtra.swlearning.com) for additional learning resources such as practice quizzes, help with graphing, and current events applications.

11·1

Exploring Further

Techniques of Foreign-Exchange Market Speculation

Speculation in the foreign-exchange market can be conducted in the spot market and the forward market. Let us examine the techniques of speculating in these markets.

Speculating in the Spot Market

Imagine that you are a currency speculator in New York, willing to risk money on your opinion about future prices of a foreign currency—say, the Swiss franc. Consider the following scenarios.

Case 1:

Speculating on a Swiss franc appreciation.
GIVEN: Today's spot price is $0.40 per franc.
ASSUMPTION: In 3 months, the spot price of the franc will rise to $0.50.
PROCEDURE:
1. Purchase francs at today's spot price of $0.40 and deposit them in a bank to earn interest.
2. In 3 months, sell the francs at the prevailing spot price of $0.50 per franc.

OUTCOME: If assumption is right, profit = $0.10 per franc. If assumption is wrong and the spot price of the franc falls instead, you incur a loss, reselling francs at a price lower than the purchase price.

Case 2:

Speculating on a Swiss franc depreciation.
GIVEN: Today's spot price is $0.40 per franc.
ASSUMPTION: In 3 months, the spot price of the franc will fall to $0.25.
PROCEDURE:
1. Borrow francs today, exchange them for dollars at the prevailing spot price of

$0.40 per franc, and deposit the dollars in a bank to earn interest.
2. In 3 months, buy francs at the prevailing spot price of $0.25 per franc and use them to pay back the loan.

OUTCOME: If assumption is right, profit = $0.15 per franc. (This return is reduced by the interest paid on borrowed money, but increased by the interest received on the bank savings account). If assumption is wrong and the spot price of the franc rises in 3 months instead, you incur a loss buying francs at a higher price than the initial selling price.

Speculating in the Forward Market

Although speculation on the spot market can lead to profits, it has a serious drawback: The speculator must have a large amount of idle cash or borrowing privileges, which require interest payments. Speculation in the forward market, however, does not require cash or credit facilities. All the speculator needs to do is sign a forward contract with a bank to either purchase or sell a specified amount of foreign currency at a specified date. The bank may impose a *margin requirement*, requiring the speculator to put up, say, 10 percent of the value of the foreign contract as security. In practice, most speculation is done in the forward market.

Forward market speculation occurs when a speculator believes that a currency's spot price at some future date will differ from today's forward price for that same date. For example, suppose the 30-day forward pound is selling at a 10 percent discount; this discount is the market's consensus (average expectation) that in 30 days the spot rate of the pound will be 10 percent lower than it is today. As a speculator, however, you feel you have better information than the market. You believe that in 30 days the pound's spot rate will be only 5 percent lower (or maybe 15 percent higher) than it is today. You are willing to bet your money that the market consensus is wrong. Your gains or losses will equal the difference between the current forward rate and the spot rate 30 days from now. Consider the following scenarios.

Case 1:
Speculating that the spot rate of the Swiss franc in 3 months will be higher than its current 3-month forward rate.
GIVEN: The current price of the 3-month forward franc is $0.40.
ASSUMPTION: In 3 months, the prevailing spot price of the franc will be $0.50.
PROCEDURE:
1. Contract to purchase a specified amount of francs in the forward market, at $0.40 per franc, for 3-month delivery.
2. After receiving delivery of the francs in 3 months, resell them in the spot market at the prevailing price of $0.50 per franc.

OUTCOME: If assumption is right, profit = $0.10 per franc. If assumption is wrong and the prevailing spot price in 3 months is lower than $0.40 per franc, you incur a loss.

Case 2:
Speculating that the spot rate of the Swiss franc in 3 months will be lower than its current 3-month forward rate.
GIVEN: The current price of the 3-month forward franc is $0.40.
ASSUMPTION: In 3 months, the prevailing spot price of the franc will be $0.30.
PROCEDURE:
1. Contract to sell a specified amount of francs (which you do not currently have) for delivery in 3 months at the forward price of $0.40 per franc.
2. In 3 months, purchase an identical amount of francs in the spot market at $0.30 per franc and deliver them to fulfill the forward contract.

OUTCOME: If assumption is right, profit = $0.10 per franc. If assumption is wrong and the prevailing spot price in 3 months is higher than $0.40 per franc, you incur a loss.

When speculators purchase foreign currency on the spot or forward market with the anticipation of selling it at a higher future spot price, they are said to take a **long position** in the currency. But when speculators borrow or sell forward a foreign currency with the anticipation of purchasing it at a future lower price to repay the foreign-exchange loan or fulfill the forward sale contract, they are said to take a **short position** (that is, they are selling what they do not currently have).

chapter 12

Exchange-Rate Determination

Since the introduction of market-determined exchange rates by the major industrial nations in the 1970s, notable shifts in exchange rates have been observed. Although changes in long-run exchange rates have tended to undergo relatively gradual shifts, if we examine shorter intervals, we see that the exchange rate is very volatile. Indeed, exchange rates can fluctuate by several percentage points even during a single day. This chapter seeks to explain the forces that underlie fluctuations of exchange rates under a system of market-determined (floating) exchange rates.

What Determines Exchange Rates?

We have learned that foreign-exchange markets are highly competitive by nature. Large numbers of sellers and buyers meet in these markets, which are located in the major cities of the world and are connected electronically to form one worldwide market. Participants in the foreign-exchange market have excellent, up-to-the-minute information about the exchange rates between any two currencies. As a result, currency values are determined by the unregulated forces of supply and demand as long as central banks do not attempt to stabilize them. The supplies and demands for a currency are those of private individuals, corporations, banks, and government agencies other than central banks. In a free market, the equilibrium exchange rate occurs at the point at which the quantity demanded of a foreign currency equals the quantity of that currency supplied.

To say that supply and demand determine exchange rates in a free market is at once to say everything and to say nothing. If we are to understand why some currencies depreciate and others appreciate, we must investigate the factors that cause the supply and demand schedules of currencies to change. These factors include **market fundamentals** (economic variables) such as productivity, inflation rates, real interest rates, consumer preferences, and government trade policy. They also include **market expectations** such as news about future market fundamentals and traders'opinion about future exchange rates.[1]

---

[1]This approach to exchange-rate determination is known as the balance-of-payments approach. It emphasizes the flow of goods, services, and investment funds and their impact on foreign-exchange transactions and exchange rates. The approach predicts that exchange-rate depreciation (appreciation) tends to occur for a nation that spends more (less) abroad in combined purchases and investments than it acquires from abroad over a sustained period of time.

Because economists believe that the determinants of exchange-rate fluctuations are rather different in the short run (a few weeks or even days), medium run (several months), and long run (1, 2, or even 5 years), we will consider these time frames when analyzing exchange rates. In the *short run*, foreign-exchange transactions are dominated by transfers of financial assets (bank deposits) that respond to differences in real interest rates and to shifting expectations of future exchange rates; such transactions have the major influence on short-run exchange rates. Over the *medium run*, exchange rates are governed by cyclical factors such as cyclical fluctuations in economic activity. Over the *long run*, foreign-exchange transactions are dominated by flows of goods, services, and investment capital, which respond to forces such as inflation rates, investment profitability, consumer tastes, productivity, and government trade pol-

icy; such transactions have the dominant impact on long-run exchange rates.

Note that day-to-day influences on foreign-exchange rates can cause the rate to move in the opposite direction from that indicated by longer-term fundamentals. Although today's exchange rate may be out of line with long-term fundamentals, this should not be construed as implying that it is necessarily inconsistent with short-term determinants— for example, interest-rate differentials, which are among the relevant fundamentals at the short end of the time dimension.

Figure 12.1 highlights the framework in which exchange rates are determined.[2] The figure views exchange rates as simultaneously determined by

[2]This figure and its analysis are adapted from Michael Rosenberg, *Currency Forecasting* (Homewood, IL: Richard D. Irwin, 1996), pp. 3–5.

FIGURE 12.1

The Path of the Yen's Exchange Rate

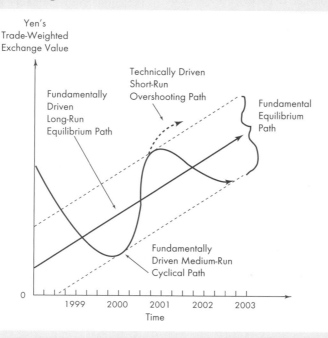

The figure views the exchange value of a nation's currency as being determined by long-run structural, medium-run cyclical, and short-run speculative forces.

long-run structural, medium-run cyclical, and short-run speculative forces. The figure illustrates the idea that there exists some equilibrium level or path to which a currency will eventually gravitate. This path serves as a long-run magnet or anchor; it ensures that exchange rates will not fluctuate aimlessly without limit but rather will tend to gravitate over time toward the long-run equilibrium path.

Medium-run cyclical forces can induce fluctuations of a currency above and below its long-run equilibrium path. However, fundamental forces serve to push a currency toward its long-run equilibrium path. Note that medium-run cyclical fluctuations from a currency's long-run equilibrium path can be large at times, if economic disturbances induce significant changes in either trade flows or capital movements.

Longer-run structural forces and medium-run cyclical forces interact to establish a currency's equilibrium path. Exchange rates may sometimes move away from this path if short-run forces (for example, changing market expectations) induce fluctuations in exchange rates beyond those based on fundamental factors. Although such overshooting behavior can persist for significant periods, fundamental forces generally push the currency back into its long-run equilibrium path.

Unfortunately, predicting exchange-rate movements is a difficult job. That is because economic forces affect exchange rates through a variety of channels—some of which may induce negative impacts on a currency's value, others of which may exert positive impacts. Some of those channels may be more important in determining short-run tendencies, whereas other channels may be more important in explaining the long-run trend that a currency follows.

To simplify our analysis of exchange rates, we divide it into two parts. First, we consider how exchange rates are determined in the long run. Then we use our knowledge of the long-run determinants of the exchange rate to help us understand how they are determined in the short run.

To gain a better understanding of these determinants, you can refer to the "Currency Trading" column that appears daily in the *The Wall Street Journal*; it is usually located in the third section,

"Money and Investing." The column typically discusses factors causing fluctuations in the dollar's exchange value. Table 12.1 provides an example of this column.

Determining Long-Run Exchange Rates

Changes in the long-run value of the exchange rate are due to reactions of traders in the foreign-exchange market to changes in four key factors: relative price levels, relative productivity levels, consumer preferences for domestic or foreign goods, and trade barriers. Note that these factors underlie trade in domestic and foreign goods and thus changes in the demand for exports and imports. Table 12.2 on page 376 summarizes the effects of these factors.

To illustrate the effects of these factors, refer to Figure 12.2 on page 377, which shows the demand and supply schedules of pounds. Initially, the equilibrium exchange rate is $1.50 per pound. We will examine each factor by itself, assuming that all other factors remain constant.

Relative Price Levels

Referring to Figure 12.2(a), suppose the domestic price level increases rapidly in the United States and remains constant in the United Kingdom. This causes U.S. consumers to desire relatively low-priced British goods. The demand for pounds thus increases to D_1 in the figure. Conversely, as the British purchase less relatively high-priced U.S. goods, the supply of pounds decreases to S_1. The increase in the demand for pounds and the decrease in the supply of pounds result in a depreciation of the dollar to $1.60 per pound. This analysis suggests that an increase in the U.S. price level relative to price levels in other countries causes the dollar to depreciate in the long run.

Relative Productivity Levels

Productivity growth measures the increase in a country's output for a given level of input. If one country becomes more productive than other countries, it can produce goods more cheaply than its

TABLE 12.1

Currency Trading: Dollar Drops Sharply on Yen After Fed Leaves Rates Steady

The dollar hit a three-week low against the yen, but was little changed against the euro after Federal Reserve policy makers signaled no shift in the outlook for interest rates.

The Federal Open Market Committee not only left its key interest rate at a 46-year low of 1 percent, as expected, but also reiterated its stance that inflationary pressures are low enough that it "can be patient in removing its policy accommodation."

Fed officials also acknowledged the recent batch of disappointing employment reports, noting in their post-meeting statement that, "Although job losses have slowed, new hiring has lagged."

The statement reaffirmed market expectations that the Fed would hold off from raising rates until at least late 2004, which may continue to weigh on the dollar. Low U.S. rates have been a major factor in the dollar's long-term downtrend because it makes it more difficult to attract enough foreign investment to fund the U.S. current-account deficit.

However, the dollar was mostly directionless in choppy trading against most currencies after the Fed's decision.

"The dollar consequences will be marginal at best," said Jason Bonanca, director and currency strategist at Credit Suisse First Boston in New York. "The Fed's still not talking about removing policy accommodation, so this is not dovish enough to reignite dollar bearishness."

Marc Chandler, chief currency strategist at HSBC Bank in New York, agreed that the statement included "nothing really new substantially to elicit much of a response in the forex market."

Instead, the biggest moves in the dollar came against the yen amid continued speculation that the Bank of Japan would ease up on large-scale intervention. The dollar fell as far as 108.65 yen, a level not seen since late February. The dollar's slide against the yen started a chain reaction during the New York session, pushing European currencies down.

That, in turn, helped the dollar recoup most of its overnight losses against the European currencies, which were due in large part to continued jitters about an increase in global terrorism.

Late yesterday afternoon, the dollar was trading at 108.84 yen, down sharply from 110.31 yen late Monday in New York. The euro was at $1.2264, down slightly from $1.2271, and was lower against the yen at 133.40 yen from 135.40 yen. Against the Swiss franc, the dollar was at 1.2784 francs, up from 1.2752 francs, while sterling remained higher on the day at $1.8110 versus $1.8057 late Monday.

In recent weeks, the Bank of Japan, which intervenes on behalf of the Ministry of Finance, had apparently switched tactics by buying dollars even when the U.S. currency was rallying. The more aggressive stance was viewed as a move to push down the yen ahead of the March 31 fiscal year end to assist Japanese exporters and others that need to repatriate money.

foreign competitors can. If productivity gains are passed forward to domestic and foreign buyers in the form of lower prices, the nation's exports tend to increase and imports tend to decrease.

Referring to Figure 12.2(b), suppose U.S. productivity growth is faster than that of the United Kingdom. As U.S. goods become relatively less expensive, the British demand more U.S. goods, which results in an increase in the supply of pounds to S_2. Also, Americans demand fewer British goods, which become relatively more expensive, causing the demand for pounds to decrease to D_2. Therefore, the dollar appreciates to $1.40 per pound. Simply put, in the long run, as a country becomes more productive relative to other countries, its currency appreciates.

TABLE 12.2

Determinants of the Dollar's Exchange Rate in the Long Run

Factor*	Change	Effect on the Dollar's Exchange Rate
U.S. price level	Increase	Depreciation
	Decrease	Appreciation
U.S. productivity	Increase	Appreciation
	Decrease	Depreciation
U.S. preferences	Increase	Depreciation
	Decrease	Appreciation
U.S. trade barriers	Increase	Appreciation
	Decrease	Depreciation

*Relative to other countries. The analysis for a change in one determinant assumes that the other determinants are unchanged.

Preferences for Domestic or Foreign Goods

Referring to Figure 12.2(c), suppose that U.S. consumers develop stronger preferences for British-manufactured goods such as automobiles and CD players. The stronger demand for British goods results in Americans' demanding more pounds to purchase these goods. As the demand for pounds rises to D_1, the dollar depreciates to $1.55 per pound. Conversely, if British consumers demanded additional American computer software, machinery, and apples, the dollar would tend to appreciate against the pound. We conclude that an increased demand for a country's exports causes its currency to appreciate in the long run; conversely, increased demand for imports results in a depreciation in the domestic currency.

Trade Barriers

Barriers to free trade also affect exchange rates. Suppose that the U.S. government imposes tariffs on British steel. By making steel imports more expensive than domestically produced steel, the tariff discourages Americans from purchasing British steel. In Figure 12.2(d), this causes the demand for pounds to decrease to D_2, which results in an appreciation of the dollar to $1.45 per pound. Simply put, trade barriers such as tariffs and quotas cause a currency appreciation in the long run for the country imposing the barriers.

Inflation Rates, Purchasing Power Parity, and Long-Run Exchange Rates

The determinants discussed earlier are helpful in understanding the long-run behavior of exchange rates. Let us now focus on the **purchasing-power-parity approach** and see how it builds on the relative price determinant of long-run exchange rates.

Law of One Price

The simplest concept of purchasing power parity is the **law of one price**. It asserts that identical goods should cost the same in all nations, assuming that it is costless to ship goods between nations and there are no barriers to trade.

Before the costs of goods in different nations can be compared, prices must first be converted into a common currency. Once converted at the going market-exchange rate, the prices of identical goods from any two nations should be identical. After converting francs into dollars, for example, machine tools purchased in Switzerland should cost the same as identical machine tools bought in the United States.

In theory, the pursuit of profits tends to equalize the price of identical products in different nations. Assume that machine tools bought in Switzerland are cheaper than the same machine tools bought in the United States, after convert-

FIGURE 12.2

Market Fundamentals that Affect the Dollar's Exchange Rate in the Long Run

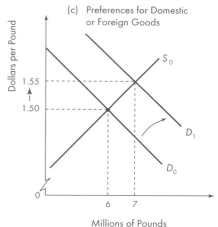

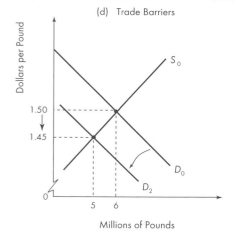

In the long run, the exchange rate between the dollar and the pound reflects relative price levels, relative productivity levels, preferences for domestic or foreign goods, and trade barriers.

ing francs into dollars. Swiss exporters could realize a profit by purchasing machine tools in Switzerland at a low price and selling them in the United States at a high price. Such transactions would force prices up in Switzerland and force prices down in the United States until the price of the machine tools would eventually become equal in both nations, whether prices are expressed in francs or dollars. As a result, the law of one price would prevail.

In practice, however, the law of one price does not always prevail. For example, tariffs and other trade barriers tend to drive a wedge between prices of identical products in different nations. Moreover, the cost of transporting goods from one nation to another restricts the potential profit from buying and selling identical products with different prices.

The "Big Mac" Index and the Law of One Price

The "Big Mac" hamburger sandwich sold by McDonald's has been viewed as an international monetary standard. Although economists generally prefer vast indexes based on thousands of commodities and prices to measure purchasing power, playful ones have opted for hamburger sandwiches. After all, the amount you pay for a Big Mac is a reflection of everything from sesame-seed prices to labor costs.

The so-called Big Mac Index is a popular stand-in for a much more serious concept, the law of one price. Based solely on the price of a Big Mac, the index is used to roughly assess which currencies are *overvalued* and which are *undervalued* relative to the U.S. dollar. *The Economist* magazine publishes Big Mac updates each year.

Consistent with the law of one price, the Big Mac Index suggests that the exchange rate between the dollar and the yen is in equilibrium when it equates the prices of hamburger sandwiches in the United States and Japan. Big Macs should thus cost the same in each country when the prices are converted to the dollar. When Big Macs do not cost the same, the yen is said to be overvalued or undervalued compared to the dollar.

Table 12.3 shows what a Big Mac cost in different countries as of May 27, 2004. The U.S. equivalent prices denote which currencies are overvalued and which are undervalued relative to the dollar. In the United States (New York), a Big Mac cost $2.90. In Norway, the dollar-equivalent price of a Big Mac was $5.18. Compared to the dollar, the Norwegian krone was *overvalued* by 79 percent ($5.18/2.90 = $1.79). The Big Mac was a bargain in Canada, however, where the U.S. dollar equivalent price was $2.33; the Canadian dollar was *undervalued* by 20 percent ($2.33/2.90 = $0.80).

To be sure, the Big Mac Index is primitive and has many flaws. However, it is widely understood by noneconomists and serves as an approximation of which currencies are too weak or strong, and by how much.

TABLE 12.3

Big Mac Index

The Price of a Big Mac, May 27, 2004

Country	Big Mac Price in Dollars	Local Currency Overvaluation (+), Undervaluation (-) (Percent)
United States	$2.90	—
Kuwait	7.33	+153%
Norway	5.18	+79
Switzerland	3.94	+69
Euro area	3.28	+13
Lebanon	2.84	−2
South Korea	2.72	−6
Canada	2.33	−20
Venezuela	1.48	−49
Ukraine	1.36	−53

Source: "Big MacCurrencies" *The Economist*, May 27, 2004, at http://www.economist.com.

Inflation Differentials and the Exchange Rate

Inflation Differentials and the Dollar's Exchange Value

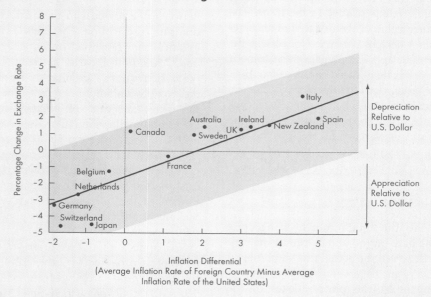

The purchasing-power-parity theory helps explain the behavior of a currency's exchange value. According to this theory, changes in relative national price levels determine changes in exchange rates over the long run. A currency would be expected to depreciate by an amount equal to the excess of domestic inflation over foreign inflation; it would appreciate by an amount equal to the excess of foreign inflation over domestic inflation.

The figure shows the relationship between inflation and the exchange rate for selected countries. The horizontal axis shows the country's average inflation minus the U.S. average inflation during the 1960–1997 period. The vertical axis shows the average percentage change in a country's exchange rate (foreign currency per dollar) over that period. Consistent with the predictions of the purchasing-power-parity theory, the figure shows that countries with relatively low inflation rates tend to have appreciating currencies, and countries with relatively high inflation tend to have depreciating currencies.

Source: International Monetary Fund, *IMF Financial Statistics*, various issues.

Relative Purchasing Power Parity

Rather than focusing on a particular good when applying the purchasing-power-parity concept, most analysts look at market baskets consisting of many goods. They consider a nation's overall inflation (deflation) rate as measured by, say, the producer price index or consumer price index.

According to the theory of **relative purchasing power parity**, changes in relative national price levels determine changes in exchange rates over the long run. The theory predicts that the foreign-exchange value of a currency tends to appreciate or depreciate at a rate equal to the difference between foreign and domestic inflation. As an example, if U.S. inflation exceeds Switzerland's inflation by 4 percentage points per year, the purchasing power of the dollar falls 4 points relative to the franc. The foreign-exchange value of the dollar should therefore depreciate 4 percent per year. Conversely, the U.S. dollar should appreciate against the franc if U.S. inflation is less than Switzerland's inflation.

The purchasing-power-parity theory can be used to predict long-run exchange rates. We'll consider an example using the price indexes (P) of the United States and Switzerland. Letting 0 be the base period and 1 represent period 1, the purchasing-power-parity theory is given in symbols as[3]

$$S_1 = S_0 \; \frac{P_{US_1} / P_{US_0}}{P_{S_1} / P_{S_0}}$$

where S_0 equals the equilibrium exchange rate existing in the base period and S_1 equals the estimated target at which the actual rate should be in the future.

For example, let the price indexes of the United States and Switzerland and the equilibrium exchange rate be as follows:

$$P_{US_0} = 100 \qquad P_{S_0} = 100 \qquad S_0 = \$0.50$$
$$P_{US_1} = 200 \qquad P_{S_1} = 100$$

[3]This chapter presents the so-called *relative version* of the purchasing-power-parity theory, which addresses changes in prices and exchange rates over a period of time. Another variant is the *absolute version*, which states that the equilibrium exchange rate will equal the ratio of domestic to foreign prices of an appropriate market basket of goods and services at a given point in time.

Putting these figures into the previous equation, we can determine the new equilibrium exchange rate for period 1:

$$S_1 = \$0.50 \left(\frac{200/100}{100/100} \right) = \$0.50(2) = \$1.00$$

Between one period and the next, the U.S. inflation rate rose 100 percent, whereas Switzerland's inflation rate remained unchanged. Maintaining purchasing power parity between the dollar and the franc requires the dollar to depreciate against the franc by an amount equal to the difference in the percentage rates of inflation in the United States and Switzerland. The dollar must depreciate by 100 percent, from $0.50 per franc to $1 per franc, to maintain its purchasing power parity. If the example assumed instead that Switzerland's inflation rate doubled while the U.S. inflation rate remained unchanged, the dollar would appreciate to a level of $0.25 per franc, according to the purchasing-power-parity theory.

An application of the purchasing-power-parity concept is provided in Table 12.4, which gives the dollar/peso exchange rate over the period 1985–1989, during which time Mexico experienced rampant inflation. From 1985 to 1989, U.S. prices rose by about 15 percent, whereas Mexico's prices skyrocketed more than 1,100 percent. Applying the purchasing-power-parity formula to these figures, we would forecast the dollar to appreciate against the peso, from $0.0039 per peso to $0.0004 per peso, owing to the relative decline in the peso's domestic purchasing power. In fact, the dollar did appreciate to $0.0004 per peso.

TABLE 12.4

Purchasing Power Parity in Action, 1985–1989

Year	U.S. Consumer Price Index	Mexican Consumer Price Index	Actual Exchange Rate: Dollars/Peso	Forecasted Exchange Rate: Dollars/Peso
1985	100.0	100.0	0.0039	—
1987	105.7	431.7	0.0007	0.0010
1989	115.2	1,109.6	0.0004	0.0004

Source: International Monetary Fund, *IMF Financial Statistics*, Washington, DC, May 1990.

Although the purchasing-power-parity theory can be helpful in forecasting appropriate levels to which currency values should be adjusted, it is not an infallible guide to exchange-rate determination. For instance, the theory overlooks the fact that exchange-rate movements may be influenced by investment flows. The theory also faces the problems of choosing the appropriate price index to be used in price calculations (for example, consumer prices or producer prices) and of determining the equilibrium period to use as a base. Moreover, government policy may interfere with the operation of the theory by implementing trade restrictions that disrupt the flow of exports and imports among nations.

The predictive power of the purchasing-power-parity theory is most evident in the long run. From 1973 to 2003, the British price level increased about 99 percent relative to the U.S. price level, as seen in Figure 12.3. As the purchasing-power-parity theory would forecast, the pound depreciated against the dollar by about 73 percent during this period, although this amount

is less than the 99 percent increase forecasted by the theory. Moreover, the figure shows that the purchasing-power-parity theory has negligible predictive power in the short run. From 1985 to 1988, for example, the British price level increased relative to the U.S. price level. Rather than depreciating, as the purchasing-power-parity theory would predict, the pound actually appreciated against the dollar. Simply put, the purchasing-power-parity theory is most appropriate for forecasting exchange rates in the long run; in the short run, it is a poor forecaster.

Determining Short-Run Exchange Rates: The Asset-Market Approach

We have seen that exchange-rate fluctuations in the long run stem from volatility in market fundamentals including relative price levels (purchasing power parity), relative productivity levels, preferences for

---

FIGURE 12.3

Purchasing Power Parity: United States–United Kingdom, 1973–2003

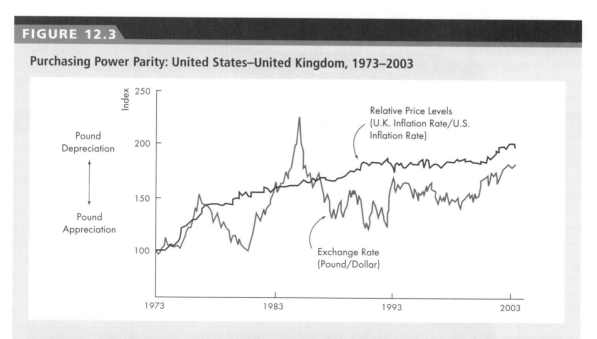

The figure suggests that the predictive power of the purchasing-power-parity theory is most evident in the long run. In the short run, the theory has negligible predictive power.

Source: *Economic Report of the President and National Statistics Online* at http://www.statistics.gov.uk.

domestic or foreign goods, and trade barriers. Fluctuations in exchange rates, however, are sometimes too large and too sudden to be explained solely by such factors. For example, exchange rates can change by 2 percentage points or more in a single day. But variations in the determinants usually do not occur frequently or significantly enough to fully account for such exchange-rate irascibility. Therefore, to understand why exchange rates can fluctuate sharply in a particular day or week, we must consider other factors besides relative price-level behavior, productivity trends, preferences, and trade barriers. We need to develop a framework that can demonstrate why exchange rates fluctuate in the short run.

To understand short-run exchange-rate behavior, it is important to recognize that foreign-exchange market activity is dominated by investors in assets such as Treasury securities, corporate bonds, bank accounts, stocks, and real property. Today, only about 2 percent of all foreign-exchange transactions are related to the financing of exports and imports. This suggests that most foreign-exchange transactions are attributable to assets being traded in global markets. Because these markets are connected by sophisticated telecommunication systems and trading occurs on a 24-hour basis, investors in financial assets can trade rapidly and modify their outlooks of currency values almost instantaneously. Simply put, over short periods such as a month, decisions to hold domestic or foreign assets play a much greater role in exchange-rate determination than the demand for imports and exports does.

According to the **asset-market approach**, investors consider two key factors when deciding between domestic and foreign investments: relative levels of interest rates and expected changes in the exchange rate itself over the term of the investment. These factors, in turn, account for fluctuations in exchange rates that we observe in the short run. Table 12.5 summarizes the effects of these factors.

Relative Levels of Interest Rates

The level of **nominal** (money) **interest rate** is a first approximation of the rate of return on assets that can be earned in a particular country. Thus, differences in the level of nominal interest rates between economies are likely to affect international investment flows, as investors seek the highest rate of return.

When interest rates in the United States are significantly higher than interest rates abroad, the foreign demand for U.S. securities and bank accounts will increase, which increases the

TABLE 12.5

Determinants of the Dollar's Exchange Rate Against the Pound in the Short Run

Change in Determinant*	Repositioning of International Financial Investment	Effect on Dollar's Exchange Rate
U.S. Interest Rate		
Increase	Toward dollar-denominated assets	Appreciates
Decrease	Toward pound-denominated assets	Depreciates
British Interest Rate		
Increase	Toward pound-denominated assets	Depreciates
Decrease	Toward dollar-denominated assets	Appreciates
Expected Future Change in the Dollar's Exchange Rate		
Appreciate	Toward dollar-denominated assets	Appreciates
Depreciate	Toward pound-denominated assets	Depreciates

*The analysis for a change in one determinant assumes that the other determinants are unchanged.

demand for the dollars needed to buy those assets, thus causing the dollar to appreciate relative to foreign currencies. In contrast, if interest rates in the United States are on average lower than interest rates abroad, the demand for foreign securities and bank accounts strengthens and the demand for U.S. securities and bank accounts weakens. This will cause the demand for foreign currencies needed to buy foreign assets to increase and the demand for the dollar to decrease, resulting in a depreciation of the dollar relative to foreign currencies.

To illustrate the effects of relative interest rates as a determinant of exchange rates, refer to Figure 12.4. It shows the demand and supply schedules of pounds. Initially, the equilibrium exchange rate is $1.50 per pound. Referring to Figure 12.4(a), assume that an expansionary monetary policy of the U.S. Federal Reserve results in a fall in interest rates to 3 percent, while interest rates in the United Kingdom are at 6 percent. U.S. investors will be attracted to the relatively high interest rates in the United Kingdom and will demand more pounds to buy British treasury bills. The demand for pounds

thus rises to D_1 in the figure. Concurrently, the British will find investing in the United States less attractive than before, so fewer pounds will be offered to buy dollars for purchases of U.S. securities. The supply of pounds thus decreases to S_1 in the figure. The combined effect of these two shifts is to cause the dollar to depreciate to $1.60 per pound. Alternatively, if interest rates were lower in the United Kingdom than in the United States, the dollar would appreciate against the pound as Americans made fewer investments in the United Kingdom and the British made more investments in the United States.

Things may not always be so simple, though, concerning the relationship between interest rates, investment flows, and exchange rates. It is important to distinguish between the nominal interest rate and the **real interest rate** (the nominal interest rate minus the inflation rate).

Real interest rate = Nominal interest rate − Inflation rate

For international investors, it is relative changes in the real interest rate that matter.

FIGURE 12.4

Factors Affecting the Dollar's Exchange Rate in the Short Run

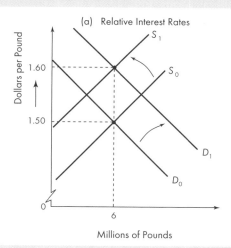 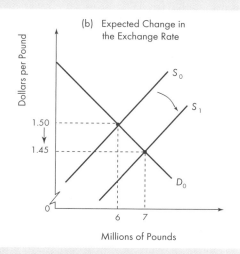

In the short run, the exchange rate between the dollar and the pound reflects interest rates and expected changes in the exchange rate.

Interest Rates and the Dollar's Exchange Value

Interest-Rate Differentials and Exchange Rates

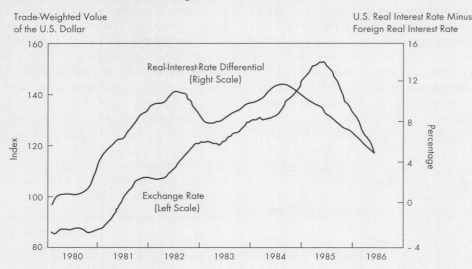

The theory of flexible exchange rates helps explain the behavior of the dollar in the 1980s. When real interest rates in the United States are increasing relative to real interest rates overseas, the U.S. dollar should appreciate as investors seek to locate their funds in the United States.

The figure shows the real-interest-rate differential between the United States and other industrial nations in the 1980s. Over the period 1980–1984, the real interest rate rose in the United States relative to the other nations. This attracted investment funds into the United States and promoted a steady appreciation in the dollar's value until early 1985. Subsequently, the dollar's exchange value decreased sharply as the real-interest-rate differential moved lower.

Source: Craig Hakkio, "Interest Rates and Exchange Rates: What Is the Relationship?" *Economic Review*, Federal Reserve Bank of Kansas City, November 1986.

If a rise in the nominal interest rate in the United States is accompanied by an equal rise in the U.S. inflation rate, the real interest rate remains constant. In this case, higher nominal interest rates do not make dollar-denominated securities more attractive to British investors. This is because rising U.S. inflation will encourage U.S. buyers to seek out low-priced British goods, which will increase the demand for pounds and cause the dollar to depreciate. British investors will expect the exchange rate of the dollar, in terms of the pound, to depreciate along with the declining purchasing power of the dollar. The higher nominal return on U.S. securities will thus be offset by the expectation of a lower future exchange rate, leaving the motivation for increased British investment in the United States unaffected. Only if higher nominal interest rates in the United States signal an increase in the real interest rate will the dollar appreciate; if they signal rising inflationary expectations and a falling real interest rate, the dollar will depreciate. Table 12.6 provides examples of short-term real interest rates for various nations.

In summary, we expect to see appreciating currencies in countries whose real interest rates are higher than abroad because these countries will attract investment funds from all over the world. Countries that experience relatively low real interest rates tend to find their currencies depreciating.

Expected Change in the Exchange Rate

Yet differences in interest rates may not be all an investor needs to know to guide her decision. One must also consider that the return actually realized from an investment is paid out over some future period. This means that the realized value of that future payment can be altered by changes in the exchange rate itself over the term of the investment. Simply put, investors must think about possible gains or losses on foreign currency transactions in addition to interest rates on assets.

Expectations about the future path of the exchange rate itself will figure prominently in the investor's calculation of what she will actually earn from an investment denominated in another currency. Even a high interest rate would not be attractive if one expects the denominating currency to depreciate at a similar or greater rate and erase all economic gain. Conversely, if the denominating currency is expected to appreciate, the realized gain would be greater than what the interest rate alone would suggest, and the asset appears more lucrative.

Figure 12.4(b) illustrates the effects of investor expectations of changes in exchange rates over the term of an investment. Assume that the equilibrium exchange rate is initially $1.50 per pound. Suppose that British investors expect that in 3 months the exchange value of the dollar will appreciate against the pound. Thus, by investing in 3-month U.S. Treasury bills, British investors can anticipate a foreign currency gain: initially selling pounds for dollars when dollars are relatively cheap, and, in 3 months, purchasing pounds with dollars when pounds are relatively cheap. The expectation of foreign currency gain will make U.S. Treasury bills seem more attractive, and the British will purchase more of them. In the figure, the supply of pounds in the foreign-exchange market will shift rightward from S_0 to S_1 and the dollar appreciates to $1.45 per pound.

TABLE 12.6

Short-Term Nominal and Real Interest Rates, 2002

Country	Nominal Interest Rate*	Inflation Rate**	Real Interest Rate
Canada	2.6	2.0	0.6
France	3.0	1.9	1.1
Germany	3.3	1.0	2.3
Japan	0.1	1.0	−0.9
Netherlands	2.8	3.5	−0.7
New Zealand	5.5	2.6	2.9
South Korea	4.2	2.7	1.5
Mexico	7.1	5.1	2.0
United States	1.6	1.0	0.6
United Kingdom	3.9	1.6	2.3

*Rates are for 3-month treasury bills.

**Measured by the consumer price index.

Source: *International Financial Statistics*, January 2004.

In this way, future expectations of an appreciation of the dollar can be self-fulfilling.

Given the importance of expectations in decision making and the speed with which many investment transactions can occur, exchange rates can be volatile. Predicting the magnitude and duration of short-run exchange-rate movements with precision is a very elusive goal.

Diversification, Safe Havens, and Investment Flows

Although relative levels of interest rates between countries and expected changes in exchange rates tend to be strong forces directing investment flows among economies, other factors can also affect these flows. For example, the size of the stock of assets denominated in a particular currency in investor portfolios can induce a change in investor preferences. Why? Investors know that it is prudent to have an appropriate degree of *diversification* across asset types, including the currencies in which they are denominated. Thus, even though dollar-denominated Treasury securities may provide a high relative return, if the accumulation has been large, at some point foreign investors, considering both risk and reward, will decide that their portfolio's share of U.S. securities is large enough. To improve the diversity of their portfolios, investors will slow or halt their purchases of U.S. securities.

There is also likely to be a significant *safe-haven* effect behind some investment flows. Some investors may be willing to sacrifice a significant amount of return if an economy offers them an especially low-risk repository for their funds. In recent decades, the United States, with a long history of stable government, steady economic growth, and large and efficient financial markets, can be expected to draw foreign investment for this reason.

The Ups and Downs of the Dollar: 1980 to 2004

Let us now apply the determinants of exchange rates to the path of the U.S. dollar since the 1980s. During this period, the dollar has experienced sustained appreciations and depreciations several times, but for different reasons. Let us examine the forces causing the ups and downs of the dollar.

The 1980s

During the 1980s, the dollar's exchange value followed a path of appreciation followed by depreciation. The dollar actually began its ascent in 1979 in response to a sharp tightening of monetary policy, which pushed up domestic interest rates. The Federal Reserve's objective at this time was not dollar appreciation, but to reign in double-digit inflation, which plagued the economy. Nevertheless, as investors became convinced of the Federal Reserve's determination in fighting inflation and the likely dual prospect of steadily increasing interest rates and decelerating inflation, the United States became an attractive destination for foreign investment. Also, the Reagan Administration enacted sizable tax cuts along with increased government spending, which resulted in large federal budget deficits. That federal borrowing increased the demand for a shrinking pool of domestic saving and added to the upward pressure on interest rates. Investment flowed into the United States and the dollar climbed higher. The dollar peaked in 1985, about 50 percent above its level in 1979.

The latter half of the 1980s witnessed a depreciation of the dollar of similar magnitude. What caused the change? One factor was a turn in the speculative belief that the dollar would continue to appreciate. At this point, a large number of investors apparently felt that the dollar was far above a sustainable level and now was more likely to depreciate than appreciate. These investor expectations were reinforced by sizable currency interventions by the United States and other major economies aimed at weakening an overvalued dollar. Investors thus developed expectations that the government wanted the dollar to depreciate and that changes in macroeconomic policy would support that desire. The Federal Reserve enacted an expansionary monetary policy that forced interest rates down. Fiscal policy began to reduce the size of budget deficits, which also fostered lower interest rates. Both factors contributed to investment outflows and a weakening dollar.

On balance, the 1980s illustrated that fluctuations in the dollar's exchange value were not haphazard, but were broadly predictable responses to changes in economic fundamentals that influence the expected rate of return on dollar-denominated assets. Also, those fluctuations were significantly caused by changes in macroeconomic policy, including monetary policy and fiscal policy.

The 1990s

The 1990s began in economic weakness for the United States. The pace of economic growth slowed sharply and the economy fell into recession in 1991. In response to the weakening economy, monetary policy turned to a more expansionary stance, and the federal budget deficit grew as fiscal policy increased government spending and dampened tax receipts. Interest rates in the United States fell. In contrast, economic activity abroad was moving relatively briskly. In this environment, the demand for dollar-denominated assets declined, and the dollar depreciated about 15 percent on average against the currencies of its major trading partners.

By the mid-1990s, however, the U.S. economy was growing rapidly. What underlaid the acceleration of growth was a sharp increase in the pace of investment spending by business and a market acceleration in productivity growth. The combination of strong consumer demand, deregulation, trade liberalization, and a rush to include computers in the production process propelled investment spending up at a record pace. But even with the federal budget's move toward surplus, the flow of domestic saving could not keep pace with investment, and interest rates edged up. Also, the United States witnessed a declining rate of inflation, while the economies of other nations such as Japan and Europe were sluggish. These factors resulted in the United States becoming an attractive destination for foreign investors. An increase in the foreign demand for dollar-denominated assets pushed the dollar steadily higher, rising over 30 percent on average against the currencies of its trading partners from 1995 through 2001.

This time, the dollar's sharp appreciation was propelled by the private sector. Economic policy moved in conflicting directions, probably making its net impact on the dollar a minor one. The government's move toward budget surpluses certainly added to national saving and lessened the dollar's appreciation. However, the Federal Reserve implemented a steadily more contractionary monetary policy that increased interest rates; this may have added to the dollar's upward momentum. But the Federal Reserve was not the main force behind the appreciation of the dollar.

Visit EconDebate Online for a debate on this topic

The 2000s

A rising dollar and the large flow of investment into the United States that pushes the currency higher could not be sustained. Borrowers and lenders alike tend to find sound reasons to reduce the size of the investment inflow. For lenders, rising risk and the imperative of adequate portfolio diversification can prompt a diminished willingness to acquire dollar-denominated assets. For the borrower, a rising burden of debt service may reduce the desire to borrow.

The depreciation of the dollar in 2002 and 2003 reflected a weakening of the demand for dollar-denominated assets on the part of foreign investors. Recession in the United States in 2001, a declining stock market, uncertainty about corporate accounting practices, and a steady decline in interest rates to levels not seen in over 30 years (and decreasing significantly more than foreign interest rates) all pointed to a likely deterioration of the attractiveness of the investment climate in the United States. Add to this the inevitable elevation of uncertainty due to the ongoing war on terrorism and the war with Iraq, and a depreciation of the dollar was not surprising.

Although the dollar continued to weaken into 2004, analysts generally felt that a crash of the dollar was not likely. This conclusion was reinforced by the fact that there seemed to be a shortage of better investment alternatives around the world. Most other major economies had lower growth rates than the United States. Also, the prospect of a series of large U.S. budget deficits in a growing economy suggested that interest rates in the United States would likely rise. Finally,

Does the Current Account Deficit Weigh on the Dollar?

U.S. Current Account Balance and Exchange Rate

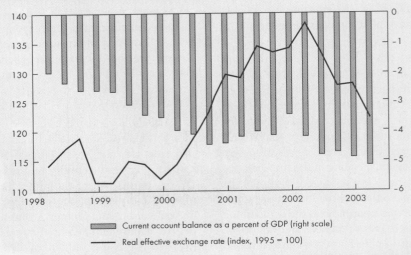

Current account balance as a percent of GDP (right scale)

Real effective exchange rate (index, 1995 = 100)

The United States has run current account deficits since the early 1980s. But only in the last couple of years have these deficits assumed extraordinary proportions. By 2003, the U.S. current account deficit was about 5 percent of GDP.

Recall from Chapter 10 that a country with a current account deficit has more imports of goods and services than exports and net receipts of transfers from abroad. Any current account deficit must be matched by a financial and capital

about three-fourths of foreign investment in the United states is long-term investment, including direct investment in plant and equipment, bonds, and stocks. These investments tend to be more stable than short-term investment flows because they are based on long-run return and are thus less sensitive to adverse short-term changes in economic conditions. However, predicting the path of the dollar is very difficult. Speculative forces can exert strong short-term effects that may not be tied to more predictable underlying fundamentals. It remains to be seen where the dollar will go in the years ahead.

Exchange-Rate Overshooting

Changes in expected future values of market fundamentals contribute to exchange-rate volatility in the short run. For example, announcements by the Federal Reserve of changes in monetary-growth targets or by the president and Congress of changes in tax or spending programs cause changes in expectations of future exchange rates that can lead to immediate changes in equilibrium exchange rates. In this manner, frequent changes in policy contribute to volatile exchange rates in a system of market-determined exchange rates.

account surplus. In other words, a country with a current account deficit surrenders claims on future income—such as physical assets, stocks, and bonds—to foreigners. In 2003, a U.S. current account deficit of 5 percent of GDP translated into an average of $1.6 billion in net capital imports per business day. That is, foreign investors were accumulating U.S. assets at an unusually high rate.

Foreign investors might become wary of holding increasingly larger portions of their wealth in U.S. assets. In order to promote continued investment in the United States, U.S. assets would then have to become more attractive. One way of attracting foreign investment is to lower the price of the asset in foreign-currency terms. A decline in the foreign-exchange value of the dollar would do just that. Therefore, a large current account deficit might be expected to depress the value of the dollar over time. But will the current account deficit decrease in response to currency depreciation? Researchers at the Federal Reserve Bank of St. Louis studied 25 episodes of current account reversals of industrial countries during the period 1980–1997. They found that, when a current account deficit approaches 5 percent of GDP, a country's real exchange rate starts depreciating. Typically, the current account starts to reverse toward balance one year after the onset of the currency depreciation. Three years after the peak deficit, most of the countries show a nearly complete reversal of a balanced current account.

The figure shows the real effective U.S. dollar exchange rate and the U.S. current account balance as a percentage of GDP for the period 1998–2003. In spite of a current account deficit in the neighborhood of 4 percent of GDP, the real effective value of the U.S. dollar appreciated considerably from 2000 to early 2002; subsequently, the dollar started declining amidst further widening of the current account deficit to about 5 percent of GDP. The researchers concluded that if the United States follows the typical pattern of current account reversals, then from 2003 to 2006 the real effective exchange rate should keep depreciating and the current account deficit will swing back to balance. It remains to be seen whether this forecast is correct.

Source: Frank Schmid, "Is the Current Account Deficit Weighing on the Dollar?" *International Economic Trends*, Federal Reserve Bank of St. Louis, August 2003, and Caroline Freund, "Current Account Adjustment in Industrialized Countries," *International Finance Discussion Paper No. 692*, Board of Governors of the Federal Reserve System, December 2000.

The volatility of exchange rates is further intensified by the phenomenon of **overshooting**. An exchange rate is said to overshoot when its short-run response (depreciation or appreciation) to a change in market fundamentals is *greater* than its long-run response. Changes in market fundamentals thus exert a disproportionately large *short-run* impact on exchange rates. Exchange-rate overshooting is an important phenomenon because it helps explain why exchange rates depreciate or appreciate so sharply from day to day.

Exchange-rate overshooting can be explained by the tendency of elasticities to be smaller in the short run than in the long run. Referring to Figure 12.5 on page 390, the short-run supply schedule and demand schedule of the British pound are denoted by S_0 and D_0, respectively, and the equilibrium exchange rate is $2 per pound. If the demand for pounds increases to D_1, the dollar depreciates to $2.20 per pound in the short run. Because of the dollar depreciation, however, there occurs a decrease in the British price of U.S. exports, an increase in the quantity of U.S. exports demanded, and thus an increase in the quantity of pounds supplied. The longer the time period, the greater the rise in the quantity of exports is likely to be, and the greater the rise in the quantity of pounds supplied will be.

FIGURE 12.5

Short-Run/Long-Run Equilibrium Exchange Rates: Overshooting

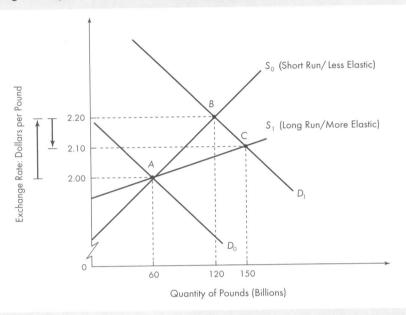

Given the short-run supply of pounds (S_0), if the demand for pounds increases from D_0 to D_1, the dollar depreciates from $2 per pound to a short-run equilibrium of $2.20 per pound. In the long run, the supply of pounds is more elastic (S_1), and the equilibrium exchange rate is lower, at $2.10 per pound. Because of the difference in these elasticities, the short-run depreciation of the dollar overshoots its long-run depreciation.

The long-run supply schedule of pounds is thus more elastic than the short-run supply schedule, as shown by S_1 in the figure. Following the increase in the demand for pounds to D_1, the long-run equilibrium exchange rate is $2.10 per pound, as compared to the short-run equilibrium exchange rate of $2.20 per pound. Because of differences in these elasticities, the dollar's depreciation in the short run overshoots its long-run depreciation.

Overshooting can also be explained by the fact that exchange rates tend to be more flexible than many other prices. Many prices are written into long-term contracts (for example, workers' wages) and do not respond immediately to changes in market fundamentals. Exchange rates, however, tend to be highly sensitive to current demand and sup-

ply conditions. Exchange rates often depreciate or appreciate more in the short run than in the long run so as to compensate for other prices that are slower to adjust to their long-run equilibrium levels. As the general price level slowly gravitates to its new equilibrium level, the amount of exchange-rate overshooting dissipates, and the exchange rate moves toward its long-run equilibrium level.

Forecasting Foreign-Exchange Rates

Previous sections of this chapter have examined various factors that determine exchange-rate movements. But even a clear understanding of how factors influence exchange rates does not guarantee that we can forecast how exchange rates will change. Not only do exchange-rate determinants often point in the opposite direction, but predicting how these determinants will change is also difficult. Forecasting exchange rates is tricky.

A major issue, as far as business is concerned, however, is whether **forecasting exchange rates** is feasible and, if so, how to do it. Because the future is unclear, participants in international financial markets are unsure what the spot rate will be in the months ahead. Exchange-rate forecasts are used by exporters, importers, investors, bankers, and foreign-exchange dealers.

Multinational enterprises need short-term currency-price forecasts for a variety of reasons. For example, corporations often have for brief periods large amounts of cash, used to make bank deposits in various currencies. Choosing a currency in which to make deposits requires some idea of what the currency's exchange rate will be in the future. Long-term corporate planning, especially concerning decisions about foreign investment, necessitates an awareness of where exchange rates will move over an extended time period—hence, the need for long-term forecasts. For multinational enterprises, short-term forecasting tends to be more widespread than long-term forecasting. Most corporations revise their currency forecasts at least every quarter.

The need of multinational enterprises and investors for forecasted currency values has resulted in the emergence of *consulting firms*, including Predex, Goldman Sachs, and Wharton Econometric Forecasting Associates. In addition, large banks such as Chase Manhattan Bank, Chemical Bank, and Citibank have provided free currency forecasts to corporate clients. Customers of consulting firms often pay fees ranging up to $100,000 per year or more for expert opinions. Consulting firms provide forecast services ranging from video screens to "listening-post" interviews with forecast service employees who provide their predictions of exchange-rate movements and respond to specific questions from the client. It has become customary for corporate managers to use home or hotel telephones to connect portable terminals to advisory services that make available foreign-exchange forecasts.

Most exchange-rate forecasting methods use accepted economic relationships to formulate a model that is then refined through statistical analysis of past data. The forecasts generated by the models are usually tempered by the additional insights or intuition of the forecaster before being offered to the final user.

In the current system of market-determined exchange rates, currency values fluctuate almost instantaneously in response to new information regarding changes in interest rates, inflation rates, money supplies, trade balances, and the like. To successfully forecast exchange-rate movements, it is necessary to estimate the future values of these economic variables and determine the relationship between them and future exchange rates. Even the most sophisticated analysis, however, can be rendered worthless by unexpected changes in government policy, market psychology, and so forth. Indeed, people who deal in the currency markets on a daily basis have come to feel that market psychology is a dominant influence on future exchange rates. Despite these problems, exchange-rate forecasters are in current demand. Their forecasting approaches are classified as judgmental, technical, or fundamental (econometric). Table 12.7 on page 392 provides examples of exchange-rate forecasting organizations and their methodologies.[4]

Judgmental Forecasts

Judgmental forecasts are sometimes known as subjective or commonsense models. They require the gathering of a wide array of political and economic data and the interpretation of these data in terms of the timing, direction, and magnitude of exchange-rate changes. Judgmental forecasters formulate projections based on a thorough examination of individual nations. They consider economic indicators, such as inflation rates and trade data; political factors, such as a future national election; technical factors, such as potential intervention by a central bank in the foreign-exchange market; and psychological factors that relate to one's "feel for the market."

[4]This section is drawn from Sam Cross, *The Foreign-Exchange Market in the United States*, Federal Reserve Bank of New York, 1998, pp. 113–115.

TABLE 12.7

Exchange-Rate Forecasters

Forecasting Organization	Methodology	Horizon
Chase Econometrics	Econometric	8 quarters
Chase Manhattan Bank	Judgmental	Under 12 months
Data Resources	Econometric	6 quarters
Exchange Rate Outlook	Judgmental	12 months ahead
Goldman Sachs	Technical	Under 12 months
	Econometric	Over 12 months
Phillips & Drew	Judgmental, econometric	6, 12 months ahead
Predex Forecast	Econometric	7 quarters
Predex Short-Term Forecast	Technical	1–3 months ahead
Wharton Econometric Forecasting Associates	Econometric	24 months ahead

Source: *Euromoney*, various issues.

Technical Forecasts

Technical analysis involves the use of historical exchange-rate data to estimate future values. The approach is technical in that it extrapolates from past exchange-rate trends and ignores economic and political determinants of exchange-rate movements. Technical analysts look for specific exchange-rate patterns. Once the beginning of a particular pattern has been determined, it automatically implies what the short-run behavior of the exchange rate will be.

Technical analysis encompasses a variety of charting techniques involving a currency's price, cycles, or volatility. A common starting point for technical analysis is a chart that plots a trading period's opening, high, low, and closing prices. These charts most often plot one trading day's range of prices, but also are created on a weekly, monthly, and yearly basis. Traders watch for new highs and lows, broken trendlines, and patterns that are thought to predict price targets and movement.

To illustrate technical analysis, assume you have formed an opinion about the yen's exchange value against the dollar based on your analysis of economic fundamentals. Now you want to look at what the markets can tell you; you're looking for price trends, and you can use charts to do it.

As shown in Figure 12.6, you might want to look at the relative highs and lows of the yen for the past several months; the trendlines in the figure connect the higher highs and the lower lows for the yen. If the yen's exchange rate moves substantially above or below the trendlines, it might signal that a trend is changing. Changes in trends help you decide when to purchase or sell yen in the foreign-exchange market.

Because technical analysis follows the market closely, it is used to forecast exchange-rate movements in the short run. Determining an exchange-rate pattern is useful only as long as the market continues to consistently follow that pattern. No pattern, however, can be relied on to continue more than a few days, perhaps weeks. A client must therefore respond quickly to a technical recommendation to buy or sell a currency. Clients require immediate communication of technical recommendations, so as to make timely financial decisions.

Although fundamental-based models have not been successful in forecasting exchange-rate movements over short-run periods, many technical-based models have been useful in explaining exchange-rate movements over short-run periods. It is not surprising that most foreign-exchange dealers use some technical model input to help

FIGURE 12.6

Technical Analysis of the Yen's Exchange Value

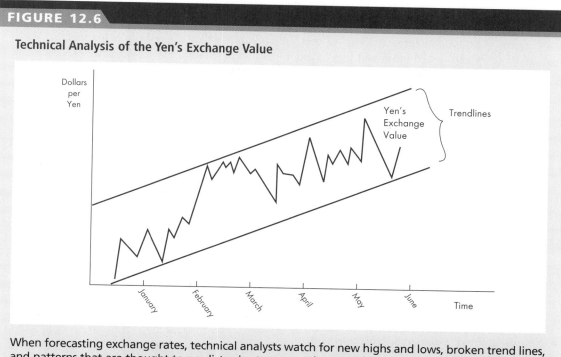

When forecasting exchange rates, technical analysts watch for new highs and lows, broken trend lines, and patterns that are thought to predict price targets and movement.

them formulate their forecast for exchange rates, especially for intraday and one-week horizons.

Fundamental Analysis

Fundamental analysis is the opposite of technical analysis. It involves consideration of economic variables that are likely to affect a currency's value. Fundamental analysis uses computer-based econometric models, which are statistical estimations of economic theories. To generate forecasts, econometricians develop models for individual nations that attempt to incorporate the fundamental variables that underlie exchange-rate movements: trade and investment flows, industrial activity, inflation rates, and the like. If you take an econometric course at your university, you might consider preparing an exchange-rate forecast as your class project. "Exploring Further 12.1" at the end of this chapter gives you an idea of the types of variables you might include in your econometric model.

Econometric models used to forecast exchange rates, however, face limitations. They often rely on predictions of key economic variables, such as inflation rates or interest rates, and obtaining reliable information can be difficult. Moreover, there are always factors affecting exchange rates that cannot easily be quantified (such as intervention by a country's central bank in currency markets). Also, the precise timing of a factor's effect on a currency's exchange rate may be unclear. For example, inflation-rate changes may not have their full impact on a currency's value until three or six months in the future. Thus, econometric models are best suited for forecasting long-run exchange-rate trends.

As we have learned, those who forecast foreign-exchange rates often are divided into those who use technical analysis and those who rely on analysis of economic determinants. Nearly all traders acknowledge their use of technical analysis and charts. According to surveys, a majority say they employ technical analysis to a greater extent than fundamental analysis and that they regard it as more useful than fundamental analysis—a contrast to 30 years ago, when most said they relied more heavily on fundamental analysis.

In spite of the appeal of technical analysis, most forecasters tend to use a combination of fundamental, technical, and judgmental analysis, with the emphasis on each shifting as conditions change. They form a general view about whether a particular currency is overvalued or undervalued in a longer-term sense. Within that framework, they assess all current economic forecasts, news events, political developments, statistical releases, rumors, and changes in sentiment, while also carefully studying the charts and technical analysis.

Forecast Performance of Advisory Services

To be successful, a forecasting model should provide better information about future exchange rates than is available to the market in general. Successful forecasters are those who can consistently profit from their forecasting activities by predicting *more accurately* than the rest of the market.

In evaluating the performance of forecasters, it is important to determine what a naive forecast would be in the absence of any specific model or information. Assuming efficient foreign-exchange markets in which prices reflect all available information, what exchange-rate prediction is implicit in market quotations? As discussed in Chapter 11, the *forward-exchange rate* (the spot rate plus the interest-rate differential) is the rational approximation of the market's expectation of the spot rate that will exist at the end of the forward period. This means that the forward *premium* or *discount* on a currency serves as a rough benchmark of the expected rate of appreciation or depreciation of a currency. The forward rate is widely considered to be useful as a forecasting device for a period of one to three months. A successful forecaster should thus be able to predict spot rates better than what is implied by the forward rate.

Summary

1. In a free market, exchange rates are determined by market fundamentals and market expectations. The former includes real interest rates, consumer preferences for domestic or foreign products, productivity, investment profitability, product availability, monetary policy and fiscal policy, and government trade policy. Economists generally agree that the major determinants of exchange-rate fluctuations are different in the long run than in the short run.

2. The determinants of long-run exchange rates differ from the determinants of short-run exchange rates. In the long run, exchange rates are determined by four key factors: relative price levels, relative productivity levels, consumer preferences for domestic or foreign goods, and trade barriers. These factors underlie trade in domestic and foreign goods and thus changes in the demand for exports and imports.

3. In the long run, a nation's currency tends to appreciate when the nation has relatively low levels of inflation, relatively high levels of productivity, relatively strong demand for its export products, and relatively high barriers to trade.

4. According to the purchasing-power-parity theory, changes in relative national price levels determine changes in exchange rates over the long run. A currency maintains its purchasing power parity if it depreciates (appreciates) by an amount equal to the excess of domestic (foreign) inflation over foreign (domestic) inflation.

5. Over short periods of time, decisions to hold domestic or foreign financial assets play a much greater role in exchange-rate determination than the demand for imports and exports does. According to the asset-market approach to exchange-rate determination, investors consider two key factors when deciding

between domestic and foreign investments: relative interest rates and expected changes in exchange rates. Changes in these factors, in turn, account for fluctuations in exchange rates that we observe in the short run.

6. Short-term interest-rate differentials between any two nations are important determinants of international investment flows and short-term exchange rates. A nation that has relatively high (low) interest rates tends to find its currency's exchange value appreciating (depreciating) in the short run.

7. In the short run, market expectations also influence exchange-rate movements. Future expectations of rapid domestic economic growth, falling domestic interest rates, and high domestic inflation rates tend to cause the domestic currency to depreciate.

8. Exchange-rate volatility is intensified by the phenomenon of overshooting. An exchange rate is said to overshoot when its short-run response to a change in market fundamentals is greater than its long-run response.

9. Currency forecasters use several methods to predict future exchange-rate movements: (a) judgmental forecasts, (b) technical analysis, and (c) fundamental analysis.

Key Concepts and Terms

- Asset-market approach *(page 382)*
- Forecasting exchange rates *(page 391)*
- Fundamental analysis *(page 393)*
- Judgmental forecasts *(page 391)*
- Law of one price *(page 376)*
- Market expectations *(page 372)*
- Market fundamentals *(page 372)*
- Nominal interest rate *(page 382)*
- Overshooting *(page 389)*
- Purchasing-power-parity approach *(page 376)*
- Real interest rate *(page 383)*
- Relative purchasing power parity *(page 379)*
- Technical analysis *(page 392)*

Study Questions

1. In a free market, what factors underlie currency exchange values? Which factors best apply to long-run exchange rates and to short-run exchange rates?

2. Why are international investors especially concerned about the real interest rate as opposed to the nominal rate?

3. What predictions does the purchasing-power-parity theory make concerning the impact of domestic inflation on the home country's exchange rate? What are some limitations of the purchasing-power-parity theory?

4. If a currency becomes overvalued in the foreign-exchange market, what will be the likely impact on the home country's trade balance? What if the home currency becomes undervalued?

5. Identify the factors that account for changes in a currency's value over the long run.

6. What factors underlie changes in a currency's value in the short run?

7. Explain how the following factors affect the dollar's exchange rate under a system of market-determined exchange rates: (a) a rise in the U.S. price level, with the foreign price level held constant; (b) tariffs and quotas placed on U.S. imports; (c) increased demand for U.S. exports and decreased U.S. demand for imports; (d) rising productivity in the United States relative to other countries; (e) rising real interest rates overseas, relative to U.S. rates; (f) an increase in U.S. money growth; (g) an increase in U.S. money demand.

8. What is meant by exchange-rate overshooting? Why does it occur?

9. What methods do currency forecasters use to predict future changes in exchange rates?

10. **Xtra!** **For a tutorial of this question, go to** http://carbaughxtra.swlearning.com
Assuming market-determined exchange rates, use supply and demand schedules for pounds to analyze the effect on the exchange rate (dollars per pound) between the U.S. dollar and the British pound under each of the following circumstances:

a. Voter polls suggest that Britain's conservative government will be replaced by radicals who pledge to nationalize all foreign-owned assets.

b. Both the British economy and U.S. economy slide into recession, but the British recession is less severe than the U.S. recession.

c. The Federal Reserve adopts a tight monetary policy that dramatically increases U.S. interest rates.

d. Britain's oil production in the North Sea decreases, and exports to the United States fall.

e. The United States unilaterally reduces tariffs on British products.

f. Britain encounters severe inflation, while price stability exists in the United States.

g. Fears of terrorism reduce U.S. tourism in Britain.

h. The British government invites U.S. firms to invest in British oil fields.

i. The rate of productivity growth in Britain decreases sharply.

j. An economic boom occurs in Britain, which induces the British to purchase more U.S.–made autos, trucks, and computers.

k. Ten-percent inflation occurs in both Britain and the United States.

11. Explain why you agree or disagree with each of the following statements:

a. "A nation's currency will depreciate if its inflation rate is less than that of its trading partners."

b. "A nation whose interest rate falls more rapidly than that of other nations can expect the exchange value of its currency to depreciate."

c. "A nation that experiences higher growth rates in productivity than its trading partners can expect the exchange value of its currency to appreciate."

12. The appreciation in the dollar's exchange value from 1980 to 1985 made U.S. products (less/more) expensive and foreign products (less/more) expensive, (decreased, increased) U.S. imports, and (decreased, increased) U.S. exports.

13. Suppose the dollar/franc exchange rate equals $0.50 per franc. According to the purchasing-power-parity theory, what will happen to the dollar's exchange value under each of the following circumstances?

a. The U.S. price level increases by 10 percent and the price level in Switzerland stays constant.

b. The U.S. price level increases by 10 percent and the price level in Switzerland increases by 20 percent.

c. The U.S. price level decreases by 10 percent and the price level in Switzerland increases by 5 percent.

d. The U.S. price level decreases by 10 percent and the price level in Switzerland decreases by 15 percent.

14. Suppose that the nominal interest rate on 3-month Treasury bills is 8 percent in the United States and 6 percent in the United Kingdom, and the rate of inflation is 10 percent in the United States and 4 percent in the United Kingdom.

a. What is the real interest rate in each nation?

b. In which direction would international investment flow in response to these real interest rates?

c. What impact would these investment flows have on the dollar's exchange value?

12.1 Historical information on exchange rates can be found at the home page of the Federal Reserve Bank of St. Louis. After going to the link, click on Economic Research, FRED II, and then U.S. Trade & International Transactions and Trade Balances. Set your browser to this URL:

http://www.stls.frb.org

12.2 The Pacific Exchange Rate Service provides information on current and past daily exchange rates, as well as exchange-rate forecasts for the Canadian dollar relative to five other major currencies. Set your browser to this URL:

http://pacific.commerce.ubc.ca/xr

To access NetLink Exercises and the Virtual Scavenger Hunt, visit the Carbaugh Web site at http://carbaugh.swlearning.com.

Xtra!

CARBAUGH

Log onto the Carbaugh Xtra! Web site (http://carbaughxtra.swlearning.com) for additional learning resources such as practice quizzes, help with graphing, and current events applications.

12·1

Fundamental Forecasting—Regression Analysis

Recall that fundamental forecasting involves estimating an exchange rate's response to changes in economic factors. By determining how these factors have influenced exchange-rate fluctuations in the past, one can get insight about the future course of the exchange rate. Regression analysis is often used to make such an assessment. Forecasting organizations, such as Chase Econometrics, construct regression models based on 20 or more economic determinants of exchange rates.

Suppose we wish to forecast the percentage change in the Swiss franc's exchange value against the dollar in the next quarter. For simplicity, assume that our forecast for the franc is dependent on only two factors that influence the franc's exchange value: (1) the inflation-rate differential between the United States and Switzerland; and (2) the income-growth differential, measured as a percentage change, between the United States and Switzerland. Assume also that these factors have a lagged effect on the franc's exchange rate. A regression model can be constructed as follows:

$$Y_t = b_0 + b_1 X1_{t-n} + b_2 X2_{t-n} + u_1$$

wherein the dependent variable, the quarterly percentage change in the franc's exchange value (Y), is related to quarterly percentage changes in the two independent variables, the U.S./Swiss inflation differential ($X1$) and the U.S./Swiss income growth differential ($X2$). In the model, b_2 is a constant, b_1 indicates the sensitivity of the franc's exchange value to

changes in the inflation differential between the United States and Switzerland, b_2 indicates the sensitivity of the franc's exchange value to changes in the income growth differential between the United States and Switzerland, t stands for the time period, n indicates the number of quarters lagged, and u_t is an error term with all assumed statistical properties.

Once the regression model is constructed, a set of historical data must be compiled for quarterly changes in the franc's exchange rate, the U.S./Swiss inflation differential, and the U.S./Swiss income-growth differential. A large time-series database is desirable, generally consisting of 30 or more quarters of information. Using these data, suppose our model estimates the following regression coefficients:

$$b_1 = 0.6$$
$$b_1 = 0.4$$

The regression coefficient $b_1 = 0.6$ implies that for every 1-unit percentage change in the U.S./Swiss inflation differential, the predicted percentage change in the franc's exchange value is 0.6 percent, the income-growth differential remaining constant. Underlying this positive relationship is the tendency for relatively high inflation in the United States to cause a rise (appreciation) in the franc's value against the dollar, and vice versa. The regression coefficient $b_2 = 0.4$ suggests that for each 1-unit percentage change in the U.S./Swiss income-growth differential, the predicted percentage change in the franc's exchange value is 0.4 percent, the inflation-rate differential remaining constant. The positive relationship suggests that relatively high income growth in the United States leads to an appreciation in the franc against the dollar, and vice versa. Once the regression coefficients have been estimated, and any potential statistical problems have been corrected, the coefficients can be tested to determine if they are statistically significant. If so, there exists a predictable relationship between a given exchange-rate determinant and the franc's exchange rate.

Our regression model can now be used for exchange-rate forecasting. Suppose that in the most recent year the U.S. inflation rate exceeded the Swiss inflation rate by 3 percentage points and that the U.S. income-growth rate exceeded the Swiss income-growth rate by 1 percentage point. Combining these data with the estimated regression coefficients, the forecast for the franc's exchange value is

$$
\begin{aligned}
Y_t &= b_0 + b_1 X1_{t-n} + b_2 X2_{t-n} + u_1 \\
&= .01 + .6(3\%) + .4(1\%) \\
&= 1\% + 1.8\% + .4\% \\
&= 3.2\%
\end{aligned}
$$

Our forecast is that the franc will appreciate by about 3.2 percent against the dollar in the next quarter.

In practice, using regression analysis to forecast exchange rates is more difficult than our simplified model suggests. Recall that our model was based on the impact of inflation differentials and income-growth differentials on trade flows and their effects on foreign-exchange market trading. In reality, much foreign-exchange market trading is related to investment flows and speculation, which requires that other variables be included in our model, such as relative interest rates and future expectations. Finally, other exchange-rate determinants, such as labor strikes, are difficult to measure and cannot be included in our model. As a result of these limitations, even the most sophisticated regression models cannot produce consistently accurate exchange-rate forecasts. Forecasters typically modify the results of regression models with their own commonsense judgments.

chapter 13

Balance-of-Payments Adjustments

In Chapter 10, we learned about the meaning of a balance-of-payments deficit and surplus. Recall that, owing to double-entry bookkeeping, total inpayments (credits) always equal total outpayments (debits) when all balance-of-payments accounts are considered. A deficit refers to an excess of outpayments over inpayments for selected accounts grouped along functional lines. For example, a current account deficit suggests an excess of imports over exports of goods, services, income flows, and unilateral transfers. A current account surplus implies the opposite.

A nation finances or covers a current account deficit out of its international reserves or by attracting investment (such as purchases of factories) or borrowing from other nations. The capacity of a *deficit nation* to cover the excess of outpayments over inpayments is limited by its stocks of international reserves and the willingness of other nations to invest in, or lend to, the deficit nation. For a surplus nation, once it believes that its stocks of international reserves or overseas investments are adequate—although history shows that this belief may be a long time in coming—it will be reluctant to run prolonged surpluses. In general, the incentive for reducing a payments surplus is not so direct and immediate as that for reducing a payments deficit.

The **adjustment mechanism** works for the return to equilibrium after the initial equilibrium has been disrupted. The process of payments adjustment takes two different forms. First, under certain conditions, there are adjustment factors that automatically promote equilibrium. Second, should the automatic adjustments be unable to restore equilibrium, discretionary government policies may be adopted to achieve this objective.

This chapter emphasizes the **automatic adjustment** of the balance-of-payments process that occurs under a fixed exchange-rate system.[1] The adjustment variables that we will examine include prices, interest rates, and income. The impact of money on the balance of payments is also considered. Subsequent chapters discuss the adjustment mechanism under flexible exchange rates and the role of government policy in promoting payments adjustment.

---

[1] Under a fixed exchange-rate system, the supply of and demand for foreign exchange reflect credit and debit transactions in the balance of payments. These forces of supply and demand, however, are not permitted to determine the exchange rate. Instead, government officials peg, or fix, the exchange rate at a stipulated level by intervening in the foreign-exchange markets to purchase and sell currencies. This topic is examined further in the next chapter.

Although the various automatic adjustment approaches have their contemporary advocates, each was formulated during a particular period and reflects a different philosophical climate. That the balance of payments could be adjusted by prices and interest rates stemmed from the *classical* economic thinking of the 1800s and early 1900s. The classical approach was geared toward the existing gold standard associated with fixed exchange rates. That income changes could promote balance-of-payments adjustments reflected the *Keynesian* theory of income determination, which grew out of the Great Depression of the 1930s. That money plays a crucial role in the long run as a disturbance and adjustment in the nation's balance of payments is an extension of domestic monetarism. This approach originated during the late 1960s and is associated with the *Chicago school* of economic thought.

Price Adjustments

The original theory of balance-of-payments adjustment is credited to David Hume (1711–1776), the English philosopher and economist.[2] Hume's theory arose from his concern with the prevailing mercantilist view that advocated government controls to ensure a continuous favorable balance of payments. According to Hume, this strategy was self-defeating over the long run because a nation's balance of payments tends to move toward equilibrium *automatically*. Hume's theory stresses the role that adjustments in national *price levels* play in promoting balance-of-payments equilibrium.

Gold Standard

The classical **gold standard** that existed from the late 1800s to the early 1900s was characterized by three conditions. (1) Each member nation's money supply consisted of gold or paper money backed by gold. (2) Each member nation defined the official price of gold in terms of its national

[2]David Hume, "Of the Balance of Trade." Reprinted in Richard N. Cooper, ed., *International Finance: Selected Readings* (Harmondsworth, England: Penguin Books, 1969), Chapter 1.

currency and was prepared to buy and sell gold at that price. (3) Free import and export of gold was permitted by member nations. Under these conditions, a nation's money supply was directly tied to its balance of payments. A nation with a balance-of-payments surplus would acquire gold, directly expanding its money supply. Conversely, the money supply of a deficit nation would decline as the result of a gold outflow.

The balance of payments can also be tied directly to a nation's money supply under a modified gold standard, requiring that the nation's stock of money be fractionally backed by gold at a constant ratio. It would also apply to a fixed exchange-rate system in which payments disequilibria are financed by some acceptable international reserve asset, assuming that a constant ratio between the nation's international reserves and its money supply is maintained.

Quantity Theory of Money

The essence of the classical price-adjustment mechanism is embodied in the **quantity theory of money**. Consider the *equation of exchange*:

$$MV = PQ$$

M refers to a nation's money supply. V refers to the velocity of money—that is, the number of times per year the average currency unit is spent on final goods. The expression MV corresponds to the aggregate demand, or total monetary expenditures on final goods. Alternatively, the monetary expenditures on any year's output can be interpreted as the physical volume of all final goods produced (Q) multiplied by the average price at which each of the final goods is sold (P). As a result, $MV = PQ$.

This equation is an identity. It says that total monetary expenditures on final goods equals the monetary value of the final goods sold; the amount spent on final goods equals the amount received from selling them.

The classical economists made two additional assumptions. First, they took the volume of final output (Q) to be fixed at the full employment level in the long run. Second, they assumed that the velocity of money (V) was constant, depending on institutional, structural, and physical factors that rarely changed. With V and Q relatively stable, a change in M must induce a *direct and proportionate change* in P. The model linking changes in M to changes in P became known as the *quantity theory of money*.

Balance-of-Payments Adjustment

The preceding analysis showed how, under the classical gold standard, the balance of payments is linked to a nation's money supply, which is linked to its domestic price level. Let us consider how the price level is linked to the balance of payments.

Suppose that, under the classical gold standard, a nation realized a balance-of-payments deficit. The deficit nation would experience a gold outflow, which would reduce its money supply and thus its price level. The nation's international competitiveness would be enhanced, so that its exports would rise and imports fall. This process would continue until its price level had fallen to the point where balance-of-payments equilibrium was restored. Conversely, a nation with a balance-of-payments surplus would realize gold inflows and an increase in its money supply. This process would continue until its price level had risen to the point where balance-of-payments equilibrium was restored. Thus, the opposite price-adjustment process would occur at the same time in each trading partner.

The price-adjustment mechanism as devised by Hume illustrated the impossibility of the mercantilist notion of maintaining a continuous favorable balance of payments. The linkages (balance of payments—money supply—price level—balance of payments) demonstrated to Hume that, over time, balance-of-payments equilibrium tends to be achieved automatically.

With the advent of Hume's price-adjustment mechanism, classical economists had a very powerful and influential theory. It was not until the Keynesian revolution in economic thinking during the 1930s that this theory was effectively challenged. Even today, the price-adjustment mechanism is a hotly debated issue. A brief discussion of some of the major criticisms against the price-adjustment mechanism is in order.

The classical linkage between changes in a nation's gold supply and changes in its money supply no longer holds. Central bankers can easily offset a gold outflow (or inflow) by adopting an expansionary (or contractionary) monetary policy. The experience of the gold standard of the late 1800s and early 1900s indicates that these offsetting monetary policies often occurred. The classical view that full employment always exists has also been challenged. When an economy is far below its full employment level, there is a smaller chance that prices in general will rise in response to an increase in the money supply than if the economy is at full employment. It has also been pointed out that, in a modern industrial world, prices and wages are inflexible in a downward direction. If prices are inflexible downward, then changes in M will affect not P but rather Q. A deficit nation's falling money supply will bring about a fall in output and employment. Furthermore, the stability and predictability of V have been questioned. Should a gold inflow that results in an increase in M be offset by a decline in V, total spending (MV) and PQ would remain unchanged.

These issues are part of the current debate over the price-adjustment mechanism's relevance. They have caused sufficient doubts among economists to warrant a search for additional balance-of-payments adjustment explanations. The most notable include the effect of interest-rate changes on capital movements and the effect of changing incomes on trade flows.

Interest-Rate Adjustments

Under the classical gold standard, the price-adjustment mechanism was not the only vehicle that served to restore equilibrium in the balance of payments. Another monetary effect of a payments surplus or deficit lay in its impact on *short-term interest rates* and hence on short-term private capital flows.

Consider a world of two countries: nation A, enjoying a surplus, and nation B, facing a deficit. The inflow of gold from the deficit to the surplus nation automatically results in an increase in nation A's money supply and a decline in the money supply of nation B. Given a constant demand for money, the increase in nation A's money supply would lower domestic interest rates. At the same time, nation B's gold outflow and declining money supply would bid up interest rates. In response to falling domestic interest rates and rising foreign interest rates, the investors of nation A would find it attractive to send additional investment funds abroad. Conversely, nation-B investors would not only be discouraged from sending money overseas, but they might also find it beneficial to liquidate foreign investment holdings and put the funds into domestic assets.

This process facilitates the automatic restoration of payments equilibrium in both nations. Because of the induced changes in interest rates, stabilizing capital movements automatically flow from the surplus to the deficit nation, thereby reducing the payment imbalances of both nations. Although this induced short-term capital movement is temporary rather than continuous, it nevertheless facilitates the automatic balance-of-payments adjustment process.

During the actual operation of the gold standard, however, central bankers were not totally passive in response to these automatic adjustments. They instead agreed to reinforce and speed up the interest-rate adjustment mechanism by adhering to the so-called **rules of the game**. This required central bankers in a *surplus* nation to *expand* credit, leading to lower interest rates; central bankers in *deficit* nations would *tighten* credit, bidding interest rates upward. Private short-term capital presumably would flow from the surplus nation to the deficit nation. Not only would the deficit nation's ability to finance its payments imbalance be strengthened, but also the surplus nation's gold inflows would be checked.

Financial Flows and Interest-Rate Differentials

The classical economists were aware of the impact of changes in interest rates on international financial movements, even though this factor was not the central focus of their balance-of-payments adjustment theory. With national financial systems closely integrated today, it is recognized that interest-rate

ECONOMIC *Applications*

Visit EconData Online

fluctuations can induce significant changes in a nation's capital and financial account, as discussed in Chapter 10.

Recall that capital and financial transactions include all international purchases or sales of assets, such as real estate, corporate stocks and bonds, commercial bank deposits, and government securities. The vast majority of transactions appearing in the capital and financial account come from financial transactions. The most important factor that causes financial assets to move across national borders is interest rates in domestic and foreign markets. However, other factors are important too, such as investment profitability, national tax policies, and political stability.

Figure 13.1 on page 404 shows hypothetical capital and financial account schedules for the United States. Capital and financial account *surpluses* and *deficits* are measured on the vertical axis. In particular, financial flows between the United States and the rest of the world are assumed to respond to *interest-rate differentials* between the two areas (U.S. interest rate minus foreign interest rate) for a particular set of economic conditions in the United States and abroad.

Referring to schedule CFA_0, the U.S. capital and financial account is in *balance* at point A, where the U.S. interest rate is equal to that abroad. Should the United States reduce its monetary growth, the scarcity of money would tend to raise interest rates in the United States compared with the rest of the world. Suppose U.S. interest rates rise 1 percent above those overseas. Investors, seeing higher U.S. interest rates, will tend to sell foreign securities to purchase U.S. securities that offer a higher yield. The 1 percent interest-rate differential leads to *net financial inflows* of $5 billion for the United States, which thus moves to point B on schedule CFA_0. Conversely, should foreign interest rates rise above those in the United States, the United States will face *net financial outflows* as investors sell U.S. securities to purchase foreign securities offering a higher yield.

Figure 13.1 assumes that interest-rate differentials are the basic determinant of financial flows for the United States. That is, movements along schedule CFA_0 are caused by changes in the interest rate

FIGURE 13.1

Capital and Financial Account Schedule for the United States

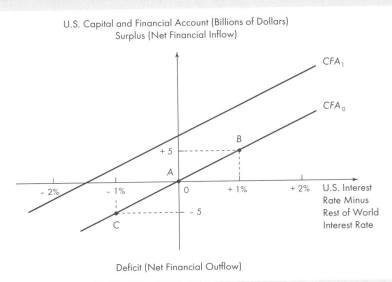

Interest-rate differentials between the United States and the rest of the world induce movements along the U.S. capital and financial account schedule. Relatively high (low) U.S. interest rates trigger net financial inflows (outflows) and an upward (downward) movement along the capital and financial account schedule. The schedule shifts upward/downward in response to changes in noninterest-rate determinants such as investment profitability, tax policies, and political stability.

in the United States relative to that in the rest of the world. However, there are certain determinants other than interest-rate differentials that might cause the United States to import (or export) more or less assets at each possible interest-rate differential and thereby change the location of schedule CFA_0.

To illustrate, assume the United States is located along schedule CFA_0 at point A. Suppose that rising U.S. income leads to higher sales and increased profits. Direct investment (in an auto-assembly plant, for example) becomes more profitable in the United States. Nations such as Japan will invest more in their U.S. subsidiaries, whereas General Motors will invest less overseas. The higher profitability of direct investment leads to a greater flow of funds into the United States at

each possible interest-rate differential and an upward shift in the schedule to CFA_1.

Suppose the U.S. government levies an *interest equalization tax*, as it did from 1964 to 1974. This tax was intended to help reverse the large financial outflows that the United States faced when European interest rates exceeded those in the United States. By taxing U.S. investors on dividend and interest income from foreign securities, the tax reduced the net profitability (that is, the after-tax yield) of foreign securities. At the same time, the U.S. government enacted a foreign-credit-restraint program, which placed direct restrictions on foreign lending by U.S. banks and financial institutions and later on foreign lending of nonfinancial corporations. By discouraging flows of funds from the United States to Europe, these policies resulted in an upward shift in the U.S. capital and financial account schedule in Figure 13.1, suggesting that less funds would flow out of the United States in response to higher interest rates overseas.

Income Adjustments

The classical balance-of-payments adjustment theory relied primarily on the price-adjustment mechanism, while delegating a secondary role to the effects of interest rates on private short-term capital movements. A main criticism of the classical theory was that it almost completely neglected the effect of *income adjustments*. The classical economists were aware that the income, or purchasing power, of a surplus nation rose relative to that of the deficit nation. This would have an impact on the level of imports in each nation. But the income effect was viewed as an accompaniment of price changes. Largely because the gold movements of the nineteenth century exerted only minor impacts on price and interest-rate levels, economic theorists began to look for alternate balance-of-payments adjustment explanations under a fixed exchange-rate system. The theory of **income determination,** developed by John Maynard Keynes in the 1930s, provided such an explanation.[3]

Keynes asserted that under a system of fixed exchange rates, the influence of income changes in surplus and deficit nations would help restore payments equilibrium *automatically*. Given a persistent payments imbalance, a surplus nation will experience rising income, and its imports will increase. Conversely, a deficit nation will experience a fall in income, resulting in a decline in imports. These effects of income changes on import levels will reverse the disequilibrium in the balance of payments. The income adjustment mechanism is more fully discussed in "Exploring Further 13.1" at the end of this chapter.

The preceding income-adjustment analysis needs to be modified to include the impact that changes in domestic expenditures and income levels have on foreign economies. This process is referred to as the **foreign repercussion effect.**

[3]John Maynard Keynes, *The General Theory of Employment, Interest, and Money* (London: Macmillan, 1936).

Assume a two-country world, the United States and Canada, in which there initially exists balance-of-payments equilibrium. Owing to changing consumer preferences, suppose the United States faces an autonomous increase in imports from Canada. This results in an increase in Canada's exports. The result is a decrease in U.S. income, and an increase in Canada's income. The fall in U.S. income induces a fall in the level of U.S. imports (and a fall in Canada's exports). At the same time, the rise in Canada's income induces a rise in Canada's imports (and a rise in U.S. exports). This feedback process is repeated again and again.

The consequence of this process is that both the rise in income of the surplus nation (Canada) and the fall in income of the deficit nation (United States) are dampened. This is because the autonomous increase in U.S. imports (and Canada's exports) will cause the U.S. income to decrease as imports are substituted for home-produced goods. The decline in U.S. income will generate a reduction in its imports. Because U.S. imports are Canada's exports, the result will be to moderate the rise in Canada's income. From the perspective of the United States, the decline in its income will be cushioned by an increase in exports to Canada stemming from a rise in Canada's income.

The importance of the foreign repercussion effect depends in part on the economic size of a country as far as international trade is concerned. A small nation that increases its imports from a large nation will have little impact on the large nation's income level. But for major trading nations, the foreign repercussion effect is likely to be significant and must be taken into account when the income-adjustment mechanism is being considered.

Disadvantages of Automatic Adjustment Mechanisms

The preceding sections have considered automatic balance-of-payments adjustment mechanisms under a system of fixed exchange rates. According to the classical school of thought, adjustments occur as prices and interest rates respond to international gold movements. Keynesian theory emphasized another adjustment process, the effect of changes in national income on a nation's balance of payments.

Although elements of price, interest rate, and income adjustments may operate in the real world, these adjustment mechanisms have a major shortcoming. The problem is that an efficient adjustment mechanism requires central bankers to forgo their use of monetary policy to promote the goal of full employment without inflation; each nation must be willing to accept inflation or recession when balance-of-payments adjustment requires it. Take the case of a nation that faces a deficit caused by an autonomous increase in imports or decrease in exports. For income adjustments to reverse the deficit, monetary authorities must permit domestic income to decrease and not undertake policies to offset its decline. The opposite applies equally to a nation with a balance-of-payments surplus.

To the classical economists, abandoning an independent monetary policy would not be considered a disadvantage. This is because classical thought envisioned a system that would automatically move toward full employment over time and placed a high priority on balance-of-payments adjustment. In today's world, *unemployment* is often the norm, and its elimination is generally given priority over balance-of-payments equilibrium. Modern nations are thus reluctant to make significant internal sacrifices for the sake of external equilibrium. The result is that reliance on an automatic payments-adjustment process is politically unacceptable.

Monetary Adjustments

The previous sections have examined how changes in national price, interest rate, and income levels automatically lead to balance-of-payments adjustment. During the 1960s and 1970s, a new theory emerged, called the *monetary approach* to the balance of payments.[4] The

---

[4]The monetary approach to the balance of payments had its intellectual background at the University of Chicago. It originated with Robert Mundell, *International Economics* (New York: Macmillan, 1968) and Harry Johnson, "The Monetary Approach to Balance-of-Payments Theory," *Journal of Financial and Quantitative Analysis*, March 1972.

---

monetary approach views disequilibrium in the balance of payments primarily as a monetary phenomenon. Money acts as both a *disturbance* and an *adjustment* to the balance of payments. As in the classical and Keynesian approaches, adjustment in the balance of payments is viewed as an automatic process.

Payments Imbalances Under Fixed Exchange Rates

The monetary approach emphasizes that disequilibrium in the balance of payments reflects an imbalance between the demand and the supply of money. A first assumption is that, over the long run, the nation's demand for money is a stable function of real income, prices, and the interest rate.

The quantity of nominal money balances demanded is *directly* related to income and prices. Increases in income or prices trigger increases in the value of transactions and an increased need for money to finance the transactions, and vice versa. The quantity of money demanded is *inversely* related to the interest rate. Whenever money is held rather than used to make an investment, the money holder sacrifices interest that could have been earned. If interest rates are high, people will try to keep as little money on hand as possible, putting the rest into interest-earning investments. Conversely, a decline in interest rates increases the quantity of money demanded.

The nation's *money supply* is a multiple of the monetary base that includes two components. The *domestic component* refers to credit created by the nation's monetary authorities (such as Federal Reserve liabilities for the United States). The *international component* refers to the foreign-exchange reserves of a nation, which can be increased or decreased as the result of balance-of-payments disequilibrium.

The monetary approach maintains that all payments *deficits* are the result of an *excess supply of money* in the home country. Under a fixed exchange-rate system, the excess supply of money results in a flow overseas of foreign-exchange reserves, and thus a reduction in the domestic money supply. Conversely, an *excess demand for money* in the home country leads to a payments *surplus*, resulting in the inflow of foreign-exchange reserves from overseas and an increase in the domestic money supply. Balance in the nation's payments position is restored when the excess supply of money, or the excess demand for money, has fallen enough to restore the equilibrium condition: *Money supply equals money demand.* Table 13.1 summarizes the conclusions of the monetary approach, given a system of fixed exchange rates.

Assume that to finance a budget deficit, the Canadian government creates additional money. Considering this money to be in excess of desired levels (excess money supply), Canadian residents choose to increase their spending on goods and services instead of holding extra cash balances. Given a fixed exchange-rate system, the rise in home spending will push up the prices of Canadian goods and services relative to those abroad. Canadian buyers will be induced to decrease purchases of Canadian-produced goods and services, as will foreign buyers. Conversely, Canadian sellers will offer more goods at home and fewer abroad, whereas foreign sellers will try to increase sales to Canada. By encouraging a rise in imports and a fall in exports, these forces tend to worsen the Canadian payments position. As Canada finances its deficit by transferring international reserves to foreign nations, the Canadian money supply will fall back toward desired levels. This, in turn, will reduce Canadian spending and demand for imports, restoring payments balance.

TABLE 13.1

Changes in the Supply of Money and Demand for Money Under Fixed Exchange Rates: Impact on the Balance of Payments According to the Monetary Approach

Change*	Impact
Increase in money supply	Deficit
Decrease in money supply	Surplus
Increase in money demand	Surplus
Decrease in money demand	Deficit

*Starting from a position at which the nation's money demand equals the money supply and its balance of payments is in equilibrium.

The monetary approach views balance-of-payments adjustment as an automatic process. Any payments imbalance reflects a disparity between actual and desired money balances that tends to be eliminated by inflows or outflows of foreign-exchange reserves, which lead to increases or decreases in the domestic money supply. This self-correcting process requires time. Except for implying that the adjustment process takes place over the long run, the monetary approach does not consider the time period needed to achieve equilibrium. The monetary approach thus emphasizes the economy's final, long-run equilibrium position.

The monetary approach assumes that flows in foreign-exchange reserves associated with payments imbalances do exert an influence on the domestic money supply. This is true as long as central banks do not use monetary policies to neutralize the impact of flows in foreign-exchange reserves on the domestic money supply. If they do neutralize such flows, payments imbalances will continue, according to the monetary approach.

Policy Implications

What implications does the monetary approach have for domestic economic policies? The approach suggests that economic policy affects the balance of payments through its impact on the domestic demand for and supply of money. Policies that *increase the supply of money* relative to the demand for money will lead to a payments *deficit*, an outflow of foreign-exchange reserves, and a reduction in the domestic money supply. Policies that *increase the demand for money* relative to the supply of money will trigger a payments *surplus*, an inflow of foreign-exchange reserves, and an increase in the domestic money supply.

The monetary approach also suggests that nonmonetary policies that attempt to influence a nation's balance of payments (such as tariffs, quotas, or currency devaluation) are unnecessary because payments disequilibria are self-correcting over time. However, in the short run, such policies may speed up the adjustment process by reducing excesses in the supply of money or the demand for money.

For example, given an initial equilibrium, suppose the Canadian government creates money in excess of that demanded by the economy, leading to a payments deficit. The monetary approach maintains that, in the long run, foreign-exchange reserves will flow out of Canada and the Canadian money supply will decrease. This automatic adjustment process will continue until the money supply decreases enough to restore the equilibrium condition: Money supply equals money demand. Suppose Canada, to speed the return to equilibrium, imposes a tariff on imports. The tariff increases the price of imports as well as the prices of nontraded goods (goods produced exclusively for the domestic market, which face no competition from imports), owing to interproduct substitution. Higher Canadian prices trigger an increase in the quantity of money demanded, because Canadians now require additional funds to finance higher-priced purchases. The increase in the quantity of money demanded absorbs part of the excess money supply. The tariff therefore results in a speedier elimination of the excess money supply and payments

deficit than would occur under an automatic adjustment mechanism.[5]

The monetary approach also has policy implications for the growth of the economy. Starting from the point of equilibrium, as the nation's output and real income expand, so do the number of transactions and the quantity of money demanded. If the government does not increase the domestic component of the money supply commensurate with the increase in the quantity of money demanded, the excess demand will induce an inflow of funds from abroad and a payments surplus. This explanation is often advanced for the German payments surpluses that occurred during the late 1960s and early 1970s, a period when the growth in German national output and money demand surpassed the growth in the domestic component of the German money supply.

[5]An import quota would also promote payments equilibrium by restricting the supply of Canadian imports and increasing their price. The quantity of money demanded by Canadians would rise, reducing the excess money supply and the payments deficit. As discussed in the next chapter, a currency devaluation also leads to higher-priced imports. This generates a higher demand for money and a shrinking payments deficit, according to the monetary approach.

Summary

1. Because persistent balance-of-payments disequilibrium—whether surplus or deficit—tends to have adverse economic consequences, there exists a need for adjustment.

2. Balance-of-payments adjustment can be classified as automatic or discretionary. Under a system of fixed exchange rates, automatic adjustments can occur through variations in prices, interest rates, and incomes. The demand for and supply of money can also influence the adjustment process.

3. David Hume's theory provided an explanation of the automatic adjustment process that occurred under the gold standard. Starting from a condition of payments balance, any surplus or deficit would automatically be eliminated by changes in domestic price levels. Hume's theory relied heavily on the quantity theory of money.

4. Another important consequence of international gold movements under the classical theory was their impact on short-term interest rates. A deficit nation suffering gold losses would face a shrinking money supply, which would force up interest rates, promoting financial inflows and payments equilibrium. The opposite held true for a surplus nation. Rather than relying on automatic adjustments in interest rates to restore payments balance, central bankers often resorted to monetary policies designed to reinforce the adjustment mechanism during the gold-standard era.

5. With the advent of Keynesian economics during the 1930s, greater emphasis was put on the income effects of trade in explaining adjustment.

6. The foreign repercussion effect refers to a situation in which a change in one nation's

macroeconomic variables relative to another nation will induce a chain reaction in both nations' economies.

7. An automatic balance-of-payments adjustment mechanism has several disadvantages. Nations must be willing to accept adverse changes in the domestic economy when required for balance-of-payments adjustment. Policy makers must forgo using discretionary economic policy to promote domestic equilibrium.

8. The monetary approach to the balance of payments is presented as an alternative, rather than a supplement, to traditional adjustment theories. It maintains that, over the long run, payments disequilibria are rooted in the relationship between the demand for and the supply of money. Adjustment in the balance of payments is viewed as an automatic process.

Key Concepts and Terms

- Adjustment mechanism *(page 400)*
- Automatic adjustment *(page 400)*
- Foreign repercussion effect *(page 405)*
- Foreign-trade multiplier *(page 413)*
- Gold standard *(page 401)*
- Income determination *(page 405)*
- Multiplier process *(page 411)*
- Quantity theory of money *(page 401)*
- Rules of the game *(page 403)*

Study Questions

1. What is meant by the term *balance-of-payments adjustment*? Why does a deficit nation have an incentive to undergo adjustment? What about a surplus nation?

2. Under a fixed exchange-rate system, what automatic adjustments promote payments equilibrium?

3. What is meant by the quantity theory of money? How did it relate to the classical price-adjustment mechanism?

4. How can adjustments in domestic interest rates help promote payments balance?

5. In the gold-standard era, there existed the so-called rules of the game. What were these rules? Were they followed in practice?

6. Keynesian theory suggests that under a system of fixed exchange rates, the influence of income changes in surplus and deficit nations helps promote balance-of-payments equilibrium. Explain.

7. When analyzing the income-adjustment mechanism, one must account for the foreign repercussion effect. Explain.

8. What are some major disadvantages of the automatic adjustment mechanism under a system of fixed exchange rates?

9. According to the monetary approach, balance in a nation's payments position is restored when the excess supply of money or the excess demand for money has fallen to restore the equilibrium condition: Money supply equals money demand. Explain.

10. What implications does the monetary approach have for domestic economic policies?

13.1 The Asian Development Bank, based in the Philippines, promotes the economic and social progress of its developing member countries. It has extensive reports and statistics on a number of Asian countries. Find it by setting your browser to this URL:

http://www.adb.org

To access NetLink Exercises and the Virtual Scavenger Hunt, visit the Carbaugh Web site at http://carbaugh.swlearning.com.

Log onto the Carbaugh Xtra! Web site (http://carbaughxtra.swlearning.com) for additional learning resources such as practice quizzes, help with graphing, and current events applications.

Income Adjustment Mechanism

To illustrate the Keynesian theory of income determination, let us first assume a *closed economy* with no foreign trade, with price and interest-rate levels constant. In this simple Keynesian model, national income (Y) is the sum of consumption expenditures (C) plus savings (S):

$$Y = C + S$$

Total expenditures on national product are C plus business investment (I). This relationship is given by

$$Y = C + I$$

Figure 13.2 on page 412 represents the familiar income-determination model found in introductory economics textbooks. Referring to Figure 13.2(a), consumption is assumed to be functionally dependent on income, whereas investment spending is autonomous—that is, independent of the level of income. The economy is in equilibrium when the level of planned expenditures equals income. This occurs at Y_E, where the 45-degree line intersects the ($C + I$) schedule. At any level of income lower (or higher) than Y_E, planned expenditure would exceed (or fall below) income and income would rise (or fall).

Combining these relationships yields the following:

$$Y = C + S = C + I$$

The basic equilibrium condition can thus be stated as

$$S = I$$

or

$$S - I = 0$$

This equivalent condition for equilibrium income is illustrated in Figure 13.2(b). Like consumption, saving is assumed to be functionally related to income. Given a constant level of investment, the ($S - I$) schedule is upward-sloping. Savings can be regarded as a leakage from the income stream, whereas investment is an injection into the income stream. At income levels below Y_E, I exceeds S, and the level of income rises. The opposite holds equally true. The economy is thus in equilibrium where $S = I$ (or $S - I = 0$). Figure 13.2(b) illustrates income determination in an open economy.

Suppose an economy that is initially in equilibrium experiences some disturbance, say, an increase in investment spending. This would bid up the level of equilibrium income. This result comes about through a **multiplier process**; that is, the initial investment sets off a chain reaction that results in greater levels of spending, so that income increases by some multiple of the initial investment. Given an autonomous injection of investment spending

FIGURE 13.2

Income Determination in a Closed Economy

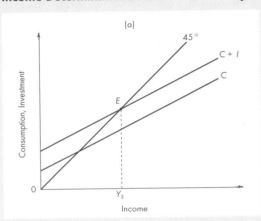
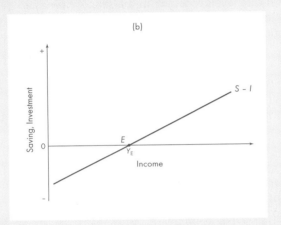

In an economy not exposed to international trade, equilibrium income occurs where the level of planned expenditures (consumption plus investment) equals income: $Y = C + I$. An equivalent condition for equilibrium income is planned saving equals planned investment: $S = I$, or $S - I = 0$.

into the economy, the induced increase in income is given by

$$\Delta Y = k\Delta I$$

where k represents some multiplier.

Let's see how the multiplier is derived for a closed economy. First, remember that in equilibrium, an economy will find planned saving equal to planned investment. It follows that any I must be matched by an equivalent S if the economy is to remain in balance. Because it has been assumed that saving is functionally

dependent on income, changes in saving will be related to changes in income. If we use s to represent the marginal propensity to save out of additional income levels, then $S = sY$. Given an autonomous increase in investment, the equilibrium condition suggests that

$$\Delta I = \Delta S = s\Delta Y$$

From the preceding expression, the multiplier can be derived as

$$\Delta Y = \frac{1}{s} \Delta I$$

Suppose, for example, a nation finds that its marginal propensity to save (s) is 0.25, and there occurs an autonomous increase in investment of $100. According to the multiplier principle, the induced change in income stemming from the initial increase in investment spending equals the increase in investment spending times the multiplier (k). Because the s is assumed to equal 0.25, $k = 1/s = 1/0.25 = 4$. The $100 increase in investment expenditure ultimately results in a $400 increase in the level of income.

Income Determination in an Open Economy

Now assume an *open economy* subject to international trade. The condition for equilibrium income, as well as the formulation of the spending multiplier, must both be modified. In an open economy, imports (M), like savings, constitute a leakage out of the income stream, whereas exports (X), like investment, represent an injection into the stream of national income. The condition for equilibrium income, which relates leakages to injections in an open economy's income stream, becomes

$$S + M = I + X$$

Rearranging terms, this becomes

$$S - I = X - M$$

Assume that exports are unrelated to the level of domestic income. Also assume that imports are functionally dependent on domestic income—that is,

$$\Delta M = m\Delta Y$$

where m represents the marginal propensity to import. We are now in a position to derive what is known as the **foreign-trade multiplier**.

First, let the injections into and leakages from the income stream rise by the same amount, so that the induced change in income will be of equilibrium magnitude. This yields

$$\Delta S + \Delta M = \Delta I + \Delta X$$

Given that

$$\Delta S = s\Delta Y$$

and

$$\Delta M = m\Delta Y$$

the induced change in income stemming from the changes in injections and leakages can be shown as follows:

$$(s + m)\Delta Y = \Delta I + \Delta X$$

Holding exports constant, ($\Delta X = 0$), the induced change in income is equal to the change in investment times the foreign trade multiplier, or

$$\Delta Y = \left(\frac{1}{s + m} \right) \times \Delta I$$

The preceding expression states that *the foreign-trade multiplier equals the reciprocal of the sum of the marginal propensities to save and to import.* In this formulation, an autonomous change in exports, investment remaining fixed, would have an impact on domestic income identical to that of an equivalent change in investment.

Implications of the Foreign-Trade Multiplier

To show the adjustment implications of the foreign-trade multiplier, we construct a diagram based on the framework of Figure 13.2. Remember that the $(S - I)$ schedule is positively sloped. This is because changes in savings are assumed to be directly related to changes in income, investment being unaffected. Subtracting investment from saving yields an upward-sloping $(S - I)$ schedule, as shown in Figure 13.3. Similarly, it has been assumed that changes in imports are directly related to changes in income, exports remaining constant. When imports are subtracted from exports, the result is a downward-sloping $(X - M)$ schedule. As before, the equilibrium condition of an open economy with no government is $(X - M) = (S - I)$.

Starting at equilibrium income level $1,000 in Figure 13.3, suppose a disturbance results in an autonomous increase in exports by, say, $200. This is shown by shifting the $(X - M)$ schedule upward by $200, resulting in the new schedule $(X' - M)$. The level of income rises, generating increases in imports and savings. Domestic equilibrium is established at income level $1,400, where $(S - I) = (X' - M)$. The trade account is no longer in balance; there is a trade surplus of $100. This trade surplus is less than the initial $200 rise in exports because part of the surplus is offset by increases in imports induced by the rise in income from $1,000 to $1,400.

In this example, we can use the concept of a foreign-trade multiplier to determine the effect of the increase in exports on the home economy. Inspection of the $(S - I)$ schedule in Figure 13.3 reveals that the slope of the schedule, which represents the marginal propensity to save, equals 0.25. The slope of the $(X - M)$ schedule indicates that the marginal propensity to import also equals 0.25. The foreign-trade multiplier is the reciprocal of the sum of the marginal propensities to save and to import—that is, 1/0.50, or 2. An autonomous increase in exports of $200 thus generates a twofold increase in domestic income, and equilibrium income rises from $1,000 to $1,400.

As for the trade account effect, the $400 rise in domestic income induces a $100 increase in imports, given a marginal propensity to import of 0.25. Part of the initial export-led surplus is neutralized, lowering it from $200 to $100. Over time, the increase in imports generated by increased domestic expenditures will tend to reduce the trade surplus, but not enough to restore balance-of-payments equilibrium.

Consider another case that illustrates the national-income and balance-of-payments effects of a change in expenditures. Assume that, owing to improved profit expectations, domestic investment rises autonomously by $200. Starting at equilibrium level $1,000 in Figure 13.3, the increase in investment will displace the $(S - I)$ schedule downward by $200 because the negative term is increased. This gives us the new schedule $(S - I')$. Domestic income rises from $1,000 to $1,400, which stimulates a rise in imports, producing a trade deficit of $100. Unlike the previous case of export-led expansion, an autonomous increase in domestic investment spending (or government expenditures) increases domestic income but at the expense of a balance-of-payments deficit. This should serve as a reminder to economic policy makers that under a system of fixed exchange rates, the impact of domestic policies on the balance of payments cannot be overlooked.

FIGURE 13.3

Domestic Income and Trade-Balance Effects of an Increase in Exports and an Increase in Investment

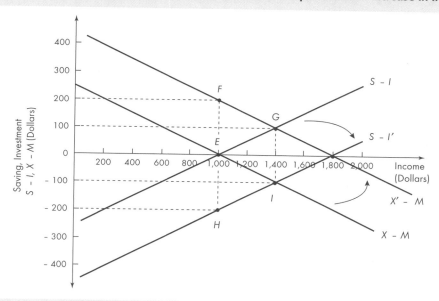

Starting at equilibrium income, an autonomous increase in domestic exports leads to a rise in domestic income, which promotes an increase in imports and savings. Because of the multiplier effect, the induced increase in income tends to be larger than the initial increase in exports. The trade account moves into surplus because the induced increase in imports tends to be less than the initial increase in exports. Again starting at equilibrium income, an autonomous increase in domestic investment generates an increase in income, which promotes additional savings and imports. Because of the multiplier effect, the increase in investment generates a magnified increase in income. As the increase in income induces a rise in imports, a trade deficit appears.

chapter 14

Exchange-Rate Adjustments and the Balance of Payments

The previous chapter demonstrated that balance-of-payments disequilibria tend to be reversed by automatic adjustments in prices, interest rates, and incomes. If these adjustments are allowed to operate, however, reversing balance-of-payments disequilibria may come at the expense of domestic recession or price inflation. The cure may be perceived as worse than the disease.

Instead of relying on adjustments in prices, interest rates, and incomes to counteract payments imbalances, governments permit alterations in exchange rates. By adopting a floating exchange-rate system, a nation permits its currency to depreciate or appreciate in a free market in response to shifts in either the demand for or supply of the currency.

Under a fixed exchange-rate system, rates are set by government in the short run. However, if the official exchange rate becomes overvalued over a period of time, a government may initiate policies to *devalue* its currency. Currency devaluation causes a depreciation of a currency's exchange value; it is initiated by government policy rather than by the free-market forces of supply and demand. When a nation's currency is undervalued, it may be *revalued* by the government; this policy causes the currency's exchange value to appreciate. Currency devaluation and revaluation will be discussed further in the next chapter.

In this chapter, we examine the impact of exchange-rate adjustments on the balance of payments. We will learn under what conditions currency depreciation and appreciation will improve/worsen a nation's payments position.

Effects of Exchange-Rate Changes on Costs and Prices

Industries that compete with foreign producers, or that rely on imported inputs in production, can be noticeably affected by exchange-rate fluctuations. Changing exchange rates influence the international competitiveness of a nation's industries through their influence on relative costs. How do exchange-rate fluctuations affect relative costs? The answer depends on the extent to which a firm's costs are denominated in terms of the home currency or foreign currency.

Case 1:

No foreign sourcing—all costs are denominated in dollars.

Table 14.1 illustrates the hypothetical production costs of Nucor, a U.S. steel manufacturer. Assume that in its production of steel, Nucor utilizes U.S. labor, coal, iron, and other inputs whose costs are denominated in dollars. In period 1, the exchange value of the dollar is assumed to be 50 cents per Swiss franc (2 francs per dollar). Assume that the firm's cost of producing a ton of steel is $500, which is equivalent to 1,000 francs at this exchange rate.

Suppose that in period 2, because of changing market conditions, the dollar's exchange value *appreciates* from 50 cents per franc to 25 cents per franc, a 100 percent appreciation (the franc depreciates from 2 to 4 francs per dollar). With the dollar appreciation, Nucor's labor, iron, coal, and other input costs remain constant in dollar terms. In terms of the franc, however, these costs rise from 1,000 francs to 2,000 francs per ton, a 100 percent increase. The 100 percent dollar appreciation induces a 100 percent increase in Nucor's franc-denominated production cost. The international competitiveness of Nucor is thus reduced.

This example assumes that all of a firm's inputs are acquired domestically and that their costs are denominated in the domestic currency.

In many industries, however, some of a firm's inputs are purchased in foreign markets (foreign sourcing), and these input costs are denominated in a foreign currency. What impact does a change in the home-currency's exchange value have on a firm's costs in this situation?

Case 2:

Foreign sourcing—some costs denominated in dollars and some costs denominated in francs.

Table 14.2 on page 418 again illustrates the hypothetical production costs of Nucor, whose costs of labor, iron, coal, and certain other inputs are assumed to be denominated in dollars. However, suppose Nucor acquires scrap iron from Swiss suppliers (foreign sourcing), and these costs are denominated in francs. Once again, assume the dollar's exchange value appreciates from 50 cents per franc to 25 cents per franc. As before, the cost in francs of Nucor's labor, iron, coal, and certain other inputs rise by 100 percent following the dollar appreciation; however, the franc cost of scrap iron remains constant. As can be seen in the table, Nucor's franc cost per ton of steel rises from 1,000 francs to 1,640 francs—an increase of only 64 percent. Thus, the dollar appreciation worsens Nucor's international competitiveness, but not as much as in the previous example.

TABLE 14.1

Effects of a Dollar Appreciation on a U.S. Steel Firm's Production Costs When All Costs Are Dollar-Denominated

	Cost of Producing a Ton of Steel			
	Period 1 $.50 per Franc (2 Francs = $1)		Period 2 $.25 per Franc (4 Francs = $1)	
	Dollar Cost	Franc Equivalent	Dollar Cost	Franc Equivalent
Labor	$160	320 francs	$160	640 francs
Materials (iron/coal)	300	600	300	1,200
Other costs (energy)	40	80	40	160
Total	$500	1,000 francs	$500	2,000 francs
Percentage change	—	—	—	100%

TABLE 14.2

**Effects of a Dollar Appreciation on a U.S. Steel Firm's Production Costs
When Some Costs Are Dollar-Denominated and Other Costs Are Franc-Denominated**

	Cost of Producing a Ton of Steel			
	Period 1 $.50 per Franc (2 Francs = $1)		Period 2 $.25 per Franc (4 Francs = $1)	
	Dollar Cost	Franc Equivalent	Dollar Cost	Franc Equivalent
Labor	$160	320 francs	$160	640 francs
Materials				
Dollar-denominated (iron/coal)	120	240	120	480
Franc-denominated (scrap iron)	180	360	90	360
Total	300	600	210	840
Other costs (energy)	40	80	40	160
Total cost	$500	1,000 francs	$410	1,640 francs
Percentage change	—	—	−18%	+64%

In addition to influencing Nucor's franc-denominated cost of steel, a dollar appreciation affects a firm's dollar cost when franc-denominated inputs are involved. Because scrap-iron costs are denominated in francs, they remain at 360 francs after the dollar appreciation; however, the dollar-equivalent scrap-iron cost falls from $180 to $90. Because the costs of Nucor's other inputs are denominated in dollars and do not change following the dollar appreciation, the firm's total dollar cost falls from $500 to $410 per ton—a decrease of 18 percent. This cost reduction offsets some of the cost disadvantage that Nucor incurs relative to Swiss exporters as a result of the dollar appreciation (franc depreciation).

The preceding examples suggest the following generalization: As franc-denominated costs become a larger portion of Nucor's total costs, a dollar appreciation (depreciation) leads to a smaller increase (decrease) in the franc cost of Nucor steel and a larger decrease (increase) in the dollar cost of Nucor steel compared to the cost changes that occur when all input costs are dollar-denominated. As franc-denominated costs become a smaller portion of total costs, the opposite conclusions apply. These conclusions have been especially significant for the world trading system during the 1980s to 2000s as industries—e.g., autos and computers—have become increasingly internationalized and utilize increasing amounts of imported inputs in the production process.

Changes in relative costs because of exchange-rate fluctuations also influence relative prices and the volume of goods traded among nations. By increasing relative U.S. production costs, a dollar *appreciation* tends to *raise* U.S. export prices in foreign-currency terms, which induces a decrease in the quantity of U.S. goods sold abroad; similarly, the dollar appreciation leads to an increase in U.S. imports. By decreasing relative U.S. production costs, a dollar *depreciation* tends to *lower* U.S. export prices in foreign-currency terms, which induces an increase in the quantity of U.S. goods sold abroad; similarly, the dollar depreciation leads to a decrease in U.S. imports.

Several factors govern the extent by which exchange-rate movements lead to relative price changes among nations. Some U.S. exporters may be able to offset the price-increasing effects of an appreciation in the dollar's exchange value by reducing profit margins to maintain competitiveness. Perceptions concerning long-term trends in exchange rates also promote price rigidity: U.S. exporters may be less willing to raise prices if the dollar's appreciation is viewed as temporary. The extent to which industries implement pricing strategies depends significantly on the substitutability of their product: The greater the degree of product differentiation (as in quality or service), the greater control producers can exercise over prices; the pricing policies of such producers are somewhat insulated from exchange-rate movements.

Is there any way in which companies can offset the impact of currency swings on their competitiveness? Suppose the exchange value of the Japanese yen appreciates against other currencies, which causes Japanese goods to become less competitive in world markets. To insulate themselves from the squeeze on profits caused by the rising yen, Japanese companies could move production to affiliates located in countries whose currencies have depreciated against the yen. This would be most likely to occur if the yen's appreciation is sizable and is regarded as being permanent. Even if the yen's appreciation is not permanent, shifting production offshore can help reduce the uncertainties associated with currency swings. Indeed, Japanese companies have resorted to offshore production to protect themselves from an appreciating yen.

Cost-Cutting Strategies of Manufacturers in Response to Currency Appreciation

For years, manufacturers have watched with dismay as the home currency surges to new heights, making it harder for them to wring profits out of exports. This tests their ingenuity to become more efficient in order to remain competitive on world markets. Let us consider how Japanese and American manufacturers responded to appreciations of their home currencies.

Appreciation of the Yen: Japanese Manufacturers

From 1990 to 1996, the value of the Japanese yen relative to the U.S. dollar increased by almost 40 percent. In other words, if the yen and dollar prices in the two nations had remained unchanged, Japanese products in 1996 would have been roughly 40 percent more expensive, compared with U.S. products, than they were in 1990. How then did Japanese manufacturers respond to a development that could have had disastrous consequences for their competitiveness in world markets?

ECONOMIC *Applications*

Visit EconNews Online
International Finance

Japanese firms remained competitive by using the yen's strength to cheaply establish integrated manufacturing bases in the United States and in dollar-linked Asia. This allowed Japanese firms to play both sides of fluctuations in the yen/dollar exchange rate: using cheaper dollar-denominated parts and materials to offset higher yen-related costs. While they maintained their U.S. markets, many Japanese companies also used the strong yen to purchase cheaper components from around the world and ship them home for assembly. That provided a competitive edge in Japan for these firms.

Consider the Japanese electronics manufacturer Hitachi, whose TV sets were a global production effort in the mid-1990s, as shown in Figure 14.1 on page 420. The small tubes that projected information onto Hitachi TV screens came from a subsidiary in South Carolina, while the TV chassis and circuitry were manufactured by an affiliate in Malaysia. From Japan came only computer chips and lenses, which amounted to 30 percent of the value of the parts used. By sourcing TV production in countries whose currencies had fallen against the yen, Hitachi was able hold down the dollar price of its TV sets in spite of the rising yen.

To limit their vulnerability to a rising yen, Japanese exporters also shifted production from commodity-type goods to high-value products. The demand for commodities—for example, metals and textiles—is quite sensitive to price changes because these goods are largely indistinguishable,

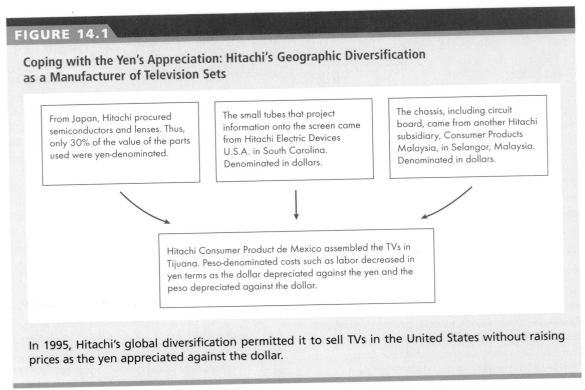

FIGURE 14.1

Coping with the Yen's Appreciation: Hitachi's Geographic Diversification as a Manufacturer of Television Sets

From Japan, Hitachi procured semiconductors and lenses. Thus, only 30% of the value of the parts used were yen-denominated.

The small tubes that project information onto the screen came from Hitachi Electric Devices U.S.A. in South Carolina. Denominated in dollars.

The chassis, including circuit board, came from another Hitachi subsidiary, Consumer Products Malaysia, in Selangor, Malaysia. Denominated in dollars.

Hitachi Consumer Product de Mexico assembled the TVs in Tijuana. Peso-denominated costs such as labor decreased in yen terms as the dollar depreciated against the yen and the peso depreciated against the dollar.

In 1995, Hitachi's global diversification permitted it to sell TVs in the United States without raising prices as the yen appreciated against the dollar.

Source: "What the Strong Yen Is Breeding: Japanese Multinationals," *Business Week,* April 10, 1995, p. 119.

except by price. Customers, therefore, could easily switch to non-Japanese suppliers if an increase in the yen shoved the dollar price of Japanese exports higher. In contrast, more sophisticated, high-value products—for example, transportation equipment and electrical machinery—are less sensitive to price increases. For these goods, factors such as embedded advanced technology and high-quality standards work to neutralize the effect on demand if prices are driven up by an appreciating yen. Shifting production from commodity-type products to high-value products from 1990 to 1996 enhanced the competitiveness of Japanese firms.

Then, there's the Japanese auto industry. To offset the rising yen, Japanese automakers cut the yen prices of their autos and thus realized falling unit-profit margins. They also reduced manufacturing costs by increasing worker productivity, importing materials and parts whose prices were denominated in currencies that had depreciated

against the yen, and by outsourcing larger amounts of a vehicle's production to transplant factories in countries whose currencies had depreciated against the yen.

In 1994, Toyota Motor Corporation announced that its competitiveness had been eroded by as much as 20 percent as a result of the yen's recent appreciation. Toyota therefore convinced its subcontractors to cut part prices by 15 percent over three years. By using common parts in various vehicles and shortening the time needed to design, test, and commercialize automobiles, Toyota was also able to cut costs. Moreover, Toyota pressured Japanese steelmakers to produce less costly galvanized sheet steel for use in its vehicles. Finally, Toyota reintroduced less expensive models with fewer options in an effort to reduce costs and prices and thus recapture sales in the mid-size-family-car segment of the market.

Foreign-made parts, once rejected by Japanese automakers as inferior to domestically produced

Cheap Imports? Not So Fast

When East Asia's currencies crashed in 1997, many analysts predicted that a flood of cheap, East Asian exports would pour into the United States. As things turned out, however, East Asia's export boom met resistance.

The crash of East Asia's currencies provided an opportunity for Vigor International President Wang Yu-len. Like many Asian middlemen who exported handicrafts and garments to big retailers in the United States, Taipei-based Vigor relied heavily on low-cost factories in China. With the Thai baht, Malaysian ringgit, Indonesian rupiah, and Philippine peso all suddenly trading at less than half their old values against the dollar—while China's renminbi remained stable—Wang anticipated that bargains would be abundant in East Asia. But after a swing through East Asia in 1998, Wang returned empty-handed. Why? Most East Asian manufacturers sought foreign orders. However, they so lacked cash that they could not purchase the imported materials needed to run their factories. That made it much more difficult to generate the exports.

To the depressed economies of East Asia, the situation was frustrating. They had anticipated that their cheaper currencies would translate into a big increase in export competitiveness in everything from computer chips to toys, thus permitting their countries to quickly recover from the economic decline. However, this expectation did not materialize for many exporters. East Asian exporters could sell at a discount, but not so much that they could steal much market share from U.S. rivals.

East Asian exporters met resistance when nervous local suppliers, fearful of more currency depreciations, demanded dollars up front. Other key suppliers went bankrupt. Moreover, the region's financial systems were so squeezed that many manufacturers could not get financing to fill exports. For many normally sound manufacturers, getting export financing from shell-shocked Asian banks was nearly impossible. A manager at a trading branch of an elite Korean conglomerate said his firm faced difficulty in all export areas, including machinery, electronics, automobiles, and textiles. Also, furniture makers noted that they were not able to purchase imported raw materials. To fill export orders, they had to draw down inventories. Financing costs also soared in East Asia after the currency crash. Interest rates in some countries tripled to around 30 percent, as panicked central banks attempted to stabilize currencies. The increases in financial costs added to the costs of goods sold abroad.

True, the depreciation in Southeast Asian currencies made the labor costs of East Asian manufacturers more competitive. However, this advantage was offset by higher import costs caused by depreciating currencies. Most East Asian producers purchased most of their raw materials and components from abroad and thus were sensitive to exchange-rate fluctuations. For example, Nike noted that 65 percent of the materials of its shoes made in Indonesia were imported. Inflation of raw-material costs thus negated most of the price cuts that would normally be expected to occur following a large depreciation in currency values.

In the United States, retailers initially expected discounts of 35 percent to 75 percent on items purchased from East Asia as a result of the currency realignment. However, East Asian manufacturers found that they could not afford to cut prices much more than 10 percent. This dampened the tidal wave of cheap exports going to the United States. Moreover, the Asian crisis amplified the commitment of U.S. producers to reduce costs and prices in an effort to protect their share of the market.

parts, became much less alien to them in the 1990s. Foreign parts steadily made their way into Japanese autos, helped by both the strong yen and Japanese automakers' urgency to slash costs. Moreover, Japanese auto-parts makers set up manufacturing operations in Southeast Asia and South America to cut costs; these parts were then exported to Japan for assembly into autos.

Appreciation of the Dollar: U.S. Manufacturers

From 1996 to 2002, U.S. manufacturers were alarmed as the dollar appreciated by 22 percent on average against the currencies of major U.S. trading partners. This resulted in U.S. manufacturers seeking ways to tap overseas markets and defend their home turf.

Take American Feed Co., a Napoleon, Ohio, company that makes machinery used in auto plants. In 2001, the firm reached a deal with a similar manufacturing company in Spain. Both companies produce machines that car factories use to unroll giant coils of steel and feed them through presses to make parts. According to the pact, when orders come in, management of the two companies meet to decide which plant should make which parts, in essence divvying up the work to keep both factories operating. As a result, American Feed can share in the benefits of having a European production base without having to take on the risks of building its own factory there. Also, the company redesigned its machines to make them more efficient and less expensive to build. These efforts chopped about 20 percent off the machines' production costs.

Then, there's Sipco Molding Technologies, a Meadville, Pennsylvania, tool-and-die maker who also had to cut costs to survive the dollar's appreciation. For years, Sipco had a partnership with an Austrian company, which designed a special line of tools that Sipco once built in the United States. Because of the strong dollar, however, the Austrian company assumed the responsibility of designing and making the tools, while Sipco simply resold them. Although these efforts helped the firm cut costs, it resulted in a loss of jobs for 30 percent of its employees.

Though officials of the U.S. government have met with manufacturing and labor groups to discuss complaints about a strong dollar, they generally insist that market forces should determine the dollar's value. As Treasury Secretary Paul O'Neill put it in 2002, "The great companies don't worry about a weak dollar or a strong dollar."

Requirements for a Successful Depreciation

We have seen that currency depreciation tends to improve a nation's competitiveness by reducing its costs and prices, while currency appreciation implies the opposite. Under what circumstances will currency depreciation succeed in reducing a payments deficit?

Several approaches to currency depreciation must be considered, and each of them will be dealt with in a separate section. The **elasticity approach** emphasizes the relative *price effects* of depreciation and suggests that depreciation works best when demand elasticities are high. The **absorption approach** deals with the *income effects* of depreciation; the implication is that a decrease in domestic expenditure relative to income must occur for depreciation to promote payments equilibrium. The **monetary approach** stresses the effects depreciation has on the *purchasing power of money* and the resulting impact on domestic expenditure levels.

The Elasticity Approach to Exchange-Rate Adjustment

Currency depreciation affects a country's balance of trade through changes in the relative prices of goods and services internationally. A trade-deficit nation may be able to reverse its imbalance by lowering its relative prices, so that exports increase and imports decrease. The nation can lower its relative prices by permitting its exchange rate to depreciate in a free market or by formally devaluing its currency under a system of fixed exchange rates. The ultimate outcome of currency depreciation depends on the price elasticity of demand for a nation's imports and the price elasticity of demand for its exports.

Recall that *elasticity of demand* refers to the responsiveness of buyers to changes in price. It indicates the percentage change in the quantity demanded stemming from a 1 percent change in price. Mathematically, elasticity is the ratio of the percentage change in the quantity demanded to the percentage change in price. This can be symbolized as

$$Elasticity = \frac{\Delta Q}{Q} \div \frac{\Delta P}{P}$$

The elasticity coefficient is stated numerically, without regard to the algebraic sign. If the preceding ratio exceeds 1, a given percentage change in price results in a larger percentage change in quantity demanded; this is referred to as relatively *elastic* demand. If the ratio is less than 1, demand is said to be relatively *inelastic*, because the percentage change in quantity demanded is less than the percentage change in price. A ratio precisely equal to 1 denotes *unitary elastic* demand, meaning that the percentage change in quantity demanded just matches the percentage change in price.

Next we investigate the effects of a currency depreciation on a nation's balance of trade—that is, the value of its exports minus imports. Suppose the British pound depreciates by 10 percent against the dollar. Whether the British trade balance will be improved depends on what happens to the dollar inpayments for Britain's exports as opposed to the dollar outpayments for its imports. This, in turn, depends on whether the U.S. demand for British exports is elastic or inelastic and whether the British demand for imports is elastic or inelastic.

Depending on the size of the demand elasticities for British exports and imports, Britain's trade balance may improve, worsen, or remain unchanged in response to the pound depreciation. The general rule that determines the actual outcome is the so-called **Marshall–Lerner condition**. The Marshall–Lerner condition states: (1) Depreciation will *improve* the trade balance if the currency-depreciating nation's demand elasticity for imports plus the foreign demand elasticity for the nation's exports exceeds 1. (2) If the sum of the demand elasticities is less than 1, depreciation will *worsen* the trade balance. (3) The trade balance will be *neither helped nor hurt* if the sum of the demand elasticities equals 1. The Marshall–Lerner condition may be stated in terms of the currency of either the nation undergoing a depreciation or its trading partner. Our discussion is confined to the currency of the currency-depreciating country, Great Britain.

Case 1:

Improved trade balance.

Referring to Table 14.3, assume that the British demand elasticity for imports equals 2.5 and the U.S. demand elasticity for British exports equals 1.5; the sum of the elasticities is 4.0. Suppose the pound depreciates by 10 percent against the dollar.

TABLE 14.3

British Pound Depreciation: Improved Trade Balance

Sector	Change in Pound Price (%)	Trade-Balance Effect Change in Quantity Demanded (%)	Net Effect (in Pounds)
Import	+10	−25	−15% outpayments
Export	0	+15	+15% inpayments

Assumptions:
British demand elasticity for imports = 2.5 ⎫ Sum = 4.0
Demand elasticity for British exports = 1.5 ⎭
Pound depreciation = 10%

An assessment of the overall impact of the depreciation on Britain's payments position requires identification of the depreciation's impact on import expenditures and export receipts.

If prices of imports remain constant in terms of foreign currency, then a depreciation increases the home-currency price of goods imported. Because of the depreciation, the pound price of British imports rises 10 percent. British consumers would thus be expected to reduce their purchases from abroad. Given an import demand elasticity of 2.5, the depreciation triggers a 25 percent decline in the quantity of imports demanded. The 10 percent price increase in conjunction with a 25 percent quantity reduction results in approximately a 15 percent decrease in British outpayments in pounds. This cutback in import purchases actually reduces import expenditures, which reduces the British deficit.

How about British export receipts? The pound price of the exports remains constant, but after depreciation of the pound, consumers in the United States find British exports costing 10 percent less in terms of dollars. Given a U.S. demand elasticity of 1.5 for British exports, the 10 percent British depreciation will stimulate foreign sales by 15 percent, so that export receipts in pounds will increase by approximately 15 percent. This strengthens the British payments position. The 15 percent reduction in import expenditures coupled with a 15 percent rise in export receipts means

that the pound depreciation will reduce the British payments deficit. *With the sum of the elasticities exceeding 1, the depreciation strengthens Britain's trade position.*

Case 2:
Worsened trade balance.

In Table 14.4, the British demand elasticity for imports is 0.2 and the U.S. demand elasticity for British exports is 0.1; the sum of the elasticities is 0.3. The 10 percent pound depreciation raises the pound price of imports by 10 percent, inducing a 2 percent reduction in the quantity of imports demanded. In contrast to the previous case, under relatively inelastic conditions the depreciation contributes to an *increase*, rather than a decrease, in import expenditures of some 8 percent. As before, the pound price of British exports is unaffected by the depreciation, whereas the dollar price of exports falls 10 percent. U.S. purchases from abroad increase by 1 percent, resulting in an increase in pound receipts of about 1 percent. With expenditures on imports rising 8 percent while export receipts increase only 1 percent, the British deficit will tend to *worsen*. As stated in the Marshall–Lerner condition, *if the sum of the elasticities is less than 1, currency depreciation will cause a deterioration in a nation's trade position.* The reader is left to verify that a nation's trade balance remains unaffected by depreciation if the sum of the demand elasticities equals 1.

TABLE 14.4

British Pound Depreciation: Worsened Trade Balance

Sector	Trade-Balance Effect		
	Change in Pound Price (%)	Change in Quantity Demanded (%)	Net Effect (in Pounds)
Import	+10	−2	+8% outpayments
Export	0	+1	+1% inpayments

Assumptions:
British demand elasticity for imports = 0.2 } Sum = 0.3
U.S. demand elasticity for British exports = 0.1
Pound depreciation = 10%

Although the Marshall–Lerner condition provides a general rule as to when a currency depreciation will be successful in restoring payments equilibrium, it depends on some simplifying assumptions. For one, it is assumed that a nation's trade balance is in equilibrium when the depreciation occurs. If there is initially a very large trade deficit, with imports exceeding exports, then a depreciation might cause import expenditures to change more than export receipts, even though the sum of the demand elasticities exceeds 1. The analysis also assumes no change in the sellers' prices in their own currency. But this may not always be true. To protect their competitive position, foreign sellers may lower their prices in response to a depreciation of the home-country's currency; domestic sellers may raise home-currency prices so that the depreciation's effects are not fully transmitted into lower foreign-exchange prices for their goods. However, neither of these assumptions invalidates the Marshall–Lerner condition's spirit, which suggests that currency depreciations work best when demand elasticities are high.

Empirical Measurement: Import/Export Demand Elasticities

The Marshall–Lerner condition illustrates the price effects of currency depreciation on the home-country's trade balance. The extent to which price changes affect the volume of goods traded depends on the elasticity of demand for imports and exports. If the elasticities were known in advance, it would be possible to determine the proper exchange-rate policy to restore payments equilibrium. Without such knowledge, nations often have been reluctant to change the par values of their currencies.

During the 1940s and 1950s, there was considerable debate among economists concerning the empirical measurement of demand elasticities. Several early studies suggested low demand elasticities. Those findings led to the formation of the *elasticity pessimist* school of thought, which contended that currency depreciations and appreciations would be largely ineffectual in promoting changes in a nation's trade balance. By the 1960s, most economists considered themselves *elasticity optimists*, estimating the demand elasticities for most nations to be rather high. Table 14.5 shows estimated price elasticities of demand for total imports and exports by country.

J-Curve Effect: Time Path of Depreciation

Empirical estimates of price elasticities in international trade suggest that, according to the Marshall–Lerner condition, currency depreciation is

TABLE 14.5

Price Elasticities of Demand for Total Imports and Exports of Selected Countries

Country	Import Price Elasticity	Export Price Elasticity	Sum of Import and Export Elasticities
United States	0.92	0.99	1.91
United Kingdom	0.47	0.44	0.91
Germany	0.60	0.66	1.26
Japan	0.93	0.93	1.86
Canada	1.02	0.83	1.85
Other developed countries	0.49	0.83	1.32
Less-developed countries	0.81	0.63	1.44
OPEC	1.14	0.57	1.71

Source: Jaime Marques, "Bilateral Trade Elasticities," *Review of Economics and Statistics* 72, No. 1, February 1990, pp. 75–76.

likely to improve a nation's trade balance. A basic problem in measuring world price elasticities, however, is that there tends to be a *time lag* between changes in exchange rates and their ultimate effect on real trade. One popular description of the time path of trade flows is the so-called **J-curve effect**. This view suggests that in the very short run, a currency depreciation will lead to a worsening of a nation's trade balance. But as time passes, the trade balance will likely improve. This is because it takes time for new information about the price effects of depreciation to be disseminated throughout the economy and for economic units to adjust their behavior accordingly.

A currency depreciation affects a nation's trade balance through its net impact on export receipts and import expenditures. Export receipts and import expenditures are calculated by multiplying the commodity's per-unit price times the quantity being demanded. Figure 14.2 illustrates the process by which depreciation influences export receipts and import expenditures.

The immediate effect of depreciation is a change in relative prices. If a nation's currency depreciates 10 percent, it means that import prices initially increase 10 percent in terms of the home currency. The quantity of imports demanded will then fall according to home demand elasticities. At the same time, exporters will initially receive 10 percent more in home currency for each unit of foreign currency they earn. This means they can

become more competitive and lower their export prices measured in terms of foreign currencies. Export sales will then rise in accordance with foreign demand elasticities. The problem with this process is that for depreciation to take effect, time is required for the pricing mechanism to induce changes in the volume of exports and imports.

The time path of the response of trade flows to a currency's depreciation can be described in terms of the J-curve effect, so called because the trade balance continues to get worse for awhile after depreciation (sliding down the hook of the J) and then gets better (moving up the stem of the J). This effect occurs because the initial effect of depreciation is an increase in import expenditures: The home-currency price of imports has risen, but the volume is unchanged owing to prior commitments. As time passes, the quantity adjustment effect becomes relevant: Import volume is depressed, whereas exports become more attractive to foreign buyers.

Advocates of the J-curve effect use the depreciation of the British pound as an example. In 1967, the British balance of trade showed a $1.3 billion deficit. This was followed by a 14.3 percent depreciation of the pound in November 1967. The initial impact of the depreciation was negative: In 1968, the British balance of trade showed a $3 billion deficit. After a lag, however, the British balance of trade improved, with a reduction in the growth of imports and a rise in the growth of exports. By 1969, the British balance of trade showed a $1 billion surplus; by 1971, the surplus was $6.5 billion.

Another example of the J-curve effect is the experience of the U.S. balance of trade during the 1980s and 1990s. As seen in Figure 14.3, between 1980 and 1987 the U.S. trade deficit expanded at a very rapid rate. The deficit decreased substantially between 1988 and 1991. The rapid increase in the trade deficit that took place during the early 1980s occurred mainly because of the appreciation of the dollar at the time, which resulted in a steady increase in imports and a drop in U.S. exports. The depreciation of the dollar that began in 1985 led to a boom in exports in 1988 and a drop in the trade deficit through 1991.

What factors might explain the time lags in a currency depreciation's adjustment process? The

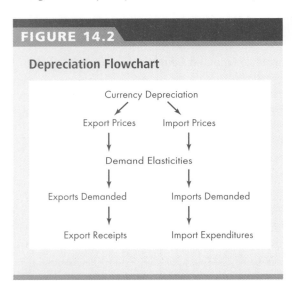

FIGURE 14.2

Depreciation Flowchart

Currency Depreciation

Export Prices   Import Prices

Demand Elasticities

Exports Demanded   Imports Demanded

Export Receipts   Import Expenditures

FIGURE 14.3

Time Path of U.S. Balance of Trade, in Billions of Dollars, in Response to Dollar Appreciation and Depreciation

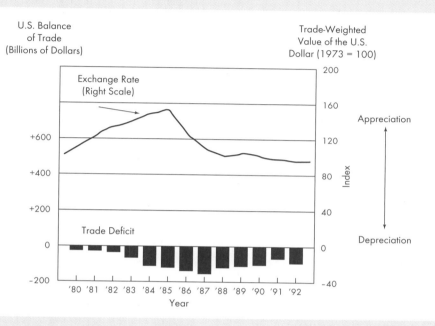

Between 1980 and 1987, the U.S. merchandise trade deficit expanded at a rapid rate. The trade deficit decreased substantially between 1988 and 1991. The rapid increase in the trade deficit that took place during the early 1980s occurred mainly because of the appreciation of the dollar at the time, which resulted in a steady increase in imports and a drop in U.S. exports. The depreciation of the dollar that began in 1985 led to a boom in exports in 1988 and a drop in the trade deficit through 1991.

types of lags that may occur between changes in relative prices and the quantities of goods traded include the following:

- *Recognition lags* of changing competitive conditions
- *Decision lags* in forming new business connections and placing new orders
- *Delivery lags* between the time new orders are placed and their impact on trade and payment flows is felt
- *Replacement lags* in using up inventories and wearing out existing machinery before placing new orders

- *Production lags* involved in increasing the output of commodities for which demand has increased

Empirical evidence suggests that the trade-balance effects of currency depreciation do not materialize until years afterward. Adjustment lags may be four years or more, although the major portion of adjustment takes place in about two years. One study made the following estimates of the lags in the depreciation adjustment process for trade in manufactured goods: (1) The response of trade flows to relative price changes stretches out over a period of some four to five years. (2) Following a price change, almost 50 percent of the full trade-flow response occurs within the first three years, and about 90 percent takes place during the first five years.[1]

Exchange Rate Pass-Through

The J-curve analysis assumes that a given change in the exchange rate brings about a proportionate change in import prices. In practice, this relationship may be less than proportionate, thus weakening the influence of a change in the exchange rate on the volume of trade.

The extent to which changing currency values lead to changes in import and export prices is known as the **exchange rate pass-through** relationship. Pass-through is important because buyers have incentives to alter their purchases of foreign goods only to the extent that the prices of these goods change in terms of their domestic currency following a change in the exchange rate. This depends on the willingness of exporters to permit the change in the exchange rate to affect the prices they charge for their goods, measured in terms of the buyer's currency.

Assume that Toyota of Japan exports autos to the United States and that the prices of Toyota are fixed in terms of the yen. Suppose the dollar's value depreciates 10 percent relative to the yen. Assuming no offsetting actions by Toyota, U.S. import prices will rise 10 percent. This is because 10 percent more dollars are needed to purchase the yen that are used to pay for the import purchases. *Complete pass-through* thus exists: Import prices in dollars rise by the full proportion of the dollar depreciation.

To illustrate the calculation of complete currency pass-through, assume that Caterpillar charges $50,000 for a tractor exported to Japan. If the exchange rate is 150 yen per U.S. dollar, the price paid by the Japanese buyer will be 7,500,000 yen. Assuming the dollar price of the tractor remains constant, a 10 percent appreciation in the dollar's exchange value will increase the tractor's yen price 10 percent, to 8,250,000 yen (165 × 50,000 = 8,250,000). Conversely, if the dollar depreciates by 10 percent, the yen price of the tractor will fall by 10 percent, to 6,750,000. So long as Caterpillar keeps the dollar price of its tractor constant, changes in the dollar's exchange rate will be fully reflected in changes in the foreign-currency price of exports. The ratio of changes in the foreign-currency price to changes in the exchange rate will be 100 percent, implying complete currency pass-through.

Empirical evidence suggests, however, that the more typical real-world situation is *partial pass-through*, with significant time lags. Table 14.6 shows the percent of a change in the dollar's exchange rate that is passed-through into prices for selected U.S. imports. For example, just 21 percent of a change in the exchange rate is passed through to prices of imported chemicals. The estimates of Table 14.6 suggest that exchange rate pass-through is usually partial rather than complete; there is also a considerable degree of variation in pass-through across different industries. The effects of exchange rate pass-through are more fully discussed on "Exploring Further 14.1" at the end of this chapter.

What Determines Currency Pass-Through?

What explains the magnitude of the pass-through effect? Data concerning U.S. trade show that changing profit margins are a significant factor in explaining the size of the pass-through effect. Researchers at the Federal Reserve analyzed prices and profit margins for the 1977–1980 period of dollar depreciation (15.5 percent) and the 1980–1985 period of dollar appreciation (74.9 percent). Table 14.7 on page 430 shows the evidence for U.S. imports and exports.

Concerning the evidence regarding U.S. *imports*, notice that during the period of dollar depreciation, foreign firms usually reduced profit margins. This meant that the dollar price of foreign goods sold in the United States did not increase by the full amount of the dollar depreciation. When the dollar appreciated during the period 1980–1985,

[1]Helen Junz and Rudolf R. Rhomberg, "Price Competitiveness in Export Trade Among Industrial Countries," *American Economic Review*, May 1973, pp. 412–419.

TABLE 14.6

Exchange Rate Pass-Through into Import Prices for the United States

Imported Product	Percent of a Change in the Exchange Rate that Is Passed Through to Import Prices*
Chemicals	.21%
Medicinal and pharmaceutical products	.36
Iron and steel	.53
Aluminum	.89
Textile and leather machinery	.59
Computer equipment	.34
Radios	.08
Telecommunications equipment	.15
Electrical machinery	.33
Road vehicles	.39
Apparel	.17
Footwear	.01
Photographic equipment	.46
CDs	.38

*Long-run.

Source: Giovanni Olivei, "Exchange Rates and the Prices of Manufacturing Products Imported into the United States," *New England Economic Review*, First Quarter 2002, p. 8.

foreign firms increased their profit margins on goods shipped to the United States. Therefore, the dollar price of such foreign goods did not decrease by the full amount of the dollar appreciation. The experience of the U.S. import sector thus shows that there was only a modest pass-through of changing currency values to changes in import prices during these periods.

The lower portion of the table considers U.S. *exports*. During the 1977–1980 period of dollar depreciation and the 1980–1985 period of dollar appreciation, the profit margins of U.S. exporters changed by small amounts compared to the changes in the dollar's exchange rate. This may have been caused by the large size of the home market in the United States: Pricing decisions by U.S. companies may have been more closely tied to domestic market conditions than to global conditions. As a result, there was significant pass-through of changing currency values to changes in export prices during these periods. Conclusion:

The foreign-currency prices of U.S. exports are more likely to have a significant pass-through of exchange-rate changes than the dollar prices of U.S. imports are. Let us consider two examples of partial currency pass-through.

Dollar Depreciation of the 1980s

Following an appreciation in value during the early 1980s, the U.S. dollar began to depreciate in 1985. By 1986, the value of the dollar had fallen more than 25 percent against the currencies of the major U.S. trading partners on a trade-weighted basis and more than 47 percent against the Japanese yen. Other things being equal, the dollar depreciation should have led to higher U.S. exports and lower U.S. imports. But other things were not equal. Foreign manufacturers, particularly the Japanese, were not willing to sacrifice their share of the U.S. market without a struggle.

TABLE 14.7

Percentage Change in Profit Margins for Selected U.S. Industries

Industry	1977–1980	1980–1985
Exchange Value of the Dollar	−15.5%	74.9%
Imports		
Leather footwear	−4.2	87.3
Textiles	−9.1	28.0
Construction machinery	−9.2	11.6
Paper products	−2.3	17.6
Apparel	−4.9	4.1
Canned fruits and vegetables	−14.1	6.8
Steel	14.6	4.1
Exports		
Semiconductors	−5.9	−9.6
Power-driven hand tools	−5.0	−6.9
Pulp mill products	4.6	−17.1
Internal combustion engines	−4.5	4.2
Valves and pipe fittings	−2.7	8.7
Oil-field and gas-field equipment	−2.0	1.0
Printing trades machinery	−3.9	5.3
Farm machinery	−2.9	4.5
Meatpacking	−3.6	17.7

Source: Catherine Mann, "Prices, Profit Margins, and Exchange Rates," *Federal Reserve Bulletin,* June 1986. See also Joseph Gagnon and Michael Knetter, "Markup Adjustment and Exchange Rate Fluctuations: Evidence from Panel Data on Automobiles," *Journal of International Money and Finance,* April 1995.

Rather than permit increases in the prices of their goods sold in the United States, Japanese firms absorbed the dollar depreciation in reduced profits—and even losses—which triggered accusations of dumping by their U.S. competitors. But Japanese companies could not cut profits or absorb losses indefinitely. Therefore, many concerns attempted to reduce manufacturing costs, either by leaving Japan for lower-cost sites such as South Korea or by overhauling products and factories in Japan. The result was only a partial pass-through of the dollar depreciation into retail price increases in the United States.

Prior to the dollar depreciation, Japanese automakers enjoyed an estimated 12 percent profit margin on their exports to the United States—nearly double that of U.S. companies. As

a way of compensating for the depreciating dollar, throughout 1986 Japanese automakers pared profits by some $518 per vehicle. Yet foreign businesses could not persistently operate on razor-thin profit margins because they would lack money for product development and sales promotion. Eventually the businesses would have to reduce their emphasis on market share, and the U.S. trade deficit would shrink. However, it was estimated that if foreigners kept profit margins thin, they could preserve their market share for two years or longer.

U.S. imports also remained strong because of pricing policies of U.S. companies. As foreign prices inched upward as a result of the dollar depreciation, many U.S. businesses followed the price increases, although at a slower rate. In

Japanese Firms Move Output Overseas to Limit Effects of Strong Yen

In 2003, the Japanese yen's exchange value was appreciating against the dollar. Japanese exporting companies realized that a more costly yen would result in smaller profits if they converted their dollar profits back into yen. How could the Japanese protect their profits? By moving production overseas and thus lessening the amount of money they convert from dollars to yen.

During the 1990s, executives at Japan's large auto and electronics companies were apprehensive about an appreciating yen that reduced their profits by slashing the value of overseas earnings when translated into yen. By 2003, however, the harm caused by an appreciating yen was not nearly as great for Japan's exporters, including consumer electronics firms and auto manufacturers, due to their increasing efforts to locate production in the United States and other offshore markets. Although the yen's appreciation hindered Japan's companies, it did not stop them in their tracks.

Toyota and other exporters began decreasing their exposure to exchange-rate fluctuations in the 1980s by expanding production abroad, a strategy that was accelerating at the turn of the century. By 2003, Honda produced 75 percent of the cars it sold in the United States in North American factories, up from 60 percent in the previous decade. Also, Nissan opened a $1 billion factory in Canton, Mississippi, to manufacture minivans, sport-utility vehicles, and pickup trucks. With the new plant, Nissan almost doubled its manufacturing capacity in North America to 1.35 million vehicles. Nissan management noted that they were attempting to take foreign exchange out of the equation as much as possible.

Back in 1996, Toshiba Corp. exported about $6 billion more in goods than it imported. This meant that the firm's sales could theoretically decline by 6 billion yen ($54 million) each time the yen appreciated against the dollar by one yen. Since then, Japan's largest semiconductor producer has succeeded in slashing its net dollar exposure by locating manufacturing abroad and increasing dollar-based imports of parts. In 1996, Toshiba started a plant in Indonesia to manufacture color-TV sets; it also opened a factory in the Philippines to produce hard-disk and optical-disk drives. Other factories in Asia followed, including a personal-computer plant in China. By 2003, Toshiba produced more than 30 percent of its goods abroad, compared with 17 percent in 1995; and it exported only $1 billion of goods more than it imported.

Besides moving production abroad, Japan's big auto and electronics companies have increasingly shifted development, engineering, and design operations abroad. That also helps reduce exchange-rate risk by keeping even more of their costs and revenues denominated in a single currency. For example, in 2004 Toyota opened a design studio in Michigan, allowing the firm to perform in the United States all the stages in the process of manufacturing new vehicles, from design to engineering and production.

In 2003, Matsushita Electric Industrial, producer of Panasonic brand equipment, increased efforts to make its overseas divisions as self-sufficient as possible. In the past, Matsushita repatriated revenue earned overseas, which exposed the firm not only to exchange-rate risk but also to high Japanese corporate taxes. Now, it strives to reinvest money earned abroad in manufacturing and research facilities located in each region. Although the strategy was mainly aimed at making Matsushita more productive and quicker in responding to local customers' needs, some of the result has been to reduce the amount of money Matsushita exchanges from dollars or euros to yen.

Source: "Japanese Firms Practice Yen Damage Control," *The Wall Street Journal*, September 26, 2003, p. A7.

April 1986, General Motors surprised the auto industry with price increases, which were matched by Ford in July. It was argued that with such price hikes, U.S. companies would fritter away a chance to increase market share and close the U.S. trade deficit.

Currency pass-through also had implications for U.S. exporters. A factor that contributed to sluggish U.S. exports was that U.S. prices in foreign markets did not fall proportionate to the dollar depreciation, implying partial pass-through. Throughout 1986, many U.S. exporters sought to restore profit margins, which had deteriorated when the dollar was so strong in the early 1980s, by maintaining or even increasing export prices.

Dollar Depreciation of 2003–2004

During 2003–2004, the U.S. dollar steadily depreciated against foreign currencies such as the yen and euro. As we have learned, the dollar decline would generally be expected to reduce U.S. imports and increase its exports, thus causing a decrease in its trade deficit. Yet the falling dollar was not doing what it was supposed to do. Why?

Part of the blame could be ascribed to the nature of the global economy. Excess capacity worldwide, sharp competition, and Asian currency intervention all restricted the dollar's effect on prices in the United States. And because the falling dollar wasn't causing more inflation, the Federal Reserve did not increase interest rates, which would limit the growth of the U.S. economy and its desire for imports.

ECONOMIC *Applications*

Visit EconData Online

Excess capacity and strong competition around the world discouraged foreign producers from attempting to increase prices in the United States, even though their costs increased in dollar terms. Rather, they tolerated decreased profit margins or tried to slash costs in other ways to maintain market share. For example, Kellwood Co., a major American marketer of garments such as Calvin Klein, noted that some of its Asian suppliers, such as sewing factories and fabric mills, inquired about increasing their prices because of higher costs. But apparel was an industry with sizable world overcapacity, and suppliers knew that if they increased prices, there were many competitors in other countries that Kellwood could turn to. These suppliers refrained from raising their prices, which allowed Kellwood's prices on Calvin Klein garments to remain unchanged.

Also, a price war in the U.S. car market contributed to flat prices. The price war resulted in German auto companies selling some luxury models in the United States at lower prices than could be obtained in Europe. For example Volkswagen AG's luxury Audi A8L listed for $68,500 in the United States in 2004, a third less than its dollar-equivalent price in Europe. VW officials noted that they did not realize much profit on the sale of this vehicle to Americans.

Moreover, Japan's Toyota Motor Corp. protected itself against dollar oscillations by manufacturing 60 percent of the vehicles it sold in North America locally. Although Toyota did increase prices on some luxury Lexus and sport-utility vehicles, they increased by only 0.4 percent. The base price of the LS430 Lexus sedan remain unchanged at $55,125.

Researchers at the New York Federal Reserve Bank have found that a fluctuation in the exchange rate has a far smaller effect on U.S. import prices than in other countries. As seen in Table 14.8, just 26 percent of a change in the exchange rate is passed through to import prices in the United States in the short run, the researchers found, compared with 53 percent in France, 59 percent in Germany, and 88 percent in Japan. That helps explain why the dollar's depreciation in the early 2000s caused far less concern in the United States than overseas.

The Dollar and U.S. Manufacturing

As we have learned, a dollar appreciation can affect the revenues and costs of U.S. manufacturers. Concerning revenues, a stronger dollar pushes up the prices of U.S. goods in export markets, making those goods less attractive to foreign buyers and ultimately resulting in reduced export sales for U.S. producers. Also a stronger dollar can jeopardize the domestic sales of U.S. manufacturers by giving the foreign producers that have penetrated U.S. markets a competitive edge in pricing. For example, if the dollar appreciates against the yen, then Japanese producers selling to U.S. markets will find that their dollar revenues

TABLE 14.8

Exchange Rate Pass-Through into Import Prices, 1999

Percent of a Change in the Exchange Rate that Is Passed Through to Import Prices*

Country	Short Run	Long Run
Australia	0.55%	0.69%
Canada	0.65	0.68
Germany	0.59	0.79
France	0.53	1.21
United Kingdom	0.39	0.47
Japan	0.88	1.26
Netherlands	0.75	0.77
New Zealand	0.47	0.62
United States	0.26	0.77
Average*	0.61	0.77

*Average of 25 countries belonging to the Organization of Economic Cooperation and Development.

Source: Jose Campa and Linda Goldberg, "Exchange Rate Pass-Through into Import Prices: A Macro or Micro Phenomenon?" Federal Reserve Bank of New York, 2002, at Internet Site http://www.newyorkfed.org/research/staff-reports/sr149.pdf.

translate into more yen than in the past. This increase in their "local currency profit" enables the Japanese producers to reduce the prices they charge in U.S. markets and thus to draw customers away from rival U.S. producers.

A stronger dollar also affects the costs of U.S. manufacturers. In recent years, U.S. firms have increasingly relied on foreign equipment and components in producing their goods. When the dollar rises, the cost of such imported inputs falls. The resulting savings can at least partially offset the revenue losses associated with a dollar appreciation and thereby help to stabilize industries' profits. Indeed, for some industries, the cost benefits of the appreciation may outweigh the adverse revenue effects.

Economists at the Federal Reserve Bank of New York have captured both the revenue and cost sides of an industry's exposure to dollar movements by constructing a measure called "net external orientation." This measure is computed as the share of an industry's total revenues that is derived from exports less the share of its total spending that is attributable to imported inputs.

An industry has a positive (negative) net external orientation when its export revenues are greater (less) than its imported input costs.

To assess the vulnerability of U.S. manufacturers to a rise in the dollar's exchange value, refer to Table 14.9 on page 434. In many industries, exports represent a large fraction of total revenues: Chemicals, industrial machinery, electronic equipment, transportation, equipment, and instruments generate more than 15 percent of their revenues through exports. This shared focus on exports would seem to suggest that the profitability of all these industries would suffer significantly under a dollar appreciation. But once we take into account the offsetting effects of imported input use, we find that these industries would not, in fact, all fare alike with a rise in the dollar.

In the electronic equipment industry, exports account for 24.2 percent of revenues, while imported inputs account for a much smaller share of costs—11.6 percent. Subtracting the imported input share from the export share yields a relatively high net external orientation of 12.6 percent. By contrast, in the transportation equipment industry,

TABLE 14.9

Trade Orientation of U.S. Manufacturing Industries in 1995

Industry	Export Revenues as a Percent of Total Revenues	Imported Input Spending as a Percent of Total Spending	Net External Orientation	
Instruments	21.3%	6.3%	15.0	Profits More Vulnerable
Industrial machinery	25.8	11.0	14.8	to a Dollar Appreciation
Electronic equipment	24.2	11.6	12.6	
Tobacco products	14.0	2.1	11.9	
Chemicals	15.8	6.3	9.5	
Apparel	7.4	3.2	4.2	
Rubber and plastics	9.2	5.3	3.9	
Lumber	7.6	4.3	3.3	
Transportation equipment	17.8	15.7	2.1	
Food products	5.9	4.2	1.7	
Stone and concrete products	5.6	4.7	0.9	Profits Less Vulnerable
Petroleum refining	3.9	5.3	-1.4	to a Dollar Appreciation
Leather products	14.4	20.5	-6.1	

Source: Linda Goldberg and Keith Crockett, "The Dollar and U.S. Manufacturing," *Current Issues in Economics and Finance*, Federal Reserve Bank of New York, November 1998, p. 3.

the share of total revenues attributable to exports is a sizable 17.8 percent, but spending on imports—15.7 percent of total spending—largely offsets the high export share, producing a net external orientation of only 2.1 percent. The contrasting net figures for the two industries indicate that a strong dollar is likely to have significant adverse effects on the profitability of U.S. electronic equipment manufacturers, while the profitability of the transportation equipment industry should be more insulated from exchange-rate effects. As Table 14.9 shows, the industries most likely to be hurt by a stronger dollar are those with high net external orientation—tobacco, industrial machinery, electronic equipment, and instruments. For some industries, such as petroleum refining and leather products, the cost benefits of a dollar appreciation outweigh and adverse revenue effects.

U.S. manufacturing industries are becoming increasingly sensitive to changes in the international value of the dollar. This increased sensitivity is large-ly attributable to the growing reliance of this sector on international trade. Firms now export a greater share of their products than in the past and make more extensive use of foreign parts and materials in the production of their goods.

The Absorption Approach to Exchange-Rate Adjustment

According to the elasticities approach, currency depreciation offers a price incentive to reduce imports and increase exports. But even if elasticity conditions are favorable, whether the home country's trade balance will actually improve may depend on how the economy reacts to the depreciation. The absorption approach[2] provides insights

[2]Sidney S. Alexander, "Effects of a Devaluation on a Trade Balance," *IMF Staff Papers*, April 1952, pp. 263–278.

into this question by considering the impact of depreciation on the spending behavior of the domestic economy and the influence of domestic spending on the trade balance.

The absorption approach starts with the idea that the value of total domestic output (Y) equals the level of total spending. Total spending consists of consumption (C), investment (I), government expenditures (G), and net exports ($X - M$). This can be written as

$$Y = C + I + G + (X - M)$$

The absorption approach then consolidates $C + I + G$ into a single term A, which is referred to as absorption, and designates net exports ($X - M$) as B. Total domestic output thus equals the sum of absorption plus net exports, or

$$Y = A + B$$

This can be rewritten as

$$B = Y - A$$

This expression suggests that the balance of trade (B) equals the difference between total domestic output (Y) and the level of absorption (A). If national output exceeds domestic absorption, the economy's trade balance will be positive. Conversely, a negative trade balance suggests that an economy is spending beyond its ability to produce.

The absorption approach predicts that a currency depreciation will improve an economy's trade balance only if national output rises relative to absorption. This means that a country must increase its total output, reduce its absorption, or do some combination of the two. The following examples illustrate these possibilities.

Assume that an economy faces *unemployment* as well as a *trade deficit*. With the economy operating below maximum capacity, the price incentives of depreciation would tend to direct idle resources into the production of goods for export, in addition to diverting spending away from imports to domestically produced substitutes. The impact of the depreciation is thus to expand domestic output as well as to improve the trade balance. It is no wonder that policy makers tend to view currency depreciation as an effective tool

when an economy faces unemployment with a trade deficit.

In the case of an economy operating at *full employment*, however, there are no unutilized resources available for additional production. National output is at a fixed level. The only way in which currency depreciation can improve the trade balance is for the economy to somehow cut domestic absorption, freeing resources needed to produce additional export goods and import substitutes. For example, domestic policy makers could decrease absorption by adopting restrictive fiscal and monetary policies in the face of higher prices resulting from the depreciation. But this would result in sacrifice on the part of those who bear the burden of such measures. Currency depreciation may thus be considered inappropriate when an economy is operating at maximum capacity.

The absorption approach goes beyond the elasticity approach, which views the economy's trade balance as distinct from the rest of the economy. Instead, currency depreciation is viewed in relation to the economy's utilization of its resources and level of production. The two approaches are therefore complementary.

The Monetary Approach to Exchange-Rate Adjustment

A survey of the traditional approaches to currency depreciation reveals a major shortcoming. According to the elasticities and absorption approaches, monetary consequences are not associated with balance-of-payments adjustment; or, to the extent that such consequences exist, they can be neutralized by domestic monetary authorities. The elasticities and absorption approaches apply only to the trade account of the balance of payments, neglecting the implications of capital movements. The *monetary approach* to depreciation addresses this shortcoming.[3] According to the monetary

[3]See Donald S. Kemp, "A Monetary View of the Balance of Payments," *Review*, Federal Reserve Bank of St. Louis, April 1975, pp. 14–22; and Thomas M. Humphrey, "The Monetary Approach to Exchange Rates: Its Historical Evolution and Role in Policy Debates," *Economic Review*, Federal Reserve Bank of Richmond, July–August 1978, pp. 2–9.

approach, currency depreciation may induce a *temporary* improvement in a nation's balance-of-payments position. For example, assume that equilibrium initially exists in the home country's money market. A depreciation of the home currency would increase the price level—that is, the domestic-currency prices of potential imports and exports. This increase would increase the demand for money, because larger amounts of money are needed for transactions. If that increased demand is not fulfilled from domestic sources, an inflow of money from overseas occurs. This inflow results in

a balance-of-payments surplus and a rise in international reserves. But the surplus does not last forever. By adding to the international component of the home-country money supply, the currency depreciation leads to an increase in spending (absorption), which reduces the surplus. The surplus eventually disappears when equilibrium is restored in the home country's money market. The effects of depreciation on real economic variables are thus temporary. *Over the long run, currency depreciation merely raises the domestic price level.*

Summary

1. Currency depreciation (devaluation) may affect a nation's trade position through its impact on relative prices, incomes, and purchasing power of money balances.

2. When all of a firm's inputs are acquired domestically and their costs are denominated in the domestic currency, an appreciation in the domestic currency's exchange value tends to increase the firm's costs by the same proportion, in terms of the foreign currency. Conversely, a depreciation of the domestic currency's exchange value tends to reduce the firm's costs by the same proportion in terms of the foreign currency.

3. Manufacturers often obtain inputs from abroad (foreign sourcing) whose costs are denominated in terms of a foreign currency. As foreign-currency-denominated costs become a larger portion of a producer's total costs, an appreciation of the domestic currency's exchange value leads to a smaller increase in the foreign-currency cost of the firm's output and a larger decrease in the domestic cost of the firm's output—compared to the cost changes that occur when all input costs are denominated in the domestic currency. The opposite applies for currency depreciation.

4. By increasing (decreasing) relative U.S. production costs, a dollar appreciation (depreciation) tends to raise (lower) U.S. export prices in terms of a foreign currency, which induces a decrease (increase) in the quantity of U.S. goods sold abroad; similarly, a dollar appreciation (depreciation) tends to raise (lower) the amount of U.S. imports.

5. According to the elasticities approach, currency depreciation leads to the greatest improvement in a country's trade position when demand elasticities are high. Recent empirical studies indicate that the estimated demand elasticities for most nations are quite high.

6. The time path of currency depreciation can be explained in terms of the J-curve effect. According to this concept, the response of trade flows to changes in relative prices increases with the passage of time. Currency depreciation tends to worsen a country's trade balance in the short run, only to be followed by an improvement in the long run (assuming favorable elasticities).

7. The extent to which exchange-rate changes lead to changes in import prices and export prices is known as the pass-through relationship. Complete (partial) pass-through occurs when a change in the exchange rate brings about a proportionate (less than proportionate) change in export prices and import prices. Empirical evidence suggests that pass-through tends to be partial rather than complete.

8. The absorption approach emphasizes the income effects of currency depreciation. According to this view, a depreciation may initially stimulate a nation's exports and production of import-competing goods. But this

will promote excess domestic spending unless real output can be expanded or domestic absorption reduced. The result would be a return to a payments deficit.

9. The monetary approach to depreciation emphasizes the effect that depreciation has on the purchasing power of money balances and the resulting impacts on domestic expenditures and import levels. According to the monetary approach, the influence of currency depreciation on real output is temporary; over the long run, depreciation merely raises the domestic price level.

Key Concepts and Terms

- Absorption approach *(page 422)*
- Elasticity approach *(page 422)*
- Exchange rate pass-through *(page 428)*
- J-curve effect *(page 426)*
- Marshall–Lerner condition *(page 423)*
- Monetary approach *(page 422)*

Study Questions

1. How does a currency depreciation affect a nation's balance of trade?

2. Three major approaches to analyzing the economic impact of currency depreciation are (a) the elasticities approach, (b) the absorption approach, and (c) the monetary approach. Distinguish among the three.

3. What is meant by the Marshall–Lerner condition? Do recent empirical studies suggest that world elasticity conditions are sufficiently high to permit successful depreciations?

4. How does the J-curve effect relate to the time path of currency depreciation?

5. What implications does currency pass-through have for a nation whose currency depreciates?

6. According to the absorption approach, does it make any difference whether a nation's currency depreciates when the economy is operating at less than full capacity versus at full capacity?

7. How can currency depreciation-induced changes in household money balances promote payments equilibrium?

8. Suppose ABC Inc., a U.S. auto manufacturer, obtains all of its auto components in the United States and that its costs are denominated in dollars. Assume the dollar's exchange value appreciates by 50 percent against the Mexican peso. What impact does the dollar appreciation have on the firm's international competitiveness? What about a dollar depreciation?

9. Suppose ABC Inc., a U.S. auto manufacturer, obtains some of its auto components in Mexico and that the costs of these components are denominated in pesos; the costs of the remaining components are denominated in dollars. Assume the dollar's exchange value appreciates by 50 percent against the peso. Compared to your answer in study question 8, what impact will the dollar appreciation have on the firm's international competitiveness? What about a dollar depreciation?

10. **Xtra!** **For a tutorial of this question, go to http://carbaughxtra.swlearning.com**
Assume the United States exports 1,000 computers at a price of $3,000 each and imports 150 British autos at a price of £10,000 each. Assume that the dollar/pound exchange rate is 2 dollars per pound.

    a. Calculate, in dollar terms, the U.S. export receipts, import payments, and trade balance prior to a depreciation of the dollar's exchange value.

    b. Suppose the dollar's exchange value depreciates by 10 percent. Assuming that the price elasticity of demand for U.S. exports equals

3.0 and the price elasticity of demand for U.S. imports equals 2.0, calculate the U.S. export receipts, import payments, and trade balance. Does the dollar depreciation improve or worsen the U.S. trade balance? Why?

c. Now assume that the price elasticity of demand for U.S. exports equals 0.3 and the price elasticity of demand for U.S. imports equals 0.2. Does this change the outcome? Why?

14.1 Changes in the exchange rate can have a significant impact on various sectors of the economy. For a detailed look at various countries' exports and imports of agricultural products to the United States, visit the home page of the U.S. Department of Agriculture/Foreign Agricultural Service. Set your browser to this URL:

http://www.fas.usda.gov

14.2 The Council on Foreign Relations is a national organization that is committed to the study and debate of America's global role. Visit its Web site to view some of their recent studies on international finance and trade. Set your browser to this URL:

http://www.cfr.org

To access NetLink Exercises and the Virtual Scavenger Hunt, visit the Carbaugh Web site at http://carbaugh.swlearning.com.

Xtra!
CARBAUGH

Log onto the Carbaugh Xtra! Web site (http://carbaughxtra.swlearning.com) for additional learning resources such as practice quizzes, help with graphing, and current events applications.

Exchange Rate Pass-Through

Exchange rate pass-through denotes the impact of a change in the exchange rate between exporting and importing countries on local-currency prices of imports. Two factors determine the extent of pass-through: the responsiveness of markups to competitive conditions and the degree of returns to scale in the production of the imported good.[4]

If the typical foreign firm sets the price of a good exported to the United States as a constant markup over marginal cost (with price and marginal cost measured in the dollar), then complete pass-through occurs when returns to scale are constant, implying constant marginal cost. In this situation, a dollar appreciation of, say, 10 percent lowers the foreign firm's marginal cost measured in dollars by the same amount. With a constant markup, the dollar price of the imported good must then decline by 10 percent.

Pass-through will be less than complete (partial) when returns to scale are decreasing, implying increasing marginal cost. Again assume that the foreign firm sets the price of a good exported to the United States as a constant markup over marginal cost. The increase in U.S. demand for the imported good brought by a dollar appreciation now puts upward pressure on the foreign firm's marginal cost. Thus when measured in dollars, marginal cost

declines by less than 10 percent in response to a 10 percent dollar appreciation. Because the markup is constant, this leads to partial pass-through; that is, a decline in the dollar price of the imported good is less than 10 percent. The reader can verify that the opposite result occurs in the presence of increasing returns to scale (declining marginal cost), where a change in the exchange rate is more than fully passed through in the import price.

A constant markup of price over cost is typical of industries with a very large number of firms, where the impact of any individual firm's price changes on the industry price is negligible. In the limiting case of a perfectly competitive industry, the markup will be constant at zero. In a setting with monopolistic competition, the markup will be positive but constant, because a firm's market share is relatively small. In an oligopoly setting, however, the markup will usually depend on the good's dollar price and the dollar price of competing goods, as well as the strength of demand for both the imported and the competing goods.

To illustrate how the markup may respond to changes in the dollar price of the imported good, let us consider an example in which a monopolist foreign firm, say, Toyota, sells all of its output to the United States. We assume that the demand curve D depicted in Figure 14.4(a) on page 440 represents the U.S. demand for Toyotas as a function of the dollar price of Toyotas. Profit maximization

[4]Giovanni Olivei, "Exchange Rates and the Prices of Manufacturing Products Imported into the United States," *New England Economic Review*, First Quarter 2002, pp. 4–6.

FIGURE 14.4

Exchange-Rate Pass-Through with a Monopolistic Foreign Firm (Toyota)

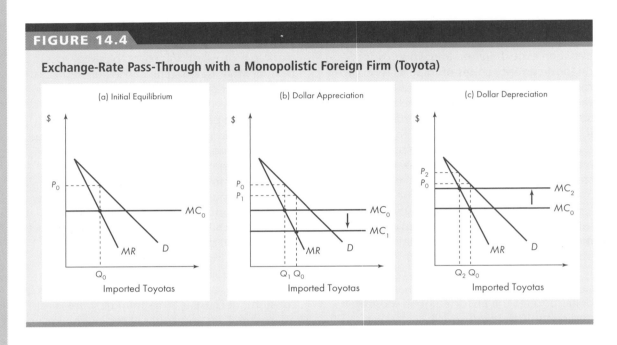

requires equalization of marginal revenue and marginal cost, both expressed in dollars, which occurs at the intersection of the schedules MR and MC_0. Note that the marginal cost schedule is horizontal, implying constant returns to scale. Toyota sets the profit-maximizing price P_0 as a markup over marginal cost, with Q_0 denoting the quantity of Toyotas demanded at price P_0.

Figure 14.4(b) illustrates how a dollar appreciation affects the dollar price of Toyotas. The appreciation lowers the dollar cost of producing Toyotas, and thus the marginal cost schedule shifts down by the same

proportion of the appreciation.[5] The graph shows that at the new equilibrium the difference between the dollar price of Toyotas, P_1, and marginal cost, MC_1, is larger than at the old equilibrium. This signals that the foreign firm charges a higher markup (in dollars) over

[5]The assumption that Toyota's costs in dollars decline by the same percentage of the dollar appreciation implies that the change in the exchange rate has no impact on the Japanese price of inputs used in the production of Toyotas. This is a reasonable approximation for labor inputs, but it is an unrealistic assumption when Toyota heavily relies on imported raw materials and energy. In this case, a dollar appreciation would raise Toyota's price of imported raw materials and energy. Allowing for this effect would lower the extent of exchange rate pass-through, other things being equal.

production cost. The graph also shows that as a consequence of the higher markup, the decline in the dollar price of Toyotas is smaller than the dollar appreciation, implying partial pass-through.

Figure 14.4(c) illustrates the opposite case of a dollar depreciation. The depreciation raises the dollar cost of producing Toyotas, and thus the marginal cost curve shifts up. At the new equilibrium, the dollar price of Toyotas increases by less than the increase in marginal cost resulting from the depreciation. This implies that the firm charges a lower markup (in dollars) over production cost, implying partial pass-through.

The example in Figure 14.4 shows that exchange rate pass-through can be less than complete even in the presence of constant returns to scale. As the reader can verify, increasing marginal cost (that is, decreasing returns to scale) would lower the extent of exchange rate pass-through. Conversely, decreasing marginal cost (increasing returns to scale) would increase the extent of pass-through.

To summarize, the two determinants of exchange rate pass-through, the responsiveness of markups to competitive conditions and the degree of return to scale in production, can interact in different ways to produce different outcomes.

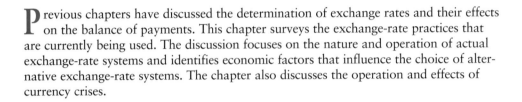

chapter 15

Exchange-Rate Systems and Currency Crises

P revious chapters have discussed the determination of exchange rates and their effects on the balance of payments. This chapter surveys the exchange-rate practices that are currently being used. The discussion focuses on the nature and operation of actual exchange-rate systems and identifies economic factors that influence the choice of alternative exchange-rate systems. The chapter also discusses the operation and effects of currency crises.

Exchange-Rate Practices

In choosing an exchange-rate system, a nation must decide whether to allow its currency to be determined by market forces (floating rate) or to be fixed (pegged) against some standard of value. If a nation adopts a floating rate, it must decide whether to float independently, to float in unison with a group of other currencies, or to crawl according to a predetermined formula such as relative inflation rates. The decision to anchor a currency includes the options of anchoring to a single currency, to a basket of currencies, or to gold. Since 1971, however, the technique of expressing official exchange rates in terms of gold has not been used; gold has been phased out of the international monetary system. The role of gold in the international monetary system will be further discussed in Chapter 17.

Members of the International Monetary Fund (IMF) have been free to follow any exchange-rate policy that conforms to three principles: (1) Exchange rates should not be manipulated to prevent effective balance-of-payments adjustments or to gain unfair competitive advantage over other members. (2) Members should act to counter short-term disorderly conditions in exchange markets. (3) When members intervene in exchange markets, they should take into account the interests of other members. Table 15.1 summarizes the exchange-rate practices used by IMF member countries; Table 15.2 highlights some of the factors that affect the choice of an exchange-rate system.

Fixed exchange rates are used primarily by small, developing nations whose currencies are anchored to a **key currency**, such as the U.S. dollar. A key currency is widely traded on world money markets, has demonstrated relatively stable values over time, and has been widely accepted as a means of international settlement. Table 15.3 on page 444 identifies the major key currencies of the world.

TABLE 15.1

Exchange-Rate Arrangements of IMF Members, 2003

Exchange Arrangement	Number of Countries
Exchange arrangements with no separate legal tender*	41
Currency-board arrangements	7
Conventional pegged (fixed) exchange rates	43
Pegged exchange rates within horizontal bands	4
Crawling pegged exchange rates	5
Exchange rates within crawling bands	5
Managed floating exchange rates	47
Independently floating exchange rates	35
	187

*The currency of another country circulates as the sole legal tender, or the member belongs to a monetary or currency union in which the same legal tender is shared by the members of the union.

Source: International Monetary Fund, *Classification of Exchange Rate Arrangements and Monetary Policy Frameworks*, June 2003, at http://www.imf.org. See also *International Financial Statistics*, various issues.

TABLE 15.2

Choosing an Exchange-Rate System

Characteristics of Economy	Implication for the Desired Degree of Exchange-Rate Flexibility
Size and openness of the economy	If trade is a large share of national output, then the costs of currency fluctuations can be high. This suggests that small, open economies may best be served by fixed exchange rates.
Inflation rate	If a country has much higher inflation than its trading partners, its exchange rate needs to be flexible to prevent its goods from becoming uncompetitive in world markets. If inflation differentials are more modest, a fixed rate is less troublesome.
Labor-market flexibility	The more rigid wages are, the greater the need for a flexible exchange rate to help the economy respond to an external shock.
Degree of financial development	In developing countries with immature financial markets, a freely floating exchange rate may not be sensible because a small number of foreign-exchange trades can cause big swings in currencies.
Credibility of policy makers	The weaker the reputation of the central bank, the stronger the case for pegging the exchange rate to build confidence that inflation will be controlled.
Capital mobility	The more open an economy to international capital, the harder it is to sustain a fixed rate.

Source: International Monetary Fund, *World Economic Outlook*, October 1997, p. 83.

TABLE 15.3

Key Currencies: Share of National Currencies in Total Identified
Official Holdings of Foreign Exchange, 2002 (in Percent)

Key Currency	All Countries	Industrial Countries	Developing Countries
U.S. dollar	64.8%	70.1%	61.3%
Japanese yen	4.5	4.8	4.3
Pound sterling	4.4	2.2	5.8
Swiss franc	0.7	0.6	0.9
Euro	14.6	11.2	16.8
Other	11.0	11.1	10.9
	100.0%	100.0%	100.0%

Source: International Monetary Fund, *Annual Report,* 2003, p. 99.

One reason why developing nations choose to anchor their currencies to a key currency is that it is used as a means of international settlement. Consider a Norwegian importer who wants to purchase Argentinean beef over the next year. If the Argentine exporter is unsure of what the Norwegian krone will purchase in one year, he might reject the krone in settlement. Similarly, the Norwegian importer might doubt the value of Argentina's peso. One solution is for the contract to be written in terms of a key currency. Generally speaking, smaller nations with relatively undiversified economies and large foreign-trade sectors have been inclined to anchor their currencies to one of the key currencies.

Maintaining an anchor to a key currency provides several benefits for developing nations. First, the prices of the traded products of many developing nations are determined primarily in the markets of industrialized nations such as the United States; by anchoring, say, to the dollar, these nations can stabilize the domestic-currency prices of their imports and exports. Second, many nations with high inflation have anchored to the dollar (the United States has relatively low inflation) in order to exert restraint on domestic policies and reduce inflation. By making the commitment to stabilize their exchange rates against the dollar, governments hope to convince their citizens that they are willing to adopt the responsible monetary policies

necessary to achieve low inflation. Anchoring the exchange rate may thus lessen inflationary expectations, leading to lower interest rates, a lessening of the loss of output due to disinflation, and a moderation of price pressures.

In maintaining fixed exchange rates, nations must decide whether to anchor their currencies to another currency or a currency basket. Anchoring to a *single currency* is generally done by developing nations whose trade and financial relationships are mainly with a single industrial-country partner.

Developing nations with more than one major trading partner often anchor their currencies to a group or *basket of currencies*. The basket is composed of prescribed quantities of foreign currencies in proportion to the amount of trade done with the nation anchoring its currency. Once the basket has been selected, the currency value of the nation is computed using the exchange rates of the foreign currencies in the basket. Anchoring the domestic-currency value of the basket enables a nation to average out fluctuations in export or import prices caused by exchange-rate movements. The effects of exchange-rate changes on the domestic economy are thus reduced.

Rather than constructing their own currency basket, some nations anchor the value of their currencies to the **special drawing right (SDR)**, a basket of four currencies established by the IMF. The IMF requires that the valuation of the SDR basket be reviewed every five years; the basket is to include, in proportional amounts, the currencies of the members having the largest exports of goods and services during the previous five years. The currencies comprising the basket as of 2003, along with their amounts and percentage weights, are listed in Table 15.4.

The idea behind the SDR basket valuation is to make the SDR's value more stable than the foreign-currency value of any single national currency. The SDR is valued according to an index based on the moving average of those currencies in the basket. Should the values of the basket currencies either depreciate or appreciate against one another, the SDR's value would remain in the center. The SDR would depreciate against those currencies that are rising in value and appreciate against currencies whose values are falling. Nations desiring exchange-rate stability are attracted to the SDR as a currency basket against which to anchor their currency values.

Fixed Exchange-Rate System

Few nations have allowed their currencies' exchange values to be determined solely by the forces of supply and demand in a free market. Until the industrialized nations adopted managed floating exchange rates in the 1970s, the practice generally was to maintain a pattern of relatively fixed exchange rates among national currencies. Changes in national exchange rates presumably were to be initiated by domestic monetary authorities when long-term market forces warranted it.

Par Value and Official Exchange Rate

Under a fixed exchange-rate system, governments assign their currencies a **par value** in terms of gold or other key currencies. By comparing the par values of two currencies, we can determine their **official exchange rate**. For example, the official exchange rate between the U.S. dollar and the British pound was $2.80 = £1 as long as the United States bought and sold gold at a fixed price of $35 per ounce and Britain bought and sold gold at £12.50 per ounce (35.00/12.50 = 2.80). The major industrial nations set their currencies' par values in terms of gold until gold was phased out of the international monetary system in the early 1970s.

Today, many developing nations choose to define their par values in terms of certain key currencies. Under this arrangement, the monetary authority first defines its official exchange rate in terms of the key currency. It then defends the fixed parity by purchasing and selling its currency for the key currency at that rate. Assume, for example, that Bolivian central bankers fix their peso at 20 pesos = US$1, whereas Ecuador's sucre is set at 10 sucres = US$1. The official exchange rate between the peso and sucre becomes 1 peso = 0.5 sucre.

TABLE 15.4

Special Drawing Right Valuation, April 30, 2003

Currency	Amount of Currency Units	Exchange Rate	U.S. Dollar Equivalent
Euro	0.4260	1.11290	0.474095
Japanese yen	21.0000	119.48000	0.175762
Pound sterling	0.0984	1.59610	0.157056
U.S. dollar	0.5770	1.00000	0.577000
			1.383913

Source: International Monetary Fund, *Annual Report,* 2003, p. 76.

Exchange-Rate Stabilization

A first requirement for a nation participating in a fixed exchange-rate system is to determine an official exchange rate for its currency. The next step is to set up an **exchange-stabilization fund** to defend the official rate. Through purchases and sales of foreign currencies, the exchange-stabilization fund attempts to ensure that the market exchange rate does not move above or below the official exchange rate.

In Figure 15.1, assume that the market exchange rate equals $2.80 per pound, seen at the intersection of the demand and supply schedules of British pounds, D_0 and S_0. Also assume that the official exchange rate is defined as $2.80 per pound. Now suppose that rising interest rates in Britain cause U.S. investors to demand additional pounds to finance the purchase of British securities; let the demand for

pounds rise from D_0 to D_1 in Figure 15.1(a). Under free-market conditions, the dollar would depreciate from $2.80 per pound to $2.90 per pound. But under a fixed exchange-rate system, the monetary authority will attempt to defend the official rate of $2.80 per pound. At this rate, there exists an excess demand for pounds equal to £40 billion; this means that the British face an excess supply of dollars in the same amount. To keep the market exchange rate from depreciating beyond $2.80 per pound, the U.S. exchange-stabilization fund would purchase the excess supply of dollars with pounds. The supply of pounds thus rises from S_0 to S_1, resulting in a stabilization of the market exchange rate at $2.80 per pound.

Conversely, suppose that increased prosperity in the United Kingdom leads to rising imports from the United States; the supply of pounds thus

FIGURE 15.1

Exchange-Rate Stabilization Under a Fixed Exchange-Rate System

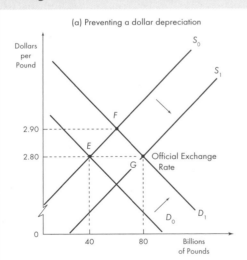

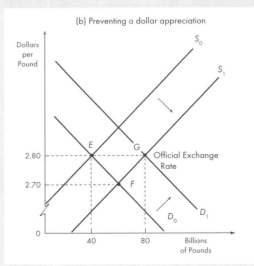

To defend the official exchange rate of $2.80 per pound, the central bank must supply all of the nation's currency that is demanded at the official rate and demand all of the nation's currency that is supplied to it at the official rate. To prevent a dollar depreciation, the central bank must purchase the excess supply of dollars with an equivalent amount of pounds. To prevent a dollar appreciation, the central bank must purchase the excess supply of pounds with an equivalent amount of dollars.

increases from, say, S_0 to S_1 in Figure 15.1(b). At the official exchange rate of $2.80 per pound, there exists an excess supply of pounds equal to £40 billion. To keep the dollar from appreciating against the pound, the U.S. stabilization fund would purchase the excess supply of pounds with dollars. The demand for pounds thus increases from D_0 to D_1, resulting in a stabilization of the market exchange rate at $2.80 per pound.

This example illustrates how an exchange-stabilization fund undertakes its pegging operations to offset short-term fluctuations in the market exchange rate. Over the long run, however, the official exchange rate and the market exchange rate may move apart, reflecting changes in fundamental economic conditions—income levels, tastes and preferences, and technological factors. In the case of a **fundamental disequilibrium**, the cost of defending the existing official rate may become prohibitive.

Consider the case of a deficit nation that finds its currency weakening. Maintaining the official rate may require the exchange-stabilization fund to purchase sizable quantities of its currency with foreign currencies or other reserve assets. This may impose a severe drain on the deficit nation's stock of international reserves. Although the deficit nation may be able to borrow reserves from other nations or from the IMF to continue the defense of its exchange rate, such borrowing privileges are generally of limited magnitude. At the same time, the deficit nation will be undergoing internal adjustments to curb the disequilibrium. These measures will likely be aimed at controlling inflationary pressures and raising interest rates to promote capital inflows and discourage imports. If the imbalance is persistent, the deficit nation may view such internal adjustments as too costly in terms of falling income and employment levels. Rather than continually resorting to such measures, the deficit nation may decide that the reversal of the disequilibrium calls for an adjustment in the exchange rate itself. Under a system of fixed exchange rates, a chronic imbalance may be counteracted by a currency devaluation or revaluation.

Devaluation and Revaluation

Under a fixed exchange-rate system, a nation's monetary authority may decide to pursue balance-of-payments equilibrium by devaluing or revaluing its currency. The purpose of **devaluation** is to cause the home currency's exchange value to *depreciate*, thus counteracting a payments *deficit*. The purpose of currency **revaluation** is to cause the home currency's exchange value to *appreciate*, thus counteracting a payments *surplus*.

The terms *devaluation* and *revaluation* refer to a legal redefinition of a currency's par value under a system of fixed exchange rates. The terms *depreciation* and *appreciation* refer to the actual impact on the market exchange rate caused by a redefinition of a par value or to changes in an exchange rate stemming from changes in the supply of or demand for foreign exchange. The legal and economic effects of devaluation and revaluation are further discussed in "Exploring Further 15.1" at the end of this chapter.

Devaluation and revaluation policies work on relative prices to divert domestic and foreign expenditures between domestic and foreign goods. By raising the home price of the foreign currency, a devaluation makes the home country's exports cheaper to foreigners in terms of the foreign currency, while making the home country's imports more expensive in terms of the home currency. Expenditures are diverted from foreign to home goods as home exports rise and imports fall. In like manner, a revaluation discourages the home country's exports and encourages its imports, diverting expenditures from home goods to foreign goods.

Before implementing a devaluation or revaluation, the monetary authority must decide (1) if an adjustment in the official exchange rate is necessary to correct a payments disequilibrium, (2) when the adjustment will occur, and (3) how large the adjustment should be. Exchange-rate decisions of government officials may be incorrect—that is, ill timed and of improper magnitude.

In making the decision to undergo a devaluation or revaluation, monetary authorities generally attempt to hide behind a veil of secrecy. Just hours before the decision is to become effective, public denials of any such policies by official government representatives are common. This is to discourage currency speculators, who try to profit by shifting funds from a currency falling in value to one rising in value. Given the destabilizing impact that massive speculation can exert on financial markets, it is hard to criticize monetary authorities for being secretive in their actions. However, the need for devaluation tends to be obvious to outsiders as well as to government officials and in the past has nearly always resulted in heavy speculative pressures. Table 15.5 summarizes the advantages and disadvantages of fixed exchange rates.

Bretton Woods System of Fixed Exchange Rates

An example of fixed exchange rates is the **Bretton Woods system.** In 1944, delegates from 44 member nations of the United Nations met at Bretton Woods, New Hampshire, to create a new international monetary system. They were aware of the unsatisfactory monetary experience of the 1930s, during which the international gold standard collapsed as the result of the economic and financial crises of the Great Depression and nations experimented unsuccessfully with floating exchange rates and exchange controls. The delegates wanted to establish international monetary order and avoid the instability and nationalistic practices that had been in effect until 1944.

The international monetary system that was created became known as the Bretton Woods system. The founders felt that neither completely fixed exchange rates nor floating rates were optimal; instead, they adopted a kind of semifixed exchange-rate system known as **adjustable pegged exchange rates.** The Bretton Woods system lasted from 1946 until 1973.

The main feature of the adjustable peg system was that currencies were tied to each other to provide stable exchange rates for commercial and financial transactions. When the balance of payments moved away from its long-run equilibrium position, however, a nation could repeg its exchange rate via devaluation or revaluation policies. Member nations agreed in principle to defend existing par values as long as possible in times of balance-of-payments disequilibrium. They were expected to use fiscal and monetary policies first to correct payments imbalances. But if reversing a persistent payments imbalance would mean severe disruption to the domestic economy in terms of inflation or unemployment, member nations could correct this *fundamental disequilibrium* by repegging their currencies up to 10 percent without permission from the IMF and by greater than 10 percent with the Fund's permission.

Under the Bretton Woods system, each member nation set the par value of its currency in terms of gold or, alternatively, the gold content of the U.S. dollar in 1944. Market exchange rates were

---

TABLE 15.5

Advantages and Disadvantages of Fixed Exchange Rates and Floating Exchange Rates

	Advantages	Disadvantages
Fixed exchange rates	Simplicity and clarity of exchange-rate target	Loss of independent monetary policy
	Automatic rule for the conduct of monetary policy	Vulnerable to speculative attacks
	Keeps inflation under control	
Floating exchange rates	Continuous adjustment in the balance of payments	Conducive to price inflation
	Operate under simplified institutional arrangements	Disorderly exchange markets can disrupt trade and investment patterns
	Allow governments to set independent monetary and fiscal policies	Encourage reckless financial policies on the part of government

almost but not completely fixed, being kept within a band of 1 percent on either side of parity for a total spread of 2 percent. National exchange-stabilization funds were used to maintain the band limits. In 1971, the exchange-support margins were widened to 2.25 percent on either side of parity to eliminate payments imbalances by setting in motion corrective trade and capital movements. Devaluations or revaluations could be used to adjust the par value of a currency when it became overvalued or undervalued.

Although adjustable pegged rates are intended to promote a viable balance-of-payments adjustment mechanism, they have been plagued with operational problems. In the Bretton Woods system, adjustments in prices and incomes often conflicted with domestic-stabilization objectives. Also, currency devaluation was considered undesirable because it seemed to indicate a failure of domestic policies and a loss of international prestige. Conversely, revaluations were unacceptable to exporters, whose livelihoods were vulnerable to such policies. Repegging exchange rates only as a last resort often meant that when adjustments did occur, they were sizable. Moreover, adjustable pegged rates posed difficulties in estimating the equilibrium rate to which a currency should be repegged. Finally, once the market exchange rate reached the margin of the permissible band around parity, it in effect became a rigid fixed rate that presented speculators with a one-way bet. Given persistent weakening pressure, for example, at the band's outer limit, speculators had the incentive to move out of a weakening currency that was expected to depreciate further in value as the result of official devaluation.

These problems reached a climax in the early 1970s. Faced with continuing and growing balance-of-payments deficits, the United States suspended the dollar's convertibility into gold in August 1971. This suspension terminated the U.S. commitment to exchange gold for dollars at $35 per ounce—a commitment that had existed for 37 years. This policy abolished the tie between gold and the international value of the dollar, thus floating the dollar and permitting its exchange rate to be set by market forces. The floating of the dollar terminated U.S. support of the Bretton Woods system of fixed exchange rates and led to the demise of that system.

Floating Exchange Rates

Instead of adopting fixed exchange rates, some nations allow their currencies to float in the foreign-exchange market. By **floating** (or flexible) **exchange rates**, we mean currency prices that are established daily in the foreign-exchange market, without restrictions imposed by government policy on the extent to which the prices can move. With floating rates, there is an equilibrium exchange rate that equates the demand for and supply of the home currency. Changes in the exchange rate will ideally correct a payments imbalance by bringing about shifts in imports and exports of goods, services, and short-term capital movements. The exchange rate depends on relative productivity levels, interest rates, inflation rates, and other factors discussed in Chapter 12.

Unlike fixed exchange rates, floating exchange rates are not characterized by par values and official exchange rates; they are determined by market supply and demand conditions rather than central bankers. Although floating rates do not have an exchange-stabilization fund to maintain existing rates, it does not necessarily follow that floating rates must fluctuate erratically. They will do so if the underlying market forces become unstable. Because there is no exchange-stabilization fund under floating rates, any holdings of international reserves serve as working balances rather than to maintain a given exchange rate for any currency.

Achieving Market Equilibrium

How do floating exchange rates promote payments equilibrium for a nation? Consider Figure 15.2 on page 450, which illustrates the foreign-exchange market in Swiss francs in the United States. The intersection of supply schedule S_0 and demand schedule D_0 determines the equilibrium exchange rate of $0.50 per franc.

Referring to Figure 15.2(a), suppose a rise in real income causes U.S. residents to demand more Swiss cheese and watches, and therefore more francs; let the demand for francs rise from D_0 to D_1. Initially the market is in disequilibrium, because the quantity of francs demanded (60 francs) exceeds the quantity supplied (40 francs) at the exchange rate of $0.50 per franc. The excess demand for

FIGURE 15.2

Market Adjustment Under Floating Exchange Rates

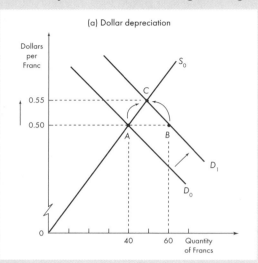

(a) Dollar depreciation

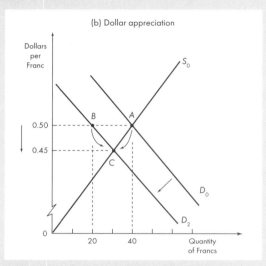

(b) Dollar appreciation

Under a floating exchange-rate system, continuous changes in currency values restore payments equilibrium at which the quantity supplied and quantity demanded of a currency are equal. Starting at equilibrium point A, an increase in the demand for francs leads to a depreciation of the dollar against the franc; conversely, a decrease in the demand for francs leads to an appreciation of the dollar against the franc.

francs leads to an increase in the exchange rate from $0.50 to $0.55 per franc; the dollar thus falls in value, or depreciates, against the franc, while the franc rises in value, or appreciates, against the dollar. The higher value of the franc prompts Swiss residents to increase the quantity of francs supplied on the foreign-exchange market to purchase more U.S. goods, which are now cheaper in terms of the franc; at the same time, it dampens U.S. demand for more expensive Swiss goods. Market equilibrium is restored at the exchange rate of $0.55 per franc, at which the quantities of francs supplied and demanded are equal.

Suppose instead that real income in the United States falls, which causes U.S. residents to demand less Swiss cheese and watches, and therefore fewer francs. In Figure 15.2(b), let the demand for francs fall from D_0 to D_2. The market is initially in dise-

quilibrium because the quantity of francs supplied (40 francs) exceeds the quantity demanded (20 francs) at the exchange rate of $0.50 per franc. The excess supply of francs causes the exchange rate to fall from $0.50 to $0.45 per franc; the dollar thus appreciates against the franc, while the franc depreciates against the dollar. Market equilibrium is restored at the exchange rate of $0.45 per franc, at which the quantities of francs supplied and demanded are equal.

This example illustrates one argument in favor of floating rates: When the exchange rate is permitted to adjust freely in response to market forces, market equilibrium will be established at a point where the quantities of foreign exchange supplied and demanded are equal. If the exchange rate promotes market equilibrium, monetary authorities will not need international reserves for the purpose of intervening in the market to maintain exchange rates at their par value. Presumably, these resources can be used more productively elsewhere in the economy.

Trade Restrictions, Jobs, and Floating Exchange Rates

During economic downturns, labor unions often lobby for import restrictions in order to save jobs for domestic workers. Do import restrictions lead to rising total employment in the economy?

As long as the United States maintains a floating exchange rate, the implementation of import restrictions to help one industry will gradually shift jobs from other industries in the economy to the protected industry, with no significant impact on aggregate employment. Short-run employment gains in the protected industry will be offset by long-run employment losses in other industries.

Suppose the United States increases tariffs on autos imported from Japan. This policy would reduce auto imports, causing a decrease in the U.S. demand for yen to pay for imported vehicles. With floating exchange rates, the yen would depreciate against the dollar (the dollar would appreciate against the yen) until balance in international transactions was attained. The change in the exchange rate would encourage Americans to purchase more goods from Japan and the Japanese to purchase fewer goods from the United States. Sales and jobs would therefore be lost in other U.S. industries. Trade restrictions thus result in a zero-sum game within the United States. Job increases in Detroit are offset by job decreases in Los Angeles and Portland, with exchange-rate changes imposing costs on unprotected workers in the U.S. economy.

Arguments for and Against Floating Rates

One advantage claimed for floating rates is their simplicity. Floating rates allegedly respond quickly to changing supply and demand conditions, clearing the market of shortages or surpluses of a given currency. Instead of having formal rules of conduct among central bankers governing exchange-rate movements, floating rates are market determined. They operate under simplified institutional arrangements that are relatively easy to enact.

Because floating rates fluctuate throughout the day, they permit continuous adjustment in the balance of payments. The adverse effects of prolonged disequilibriums that tend to occur under fixed exchange rates are minimized under floating rates. It is also argued that floating rates partially insulate the home economy from external forces. This means that governments will not have to restore payments equilibrium through painful inflationary or deflationary adjustment policies. Switching to floating rates frees a nation from having to adopt policies that perpetuate domestic disequilibrium as the price of maintaining a satisfactory balance-of-payments position. Nations thus have greater freedom to pursue policies that promote domestic balance than they do under fixed exchange rates.

Although there are strong arguments in favor of floating exchange rates, this system is often considered to be of limited usefulness for bankers and businesspeople. Critics of floating rates maintain that an unregulated market may lead to wide fluctuations in currency values, discouraging foreign trade and investment. Although traders and investors may be able to hedge exchange-rate risk by dealing in the forward market, the cost of hedging may become prohibitively high.

Floating rates in theory are supposed to allow governments to set independent monetary and fiscal policies. But this flexibility may cause a problem of another sort: *inflationary bias*. Under a system of floating rates, monetary authorities may lack the financial discipline required by a fixed exchange-rate system. Suppose a nation faces relatively high rates of inflation compared with the rest of the world. This domestic inflation will have no negative impact on the nation's trade balance under floating rates because its currency will automatically depreciate in the exchange market. However, a protracted depreciation of the currency would result in persistently increasing import prices and a rising price level, making inflation self-perpetuating and the depreciation continuous. Because there is greater freedom for domestic financial management under floating rates, there may be less resistance to overspending and to its subsequent pressure on wages and prices. Table 15.5 summarizes the advantages and disadvantages of floating exchange rates.

Is It China's Fault?

In 2003, a coalition of business groups, led by the 14,000-strong National Association of Manufacturers (NAM), requested that President George W. Bush take steps to weaken the dollar against currencies of major export-driven economies of Asia. They especially wanted Bush to convince China to revalue its yuan so as to reduce its trade surplus with the United States. What especially irritated NAM was that China, Japan, and other Asian exporting nations were massively intervening in the markets to keep the dollar high against their own currencies.

Since hitting its low point in 1995, by 2002 the dollar has risen about 40 percent in real terms against the currencies of its major trading partners. As the value of the dollar rises, foreign buyers must spend more of their currency to purchase U.S. exports. This causes foreign buyers to decrease their consumption of U.S. commodities or to buy from U.S. competitors instead. An appreciating dollar also causes Americans to purchase more imported goods.

According to NAM, the value of the dollar rose above the level consistent with economic fundamentals, resulting in an "overvalued" dollar. It noted that the dollar continued to appreciate in spite of fluctuations in economic growth, interest rates, and trade balances that would normally warrant a dollar depreciation. NAM contended that the overvalued dollar is one of the most serious economic problems facing manufacturers in the United States. They noted that the strong dollar is decimating U.S. manufactured goods exports, artificially stimulating imports, and putting hundreds of thousands of American workers out of work. Because of the overvalued dollar, the foreign-currency price of U.S. products increased by 25 to 30 percent relative to foreign products during 1995–2002. As a result:

- Japanese auto companies can more easily penetrate the U.S. auto market.
- Boeing is losing market share to Europe's Airbus.
- U.S. tourism and hotels are hurt, and film production is moving offshore.
- Caterpillar has been forced to cut prices of tractors to protect its overseas markets.
- International Paper Company sees its sales falling as foreign paper products enter the United States.
- U.S. exports of corn, wheat, soybeans, and meats decline in Europe and Asia.

Although NAM requested that Bush convince China to revalue its yuan, critics maintained that such action would not help. For starters, a weaker currency could scare off foreign investors, depressing the stock market and sending interest rates soaring. Also, currency manipulation would do nothing to fix the fundamental problem: Much of U.S. manufacturing has simply not been innovating and boosting productivity fast enough to compete effectively in the global marketplace.

As things turned out, China rejected Bush's calls for an immediate rise in the value of its currency against the dollar. Instead, China pledged only to let the yuan float more freely at some undefined point in the distant future. At the writing of this text, future of the yuan–dollar exchange ratio is not clear.

Managed Floating Rates

The adoption of managed floating exchange rates by the United States and other industrial nations in 1973 followed the breakdown of the international monetary system based on fixed rates. Before the 1970s, only a handful of economists gave serious consideration to a general system of floating rates. Because of defects in the decision-making process caused by procedural difficulties and political biases, however, adjustments of par values under the Bretton Woods system were often delayed and discontinuous. It was recognized that exchange rates should be adjusted more promptly and in small but continuous amounts in response to evolving market forces. In 1973, a **managed floating system** was adopted, under which informal guidelines were established by the IMF for coordination of national exchange-rate policies.

The motivation for the formulation of guidelines for floating arose from two concerns. The first was that nations might intervene in the exchange markets to avoid exchange-rate alterations that would weaken their competitive position. When the United States suspended its gold-convertibility pledge and allowed its overvalued dollar to float in the exchange markets, it hoped that a free-market adjustment would result in a depreciation of the dollar against other, undervalued currencies. Rather than permitting a **clean float** (a market solution) to occur, foreign central banks refused to permit the dollar depreciation by intervening in the exchange market. The United States considered this a **dirty float**, because the free-market forces of supply and demand were not allowed to achieve their equilibrating role. A second motivation for guidelines was the concern that floats over time might lead to disorderly markets with erratic fluctuations in exchange rates. Such destabilizing activity could create an uncertain business climate and reduce the level of world trade.

Under managed floating, a nation can alter the degree to which it intervenes on the foreign-exchange market. Heavier intervention moves the nation nearer the fixed exchange-rate case, whereas less intervention moves the nation nearer the floating exchange-rate case. Concerning day-to-day and week-to-week exchange-rate movements, a main objective of the floating guidelines has been to prevent the emergence of erratic fluctuations. Member nations should intervene on the foreign-exchange market as necessary to prevent sharp and disruptive exchange-rate fluctuations from day to day and week to week. Such a policy is known as **leaning against the wind**—intervening to reduce short-term fluctuations in exchange rates without attempting to adhere to any particular rate over the long run. Members should also not act aggressively with respect to their currency exchange rates; that is, they should not enhance the value when it is appreciating or depress the value when it is depreciating.

Under the managed float, some nations choose **target exchange rates** and intervene to support them. Target exchange rates are intended to reflect long-term economic forces that underlie exchange-

rate movements. One way for managed floaters to estimate a target exchange rate is to follow statistical indicators that respond to the same economic forces as the exchange-rate trend. Then, when the values of indicators change, the exchange-rate target can be adjusted accordingly. Among these indicators are rates of inflation in different nations, levels of official foreign reserves, and persistent imbalances in international payments accounts. In practice, defining a target exchange rate can be difficult in a market based on volatile economic conditions.

Managed Floating Rates in the Short Run and Long Run

Managed floating exchange rates attempt to combine market-determined exchange rates with foreign-exchange market intervention in order to take advantage of the best features of floating exchange rates and fixed exchange rates. Under a managed float, market intervention is used to stabilize exchange rates in the short run; in the long run, a managed float allows market forces to determine exchange rates.

Figure 15.3 on page 454 illustrates the theory of a managed float in a 2-country framework, Switzerland and the United States. The supply and demand schedules for francs are denoted by S_0 and D_0; the equilibrium exchange rate, at which the quantity of francs supplied equals the quantity demanded, is $0.50 per franc.

Suppose there occurs a permanent increase in U.S. real income, as a result of which U.S. residents demand additional francs to purchase more Swiss chocolate. Let the demand for francs rise from D_0 to D_1, as shown in Figure 15.3(a). Because this increase in demand is the result of long-run market forces, a managed float permits supply and demand conditions to determine the exchange rate. With the increase in the demand for francs, the quantity of francs demanded (180 francs) exceeds the quantity supplied (100 francs) at the exchange rate of $0.50 per franc. The excess demand results in a rise in the exchange rate to $0.60 per franc, at which the quantity of francs supplied and the quantity demanded are equal. In this manner, long-run movements in

FIGURE 15.3

Managed Floating Exchange Rates

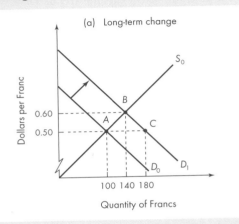

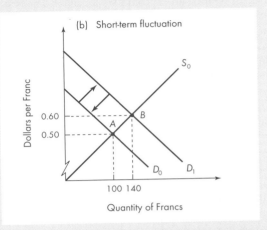

Under this system, central-bank intervention is used to stabilize exchange rates in the short run; in the long run, market forces are permitted to determine exchange rates.

exchange rates are determined by the supply and demand for various currencies.

Figure 15.3(b) illustrates the case of a short-term increase in the demand for francs. Suppose U.S. investors demand additional francs to finance purchases of Swiss securities, which pay relatively high interest rates; again, let the demand for francs rise from D_0 to D_1. In a few weeks, suppose Swiss interest rates fall, causing the U.S. demand for francs to revert to its original level, D_0. Under floating rates, the dollar price of the franc would rise from $0.50 per franc to $0.60 per franc and then fall back to $0.50 per franc. This type of exchange-rate irascibility is widely considered to be a disadvantage of floating rates because it leads to uncertainty regarding the profitability of international trade and financial transactions; as a result, the pattern of trade and finance may be disrupted.

Under managed floating rates, the response to this temporary disturbance is exchange-rate intervention by the Federal Reserve to keep the exchange rate at its long-term equilibrium level of

$0.50 per franc. During the time period in which demand is at D_1, the central bank will sell francs to meet the excess demand. As soon as the disturbance is over, and demand reverts back to D_0, exchange-market intervention will no longer be needed. In short, central bank intervention is used to offset temporary fluctuations in exchange rates that contribute to uncertainty in carrying out transactions in international trade and finance.

Since the advent of managed floating rates in 1973, the frequency and size of U.S. foreign-exchange interventions have varied. Intervention was substantial from 1977 to 1979, when the dollar's exchange value was considered to be unacceptably low. U.S. stabilization operations were minimal during the Reagan Administration's first term, consistent with its goal of limiting government interference in markets; they were directed at offsetting short-run market disruptions. Intervention was again substantial in 1985, when the dollar's exchange value was deemed unacceptably high, hurting the competitiveness of U.S. producers. The most extensive U.S. intervention operations took place after the Louvre Accord of 1987, when the major industrial nations reached informal understandings about the limits of tolerance for exchange-rate fluctuations.

Exchange-Rate Stabilization and Monetary Policy

We have seen how central banks can buy and sell foreign currencies to stabilize their values under a system of managed floating exchange rates. Another stabilization technique involves a nation's *monetary policy*. As we shall see, stabilizing a currency's exchange value requires the central bank to adopt (1) an *expansionary* monetary policy to offset currency *appreciation*, and (2) a *contractionary* monetary policy to offset currency *depreciation*.

Figure 15.4 illustrates the foreign-exchange market for the United States. Assume the supply schedule of British pounds is denoted by S_0 and the demand schedule of pounds is denoted by D_0. The equilibrium exchange rate, at which the quantity of pounds supplied and the quantity demanded are equalized, is $2 per pound.

Suppose that as a result of production shutdowns in Britain, caused by labor strikes, U.S. residents purchase fewer British products and therefore demand fewer pounds. Let the demand for pounds decrease from D_0 to D_1 in Figure 15.4(a). In the absence of central-bank intervention, the dollar price of the pound falls from $2 to $1.80; the dollar thus appreciates against the pound.

To offset the appreciation of the dollar, the Federal Reserve can increase the supply of money in the United States, which will decrease domestic interest rates in the short run. The reduced interest rates will cause the foreign demand for U.S. securities to decline. Fewer pounds will thus be supplied to the foreign-exchange market to buy dollars with which to purchase U.S. securities. As the supply of pounds shifts leftward to S_1, the dollar's exchange value reverts to $2 per pound. In this manner, the expansionary monetary policy has offset the dollar's appreciation.

FIGURE 15.4

Exchange-Rate Stabilization and Monetary Policy

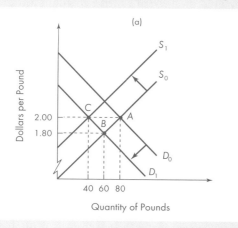
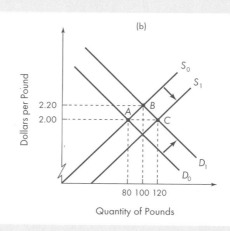

In the absence of international policy coordination, stabilizing a currency's exchange value requires a central bank to initiate (a) an expansionary monetary policy to offset an appreciation of its currency, and (b) a contractionary monetary policy to offset a depreciation of its currency.

Referring now to Figure 15.4(b), suppose a temporary surge in British interest rates causes U.S. investors to demand additional pounds with which to purchase additional British securities. Let the demand for pounds rise from D_0 to D_1. In the absence of central-bank intervention, the dollar's exchange value would rise from \$2 to \$2.20 per pound; the dollar has depreciated against the pound.

To offset this dollar depreciation, the Federal Reserve can decrease the supply of money in the United States, which will increase domestic interest rates and attract British investment. More pounds will thus be supplied to the foreign-exchange market to purchase dollars with which to buy U.S. securities. As the supply of pounds increases from S_0 to S_1, the dollar's exchange value reverts to \$2 per pound. The contractionary monetary policy thus helps offset the dollar depreciation.

These examples illustrate how domestic monetary policies can be used to stabilize currency values. Such policies are not without costs, however, as seen in the following example.

Suppose the U.S. government increases federal spending without a corresponding increase in taxes. To finance the resulting budget deficit, assume the government borrows funds from the money market, which raises domestic interest rates. High U.S. interest rates enhance the attractiveness of dollar-denominated securities, leading to increased foreign purchases of these assets, an increased demand for dollars, and an appreciation in the dollar's exchange value. The appreciating dollar makes U.S. goods more expensive overseas and foreign goods less expensive in the United States, thus causing the U.S. trade account to fall into deficit.

Now suppose the Federal Reserve intervenes and adopts an expansionary monetary policy. The resulting increase in the supply of money dampens the rise in U.S. interest rates and the dollar's appreciation. By restraining the increase in the dollar's exchange value, the expansionary monetary policy enhances the competitiveness of U.S. businesses and keeps the U.S. trade account in balance.

However, the favorable effects of the expansionary monetary policy on the domestic economy are temporary. When pursued indefinitely (over the long run), a policy of increasing the domestic money supply leads to a *weakening* in the U.S.

trade position, because the monetary expansion required to offset the dollar's appreciation eventually promotes higher prices in the United States. The higher prices of domestic goods offset the benefits to U.S. competitiveness that initially occur under the monetary expansion. U.S. spending eventually shifts back to foreign products and away from domestically produced goods, causing the U.S. trade account to fall into deficit.

This example shows how monetary policy can be used to stabilize the dollar's exchange value in the short run. But when monetary expansion occurs on a sustained, long-run basis, it brings with it eventual price increases that nullify the initial gains in domestic competitiveness. The long-run effectiveness of using monetary policy to stabilize the dollar's exchange value is limited, because the increase in the money supply to offset the dollar's appreciation does not permanently correct the underlying cause of the trade deficit—the increase in domestic spending.

Attempting to stabilize both the domestic economy and the dollar's exchange value can be difficult for the Federal Reserve. In early 1995, for example, the dollar was taking a nosedive against the yen, and the U.S. economy showed signs of slowing. To boost the dollar's exchange value would have required the Federal Reserve to adopt a restrictive monetary policy, which would have led to higher interest rates and net investment inflows. However, further increases in domestic interest rates would heighten the danger that the U.S. economy would be pushed into a recession by the next year. The Federal Reserve thus had to choose between supporting domestic economic expansion or the dollar's exchange value. In this case, the Federal Reserve adopted a policy of lower interest rates, thus appearing to respond to U.S. domestic needs.

Is Exchange-Rate Stabilization Effective?

Many governments have intervened on foreign-exchange markets to try to dampen volatility and to slow or reverse currency movements.[1] Their

---

[1]This section is drawn from Michael Hutchinson, "Is Official Foreign Exchange Intervention Effective?" *Economic Letter*, Federal Reserve Bank of San Francisco, July 18, 2003.

concern is that excessive short-term volatility and longer-term swings in exchange rates that "overshoot" values justified by fundamental conditions may hurt their economies, particularly sectors heavily involved in international trade. And, the foreign-exchange market can be volatile. For example, one euro cost about $1.15 in January 1999, then dropped to $0.85 by the end of 2000, only to climb to over $1.18 in June 2003. Over this same period, one U.S. dollar bought as much as 133 yen and as little as 102 yen, a 30 percent fluctuation. Many other currencies have also experienced similarly large price swings in recent years.

Many central banks intervene in foreign-exchange markets. The largest player is Japan. Between 1991 and 2000, for example, the Bank of Japan bought U.S. dollars on 168 occasions for a cumulative amount of $304 billion and sold U.S. dollars on 33 occasions for a cumulative amount of $38 billion. A typical case: On April 3, 2000, the Bank of Japan purchased $13.2 billion in the foreign-exchange market in an attempt to stop the more than 4 percent depreciation of the dollar against the yen that had occurred during the previous week. Japan's intervention magnitudes dwarf all other countries' official intervention in the foreign-exchange market. For example, it exceeded U.S. intervention in the 1991–2000 period by a factor of more than 30. However, compared to overall market transactions in the foreign-exchange market, the magnitude of Japan's interventions has been quite small.

Not surprisingly, intervention supported by central-bank interest-rate changes tends to have an even larger impact on exchange rates than intervention alone. Moreover, cases where intervention was coordinated between two central banks, such as the Federal Reserve and the Bank of Japan, had a larger impact on exchange rates than unilateral foreign-exchange operations. However, episodes of coordinated intervention are rather rare.

Academic researchers have often questioned the usefulness of official foreign-exchange intervention. However, proponents of foreign-exchange intervention note that it may be useful when the exchange rate is under speculative attack—that is, when a change in the exchange rate is not justified by fundamentals. It may also be helpful in coordi-

nating private-sector expectations. Recent research provides some support for the short-run effectiveness of intervention. However, this should not be interpreted as a rationale for intervention as a longer-term management tool.[2]

The Crawling Peg

Instead of adopting fixed or floating rates, why not try a compromise approach, the **crawling peg**. This system has been used by nations including Bolivia, Brazil, Costa Rica, Nicaragua, Solomon Islands, and Peru. The crawling-peg system means that a nation makes small, frequent changes in the par value of its currency to correct balance-of-payments disequilibriums. Deficit and surplus nations both keep adjusting until the desired exchange-rate level is attained. The term *crawling peg* implies that par-value changes are implemented in a large number of small steps, making the process of exchange-rate adjustment continuous for all practical purposes. The peg thus crawls from one par value to another.

The crawling-peg mechanism has been used primarily by nations having high inflation rates. Some developing nations, mostly South American, have recognized that a pegging system can operate in an inflationary environment only if there is provision for frequent changes in the par values. Associating national inflation rates with international competitiveness, these nations have generally used price indicators as a basis for adjusting crawling pegged rates. In these nations, the primary concern is the criterion that governs exchange-rate movements, rather than the currency or basket of currencies against which the peg is defined.

The crawling peg differs from the system of adjustable pegged rates. Under the adjustable peg, currencies are tied to a par value that changes infrequently (perhaps once every several years) but suddenly, usually in large jumps. The idea behind the crawling peg is that a nation can make small, frequent changes in par values, perhaps several times a year, so that they creep along slowly in response to evolving market conditions.

[2]Michael Hutchinson, "Intervention and Exchange Rate Stabilization Policy in Developing Countries," *International Finance* 6, 2003, pp. 41–59.

Supporters of the crawling peg argue that the system combines the flexibility of floating rates with the stability usually associated with fixed rates. They contend that a system providing continuous, steady adjustments is more responsive to changing competitive conditions and avoids a main problem of adjustable pegged rates—that changes in par values are frequently wide of the mark. Moreover, small, frequent changes in par values made at random intervals frustrate speculators with their irregularity.

In recent years, the crawling-peg formula has been used by developing nations facing rapid and persistent inflation. However, the IMF has generally contended that such a system would not be in the best interests of nations such as the United States or Germany, which bear the responsibility for international currency levels. The IMF has felt that it would be hard to apply such a system to the industrialized nations, whose currencies serve as a source of international liquidity. Although even the most ardent proponents of the crawling peg admit that the time for its widespread adoption has not yet come, the debate over its potential merits is bound to continue.

Currency Crises

A shortcoming of the international monetary system is that major currency crises have been a common occurrence in recent years. A **currency crisis**, also called a **speculative attack**, is a situation in which a weak currency experiences heavy selling pressure. There are several possible indications of selling pressure. One is sizable losses in the foreign reserves held by a country's central bank. Another is depreciating exchange rates in the forward market, where buyers and sellers promise to exchange currency at some future date rather than immediately. Finally, in extreme cases where inflation is running rampant, selling pressure consists of widespread flight out of domestic currency into foreign currency or into goods that people think will retain value, such as gold or real estate. Experience shows that currency crises can decrease the growth of a country's gross domestic product by

6 percent, or more. That is like losing one or two years of economic growth in most countries. Table 15.6 provides examples of currency crises.

A currency crisis ends when selling pressure stops. One way to end pressure is to devalue; that is, establish a new exchange rate at a sufficiently depreciated level. For example, Mexico's central bank might stop exchanging pesos for dollars at the previous rate of 10 pesos per dollar and set a new level of 20 pesos per dollar. Another way to end selling pressure is to adopt a floating exchange rate. Floating permits the exchange rate to "find its own level," which is almost always depreciated compared to the previous pegged rate. Devaluation and allowing depreciation make foreign currency and foreign goods more costly in terms of domestic currency, which tends to decrease demand for foreign currency, ending the imbalance that triggered selling pressure. However, in some cases, especially when confidence in the currency is low, the crisis continues, and further rounds of devaluation or depreciation occur.

Currency crises that end in devaluations or accelerated depreciations are sometimes called **currency crashes**. Not all crises end in crashes. A way of trying to end the selling pressure of a crisis without suffering a crash is to impose restrictions on the ability of people to buy and sell foreign currency. These controls, however, create profit opportunities for people who discover how to evade them, so over time controls lose effectiveness unless enforced by an intrusive bureaucracy. Another way to end selling pressure is to obtain a loan to bolster the foreign reserves of the monetary authority. Countries that wish to bolster their foreign reserves often ask the IMF for loans. Although the loan can help temporarily, it may just delay rather than end selling pressure. The final way to end selling pressure is to restore confidence in the existing exchange rate, such as by announcing appropriate and credible changes in monetary policy.

Sources of Currency Crises

Why do currency crises occur?[3] A popular explanation is that big currency speculators instigate the

[3]Kurt Schuler, *Why Currency Crises Happen*, Joint Economic Committee, U.S. Congress, January 2002.

TABLE 15.6

Examples of Currency Crises

- **European Monetary System, 1992–1993.** As a result of monetary policy decisions related to German reunification in 1989–1990, Germany raised interest rates to high levels. Also, Denmark decided not to commit to joining the European Monetary Union, creating doubts about the political viability of the union. As a result, currencies anchored to the German mark suffered speculative attacks. The crisis ended when major European countries either devalued their currencies or adopted floating exchange rates. The crisis resulted in mild recessions in these countries in 1993.

- **Mexico, December 1994–1995.** Mexico's central bank maintained the value of the peso within a band that depreciated 4 percent a year against the U.S. dollar. In order to reduce interest rates on its debt, the Mexican government in April 1994 began issuing debt linked to the dollar. The amount of this debt soon exceeded the central bank's falling foreign-exchange reserves. Unrest in the province of Chiapas led to a speculative attack on the peso. Although the government devalued the peso by 15 percent by widening the band, the crisis continued. The government then let the peso float; it depreciated from 3.46 per dollar before the crisis to more than 7 per dollar. To end the crisis, Mexico received pledges for $49 billion in loans from the U.S. government and the IMF. Mexico's economy suffered a depression and banking problem that led to government rescues.

- **Russia, 1998.** The Russian government was paying high interest rates on its short-term debt. Falling prices for oil, a major export, and a weak economy also contributed to speculative attacks against the ruble, which had an official crawling band with the U.S. dollar. Although the IMF approved loans for Russia of about $11 billion and the Russian government widened the band for the ruble by 35 percent, the crisis continued. This led to the floating of the ruble and its depreciating against the dollar of about 20 percent. Russia then went into recession and experienced a burst of inflation. Many banks became insolvent. The government defaulted on its ruble-denominated debt and imposed a moratorium on private-sector payments of foreign debt.

- **Turkey, 2001.** The Turkish lira had an IMF-designed official crawling peg against the U.S. dollar. In November 2000, rumors about a criminal investigation into 10 government-run banks led to a speculative attack on the lira. Interbank interest rates rose to 2,000 percent. The central bank then intervened. Eight banks became insolvent and were taken over by the government. The central bank's intervention had violated Turkey's agreement with the IMF, yet the IMF lent Turkey $10 billion. In February 2001, a public dispute between the president and prime minister caused investors to lose confidence in the stability of Turkey's coalition government. Interbank interest rates rose to 7,500 percent. Thus, the government let the lira float. The lira depreciated from 668,000 per dollar before the crisis to 1.6 million per dollar by October 2001. The economy of Turkey stagnated and inflation skyrocketed to 60 percent.

Source: Kurt Schuler, *Why Currency Crises Happen*, Joint Economic Committee, U.S. Congress, January 2002.

crises for their own profit. The world's best-known currency speculator, George Soros, made $2 billion in 1992 by speculating against European currencies. However, speculation can also result in substantial losses. George Soros retired in 2000 after suffering the effects of losing almost $2 billion as the result of unsuccessful speculations. However, currency speculation is not just an activity of big speculators.

Millions of ordinary people also speculate in the form of holding foreign currency in their wallets, under their mattresses, and the like. Millions of small speculators can move markets like the big speculators do. Simply put, currency crises are not simply caused by big currency speculators who arise out of nowhere. There must be an underlying reason for a currency crisis to occur.

One source for a currency crisis is budget deficits financed by inflation. If the government cannot easily finance its budget deficits by raising taxes or borrowing, it may pressure the central bank to finance them by creating money. Creating money can increase the supply of money faster than demand is growing, thus causing inflation. Budget deficits financed by inflation seemed to capture the essentials of many currency crises up through the 1980s. By the 1990s, however, this explanation appeared to be lacking. During the currency crises in Europe in 1992–1993, budget deficits in most adversely affected countries were small and sustainable. Moreover, most East Asian countries affected by the currency crisis of 1997–1998 were running budget surpluses and realizing strong economic growth. Economists have thus looked for other explanations of currency crises.

Currency crisis may also be caused by weak financial systems. Weak banks can trigger speculative attacks if people think the central bank will rescue the banks even at the cost of spending much of its foreign reserves to do so. The explicit or implicit promise to rescue the banks is a form of moral hazard—a situation in which people do not pay the full cost of their own mistakes. As people become apprehensive about the future value of the local currency, they sell it to obtain more stable foreign currencies.

Some of the major currency crises of the last 20 years have occurred in countries that had recently deregulated their financial systems. Many governments formerly used financial regulations to channel investment into politically favored outlets. In return, they restricted competition among banks, life insurance companies, and the like. Profits from restricted competition subsidized unprofitable government-directed investments. Deregulation altered the picture by reducing government direction of investments and allowing more competition among institutions. However, governments failed to ensure that in the new environment of greater freedom to reap the rewards of success, financial institutions also bore greater responsibility for failure. Therefore, financial institutions made mistakes in the unfamiliar environment of deregulation, failed, and were rescued at public expense. This resulted

in public fears about the future value of local currency and the selling of local currency to obtain more stable foreign currencies.

A weak economy can trigger a currency crisis by creating doubt about the determination of the government and the central bank to continue with the current monetary policy if weakness continues. A weak economy is characterized by falling GDP growth per person, a rising unemployment rate, a falling stock market, and falling export growth. If the public expects the central bank to increase the money supply to stimulate the economy, it may become apprehensive about the future value of the local currency and beginning selling it on currency markets.

Political factors can also cause currency crises. Developing countries have historically been more prone to currency crises than developed countries because they tend to have a weaker rule of law, governments more prone to overthrow by force, central banks that are not politically independent, and other characteristics that create political uncertainty about monetary policy.

External factors can be another source for a currency crisis. For example, an increase in interest rates in major international currencies can trigger a currency crisis if a central bank resists increasing the interest rate it charges. Funds may flow out of the local currency into foreign currency, decreasing the central bank's reserves to unacceptably low levels and therefore putting pressure on the government to devalue its currency if the currency is pegged. Moreover, a big external shock that disrupts the economy, such as war or a spike in the price of imported oil, can likewise trigger a currency crisis. External shocks have been key features in many currency crises historically.

Finally, the choice of an exchange-rate system also affects whether and how currency crises occur. In recent years, fixing the value of the domestic currency to that of a large, low-inflation country has become popular. It helps to keeping inflation under control by linking the inflation rate for internationally traded goods to that found in the anchor country. For example, prior to 2002, the exchange rate for the Argentine peso was pegged at one peso per U.S. dollar. Thus, a bushel of corn sold on the world market at $4 had its price set at 4 pesos. If the public expects this exchange rate to be unchangeable, the fixed rate has the extra advantage of anchoring inflation expectations for Argentina to the inflation rate in the United States, a relatively low-inflation country.

In spite of the advantage of promoting relatively low inflation, a fixed exchange-rate system makes countries vulnerable to speculative attacks on their currencies. Recall that preservation of fixed exchange rates requires the government to purchase or sell domestic currency for foreign currency at the target rate of exchange. This forces the central bank to maintain a sufficient quantity of international reserves in order to fulfill the demand by the public to sell domestic currency for foreign currency at the fixed exchange rate. If the public thinks that the central bank's supply of international reserves has decreased to the level where the ability to fulfill the demand to sell domestic currency for foreign currency at a fixed exchange rate is doubted, then a devaluation of the domestic currency is anticipated. This anticipation can result in a speculative attack on the central bank's remaining holdings of international reserves. The attack consists of huge sales of domestic currency for foreign currency so that the decrease of international reserves is expedited, and devaluation results from the decline of reserves. In is no wonder that the most important recent currency crises have happened to countries having fixed exchange rates but demonstrating lack of political will to correct previous economic problems.

Next, we will examine two cases of currency crisis: the speculative attack on the Swedish krona and the speculative attacks on East Asian currencies.

Speculators Attack the Krona

In May 1991, Sweden applied to enter the Exchange Rate Mechanism of the European Union in a bid to stabilize its currency.[4] To stabilize the krona–mark exchange rate, interest rates in Sweden and Germany had to be the same. Thus, the Swedish and German central banks couldn't independently use changes in short-term interest rates if they wanted to keep the exchange rates stable. If Sweden wanted to act independently, it had

to use fiscal policy (tax and government spending policies) to stimulate the country's growth rate.

However, a weak Swedish economy provoked speculators, who mounted an attack on the krona in September 1992. Speculators knew that the weak economy would tempt Sweden to abandon its fixed exchange rate and use monetary policy to cut short-term interest rates, especially since the new Swedish government was adopting restrictive fiscal policy. Speculators believed that if the Swedish central bank cut the short-term interest rate, the krona wouldn't be as attractive to investors. Thus, the speculators thought that after interest rates were cut, the currency would depreciate with respect to other European currencies. But because speculators expected the depreciation to happen, they decided to sell the krona immediately and thus mount a speculative attack on the currency.

This attack put the Swedish central bank in an uncomfortable position. To combat the currency's depreciation, the central bank raised short-term interest rates temporarily to repel the speculative attack—exactly the policy it didn't want in the face of sluggish economic growth. In fact, the Swedish central bank raised the short-term interest rate to an astonishing 500 percent and held it there for four days. The speculators were deterred, but not for long.

The speculators understood that the Swedish central bank had to raise short-term interest rates temporarily to support the currency. But they were betting that the central bank wouldn't fight off the attack for long, especially in the face of disquiet in the country resulting from weak economic growth and the higher interest rates needed to fight the speculative attack. The high short-term interest rates had made the economic situation in Sweden even more precarious so, in November, the speculators attacked again, selling the krona in favor of other European currencies. This time the Swedish central bank did not aggressively raise interest rates, and the krona depreciated.

Speculators Attack East Asian Currencies

After more than a decade of maintaining the Thai baht's peg to the U.S. dollar, Thai authorities

[4]Gregory Hopper, "What Determines the Exchange Rate: Economic Factors or Market Sentiment?" *Business Review*, Federal Reserve Bank of Philadelphia, September/October 1997, p. 23.

abandoned the peg in July 1997.[5] By October, market forces had led the baht to depreciate by 60 percent against the dollar. The depreciation triggered a wave of speculation against other Southeast Asian currencies. Over the same period, the Indonesian rupiah, Malaysia ringgit, Philippine peso, and South Korean won abandoned links to the dollar and depreciated 47, 35, 34, and 16 percent, respectively. This episode reopened one of the oldest debates in economics: whether a currency should have a fixed or floating exchange rate. Consider the case of Thailand.

Although Thailand was widely regarded as one of Southeast Asia's outstanding performers throughout the 1980s and 1990s, it relied heavily on inflows of short-term foreign capital, attracted both by the stable baht and by Thai interest rates, which were much higher than comparable interest rates elsewhere. The capital inflow supported a broad-based economic boom that was especially visible in the real estate market.

By 1996, however, Thailand's economic boom fizzled. As a result, both local and foreign investors got nervous and began withdrawing funds from Thailand's financial system, which put downward pressure on the baht. However, the Thai government resisted the depreciation pressure by purchasing baht with dollars in the foreign-exchange market and also raising interest rates, which increased the attractiveness of the baht. But the purchases of the baht greatly depleted Thailand's reserves of hard currency. Moreover, raising interest rates adversely affected an already weak financial sector by dampening economic activity. These factors ultimately contributed to the abandonment of the baht's link to the dollar.

Although Thailand and other Southeast Asian countries abandoned fixed exchange rates in 1997, some economists questioned whether such a policy would be in their best interest in the long run. Their reasoning was that these economies were relatively small and wide open to international trade and investment flows. Moreover, inflation rates were modest by the standards of a developing country, and labor markets were relatively flexible. In other words, floating exchange rates were probably not the best long-run option. Indeed, these economists maintained that unless the Southeast Asian governments anchored their currencies to something, currencies might drift into a vicious cycle of depreciation and higher inflation. There was certainly a concern that central banks in the region lacked the credibility to enforce tough monetary policies without the external constraint of a fixed exchange rate. Simply put, neither fixed exchange rates nor floating exchange rates offer a magical solution. What really makes a difference to a country's prospects is the quality of the overall economic policies that are pursued.

Capital Controls

Because capital flows have often been an important element in currency crises, controls on capital movements have been established to support fixed exchange rates and thus avoid speculative attacks on currencies. **Capital controls**, also known as **exchange controls**, are government-imposed barriers to foreign savers investing in domestic assets (for example, government securities, stock, or bank deposits) or to domestic savers investing in foreign assets. At one extreme, a government may seek to gain control over its payments position by directly circumventing market forces through the imposition of direct controls on international transactions. For example, a government that has a virtual monopoly over foreign-exchange dealings may require that all foreign-exchange earnings be turned over to authorized dealers. The government then allocates foreign exchange among domestic traders and investors at government-set prices.

The advantage of such a system is that the government can influence its payments position by regulating the amount of foreign exchange allocated to imports or capital outflows, limiting the extent of these transactions. Capital controls also permit the government to encourage or discourage certain transactions by offering different rates for foreign currency for different purposes. Furthermore, capital controls can give domestic monetary and fiscal policies greater freedom in their stabilization roles. By controlling the balance of payments through

---

[5]Ramon Moreno, "Lessons from Thailand," *Economic Letter*, Federal Reserve Bank of San Francisco, November 7, 1997.

capital controls, a government can pursue its domestic economic policies without fear of balance-of-payments repercussions.

Speculative attacks in Mexico and East Asia were fueled in part by large changes in capital outflows and capital inflows. As a result, some economists and politicians argued for restrictions on capital mobility in developing countries. For example, Malaysian Prime Minister Mahathir imposed limits on capital outflows in 1998 to help his economy regain financial stability.

Although restrictions on capital outflows may seem attractive, they suffer from several problems. Evidence suggests that capital outflows may further increase after the controls are implemented, because confidence in the government is weakened. Also, restrictions on capital outflows often result in evasion, as government officials get paid to ignore domestic residents who shift funds overseas. Finally, capital controls may provide government officials the false sense of security that they do not have to reform their financial systems to ameliorate the crisis.

Although economists are generally dubious of controls on capital outflows, controls on capital inflows often receive more support. Supporters contend that if speculative capital cannot enter a country, then it cannot suddenly leave and create a crisis. They note that the financial crisis in East Asia in 1997–1998 illustrated how capital inflows can result in a lending boom, excessive risk taking by domestic banks, and ultimately financial collapse. However, restrictions on the inflow of capital are problematic because they can prevent funds that would be used to finance productive investment opportunities from entering a country. Also, limits on capital inflows are seldom effective because the private sector finds ways to evade them and move funds into the country.[6]

Should Foreign-Exchange Transactions Be Taxed?

The 1997–1998 financial crises in East Asia, in which several nations were forced to abandon their fixed exchange-rate regimes, produced demands for more stability and government regu-

lation in the foreign-exchange markets. Indeed, market volatility was blamed for much of the trouble sweeping the region.

Economists generally argue that the free market is the best device for determining how money should be invested. Global capital markets provide needy countries with funds to grow, while permitting foreign investors to diversify their portfolios. If capital is allowed to flow freely, they contend, markets will reward countries that pursue sound economic policies and will pressure the rest to do the same. Indeed, most countries welcome and even encourage capital inflows such as foreign direct investment in factories and businesses, which represent long-lasting commitments. But some have become skeptical of financial instruments such as stocks and bonds, bank deposits, and short-term debt securities, which can be pulled out of a country with a stroke of a computer key. That's what occurred in East Asia in 1997, in Mexico in 1994 and 1995, and in the United Kingdom and Italy in 1992 and 1993.

To prevent international financial crises, several notable economists have called for sand to be thrown in the wheels of international finance by imposing a tax on foreign-exchange transactions. The idea is that a tax would increase the cost of these transactions, which would discourage massive responses to minor changes in information about the economic situation and thus dampen volatility in exchange rates. Proponents argue that such a tax would give traders an incentive to look at long-term economic trends, not short-term hunches, when buying and selling foreign exchange and securities. Traders must pay a small tax, say, 0.1 percent for every transaction, so they won't buy or sell unless expected returns justify the additional expense. Fewer transactions suggest less volatility and more stable exchange rates.

Proponents of a tax may well contend that they are not trying to interfere with free markets, but only to prevent excess volatility. However, we do not know how much volatility is excessive or irrational. It's true that economists cannot explain all exchange-rate volatility in terms of changes in the economic fundamentals of nations, but it does not follow from this that we should seek to regulate such fluctuations. Indeed,

[6]Sebastian Edwards, "How Effective Are Capital Controls?" *Journal of Economic Perspective,* Winter 2000, Vol. 13, No. 4, pp. 65–84.

some of the volatility may be produced by uncertainty about government policies.

There are other drawbacks to the idea of taxing foreign-exchange transactions. Such a tax could impose a burden on countries that are quite rationally borrowing overseas. By raising the cost of capital for these countries, it would discourage investment and hinder their development. Also, a tax on foreign-exchange transactions would be difficult to implement. Foreign-exchange trading can be conducted almost anywhere in the world, and a universal agreement to impose such a tax seems extremely unlikely. Those countries that refused to implement the tax would become centers for foreign-exchange trading.

Increasing the Credibility of Fixed Exchange Rates

As we have learned, when speculators feel that a central bank is unable to defend the exchange rate for a weakening currency, they will sell the local currency to obtain more stable foreign currencies. Are there ways to convince speculators that the exchange rate is unchangeable? Currency boards and dollarization are explicitly intended to maintain fixed exchange rates and thus prevent currency crises.

Currency Board

A **currency board** is a monetary authority that issues notes and coins convertible into a foreign anchor currency at a *fixed exchange rate*. The anchor currency is a currency chosen for its expected stability and international acceptability. For most currency boards, the U.S. dollar or British pound has been the anchor currency. Also, a few currency boards have used gold as the anchor. Usually, the fixed exchange rate is set by law, making changes to the exchange rate very costly for governments. Put simply, currency boards offer the strongest form of a fixed exchange rate that is possible short of full currency union.

The commitment to exchange domestic currency for foreign currency at a fixed exchange rate requires that the currency board have sufficient foreign exchange to honor this commitment. This means that its holdings of foreign exchange must at least equal 100 percent of its notes and coins in circulation, as set by law. A currency board can operate in place of a central bank or as a parallel issuer alongside an existing central bank. Usually, a currency board takes over the role of a central bank in strengthening the currency of a developing country.

By design, a currency board has no discretionary powers. Its operations are completely passive and automatic. The sole function of a currency board is to exchange its notes and coins for the anchor at a fixed rate. Unlike a central bank, a currency board does not lend to the domestic government, to domestic companies, or to domestic banks. In a currency-board system, the government can finance its spending only by taxing or borrowing, not by printing money and thereby creating inflation. This results from the stipulation that the backing of the domestic currency must be at least 100 percent.

A country that adopts a currency board thus puts its monetary policy on autopilot. It is as if the chairman of the board of governors of the Federal Reserve System were replaced by a personal computer. When the anchor currency flows in, the board issues more domestic currency and interest rates fall; when the anchor currency flows out, interest rates rise. The government sits back and watches, even if interest rates skyrocket and a recession ensues.

Many economists maintain that, especially in the developing world, central banks are incapable of retaining nonpolitical independence and thus instill less confidence than is necessary for the smooth functioning of a monetary system. They are answerable to the prerogatives of populism or dictatorship and are at the beck and call of political changes. The bottom line is that central banks should not be given the onerous responsibility of maintaining the value of currencies. This job should be left to an independent body whose sole mandate is to issue currency against a strict and inalterable set of guidelines that require a fixed amount of foreign exchange or gold to be deposited for each unit of domestic currency issued.

Currency boards can confer considerable credibility on fixed exchange-rate regimes. The most vital contribution a currency board can make to exchange-rate stability is by imposing discipline on the process of money creation. This results in greater stability of domestic prices, which, in turn, stabilizes the value of the domestic currency. In short, the major benefits of the currency-board system are:

- making a nation's currency and exchange-rate regimes more rule-bound and predictable
- placing an upper bound on the nation's base money supply
- arresting any tendencies in an economy toward inflation
- forcing the government to restrict its borrowing to what foreign and domestic lenders are willing to lend it at market interest rates
- engendering confidence in the soundness of the nation's money, thus assuring citizens and foreign investors that the domestic currency can always be exchanged for some other strong currency
- creating confidence and promoting trade, investment, and economic growth

Proponents cite Hong Kong as a country that has benefited from a currency board. In the early 1980s, Hong Kong had a floating exchange rate. The immediate cause of Hong Kong's economic problems was uncertainty about its political future. In 1982, the United Kingdom and China began talks about the fate of Hong Kong after the U.K.'s lease on the territory expired in 1997. Fear that China would abandon Hong Kong's capitalist system sent Hong Kong's stock market down by 50 percent. Hong Kong's real estate market weakened also, and small banks with heavy exposure in real estate suffered runs. The result was a 16 percent depreciation in the Hong Kong dollar against the U.S. dollar. With this loss of confidence, many merchants refused to accept Hong Kong dollars and quoted prices in U.S. dollars instead. Panic buying of vegetable oil, rice, and other staples emptied merchants' shelves.

In 1983, the government of Hong Kong ended its economic crises by announcing that Hong Kong would adopt a currency-board system. It pegged its exchange rate at HK$7.8 = US$1. The currency reform immediately reversed the loss of confidence about Hong Kong's economy despite continuing troubles in the U.K.–China discussions.

A stable currency provided the basis for Hong Kong to continue its rapid economic growth.

By maintaining a legal commitment to exchange domestic currency for a foreign currency at a fixed exchange rate, and a commitment to issue currency only if it is backed by foreign reserves, a currency board can be a good way of restoring confidence in a country gripped by economic chaos. Although a currency board cannot solve all of a country's economic problems, it may achieve more financial credibility than a domestic central bank can.

Although currency boards help discipline government spending, therefore reducing a major source of inflation in developing countries, there are concerns about currency boards. Perhaps the most common objection is that a currency board prevents a country from pursuing a discretionary monetary policy and thus reduces its economic independence. Also, it is sometimes said that a currency-board system is susceptible to financial panics because it lacks a lender of last resort. Another objection is that a currency-board system creates a colonial relationship with the anchor currency. Critics cite the experiences of British colonies, which operated under currency-board systems in the early 1900s.

It is possible for a nation's monetary system to be orderly and disciplined under either a currency board or a central banking system. But neither system by itself guarantees either order or discipline. The effectiveness of both systems depends on other factors, such as fiscal discipline and a sound banking system. In other words, it is a whole network of responsible and mutually supporting policies and institutions that make for sound money and stable exchange rates. No monetary regime, however well conceived, can bear the entire burden alone.

For Argentina, No Panacea in a Currency Board

For much of the post–World II era, when the financial press focused on Argentina, it was to highlight bouts of very high inflation and failed stabilization efforts. Hyperinflation was rampant in the 1970s and 1980s, and prices increased by more than 1,000 percent in both 1989 and 1990.

In 1991, to tame its tendency to finance public spending by printing pesos, Argentina introduced convertibility of its peso into dollars at a fixed one-to-one exchange rate. To control the issuance of money, the Argentines abandoned their central-bank–based monetary regime, which they felt lacked credibility, and established a currency board. Under this arrangement, currency could be issued only if the currency board had an equivalent amount of dollars.

The fixed exchange rate and the currency board were designed to ensure that Argentina would have a low inflation rate, one similar to that in the United States. At first, this program appeared to work: By 1995, prices were rising at less than 2 percent per year.

During the late 1990s, however, the Argentine economy was hit with four external shocks: (1) the appreciation of the dollar, which had the same negative effect on Argentine export- and import-competing industries that it had on similar industries in the United States; (2) rising U.S. interest rates that spilled over into the Argentine economy, resulting in a decrease in spending on capital goods; (3) falling commodity prices on world markets, which significantly harmed Argentina's commodity-exporting industries; and (4) the depreciation of Brazil's real, which made Brazil's goods relatively cheaper in Argentina and Argentina's goods relatively more expensive in Brazil. These external shocks had a major deflationary effect on the Argentine economy, resulting in falling output and rising unemployment.

Argentina dealt with its problems by spending much more than it collected in taxes to bolster its economy. To finance its budget deficits, Argentina borrowed dollars on the international market. When further borrowing became impossible in 2001, Argentina defaulted, ended convertibility of pesos into dollars, and froze most deposits at banks. Violence and other protests erupted as Argentinians voiced their displeasure with politicians.

Some economists have questioned whether the establishment of a currency board was a mistake for Argentina. They note that although Argentina tied itself to the American currency area as if it were Utah or Massachusetts, it did not benefit from adjustment mechanisms that enable the American currency area to work smoothly in the face of neg-ative external shocks. For example, when unemployment rose in Argentina, its people could not move to the United States were jobs were relatively plentiful. Also, Federal Reserve policy was geared to the conditions of the United States rather than to Argentina. Moreover, the U.S. Congress did not target American fiscal policy on problem areas in Argentina. As a result, the negative shocks to the Argentine economy were dealt with by wage and price deflation. It was a consequence of having fixed its currency rigidly to the dollar.

Dollarization

Instead of using a currency board to maintain fixed exchange rates, why not "dollarize" an economy? **Dollarization** occurs when residents of, say, Ecuador, use the U.S. dollar alongside or instead of the sucre. Partial dollarization occurs when Ecuadoreans hold dollar-denominated bank deposits or Federal Reserve notes to protect against high inflation in the peso. Partial dollarization has existed for years in many Latin American and Caribbean countries, where the United States is a major trading partner and a major source of foreign investment.

Full dollarization means the elimination of the Ecuadorean sucre and its complete replacement with the U.S. dollar. The monetary base of Ecuador, which initially consisted entirely of sucre-denominated currency, would be converted into U.S. Federal Reserve notes. To replace its currency, Ecuador would sell foreign reserves (mostly U.S. Treasury securities) to buy dollars and exchange all outstanding sucre notes for dollar notes. The U.S. dollar would be the sole legal tender and sole unit of account in Ecuador. Full dollarization has occurred in the U.S. Virgin Islands, the Marshall Islands, Puerto Rico, Guam, Ecuador, and other Latin American countries.

Full dollarization is rare today because of the symbolism countries attach to a national currency and the political impact of a perceived loss of sovereignty associated with the adoption of another country's unit of account and currency. When it does occur, it is principally implemented by small countries or territories that are closely associated politically, geographically, and/or through extensive economic and trade ties with the country whose currency is adopted.

Why Dollarize?

Why would a small country want to dollarize its economy? Benefits to the dollarizing country include the credibility and policy discipline that is derived from the implicit irrevocability of dollarization. Behind this lies the promise of lower interest and inflation rates, greater financial stability, and increased economic activity. Countries with a history of high inflation and financial instability often find the potential offered by dollarization to be quite attractive. Dollarization is considered to be one way of avoiding the capital outflows that often precede or accompany an embattled currency situation.

A major benefit of dollarization is the decrease in transaction costs as a result of a common currency. The elimination of currency risk and hedging allows for more trade and more investment within the unified currency zone to occur. Another benefit is in the area of inflation. The choice of another currency necessarily means that the rate of inflation in the dollarized economy will be tied to that of the issuing country. To the extent that a more accepted, stable, recognized currency is chosen, lower inflation now and in the future can be expected to result from dollarization. Finally, greater openness results from a system where exchange controls are unnecessary and balance of payments crises are minimized. Dollarization will not assure an absence of balance of payments difficulties, but it does ensure that such crises will be handled in a way that forces a government to deal with events in an open manner, rather than by printing money and contributing to inflation.

Effects of Dollarization

A convenient way to think about any country that plans to adopt the dollar as its official currency is to treat it as one would treat any of the 50 states in the United States. Thus, in discussions about monetary policy in the United States, it is assumed that the Federal Reserve conducts monetary policy with reference to national economic conditions rather than the economic conditions in an individual state or region, even though economic conditions are not uniform throughout the country. The reason for this is that monetary policy works through interest rates on credit markets that are national in scope. Thus, monetary policy cannot be tailored to deal with business conditions in an individual state or region that is different from the national economy. When Ecuador dollarized its economy, it essentially accepted the monetary policy of the Federal Reserve.

With dollarization in Ecuador, U.S. monetary policy would presumably be carried out as it is now. If Ecuadorean business cycles do not coincide with those in the United States, Ecuador could not count on the Federal Reserve to come to its rescue, just as any state in the United States cannot count on the Federal Reserve to come to its rescue if its business conditions are out of sync with the national pattern. This may be a major downside for the Ecuadoreans. Despite this, Ecuador might still be better off without the supposed safety valve of an independent monetary policy.

Another limitation facing the Ecuadoreans is that the Federal Reserve is not their lender of last resort as it is for Americans. That is, if the U.S. financial system should come under stress, the Federal Reserve could use its various monetary powers to aid these institutions and contain possible failures. Without the consent of the U.S. Congress, the Federal Reserve could not perform this function for Ecuador or for any other country that decided to adopt the dollar officially as its currency.

A third shortcoming arising from the adoption of the dollar as the official currency is that Ecuador could no longer get any **seigniorage** from its monetary system. This cost for Ecuador stems from the loss of the foreign reserves (mainly U.S. Treasury securities) that Ecuador would have to sell in exchange for dollars. These reserves bear interest and, therefore, are a source of income for Ecuador. This income is called *seigniorage*. But once Ecuador's reserves are replaced by dollar bills, this source of income disappears.

With dollarization, Ecuador would enjoy the same freedom that the 50 states in the United States enjoy as to how to spend its tax dollars. Ecuador state expenditures for education, police protection, social insurance, and the like would not be affected by its use of the U.S. dollar. Also, Ecuador could establish its own tariffs, subsidies, and other trade policies. Therefore, Ecuador's sovereignty would not be compromised in these areas. There would, however, be an overall constraint on Ecuador fiscal policy: Ecuador would not have recourse to printing more pesos to finance budget deficits and would thus have to exercise caution in its spending policies.

Official dollarization of Ecuador's economy also has implications for the United States. First, when Ecuadoreans acquire dollars they surrender goods and services to Americans. Thus, for each dollar sent abroad, Americans enjoy a one-time increase in the amount of goods and services they are able to consume. Second, by opting to hold dollars rather than the interest-bearing debt of the United States, the United States, in effect, gets an interest-free loan from Ecuador. The interest that does not have to be paid is a measure of seigniorage that accrues on an annual basis to the United States. On the other hand, use of U.S. currency abroad might hinder the formulation and execution of monetary policy by the Federal Reserve. Also, by making Ecuador more dependent on U.S. monetary policy, dollarization could result in more pressure on the Federal Reserve to conduct policy according to the interests of Ecuador rather than those of the United States.

Summary

1. Most nations maintain neither completely fixed nor floating exchange rates. Contemporary exchange-rate systems generally embody some features of each of these standards.

2. Small, developing nations often anchor their currencies to a single currency or a currency basket. Anchoring to a single currency is generally used by small nations whose trade and financial relationships are mainly with a single trading partner. Small nations with more than one major trading partner often anchor their currencies to a basket of currencies.

3. The special drawing right (SDR) is a currency basket composed of five currencies of IMF members. The basket-valuation technique attempts to make the SDR's value more stable than the foreign-currency value of any single currency in the basket. Developing nations often choose to anchor their exchange rates to the SDR.

4. Under a fixed exchange-rate system, a government defines the official exchange rate for its currency. It then establishes an exchange-stabilization fund, which buys and sells foreign currencies to prevent the market exchange rate from moving above or below the official rate. Nations may officially devalue/revalue their currencies to restore trade equilibrium.

5. With floating exchange rates, market forces of supply and demand determine currency values. Among the major arguments for floating rates are (a) simplicity, (b) continuous adjustment, (c) independent domestic policies, and (d) reduced need for international reserves. Arguments against floating rates stress (a) disorderly exchange markets, (b) reckless financial policies on the part of governments, and (c) conduciveness to price inflation.

6. With the breakdown of the Bretton Woods system of fixed exchange rates, major industrial nations adopted a system of managed floating exchange rates. Under this system, central-bank intervention in the foreign-exchange market is intended to prevent disorderly market conditions in the short run. In the long run, exchange rates are permitted to float in accordance with changing supply and demand.

7. To offset a depreciation in the home currency's exchange value, a central bank can (a) use its international reserves to purchase quantities of that currency on the foreign-exchange market; (b) initiate a contractionary monetary policy, which leads to higher domestic interest rates, increased investment inflows, and increased demand for the home currency. To offset an appreciation in the home currency's exchange value, a central bank can sell additional quantities of its currency on the foreign-exchange market or initiate an expansionary monetary policy.

8. Under a crawling-peg exchange-rate system, a nation makes frequent devaluations (or

revaluations) of its currency to restore payments balance. Developing nations suffering from high inflation rates have been major users of this mechanism.

9. A currency crisis, also called a speculative attack, is a situation in which a weak currency experiences heavy selling pressure. Among the causes of currency crises are budget deficits financed by inflation, weak financial systems, political uncertainty, and changes in interest rates on world markets. Although a fixed exchange-rate system has the advantage of promoting low inflation, it is especially vulnerable to speculative attacks.

10. Capital controls are sometimes used by governments in an attempt to support fixed exchange rates and prevent speculative attacks on currencies. However, capital controls are hindered by the private sector's finding ways to evade them and move funds into or out of a country.

11. Currency boards and dollarization are explicitly intended to maintain fixed exchange rates and thus prevent currency crises. A currency board is a monetary authority that issues notes and coins convertible into a foreign currency at a fixed exchange rate. The most vital contribution a currency board can make to exchange-rate stability is to impose discipline on the process of money creation. This results in greater stability on domestic prices which, in turn, stabilizes the value of the domestic currency. Dollarization occurs when residents of a country use the U.S. dollar alongside or instead of their own currency. Dollarization is seen as a way to protect a country's growth and prosperity from bouts of inflation, currency depreciation, and speculative attacks against the local currency.

Key Concepts and Terms

- Adjustable pegged exchange rates *(page 448)*
- Bretton Woods system *(page 448)*
- Capital controls *(page 462)*
- Clean float *(page 453)*
- Crawling peg *(page 457)*
- Currency board *(page 464)*
- Currency crashes *(page 458)*
- Currency crisis *(page 458)*
- Devaluation *(page 447)*
- Dirty float *(page 453)*

- Dollarization *(page 466)*
- Exchange controls *(page 462)*
- Exchange-stabilization fund *(page 446)*
- Fixed exchange rates *(page 442)*
- Floating exchange rates *(page 449)*
- Fundamental disequilibrium *(page 447)*
- Key currency *(page 442)*
- Leaning against the wind *(page 453)*

- Managed floating system *(page 452)*
- Official exchange rate *(page 445)*
- Par value *(page 445)*
- Revaluation *(page 447)*
- Seigniorage *(page 467)*
- Special drawing right (SDR) *(page 444)*
- Speculative attack *(page 458)*
- Target exchange rates *(page 453)*

Study Questions

1. What factors underlie a nation's decision to adopt floating exchange rates or fixed exchange rates?

2. How do managed floating exchange rates operate? Why were they adopted by the industrialized nations in 1973?

3. Why do some developing countries adopt currency boards? Why do others dollarize their monetary systems?

4. Discuss the philosophy and operation of the Bretton Woods system of adjustable pegged exchange rates.

5. Why do nations use a crawling-peg exchange-rate system?

6. What is the purpose of capital controls?

7. What factors contribute to currency crises?

8. Why do small nations adopt currency baskets against which to peg their exchange rates?

9. What advantage does the SDR offer to small nations seeking to peg their exchange rates?

10. Present the case for and the case against a system of floating exchange rates.

11. What techniques can a central bank use to stabilize the exchange value of its currency?

12. What is the purpose of a currency devaluation? What about a currency revaluation?

netlink

15.1 The Federal Reserve Bank of New York regularly reports on its intervention in foreign-exchange markets. Set your browser to this URL:

http://www.ny.frb.org/markets/foreignex.htm

15.2 Throughout the world, central banks intervene in the foreign market. For a quick link to numerous central banks, go to the Bank for International Settlements Web page at this URL:

http://www.bis.org/cbanks.htm

15.3 The International Monetary Fund (IMF) provides loans, technical assistance, and policy guidance to developing members in order to reduce poverty, improve living standards, and safeguard the stability of the international monetary system. Learn about exchange-rate practices by setting your browser to this URL:

http://www.imf.org

To access NetLink Exercises and the Virtual Scavenger Hunt, visit the Carbaugh Web site at http://carbaugh.swlearning.com.

Xtra! Log onto the Carbaugh Xtra! Web site (http://carbaughxtra.swlearning.com) for additional learning resources such as practice quizzes, help with graphing, and current events applications.

Legal and Economic Implications of Devaluation and Revaluation

Currency devaluations and revaluations are used in conjunction with a *fixed* exchange-rate system. The monetary authority changes a currency's exchange rate by decree, usually by a sizable amount at one time. How is such a policy implemented?

Recall that under a fixed exchange-rate system, the home currency is assigned a par value by the nation's monetary authorities. The par value is the amount of a nation's currency that is required to purchase a fixed amount of gold, a key currency, or the special drawing right. These assets represent the legal *numeraire*, or the unit of contractual obligations. By comparing various national currency prices of the numeraire, monetary authorities determine the official rate of exchange for the currencies.

In the *legal* sense, a devaluation or revaluation occurs when the home country redefines its currency price of the official numeraire, changing the par value. The *economic* effect of the par value's redefinition is the impact on the market rate of exchange. Assuming that other trading nations retain their existing par values, one would expect (1) a devaluation to result in a depreciation in the currency's exchange value; (2) a revaluation to result in an appreciation in the currency's exchange value.

Figure 15.5 on page 472 illustrates the legal and economic implications of devaluation/

revaluation policies. Assume that the SDR serves as the numeraire by which the value of individual currencies can be defined relative to each other—Burundi's franc and Uganda's shilling. The diagram's vertical axis denotes the shilling price of an SDR, and the horizontal axis depicts the franc price of an SDR. Three price ratios are illustrated by each point in the figure: (1) the shilling price of the SDR, (2) the franc price of the SDR, and (3) the shilling price of the franc, indicated by the slope of a ray connecting the origin with any point in the figure.

Referring to Figure 15.5(a), suppose Uganda sets its par value at 700 shillings per SDR, whereas Burundi's par value equals 350 francs per SDR. Connecting these two prices yields point *A* in the diagram. Relative to each other, the official exchange rate between the shilling and the franc is 2 shillings = 1 franc, denoted by the slope of the ray *0A* (700/350 = 2.0).

Assume that Uganda wishes to devalue the shilling by, say, 10 percent to correct a payments deficit. Starting at point *A*, Uganda would raise the shilling price of the SDR from 700 to 770 shillings per SDR, a 10 percent increase. This results in a movement from point *A* to point *B* in the figure. Corresponding to the slope of ray *0B*, the new exchange rate is 2.2 shillings = 1 franc (770/350 = 2.2). Uganda's devaluation results in a depreciation in the shilling's exchange value from 2 shillings = 1 franc to 2.2 shillings = 1 franc, a 10 percent

FIGURE 15.5

Devaluation/Revaluation: Legal Versus Economic Implications

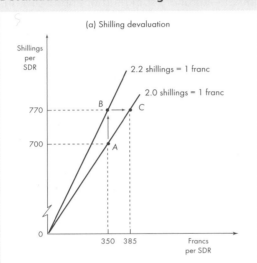

(a) Shilling devaluation

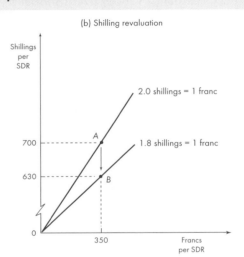

(b) Shilling revaluation

Starting at the official exchange rate of 2 Uganda shillings per Burundi franc, a 10 percent devaluation of the shilling results in the shilling's depreciating 10 percent against the franc, to 2.2 shillings per franc; if Burundi retaliates and devalues its franc by 10 percent, the exchange rate will revert back to 2 shillings per franc. A 10 percent revaluation of the Uganda shilling, unaccompanied by an offsetting currency revaluation by Burundi, leads to a 10 percent appreciation of the shilling against the franc.

change. Conversely, suppose that Uganda revalues the shilling by 10 percent to reverse a payments surplus. Starting at point *A* in Figure 15.5(b), Uganda would lower the official price of the SDR from 700 shillings to 630 shillings, a 10 percent decrease. The exchange value of the shilling would increase from 2 shillings = 1 franc to 1.8 shillings = 1 franc, a 10 percent change.

To change the shilling/franc exchange rate, it is not sufficient for Uganda to redefine the shilling's par value. It is also necessary that the par value of the Burundi franc remain constant or be altered by a smaller fraction. In Figure 15.5(a), a change in the shilling/franc exchange rate requires a change in the *slope* of ray *OA*. Acting by itself, Uganda can establish only the vertical position in the diagram. Because Burundi determines the horizontal position, any redefinition of Uganda's par value can be neutralized by an equivalent change in Burundi's par value. In other words, Burundi can offset any change in the slope of the ray that Uganda may wish to undertake.

Let us start again at point *A* in Figure 15.5(a), where the exchange rate is set at 2 shillings = 1 franc. Facing a payments deficit, suppose Uganda devalues the shilling 10 percent by increasing the official price of the SDR from 700 to 770 shillings. This would cause a movement from point *A* to point *B*, where the exchange rate is 2.2 shillings = 1 franc. But what if Burundi determines that the shilling's devaluation gives Uganda an unfair competitive advantage? Suppose Burundi retaliates by devaluing the franc 10 percent, thus increasing the official price of the SDR from 350 to 385 francs. A movement from point *B* to point *C* in the diagram would result. Although both currencies have been officially devalued by 10 percent, the exchange rate between them remains constant at 2 shillings = 1 franc. The conclusion is that a devaluation in the legal sense does not necessarily ensure a devaluation in the economic sense—that is, a depreciation in the exchange rate. This occurs only if other nations do not retaliate by initiating offsetting devaluations of their own.

Currency devaluations do have foreign repercussions similar to those of domestic economic policies. The larger and more significant the devaluing nation, the greater the economic effects transmitted abroad. A nation that devalues to initiate an export-led economic recovery may be the cause of recession in its trading partners. This was often the case during the Great Depression of the 1930s, when competitive devaluations were widespread. It is no wonder that when currency realignments involving devaluations and revaluations are called for, they usually require intense negotiations and the harmonization of economic interests among participating nations.

chapter 16

Macroeconomic Policy in an Open Economy

A nation with a closed economy can select its economic policies in view of its own goals. In an open world economy, however, consequences of a nation's activities are felt by its trading partners. The result has been efforts among nations to coordinate their economic policies. This chapter examines government policies designed to achieve full employment with price stability and equilibrium in the balance of payments. The importance of international economic-policy cooperation is emphasized throughout the discussion.

Economic Policy in an Open Economy

International economic policy refers to activities of national governments that affect the movement of trade and factor inputs among nations. Included are not only the obvious measures such as import tariffs and quotas, but also domestic measures such as monetary policy and fiscal policy. Policies that are undertaken to improve the conditions of one sector in a nation tend to have repercussions that spill over into other sectors. Because an economy's *internal* (domestic) sector is tied to its *external* (foreign) sector, one cannot designate economic policies as being purely domestic or purely foreign. Rather, the effects of economic policy should be viewed as being located on a continuum between two poles— an internal-effects pole and an external-effects pole. Although the primary impact of an import restriction is on a nation's trade balance, for example, there are secondary effects on national output, employment, and income. Most economic policies are located between the external and internal poles rather than falling directly on either one.

Economic Objectives of Nations

What are the basic objectives of economic policies? Since the Great Depression of the 1930s, governments have actively pursued the goal of economic stability at full employment. Known as **internal balance**, this objective has two dimensions: (1) a fully employed economy, and (2) no inflation—or, more realistically, a reasonable amount of inflation. Nations traditionally have considered internal balance to be of primary importance and have formulated economic policies to attain this goal.

ECONOMIC *Applications*

Visit EconNews Online
International Trade

474

Policy makers are also aware of a nation's balance-of-payments (BOP) position. A nation is said to be in **external balance** when it realizes neither BOP deficits nor BOP surpluses.[1] In practice, policy makers usually express external balance in terms of a BOP subaccount, such as the current account. In this context, external balance occurs when the current account is neither so deeply in deficit that the home nation is incapable of repaying its foreign debts in the future nor so strongly in surplus that foreign nations cannot repay their debts to it. Although nations usually consider internal balance to be the highest priority, they are sometimes forced to modify priorities when confronted with large and persistent external imbalances.

Nations have economic targets other than internal balance and external balance, such as long-run economic development and a reasonably equitable distribution of national income. Although these and other commitments may influence international economic policies, the discussion in this chapter is confined to the pursuit of internal balance and external balance.

▌Policy Instruments

To attain the objectives of external balance and internal balance, policy makers enact expenditure-changing policies, expenditure-switching policies, and direct controls. **Expenditure-changing policies** alter the level of aggregate demand for goods and services, including those produced domestically and those imported. They include **fiscal policy**, which refers to changes in government spending and taxes,

and **monetary policy**, which refers to changes in the money supply by a nation's central bank (such as the Federal Reserve). Depending on the direction of change, expenditure-changing policies are either expenditure increasing or expenditure reducing.

If *inflation* is a problem, it is likely to be because the level of aggregate demand (total spending) is too high for the level of output that can be sustained by the nation's resources at constant prices. The standard recommendation in this case is for policy makers to reduce aggregate demand by implementing *expenditure-decreasing* policies such as reductions in government expenditures, tax increases, or decreases in the money supply; these policies offset the upward pressure on prices resulting from excess aggregate demand. If *unemployment* is excessive, the standard recommendation is for policy makers to increase aggregate demand for goods and services by initiating *expenditure-increasing* policies.

Expenditure-switching policies modify the direction of demand, shifting it between domestic output and imports. Under a system of fixed exchange rates, a trade-deficit nation could devalue its currency to increase the international competitiveness of its industries, thus diverting spending from foreign goods to domestic goods. To increase its competitiveness under a managed floating exchange-rate system, the nation could purchase other currencies with its currency, thereby causing the exchange value of its currency to depreciate. The success of these policies in promoting trade balance largely depends on switching demand in the proper direction and amount, as well as on the capacity of the home economy to meet the additional demand by supplying more goods. Exchange-rate adjustments are general switching policies that influence the balance of payments indirectly, through their effects on the price mechanism and national income.

Direct controls consist of government restrictions on the market economy. They are selective expenditure-switching policies whose objective is to control particular items in the balance of payments. Direct controls, such as automobile tariffs and dairy quotas, are levied on imports in an attempt to switch domestic spending away from foreign goods to domestic goods. Similarly, the object of an export subsidy is to enhance exports

---

[1]Recall from Chapter 10 that BOP transactions are grouped into two categories: the current account and the capital and financial account. Private-sector transactions and official (central bank) transactions are included in the capital and financial account. With double-entry accounting, total debits equal total credits in the BOP statement. This implies that a current account deficit (surplus) will equal a capital and financial account surplus (deficit).

In this chapter, we assume that BOP equilibrium occurs when the current-account deficit (surplus) is equal to the surplus (deficit) on private-sector financial and capital transactions; the balance on official financial and capital transactions thus equals zero. This measure is known as the official reserve transaction balance; it emphasizes the role of all private-sector transactions in a nation's international payments position. It follows that a BOP deficit (surplus) occurs if the deficit (surplus) on current-account transactions exceeds the surplus (deficit) on private-sector financial and capital transactions.

by switching foreign spending to domestic output. When a government wishes to limit the volume of its overseas sales, it may impose an export quota (such as Japan's automobile export quotas of the 1980s). Direct controls may also be levied on capital flows so as to either restrain excessive capital outflows or stimulate capital inflows.

Economic-policy formation is subject to **institutional constraints** that involve considerations of fairness and equity.[2] Policy makers are aware of the needs of groups they represent, such as labor

[2]See A.C. Day, "Institutional Constraints and the International Monetary System," in R. Mundell and A. Swoboda, eds., *Monetary Problems of the International Economy* (Chicago: University of Chicago Press, 1969), pp. 333–342.

and business, especially when pursuing conflicting economic objectives. For example, to what extent are policy makers willing to permit reductions in national income, output, and employment at the cost of restoring BOP equilibrium? The outcry of adversely affected groups within the nation may be more than sufficient to convince policy makers not to pursue external balance as a goal. During election years, government officials tend to be especially sensitive to domestic economic problems. Reflecting perceptions of fairness and equity, policy formation tends to be characterized by negotiation and compromise.

Figure 16.1 illustrates the two basic policy dimensions of internal balance and external bal-

---

FIGURE 16.1

Economic Objectives and Macroeconomic Policy

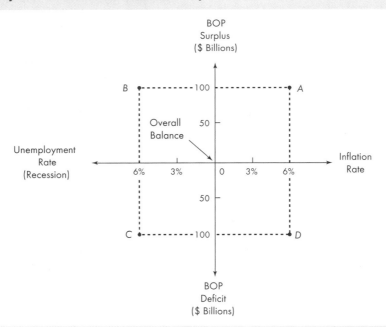

A nation attains overall balance when it simultaneously achieves internal balance and external balance. When overall balance is not realized, nations can implement expenditure-changing policies (such as monetary/fiscal policy) or expenditure-switching policies (such as currency devaluation/revaluation) to help eliminate internal disequilibrium and/or external disequilibrium, thus pushing the economy toward overall balance.

ance. The vertical axis of the diagram depicts the size of a nation's BOP deficit or surplus. External balance is reached at the diagram's origin, with neither BOP surplus nor BOP deficit. The horizontal axis indicates the extent of domestic recession or inflation. Full employment (zero recession) without inflation, or internal balance, is also achieved at the diagram's origin. An economy reaches **overall balance** when it attains internal balance and external balance.

Exchange-Rate Policies and Overall Balance

As noted previously, expenditure-switching policies can help a nation attain overall balance. Although these measures are designed primarily to influence the nation's external sector, they have secondary impacts on its internal sector. Let us examine one expenditure-switching instrument, the exchange rate, and its impact on a nation's external sector and internal sector.

Referring to Figure 16.1, suppose a nation is located in the disequilibrium zone of *BOP deficit with recession*, indicated by point C in the figure. A depreciation (devaluation) of the nation's currency increases the international competitiveness of its goods; this leads to rising exports and a reduction in the BOP deficit. Additional export sales provide an injection of spending into the economy, which encourages additional production and thus reduces the level of unemployment. In terms of the figure, the currency depreciation induces movement in a northeasterly direction, promoting both internal balance and external balance.

Conversely, suppose that a nation experiences *BOP surplus with inflation*, indicated by point A in Figure 16.1. If this nation permits an appreciation (revaluation) of its currency, the international competitiveness of its goods will decline, causing exports to fall. Falling export sales decrease the level of spending in the economy, thus reducing its inflation rate. By promoting internal balance and external balance, the currency's appreciation induces a southwesterly movement in the figure.

As these examples suggest, the ability to implement exchange-rate policies is subject to interna-

tional policy cooperation for several reasons. A *depreciation* of one nation's currency implies an *appreciation* for its trading partners. If the dollar depreciates by 30 percent, this can be equivalent to a 30 percent subsidy on U.S. exports and a 30 percent tax on U.S. imports. Furthermore, changes in the exchange rate influence the external sectors and internal sectors of both the home country and its trading partners. In a global system, one nation cannot achieve overall balance single-handedly by means of its own policy tools. Other nations can implement retaliatory policies—such as tariffs and currency devaluations—that offset the nation's pursuit of overall balance, as occurred during the Great Depression of the 1930s.

Monetary Policy and Fiscal Policy: Effects on Internal Balance

The previous section suggested that exchange-rate policies primarily affect the economy's external sector, while having secondary effects on its internal sector. Let us now consider monetary policy and fiscal policy as stabilization tools. These tools are generally used to stabilize the economy's internal sector, while having secondary effects on its external sector. How successful are monetary policy and fiscal policy in achieving full employment and price stability?

Let us assume that the mobility of international capital is high. This suggests that a small change in the relative interest rate across nations induces a large international flow of capital (investment funds). This assumption is consistent with capital movements among many industrial nations, such as the United States and Germany, and the conclusions of many analysts that capital mobility is increasing as national financial markets have become internationalized.

Two conclusions will emerge from our discussion: (1) Under a fixed exchange-rate system, fiscal policy is successful in promoting internal balance, whereas monetary policy is unsuccessful. (2) Under a floating rate system, monetary policy is successful in promoting internal balance, whereas fiscal policy is unsuccessful. These conclusions are summarized in Table 16.1.

In practice, most industrial nations maintain neither rigidly fixed exchange rates nor freely floating exchange rates. Rather, they maintain managed floating exchange rates in which central banks buy and sell currencies in an attempt to prevent exchange-rate movements from becoming disorderly. Heavier exchange-rate intervention moves a nation closer to our fixed exchange-rate conclusions for monetary and fiscal policy; less intervention moves a nation closer to our floating exchange-rate conclusions.

Fiscal Policy with Fixed Exchange Rates and Floating Exchange Rates

Assume that a nation operates under a fixed exchange-rate system and encounters high unemployment. Let us follow the case of an expansionary fiscal policy—say, an increase in government purchases of goods and services. The rise in government spending increases aggregate demand, which leads to higher output, employment, and income, as seen in the upper portion of Figure 16.2(a).

Now refer to the lower portion of Figure 16.2(a). As total spending rises, so does the demand for money. Given the supply of money, interest rates increase; this encourages foreigners to invest more in the home nation and discourages its residents from investing abroad. The resulting net capital inflows push the nation's capital account into surplus. Concurrently, the increase in spending results in higher imports and a trade deficit. If investment flows are highly mobile, it is likely that the capital-account surplus will exceed the trade-account deficit; the overall BOP thus moves into surplus. Because the nation is committed to fixed exchange rates, its central bank buys foreign currency, thus preventing an appreciation of the home currency. This increases the money supply, which leads to additional spending, output, and employment. In this manner, the expansionary fiscal policy promotes internal balance.

If capital mobility is low, however, the trade-account deficit may more than offset the capital-account surplus, pulling the overall BOP into deficit. To prevent the home currency from depreciating, central bankers would purchase it on the foreign-exchange market. This would cause a decrease in the money supply, an increase in interest rates, a decline in investment spending, and a decrease in output. The attempt to use expansionary fiscal policy to jumpstart the economy could backfire.

The result is different if the country has floating exchange rates. As before, fiscal expansion leads to higher output and income as well as higher interest rates. Higher income induces rising imports, which push the trade account into deficit. Higher interest rates lead to net investment inflows and a surplus in the capital account. With highly mobile capital, it is likely that the surplus in the capital account will exceed the deficit in the trade account, so that the overall BOP moves into surplus. This leads to an appreciation in the home currency's exchange value. With a

---

TABLE 16.1

The Effectiveness of Fiscal Policy and Monetary Policy in Promoting Internal Balance[*]

Exchange-Rate Regime	Monetary Policy	Fiscal Policy
Floating exchange rates	Effective	Ineffective
Fixed exchange rates	Ineffective	Effective

*Assuming a high degree of capital mobility.

FIGURE 16.2

Fiscal Policy: Short-Run Effects on a Nation's Internal Sector

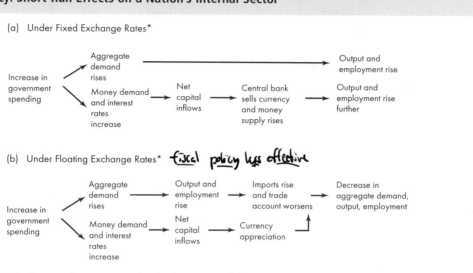

(a) Under Fixed Exchange Rates*

(b) Under Floating Exchange Rates*   *fiscal policy less effective*

*For the case of contractionary fiscal policy, reverse all changes.

(a) Under fixed exchange rates, an expansionary (contractionary) fiscal policy helps correct the problem of recession (inflation). (b) Under floating exchange rates, an expansionary (contractionary) fiscal policy is unsuccessful in correcting the problem of recession (inflation).

floating exchange-rate system, however, the central bank does nothing to offset this appreciation. By making the nation less competitive, the appreciation leads to falling exports and rising imports; the ensuing decrease in aggregate demand, output, and employment offsets the initial gains of the fiscal expansion. The expansionary fiscal policy is thus unable to mitigate the economy's recession. Adjustment following an increase in government spending under floating exchange rates is summarized in Figure 16.2(b).

Monetary Policy with Fixed Exchange Rates and Floating Exchange Rates

Suppose that a nation experiences domestic recession and that it allows its currency to float in the foreign-exchange market. To stimulate domestic output, assume that the central bank adopts an expansionary monetary policy. By increasing the supply of money relative to the money demand, the monetary policy leads to lower interest rates, which stimulate aggregate demand and output. Lower interest rates also discourage foreigners from investing in the home country and encourage its residents to invest abroad. The resulting net capital outflows induce a depreciation of the nation's currency and an improvement in its international competitiveness. The subsequent rise in exports and fall in imports lead to further increases in output and employment; the expansionary monetary policy thus promotes internal balance. Adjustment following an expansionary monetary policy under floating exchange rates is summarized in Figure 16.3(a) on page 480.

FIGURE 16.3

Monetary Policy: Short-Run Effects on a Nation's Internal Sector

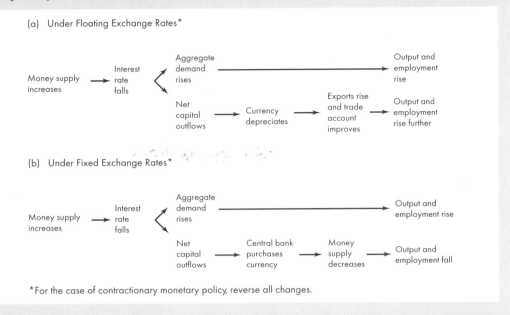

(a) Under Floating Exchange Rates*

(b) Under Fixed Exchange Rates*

*For the case of contractionary monetary policy, reverse all changes.

(a) Under floating exchange rates, an expansionary (contractionary) monetary policy is successful in correcting the problem of recession (inflation). (b) Under fixed exchange rates, an expansionary (contractionary) monetary policy is unsuccessful in correcting the problem of recession (inflation).

Contrast this outcome with the effects of monetary policy under a system of fixed exchange rates. The monetary expansion reduces interest rates, leading to rising aggregate demand, output, and employment. Lower interest rates result in net capital outflows and a depreciation in the currency's exchange value. To maintain a fixed exchange rate, however, the central bank intervenes on the foreign-exchange market and purchases the home currency with foreign currency. This decreases the money supply and offsets the initial increase in the money supply. The initial output and employment expansion resulting from the expansionary monetary policy is thus blunted, and internal balance is not attained. Adjustment following an expansionary monetary policy under fixed exchange rates is summarized in Figure 16.3(b).

Monetary and Fiscal Policies: Effects on External Balance

What are the effects of monetary policy and fiscal policy on a nation's external balance? We assume that the exchange rate is fixed, because BOP surpluses and BOP deficits are issues only when the exchange rate is fixed; recall that floating exchange rates automatically adjust to promote BOP equilibrium.

The short-run effects of monetary policy on the BOP are definite: An expansion in the money supply worsens the BOP, whereas a contraction in the money supply improves the BOP. These effects are illustrated in Figure 16.4.

FIGURE 16.4

Monetary Policy and Fiscal Policy Under Fixed Exchange Rates: Short-Run Effects on a Nation's External Sector

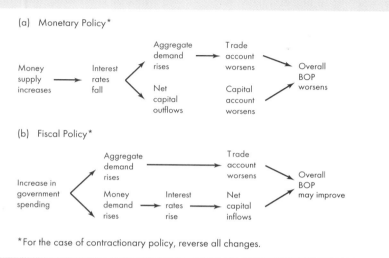

*For the case of contractionary policy, reverse all changes.

(a) An expansionary (contractionary) monetary policy leads to a worsening (improving) trade account and capital account, thus worsening (improving) the overall balance of payments. (b) An expansionary (contractionary) fiscal policy leads to a worsening (improving) trade account and an improving (worsening) capital account. The overall balance of payments improves (worsens) depending on the relative strength of these two opposing forces.

To illustrate, assume the central bank increases the money supply, relative to the money demand, which pushes interest rates downward. Falling interest rates encourage additional investment spending, which leads to an increase in aggregate demand, output, and income. The rise in income, in turn, increases imports and worsens the trade balance. At the same time, falling interest rates (relative to those abroad) induce net investment outflows and a deterioration in the capital account. By worsening the trade balance and the capital account balance, the monetary expansion worsens overall BOP. In the long run, the overseas investments will be repaid with interest, resulting in a positive feedback into the BOP; however, the negative effect on the trade balance will persist.

The short-run effects on the BOP of expansionary fiscal policy are not as clear as those of monetary policy. Assume the government increases its purchases of goods and services, leading to increases in aggregate demand, output, and income. Rising income, in turn, induces rising imports and a worsening trade balance. Meanwhile, increased government spending leads to increased money demand and rising interest rates. The higher interest rates, in turn, induce net investment inflows and an improvement in the capital account. If capital mobility is sufficiently high, the improvement in the capital account more than offsets the trade-account deterioration, and the overall BOP improves. Eventually, however, foreign investors must be repaid with interest, and this more than offsets the investment inflows caused by higher interest rates. As a result, the fiscal expansion probably worsens the overall BOP in the long run, albeit improving it in the short run if enough investment inflows occur in response to higher interest rates.

Monetary Policy and Fiscal Policy: Policy Agreement and Policy Conflict

With fixed exchange rates, let us consider monetary policy and fiscal policy and see what effects they have on a nation's internal balance and external balance.

Consider monetary policy first. Referring to Figure 16.1, suppose that a nation experiences *unemployment with BOP surplus*, shown by point B. The previous section suggested that if the central bank increases the money supply, which leads to rising aggregate demand, unemployment will fall and the BOP surplus will decrease. In this case, the expansionary monetary policy clearly promotes overall balance. Alternatively, suppose that a country experiences *inflation with BOP deficit*, shown by point D in Figure 16.1. A reduction in the money supply, which reduces aggregate demand, decreases the inflation rate as well as the BOP deficit, thus promoting overall balance. These two disequilibrium zones illustrate **policy agreement** for monetary policy. Changes in the money supply move the economy toward both internal balance and external balance.

Not all disequilibrium zones, however, are as favorable for monetary policy. Suppose now that a nation experiences *unemployment with BOP deficit*, shown by point C in Figure 16.1. The previous section suggested that an expansionary monetary policy, which raises aggregate demand, will reduce unemployment—but at the cost of a larger BOP deficit (southeast from point C). If a country experiences *inflation with BOP surplus*, shown by point A in Figure 16.1, a contractionary monetary policy leads to less inflation but increased BOP surplus (northwest from point A). These disequilibrium zones imply **policy conflict** for monetary policy. Although changes in the money supply improve one economic objective, they detract from another objective. A dilemma thus exists for monetary authorities concerning which objective to pursue.

Instead of utilizing monetary policy in policy-conflict zones, suppose a nation resorts to fiscal policy. Assume, for example, that a country experiences *unemployment and BOP deficit*, as shown by point C in Figure 16.1. Recall that an expansionary fiscal policy, which raises aggregate demand, promotes full employment; however, it reduces a nation's BOP deficit only if the ensuing improvement in the capital account more than offsets the deterioration in the trade account. If a country experiences *inflation and BOP surplus*, shown by point A in Figure 16.1, a contractionary fiscal policy lessens inflation; whether the BOP surplus rises or falls depends on whether the worsening of its capital account more than offsets the improvement of its trade account. It is thus not clear whether fiscal policy is able to promote overall balance for a nation situated in one of these policy-conflict zones.

When a nation finds itself in a policy-conflict zone, fiscal policy or monetary policy alone will not necessarily restore both internal and external balance. A combination of policies is generally needed. Suppose, for example, that a nation experiences *unemployment with BOP deficit*, shown by point C in Figure 16.1. An expansionary monetary policy to combat unemployment might be accompanied by tariffs or quotas, or possibly currency devaluation, to reduce imports and improve the BOP. Each economic objective is matched with an appropriate policy instrument so that both objectives can be attained at the same time.

In U.S. history, the Federal Reserve has attempted to line up policy instruments with targets during conflict situations. During the early 1960s, the conflict was *domestic recession with BOP deficit*. The Federal Reserve attempted to match instruments with targets by manipulating the structure of domestic interest rates in a program called **Operation Twist**. Under this program, the U.S. interest-rate structure was modified so that short-term rates were used primarily to promote external balance whereas long-term rates were used primarily for internal balance. By keeping short-term interest rates high, the United States could expect to experience net investment inflows, thereby improving its BOP position. Low long-term rates would presumably stimulate domestic investment, output, and employment, thus correcting the recession. At best, Operation Twist was only partially successful in promoting overall balance. The policy was initially successful in keeping short-term rates above long-term rates. As time passed, however, the differential between them disappeared as inflation pushed both short-term and long-term rates upward, thus moderating the program's success.

Inflation with Unemployment

The analysis so far has looked at internal balance under special circumstances. It has been assumed that as the economy advances to full employment, domestic prices remain unchanged until full employment is reached. Once the nation's capacity to produce has been achieved, further increases in aggregate demand pull prices upward. This type of inflation is known as **demand-pull inflation**. Under these conditions, internal balance (full employment with stable prices) can be viewed as a single target that requires but one policy instrument: reductions in aggregate demand via monetary policy or fiscal policy.

A more troublesome problem is the appropriate policy to implement when a nation experiences *inflation with unemployment*. Here the problem is that internal balance cannot be achieved just by manipulating aggregate demand. To decrease inflation, a reduction in aggregate demand is required; to decrease unemployment, an expansion in aggregate demand is required. Thus, the objectives of full employment and stable prices cannot be considered as one and the same target; rather, they are two independent targets, requiring two distinct policy instruments.

Achieving overall balance thus involves three separate targets: (1) BOP equilibrium, (2) full employment, and (3) price stability. To ensure that all three objectives can be achieved simultaneously, monetary/fiscal policies and exchange-rate adjustments may not be enough; direct controls may also be needed.

Inflation with unemployment has been a problem for the United States. In 1971, for example, the U.S. economy experienced *inflation with recession and BOP deficit*. Increasing aggregate demand to achieve full employment would presumably intensify inflationary pressures. The president therefore implemented a comprehensive system of **wage and price controls** to remove the inflationary constraint. Later the same year, the United States entered into exchange-rate realignments that resulted in a depreciation of the dollar's exchange value by 12 percent against the trade-weighted value of other major currencies. The dollar depreciation was intended to help the United States reverse its BOP deficit. In short, it was the president's view that the internal and external problems of the United States could not be eliminated through expenditure-changing policies alone.

International Economic-Policy Coordination

Policy makers have long been aware that the welfare of their economies is linked to that of the world economy. Because of the international mobility of goods, services, capital, and labor, economic policies of one nation have spillover effects on others. This spillover is especially true for the larger industrial economies, but even here, the linkages are stronger among some nations, such as those within Western Europe, than for others. Recognizing these spillover effects, governments have often made attempts to coordinate their economic policies.

Economic relations among nations can be visualized along a spectrum, illustrated in Figure 16.5 on page 484, ranging from *open conflict* to *integration*, where nations implement policies jointly in a supranational forum to which they have ceded a large degree of authority, such as the European Union. At the spectrum's midpoint lies *policy independence*: Nations take the actions of other nations as a given; they do not attempt to

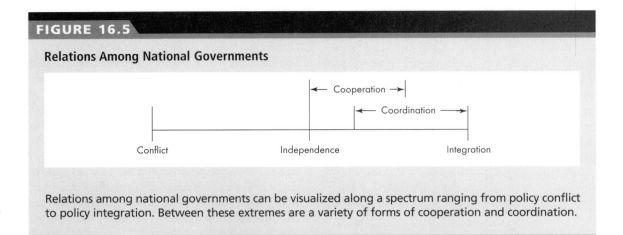

FIGURE 16.5

Relations Among National Governments

Relations among national governments can be visualized along a spectrum ranging from policy conflict to policy integration. Between these extremes are a variety of forms of cooperation and coordination.

influence those actions or be influenced by them. Between independence and integration lie various forms of policy coordination and cooperation.

Cooperative policy making can take many forms, but in general it occurs whenever officials from different nations meet to evaluate world economic conditions. During these meetings, policy makers may present briefings on their individual economies and discuss current policies. Such meetings represent a simple form of cooperation. A more involved format might consist of economists' studies on a particular subject, combined with an in-depth discussion of possible solutions. True policy coordination, however, goes beyond these two forms of cooperation; policy coordination is a formal agreement among nations to initiate particular policies.

International economic-policy coordination is the attempt to significantly modify national policies—monetary policy, fiscal policy, exchange-rate policy—in recognition of international economic interdependence. Policy coordination does not necessarily imply that nations give precedence to international over domestic concerns. It does recognize, however, that the policies of one nation can spill over to influence the objectives of others; nations should therefore communicate with one another and attempt to coordinate their policies so as to take these linkages into account. Presumably, they will be better off than if they had acted independently.

There are many examples of international economic-policy coordination. The Smithsonian Agreement of 1971 was a coordinated attempt by the major industrial nations to realign the exchange values of their currencies using currency devaluations and revaluations. The 1978 Bonn Summit resulted in the enactment by Germany and Japan of expansionary fiscal and monetary policies to stimulate their demand for U.S. goods and reduce the U.S. trade deficit; in return, the United States raised its price of oil to the world level.

To facilitate policy coordination, economic officials of the major governments talk with one another frequently in the context of the International Monetary Fund (IMF) and the Organisation for Economic Cooperation and Development (OECD). Also, central-bank senior officials meet monthly at the Basel meetings of the **Bank for International Settlements (BIS)**. Since 1975, government officials of the seven largest industrial economies (United States, Canada, Japan, United Kingdom, Germany, France, and Italy), known as the **Group of Seven (G-7)**, have met in annual economic summits to discuss economic issues of common concern. Not only do the G-7 nations initiate dialogues concerning economic objectives and policy, but they also devise economic indicators that provide a framework for multilateral surveillance of their economies and help monitor the international consequences of domestic policies.

Policy Coordination in Theory

If economic policies in each of two nations affect the other, then the case for policy coordination would appear to be obvious. Policy coordination is considered important in the modern world because economic disruptions are transmitted rapidly from one nation to another. Without policy coordination, national economic policies can destabilize other economies. The logic of policy coordination is illustrated in the following basketball-spectator problem.[3]

Suppose you are attending a basketball game between the Seattle Supersonics and the Chicago Bulls. If everyone is sitting, someone who stands has a superior view. Spectators usually can see well if everyone sits or if everyone stands. Sitting in seats is more comfortable than standing. When there is no cooperation, everyone stands; each spectator does what is best for herself/himself given the actions of other spectators. If all spectators sit, someone, taking what the others will do as a given, will stand. If all spectators are standing, then it is best to remain standing. With spectator cooperation, the solution is for everyone to sit. The problem is that each spectator may be tempted to get a better view by standing. The cooperative solution will not be attained, therefore, without an outright agreement on coordination—in this situation, everyone remains seated.

Consider the following economic example. Suppose the world consists of just two nations, Germany and Japan. Although these nations freely trade goods with each other, they desire to pursue their own domestic economic priorities. Germany wants to avoid trade deficits with Japan, while achieving full employment for its economy; Japan desires full employment for its economy, while avoiding trade deficits with Germany. Assume that both nations achieve balanced trade with each other, but each nation's economy operates below full employment. Germany and Japan contemplate enacting expansionary government spending policies that would stimulate demand, output, and employment. But each nation rejects the idea, recognizing the policy's adverse impact on the trade balance. Germany and Japan realize that bolstering domestic income to increase jobs has the side effect of stimulating the demand for imports, thus pushing the trade account into deficit.

The preceding situation is *favorable* for successful policy coordination. If Germany and Japan agree to simultaneously expand their government spending, then output, employment, and incomes will rise concurrently. While higher German income promotes increased imports from Japan, higher Japanese income promotes increased imports from Germany. An appropriate increase in government spending results in each nation's increased demand for imports being offset by an increased demand for exports, which leads to balanced trade between Germany and Japan. In our example of mutual implementation of expansionary fiscal policies, policy coordination permits each nation to achieve full employment and balanced trade.

This is an optimistic portrayal of international economic-policy coordination. The synchronization of policies appears simple because there are only two economies and two objectives. In the real world, however, policy coordination generally involves many countries and many diverse objectives, such as low inflation, high employment, economic growth, and trade balance.

If the benefits of international economic-policy coordination are really so obvious, it may seem odd that agreements do not occur more often than they do. Several obstacles hinder successful policy coordination. Even if national economic objectives are harmonious, there is no guarantee that governments can design and implement coordinated policies. Policy makers in the real world do not always have sufficient information to understand the nature of the economic problem or how their policies will affect economies. Implementing appropriate policies when governments disagree about economic fundamentals is difficult.

Policy coordination is also complicated by different national starting points:[4]

[3]See S. Fischer, "International Macroeconomic Policy Coordination," in M. Feldstein, *International Economic Cooperation* (Chicago: University of Chicago Press, 1988), p. 19.

[4]See R. Putnam and C. R. Henning, "The Bonn Summit of 1978: A Case Study in Coordination," in R. Cooper et al., *Can Nations Agree?* (Washington, DC: The Brookings Institution, 1989), p. 17.

Different economic objectives. Some nations give higher priority to price stability, for instance, or to full employment, than others.

Different national institutions. Some nations have a stronger legislature, or weaker trade unions, than others.

Different national political climates. The party pendulums in different nations, for example, shift with elections occurring in different years.

Different phases in the business cycle. One nation may experience economic recession while another nation experiences rapid inflation.

Although the theoretical advantages of international economic-policy coordination are fairly clearly established, attempts to quantify their gains are rare. Skeptics point out that in practice, the gains from policy coordination are smaller than what is often suggested. Let us consider some examples of international economic-policy coordination.

Does Policy Coordination Work?

Does coordination of economic policies improve the performance of nations? Proponents of policy coordination cite the examples of the Plaza Agreement of 1985 and the Louvre Accord of 1987.

By early 1984, the U.S. economy was recovering from the recession of 1981–1983; domestic output was rising and unemployment was falling. While an expansionary fiscal policy contributed to economic recovery, growing U.S. government budget deficits were causing concern about the stability of the world financial system. Equally problematic was the appreciation in the dollar's exchange value, which encouraged U.S. consumers to purchase cheaper imports, and resulted in large U.S. current account deficits. By 1985, it was estimated that the dollar was overvalued by about 30 to 35 percent. As the U.S. recovery slowed, protectionist pressures skyrocketed in the U.S. Congress.

Fearing a disaster in the world trading system, government officials of the **Group of Five (G-5)** nations—the United States, Japan, Germany, Great Britain, and France—met at New York's Plaza Hotel in 1985. There was widespread agreement

that the dollar was overvalued and that the twin U.S. deficits (trade and federal budget) were too large. Each country made specific pledges on economic policy: The United States promised to reduce the federal deficit, Japan pledged a more expansionary monetary policy and a host of financial-sector reforms, and Germany offered tax reductions. All countries agreed to intervene in currency markets as needed to shove the dollar downward. Although not all the pledges were fully honored, especially the United States on deficit reduction, the plan turned out to be successful. By 1988, the dollar had fallen by 54 percent against the currencies of Germany and Japan from its peak of 1985.

However, the sharp decline in the dollar's exchange value set off a new concern, an uncontrolled dollar plunge. So in 1987 another round of policy coordination occurred to stabilize the dollar. At the Louvre Accord, specific policy promises were made: the United States to adopt a restrictive fiscal policy and Japan to ease monetary policy. Meanwhile, the current-account deficit of the United States began to decline, aided by the large depreciation of the dollar and even more by relatively faster economic growth overseas. In the late 1980s, domestic demand slowed in the United States but remained strong in Japan and Germany. In 1990, the current-account deficit of the United States was down to 1 percent of GDP and a year later, after a modest recession, it was in surplus.

Although the episodes of the Plaza Agreement and Louvre Accord point to the success of policy coordination, by the early 2000s government officials were showing less enthusiasm for policy coordination. They felt that coordinating policy had become much more difficult because of the way policy is made, especially given the rise of independent central banks. Back in the 1980s, the governments of Japan and Germany could dictate what their central banks would do. Now, the Bank of Japan and the European Central Bank maintain their independence and see themselves as protectors of discipline against high-spending government officials. That makes domestic fiscal and monetary coordination difficult, and international efforts to coordinate policies even more difficult. Also, the huge growth in global financial markets has made currency intervention much less effective. Today, more than $1 trillion in foreign exchange crosses borders every day, up from $200 billion in 1985. Economists generally think that official currency intervention works at best at the margin, and then only if it is used to reinforce existing economic trends. Moreover, major changes in the structure of U.S. trade patterns mean that more countries would have to be involved in any adjustment process. During the 1980s, Japan accounted for 16 percent of U.S. trade; today, that share is about 9 percent. Meanwhile, Mexico, China, and other Asian coun-tries have become much more important trading partners. Generally speaking, the more nations involved in policy coordination, the more difficult it is to achieve. Finally, the sluggish economies of Japan and Germany in the early 2000s prevented them from being engines of economic growth for the world, while Asian countries refused to allow their currencies to appreciate against the dollar. That made the prospects of policy coordination much dimmer than they were earlier.

Summary

1. International economic policy refers to various government activities that influence trade pat-terns among nations, including (a) monetary and fiscal policies, (b) exchange-rate adjust-ments, (c) tariff and nontariff trade barriers, (d) foreign-exchange controls and investment controls, and (e) export-promotion measures.

2. Since the 1930s, nations have actively pur-sued internal balance (full employment without inflation) as a primary economic objective. Nations also consider external balance (balance-of-payments equilibrium) as an economic objective. A nation realizes overall balance when it attains internal bal-ance and external balance.

3. To achieve overall balance, nations implement expenditure-changing policies (monetary and fiscal policies), expenditure-switching policies (exchange-rate adjustments), and direct con-trols (price and wage controls).

4. Although exchange-rate adjustments primari-ly influence a nation's BOP position, they have secondary impacts on the domestic economy. A nation with a BOP deficit and high unemployment could devalue its curren-cy to resolve these problems; a nation with a BOP surplus and inflation could revalue its currency. Such policies are dependent upon the willingness of other nations to refrain from implementing offsetting exchange-rate adjustments. International economic-policy cooperation is thus essential when nations are economically interdependent.

5. Under a fixed exchange-rate system, fiscal pol-icy is successful in promoting internal balance, whereas monetary policy is unsuccessful. Under a floating exchange-rate system, mone-tary policy is successful in promoting internal balance, whereas fiscal policy is unsuccessful.

6. Given a fixed exchange-rate system, in the short run, an expansionary monetary policy worsens the BOP position, and a contrac-tionary monetary policy improves the BOP position. An expansionary fiscal policy leads to a worsening of the trade account and an improvement in the capital account; the impact on the overall BOP depends on the relative strength of these opposing forces.

7. Policy agreement occurs when an economic pol-icy helps eliminate internal disequilibrium and external disequilibrium, thus promoting overall balance for the nation. Policy conflict occurs when an economic policy helps eliminate one economic problem (such as internal disequilib-rium), but aggravates another economic prob-lem (such as external disequilibrium).

8. Given a fixed exchange-rate system, for mon-etary policy the disequilibrium zones of unem-ployment-with-BOP-surplus and inflation-with-BOP-deficit are zones of policy agreement. The disequilibrium zones of unemployment-with-BOP-deficit and inflation-with-BOP-sur-plus are zones of policy conflict; a dilemma exists for monetary authorities concerning which objective to pursue. A combination of policies may be needed to resolve these eco-nomic problems.

9. When a nation experiences inflation with unemployment, achieving overall balance involves three separate targets: BOP equilibrium, full employment, and price stability. Three policy instruments may be needed to achieve these targets.

10. International economic-policy coordination is the attempt to significantly modify national policies in recognition of international economic interdependence. Nations regularly consult with each other in the context of the IMF, OECD, Bank for International Settlements,

and Group of Seven. The Plaza Agreement and Louvre Accord are examples of international economic-policy coordination.

11. Several problems confront international economic-policy coordination: (a) different national economic objectives, (b) different national institutions, (c) different national political climates, (d) different phases in the business cycle. Moreover, there is no guarantee that governments can design and implement policies that are capable of achieving the intended results.

Key Concepts and Terms

- Bank for International Settlements (BIS) *(page 484)*
- Demand-pull inflation *(page 483)*
- Direct controls *(page 475)*
- Expenditure-changing policies *(page 475)*
- Expenditure-switching policies *(page 475)*
- External balance *(page 475)*
- Fiscal policy *(page 475)*
- Group of Five (G-5) *(page 486)*
- Group of Seven (G-7) *(page 484)*
- Institutional constraints *(page 476)*
- Internal balance *(page 474)*
- International economic policy *(page 474)*
- International economic-policy coordination *(page 484)*
- Monetary policy *(page 475)*
- Operation Twist *(page 482)*
- Overall balance *(page 477)*
- Policy agreement *(page 482)*
- Policy conflict *(page 482)*
- Wage and price controls *(page 483)*

Study Questions

1. Distinguish among external balance, internal balance, and overall balance.
2. What are the most important instruments of international economic policy?
3. What is meant by the terms *expenditure-changing policy* and *expenditure-switching policy*? Give some examples of each.
4. What institutional constraints bear on the formation of economic policies?
5. Assume that a nation faces a BOP deficit with high unemployment. What exchange-rate adjustment can be made to resolve these problems? What if the nation experiences a BOP surplus with inflation?
6. Under a system of fixed exchange rates, is monetary policy or fiscal policy better suited for promoting internal balance? Why?
7. Under a system of floating exchange rates, is monetary policy or fiscal policy better suited for promoting internal balance? Why?
8. With fixed exchange rates, what impact does an expansionary monetary policy have on the nation's BOP? What about a contractionary monetary policy?
9. With fixed exchange rates, when does an expansionary fiscal policy improve the nation's BOP? When does it worsen the BOP?
10. What is meant by the terms *policy agreement* and *policy conflict*?
11. Given a system of fixed exchange rates, for monetary policy, is unemployment-with-BOP-surplus a zone of policy agreement or policy conflict? What about inflation-with-BOP-deficit, unemployment-with-BOP-deficit, or inflation-with-BOP-surplus?
12. What are some obstacles to successful international economic-policy coordination?

16.1 The Bank for International Settlements, founded in 1930, facilitates international policy coordination through its monthly meetings of central bank officials. Set your browser to this URL:

http://www.bis.org

16.2 The Organisation for Economic Cooperation and Development (OECD) is a Paris-based organization of 29 countries. Its goal is to develop compatible, wide-ranging policies that boost prosperity. Visit its Web page by setting your browser to this URL:

http://www.oecd.org

16.3 The National Bureau of Economic Research (NBER) provides online data and summaries of research studies relating to international finance, trade, and investment at its Web site. Set your browser to this URL:

http://www.nber.org

To access NetLink Exercises and the Virtual Scavenger Hunt, visit the Carbaugh Web site at http://carbaugh.swlearning.com.

Log onto the Carbaugh Xtra! Web site (http://carbaughxtra.swlearning.com) for additional learning resources such as practice quizzes, help with graphing, and current events applications.

chapter 17

International Banking: Reserves, Debt, and Risk

The world's banking system plays a vital role in facilitating international transactions and maintaining economic prosperity. Commercial banks, such as Citicorp, help finance trade and investment and provide loans to international borrowers. Central banks, such as the Federal Reserve, serve as a lender of last resort to commercial banks and sometimes intervene in foreign-currency markets to stabilize currency values. Finally, the International Monetary Fund (discussed in Chapter 7) serves as a lender to nations having deficits in their balance of payments. This chapter concentrates on the role that banks play in world financial markets, the risks associated with international banking, and strategies employed to deal with these risks.

We'll begin with an investigation of the nature of international reserves and their importance for the world financial system. This is followed by a discussion of banks as international lenders and the problems associated with international debt.

Nature of International Reserves

The need of a central bank, such as the Bank of England, for international reserves is similar to an individual's desire to hold cash balances (currency and checkable deposits). At both levels, monetary reserves are intended to bridge the gap between monetary receipts and monetary payments.

Suppose that an individual receives income in equal installments every minute of the day and that expenditures for goods and services are likewise evenly spaced over time. The individual will require only a minimum cash reserve to finance purchases, because no significant imbalances between cash receipts and cash disbursements will arise. In reality, however, individuals purchase goods and services on a fairly regular basis from day to day, but receive paychecks only at weekly or longer intervals. A certain amount of cash is therefore required to finance the discrepancy that arises between monetary receipts and payments.

When an individual initially receives a paycheck, cash balances are high. But as time progresses, these holdings of cash may fall to virtually zero just before the next paycheck is received. Individuals are thus concerned with the amount of cash balances that, on average, are necessary to keep them going until the next paycheck arrives.

Although individuals desire cash balances primarily to fill the gap between monetary receipts and payments, this desire is influenced by a number of other factors. The need for cash balances may become more acute if the absolute dollar volume of transactions increases, because larger imbalances may result between receipts and payments. Conversely, to the extent that individuals can finance their transactions on credit, they require less cash in hand.

Just as an individual desires to hold cash balances, national governments have a need for **international reserves**. The chief purpose of international reserves is to enable nations to finance disequilibrium in their balance-of-payments positions. When a nation finds its monetary receipts falling short of its monetary payments, the deficit is settled with international reserves. Eventually, the deficit must be eliminated, because central banks tend to have limited stocks of reserves.

From a policy perspective, the advantage of international reserves is that they enable nations to sustain *temporary* balance-of-payments deficits until acceptable adjustment measures can operate to correct the disequilibrium. Holdings of international reserves facilitate effective policy formation because corrective adjustment measures need not be implemented prematurely. Should a deficit nation possess abundant stocks of reserve balances, however, it may be able to resist unpopular adjustment measures, making eventual adjustments even more troublesome.

Demand for International Reserves

When a nation's international monetary payments exceed its international monetary receipts, some means of settlement is required to finance its payments deficit. Settlement ultimately consists of transfers of international reserves among nations. Both the magnitude and the longevity of a balance-of-payments deficit that can be sustained in the absence of equilibrating adjustments are limited by a nation's stock of international reserves.

On a global basis, the **demand for international reserves** depends on two related factors: (1) the monetary value of international transactions and

(2) the disequilibrium that can arise in balance-of-payments positions. The demand for international reserves is also contingent on such things as the speed and strength of the balance-of-payments adjustment mechanism and the overall institutional framework of the world economy.

Exchange-Rate Flexibility

One determinant of the demand for international reserves is the *degree of exchange-rate flexibility* of the international monetary system. This is because exchange-rate flexibility in part underlies the efficiency of the balance-of-payments adjustment process.

Figure 17.1 on page 492 represents the exchange-market position of the United States in trade with Great Britain. Starting at equilibrium point E, suppose that an increase in imports increases the U.S. demand for pounds from D_0 to D_1. The prevailing exchange-rate system will determine the quantity of international reserves needed to bridge the gap between the number of pounds demanded and the number supplied.

If exchange rates are fixed or pegged by the monetary authorities, international reserves play a crucial role in the exchange-rate stabilization process. In Figure 17.1, suppose the exchange rate is pegged at $2 per pound. Given a rise in the demand for pounds from D_0 to D_1, the United States would face an excess demand for pounds equal to £100 at the pegged rate. If the U.S. dollar is not to depreciate beyond the pegged rate, the monetary authorities—that is, the Federal Reserve—must enter the market to supply pounds, in exchange for dollars, in the amount necessary to eliminate the disequilibrium. In the figure, the pegged rate of $2 per pound can be maintained if the monetary authorities supply £100 on the market. Coupled with the existing supply schedule S_0, the added supply will result in a new supply schedule at S_1. Market equilibrium is restored at the pegged rate.

Rather than operating under a rigidly pegged system, suppose a nation makes an agreement to foster some automatic adjustments by allowing market rates to float within a narrow band around the official exchange rate. This limited exchange-rate flexibility would be aimed at correcting minor

FIGURE 17.1

The Demand for International Reserves and Exchange-Rate Flexibility

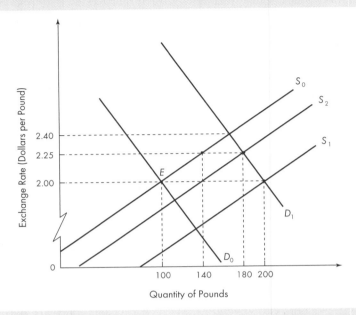

When exchange rates are fixed (pegged) by monetary authorities, international reserves are necessary for the financing of payments imbalances and the stabilization of exchange rates. With floating exchange rates, payments imbalances tend to be corrected by market-induced fluctuations in the exchange rate; the need for exchange-rate stabilization and international reserves disappears.

payments imbalances, whereas large and persistent disequilibrium would require other adjustment measures.

Referring to Figure 17.1, assume that the U.S. official exchange rate is $2 per pound, but with a band of permissible exchange-rate fluctuations whose upper limit is set at $2.25 per pound. Given a rise in the U.S. demand for pounds, the value of the dollar will begin to decline. Once the exchange rate depreciates to $2.25 per pound, domestic monetary authorities will need to supply £40 on the market to defend the band's outer limit. This will have the effect of shifting the market supply schedule from S_0 to S_2. Under a system of limited exchange-rate flexibility, then, movements in the exchange rate serve to reduce the

payments disequilibrium. Smaller amounts of international reserves are required for exchange-rate stabilization purposes under this system than if exchange rates are rigidly fixed.

A fundamental purpose of international reserves is to facilitate government intervention in exchange markets to stabilize currency values. The more active a government's stabilization activities, the greater is the need for reserves. Most exchange-rate standards today involve some stabilization operations and require international reserves. However, if exchange rates were allowed to float freely without government interference, theoretically there would be no need for reserves. This is because a floating rate would serve to eliminate an incipient payments imbalance, negating the need for stabilization operations. Referring again to Figure 17.1, suppose the exchange market is initially in equilibrium at a rate of $2 per pound. Given an increase in the demand for foreign exchange from D_0 to D_1, the home currency would begin to depreciate. It would continue to weaken until it reached an exchange value of $2.50 per pound, at which point market equilibrium would be restored. The need for international reserves would thus be nonexistent under freely floating rates.

Other Determinants

The lesson of the previous section is that changes in the degree of exchange-rate flexibility are inversely related to changes in the quantity of international reserves demanded. In other words, a monetary system characterized by more rapid and flexible exchange-rate adjustments requires smaller reserves, and vice versa.

In addition to the degree of exchange-rate flexibility, several other factors underlie the demand for international reserves, including (1) automatic adjustment mechanisms that respond to payments disequilibrium, (2) economic policies used to bring about payments equilibrium, and (3) the international coordination of economic policies.

Our earlier analysis has shown that adjustment mechanisms involving prices, interest rates, incomes, and monetary flows automatically tend to correct balance-of-payments disequilibrium. A payments deficit or surplus initiates changes in each of these variables. The more efficient each of these adjustment mechanisms is, the smaller and more short-lived market imbalances will be and the fewer reserves will be needed. The demand for international reserves therefore tends to be smaller with speedier and more complete automatic adjustment mechanisms.

The demand for international reserves is also influenced by the choice and effectiveness of government policies adopted to correct payments imbalances. Unlike automatic adjustment mechanisms, which rely on the free market to identify industries and labor groups that must bear the adjustment burden, the use of government policies involves political decisions. All else being equal, the greater a nation's propensity to apply commercial policies (including tariffs, quotas, and subsidies) to key sectors, the less will be its need for international reserves. This assumes, of course, that the policies are effective in reducing payments disequilibrium. Because of uncertainties about the nature and timing of payments disturbances, however, nations are often slow to initiate such trade policies and find themselves requiring international reserves to weather periods of payments disequilibrium.

The international coordination of economic policies is another determinant of the demand for international reserves. A primary goal of economic cooperation among finance ministers is to reduce the frequency and extent of payments imbalances and hence the demand for international reserves. Since the end of World War II, nations have moved toward the harmonization of national economic objectives by establishing programs through such organizations as the IMF Fund and the Organisation for Economic Cooperation and Development. Another example of international economic organization has been the European Union, whose goal is to achieve a common macroeconomic policy and full monetary union. By reducing the intensity of disturbances to payments balance, such policy coordination reduces the need for international reserves.

Other factors influence the demand for international reserves. The quantity demanded is positively related to the level of world prices and income. One would expect rising price levels to inflate the market value of international transactions and, therefore, to increase the potential demand for reserves. The need for reserves would also tend to rise with the level of global income and trade activity.

In summary, central banks need international reserves to cover possible or expected excess payments to other nations at some future time. The quantity of international reserves demanded is directly related to the size and duration of these payment gaps. If a nation with a payments deficit is willing and able to initiate quick actions to increase receipts or decrease payments, the amount of reserves needed will be relatively small. Conversely, the demand for reserves will be relatively large if nations initiate no actions to correct payments imbalances or adopt policies that prolong such disequilibrium.

Supply of International Reserves

The analysis so far has emphasized the demand for international reserves. But what about the **supply of international reserves?**

The total supply of international reserves consists of two distinct categories: *owned reserves* and *borrowed reserves*. Reserve assets such as gold, acceptable foreign currencies, and SDRs are generally considered to be directly owned by the holding nations. But if nations with payments deficits find their stocks of owned reserves falling to unacceptably low levels, they may be able to borrow international reserves as a cushioning device. Lenders may be foreign nations with excess reserves, foreign financial institutions, or international agencies such as the IMF.

Foreign Currencies

International reserves are a means of payment used in financing foreign transactions. One such asset is holdings of *national currencies* (foreign exchange). As seen in Table 17.1, the largest share of international reserves today consists of holdings of national currencies.

Over the course of the 1800s–1900s, two national currencies in particular have gained promi-

---

TABLE 17.1

International Reserves, 2003, All Countries (in Billions of SDRs*)

Item	Amount	Percentage
Foreign exchange	1,974.1	94.1%
IMF reserve positions	71.0	3.4
Gold**	32.4	1.5
SDRs	20.3	1.0
Total	2,097.8	100.0%

*For 2003, 1 SDR = $1.43.

**At 35 SDRs per ounce.

Source: International Monetary Fund, *International Financial Statistics*, May 2004.

---

nence as means of financing international transactions. These currencies, the U.S. dollar and the British pound, have been considered *reserve currencies* (or *key currencies*), because trading nations have traditionally been willing to hold them as international reserve assets. Since World War II, the U.S. dollar has been the dominant reserve currency. Other reserve currencies are the Japanese yen and a few other currencies that are acceptable in payment for international transactions.

The role of the pound as a reserve currency is largely due to circumstances of the late 1800s and early 1900s. Not only did Britain at that time play a dominant role in world trade, but the efficiency of London as an international money market was also widely recognized. This was the golden age of the gold standard, and the pound was freely convertible into gold. Traders and investors felt confident financing their transactions with pounds. With the demise of the gold standard and the onset of the Great Depression during the 1930s, Britain's commercial and financial status began to deteriorate, and the pound lost some of its international luster. Today, the pound still serves as an important international reserve asset, but it is no longer the most prestigious reserve currency.

The emergence of the U.S. dollar as a reserve currency stems from a different set of circumstances. Emerging from World War II, the U.S. economy was not only unharmed but actually stronger. Because of the vast inflows of gold into the United States during the 1930s and 1940s, the dollar was in a better position than the pound to assume the role of a reserve currency.

The mechanism that supplied the world with dollar balances was the balance-of-payments deficits of the United States. These deficits stemmed largely from U.S. foreign aid granted to Europe immediately after World War II, as well as from the flow of private investment funds abroad from U.S. residents. The early 1950s were characterized as a *dollar-shortage era*, when the massive development programs of the European nations resulted in an excess demand for the dollars used to finance such efforts. As the United States began to run modest payments deficits during the early 1950s, the dollar outflow was appreciated by the recipient nations.

By the late 1950s, the U.S. payments deficits had become larger. As foreign nations began to accumulate larger dollar balances than they were accustomed to, the dollar-shortage era gave way to a *dollar glut*. Throughout the 1960s, the United States continued to provide reserves to the world through its payments deficits. However, the persistently weak position of the U.S. balance of payments increasingly led foreigners to question the soundness of the dollar as a reserve currency. By 1970, the amount of dollar liabilities in the hands of foreigners was several times as large as U.S. reserve assets. Lack of confidence in the soundness of the dollar inspired several European nations to exercise their rights to demand that the U.S. Treasury convert their dollar holdings into gold, which in turn led the United States to suspend its gold convertibility pledge to the rest of the world in 1971.

Using the dollar as a reserve currency meant that the supply of international reserves varied with the payments position of the United States. During the 1960s, this situation gave rise to the so-called **liquidity problem**. To preserve confidence in the dollar as a reserve currency, the United States had to strengthen its payments position by eliminating its deficits. But correction of the U.S. deficits would mean elimination of additional dollars as a source of reserves for the international monetary system. The creation in 1970 of SDRs as reserve assets and their subsequent allocations have been intended as a solution for this problem.

Gold

The historical importance of gold as an international reserve asset should not be underemphasized. At one time, gold served as the key monetary asset of the international payments mechanism; it also constituted the basis of the money supplies of many nations.

As an international money, gold fulfilled several important functions. Under the historic **gold standard**, gold served directly as an international means of payments. It also provided a unit of account against which commodity prices as well as the parities of national currencies were quoted. Although

gold holdings do not yield interest income, gold has generally served as a viable store of value despite inflation, wars, and revolutions. Perhaps the greatest advantage of gold as a monetary asset is its overall acceptability, especially when compared with other forms of international monies.

Today, the role of gold as an international reserve asset has declined. Over the past 30 years, gold has fallen from nearly 70 percent to less than 3 percent of world reserves. Private individuals rarely use gold as a medium of payment and virtually never as a unit of account. Nor do central banks currently use gold as an official unit of account for stating the parities of national currencies. The monetary role of gold is currently recognized by only a few nations, mostly in the Middle East. In most nations outside the United States, private residents have long been able to buy and sell gold as they would any other commodity. On December 31, 1974, the U.S. government revoked a 41-year ban on U.S. citizens' ownership of gold. The monetary role of gold today is only that of a glittering ghost haunting efforts to reform the international monetary system.

International Gold Standard

Under the international gold standard, whose golden age was about 1880 to 1914, the values of most national currencies were anchored in gold. Gold coins circulated within these countries as well as across national boundaries as generally accepted means of payment. Monetary authorities were concerned about maintaining the public's confidence in the paper currencies that supplemented gold's role as money. To maintain the integrity of paper currencies, governments agreed to convert them into gold at a fixed rate. This requirement was supposed to prevent monetary authorities from producing excessive amounts of paper money. The so-called *discipline* of the gold standard was achieved by having the money supply bear a fixed relation to the monetary stock of gold. Given the cost of producing gold relative to the cost of other commodities, a monetary price of gold could be established to produce growth in monetary gold—and thus in the money supply—at a rate that corresponded to the growth in real national output.

Over the course of the gold standard's era, the importance of gold began to decline, whereas both paper money and demand deposits showed marked increases. From 1815 to 1913, gold as a share of the aggregate money supply of the United States, France, and Britain fell from about 33 percent to 10 percent. At the same time, the proportion of bank deposits skyrocketed from a modest 6 percent to about 68 percent. By 1913, paper monies plus demand deposits accounted for approximately 90 percent of the U.S. money supply.

After World War I, popular sentiment favored a return to the discipline of the gold standard, in part because of the inflation that gripped many economies during the war years. The United States was the first to return to the gold standard, followed by several European nations. Efforts to restore the prewar gold standard, however, ended in complete collapse during the 1930s. In response to the economic strains of the Great Depression, nations one by one announced that they could no longer maintain the gold standard.

In the United States, the Great Depression brought an important modification of the gold standard. In 1934, the Gold Reserve Act gave the U.S. government title to all monetary gold and required citizens to turn in their private holdings to the U.S. Treasury. This was done to end the pressure on U.S. commercial banks to convert their liabilities into gold. The U.S. dollar was also devalued in 1934, when the official price of gold was raised from $20.67 to $35 per ounce. The dollar devaluation was not specifically aimed at defending the U.S. trade balance. The rationale was that a rise in the domestic price of gold would encourage gold production, adding to the money supply and the level of economic activity. The Great Depression would be solved! In retrospect, the devaluation may have had some minor economic effects, but there is no indication that it did anything to lift the economy out of its depressed condition.

Gold Exchange Standard

Emerging from the discussions among the world powers during World War II was a new international monetary organization, the International Monetary Fund (IMF). A main objective of the IMF was to reestablish a system of fixed exchange rates, with gold serving as the primary reserve asset. Gold became an international unit of account when member nations officially agreed to state the par values of their currencies in terms of gold or, alternatively, the gold content of the U.S. dollar.

The post–World War II international monetary system as formulated by the fund nations was nominally a **gold exchange standard**. The idea was to economize on monetary gold stocks as international reserves, because they could not expand as fast as international trade was growing. This required the United States, which emerged from the war with a dominant economy in terms of productive capacity and national wealth, to assume the role of world banker. The dollar was to become the chief reserve currency of the international monetary system. The coexistence of both dollars and gold as international reserve assets led to this system's being dubbed the *dollar-gold system*.

As a world banker, the United States assumed responsibility for buying and selling gold at a fixed price to foreign official holders of dollars. The dollar was the only currency that was made convertible into gold; other national currencies were pegged to the dollar. The dollar was therefore regarded as a reserve currency that was as good as gold because it was thought that the dollar would retain its value relative to other currencies and remain convertible into gold.

As long as the monetary gold stocks of the United States were large relative to outstanding dollar liabilities abroad, confidence in the dollar as a viable reserve currency remained intact. Immediately following World War II, the U.S. monetary gold stocks peaked at $24 billion, about two-thirds of the world total. But as time passed, the amount of foreign dollar holdings rose significantly because of the U.S. payments deficits, whereas the U.S. monetary gold stock dwindled as some of the dollars were turned back to the U.S. Treasury for gold. By 1965, the total supply of foreign-held dollars exceeded the U.S. stock of monetary gold. With the United States unable to redeem all outstanding dollars for gold at $35 per ounce, its ability as a world banker to deliver on demand was questioned.

These circumstances led to speculation that the United States might attempt to solve its gold-shortage problem by devaluing the dollar. By increasing the official price of gold, a dollar devaluation would lead to a rise in the value of U.S. monetary gold stocks. To prevent speculative profits from any rise in the official price of gold, the United States along with several other nations in 1968 established a *two-tier gold system*. This consisted of an *official tier*, in which central banks could buy and sell gold for monetary purposes at the official price of $35 per ounce, and a *private market*, where gold as a commodity could be traded at the free-market price. By separating the official gold market from the private gold market, the two-tier system was a step toward the complete demonetization of gold.

Demonetization of Gold

The formation of the two-tier gold system was a remedy that could only delay the inevitable collapse of the gold exchange standard. By 1971, the U.S. stock of monetary gold had declined to $11 billion, only a fraction of U.S. dollar liabilities to foreign central banks. The U.S. balance-of-payments position was also deteriorating. In August 1971, U.S. President Richard Nixon announced that the United States was suspending its commitment to buy and sell gold at $35 per ounce. The closing of the gold window to foreign official holders brought an end to the gold exchange standard, and the last functional link between the dollar and monetary gold was severed.

It took several years for the world's monetary authorities to formalize the **demonetization of gold** as an international reserve asset. On January 1, 1975, the official price of gold was abolished as the unit of account for the international monetary system. National monetary authorities could enter into gold transactions at market-determined prices, and the use of gold was terminated by the IMF. It was agreed that one-sixth of the fund's gold would be auctioned at prevailing prices and the profits distributed to the less-developed nations.

As for the United States, the 41-year ban on gold ownership for U.S. residents was ended on January 1, 1975. Within a few weeks, the U.S. Treasury was auctioning a portion of its gold on the commodity markets. These actions were a signal by the United States that it would treat gold in the same way it treats any other commodity.

Special Drawing Rights

The liquidity and confidence problems of the gold exchange standard that resulted from reliance on the dollar and gold as international monies led in 1970 to the creation by the IMF of a new reserve asset, termed **special drawing rights (SDRs)**. The objective was to introduce into the payments mechanism a *new* reserve asset, in addition to the dollar and gold, that could be transferred among participating nations in settlement of payments deficits. With the IMF managing the stock of SDRs, world reserves would presumably grow in line with world commerce.

SDRs are unconditional rights to draw currencies of other nations. When the fund creates a certain number of SDRs, they are allocated to the member nations in proportion to the relative size of their fund quotas. Nations can then draw on their SDR balances in financing their payments deficits. The key point is that certain surplus nations are designated by the fund to trade their currencies for an equivalent amount in SDRs to deficit nations in need of foreign-exchange reserves. Nations whose currencies are acquired as foreign exchange are not required to accept more than three times their initial SDR allotments.

SDRs pay interest to surplus nations on their net holdings (the amount by which a nation's SDR balance exceeds its allocation as determined by its fund quota). Interest payments come from deficit nations that draw their SDR balances below their original allotments. The SDR interest rate is adjusted periodically in line with the short-term interest rates in world money markets. It is reviewed quarterly and adjusted on the basis of a formula that takes into account the short-term interest rates of the United States, the United Kingdom, Germany, France, and Japan.

When the SDR was initially adopted, it was agreed that its value should be maintained at a fixed tie to the U.S. dollar's par value, which was then expressed in terms of gold. The value of the SDR was originally set at US$1. After several monetary developments, this linkage became unacceptable. With the suspension of U.S. gold convertibility in 1971, it was doubted whether the gold value of the dollar should serve as the official unit of account for international transactions. The United States was making it known that it wished to phase out gold as an international monetary instrument. Furthermore, the dollar's exchange rate against gold fell twice as the result of U.S. devaluations in 1971 and 1973. Finally, under the system of managed floating exchange rates, adopted by the industrialized nations in 1973, it became possible for the SDR's value to fluctuate against other currencies while still bearing a fixed tie to the dollar's value. In view of these problems, in 1974, a new method of SDR valuation was initiated—the **basket valuation.**

Basket valuation is intended to provide stability for the SDR's value under a system of fluctuating exchange rates, making the SDR more attractive as an international reserve asset. The SDR is called a basket currency because it is based on the value of four currencies: the U.S. dollar, European euro, Japanese yen, and British pound. An appreciation, or increase in value, of any one currency in the basket in terms of all other currencies will raise the value of the SDR in terms of each of the other currencies. Conversely, a depreciation, or decline in value, of any one currency will lower the value of the SDR in terms of each other currency. Because the movements of some currencies can be offset or moderated by the movements of other currencies, the value of the SDR in terms of a group of currencies is likely to be relatively stable.

Besides helping nations finance balance-of-payments deficits, SDRs have a number of other uses. Some of the fund's member nations peg their currency values to the SDR. The SDR is the unit of account for IMF transactions and is used as a unit of account for individuals (such as exporters, importers, or investors) who desire protection against the risk of fluctuating exchange rates.

Facilities for Borrowing Reserves

The discussion so far has considered the different types of *owned reserves*—national currencies, gold, and SDRs. Various facilities for *borrowing reserves* have also been implemented for nations with weak balance-of-payments positions. Borrowed reserves do not eliminate the need for owned reserves, but they do add to the flexibility of the international monetary system by increasing the time available for nations to correct payments disequilibrium. Let's examine the major forms of international credit.

IMF Drawings

One of the original purposes of the IMF was to help member nations finance balance-of-payments deficits. The fund has furnished a pool of revolving credit for nations in need of reserves. Temporary loans of foreign currency are made to deficit nations, which are expected to repay them within a stipulated time. The transactions by which the fund makes foreign-currency loans available are called **IMF drawings.**

Deficit nations do not borrow from the fund. Instead, they purchase with their own currency the foreign currency required to help finance deficits. When the nation's balance-of-payments position improves, it is expected to reverse the transaction and make repayment by repurchasing its currency from the fund. The fund currently allows members to purchase other currencies at their own option up to the first 50 percent of their fund quotas, which are based on the nation's economic size. Special permission must be granted by the fund if a nation is to purchase foreign currencies in excess of this figure. The fund extends such permission once it is convinced that the deficit nation has enacted reasonable measures to restore payments equilibrium.

Since the early 1950s, the fund has also fostered liberal exchange-rate policies by entering into *standby arrangements* with interested member nations. These agreements guarantee that a member nation may draw specified amounts of foreign currencies from the fund over given time periods. The advantage is that participating nations can count on credit from the fund should it be needed. It also saves the drawing nation from administrative time delays when the loans are actually made.

General Arrangements to Borrow

During the early 1960s, the question was raised whether the IMF had sufficient amounts of foreign currencies to meet the exchange-stabilization needs of its deficit member nations. Owing to the possibility that large drawings by major nations might exhaust the fund's stocks of foreign currencies, the **General Arrangements to Borrow** were initiated in 1962. Ten leading industrial nations, called the Group of Ten, originally agreed to lend the fund up to a maximum of $6 billion. In 1964, the Group of Ten expanded when Switzerland joined the group. By serving as an intermediary and guarantor, the fund could use these reserves to offer compensatory financial assistance to one or more of the participating nations. Such credit arrangements were expected to be used only when the deficit nation's borrowing needs exceeded the amount of assistance that could be provided under the fund's own drawing facilities.

The General Arrangements to Borrow do *not* provide a permanent increase in the supply of world reserves once the loans are repaid and world reserves revert back to their original levels. However, these arrangements have made world reserves more flexible and adaptable to the needs of deficit nations.

Swap Arrangements

During the early 1960s, there occurred a wave of speculative attacks against the U.S. dollar, based on expectations that it would be devalued in terms of other currencies. To help offset the flow of short-term capital out of the dollar into stronger foreign currencies, the U.S. Federal Reserve agreed with several central banks in 1962 to initiate reciprocal currency arrangements, commonly referred to as **swap arrangements**. Today, the swap network on which the United States depends to finance its interventions in the foreign-exchange market includes the central banks of Canada and Mexico.[1]

Swap arrangements are bilateral agreements between central banks. Each government provides for an exchange, or swap, of currencies to help finance temporary payments disequilibrium. If Mexico, for example, is short of dollars, it can ask the Federal Reserve to supply them in exchange for pesos. A drawing on the swap network is usually initiated by telephone, followed by an exchange of wire messages specifying terms and conditions. The actual swap is in the form of a foreign-exchange contract calling for the sale of dollars by the Federal Reserve for the currency of a foreign central bank. The nation requesting the swap is expected to use the funds to help ease its payments deficits and discourage speculative capital outflows. Swaps are to be repaid (reversed) within a stipulated period of time, normally within 3 to 12 months.

Visit EconDebate Online for a debate on this topic

International Lending Risk

In many respects, the principles that apply to international lending are similar to those of domestic lending: The lender needs to determine the credit risk that the borrower will default. When making international loans, however, bankers face two additional risks: country risk and currency risk.

Credit risk is financial and refers to the probability that part or all of the interest or principal of a loan will not be repaid. The larger the potential for default on a loan, the higher the interest rate that the bank must charge the borrower.

Assessing credit risk on international loans tends to be more difficult than on domestic loans. U.S. banks are often less familiar with foreign business practices and economic conditions than those in the United States. Obtaining reliable information to evaluate foreign credit risk can be

---

[1]Because of the formation of the European Central Bank and in light of 15 years of disuse, the bilateral swap arrangements of the Federal Reserve with many European central banks, such as Austria, Germany, and Belgium, were jointly deemed no longer necessary in view of the well-established, present-day arrangements for international monetary cooperation. Accordingly, the respective parties to the arrangements mutually agreed to allow them to lapse in 1998.

time-consuming and costly. Many U.S. banks, therefore, confine their international lending to major multinational corporations and financial institutions. To attract lending by U.S. banks, a foreign government may provide assurances against default by a local private borrower, thus reducing the credit risk of the loan.

Country risk is political and is closely related to political developments in a country, especially the government's views concerning international investments and loans. Some governments encourage the inflow of foreign funds to foster domestic economic development. Fearing loss of national sovereignty, other governments may discourage such inflows by enacting additional taxes, profit restrictions, and wage/price controls that can hinder the ability of local borrowers to repay loans. In the extreme, foreign governments can expropriate the assets of foreign investors or make foreign loan repayments illegal.

Currency risk is economic and is associated with currency depreciations and appreciations as well as exchange controls. Some loans of U.S. banks are denominated in foreign currency instead of dollars. If the currency in which the loan is made depreciates against the dollar during the period of the loan, the repayment will be worth fewer dollars. If the foreign currency has a well-developed forward market, the loan may be hedged. But many foreign currencies, especially of the developing nations, do not have such markets, and loans denominated in these currencies cannot always be hedged to decrease this type of currency risk. Another type of currency risk arises from exchange controls, which are common in developing nations. Exchange controls restrict the movement of funds across national borders or limit a currency's convertibility into dollars for repayment, thus adding to the risk of international lenders.

When lending overseas, bankers must evaluate credit risk, country risk, and currency risk. Evaluating risks in foreign lending often results in detailed analyses, compiled by a bank's research department, that are based on a nation's financial, economic, and political conditions. When international lenders consider detailed analyses too expensive, they often use reports and statistical indicators to help them determine the risk of lending.

The Problem of International Debt

Much concern has been voiced over the volume of international lending in recent years. At times, the concern has been that international lending was insufficient. Such was the case after the oil shocks in 1974–1975 and 1979–1980, when it was feared that some oil-importing developing nations might not be able to obtain loans to finance trade deficits resulting from the huge increases in the price of oil. It so happened that many oil-importing nations were able to borrow dollars from commercial banks. They paid the dollars to OPEC nations, who redeposited the money in commercial banks, which then re-lent the money to oil importers, and so on. In the 1970s, the banks were part of the solution; if they had not lent large sums to the developing nations, the oil shocks would have done far more damage to the world economy.

By the 1980s, however, commercial banks were viewed as part of an international debt problem because they had lent so much to developing nations. Flush with OPEC money after the oil price increases of the 1970s, the banks actively sought borrowers and had no trouble finding them among the developing nations. Some nations borrowed to prop up consumption because their living standards were already low and hit hard by oil-price hikes. Most nations borrowed to avoid cuts in development programs and to invest in energy projects. It was generally recognized that banks were successful in recycling their OPEC deposits to developing nations following the first round of oil-price hikes in 1974 and 1975. But the international lending mechanism encountered increasing difficulties beginning with the global recession of the early 1980s. In particular, some developing nations were unable to pay their external debts on schedule.

Table 17.2 summarizes the magnitude of the international debt problem of the developing nations. As of 1997, the external debt of the non–oil-developing nations stood at $1,966.5 billion; this was a sharp increase from the $328 billion level of the late 1970s. Much of this debt was incurred by Latin American nations, including Mexico and Brazil. As a percentage of the gross

TABLE 17.2

Developing Nations' External Debt

	1987	1997	2003
Outstanding debt (billions)	$1,156.5	$1,966.5	$2,219.2
Outstanding debt by area (billions)			
Africa	$203.0	$292.8	$267.9
Asia	317.6	660.5	683.8
Middle East/Europe	209.3	342.6	508.9
Western Hemisphere	426.7	670.1	758.6
Ratio of external debt to gross domestic product	40.6%	37.9%	37.7%
Debt service/export ratio	9.1%	7.5%	5.6%

Source: International Monetary Fund, *World Economic Outlook*, September 2003, pp. 228, 240.

domestic product of developing nations, external debt stood at 37.9 percent in 1997. From 1997 to 2003, the external debt of the developing nations leveled off, amounting to 37.7 percent of gross domestic product in 2003.

Another indicator of debt burden is the **debt service/export ratio**, which refers to scheduled interest and principal payments as a percentage of export earnings. The debt service/export ratio permits one to focus on two key indicators of whether a reduction in the debt burden is possible in the short run: (1) the interest rate that the nation pays on its external debt and (2) the growth in its exports of goods and services. All else being constant, a rise in the interest rate increases the debt service/export ratio, while a rise in exports decreases the ratio. It is a well-known rule of international finance that a nation's debt burden rises if the interest rate on the debt exceeds the rate of growth of exports. From 1987 to 2003, the developing nations' debt service/export ratio fell from 9.1 percent to 5.6 percent, as seen in Table 17.2.

Dealing with Debt-Servicing Difficulties

A nation may experience debt-servicing problems for a number of reasons: (1) it may have pursued improper macroeconomic policies that contribute to large balance-of-payments deficits, (2) it may have borrowed excessively or on unfavorable terms, or (3) it may have been affected by adverse economic events that it could not control.

Several options are available to a nation facing debt-servicing difficulties. First, it can cease repayments on its debt. Such an action, however, undermines confidence in the nation, making it difficult (if not impossible) for it to borrow in the future. Furthermore, the nation might be declared in default, in which case its assets (such as ships and aircraft) might be confiscated and sold to discharge the debt. As a group, however, developing nations in debt may have considerable leverage in winning concessions from their lenders.

A second option is for the nation to try to service its debt at all costs. To do so may require the restriction of other foreign-exchange expenditures, a step that may be viewed as socially unacceptable.

Finally, a nation may seek debt rescheduling, which generally involves stretching out the original payment schedule of the debt. There is a cost because the debtor nation must pay interest on the amount outstanding until the debt has been repaid.

When a nation faces debt-servicing problems, its creditors seek to reduce their exposure by collecting all interest and principal payments as they come due, while granting no new credit. But there is an old adage that goes as follows: When a man owes a bank $1,000, the bank owns him; but when a man owes the bank $1 million, he owns the bank. Banks with large amounts of international loans find it in their best interest to help the debtor recover financially. To deal with debt-servicing problems, therefore, debtor nations and their creditors generally attempt to negotiate rescheduling agreements. That is, creditors agree to lengthen the time period for repayment of the principal and sometimes part of the interest on existing loans. Banks have little option but to accommodate demands for debt rescheduling because they do not want the debtor to officially default on the loan. With default, the bank's assets become nonperforming and subject to markdowns by government regulators. This could lead to possible withdrawals of deposits and bank insolvency.

Besides rescheduling debt with commercial banks, developing nations may obtain emergency loans from the IMF. The IMF provides loans to nations experiencing balance-of-payments difficulties provided that the borrowers initiate programs to correct these difficulties. By insisting on **conditionality**, the IMF asks borrowers to adopt austerity programs to shore up their economies and put their muddled finances in order. Such measures have resulted in the slashing of public expenditures, private consumption, and, in some cases, capital investment. Borrowers must also cut imports and expand exports. The IMF views austerity programs as a necessity because with a sovereign debtor, there is no other way to make it pay back its loans. The IMF faces a difficult situation in deciding how tough to get with borrowers. If it goes soft and offers money on easier terms, it sets a precedent for other debtor nations. But if it miscalculates and requires excessive austerity measures, it risks triggering political turmoil and possibly a declaration of default.

The IMF has been criticized, notably by developing nations, for demanding austerity policies that excessively emphasize short-term improvements in the balance of payments rather than fostering long-run economic growth. Developing nations also contend that the IMF austerity programs promote downward pressure on economic activity in nations that are already exposed to recessionary forces. The crucial issue faced by the IMF is how to resolve the economic problems of the debtor nations in a manner most advantageous to them, to their creditors, and to the world as a whole. The mutually advantageous solution is one that enables these nations to achieve sustainable, noninflationary economic growth, thus assuring creditors of repayment and benefiting the world economy through expansion of trade and economic activity.

Reducing Bank Exposure to Developing-Nation Debt

When developing nations cannot meet their debt obligations to foreign banks, the stability of the international financial system is threatened. Banks may react to this threat by increasing their capital base, setting aside reserves to cover losses, and reducing new loans to debtor nations.

Banks have additional means to improve their financial position. One method is to liquidate developing-nation debt by engaging in outright *loan sales* to other banks in the secondary market. But if there occurs an unexpected increase in the default risk of such loans, their market value will be less than their face value. The selling bank thus absorbs costs because its loans must be sold at a discount. Following the sale, the bank must adjust its balance sheet to take account of any previously unrecorded difference between the face value of the loans and their market value. Many small and medium-sized U.S. banks, eager to dump their bad loans in the 1980s, were willing to sell them in the secondary market at discounts as high as 70 percent, or 30 cents on the dollar. But many banks could not afford such huge discounts. Even worse, if the banks all rushed to sell bad loans at once, prices would fall further. Sales of loans in the secondary market were often viewed as a last-resort measure.

Another debt-reduction technique is the *debt buyback*, in which the government of the debtor nation buys the loans from the commercial bank at a discount. Banks have also engaged in *debt-for-debt swaps*, in which a bank exchanges its loans for securities issued by the debtor nation's government at a lower interest rate or discount.

How a Debt/Equity Swap Works

Brazil owes Manufacturers Hanover Trust (of New York) $1 billion. Manufacturers Hanover decides to swap some of the debt for ownership shares in Companhia Suzano del Papel e Celulose, a pulp-and-paper company. Here is what occurs:

- Manufacturers Hanover takes $115 million in Brazilian government-guaranteed loans to a Brazilian broker. The broker takes the loans to the Brazilian central bank's monthly debt auction, where they are valued at an average of 87 cents on the dollar.

- Through the broker, Manufacturers Hanover exchanges the loans at the central bank for $100 million worth of Brazilian cruzados. The broker is paid a commission, and the central bank retires the loans.
- With its cruzados, Manufacturers Hanover purchases 12 percent of Suzano's stock, and Suzano uses the bank's funds to increase capacity and exports.

Cutting losses on developing-nation loans has sometimes involved banks in **debt/equity swaps**. Under this approach, a commercial bank sells its loans at a discount to the developing-nation government for local currency, which it then uses to finance an equity investment in the debtor nation. In the late 1980s, Citicorp converted some of its Chilean loans into pesos, which were used to purchase ownership shares in Chilean gold mines and pulp mills. Citicorp maintained that it could get better value by selling and swapping the loans without using the secondary market. In Chile, Citicorp typically converted debt at about 87 cents worth of local currency for each $1 of debt. Although debt/equity swaps enhance a bank's chances of selling developing-nation debt, they do not necessarily decrease its risk. Some equity investments in developing nations may be just as risky as the loans that were swapped for local factories or land. Moreover, banks that acquire an equity interest in developing-nation assets may not have the knowledge to manage those assets. Debtor nations also worry that debt/equity swaps will allow major companies to fall into foreign hands.

Debt Reduction and Debt Forgiveness

Another method of coping with developing-nation debt involves programs enacted for debt reduction and debt forgiveness. **Debt reduction** refers to any

voluntary scheme that lessens the burden on the debtor nation to service its external debt. Debt reduction is accomplished through two main approaches. The first is the use of negotiated modifications in the terms and conditions of the contracted debt, such as debt reschedulings, retiring of interest payments, and improved borrowing terms. Debt reduction may also be achieved through measures such as debt/equity swaps and debt buybacks. The purpose of debt reduction is to foster comprehensive policies for economic growth by easing the ability of the debtor nation to service its debt, thus freeing resources that will be used for investment.

Some proponents of debt relief maintain that the lending nations should permit **debt forgiveness**. Debt forgiveness refers to any arrangement that reduces the value of contractual obligations of the debtor nation; it includes schemes such as markdowns or write-offs of developing-nation debt or the abrogation of existing obligations to pay interest.

Debt-forgiveness advocates maintain that the most heavily indebted developing nations are unable to service their external debt and maintain an acceptable rate of per capita income growth because their debt burden is overwhelming. They contend that if some of this debt were forgiven, a debtor nation could use the freed-up foreign-exchange resources to increase its imports and invest domestically, thus increasing domestic economic growth rates. The release of the limitation on foreign exchange would provide the debtor nation additional incentive to invest because it would not have to share as much of the benefits of its increased growth and investment with its creditors in the form of interest payments. Moreover, debt forgiveness would allow the debtor nation to service its debt more easily; this would reduce the debt-load burden of a debtor nation and could potentially lead to greater inflows of foreign investment.

Debt-forgiveness critics question whether the amount of debt is a major limitation on developing-nation growth and whether that growth would in fact resume if a large portion of that debt were forgiven. They contend that nations such as Indonesia and South Korea have experienced large amounts of external debt relative to national output but have not faced debt-servicing problems. Also, debt forgiveness does not guarantee that the freed-up foreign-exchange resources will be used productively—that is, invested in sectors that will ultimately generate additional foreign exchange.

The Eurocurrency Market

One of the most widely misunderstood topics in international finance is the nature and operation of the **eurocurrency market**. This market operates as a financial intermediary, bringing together lenders and borrowers. It serves as one of the most important tools for moving short-term funds across national borders. When the eurocurrency market first came into existence in the 1950s, its volume was estimated to be approximately $1 billion. The size of the eurocurrency market in the mid-1990s was estimated to be more than $5 trillion.

Eurocurrencies are deposits, denominated and payable in dollars and other foreign currencies—such as the Swiss franc—in banks outside the United States, primarily in London, the market's center. The term *eurocurrency market* is something of a misnomer because much eurocurrency trading occurs in non-European centers, such as Hong Kong and Singapore. Dollar deposits located in banks outside the United States are known as *eurodollars*, and banks that conduct trading in the markets for eurocurrencies (including the dollar) are designated *eurobanks*.

Eurocurrency depositors may be foreign exporters who have sold products in the United States and have received dollars in payment. They may also be U.S. residents who have withdrawn funds from their accounts in the United States and put them in a bank overseas. Foreign-currency deposits in overseas banks are generally for a specified time period and bear a stated yield, because most eurocurrency deposits are held for investment rather than as transaction balances.

Borrowers go to eurocurrency banks for a variety of purposes. When the market was first developed, borrowers were primarily corporations that required financing for international trade. But other lending opportunities have evolved with the market's development. Borrowers currently include the British government and U.S. banks.

Development of the Eurocurrency Market

Although several hundred banks currently issue eurocurrency deposits on investor demand, it was not until the late 1950s and early 1960s that the market began to gain prominence as a major source of short-term capital. Several factors contributed to the eurocurrency market's growth.

One factor was fear that deposits held in the United States would be frozen by the government in the event of an international conflict. The Eastern European countries, notably Russia, were among the first depositors of dollars in European banks, because during World War II the United States had impounded Russian dollar holdings located in U.S. banks. Russia was thus motivated to maintain dollar holdings free from U.S. regulation.

Ceilings on interest rates that U.S. banks could pay on savings deposits provided another reason for the eurocurrency market's growth. These ceilings limited the U.S. banks in competing with foreign banks for deposits. During the 1930s, the Federal Reserve system under Regulation Q established ceiling rates to prevent banks from paying excessive interest rates on savings accounts and thus being forced to make risky loans to generate high earnings. By the late 1950s, when London was paying interest rates on dollar deposits that exceeded the levels set by Regulation Q, it was profitable for U.S. residents and foreigners to transfer their dollar balances to London. Large U.S. banks directed their foreign branches to bid for dollars by offering higher interest rates than those allowed in the United

States. The parent offices then borrowed the money from their overseas branches. To limit such activity, the Federal Reserve in 1969 established high reserve requirements on head-office borrowings from abroad. In 1973, the Federal Reserve system made large-denomination certificates of deposit exempt from Regulation Q ceilings, further reducing the incentive to borrow funds from overseas branches.

In recent decades, the eurocurrency market has continued to grow. A major factor behind the sustained high growth of the market has been the risk-adjusted interest-rate advantage of eurocurrency deposits relative to domestic deposits, reflecting increases in the level of dollar interest rates and reductions in the perceived riskiness of euromarket deposits.

Financial Implications

Eurocurrencies have significant implications for international finance. By increasing the financial interdependence of nations involved in the market, eurocurrencies facilitate the financing of international trade and investment. They may also reduce the need for official reserve financing, because a given quantity of dollars can support a large volume of international transactions. On the other hand, it is argued that eurocurrencies may undermine a nation's efforts to implement its monetary policy. Volatile movements of these balances into and out of a nation's banking system complicate a central bank's attempt to hit a monetary target.

Another concern is that the eurocurrency market does not face the same financial regulations as do the domestic banking systems of most industrialized nations. Should the eurocurrency banks not maintain sound reserve requirements or enact responsible policies, the pyramid of eurocurrency credit might collapse. Such fears became widespread in 1974 with the failure of the Franklin National Bank in the United States and the Bankus Herstatt of Germany, both of which lost huge sums speculating in the foreign-exchange market.

Summary

1. The purpose of international reserves is to permit nations to bridge the gap between monetary receipts and payments. Deficit nations can use international reserves to buy time in order to postpone adjustment measures.

2. The demand for international reserves depends on two major factors: (a) the monetary value of international transactions and (b) the size and duration of balance-of-payments disequilibrium.

3. The need for international reserves tends to become less acute under a system of floating exchange rates than under a system of fixed rates. The more efficient the international adjustment mechanism and the greater the extent of international policy coordination, the smaller the need for international reserves.

4. The supply of international reserves consists of owned and borrowed reserves. Among the major sources of reserves are (a) foreign currencies, (b) monetary gold stocks, (c) special drawing rights, (d) IMF drawing positions, (e) the General Arrangements to Borrow, and (f) swap arrangements.

5. When making international loans, bankers face credit risk, country risk, and currency risk.

6. Among the indicators used to analyze a nation's external debt position are its debt-to-export ratio and debt service/export ratio.

7. A nation experiencing debt-servicing difficulties has several options: (a) cease repayment on its debt, (b) service its debt at all costs, or (c) reschedule its debt. Debt rescheduling has been widely used by borrowing nations in recent years.

8. A bank can reduce its exposure to developing-nation debt through outright loan sales in the secondary market, debt buybacks, debt-for-debt swaps, and debt/equity swaps.

9. Eurocurrencies are deposits, denominated and payable in dollars and other foreign currencies, in banks outside the United States. Dollar deposits located in banks outside the United States are called eurodollars, and banks that conduct trading in markets for eurocurrencies are known as eurobanks.

Key Concepts and Terms

- Basket valuation *(page 498)*
- Conditionality *(page 502)*
- Country risk *(page 500)*
- Credit risk *(page 499)*
- Currency risk *(page 500)*
- Debt/equity swaps *(page 503)*
- Debt forgiveness *(page 503)*
- Debt reduction *(page 503)*
- Debt service/export ratio *(page 501)*
- Demand for international reserves *(page 491)*
- Demonetization of gold *(page 497)*
- Eurocurrency market *(page 504)*
- General Arrangements to Borrow *(page 499)*
- Gold exchange standard *(page 496)*
- Gold standard *(page 495)*
- IMF drawings *(page 498)*
- International reserves *(page 491)*
- Liquidity problem *(page 495)*
- Special drawing rights (SDRs) *(page 497)*
- Supply of international reserves *(page 494)*
- Swap arrangements *(page 499)*

Study Questions

1. A nation's need for international reserves is similar to an individual's desire to hold cash balances. Explain.
2. What are the major factors that determine a nation's demand for international reserves?
3. The total supply of international reserves consists of two categories: (a) owned reserves and (b) borrowed reserves. What do these categories include?
4. In terms of volume, which component of world reserves is currently most important? Which is currently least important?
5. What is meant by a reserve currency? Historically, which currencies have assumed this role?
6. What is the current role of gold in the international monetary system?
7. What advantages does a gold exchange standard have over a pure gold standard?
8. What are special drawing rights? Why were they created? How is their value determined?
9. What facilities exist for trading nations that wish to borrow international reserves?
10. What caused the international debt problem of the developing nations in the 1980s? Why did this debt problem threaten the stability of the international banking system?
11. What is a eurocurrency? How did the eurocurrency market develop?
12. What risks do bankers assume when making loans to foreign borrowers?
13. Distinguish between debt-to-export ratio and debt service/export ratio.
14. What options are available to a nation experiencing debt-servicing difficulties? What limitations apply to each option?
15. What methods do banks use to reduce their exposure to developing-nation debt?
16. How can debt/equity swaps help banks reduce losses on developing-nation loans?

netlink

17.1 The World Bank Group provides various forms of assistance to developing countries in order to promote economic growth and investment in people. Learn more about the World Bank by setting your browser to this URL:

http://www.worldbank.org

17.2 The European Central Bank was formed in June 1998 with 11 member states. Information can be found at this home page:

http://www.ecb.int

17.3 The Stern School of Business at New York University maintains a Web site that provides extensive information and articles relating to instability in Asian financial markets. Visit this site by setting your browser to this URL:

http://www.stern.nyu.edu

17.4 The NYU Salomon Center for Research in Financial Institutions and Markets, a center within New York University's Stern School of Business, supports academic research for the study of problems and issues related to the U.S. and global financial structure. Log onto their Web page at this URL:

http://www.stern.nyu.edu/salomon

To access NetLink Exercises and the Virtual Scavenger Hunt, visit the Carbaugh Web site at http://carbaugh.swlearning.com.

Log onto the Carbaugh Xtra! Web site (http://carbaughxtra.swlearning.com) for additional learning resources such as practice quizzes, help with graphing, and current events applications.

Glossary

Glossary

A

absorption approach an approach to currency depreciation that deals with the income effects of depreciation; a decrease in domestic expenditures relative to income must occur for depreciation to promote payments equilibrium, according to the absorption approach

adjustable pegged exchange rates a system of semifixed exchange rates where it is understood that the par value of the currency will be changed occasionally in response to changing economic conditions

adjustment mechanism a mechanism that works to return a balance of payments to equilibrium after the initial equilibrium has been disrupted; the process takes two different forms: automatic (economic processes) and discretionary (government policies)

ad valorem tariff a tariff expressed as a fixed percentage of the value of the imported product

advanced nations include those of North America and Western Europe, plus Australia, New Zealand, and Japan

agglomeration economies a rich country specializes in manufacturing niches and gains productivity through groups of firms clustered together, some producing the same product and others connected by vertical linkages

antidumping duty a duty levied against commodities a home nation believes are being dumped into its markets from abroad

appreciation (as applied to currency markets) when, over time, it takes fewer units of a nation's currency to purchase a unit of some foreign currency

asset-market approach a method of determining short-run exchange rates where investors consider two key factors when deciding between domestic and foreign investments; relative levels of interest rates and expected changes in the exchange rate itself over the term of the investment

autarky a case of national self-sufficiency or absence of trade

automatic adjustment (of the balance-of-payments process) a mechanism that works to return a balance of payments to equilibrium automatically through the adjustments in economic variables

B

balance of international indebtedness a statement that summarizes a country's stock of assets and liabilities against the rest of the world at a fixed point in time

balance of payments a record of the flow of economic transactions between the residents of one country and the rest of the world

bank claims and liabilities bank claims consist of loans, overseas deposits, acceptances, foreign commercial paper, claims on affiliated banks abroad, and foreign government obligations; bank liabilities include demand deposits and NOW accounts, passbook savings deposits, certificates of deposit, and liabilities to affiliated banks abroad

basis for trade why nations export and import certain products

basket valuation the valuation of the special drawing right based on the values of several countries' currencies

beggar-thy-neighbor policy the practice of imposing protectionist policies to achieve gains from trade at the expense of other nations

bid rate the price that the bank is willing to pay for a unit of foreign currency

bonded warehouse a storage facility operated under the lock and key of (in the case of the United States) the U.S. Customs Service

brain drain emigration of highly educated and skilled people from developing nations to industrial nations

buffer stock supplies of a commodity financed and held by a producers' association; used to limit commodity price swings

business services in many cases, nonstorable or intangible products, such as tourism, consulting, banking, construction, and freight transportation

buy-national policies when a home nation's government, through explicit laws, openly discriminates against foreign suppliers in its purchasing decisions

C

call option gives the holder the right to *buy* foreign currency at a specified price

capital controls government-imposed barriers to foreign savers investing in domestic assets or to domestic savers investing in foreign assets; also known as *exchange controls*

capital and financial account the net result of both private-sector and official capital and financial transactions

capital/labor ratio a country's ratio of capital inputs to labor inputs

cartel a group of firms or nations that attempts to support prices higher than would exist under more competitive conditions

clean float when free-market forces of supply and demand are allowed to determine the exchange value of a currency

commodity terms of trade measures the relationship between the prices a nation gets for its exports and the prices it pays for its imports

common agricultural policy members of the European Union agree to maintain identical governmental agricultural policies to support farmers

common market a group of trading nations that permits the free movement of goods and services among member nations, the initiation of common external trade restrictions against nonmembers, and the free movement of factors of production across national borders within the economic bloc

community indifference curve the indifference curve that represents the tastes and preferences of all of the households of a nation

comparative advantage ability to produce a good or service at a lower opportunity cost than others can produce it

complete specialization a situation in which a country produces only one good

compound tariff a tariff that is a combination of a specific tariff and an ad valorem tariff

conditionality the standards imposed by the IMF on borrowing countries to qualify for a loan, which can include requirements that the borrowers initiate programs to correct economic difficulties, adopt austerity programs to shore up their economies, and put their muddled finances in order

conglomerate integration in the case of an MNE, diversification into nonrelated markets

constant opportunity costs a constant rate of sacrifice of one good for another as a nation slides along its production possibilities schedule

consumer surplus the difference between the amount that buyers would be willing and able to pay for a good and the actual amount they do pay

consumption effect a trade restriction's loss of welfare that occurs because of increased prices and lower consumption

consumption gains posttrade consumption points *outside* a nation's production possibilities schedule

convergence criteria economic standards required of all nations in a monetary union; in the instance of the Maastricht Treaty, these standards included price stability, low long-term interest rates, stable exchange rates, and sound public finances

corporate average fuel economy standards (CAFÉ) fuel economy standards imposed by the U.S. government on automobile manufacturers

cost-based definition a method of calculating the fair market value of a product in dumping cases; the U.S. Commerce Department "constructs" fair market value equal to the sum of (1) the cost of manufacturing the merchandise, (2) general expenses, (3) profit on home-market sales, and (4) the cost of packaging the merchandise for shipment to the United States

cost-insurance-freight (CIF) valuation when ad valorem tariffs are levied as a percentage of the imported commodity's total value as it arrives at its final destination

countertrade international trade in which goods are exchanged for goods

countervailing duty a levy imposed by importing countries to counteract foreign export subsidies;

the size of the duty is limited to the amount of the export subsidy

country risk risk associated with political developments in a country, especially the government's views concerning international investments and loans

covered interest arbitrage the process of moving funds into foreign currencies to take advantage of higher investment yields abroad, while avoiding exchange rate risk

crawling peg a system in which a nation makes small, frequent changes in the par value of its currency to correct balance-of-payments disequilibriums

credit risk the probability that part or all of the interest or principal of a loan will not be repaid

credit transaction a balance of payments transaction that results in a *receipt* of a payment from foreigners

cross exchange rate the resulting rate derived when the exchange rate between any two currencies can be derived from the rates of these two currencies in terms of a third currency

currency board a monetary authority that issues notes and coins convertible into a foreign anchor currency at a fixed exchange rate

currency crashes financial crises that often end in currency devaluations or accelerated depreciations

currency crisis a situation in which a weak currency experiences heavy selling pressure, also called a *speculative attack*

currency risk investment risk associated with currency depreciations and appreciations as well as exchange controls

currency swap the conversion of one currency to another currency at one point in time, with an agreement to reconvert it to the original currency at a specified time in the future

current account the net value of monetary flows associated with transactions in goods and services, investment income, employee compensation, and unilateral transfers

customs union an agreement among two or more trading partners to remove all tariff and nontariff trade barriers among themselves; each member nation imposes identical trade restrictions against nonparticipants

customs valuation the process of determining the value of an imported product

D

deadweight loss the net loss of economic benefits to a domestic economy due the protective effect and the consumption effect of a trade barrier

debit transaction a balance of payments transaction that leads to a *payment* to foreigners

debt/equity swaps when a commercial bank sells its loans at a discount to the debtor-nation's government for local currency, which it then uses to finance an equity investment in the debtor nation

debt forgiveness any arrangement that reduces the value of contractual obligations of the debtor nation

debt reduction any voluntary scheme that lessens the burden on the debtor nation to service its external debt

debt service/export ratio the scheduled interest and principal payments as a percentage of export earnings

demand for international reserves the requirement for international reserves; depends on two related factors: (1) the monetary value of international transactions and (2) the disequilibrium that can arise in balance-of-payments positions; the requirement for international reserves include assets such as key foreign currencies, special drawing rights, and drawing rights at the International Monetary Fund

demand-pull inflation when a nation's capacity to produce has been achieved, and further increases in aggregate demand pull prices upward

demonetization of gold occurred in the 1970s when the official price of gold was abolished as the unit of account for the international monetary system

depreciation (as applies to currency markets) when, over time, it takes more units of a nation's currency to purchase a unit of some foreign currency

destabilizing speculation speculation that occurs when speculators expect a current trend in exchange rates to continue and their transactions accelerate the rise or fall of the target currency's value

devaluation an official change in a currency's par value, which causes the currency's exchange value to depreciate

developing nations most nations in Africa, Asia, Latin America, and the Middle East

direct controls consist of government restrictions on the market economy

direct foreign investment when residents of one country acquire a controlling interest in a business enterprise in another country

dirty float a condition under a managed floating system when free-market forces of supply and demand are not allowed to achieve their equilibrating role; countries may manage their exchange rates to improve the competitiveness of their producers

discount the valuation of a currency when it is worth less in the forward market than in the spot market

distribution of income the distribution of wages earned across a country

domestic content requirements requirements that stipulate the minimum percentage of a product's total value that must be produced domestically if the product is to qualify for zero tariff rates

domestic revenue effect the amount of tariff revenue shifted from domestic consumers to the tariff-levying government

domestic subsidy a subsidy that is sometimes granted to producers of import-competing goods

double-entry accounting a system of accounting in which each credit entry is balanced by a debit entry, and vice versa, so that the recording of any transaction leads to two offsetting entries

dumping when foreign buyers are charged lower prices than domestic buyers for an identical product, after allowing for transportation costs and tariff duties

dynamic comparative advantage a changing pattern in comparative advantage; governments can establish policies to promote opportunities for changes in comparative advantage over time

dynamic effects of economic integration effects that relate to member nations' long-run rates of growth, which include economies of scale, greater competition, and investment stimulus

dynamic gains from international trade the effect of trade on the country's growth rate and thus on the volume of additional resources made available to, or utilized by, the trading country

E

economic integration a process of eliminating restrictions on international trade, payments, and factor mobility

economic interdependence all aspects of a nation's economy are linked to the economies of its trading partners

economic sanctions government-mandated limitations placed on customary trade or financial relations among nations

economic union where national, social, taxation, and fiscal policies are harmonized and administered by a supranational institution

economies of scale when increasing all inputs by the same proportion results in a greater proportion of total output

effective exchange rate a weighted average of the exchange rates between a domestic currency and that nation's most important trading partners, with weights given by relative importance of the nation's trade with each trade partner

effective tariff rate measures the total increase in domestic production that a tariff makes possible, compared to free trade

elasticity approach an approach to currency depreciation that emphasizes the relative *price effects* of depreciation and suggests that depreciation works best when demand elasticities for a nation's imports and exports are high

environmental regulation regulations imposed on the production process to limit environmental impact

escape clause allows the president to temporarily terminate or make modifications in trade concessions granted foreign nations and to temporarily levy restrictions on surging imports

euro the official currency of the EMU

exchange arbitrage the *simultaneous* purchase and sale of a currency in different foreign-exchange markets in order to profit from exchange-rate differentials in the two locations

exchange rate the price of one currency in terms of another

exchange-rate index a weighted average of the exchange rates between a domestic currency and that nation's most important trading partners, with weights given by relative importance of the nation's trade with each trade partner

exchange-rate pass-through (relationship) the extent to which changing currency values lead to changes in import and export prices

exchange-stabilization fund a government entity that attempts to ensure that the market exchange rate does not move above or below the official exchange rate through purchases and sales of foreign currencies

exit barriers cost conditions that make lengthy industry exit a rational response by companies

expenditure-changing policies policies that alter the level of aggregate demand for goods and services, including those produced domestically and those imported

expenditure-switching policies policies that modify the direction of demand, shifting it between domestic output and imports

export controls enacted to stabilize export revenues, these measures offset a decrease in the market demand for the primary commodity by assigning cutbacks in the market supply

export quotas limitations on export sales administered by one or more exporting nations or industries

export subsidies a subsidy paid to exporters so they can sell goods abroad at the lower world price but still receive the higher support price

export-led growth (export-oriented policy) involves promoting economic growth through the export of manufactured goods—trade controls are either nonexistent or very low, in the sense that any disincentives to export resulting from import barriers are counterbalanced by export subsidies

export-revenue effect an increase in home country export revenue due to an export subsidy and the corresponding drop in foreign price of home-nation exports

external balance when a nation realizes neither BOP deficits nor BOP surpluses

F

factor-endowment theory asserts that a country exports those goods that use its abundant factor more intensively

factor-price equalization free trade's tendency to cause cheap factors of production to become more expensive, and the expensive factors of production to become cheaper

fast-track authority devised in 1974, this provision commits the U.S. Congress to consider trade agreements without amendment; in return, the president must adhere to a specified timetable and several other procedures

fiscal policy refers to changes in government spending and taxes

fixed exchange rates a system used primarily by small developing nations whose currencies are anchored to a key currency, such as the U.S. dollar

floating exchange rates when a nation allows its currency to fluctuate according to the free-market forces of supply and demand

flying-geese pattern of economic growth where countries gradually move up in technological development by following in the pattern of countries ahead of them in the development process

forecasting exchange rates attempts to predict future rates of exchange

foreign direct investment foreign acquisition of a controlling interest in an overseas company or facility

foreign repercussion effect the impact that changes in domestic expenditures and income levels have on foreign economies; a rise in domestic income stimulates imports, causing a foreign expansion that in turn raises demand for domestic exports

foreign-currency options provide an options holder the right to buy or sell a fixed amount of foreign currency at a prearranged price, within a few days or several years

foreign-exchange market the organizational setting within which individuals, businesses, governments, and banks buy and sell foreign currencies and other debt instruments

foreign-trade multiplier when an increase in exports sets off a chain reaction that results in greater levels of spending so that domestic income increases by some multiple of the export increase

foreign-trade zone (FTZ) special zones that enlarge the benefits of a bonded warehouse by eliminating the restrictive aspects of customs surveillance and by offering more suitable manufacturing facilities; FTZs are intended to stimulate international trade, attract industry, and create jobs by providing an area that gives users tariff and tax breaks

forward market where foreign exchange can be traded for future delivery

forward rate the rate of exchange used in the settlement of forward transactions

forward transaction an outright purchase and sale of foreign currency at a fixed exchange rate but with payment or delivery of the foreign currency at a future date

free trade a system of open markets between countries in which nations concentrate their production on goods they can make most cheaply, with all the consequent benefits of the division of labor

free-on-board (FOB) valuation when a tariff is applied to a product's value as it leaves the exporting country

free-trade area an association of trading nations whose members agree to remove all tariff and nontariff barriers among themselves

free-trade argument if each nation produces what it does best and permits trade, over the long run each party will enjoy lower prices and higher levels of output, income, and consumption than could be achieved in isolation

free-trade-biased sector generally comprises exporting companies, their workers, and their suppliers; it also consists of consumers, including wholesalers and retail merchants of imported goods

fundamental analysis the opposite of technical analysis; involves consideration of economic variables that are likely to affect a currency's value

fundamental disequilibrium when the official exchange rate and the market exchange rate may move apart, reflecting changes in fundamental economic conditions—income levels, tastes and preferences, and technological factors

futures market a market in which contracting parties agree to future exchanges of currencies and set applicable exchange rates in advance; distinguished from the forward market in that only a limited number of leading currencies are traded; trading takes place in standardized contract amounts and in a specific geographic location

G

gains from international trade gains trading partners simultaneously enjoy due to specialization and the division of labor

generalized system of preferences (GSP) a system in which industrialized nations attempt to promote economic development in developing countries through lower tariffs and increased trade, rather than foreign aid

globalization the process of greater interdependence among countries and their citizens

global quota a technique permitting a specified number of goods to be imported each year, but does not specify where the product is shipped from or who is permitted to import

gold exchange standard a system of fixed exchange rates, with gold serving as the primary reserve asset; member nations officially agreed to state the par values of their currencies in terms of gold or, alternatively, the gold content of the U.S. dollar

gold standard a monetary system in which each member nation's money supply consisted of gold or paper money backed by gold, where each member nation defined the official price of gold in terms of its national currency and was prepared to buy and sell gold at that price; free import and export of gold was permitted by member nations

goods and services balance the result of combining the balance of trade in services and the merchandise trade balance

guest workers foreign workers, when needed, allowed to immigrate on a temporary basis

H

Heckscher–Ohlin theory differences in relative factor endowments among nations underlie the basis for trade

hedging the process of avoiding or covering a foreign-exchange risk

home market effect countries will specialize in products for which there is large domestic demand

horizontal integration in the case of an MNE, occurs when a parent company producing a commodity in the source country sets up a subsidiary to produce the identical product in the host country

I

importance of being unimportant when one trading nation is significantly larger than the other, the *larger* nation attains *fewer* gains from trade while the *smaller* nation attains *most* of the gains from trade

import license used to administer an import quota; a license specifying the volume of imports allowed

import quota a physical restriction on the quantity of goods that may be imported during a specific time period

import substitution a policy that involves extensive use of trade barriers to protect domestic industries from import competition

income determination a theory developed by John Maynard Keynes in the 1930s; asserted that under a system of fixed exchange rates, the influence of income changes in surplus and deficit nations will help restore payments equilibrium *automatically*

increasing opportunity costs when each additional unit of one good produced requires the sacrifice of increasing amounts of the other good

increasing returns to scale when increasing all inputs by the same proportion results in a total output to increase by a greater proportion

indifference curve a curve depicting the various combinations of two commodities that are equally preferred in the eyes of the consumer

industrial policy government policy that is actively involved in creating comparative advantage

infant-industry argument a tariff that temporarily shields newly developing industries from foreign competition

institutional constraints policy considerations that involve issues of fairness and equity

intellectual property rights (IPRs) the exclusive rights to use an invention, idea, product, or process for a given time awarded to the inventor (or author) through registration with the government of that invention, idea, product, or process

interbank market bank transactions with other banks

interest arbitrage the process of moving funds into foreign currencies to take advantage of higher investment yields abroad

interindustry specialization when each nation specializes in a particular industry in which it enjoys a comparative advantage

interindustry trade the exchange between nations of products of different industries

internal balance the goal of economic stability at full employment

international commodity agreements (ICAs) agreements between leading producing and consuming nations of commodities about matters such as stabilizing prices, assuring adequate supplies to consumers, and promoting the economic development of producers

international economic policy activities of national governments that affect the movement of trade and factor inputs among nations

international economic-policy coordination the attempt to coordinate national policies—monetary, fiscal, or exchange-rate policy—in recognition of international economic interdependence

international joint ventures an example of multinational enterprise in which a business organization established by two or more companies combines their skills and assets

international reserves assets held to enable nations to finance disequilibrium in their balance-of-payments positions

intraindustry specialization the focusing on the production of particular products or groups of products within a given industry

intraindustry trade two-way trade in a similar commodity

J

judgmental forecasts subjective or common-sense exchange-rate forecasts based on economic, political, and other data for a country

K

key currency a currency that is widely traded on world money markets, has demonstrated relatively stable values over time, and has been widely accepted as a means of international settlement

L

labor mobility a measure of how labor migration responds to wage differentials

labor theory of value the cost or price of a good depends exclusively upon the amount of labor required to produce it

large nation an importing nation that is large enough so that changes in the quantity of its imports, by means of tariff policy, influence the world price of the product

law of comparative advantage when each nation specializes in the production of that good in which it has a relative advantage, the total output of each good increases; thus, all countries can realize welfare gains

law of one price part of the purchasing-power-parity approach to determining exchange rates; asserts that identical goods should cost the same in all nations, assuming that it is costless to ship goods between nations and there are no barriers to trade

leaning against the wind intervening to reduce short-term fluctuations in exchange rates without attempting to adhere to any particular rate over the long run

level playing field a condition in which domestic and foreign producers can compete on equal terms

license on demand allocation a system in which licenses are required to import at the within-quota tariff

liquidity problem when a government or central bank runs short of needed international reserves

long position the position speculators take when they purchase foreign currency on the spot or forward market with the anticipation of selling it at a higher future spot price

M

managed floating system an exchange-rate system in which the rate is usually allowed to be determined by the free-market forces of supply and demand, while sometimes entailing some degree of government (central bank) intervention

maquiladoras manufacturing facilities or industrial parks in northern Mexico, typically the result of direct foreign investment; typically host an assemblage of U.S.–owned companies that combine U.S. parts and supplies and Mexican assembly to manufacture goods that are exported to the United States

margin of dumping the amount by which the domestic price of a firm's product exceeds its foreign price, or the amount by which the foreign price of a firm's product is less than the cost of producing it

marginal rate of transformation (MRT) the slope of the production possibilities schedule that shows the amount of one product a nation must sacrifice to get one additional unit of the other product

market economy where the commercial decisions of independent buyers and sellers acting in their own interest govern both domestic and international trade

market expectations examples include news about future market fundamentals and traders' opinions about future exchange rates

market fundamentals economic variables such as productivity, inflation rates, real interest rates, consumer preferences, and government trade policy

mercantilist an advocate or practitioner of mercantilism; a national economic system in which a nation could regulate its domestic and international affairs so as to promote its own interests through a strong foreign-trade sector

merchandise trade balance the result of combining the dollar value of merchandise exports recorded as a plus (credit) and the dollar value of merchandise imports recorded as a minus (debit)

migration moving from one country to settle in another

monetary approach an approach to currency depreciation that stresses the effects depreciation has on the purchasing power of money and the resulting impact on domestic expenditure levels

monetary policy refers to changes in the money supply by a nation's central bank

monetary union the unification of national monetary policies and the acceptance of a common currency administered by a supranational monetary authority

most-favored nation (MFN) an agreement between two nations to apply tariffs to each other at rates as low as those applied to any other nation

multilateral contracts contracts that stipulate a *minimum price* at which importers will purchase guaranteed quantities from the producing nations and a *maximum price* at which producing nations will sell guaranteed amounts to importers

multinational enterprise (MNE) an enterprise that cuts across national borders and is often directed from a company planning center that is distant from the host country

multiplier process when an initial increase in investment spending sets off a chain reaction that results in greater levels of spending, so that income increases by some multiple of the initial investment increase

N

net creditor the status of a nation when that country's claims on foreigners exceed foreign claims on that country at a particular time

net debtor the status of a nation when foreign claims on a country exceed that country's claims on foreigners at a particular time

net foreign investment in national income accounting, is synonymous with the current account balance

nominal exchange rate exchange-rate quotes published in newspapers that are not adjusted inflation rates in trading partners

nominal exchange-rate index the average value of a currency, not adjusted for changes in price levels of that country and its trading partners

nominal interest rate the rate of return on assets that can be earned in a particular country, not adjusted for the rate of inflation

nominal tariff rate the tariff rate published in a country's tariff schedule

nonmarket economy where state planning and control govern foreign and sometimes domestic trade

nonrestrained suppliers a trading partner that is not restrained by a voluntary export agreement

nontariff trade barriers (NTBs) policies other than tariffs that restrict international trade

normal trade relations the U.S. government's replacement for the term *most-favored nation*

no-trade boundary the terms-of-trade limit at which a country will cease to export a good

O

offer rate the price at which the bank is willing to sell a unit of foreign currency

official exchange rate the exchange rate determined by comparing the par values of two currencies

official reserve assets holding key foreign currencies, special drawing rights, and reserve positions in the IMF by official monetary institutions

official settlements transactions the movement of financial assets among official holders; these financial assets fall into two categories: official reserve assets and liabilities to foreign official agencies

offshore-assembly provision when import duties apply only to the value added in the foreign assembly process, provided that domestically made components are used by overseas companies in their assembly operations

openness the ratio of a nation's exports and imports as a percentage of its gross domestic product (GDP)

optimum currency area a region in which it is economically preferable to have a single official currency rather than multiple official currencies

optimum tariff a tariff rate at which the positive difference between the gain of improving terms of trade and the loss of declining import volume is maximized

option an agreement between a holder (buyer) and a writer (seller) that gives the holder the right, but not the obligation, to buy or sell financial instruments at any time through a specified date

orderly marketing agreement a market-sharing pact negotiated by trading partners

outer limits for the equilibrium terms of trade defined by the domestic cost ratios of trading nations

overall balance when an economy attains internal balance and external balance

overshooting an instance of an exchange rate's short-run response to a change in market fundamentals is *greater* than its long-run response

P

par value a central value in terms of a key currency that governments participating in a fixed-exchange rate system set their currencies

partial specialization when a country specializes only partially in the production of the good in which it has a comparative advantage

persistent dumping when a producer consistently sells products abroad at lower prices than at home

predatory dumping when a producer temporarily reduces the prices charged abroad to drive foreign competitors out of business

premium the valuation of a currency when it is worth more in the forward market than in the spot market

price-specie-flow doctrine David Hume's theory that a favorable trade balance was possible only in the short run, and that over time, it would automatically be eliminated via changes in product prices

priced-based definition a method of calculating fair market value in dumping cases; dumping occurs when a company sells a product in its home market at a price above that for which the same product sells in the foreign market

primary products agricultural goods, raw materials, and fuels

principle of absolute advantage in a two-nation, two-product world, international specialization and trade will be beneficial when one nation has an absolute cost advantage in one good and the other nation has an absolute cost advantage in the other good

producer surplus the revenue producers receive over and above the minimum amount required to induce them to supply the good

product life cycle theory many manufactured goods undergo a predictable *trade cycle*; during this cycle, the home country initially is an exporter, then loses its competitive advantage vis-à-vis its trading partners, and eventually may become an importer of the commodity

production controls artificial curtailments in the production of a commodity

production gains increases in production resulting from specialization in the product of comparative advantage

production possibilities schedule a schedule that shows various alternative combinations of two goods that a nation can produce when *all* of its factor inputs are used in their most efficient manner

production sharing when certain aspects of a product's manufacture are performed in more than one country

protection-biased sector generally consists of import-competing companies, the labor unions representing workers in that industry, and the suppliers to the companies in the industry

protective effect a tariff's loss to the domestic economy resulting from wasted resources when less efficient domestic production is substituted for more efficient foreign production

protective tariff a tariff designed to insulate import-competing producers from foreign competition

policy agreement when changes in economic policies move an economy toward internal balance and external balance

policy conflict when changes in economic policy improve one economic objective but detract from another objective

purchasing-power-parity theory a method of determining the equilibrium exchange rate by means of the price levels and their variations in different nations

put option gives the holder the right to *sell* foreign currency at a specified price

Q

quantity theory of money states that increases in the money supply lead directly to an increase in overall prices, and a shrinking money supply causes overall prices to fall

R

real exchange rate the nominal exchange rate adjusted for changes in relative price levels

real exchange-rate index the average value of a currency based on real exchange rates

real interest rate the nominal interest rate minus the inflation rate

redistributive effect with a tariff, the transfer of consumer surplus, in monetary terms, to the domestic producers of the import-competing product

region of mutually beneficial trade the area that is bounded by the cost ratios of the two trading countries

regional trading arrangement where member nations agree to impose lower barriers to trade within the group than to trade with nonmember nations

relative purchasing power parity a method of determining exchange rates that states that changes in relative national price levels determine changes in exchange rates over the long run

revaluation an official change in a currency's par value, which causes the currency's exchange value to appreciate

revenue effect represents the government's collections of tariff revenue; found by multiplying the number of imports times the tariff

revenue tariff a tariff imposed for the purpose of generating tax revenues and may be placed on either exports or imports

rules of the game an agreement among gold standard nations to reinforce and speed up interest-rate adjustment, requiring central bankers in a *surplus* nation to *expand* credit, leading to lower interest rates; central bankers in *deficit* nations would *tighten* credit, bidding interest rates upward

S

scientific tariff a tariff that eliminates foreign cost advantages over domestic firms

securities private-sector purchases of short- and long-term debt securities such as Treasury bills, Treasury notes, Treasury bonds, and securities of private enterprises

seigniorage profit from issuing money

selective quota an import quota allocated to specific countries

short position the position speculators take when they borrow or sell forward a foreign currency with the anticipation of purchasing it at a future lower price to repay the foreign-exchange loan or fulfill the forward sale contract

small nation a nation whose imports constitute a very small portion of the world market supply

social regulation governmental attempts to correct a variety of undesirable side effects in an economy that relate to health, safety, and the environment

special drawing right (SDR) an artificial currency unit based on a basket of four currencies established by the IMF

specific tariff a tariff expressed in terms of a fixed amount of money per unit of the imported product

specific-factors theory considers the income-distribution effects of trade when when factor inputs are immobile among industries in the short run

speculation the attempt to profit by trading on expectations about prices in the future

speculative attack see *currency crisis*

sporadic dumping (distress dumping) when a firm disposes of excess inventories on foreign markets by selling abroad at lower prices than at home

spot market where foreign exchange can be traded for immediate delivery

spot transaction an outright purchase and sale of foreign currency for cash settlement not more than two business days after the date the transaction

spread the difference between the bid rate and the offer rate

stabilizing speculation occurs when speculators expect a current trend in an exchange rate's movement to change and their purchase or sale of the currency moderates movements of the exchange rate

static effects of economic integration include the trade-creation effect and the trade-diversion effect

statistical discrepancy a correcting entry inserted into the balance-of-payments statement to make the sum of the credits and debits equal

strategic trade policy the policy that government can assist domestic companies in capturing economic profits from foreign competitors

strike price the price at which an option can be exercised

subsidies granted by governments to domestic producers to improve their trade competitiveness; include outright cash disbursements, tax concessions, insurance arrangements, and loans at below-market interest rates

supply of international reserves includes owned reserves, such as key currencies and special drawing rights, and borrowed reserves, which can come from the IMF and other official arrangements or can be obtained from major commercial banks

swap arrangements bilateral agreements between central banks where each government provides for an exchange, or swap, of currencies to help finance temporary payments disequilibrium

T

target exchange rates desired exchange rates for a currency set by the host country and supported by intervention

tariff a tax levied on a product when it crosses national boundaries

tariff escalation occurs when tariff structures of industrialized nations are characterized by rising rates that give greater protection to intermediate and finished products than to primary commodities

tariff-rate quota a device that allows a specified number of goods to be imported at one tariff rate (the *within-quota rate*), and any imports above that specified number to be imported at a higher tariff rate (the *over-quota rate*)

technical analysis a method of exchange-rate forecasting that involves the use of historical exchange-rate data to estimate future values

technology transfer the transfer to other nations of knowledge and skills applied to how goods are produced

terms of trade the relative prices at which two products are traded in the marketplace

terms-of-trade effect the tariff revenue extracted from foreign producers in the form of a lower supply price

theory of overlapping demands nations with similar per capita incomes will have overlapping demand structures and will likely consume similar types of manufactured goods; wealthy nations will likely trade with other wealthy nations, and poor nations will likely trade with other poor nations

theory of reciprocal demand relative demand conditions determine what the actual terms of trade will be within the outer limits of the terms of trade

three-point arbitrage a more intricate form of arbitrage, involving three currencies and three financial centers; also called *triangular arbitrage*

trade adjustment assistance government assistance granted to domestic workers displaced by increased imports

trade balance derived by computing the net exports (imports) in the merchandise accounts; also called *merchandise trade balance*

trade promotion authority (also known as *fast-track authority*) devised in 1974, this provision commits U.S. Congress to consider trade agreements without amendment; in return, the president must adhere to a specified timetable and several other procedures

trade remedy laws laws designed to produce a fair trading environment for all parties engaging in international business; these laws include the escape clause, countervailing duties, antidumping duties, and unfair trading practices

trade triangle an area in a production possibilities diagram showing a country's exports, imports, and equilibrium terms of trade

trade-creation effect a welfare gain resulting from increasing trade caused by the formation of a regional trade bloc

trade-diversion effect a welfare loss resulting from the formation of a regional trade bloc; it occurs when imports from a low-cost supplier outside the trade bloc are replaced by purchases from a higher-cost supplier within the trade bloc

trade-weighted dollar a weighted average of the exchange rates between a domestic currency and the currencies of the nation's most important trading partners, with weights given by relative importance of the nation's trade with each trade partner

trading possibilities line a line in a production possibilities diagram representing the equilibrium terms-of-trade ratio

transfer pricing a technique where an MNE reports most of its profits in a low-tax country, even though the profits are earned in a high-tax country

transition economies national economies making the transition from a centrally planned economy to a market economy

transplants the assembly plants of Japanese companies that produce automobiles in the United States

transportation costs the costs of moving goods from one nation to another

two-point arbitrage the simultaneous purchase and sale of a currency in two foreign-exchange markets in order to profit from exchange-rate differentials in different locations

U

uncovered interest arbitrage when an investor does not obtain exchange-market cover to protect investment proceeds from foreign-currency fluctuations

unilateral transfers include transfers of goods and services (gifts in kind) or financial assets (money gifts) between the United States and the rest of the world

V

variable levies an import tariff that increases or decreases as domestic or world prices change to guarantee that the price of the imported product after payment of duty will equal a predetermined price

vertical integration in the case of an MNE, occurs when the parent MNE decides to establish foreign subsidiaries to produce intermediate goods or inputs that go into the production of the finished good

voluntary export restraints (VER) voluntary quotas applied to exports; sometimes supplemented by backup import controls to ensure that the restraints are effective

W

wage insurance after finding new jobs, a temporary government subsidy of wages granted to domestic workers displaced by foreign trade and increased imports

wage and price controls intervention by the government to set price and wage levels

Index

Index